The Young Child

Development from Prebirth Through Age Eight

The Young Child

Development from Prebirth Through Age Eight

Janet K. Black
University of North Texas

Margaret B. Puckett
Texas Wesleyan University

Michael J. Bell
University of North Texas

Merrill, an imprint of
Macmillan Publishing Company
New York

Maxwell Macmillan Canada
Toronto

Maxwell Macmillan International
New York   Oxford   Singapore   Sydney

Cover photo: © Myrleen Ferguson/Photo Edit
Editor: Linda A. Sullivan
Developmental Editor: Linda Kauffman Peterson
Production Editor: Jonathan Lawrence
Art Coordinator: Ruth A. Kimpel
Photo Editor: Gail L. Meese
Text Designer: Anne Flanagan
Cover Designer: Russ Maselli
Production Buyer: Patricia A. Tonneman
Illustrations: Accurate Art, Inc.

This book was set in Century by Waldman Graphics, Inc., and was printed and bound by R. R. Donnelley & Sons Company. The cover was printed by New England Book Components.

Macmillan Publishing Company
866 Third Avenue
New York, NY 10022

Macmillan Publishing Company is part of the
Maxwell Communication Group of Companies.

Maxwell Macmillan Canada, Inc.
1200 Eglinton Avenue East, Suite 200
Don Mills, Ontario M3C 3N1

Library of Congress Cataloging-in-Publication Data
Black, Janet.
      The young child: development from prebirth through age eight / Janet
Black, Margaret Puckett, Michael Bell.
        p. cm.
     Includes bibliographical references and index.
     ISBN 0-675-20673-1
     1. Child development. 2. Infants—Development. 3. Child psychology. I.
Puckett, Margaret. II. Bell, Michael, (date). III. Title.
HQ767.9.B56   1992
305.23′1—dc20   91-18570

Printing: 2 3 4 5 6 7 8 9   Year: 2 3 4 5

Photo credits: p. 11 by Bettman Newsphotos; pp. 64, 73, 95, 106, 140, 144, 174, 312, 350 by Cathy Watterson; pp. 66, 351 by James Campbell; p. 92 by Vince Leo; p. 103 Courtesy Children's Hospital, Columbus, OH; pp. 114, 170, 180, 207, 390, 428, 473 by Gale Zucker; pp. 117, 124, 153 by Allen Zak; p. 190 by Andy Brunk/Macmillan; p. 204 by Rohn Engh/Sunrise Trinity Photos; p. 212 by Nancy Alexander; p. 232 by Michael Siluk; p. 269 by Randall Williams/Macmillan; pp. 318, 416, 483 by Gail Meese/Macmillan; pp. 324, 370, 371, 424, 446 by Jean-Claude Lejeune; p. 345 by Timothy O'Leary/Macmillan; p. 364 by Bruce Johnson/Macmillan; pp. 382, 464 by Macmillan; p. 406 by Ulrike Welsch; pp. 457, 485 by Paul Conklin; p. 461 by David Napravnik/Macmillan; and p. 479 by Charles Quinlan. All other photos supplied by the authors.

To those who helped us with our "roots and wings" . . .

Our parents
Wilson LaMar and Lelah Knisely Knecht
H. B. and Neutie L. Brous
Joseph Eston and Josephine Clark Bell

Our spouses
Clifford M. Black
J. Wesley Puckett
Candace K. Bell

Our children
Jonathan Andrew Black
John Wesley Puckett, Jr.
Dan William Puckett
Paula Puckett Jeffers
Daniel Eston Bell
Caitlin Jean Bell

And last but not least, our mentors
Martha L. King
Velma E. Schmidt
Marion Wilson Brous
Joe L. Frost

Preface

The earliest growth and development, that which occurs from conception through the eighth year, is dynamic. The progression from an energetic cell mass to a child of infinite characteristics and abilities at age eight is a story of such complexity and magnitude that few, if any, authors fully capture its totality.

We recognize the first eight years as being critical to later development and have attempted to present a "whole child" perspective and emphasize that understanding the development of infants and young children is a prerequisite to becoming a competent early childhood professional. In this context, we bridge theory and practice by juxtaposing research and theories of early growth and development with the role of the adult in facilitating this development.

In this text, the development of young children is presented from an ecological perspective, addressing the young child in the global context of family, school, community, and society. Major theories are interrelated with all aspects of development including physical/motor, psychosocial, cognition, language, and literacy. The long-term benefits of developmentally appropriate practice in the early years are presented. To further help the reader make the association between theory and practice, ongoing vignettes about two children appear throughout the chapters. A unique feature of this text is the interfacing of adult and professional development in the context of the developing child. Ethical responsibility in promoting developmentally appropriate practice and the role of advocacy are emphasized.

Organization of the Text

The text is divided into seven parts. Part One, An Overview of Early Childhood Development, outlines historical viewpoints and the evolution of the study of early childhood. Current theories of early childhood development and discussions of the importance of this information to the developing professional are also presented. Early and classical research in the fields of child development

and early education are described, as are various approaches and resources for studying young children.

Part Two, The Child's Life Begins, discusses the family before birth, with attention to educational, sociocultural, and economic antecedents to parenting. Prenatal development is described with emphasis on health, nutrition, and medical supervision of pregnancy. Childbirth and the family dynamics of the newborn are described.

Parts Three, Four, Five, and Six trace physical/motor, psychosocial, and cognitive/language/literacy development during infancy, ages 1 through 3, 4 through 5, and 6 through 8, respectively. This organization facilitates either chronological or topical discussion and study.

Part Seven, A Brief Look Beyond the Early Years, provides a brief overview of child development beyond the early years and projects the effects of early development upon later development. The last portion of this section focuses primarily on the developing professional's self-understanding, adult developmental patterns, and professional development, including dimensions of responsibility, developmentally appropriate practice, ethical behavior, interpersonal relationships, advocacy, and continuing study.

At the end of each chapter the reader will find Review Strategies/Activities which include relevant, hands-on suggestions. In addition, annotated bibliographies of timely topics are provided.

Angela and Jeremy

Two young children, Angela and Jeremy, are waiting in print to greet the reader. These two individuals are composites of many children we have known and will illustrate the uniqueness of growth and development in young children and their families. The readers are introduced to Angela and Jeremy at the moment of their births in Part Two.

Acknowledgments

The inspiration for this text is derived from the children, parents, teachers, and researchers who, over the years, have engendered our interest in the remarkable development of young children. Philosophical support for the text comes from the efforts and accomplishments of professional organizations that work to promote the well-being of children and the adults who nurture their development and learning. The contributions of these groups are acknowledged throughout this text.

We are grateful to many college and university students, in particular those who field-tested the text: Tanya Crossen, Brenda Smoot, Denise Bolin, Sharon Rothberg, Karen Anderson, Paula Layton, Teresa Martin, Paige Fletcher, Melody Kramer, Denise Butler, Christi Bisoni-Lais, Sue Jenkins, Tana Hansen, Stephanie Wheeler, Pam Beckemeyer, and Vanessa Sullivan. Special thanks to doctoral student Deborah Diffily for preliminary editing of the manuscript.

We also wish to thank the late Marion Wilson Brous, M.D., for serving as pediatric consultant, and Cathy Cowan, Ph.D., for suggesting resources from the field of psychology. We wish to acknowledge Rebecca Althous, R.N., M.S., of the Texas Department of Mental Health and Mental Retardation, Genetic Screening and Counseling Service for comments and suggestions on genetics and prenatal development. Appreciation is also extended to Sue Gainer, Child Care Dallas; Irene Rodriguez, Ph.D., Laredo State University; the late Velma Schmidt, Ed.D., University of North Texas, for critique of the manuscript for ethnic and cultural integrity. Gratitude is also expressed to Sandra Terrell, Ph.D., University of North Texas, for sharing expertise in speech production; Sharon Naylor, Ph.D., for her contributions regarding professional development; and Juane Heflin, Ph.D., for sharing her knowledge of the field of special education.

We are also indebted to those who reviewed the manuscript and provided valuable suggestions, many of which were incorporated into the text and helped refine its final form: Sandra Graham, Springfield Technical Community College; Barbara Harkness, San Bernardino Valley College; Craig Hart, Louisiana State University; Elizabeth Hasson, West Chester University of Pennsylvania; John Hranitz, Bloomsburg University of Pennsylvania; Jacqueline Paulson, The College of Staten Island/CUNY; Cosby Rogers, Virginia Polytechnic Institute; Edythe Schwartz, California State University/Sacramento; Deborah Smith, Appalachian State University; and Mary Knox Weir, Long Beach City College.

Last, we wish to acknowledge the constant support and encouragement of our editors—David Faherty, Linda Sullivan, Linda Peterson, and Jonathan Lawrence.

Janet Black
Margaret Puckett
Michael Bell

Contents in Brief

Contents

PART ONE

An Overview of Early Childhood Development

CHAPTER 1

There are two lasting gifts we can give our children—one is roots; the other is wings.

(Author unknown)

The What and Why of Early Childhood Development

After reading and studying this chapter, you will demonstrate comprehension by:

- Reflecting upon personal goals as a developing early childhood professional.
- Defining early childhood development.
- Stating the importance of understanding early childhood development.
- Outlining the historical viewpoints of childhood.
- Describing the evolution of early childhood development study.
- Outlining the current theories in early childhood development.

If you are reading this book, you at some time or another must have noticed young children and found them interesting, perhaps even fascinating. Just where and when did *your* interest in young children begin? Perhaps it was while babysitting, helping in classrooms, counseling at summer camps, or parenting your own children. Wherever it was, did you notice young children's general zest for life? Did you find their insatiable curiosity intriguing? Did you find some of their perceptions of the world quite different from yours and at times humorous? Did you receive inner satisfaction in helping young children learn or in providing security and nurturance in their times of need? If you said "yes" to some of these questions, you are like many others who have chosen to become early childhood professionals.

The Early Childhood Development Profession

Professionals—individuals who have internalized the knowledge base of their particular field and can implement this knowledge in appropriate practice.

Developmentally appropriate—pertains to (1) age appropriateness, the universal and predictable patterns of growth and development which occur in children from birth through age eight; and (2) individual appropriateness, the individual rates and patterns of physical/motor, psychosocial, cognition, language and literacy development, personality and learning style, and family and cultural background of each young child.

At-risk—Children who have been or are in prebirth or after-birth environments which do not promote typical physical/motor, psychosocial, cognitive, language, and literacy development.

Low-risk—Children who have been and continue to be in settings which facilitate normal physical/motor, psychosocial, cognitive, language, and literacy development.

Professionals learn the knowledge base of their particular field. This knowledge base coupled with practice in the field facilitates the development of competent practitioners and professionals.

Becoming a competent early childhood professional begins with learning about the growth and development of young children. The idea that anyone can teach young children is no longer viable for several reasons.

First, within the last 25 to 30 years a substantial body of knowledge has been added to the previous study of young children, which had its beginning in the late 1700s. This information suggests that young children's development, particularly in the area of cognition, is quite different from that of older children and adults. Therefore, teachers who work with young children need to know how they develop and learn so that **developmentally appropriate** learning environments can be provided. Currently, most of the 50 states require teachers who work with young children to have specialized training in early childhood development and related areas. The National Association for the Education of Young Children (NAEYC) has developed guidelines for the training of teachers who work with young children. These *Early Childhood Teacher Education Guidelines* were formally adopted by the National Council for the Accreditation of Teacher Education (NCATE) in 1982. These standards for teacher preparation are based upon the following premise:

The professional foundations and instructional knowledge areas provide candidates with theoretical and research knowledge and practical skills in:

1. Human development through the life span, with special emphasis on cognitive, language, physical, social and emotional development, both typical and atypical, from birth through age eight.
2. Historical, philosophical, psychological and social foundations in Early Childhood Education. (Brady et al., 1982, p. 4)

A second reason for the recognition of the importance of training for those who work with young children arises from the results of longitudinal studies on various early childhood programs for **at-risk** children (Lazar & Darlington, 1982; Schweinhart & Weikart, 1985). These studies indicate that quality educational experiences during the early years of life have long-term benefits both in terms of human potential and in cost to school systems and society in general. These successful programs had a planned curriculum implemented by trained teachers. At present, well over half of the states are providing prekindergarten programs for at-risk children. **Low-risk** children also benefit from quality early education (Larsen & Robinson, 1989). Thus, there is growing recognition that quality programs are achieved through developmentally appropriate curriculum, that is, curriculum based upon knowledge of how young children develop and learn, and implemented by trained teachers.

A third reason for increased attention to the qualifications of teachers of young children relates to change in economic patterns and the evolving nature of family structure. The necessity for more than one income to meet family

Becoming a competent early childhood professional begins with learning about the growth and development of young children.

economic needs and the increased number of single parent families have created a demand for the care and education of many young children, including infants and toddlers, in settings outside the home. Many parents now need quality programs with trained teachers for their children, and are becoming increasingly aware of the importance of quality in their children's early experiences. They are selecting environments for their children with greater attention and asking if programs have been accredited by NAEYC (1984).

A fourth reason for the emphasis upon the training of teachers of young children arises from the growing public awareness of the importance of the early years in the learning process. Many well-intentioned adults, due to their lack of training in early childhood development, incorrectly assume that education in the early years needs to emphasize more formal learning experiences usually reserved for older children. Because of the demand for so many early childhood classrooms, there are not enough trained teachers available. Unfortunately, young children, at times, are in settings which are **developmentally inappropriate** because the teacher lacks training in working with young children. A number of state, regional, and national organizations have attempted to encourage broader public awareness of developmentally appropriate learning environments through media presentations and position statements. The National Association for the Education of Young Children has developed two pub-

Developmentally inappropriate—pertains to adult expectations which are not age-appropriate or individually appropriate for children from birth through age eight.

lications to meet this need, *Developmentally Appropriate Practice in Early Childhood Programs Serving Children from Birth Through Age 8* (1987), and *Guidelines for Appropriate Curriculum Content and Assessment in Programs Serving Children Ages 3 Through 8* (1992). (See the Further Reading section in Chapter 2 for more information.)

The growing recognition of the unique nature of young children's development and of the importance of the early years in terms of lifelong productivity has created a great demand for trained early childhood professionals. It is the goal of this text to provide you with the necessary background information to develop into a competent early childhood professional.

Since much information on early childhood development is relatively recent and since early childhood professionals are in limited numbers, it is important to remember that the information in this text is important not only for providing appropriate educational and developmental experiences for young children, but also for educating other adults such as parents, teachers, directors, administrators, and policy-makers about developmentally appropriate experiences for young children. Working with young children means being in a position of *power*, power in facilitating the learning and development of young children. Working with young children also means being in a position of *responsibility*, responsibility for providing developmentally appropriate experiences to facilitate the maximum potential of each child. The authors hope this text encourages the appropriate and wise use of this power and responsibility.

Definition of Early Childhood Development

Early childhood development—the study of the physical/motor, psychosocial, cognitive, language, and literacy development in children, prebirth through age eight.

Early childhood development is the study of how children from prebirth through age eight grow and develop in the physical/motor, psychosocial, and cognitive/language and literacy domains. For convenience, this book will discuss the various domains separately. Nevertheless, it should be noted that development is interactive and that development in one area affects development or behavior in another area. This text also recognizes the uniqueness of each individual. In other words, while the pattern of development is generally the same for all children, the rate may vary from child to child, and from one developmental area to another.

Finally, this book acknowledges the multicultural nature of our society. Therefore, attention will be given to the diverse behaviors and development of children in early childhood settings whose presence contributes to the richness of those classroom environments.

The Importance of Understanding Early Childhood Development

There are several reasons why it is important to know about early childhood development. First, a knowledge of growth and development in the early years

All children are unique in their development.

can facilitate your self-understanding. Second, the knowledge of early childhood development by parents and professionals can facilitate the optimum growth and learning in young children. Finally, it is important to recognize that learning about early childhood development is an ongoing process.

Facilitating Self-Understanding

It is generally recognized that the experiences during the early years have an impact on later life. Learning about young children's development and the effect of this development years later can provide the opportunity for adults who wish to work with young children to do some perceptive reflection about their own experiences and development as a young child. Tapping back into your early life history can help you get in touch with feelings and experiences which are a part of the lives of young children. This increased or reawakened awareness of what it is like to be a young child can serve to foster more empathetic and appropriate reactions to young children's behavior.

Facilitating Optimal Development and Learning in Young Children

A knowledge of how young children develop and learn provides information that helps teachers and parents make informed decisions about what to do in particular situations. Appropriate responses to young children's behaviors and learning serve to encourage children's development in positive ways. Knowing how to encourage and foster healthy self-concepts and autonomy in young children facilitates optimal development and learning. Likewise, a knowledge of how young children develop and learn helps early childhood professionals recognize atypical development and know when to seek help from other professionals.

Recognizing that Learning about Early Childhood Development is an Ongoing Process

While this text can provide the foundation for learning about the behavior and development of young children, competent early childhood professionals continue to discover new information about young children throughout their professional careers. As teachers work with young children, patterns of behavior or reasons for behavior become apparent. Early childhood professionals become more skilled at dealing with and recognizing atypical patterns of behavior over a period of time. Professionals with decades of experience are often quick to say that they continue to learn about young children. Thus, learning about the development and behavior of young children is an ongoing process.

The Roots of Early Childhood Development and Study

Recognition of the early years as separate and different from other phases of life is relatively recent. Likewise, the responsibility of parents in the rearing of young children and the importance of the need for quality care and education are also relatively new concepts. The study of young children in depth and breadth did not begin until the early years of the 20th century. A brief discussion from the Western cultural perspective of the historical perceptions of children, the role of parents, and the evolving nature of the study of young children will facilitate understanding of the current status of young children and of early childhood development.

Historical Viewpoints of Young Children and of the Role of Parents

DeMause (1974) gathered a team of researchers who examined the visual arts and various written materials to determine prevalent attitudes about young children throughout the history of Western societies. Their analysis suggests

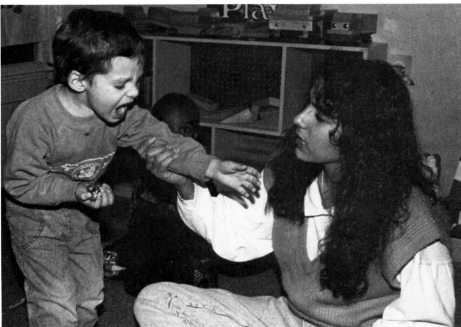

Knowledge of how children develop and learn helps parents and teachers make in-formed decisions about what to do in particular situations, such as crying or tem-per tantrums.

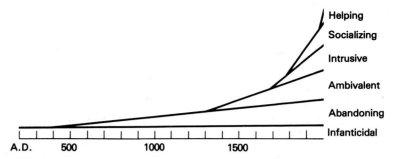

FIGURE 1.1
DeMause's child rearing modes categorize adult attitudes toward children throughout history. (From *Foundations of Psychohistory* (p. 61) by Lloyd deMause, 1982, New York: Psychohistory Press. Copyright 1982 by Lloyd deMause. Reprinted by permission.)

that "the history of childhood is a nightmare from which we only have recently begun to 'awake' " (deMause, 1974, p. 1). As shown in Figure 1.1, deMause categorized the findings into six historical periods from antiquity to the present. It should be noted that these findings describe generalized patterns and that there were exceptions to these parental attitudes and behaviors.

Infanticidal: B.C. to the 4th Century A.D.   During this period in history, there was apparently no conception of childhood as we know it today. Children, particularly the firstborn males, were sometimes sacrificed to the gods. Infanticide was also a common practice with females and later-born males. At times, healthy abandoned infants were rescued, mutilated, and then put on the streets for the purpose of begging. Unhealthy children were usually destroyed at birth. Parents had no concept of responsibility for their children. They routinely killed healthy children by abandonment in the countryside or in latrines, drowning, or enclosing in large vessels. The high rate of infant mortality is evidence that parents placed little or no value on the lives of young children. Other explanations for this lack of parental responsibility include population control, economic need, or that parents simply did not want to be bothered.

Abandoning: 4th to 13th Centuries.   During this period in history, there appears to be a shift in the attitudes of parents regarding their responsibility toward their children. Parents gradually begin to accept the right of children to live. Nevertheless, actual parental care and nurturance of children was not a universal practice. Many children were abandoned to wet nurses, foster families, monasteries, and nunneries. Children who were not physically abandoned by their parents, however, were often abandoned emotionally through lack of attention and severe neglect.

Ambivalent: 14th to 17th Centuries.   During the time of the Renaissance or Great Awakening many new ideas, including the concept of childhood, began to emerge. Parents assumed a closer relationship with their children. They began to express love and in some instances to appreciate the joy children could bring to their lives. However, children were also viewed as inherently evil. One common practice of "driving the devil" out of children was to purge them with enemas. These conflicting perceptions of children during this period produced generations of ambivalent parents.

During the 1600s, English philosopher John Locke began to speak out, promoting a more compassionate attitude toward young children. He encouraged parents to stop the commonly accepted practice of swaddling their infants—tightly binding them with strips of cloth—into the second year of life. Parents believed that swaddling would keep children from tearing off their ears, touching their genitals, or walking like animals. Swaddling also kept children immobile and easy to care for as they could be conveniently hung on pegs in homes and business establishments. Swaddled babies were sometimes used for

In the past, children have been viewed as miniature adults. This perception is still in evidence today.

sport and amusement. DeMause (1974) tells of how the brother of King Henry IV of France was dropped and killed while being "customarily" tossed.

Locke advocated dressing children in loose-fitting clothes, allowing them to play, and avoiding physical punishment. The efforts of Locke and others, coupled with the influence of new religious thought, seemed to encourage a new compassionate concern for children. Thus, these ideas encouraged the notion that the early years of life are special and important.

Intrusive: The 18th Century.

During the eighteenth century, there was a growing acceptance of the importance of the early years in the preparation for the life hereafter. Children were perceived as born with sin, so only through harsh and vigorous training could they be made acceptable for the kingdom of God. It now became the responsibility of the parent to "train a child in the ways of the Lord." Children were severely punished for their transgressions. However, punishment also occurred by a new method, guilt induction. There are accounts of children taken to hangings and to view rotting corpses and being told, "If you are not good, the same thing will happen to you."

Toilet learning involved severe punishment for the young child's lack of bowel and bladder control. Children were also sent to anti-masturbation sanitoria, made to wear spiked cages, or given circumcisions or clitoridectomies without anesthetic for exploring their genitals. These harsh measures reflected the puritanical view that sexuality is inherently evil.

Some of the more positive developments during the 1700s included the development of pediatrics as a specialized branch of medicine. This, coupled with the general improvement in child care, greatly reduced the rate of infant mortality. Nevertheless, pediatrician William Buchan suggested that one-half of all of the human species died in infancy because of improper management or neglect (deMause, 1974, p. 32).

While the Puritans viewed children as inherently evil, another idea regarding the nature of young children also emerged in the 1700s. Jean Jacques Rousseau (1712–78) wrote in his famous book *Emile* (1762/1955) that children are not born evil, but that the nature of the environment contributes to the relative goodness or evil in children. Much of what Rousseau espoused in *Emile* is considered valid for early childhood development today—the importance of play, the primacy of direct experience and discovery learning, the freedom to explore, supportive adults, and humane treatment.

Socializing: 19th to mid-20th Century.

Rousseau's concept that the first five years of life are unique paved the way for the development of new approaches to educating young children. The idea of educational programs for young children came at a time of great change in society. The Industrial Revolution and vast migration moved many families from rural to urban settings. Parents working in factories were not available to care for young children. Increasing concern was expressed for children on the streets and for children forced to work long hours in unhealthy industrial environments. As a result nursery schools, kindergartens, and the public school system were created to help protect and socialize young children. This socialization model is the source of many of the current ideas regarding child rearing, from the psychoanalytical to the behavioral. These ideas reflect the perception that young children need continuous training and guidance so that they can become socialized. During the later part of this period, abuse of children began to be considered inappropriate and the first child abuse laws appeared.

Helping: Mid-20th Century.   DeMause suggests that the Helping mode is just beginning. Characteristics of this phase include the realization that good parenting skills do not develop without education, enormous time, energy, and emotional maturity. Effective parenting requires the full commitment of both parents in the child's daily life. Some results of these new ideas include parent training seminars on how to parent effectively, the increasing availability of parenting literature, and the decisions of some persons not to have children or to limit the size of their families. DeMause proposes that the role of the parents is to facilitate children's development. He also suggests that "the child knows better than the parents what it needs at each stage of life" (deMause, 1974, p. 52). Just as Rousseau's statements about the nature of young children seemed outlandish in the 1700s, this notion may seem radical to the general population today.

Through true understanding of young children's behavior and development, parents can better understand and comprehend the needs the child is expressing. Adults tend to attribute bad motives to behavior that is not understood. Rather than punishing the child for his developmentally appropriate behavior, parents who know early childhood development understand the reasons for behavior and thereby can react and provide help and support. An example could be the 2-year-old who has a temper tantrum. Knowledgeable adults know that temper tantrums are a natural and appropriate mode of behavior for children around this age. They realize that it is necessary for young children to begin to assert their independence and express their own ideas. Child development research suggests that overly harsh punishment of young children can pave the way for either extremely passive older children and adults, or can set the stage for rebellion (Maccoby & Levin, 1957). Understanding temper tantrums as a normal and necessary part of development encourages the parent to accept the behavior, to not feel threatened by the child's assertive behavior, and to respond appropriately rather than overreacting in a harsh and punitive manner. Preparing children for a change, providing them with choices, redirecting their attention, and calmly empathizing with their distress are all considered appropriate helping strategies for handling temper tantrums.

DeMause concludes that while we have come a long way, some parents still function in one or more of the earlier stages. Reports in the media tell of children who are abandoned, killed, or physically abused and neglected. Some parents continue to psychologically manipulate and emotionally neglect their children. *One of the major roles of the early childhood professional is to help parents understand young children's development and appropriate parenting techniques.*

Evolution of the Study of Young Children

As mentioned earlier, John Locke (1632–1704) was one of the first people to advocate more humane treatment of young children. He also was one of the first to suggest that the environmental experience of the child may influence the development of the child's knowledge. Locke described the newborn's mind as a *tabula rasa,* an "empty slate," upon which knowledge is written based on children's sensory experiences in their environment.

In 1774 Johann Pestalozzi (1746–1827) published a study of his son that was the first serious attention given to the nature of development during the early years of life. Nearly a century later, Charles Darwin (1809–82) published a day-to-day record of the development of his young son. Darwin's publication of *The Origin of the Species* (1859) had far-reaching effects upon many aspects of knowledge, including the study of children.

As a biologist, Darwin took a trip to the Galapagos Islands in the South Pacific where he collected birds and animals that were virtually unknown and therefore had not been classified according to any designated species. Darwin used these birds and animals to disprove the idea of a fixed nature of species. His development of the scientific method and conceptualization that the world was dynamic and not static set the stage for the scientific study of children.

Darwin's notion that animals adapted to their particular environment over time caused biologists, psychologists, and others to begin studying the adaptive characteristics of humans. One of these psychologists, G. Stanley Hall (1846–1924), was instrumental in implementing the scientific method to study the change and development of children. In 1893, Hall published *The Contents of Children's Minds.* This book was one of the first texts to be used in colleges and universities for training students who wanted to learn about young children. Another of Hall's important contributions to the study of child development was the establishment of the first child development research journal, *The Journal of Genetic Psychology.* Some of Hall's more illustrious students included Arnold Gesell, who developed norms regarding the physical maturation of children; John Dewey, whose democratic ideas concerning the learning process created major educational reform; and Lewis Terman, who developed the idea of the intelligence quotient. Hall's international reputation and influence enabled him to convince Sigmund Freud to come to Clark University to lecture on psychoanalysis.

After World War I, Lawrence K. Frank (1890–1968) was influential in obtaining foundation monies to establish various institutes to study child development. The Society for Research in Child Development was founded in 1933. During the World War II years, child development research and study declined. With the conclusion of World War II, however, there was a substantial increase in the number of investigations concerning the nature of children. This intense interest in learning about young children continues today.

The Nature of a Theory

In the area of early childhood development, there are a number of individuals who have proposed ideas or **theories** that attempt to explain in an organized or systematic manner how young children develop and learn. The personal backgrounds of these theorists, as well as political and sociological events, often influence the development of ideas and the nature of research. At times, radical thinkers propose such new ideas that they change previous accepted theories. Rousseau is such an example. Thus, as new information is added, a theory may change. If research continues to support a theory, it will continue to be useful, but if new information does not support a theory, it will be modified or discarded.

Theories in Early Childhood Development

There are a number of theories that attempt to explain early childhood development. These include psychoanalytic, maturation, behaviorist, cognitive, and ecological systems. Some of these theories attempt to explain only one aspect of development, while others are more comprehensive. Attention to all theories can be helpful in providing information about the total development of children. The following sections provide an overview of the various theories that have influenced the body of information on early childhood development. In-depth discussion will be presented throughout the text.

Psychoanalytic, Psychosexual, Psychosocial, and Related Theories

Psychoanalytic theory attempts to explain the inner thoughts and feelings—at both the conscious and subconscious levels—that influence behavior (Freud, 1938). Sigmund Freud (1856–1939) laid the foundations for psychoanalytic or **psychosexual theory.** As a physician in Vienna specializing in nervous or mental conditions, he became intrigued with the problems adults were having that seemed to have begun in childhood. Freud developed a stage theory that suggested that there are certain drives and instincts that emerge at various times of development through various biological systems such as the mouth, the anus, and the sex organs. This theory is presently viewed as simplistic and too focused upon sexual feelings and erogenous zones. However, Freud's basic premise that children's early experiences can influence their later lives has remained viable.

Erik Erikson (1902–   ) built upon Freud's theories and studied with Freud's daughter, Anna. Erikson felt that Freud's exploration of sexuality as the main explanation for behavior was rather limiting. He thought that the broader social context of the child and family was also influential upon behavior and incorporated this idea into his **psychosocial theory** (1963). Erikson also

Theories—*ideas that are organized in a systematic manner based upon observations or other kinds of evidence and are used to explain and predict the behaviors and development of young children, older children, and adults.*

Psychoanalytic theory—*the ideas of personality development as presented in Freud's psychosexual and Erikson's psychosocial theories.*

Psychosexual theory—*Freud's theory that suggests that sexual drives play an important role in personality development.*

Psychosocial theory—*Erikson's theory that argues that social interactions are more important than sexual drives in personality development.*

developed a stage theory but extended his theory to encompass the total life span.

Erikson provided the impetus for a number of individuals to focus their thought upon the nature of adult developmental stages. This fairly recent information will be discussed in more detail in Chapter 18 and should provide you with information about your own continued development as an adult and that of other adults with whom you will live and work. For a description of Erikson's development stages and a comparison with Freud's, see Table 1.1. Erikson's stages as they relate to young children will be discussed in depth in chapters 6, 9, 12, and 15.

Two contemporary theorists whose ideas are rooted in Freud and Erikson are Carl Rogers and Abraham Maslow. Rogers and Maslow believe that individuals have the capacity to be creative in their decisions about life. Therefore, life is not viewed as determined by negative early events, as in Freud's theory, but can be changed or influenced by the individual's choice.

Self-actualiza-tion—according to Maslow, the process of having basic physical and so-cial/emotional needs met so that individuals can be-come creative, con-tributing members of society and feel positive about themselves.

Unlike Freud, Maslow studied people with healthy personalities. Maslow developed the notion of **self-actualization,** the process of individual growth resulting in the culmination of a fulfilled person (Maslow, 1970). Maslow suggests that feelings and aspirations must be considered in order to understand behavior. Self-actualized persons are continually in the process of "becoming," are in touch with and accepting of reality, are confident yet aware of their limitations, and have commitment to a meaningful project or goal. In order for self-actualization to occur, Maslow suggests that there are certain needs which must be met. These needs are in hierarchical order.

Carl Rogers (1902–87) has notions similar to Maslow's, including the importance of developing a positive self-concept and the interaction of development and environment (Rogers, 1961). Rogers' and Maslow's ideas will be discussed in more detail in chapters 9, 12, and 15.

Evaluation of Psychoanalytic and Related Theories.   Some positive aspects of psychoanalytical and related theories include:

1. Psychosexual theory was the first theory to examine in detail the nature of early experience as an explanation for adult behavior (Freud).

TABLE 1.1
A comparison of Freud's psychosexual and Erikson's psychosocial stages of development

Freud's 5 Stages and Related Conflicts		Approximate Ages	Erikson's 8 Stages
Oral	Weaning	Birth–$1\frac{1}{2}$	Basic Trust vs. Mistrust
Anal	Toilet Learning	$1\frac{1}{2}$–3	Autonomy vs. Shame/Doubt
Phallic	Oedipal and Electra	3–5	Initiative vs. Guilt
Latency	—	$5\frac{1}{2}$–12	Industry vs. Inferiority
Genital	—	Adolescence	Identity vs. Role Confusion
—	—	Young Adulthood	Intimacy vs. Isolation
—	—	Middle Adulthood	Generativity vs. Stagnation
—	—	Late Adulthood	Ego Integrity vs. Despair

Source: Erikson (1963) and Freud (1938).

2. Freud also helped people to understand that certain behaviors such as thumbsucking and masturbation are not bad but are normal behaviors.
3. Erikson expanded upon Freud and included the social experiences in home, school and community as important in development (psychosocial theory).
4. Erikson also introduced the notion that development does not just stop at the conclusion of adolescence, but is a lifelong process.
5. Freud's deterministic view was modified by Maslow's idea that individuals can change or have control over their lives (self-actualization).
6. The influence of the environment on behavior and development and of behavior and development on the environment suggests the importance of the interactive process (Rogers).

Some criticisms of psychoanalytic and related theories include:

1. Internal forces governing libidinal energy (Freud) and self-actualization (Maslow) cannot be seen or measured.
2. Some of the various stages described by Freud, particularly the oedipal and latency, do not apply to all cultures.

Examples of Psychoanalytic and Related Theories.

- **Psychosexual**—Jason's parents used harsh and punitive measures during toilet learning. His rebellious nature as an adolescent was attributed to the severity of his experience during the Anal Stage.
- **Psychosocial**—Allison's father was sent to Vietnam when she was 18 months old. Her mother then developed a serious illness which required numerous hospitalizations. Allison was cared for by a variety of friends and relatives. When she became an adolescent Allison developed agoraphobia, the fear of being in open places. Allison's reluctance to attend school and engage in other typical teenage activities outside her home was attributed to her basic mistrust, which developed due to the unstable environment of her early years (Basic trust vs. mistrust, Erikson).
- **Related Theories**—Many schools across the United States now offer free meals to students from low-income families. These programs are based upon the realization that children who lack nutritious meals and are hungry cannot perform well in school. One of these programs, Head Start, also provides low-income children with medical and dental evaluations. (Basic physical needs must be met first before learning can occur, Maslow).

Maturation Theory

Arnold Gesell (1880–1961) was a student of G. Stanley Hall. Under Hall he learned much about the use of the scientific method in child study. Gesell founded the Clinic of Child Development at Yale University in 1911. There he and his associates observed thousands of children in order to begin to chart the **norms** or typical behavior in the areas of social interaction, physical, motor, and vocabulary development. Gesell attributed the changes in development to a biological process influenced by heredity called **maturation** (Gesell & Ama-

Norms—average ages of important developmental behaviors or average scores on tests, which according to statistical procedures should be based upon large samples, representative of the whole population.

Maturation theory—usually refers to Gesell's theory that suggests that the patterns of growth and development are genetically predetermined and cannot be influenced by environmental stimulation or training to any great degree.

truda, 1941). Maturationists, unlike some of the other theorists, give little if any support to the role of the environment in influencing development and learning.

In 1950, colleagues of Arnold Gesell founded the Gesell Institute of Human Development. The Institute has been influential in applying Gesell's maturation theory to the concept of readiness for learning. Training public school personnel in child development, child observation, and screening for school readiness has been accomplished primarily through the use of the Gesell School Readiness Assessment. This instrument is used on prekindergarten and kindergarten children to determine readiness for kindergarten or first grade (Bredekamp & Shepard, 1989; Charlesworth, 1989). For those children diagnosed as not ready, it is suggested that they enter a prekindergarten program, delay entry into kindergarten or first grade, or enter a transition program between kindergarten and entry into first grade. Recent school reform and pressure from some parents have created more formal academic expectations on kindergarten and first grade children. Chapter 2 will provide more discussion regarding the influence of maturation theory and the appropriateness of readiness tests in determining the placement of young children in various educational settings.

Evaluation of Maturationist Theory.   A positive aspect of maturation theory includes the development of norms for growth and behavior that provides guidelines to help parents and early childhood professionals determine whether children's behavior was typical or atypical. Some concerns regarding maturation theory include:

1. The norms established for various developmental behaviors caused some parents and early childhood professionals to become unduly worried about their children's somewhat slow development.
2. The predictive validity, or high percentage of correct placements and a low percentage of incorrect placements, based on the use of the Gesell School Readiness Assessment has yet to be determined (Bradley, 1985; Kaufman, 1985; Naglieri, 1985; Waters, 1985).
3. The assessment discriminates against children whose first language is not English. Some non-English speaking children acquire English rapidly, but these children often remain in inappropriate placements because their assessment took place when they were not proficient in English (Medina & Neill, 1988).
4. Research on the **reliability** and **validity** of reading readiness tests indicates that these measures are not always true indicators of reading ability (Durkin, 1966; Goodman, 1980; Teale, Hiebert, & Chittenden, 1987).
5. Recent research on the literacy development of young children suggests that many of the earlier ideas of readiness for reading are no longer valid (Teale, Hiebert, & Chittenden, 1987).

Examples of Maturationist Theory.

- Lisa, at age three, could zip, tie her shoes, and even diaper her baby brother. Her friend Jonathan did not learn to tie his shoes until age seven, even though his mother, a former kindergarten teacher, provided him with patient instruction and many opportunities to develop fine motor skills.

Reliability—the consistency with which various research methods produce the same results or relatively similar results for each individual from one administration to the next.

Validity—the degree to which an instrument or procedure measures what it is intended to measure.

• One identical twin was given practice in learning to climb stairs. The other identical twin was not. The trained twin learned to climb the stairs more quickly. However, the untrained twin learned to climb the stairs on her own within two weeks of the trained twin (Gesell & Thompson, 1929). This study indicates that identical twins will learn skills at approximately the same time and that when children are biologically ready they can learn skills within a very short period of time. Thus, attempts at training to develop various skills can be considered a waste of time.

Behavioral Theory

Behaviorists concentrate on observable behavior, rather than examining and explaining the internal processes of behavior. They do not classify behavior into stages but suggest that learning is a gradual and continuous process. Experience is considered most important and heredity is given little or no attention. **Behavioral theory** is generally classified into three types—classical conditioning, operant conditioning, and social learning theory.

Behavioral theory—*the theory that emphasizes the importance of directly observable behavior as influenced by the environment rather than genetic factors or other unobservable forces such as motivation.*

Classical Conditioning Theory.   The principles of **classical conditioning theory** were developed by Russian Ivan P. Pavlov (1849–1936). He paired two events, the placing of meat powder on a dog's tongue and the ringing of a bell, a conditioned stimulus. Over a period of time, these repeated events created a conditioned response of salivation. In other words, the stimulus of the sound of the bell alone caused the dog to salivate even if no meat powder was present. The dog's association of the meat powder with the sound of the bell stimulated a response.

Classical conditioning theory—*the first idea regarding behavior theory, based upon Pavlov's experiment in which repeated pairing of two events conditioned the same response to either event.*

In this country, E. L. Thorndike conducted numerous animal experiments and is considered the "father of behaviorism." However, John B. Watson (1878–1958) was the person responsible for implementing the ideas of classical conditioning. Watson's famous experiment with an eleven-month-old infant, Albert, was used to justify the notion that certain behavioral responses could be created through conditioning. Watson believed he could take a baby at random and produce "any type of specialist I might select—doctor, lawyer, artist, merchant-chief, and yes beggar-man and thief, regardless of his talents, penchants, tendencies, abilities, vocations and race of his ancestors" (Watson, 1928, p. 104).

In Watson's experiment (Watson & Rayner, 1920), Albert was shown a white rat at the same time a loud noise was made. Initially, Albert was not afraid of the rat but was distressed at the loud noise. Eventually, Albert's association of the loud noise with the rat produced a fear of many white furry objects such as his mother's muff, rabbits, and Santa's beard. Unfortunately, Albert left the hospital where this experiment was conducted before Watson could **extinguish** his fear.

Extinguish—*stopping a behavior or response by not reinforcing it over a period of time.*

While Watson is generally associated with the Albert experiment, his notions on child-rearing were widespread and are still evident in the behaviors of some parents today. Watson suggested that showing affection for young children would spoil them. He advocated the feeding of infants every four hours, advised parents against rocking their children, and suggested that a handshake was more appropriate than a good night hug and kiss (Watson, 1928).

Operant Conditioning Theory.   A later proponent of behaviorism was Harvard psychologist B. F. Skinner. He explained Watson's views in a well-known book, *Walden Two* (1948). Skinner's thoughts and experiments expanded on classical conditioning theory and evolved into the theory of **operant conditioning,** in which the operant is the voluntary action on the part of an individual. Desired behavior is reinforced or rewarded after the behavior occurs. It is expected that the reinforcement over a period of time will make the desired behavior more frequent. Punishment is used to decrease the frequency of undesirable behavior. However, Skinner felt that punishment is generally an ineffective way to control undesirable behavior. Instead, he suggested extinguishing behavior or ceasing to reinforce the behavior until it stops. Skinner and his wife decided to try this technique on their five-year-old daughter, Julie (Skinner, 1979). Skinner reported that it took a month or two to accomplish. At first, Julie would behave in ways that in the past would have brought her punishment and she watched her parents closely for their reactions. In time, the desired behaviors emerged. Skinner indicated that he and his wife found various reinforcement techniques more effective than punishment (Skinner, 1979, p. 279).

Operant conditioning—*Skinner's term for the voluntary change or modification in behavior as a result of reinforcement or punishment.*

Social Learning Theory.   **Social learning theory** is another adaptation on classical and operant conditioning. This theory emphasizes the importance of role models and significant adults in children's lives. Social learning theorists propose that children learn and imitate behaviors from people who are important to them, and that children do not always need reinforcement to learn. This theory was introduced in 1941 by Neil Miller and John Dollard in *Social Learning and Imitation.* However, Albert Bandura is the current leading proponent of social learning theory. His research (1965) demonstrated that children learn behavior from observation. In other words, learning is not dependent upon direct personal experience. In Bandura's classic research, two different groups of children observed two versions of a film where a large plastic inflatable doll called a "Bobo doll" was hit by an adult model. In one version the model's behavior was rewarded with adult praise, candy, and soft drinks. The second version concluded with another adult model hitting the first model with a rolled up newspaper. After viewing the films, the children who saw the version with the reward were more likely to engage in the imitation of aggressive behavior than the children who viewed the version where the model was punished. Bandura concluded that children learn from observing others. Whether they act on what they observe depends on the particular circumstances.

Social learning theory—*a behavioral theory that argues that learning can also occur through observing others, thus emphasizing the role modeling of other persons the child observes directly and in various types of media.*

Evaluation of Behaviorist Theory.   Some positive aspects of behavioral theory include:

1. Behavior can be observed. Therefore, it can be scientifically measured.

2. Behavioral theory attempts to be universal by explaining behaviors that are common to all cultures.
3. Behavioral theory provides guidelines for behavior management to parents and early childhood professionals.

Some criticisms regarding behavioral theory include:

1. Much of the behavioral theory is based upon animal studies that cannot always explain the behavior of humans.
2. Behavioral theory does not consider the influence of heredity.
3. Behavioral theory does not take into account individual free will, hopes, and aspirations.
4. Behavioral theory does not seek to determine the underlying reasons for behavior.
5. Behavioral management techniques may not work unless applied consistently over a substantial period of time.

Examples of Behavioral Theory.   Sometimes aspects of behavioral theory can produce unwanted effects. Following are two fairly common examples.

- Stanley and Carol Jones are the parents of a new baby. They are reluctant to pick up Timothy when he cries for fear that they may reinforce his crying. They have decided to let him "cry it out." What the Joneses fail to realize is that allowing the baby to cry for long periods of time actually reinforces the crying behavior. A more desirable procedure would be to try to determine the reasons (hunger, soiled diapers, gas, boredom, and so on) for Timothy's cries. Responding to a baby's cries within a reasonable period of time has other long-term benefits as well, which will be discussed in more detail in chapters 6 and 7.
- The Joneses take their children to the zoo. Michael, their oldest son, hits his sister for eating some of his popcorn. Mr. Jones takes Michael aside, gives him a swat on the behind and says, "How many times do I have to tell you, we don't hit other people?" Michael probably fails to see the logic in his father's reasoning. Physical punishment does not seem to be working with Michael, much to his father's dismay. Perhaps, Mr. Jones could change Michael's behavior if he used positive reinforcement or modeled appropriate behavior himself by not hitting Michael.

Cognitive Theory

Cognitive theory attempts to explain how young children think and process information. Jean Piaget (1896–1980) developed the major theory of cognition in child development. Piaget's theory eventually achieved recognition in the United States during the 1960s for several reasons. First, the insistence of the behaviorists on quantifiable research with large populations was beginning to be questioned. Second, Piaget's theory on the nature of how young children

Cognitive theory—*the theory that explains the development of learning in terms of how children think and process information, usually associated with Piaget and more recently, the information processing theorists.*

learn came into acceptance during a time of great interest in the development of cognitively oriented experiences for young children. Finally, Piaget's theory readily explained what perceptive parents and teachers of young children had already observed, that young children's processing of knowledge is different from that of older children and adults.

Piaget worked in France to establish norms on Binet's Intelligence Test. In that process, he observed that many young children gave similar incorrect answers. Piaget began to wonder if there were different stages in the development of cognition. Using the clinical interview, Piaget questioned children to determine their thought processes. This approach, coupled with the detailed observations of his own three children, provided the basis for Piaget's theory (Piaget, 1952).

Piaget suggests that thinking develops sequentially in four stages: sensorimotor, preoperational, concrete operations, and formal operations. Table 1.2 provides an overview of each stage. The first three stages will be more thoroughly discussed later in this book.

Piaget grew up around Lake Neuchatel in Switzerland. He became intrigued with the differences in behavior in mollusks at various locations around the lake. This fascination created a lifelong interest in the relationship of the effects of the environment upon living organisms and their subsequent adaptations to the environment.

Piaget proposed that children order their interactions with the environment and then adapt to or change this order if they have new insights or information. The ordering of thought was termed **schemata. Assimilation** represents the child's attempts to fit new ideas and concepts into existing schemata. **Accommodation** is the change in schemata that a child makes as a result of new information. As children grow older and have more experience with their en-

Schemata—mental concepts or categories; plural for schema (Piaget).

Assimilation—the process of incorporating new motor or conceptual learning into existing schemata (Piaget).

Accommodation— the cognitive process by which patterns of thought (schemata) and related behaviors are modified to conform to new information or experience (Piaget).

TABLE 1.2
Piaget's stages of cognitive development

Stage	Approximate Age	Characteristics
Sensorimotor Period	Birth to 2 years	Infant develops concepts regarding object identity and object permanence
Preoperational Period	2 to 7 years	Reliant on personal perceptions of the environment; egocentric thought
Concrete Operations	7 to 11 years	Children can focus on more than one attribute through manipulation of concrete objects
Formal Operations	11 years through adulthood	Abstract reasoning; hypothesis testing/experimentation, and critical thinking.

vironment their **equilibration** or balance in thinking is often disturbed. Piaget says that this dissatisfaction or **disequilibrium** with present ideas motivates the child to accommodate new information and change schemata. An example of this process is shown in Figure 1.2.

While Piaget claims that cognitive development influences language development, another theorist, Lev Vygotsky (1899–1934) suggests that thought and language eventually converge into meaning, particularly in those cultures where verbal interaction is important and verbal language is used for problem solving (Vygotsky, 1962).

Recently, Vygotsky has received considerable attention in the United States. Vygotsky was a Russian psychologist who produced some major works during a relatively short life. Two of his books, *Thought and Language* (1962) and *Mind and Society* (1978) have been translated into English.

Much of Vygotsky's research looked at children's ability to acquire a concept for a set of characteristics regarding color, shape, and size. He determined that when children are provided with words, they are better able to form concepts than when they are not provided with words.

As young children interact with others, they observe action, become familiar with objects, and through the labeling of these objects and actions by older children and adults learn the **tools of the world.** These tools are organized over a period of time into **concept clusters** or thought categories. Eventually, these categories become internalized representations or **signs.** Vygotsky's ideas will be discussed further throughout this text, particularly in the areas of oral language and literacy development.

Equilibration—the process of establishing a balance in thinking (Piaget).

Disequilibrium—the imbalance in thinking causing the child to assimilate or accommodate (Piaget).

Tools of the world—the language and objects of the external world (Vygotsky, 1978).

Concept clusters—organization of the tools of the world into categories or patterns of thinking (Vygotsky).

Signs—internalized representations which are later associated with tools of the world (Vygotsky).

Sometimes you just have to accommodate!

FIGURE 1.2
As young children absorb new information, they often find it necessary to change or accommodate their initial concepts. (From *Piaget's Theory of Cognitive and Affective Development* by Barry J. Wadsworth. Copyright © 1979 by Longman Publishing Group. Reprinted by permission of Longman Publishing Group.)

Information processing theory—*a theory of cognitive development that suggests that the mind is similar to the information processing system of a computer, and unlike Piaget, emphasizes similarities of the thinking of children and adults.*

In the early 1970s dissatisfaction with Piaget's ideas led to the development of the **information processing theory.** This theory suggests that a child's mind operates on the same principle as a computer (Newell & Simon, 1972). This theoretical approach will also be discussed in chapters 7, 10, 13, and 16.

Evaluation of Cognitive Theory.   Some positive aspects of cognitive theory include:

1. Understanding how young children develop in their thinking helps parents and early childhood professionals know how to respond to young children's thinking and behavior.
2. Knowing how young children learn provides guidelines for parents and early childhood professionals to create appropriate learning environments.

Some criticisms commonly expressed regarding cognitive theory include:

1. Much of Piaget's research was done on small populations and cannot be applied to children from all cultures.
2. The various internal forces which are often part of Piaget's cognitive theory, such as assimilation and accommodation, cannot be scientifically measured.
3. Piaget's findings, in certain contexts, appear not to be true. This information will be discussed in later chapters on cognitive development.

Examples of Cognitive Theory.

- Two-year-old Jonathan, his parents, and neighbors are enjoying a Memorial Day picnic in the backyard. The adults happen to notice that the Goodyear blimp is overhead for a sports event. Jonathan observes the blimp, points to the sky and says, "Truck, truck." He is obviously assimilating the blimp into his truck schema.
- Aaron writes the following story to go with his painting: "misnacsiyaloeslog". As you can see in the photo, Aaron's writing is not just a string of letters. Rather, he has written a two-sentence story: "My snake is yellow. He is long." Vygotsky would suggest that the appropriate teacher response to this emergent writing is not to correct but rather to analyze what Aaron's behavior is saying about his knowledge of written language. This analysis then provides direction for the teacher in encouraging Aaron's further development in written language.

Intrafamilial—*actions and behaviors within the immediate family.*

Extrafamilial—*actions and behaviors occurring outside the immediate family.*

Ecological systems theory—*the theory that argues that a variety of social systems influences the development of children. (Bronfenbrenner)*

Ecological Systems Theory

In the past, much of child development research has focused on parent-child interactions or **intrafamilial** processes. Urie Bronfenbrenner (1979, 1986) argues that the factors influencing development are much more complex, in that intrafamilial processes are affected by **extrafamilial** forces. He explains this idea in his **ecological systems theory** as represented in Figure 1.3.

Each of the four systems in this figure interacts with the others and all of them influence the child's development. The child is at the core of the four systems. The system closest to the child is called the *microsystem*. The micro-

Analysis of Aaron's writing indicates that he has written a two-sentence story: "My snake is yellow. He is long."

system focuses upon the roles, relationships, and experiences in the child's immediate environment. The *mesosystem* pertains to the interrelationships of various microsystem environments, such as home, school or child care center, neighborhood, and religious groups. The *exosystem* consists of formal and informal social groups which impact children in the microsystem. Formal groups would include the workplace of the parents, and legal and community services. Examples of informal social networks include friends of the parents, neighbors, and extended family. Mass media are also included as part of the exosystem. The fourth system, the *macrosystem* refers to the attitudes, values, customs, laws, regulations, and rules of the culture at large that impact the child.

Evaluation of Ecological Systems Theory.   Some positive aspects of ecological systems theory include:

1. Children's development is viewed in a more complex and holistic manner.
2. Children are studied in natural environments rather than artificial laboratory settings.
3. Attention is focused upon public policy and other aspects of the society at large that impact children and families.

Some criticisms of ecological systems theory include:

1. Ecological studies do not always identify the cause of their findings.
2. The methodology used in many ecological studies can be time-consuming,

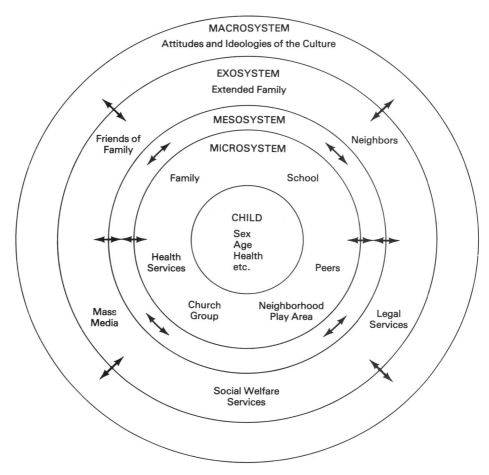

FIGURE 1.3

Bronfenbrenner's ecological systems theory emphasizes that there are a variety of influences upon the development of children. (Reprinted by permission of the publishers from *The Ecology of Human Development: Experiments by Nature and Design* by Urie Bronfenbrenner, Cambridge, Mass.: Harvard University Press, Copyright © 1979 by the President and Fellows of Harvard College.)

costly, and limited by observer bias, inability to record all detail, and selective memory of the observer.

Examples of Ecological Systems Theory

• Recent school reform included mandated testing of young children in a number of states, a policy coming from the macrosystem that ultimately had an impact on the other components of the ecological system. Some school boards (exosystem) implemented policies regarding the retention and placement of kindergarten children in transition classes to make certain they were "ready" to handle a more academically rigorous curriculum and to pass the mandated tests. Pressure upon teachers to place young children in alternative settings caused a number of problems in the relationships between home and school (microsystem). As a result of these concerns, parents, teachers, and professional organizations have lobbied successfully in several states to change these testing policies pertaining to young children (Center for Law and Education, 1988; National Center for Fair and Open Testing, Fall 1987).

- Mary and Jim Jones work at corporations that have paid maternity and paternity leaves. Both Mary and Jim took advantage of these leaves when their son Nathan was born. Upon returning to work, Mary decided to participate in the company's flexible work schedule. While she was at work on Mondays, Wednesdays, and Fridays, Nathan stayed in the corporate child care center where Mary could breastfeed on her breaks and at lunch. The policies of these corporations (mesosystems) directly supported the quality of family life for the Joneses and promoted the positive early development of Nathan.

The authors hope that you have discovered that early childhood development is an interesting, important, and complex field of study. The next chapter will provide you with additional information on how researchers study children and on how you can learn about young children through your own study.

Did you notice the quote at the beginning of this chapter? It says, "There are two lasting gifts we can give our children—one is roots; the other is wings." A knowledge of how young children develop and learn helps early childhood development professionals (and parents) to provide the conditions necessary for young children to develop deep roots and strong wings—two prerequisites for leading happy and productive lives. The authors hope the following chapters are of help to you in learning how to provide both the "roots and wings" that are necessary in facilitating optimal development in young children.

Key Terms

professionals
developmentally appropriate
at-risk
low-risk
developmentally inappropriate
early childhood development
theories
psychoanalytical theory
psychosexual theory
psychosocial theory
self-actualization
norms
maturation theory
reliability
validity
behavioral theory
classical conditioning theory

extinguish
operant conditioning
social learning theory
cognitive theory
schemata
assimilation
accommodation
equilibration
disequilibrium
tools of the world
concept clusters
signs
information processing theory
intrafamilial
extrafamilial
ecological systems theory

Review Strategies/Activities

1. Think back to your early childhood years, through age eight. Try to recall your earliest memory. At what age did it occur? Are there other recollections you have from your early childhood years?
   a. Chart out a life line. List how old you were at the time of your earliest recollection. Describe that recollection and others that took place during that year. Continue this process up through age 8 or to your current age.
   b. Discuss these recollections with other students in your early childhood development class. Your classmates probably have had similar experiences or their recollections will help you remember some events you have forgotten.
   c. Relate events in your life to the various developmental theories discussed in Chapter 1.
2. Why do you wish to become an early childhood professional?
   a. List those persons or events that have encouraged your interest in the profession.
   b. What are your concerns about becoming an early childhood professional?
   c. What are your short- and long-term professional goals?
   d. Discuss your responses with students in your class.
3. Observe early childhood classrooms in a variety of settings: child care, infants and toddlers, pre-primary classrooms for children ages 3–5, and primary grade classrooms for children ages 6–8. Talk with the teachers about what working with young children is really like.
4. A mother, father, and their thirty-month-old son are shopping at a large discount store. For a moment the son becomes separated from his parents. He runs to catch up with his parents shouting, "Don't leave me!" His father responds, "We will stay with you. You are very special to Mommy and me."
   a. What behaviors and development are being fostered by the parents?
   b. Under which of deMause's child rearing modes would you classify these parental perceptions of the child?
5. A mother, a grandmother, a two-year-old boy, and a four-year-old girl leave a fast food restaurant. The four year old starts to run onto the parking lot to the car. Her mother yells, "Go ahead and get run over and killed. We don't care."
   a. How can remarks such as this affect development?
   b. Under which of deMause's modes would you classify this type of parental behavior?
   c. What would have been some more appropriate developmental responses to the child?

Further Readings

History of Childhood

deMause, L. (Ed.). (1974). *The history of childhood.* New York: Harper & Row.

deMause, L. (1982). *Foundations of psychohistory.* New York: Creative Roots, Inc.
   These books present information regarding the perceptions of childhood from the beginnings of written history to the present. An awareness of the historical viewpoints of children helps to explain many of the attitudes and behaviors regarding young children today.

Psychoanalytical, Psychosocial, and Related Theories

Freud, S. (1938). The history of the psychoanalytic movement. In A. A. Brill (Ed. & trans.), *The basic writings of Sigmund Freud.* New York: Modern Library.

Erikson, E. H. (1963). *Childhood and society* (2nd ed.). New York: W. W. Norton.

Maslow, A. H. (1970). *Motivation and personality* (2nd ed.). New York: Harper & Row.

Rogers, C. R. (1961). *On becoming a person.* Boston: Houghton Mifflin.
> The above books provide in-depth information regarding the various psychoanalytic theories including Freud's psychosexual theory, Erikson's psychosocial theory, and the ideas of Maslow and Rogers concerning the dynamic and interactive nature of behavior.

Maturation Theory

Ames, L. B., Gillespie, C., Haines, J., & Ilg, F. L. (1979). *The Gesell Institute's child from one to six.* New York: Harper & Row.

Gesell, A., Ilg, F. L., & Ames, L. B. (1974). *The child from five to ten.* (rev. ed.). New York: Harper & Row.
> These references are helpful in broadening the reader's background information regarding maturation theory and the norms or average ages of various behaviors and aspects of development in young children.

Behavioral Theory

Skinner, B. F. (1974). *About behaviorism.* New York: Knopf.

Skinner, B. F. (1948). *Walden two.* New York: Macmillan.

Bandura, A. (1977). *Social learning theory.* Englewood Cliffs, NJ: Prentice Hall.
> These sources provide detailed information about the three major theories associated with behaviorism.

Cognitive Theory

Case, R. (1985). *Intellectual development: A systematic reinterpretation.* New York: Freeman.

Piaget, J., & Inhelder, B. (1969). *The psychology of the child.* New York: Basic Books.

Wadsworth, B. J. (1984). *Piaget's theory of cognitive and affective development* (3rd ed.). New York: Longman.

Vygotsky, L. (1978). *Mind in society.* Cambridge: Harvard University Press.
> These references provide the reader with more in-depth information regarding the ideas of the information process theorists, Piaget and Vygotsky. Wadsworth's book is particularly helpful in explaining Piaget's concepts.

The Early Childhood Profession

Brady, E., Bowman, B., Cruz, J., Hillard, A., & Katz, L. (1982). *Early childhood education teacher education guidelines.* Washington, DC: The National Association for Education of Young Children.
> This publication outlines the specific course content necessary for the training of an early childhood professional.

National Academy of Early Childhood Programs. (1984). *Accreditation Criteria and Procedures.* Washington, DC: The National Association for the Education of Young Children.
> This publication describes in detail the components of a quality early childhood program and how to obtain program accreditation from NAEYC.

CHAPTER 2

More often, teachers find as they study children, they themselves change. Thus (through child study), we often gain insight and understanding not only of the children but of ourselves as well. . . . But "understanding" alone, whether of the children or of ourselves, is not enough. The crucial question is whether such understanding improves the teacher's ability to help children learn, whether it facilitates provision of the experiences children need.

Millie Almy and Celia Genishi

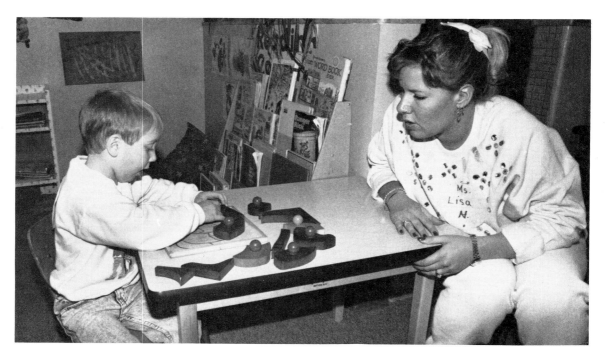

The Where, When, and How
of Early Childhood Study

After reading and studying this chapter, you will demonstrate comprehension by:

- Describing the contribution of early childhood development research in the training of the early childhood professional.
- Outlining the various types of child development research studies.
- Identifying ethical considerations in conducting research on young children.
- Justifying the importance of the ongoing study of young children in a variety of contexts.
- Outlining the various approaches the early childhood professional can use in studying young children.
- Identifying related resources that help in the study of young children.
- Describing the process of documenting the growth and development of young children.

■ It is the first day of kindergarten and Cathleen seems upset at having her mother leave her at the classroom door. Ms. Schwartz, Cathleen's teacher, invites her mother to stay awhile. This relieves Cathleen's anxiety and eventually she begins to participate in the sociodramatic (pretend play) area of the classroom. Periodically she returns to her mother and then rejoins other children in the sociodramatic center. Eventually, Cathleen's mother tells her that she has some errands to run and that she will be back at 11:30 to pick her up. Cathleen seems to accept her mother's departure. This pattern is repeated for three days with Cathleen's mother spending less and less time in the classroom. On the fourth day of kindergarten, Cathleen enters the classroom without hesitation and gives her mother a confident, "goodbye." Later, Ms. Schwartz observes Cathleen in the sociodramatic area. Ms. Schwartz suggests that she "call" her mother on the phone and tell her what she is doing. ■

■ Juan is 18 months old. His mother is planning to return to her job as a buyer for a large department store. She has enrolled Juan in a child care center. The director, Mr. Hubbard, has encouraged Juan's parents to visit the center with Juan several times a few days before Juan is to begin attending. Mr. Hubbard also suggests that Juan's parents send Juan's favorite stuffed toy and blanket every day. A picture of Juan's mother and father is also posted on a low-level bulletin board along with pictures of the other toddler's parents. ■

What would you have done if you had been Cathleen's or Juan's teachers? Typical responses include telling Cathleen's mother to leave her and not allowing favorite blankets and stuffed animals to be brought into the child care center. Why did Ms. Schwartz and Mr. Hubbard act in the ways they did?

The Contribution of Research Literature in the Development of the Early Childhood Professional

Ms. Schwartz and Mr. Hubbard acted upon their knowledge of child growth and development research. Their training included many opportunities to read the professional early childhood development research and literature. Their training also provided them with opportunities to observe and study young children's behavior as well as the responses and behavior of teachers of young children.

Through their reading and study of young children and observation of other early childhood professionals, Ms. Schwartz and Mr. Hubbard have learned that a major developmental task of young children is to separate from parents and to move into other social settings. Both Ms. Schwartz and Mr. Hubbard are familiar with the research on attachment and separation-individuation (see Chapters 6 and 9). They have observed the techniques and strategies that early childhood professionals have used to facilitate young children's adjustment to a new setting. Therefore, they make appropriate decisions about what to do to help children form new attachments and to assist in the separation from their parents.

Preservice—individuals who are in training to teach or serve young children.

Inservice—individuals who have completed teacher training programs and have accepted jobs teaching or serving young children.

Early childhood professionals learn about young children both at the **preservice** and **inservice** levels by reading about the studies of researchers in the area of early childhood development. This is why you are reading this book. You also need to learn about young children through your own observation and study of young children. First-hand experiences with young children can reinforce previously read child development information or can facilitate further reading about the nature of behavior in young children. This chapter provides information about the study of children through the professional research literature on early childhood development and your own study and investigation of young children and of the adults who work with them.

Types of Child Development Research Studies

Like you, there are other people who find the growth and development of children very interesting. These people may be affiliated with colleges or univer-

Early childhood professionals learn about young children by reading child development research studies.

sities, research centers, public agencies, or private groups. They often have hunches or **hypotheses** about the development of young children. They design research studies to determine if their hunches are correct. The results of these studies may be published in journals, books, theses, dissertations, and mass media, or presented in papers at professional conferences.

A brief overview of some of the more common types of research in the area of childhood development study follows. While presented separately for purposes of discussion, it should be noted that these research methods are not mutually exclusive categories. For example, correlational techniques can be used with longitudinal, cross-sectional, and descriptive studies. If you would like more in-depth information about various research techniques, check the Further Reading section at the end of this chapter.

Hypotheses—hunches about the development of young children, usually examined through research.

Descriptive Studies

Descriptive studies generally attempt to describe behavior. Many early studies in child development, particularly the maturation theory studies, were descriptive in nature. Researchers (Gesell & Amatruda, 1941) would observe many

Descriptive study—research that is collected by observing and recording behavior, providing a description of the observed behavior.

children at various ages in a particular area of development, such as physical development. This information was then converted into norms or averages so that teachers, parents, and physicians would have some guidelines as to the approximate age that various aspects of physical development occurred. For example, research of this nature described the average age that infants would sit, stand, and walk (Gesell & Amatruda, 1941). See Figure 2.1 for the results of a sample of a descriptive study.

A more recent trend in descriptive research is to utilize some of the techniques and approaches from the field of anthropology. Shirley Brice Heath's study (1983) into the nature of oral and written language used in three fictitiously named communities is an example of this type of research. Unlike earlier studies, this type of descriptive research examines smaller populations and attempts to describe individual behavior based upon the context of the environment. For example, Heath found that families in Roadville, a white working-class community, used alphabet and number books, Bible stories, real-life stories, and nursery rhymes with their children. Families in Trackton, an African-American working-class community, told fictional stories incorporating common events into new situations and rarely read books to their children. Maintown, a mainstream middle-class community, had parents who began reading books to their children during the first year of life, asking questions about the books, relating the book stories to their children's daily experiences and encouraging their children to tell both real and made-up stories.

Cross-Sectional and Longitudinal Studies

Cross-sectional study—research that studies children of different ages at the same time.

Cross-sectional studies look at an aspect of development or behavior at various ages or stages at the same time. For example, a **representative sample** of children at ages from 2 to 18 had their height and weight recorded at the same time. This information was converted to charts that pediatricians use to predict young children's weight and height at later ages. Cross-sectional research can provide information about certain types of development, such as height and weight, within a relatively short period of time. However, this type of study cannot determine exactly when an individual changes.

Representative sample—a sample of children in approximately the same proportions as are in the population as a whole regarding age, gender, racial and ethnic background, geographic location, and socioeconomic level.

A way to study change in the development of individuals is the **longitudinal study.** This type of study looks at the same children over a period of time. An important example of this type of study is the research conducted on a number of the at-risk young children who were enrolled in early childhood education programs in the 1960s (Berreuta-Clement, Schweinhart, Barnett, Epstein, & Weikart, 1984; Lazar & Darlington, 1982). In the Perry Preschool Program, subjects from age 4 through 19 years were tested and interviewed to determine if there were long-term effects of their participation in early childhood programs. They were then compared with children who had not attended any program. Generally, these studies indicated that at-risk **pre-primary** children who were in high-quality early childhood programs were better students and more productive as young adults than at-risk children who were not enrolled in early childhood programs. Chapter 17 discusses these studies in greater detail. See Figure 2.2 for a comparison of cross-sectional and longitudinal studies.

Longitudinal study—research that collects information about the same subjects at different ages over a period of time.

Pre-primary—the time in young children's lives before they enter primary (first, second, or third) grades.

FIGURE 2.1
These are typical responses at successive age levels to Gesell's Incomplete Man Test. (From *School Readiness* by Francis L. Ilg, Tordis Kristin Ilg, Louise B. Ames, and the Gesell Institute of Child Development, Inc. Copyright © 1978 by the Gesell Institute of Child Development, Inc. Reprinted by permission of Harper-Collins Publishers, p. 99.)

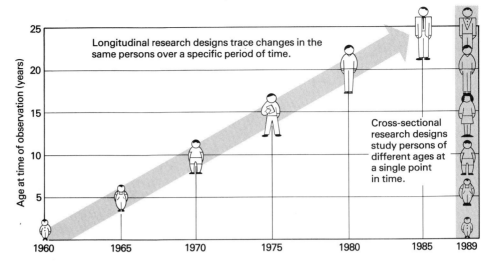

FIGURE 2.2
This graph demonstrates the difference between cross-sectional and longitudinal research. (From *The Development of Children.* By Michael Cole and Sheila R. Cole. Copyright © 1989 by Michael Cole, Sheila R. Cole and Judith Boies. Reprinted with permission by W. H. Freeman and Company.)

Correlational Studies

Correlational study—research that attempts to determine a relationship between two or more sets of measurements.

Correlational studies are designed to look at the nature of the relationship between two sets of measurements. For example, in a study by Ackerman-Ross and Khanna (1989) one finding indicated that there was a positive relationship between language performance of 3-year-old children and the amount of time parents engaged in language activities with their child, as well as the parent's economic status. Correlational studies only indicate relationships—they do not indicate causes. Thus, it *cannot* be said that the higher economic status of parents and more time spent in language activities with their 3-year-old caused the improved language performance in their child. It can only be said that there is a positive relationship between parental income, parent-child language activities, and the language performance of their 3-year-old child.

Experimental Studies

Experimental study—research that involves treating two or more groups, each in different ways to determine cause-and-effect relationships.

Random—assigning children to experimental and control groups so that each child has the same chance of being selected.

Experimental studies usually involve the researcher **randomly** dividing the population under study into two groups. One group is designated as the control group and this group usually does not receive any treatment; the second group is called the experimental group and does receive special treatment. Sometimes the two groups receive two different types of treatment. The researcher then employs statistical analysis to determine if the differences between the groups were of significance. Subjects are given pre- and post-tests to eliminate the possibility of outside influence.

An interesting example of experimental research is the study by Webster et al. (1989) to determine if intensive tutoring would improve the language skills of language-poor children. The children identified as language-poor in a Head Start early childhood program were given the Peabody Picture Vocabulary Test (PPVT) as a pre-test. One-half of the children were then randomly assigned to the control group and the other half to the experimental group. The experimental group children were then randomly assigned to university students who provided 3 to 4 hours a week of informal experiences that involved constant verbal interaction. The control group did not engage in any of these activities.

At the end of the experiment, the PPVT was administered again. Surprisingly, the control group achieved a mean gain of 4.6 months in language growth while the experimental group only recorded a mean gain of 2.6 months. The researchers explored possible reasons for this unexpected finding. More in-depth analysis of the children in the experimental group indicated that many of the children came from families characterized as disorganized. This family disorganization made it impossible for a number of children in the experimental group to participate in the tutoring experiences on a regular basis. The researchers concluded that family support appears to be essential in such a language tutoring project.

Ethics of Early Childhood Development Research

Remember little Albert, who left the hospital with a fear of white furry objects as the result of Watson & Rayner's (1920) classical conditioning experiment? Did you wonder what happened to him as a result of this experiment?

Because of the increasing awareness regarding the rights and feelings of young children, careful attention is now being given to ensure that there is no psychological or physical damage to children during the research process. Both the American Psychological Association (1972) and the Society for the Research in Child Development (1975) have developed procedures for conducting research with human subjects. These standards outline the rights of children and the responsibilities of researchers and stipulate that parental or guardian permission must be obtained before any research can begin (see Figure 2.3).

Another area of ethics involves the honesty of the researcher in reporting the study. Most researchers plan well-designed studies. However, the unpredictable nature of children and other complications sometimes prevent the researcher from completing the study as originally intended. It is the responsibility of the researcher to acknowledge these limitations when publishing the study. At times, pilot studies or smaller preliminary studies can help identify some potential problems with the research design.

Sociocultural Perspectives in Studying Young Children

Much of the early child development research information comes from studies conducted by researchers who have the same economic and sociocultural back-

March 10, 1991

Dear Parents,

I will be conducting a research project designed to study the outdoor play activities of young children and the leadership-followership relationships that develop during play time. I request permission for your child to participate. The study consists of (1) video-recordings of the daily outdoor play sessions, (2) several observers recording patterns of social interaction and (3) a brief interview with children concerning what games they prefer and who they play with during outdoor play time. The goals of the study are to determine the activities of preschool children during outdoor play time, to identify leadership behavior among the children during play activities, and what behaviors characterize leaders among young children.

At first, contact with children will be limited to a video tape camera recording the regularly scheduled outdoor play time. Occasionally, observers will be on the playground to randomly record the games and activities of all of the children. Toward the end of the study, children will have the opportunity to discuss their favorite play activities, what equipment or games they prefer, and to identify their playmates. The five to ten minute interview sessions will be supervised by the Child Development Laboratory staff and will be conducted at the center.

To preserve confidentiality, I will not use your child's name at any time during presentations or in written work of the research findings. Family information is not needed for this study. The only personal information that will be needed is your child's date of birth.

Your decision whether or not to allow your child to participate will in no way affect your child's standing in his or her class. At the conclusion of the study, a summary of group results will be made available to all interested parents and teachers. Should you have any questions or desire further information, please call me at 565-XXXX. Thank you in advance for your cooperation and support.

Best wishes,

Michael J. Bell

Michael J. Bell
Assistant Professor, Early Childhood

This project has been reviewed by University of North Texas Committee for the Protection of Human Subjects. (Phone 565-XXXX)

FIGURE 2.3
This is an example of a letter obtaining parents' permission for their child to participate in a research project.

grounds as the children they have studied. Therefore, the universal application of the research to all groups of children must be interpreted with caution. Researchers need to include children from a variety of socioeconomic and cultural groups before attempts at universal application can be made, or they need to acknowledge the lack of broad representation in their study. Researchers also need to be aware of various culturally distinct behaviors when they attempt to design their research or interpret their findings.

One of the researchers who helped create awareness of the importance of taking sociocultural considerations into account is William Labov. Labov (1970, 1972) examined the effects of a variety of social situations and their effects upon the nature of language produced by African-American speakers. He determined that in more formal contexts such as test-like settings, some children produced little verbalization. However, in more informal and relaxed situations the children were more verbal. When 8-year-old Leon, his best friend, and an Anglo male sat on the floor eating a bag of potato chips and talking about taboo subjects, Leon demonstrated that he was highly verbal. In contrast, Leon verbalized very little in test-like settings. Thus, certain research contexts can convey that children from various linguistic and cultural groups are nonverbal, when in reality they are highly verbal. Sensitivity to cultural behaviors and the effects of some research designs upon certain behaviors can help prevent biased and incorrect information about various cultural groups. The following section provides information about how you can learn about young children through your own study and observation.

Your Own Study and Observation of Young Children

Along with reading of professional child development research and literature, your own study of young children can help you develop a knowledge base regarding the unique nature of young children's development and behavior. This base fosters an awareness of typical and atypical behavior. It helps the early childhood professional select materials and strategies for working with young children. Informed study can also help prevent teacher bias and help early childhood professionals become more objective in looking at children. However, it is important to acknowledge biases and to realize that early childhood professionals bring their own backgrounds, experiences, belief systems, and values to the interpretation of children's behavior. At times, it may be helpful to have other professionals use the same procedures and tools to verify your information and ensure objectivity.

The Importance of the Ongoing Study of Young Children in Many Contexts

Competent early childhood professionals realize the importance of studying children in a variety of situations, including settings within the classroom, in

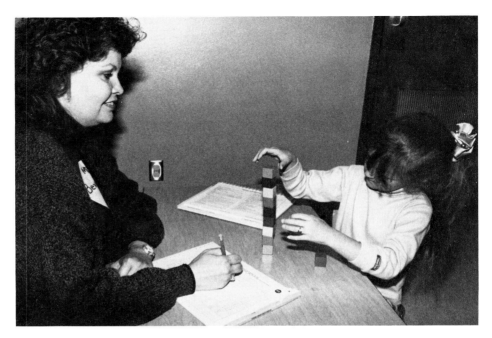

Controlled laboratory experiments do not always indicate how young children act in real life.

Disabilities—*conditions in children such as mental retardation, hearing impairments, visual impairments, emotional disturbances, orthopedic impairments, other health impairments, learning disabilities, or multiple disabilities which require special education and services.*

Least restrictive environment—*the least specialized classroom, or "regular" classroom, which is viewed as the best learning environment for the student.*

outdoor learning areas, at lunch, and during rest or quiet times, as well as in the wider context of the family and community settings. Complete understanding of young children involves study of their behavior in a variety of contexts, in real-life situations over a period of time, as children's behavior changes from one setting to another. The nature of the setting, the people in the setting, and the time all influence the way children behave. In addition, artificial, unfamiliar, or laboratory-type environments can convey misleading information about children, their behaviors, and their competencies (Ceci & Bronfenbrenner, 1985).

Studying children in a variety of settings over a period of time helps the early childhood professional see the common characteristics of young children, as well as individual behaviors. The study of young children can also help the early childhood professional provide specific examples of children's behavior when in conference with parents. Finally, the study of young children can serve as a means of documenting that program goals for facilitating young children's development and learning are being accomplished. Appropriate, reliable, and valid strategies for studying young children are increasingly important as many early childhood programs are dependent upon private, state, or federal funding and often require documentation of performance or achievement of goals and objectives.

Public Law (P.L.) 101–476 (1990) requires that all children with **disabilities** between the ages of 3 and 21 years have access to public education in the **least restrictive environment.** This means that many early childhood professionals are involved in teams of health professionals, diagnosticians, and administrators who use a variety of measures to identify the nature of the disabling condition of the child. These educational decision-making committees plan for appropriate learning experiences. Unless the disabling condition is severe, children are to be maintained in the regular classroom. Children with profound disabilities are to be **mainstreamed** into the regular classroom as much as possible.

In 1986, P.L. 99–457 was passed. This law requires that states opting to continue to acquire federal funding for special services must provide programs for infants and toddlers who have disabilities. In addition, states must document that they are providing programs for children with disabilities ages 3 to 5. As a result of these two laws, there has been a great need for measurement and evaluation strategies which are appropriate for studying young children.

Mainstream—the practice of incorporating children with disabilities into the regular classroom.

Various Approaches to Studying Young Children

There are a variety of tools and techniques that can be of help to the early childhood professional in the study of young children. Generally, these can be classified into two types, **formal** and **informal** (see Table 2.1).

Formal—refers to information gathered about young children, usually through standardized tests.

Formal Approaches to Child Study

Formal approaches in the study of young children usually refer to the use of a **standardized test.** Wortham states, "The increased use of standardized testing at all levels has been criticized, but the testing of young children is of particular concern" (Wortham, 1990, p. 8). According to the NAEYC position statement on testing (1988), increased use of standardized testing with young children is indicative of the "escalating trend toward curriculum . . . that is inappropriate for the age and developmental level of the children." In other words, kindergartens are what used to be first grades and prekindergartens are what used to

Informal—refers to information gathered about young children through approaches other than standardized tests.

Standardized test—a test which is administered and scored according to set procedures and has scores which can be interpreted according to statistical measures representative of the group for which the test was designed.

TABLE 2.1
Formal and informal approaches to studying young children

Formal	Informal
Achievement tests	Narrative observations: running records, specimen records, anecdotal records
Readiness tests	
Developmental screening tests	Checklists
Diagnostic tests	Rating scales
Intelligence tests	Time sampling
	Event sampling
	Interviews/conferences: child, parents, support staff, resource persons, peers
	Children's products: art, writings, class work, projects

Many standardized tests cause stress behaviors and are not appropriate to use with young children.

be kindergartens. Nevertheless, there is no research information to indicate that the way young children learn, or their developmental needs, has changed.

The end result of this curricular escalation is increased school failure among young children. Raising the legal age for school entry, beginning school a year later for those children whose birth date falls well into the school year, and using standardized tests to more accurately place children in hopes of preventing school failure are some of the inappropriate attempts to solve this problem (Bredekamp & Shepard, 1989; Charlesworth, 1989).

In response to a growing national concern about the inappropriate uses of standardized testing with young children, NAEYC developed its position statement entitled "Testing of Young Children: Concerns and Cautions" (1988). In it, NAEYC states that standardized tests "are designed for a specific purpose and should be used only for the purpose for which they were designed." According to NAEYC, some of the more common types of standardized tests include **achievement tests** and **readiness tests.** These two kinds of tests are designed to provide teachers with information so they can individualize instruction. These tests should *not* be used to make school entry, promotion, or retention decisions. Other frequently used tests include **developmental screening tests.** It is recommended that these tests be used only as the first step in identifying children who may be in need of further evaluation. **Diagnostic** and **intelligence tests** are also common types of standardized tests. Children should not be placed in special education programs solely on the basis of such tests. Placement decisions should be made *only* through the use of multiple measures of assessment, both informal and formal, with input by parents.

NAEYC (1988) cites the following reasons that standardized testing is "potentially harmful to young children" and their learning:

- Testing narrows the curriculum as teachers begin to focus on specific test items. They begin to "teach the test."
- Many important skills that young children need to acquire—self-esteem, social competence, desire to learn, self-discipline—are not easily measured by standardized tests.
- Standardized testing encourages the learning of rote information. Reading for information, composing stories, problem solving, and creative thinking are not emphasized. Yet these are the skills that children need to learn if they are "to function in an ever-changing American society."
- Testing can lead to labeling, mislabeling, and inappropriate placement of young children. The end result is that teacher and parent perceptions of children's ability create negative feelings of self-concept and of the child as a competent learner.
- Testing puts stress on young children, even those who perform well on tests.

A study by Fleege (1990) documents the stress behaviors of both able and less competent learners in a kindergarten classroom during the administration of a standardized test. This study indicates that kindergarten teachers may respond to the observed stress in their students by using a variety of techniques that violate standardized testing procedures.

The NAEYC position paper (1988) states that standardized testing of young children is inappropriate for several reasons:

- *Young children are not good test takers.* The younger the child, the more difficult it is to obtain reliable information (consistent over time) and valid (accurate) results from tests. Results are easily influenced by a young child's test taking skills: the ability to sit down, be quiet, and make a mark in the correct place. Such behavior does not necessarily reflect children's level of learning.
- *Young children are growing and learning rapidly.* Just how quickly children grow and learn is reflected in the fact that a school year constitutes one fourth of the lifetime of a 4-year-old.

Achievement test—*a test that measures what children have learned as a result of instruction.*

Readiness test—*a test that measures what beginning skills children have in order to predict whether they will succeed in a new learning task, e.g., reading.*

Developmental screening test—*a test that determines if a child is developing normally.*

Diagnostic test—*a test that identifies a child's strengths or weaknesses in a certain area.*

Intelligence test—*a test that measures those abilities which have been designated as a sign of intelligence.*

Decisions about placement of young children should be made using many sources of information, including the observations of parents and teachers.

- *There is no such thing as a culture-free test.* Test bias has been well-documented. Test developers ignore language and culture variations too often. Any test in English given to non-native English speakers, or children who speak a dialect of English, is first and foremost a language test, regardless of its intent. With young children, language and culture are essential aspects of children's learning and development. For example, when asked on a test, "Where do lions live?," a child who had spent his early years in Kenya might answer "in the park." From his experiences, the answer is correct; however, the test manual says that the correct answer is "in the zoo," and the teacher would record his answer as an error.

According to the NAEYC position statement (1988), standardized tests should only be administered by "qualified professionals." These tests need to be "carefully selected and used only for the purposes for which they were designed and for which there are data demonstrating the accuracy of the measures." If beneficial treatment does not exist, standardized tests do not serve a useful purpose.

The NAEYC position statement (1988) proposes the following solutions to the standardized testing dilemma.

1. Children should enter school on the basis of their chronological age and legal right to enter, not on the basis of what they already know.
2. In the primary grades, group sizes should be small (preferably no more than 20) and teacher-child ratios low so that teachers can individualize instruction. All children should not be expected to accomplish the same task at the same time.
3. Groupings of children for individual activities should be flexible and change

frequently so that children do not have to conform to rigid group expectations and can work at their own pace.

4. Children's development and learning should be assessed through ongoing and systematic observation by qualified teachers and other professionals. Developmental screening should be used to identify those children who may be in need of further testing to diagnose a specific learning problem and suggest remediation strategies.

5. Curriculum and teaching methods should be appropriate to the age and development of the children. The curriculum should be rich in all content areas, not dictated by the need to produce pre-determined test scores.

6. Decisions about promotion to the next grade or placement in special or remedial education should be based on multiple sources of information, including parents' and teachers' observations and *never* on the basis of a single test score.

The above discussion indicates that formal methods of studying young children need to be used with caution. Informal approaches generally are more appropriate techniques.

Informal Approaches to Child Study

Informal approaches of child study are more frequently used with children up through the kindergarten year. With entry into first grade, more formal approaches are usually used. In light of the previously discussed concerns regarding the use of standardized testing, continued use of informal approaches should be extended into the primary grades (Wortham, 1990).

Most informal approaches to child study can be classified under narrative observation of children's spontaneous behaviors and observation using predefined instruments. Regardless of the technique used, it is important to remember to study and be aware of the child's total development and behavior. This study of the whole child may include self-identity, emotional development, social development and prosocial behavior, gross and fine motor development, cognitive development, communicative competence, written language and print awareness, and creative and aesthetic development (Beaty, 1990).

Narrative Observations

Narrative observations are records of behaviors as they occur. The period of time may vary from several minutes to hours at a time. Notepads and pencil are all that is needed. Running records, specimen records, and anecdotal records are three types of narrative observations (Beaty, 1990).

Narrative observation—a written observation of behavior as it occurs.

Running Records.   **Running records** are accounts of *all* behavior as it occurs. A collection of these observations can be helpful in describing and documenting young children's behavior and development. This type of observation is used most frequently in preservice settings. If there is only one teacher in a classroom with no aide, running records can be difficult to accomplish because

Running record—a type of narrative observation that records all behavior as it occurs.

teachers need to be available to young children. However, using parent volunteers or planning for a time when the children are involved in independent activity can give the classroom teacher some time for conducting running records.

Procedures for using running records include:

1. *Description of the setting*—including the time the observation begins and the activity taking place.
2. *Recording information*—taking down information in a detailed sequential manner. Information needs to be factual and objective, not biased by personal opinions. Time can be jotted down in 1-minute intervals in the margin.
3. *Comments and analysis*—writing down inferences and conclusions. The comments and analysis should be related to child development information.

See Figure 2.4 for an example of a running record.

FIGURE 2.4
A running record

| Child's Name: Daniel | Age: $3\frac{1}{2}$ | Date: 3/10 |
| Observer: Veronica | Place: Lab | Time: 9:36 |

Observation	**Comments**
Daniel is sitting at a table in the classroom rolling out clay. He is making primarily flat shapes with a rolling pin.	Daniel has excellent arm strength and good coordination of his movements.
He stands while rolling out the clay and sits to cut the shapes.	The table is evidently too high for Daniel because he had to stand while rolling out the clay.
After rolling each piece of clay out completely, he takes a cookie-cutter and cuts circles out of the clay.	Daniel is cutting out circles exclusively, because no other shapes are available. Other children working with clay are using other cutters.
Taking two of the cut-out circles, he places them over his eyes, and says "I have new glasses, like my daddy."	Daniel has used the objects he created to move into fantasy and socialize with the other children.
Teacher asks, "What can you see with your new glasses?"	
Daniel: "Dark."	
Teacher: "No, what can you see?"	Teacher is attempting to draw language from Daniel. He may not be certain of the teacher's intent or the actual meaning of the question, due to his response.
Daniel: "I can't see anything with my new glasses, it's just dark . . . they're just *pretend* glasses!"	

Specimen Records.   **Specimen records** are narrative observations that are more detailed than running records. Specimen records are usually used to focus upon a particular time of day, setting, or child. Specimen records can be helpful in providing *detailed* information to early childhood professionals about the effects of scheduling, the influence of certain curricular and management strategies, and certain children and their behavior. The format used for running records can be used for specimen records. At times, audiotape recorders or video cameras may prove helpful in providing more complete and detailed information. See Figure 2.5 for an example of a specimen record.

Specimen record—a type of narrative observation that provides detailed information about a particular event, child, or time of day.

Anecdotal Records.   **Anecdotal records** differ from running and specimen records in that they are usually written *after* the incident occurs. They are brief and describe only one incident at a time that the early childhood professional

*Anecdotal record—a type of narrative observation describing in detail an incident **after** it occurs.*

FIGURE 2.5
A specimen record

A group of preschool-age boys were beginning an outdoor play activity. There was a disagreement about who was going to enact the more desirable characters. Their language characterizes the overt organizational behaviors of the fantasy theme among the frustrated subjects.

John (M1):	There will be three "Lukes" today.
All:	I want to be "Luke" today! (competing for the role)
Jim (M6):	I'll be "Luke."
Bruce (M4):	There can't be all "Lukes." (frustrated)
Kevin (M3):	I'll be "Chewy."
Paul (M5):	Who else is "Luke"?
Chuch (M2):	He is. (pointing to Bruce)
Dan (M7):	What?
Bruce (M4):	We got our whole game mixed up!
Kevin (M3):	Right, I'm "Chewy."
Bruce (M4):	Two people are "Lukes," all right?
Jim (M6):	I'm "Luke"!
Bruce (M4):	No, I'm "Luke"!
Chuck (M2):	I wanna . . .
Bruce (M4):	All right!
Jim (M6):	Let's have a converse (conference?), let's hold hands. Let's hold hands . . . we are having a converse, right? (looking for agreement among the play group members)
Paul (M5):	Right now?
Bruce (M4):	Hold onto my sleeve. (to Paul)
John (M1):	The game's mixed up. (directed to the adult observer)
Inv:	The game's mixed up? (responding to John's statement)
Bruce (M4):	Yeah, we get it mixed up all of the time.

The boys formed a circle and held hands during the "converse" (conference). The discussion developed out of frustration and lack of cooperation at the onset of the play activity. This specimen of linguistic behavior provides a source of information regarding play theme management and status hierarchies in play groups.

---

believes is of significance. Anecdotal records are cumulative in nature and describe in a factual manner what happened, how it happened, when and where it happened, and what was said and done. Commentaries can be written in the margin or at the conclusion of the anecdote. Anecdotal records can be particularly helpful to the busy classroom teacher who finds it somewhat difficult to

FIGURE 2.6
An anecdotal record

Date: February 19, 1991

Observer: Schwartz

Child: Ann S.

Time: 8:38 a.m.   During center time this morning, Ann was playing in the dramatic play center with a rag doll. While sitting on the floor, Ann began to repeatedly beat the floor with the head and upper torso of the doll, while holding on to the doll's legs and feet. At first she hit the floor lightly and sporadically. Then the intensity and frequency of the activity increased to the extent that the arm of the doll began to tear away. I intervened at this point and redirected Ann to another activity with the teacher assistant.

Time: 9:20 a.m.   During the transition time from centers to story time, Ann walked past the block area and knocked down Daniel's tower of blocks that he had built during today's center time. Daniel screamed as the tower fell and Ann watched passively as he called for me. Ann was unable to verbalize what had happened, but did manage to apologize to Daniel for this "accident."

Time: 10:30 a.m.   On the playground, I observed Ann push her way past children on three separate occasions. Twice, she pushed past children to gain access to the slide and once she pushed a child from behind to get a tricycle. The latter incident caused the child to skin her knee, requiring a trip to the school nurse. Ann was unable to verbalize what had happened and denied any responsibility for the incident.

Time: 11:15 a.m.   As the children were washing their hands and getting drinks of water, I saw Ann purposefully tear her painting as it was hanging up on the drying rack. Her expression was passive, a blank stare, as she tore the wet painting in two pieces. As both halves hung on the rack, she had no explanation for how the "accident" occurred.

Summary: While observing Ann throughout this morning, it was clear that something was bothering her. The aggressive incidents were uncharacteristic of Ann and appeared to occur without premeditation. Despite efforts by the classroom teaching team to involve Ann in guided group activities this morning, she tended to lose interest and find solitary activities. Typically, when she was working or playing independently this morning she had difficulty or acted aggressively. Further attention must be given to these behaviors for the next several days. A closer observation may be warranted. If this continues I may need to contact Ann's parents.

do the more time-consuming running record and the more detailed specimen record. Ms. Schwartz, a kindergarten teacher, became concerned about 5-year-old Ann's periodic aggressive behavior. Ms. Schwartz began to take anecdotal records after these episodes occurred. These notes were then analyzed according to time, activity, and children involved. See Figure 2.6 for an example of an anecdotal record.

FIGURE 2.7
Checklist for studying children when there are many specific behaviors to be observed

Level III	Introduced	Progress	Mastery
1. Imitates grownups (plays house, store, and so forth)			
2. Expresses frustrations in play			
3. Creates imaginary playmates			
4. Engages in housekeeping			
5. Paints and draws symbolic figures on large paper			
6. Builds simple structures with blocks			
7. Uses transportation toys, people, and animals to enrich block play			
8. Imagines any object as the object he or she wants (symbolic function)			
Level IV			
1. Role plays in the housekeeping center			
2. Role plays some adult occupations			
3. Participates in dramatization of familiar stories			
4. Uses puppets in self-initiated dialogues			
5. Differentiates between real and make-believe			
6. Pretends dolls are real people			
7. Constructs (paints, molds, and so forth) recognizable figures			
8. Participates in finger plays			
Level V			
1. Role plays a wide variety of roles in the housekeeping center and in other centers			
2. Role plays on the playground			
3. Role plays a variety of adult occupations			
4. Recognizes that pictures represent real objects			
5. Participates in a wide variety of creative activities: finger plays, rhythm band, working with clay, painting, outdoor play, housekeeping, singing, and so forth			
6. Produces objects at the carpentry table and tells about them			

Source: From the *Frost-Wortham Developmental Checklist* by J. L. Frost and S. C. Wortham. Reprinted with permission from the authors.

Observation with Predefined Instruments

Predefined instruments frequently used in studying young children include checklists, rating scales, time sampling, event sampling, and interviews. As with narrative observations, there are advantages and disadvantages to these techniques.

Checklists.   A **checklist** is a list of developmental behaviors that have been identified as important to look for in young children. They are helpful tools in studying children when there are many easily specified behaviors that need to be observed and recorded. Checklists are usually used with one child at a time and need to be prepared in an objective manner. See Figure 2.7 (p. 49) for an example of a checklist.

Rating Scales.   **Rating scales** are similar to checklists in that they include large numbers of traits or behaviors to observe. They provide more detailed information about the quality of traits or behaviors than checklists. However, the use of rating scales is dependent upon the observer's judgment, so objectivity must be maintained. See Figure 2.8 for an example of a rating scale.

Time Sampling and Event Sampling.   Two other techniques used to observe and record behavior of young children are time sampling and event sampling. **Time sampling** is used to record how often certain types of behavior

Checklist—a list of developmental behaviors that the observer identifies as present or absent.

Rating scale—a scale with various traits or categories that allows the observer to indicate the importance of the observed behaviors.

Time sampling—an observation technique for recording how often certain behaviors occur over time.

FIGURE 2.8
Rating scale

Your Child's Sleep Behaviors
(Circle the appropriate response)

1. **My child always sleeps through the night:**
   Little body movement; regular breathing; no response to mild stimulation.

2. **My child often sleeps through the night:**
   Increased body movements; irregular breathing; more easily aroused by external stimuli.

3. **My child sometimes sleeps through the night:**
   Between regular and irregular sleep, accompanied by muscle movements, rapid breathing, and then short periods of calm activity.

4. **My child seldom sleeps through the night:**
   Wakefulness; scans the environment; large motor activity (head, trunk, arms and legs), alert but relaxed.

5. **My child never sleeps through the night:**
   Intense motor activity may signal physiological need; whimpering, crying states, becoming louder as distress increases.

Application of Wolff, 1966; see Table 5.2, p. 119.

occur over a period of time. The behavior observed needs to be obvious and frequent in occurrence for this type of observation to be effective.

In **event sampling** the observer decides upon an event to study, waits for the event to occur and then records it. If narratives or time sampling do not seem to be appropriate ways to get information, event sampling could be helpful to the early childhood professional. See Figures 2.9 and 2.10 for examples of

Event sampling— an observation technique for recording when certain events occur.

FIGURE 2.9
Time sampling

Behavior:	Biting other children
Subject(s):	Jimmy (2 years, 6 months)
Observer:	Ms. Gilliam
Observation Begins:	8:00 a.m.
Observation Ends:	4:00 p.m.
Date:	6/7/91

Hour of the Day	Time of Incident	Observer Notes
8:00		Observation begins
	8:09	
	8:35	
9:00		Morning snack
		Group time
10:00		Centers
	10:32	
11:00		Begin lunch routine
12:00		
1:00		Nap time begins 12:30
		Nap time
2:00		Nap time
		Child awake: 2:36 p.m.
3:00	3:02	Selected centers
	3:48	
4:00		Observation ends

Findings: 5 biting incidents during observation period

FIGURE 2.10
Event sampling

Behavior:	Biting other children	
Subject(s):	Jimmy (2 years, 6 months)	
Observer:	Ms. Koth	
Observation Begins:	8:00 a.m.	
Observation Ends:	4:00 p.m.	
Date:	6/7/91	

Time	Observed Behavior	Observer Comments
8:09 a.m.	Jimmy and Josh are pulling on a large unit block. Both are kneeling facing each other. They are each using two hands to hold on to the block. Jimmy has lowered his head, as a wedge between Josh's body and the block. After a brief pause, Josh screams, releasing the block and grasps his left forearm. Josh runs to the classroom teacher, still grasping his arm, crying, and unable to speak.	The physical behavior of biting appears to be Jimmy's strategy for gaining materials and objects that are held or claimed by other children. No audible language was observed during the confrontation.
8:35 a.m.	Jimmy repeats a similar conflict with Kenneth over a pair of headphones in listening center. Same physical posture and strategy to gain control of a disputed object.	Similar circumstances—No language observed, physical posture was similar, confrontation was brief with no amiable solution.

time sampling and event sampling. Table 2.2 summarizes the informal observation and recording techniques.

Other Methods of Gathering Information about Young Children

Interview—asking the child predetermined questions on a one-to-one basis to find out more about the child.

At times, **interviews** can be helpful in gaining information about young children. During an interview, an adult verbally questions or interacts with a child on a one-to-one basis using predetermined questions. The purpose of an interview is to find out how and why children think the way they do. It is important for a successful interview that the interviewer spend time establishing rapport with the young child.

When using this technique there are several other preconditions that are necessary: (1) children must be able to express themselves verbally; (2) children must be comfortable with the interviewer; (3) the interviewer must be sensitive to the child's level of receptive language and cognitive development, as many responses may not be incorrect but are in reality developmentally appropriate;

TABLE 2.2
Methods for observing and recording data about child development (pp. 53–54)

Method	Purpose	Advantages	Disadvantages
Anecdotal Record: A narrative of descriptive paragraphs, recorded *after behavior occurs.*	To detail specific behavior for child's record; for case conferences; to plan for individuals	Open-ended; rich in details; no special observer training	Depends on observer's memory; behavior taken out of context; difficult to code or analyze for research
Running Record: A narrative written in sequence over a specified time, recorded *while behavior is occurring*	To discover cause and effects of behavior; for case conferences; to plan for individuals	Open-ended; comprehensive; no special observer training	Time-consuming; difficult to use for more than one child at a time; time-consuming to code and analyze for research
Specimen Record: A detailed narrative written in sequence over a specified time, recorded *while behavior is occurring*	To discover cause and effects of behavior; for child development research	Open-ended; comprehensive and complete; rich in details	Time-consuming to record; time-consuming to code or analyze for research; difficult to observe more than one child at a time
Time sampling: Tallies or symbols showing the presence or absence of specified behavior during short time periods, recorded *while behavior is occurring*	For behavior modification baseline data; for child development research	Objective and controlled; not time-consuming; efficient for observing more than one child at a time; provides quantitative data for research	Closed; limited to observable behaviors that occur frequently; no description of behavior; takes behavior out of context

TABLE 2.2
continued

Method	Purpose	Advantages	Disadvantages
Event Sampling: A brief narrative of conditions preceding and following specified behavior, recorded *while behavior is occurring*	For behavior modification input; for child development research	Objective; helpful for in-depth diagnosis of infrequent behavior	Closed; takes event out of context; limited to specified behavior
Rating Scale: A scale of traits or behaviors with check marks, recorded *before, during, and after behavior occurs*	To judge degree to which child behaves or possesses certain traits; to diagnose behavior or traits; to plan for individuals	Not time-consuming; easy to design; efficient for observing more than one child at a time for many traits; useful for several observers watching same child	Closed; subjective; limited to specified traits or behaviors
Checklist: A list of behaviors with check marks, recorded *before, during, and after behavior occurs*	To determine presence or absence of specified behaviors; to plan for individuals; to give observer an overview of child's development or progress	Efficient for observing more than one child at a time for many behaviors; useful for an individual over a period of time; a good survey or inventory tool; useful for several observers at once; no special training needed	Closed; limited to specified behaviors; no information on quality of behavior

and (4) interviews are best conducted in familiar settings without other distractions.

Other methods of gathering information about young children include samples of children's products such as artistic creations, writings, and daily class work; informal and formal meetings including conferences and home visits with the child's parents; school records, if objective and factual; and other teachers, **support staff, resource persons** and **peers.**

Technology can be helpful in recording various types of information. Audiotapes can help teachers study children's oral language including oral reading. Videotapes can be helpful in documenting and analyzing a wide range of behaviors. Videotapes can also be used to aid discussion about a child with parents and other support personnel who find it difficult to observe the child on a regular basis. Computers can also be useful in storing and quickly retrieving information about children. See Figure 2.11 for guidelines for conducting observations.

Related Resources That Help in the Study of Young Children

There are a number of other resources which can be of help in studying young children. These include:

1. Child development research journals such as *Early Childhood Research Quarterly, Journal of Research in Childhood Education, Child Development, Developmental Psychology, Society for Research in Child Development Monographs, American Educational Research Journal, Research in the Teaching of English,* and *Journal of Experimental Psychology.*
2. Journals from professional organizations and related groups such as *Young Children, Childhood Education, Dimensions, The Reading Teacher, Language Arts, Science and Children, Mathematics Teachers, Arithmetic Teacher, Teaching Exceptional Children, Journal of Special Education, Gifted Child Quarterly, Elementary School Journal, Journal of Negro Education, Journal of Ethnic Studies, Journal of Children in Contemporary Society, Phi Delta Kappan, Educational Leadership,* and *Journal of Teacher Education.*
3. Professional magazines such as *Day Care and Early Education, Child Care Information Exchange, Learning, Instructor, Prekindergarten* and *Early Years.*
4. Professional organization position statements. See the Further Reading section at the end of this chapter.

Record Keeping to Document and Record Behavior and Development

All quality early childhood programs have some process by which records are kept to document the behavior and development of young children. All ap-

Support staff—other persons within the educational setting who support the learning and development of young children; e.g., nurses, social workers, diagnosticians, psychologists, secretaries, cooks, and custodians.

Resource persons—persons outside the educational setting who can provide information about young children's development and learning, usually from health-related fields.

Peers—other children who are the same age as a particular child.

FIGURE 2.11
Effectively observing young children's behavior

An observer of young children has two responsibilities: (1) not to interfere with the normal operations of the early childhood setting they are studying, and (2) to accurately characterize the children's behavior in any reports, term papers, or academic reports. The following guidelines will help observers fulfill these responsibilities.

Be quiet. Any behavior that draws children's attention will upset the classroom routine and will affect the behavior of the children, thus influencing any observation procedures. Good observers are able to move about the early childhood setting without drawing attention to themselves, but getting a good view of activities.

Sit low and to the side of activities. Unobtrusiveness is essential to good observations in early childhood settings. Observers should sit with their backs to exterior walls or in corners, so all activities are easily observable.

Honesty is the best policy. When observers are approached by children in the classroom, classroom assistants or children's parents respond to their questions with honesty and simplicity. Children are sensitive to evasive or vague answers to their questions and they will insist on a clear answer. Observers should try to avoid prolonged or unnecessary conversations with children and adults in the observation site, so they should use simple, clear, and honest answers to any questions about their activities.

Don't let your emotions get the best of you. Sometimes young children will make funny or amusing statements, and it is natural to respond with a laugh or chuckle. Observers should remember that they are technically not a part of the social climate in the classroom and should avoid "normal" emotional responses. However, observers should respond to statements or activities that are specifically directed to them. Observers should always remember to be polite.

Be quick on your feet. Observers will be asked to move from their observation position to make room for children's activities or to follow the group of children out to the play area. Observers should bring minimal materials, that can be easily and quickly packed and moved to another observation location. Observers of young children should remember to not "lose themselves in their work." Any guest in an early childhood setting should be sensitive to the needs and well-being of the adults and the children and be alert and ready to quietly respond if necessary.

proaches including those developed by the early childhood professional need to be evaluated for (1) developmental appropriateness, (2) objectivity, and (3) usefulness to early childhood professionals and parents in helping them understand and facilitate the child's growth and development.

    Child study and appropriate record keeping at the preservice level help future professionals learn more about children and ways of documenting children's behavior. Both these skills will help the beginning teacher develop into a competent early childhood professional.

Competent early childhood professionals realize the importance of continuing their study of young children throughout their careers.

Early childhood professionals need to continue their child study and observation skills. NAEYC states in their position statement, "Testing of Young Children: Concerns and Options," that "the systematic observations of trained teachers and other professionals in conjunction with information obtained from parents and other family members are the best sources of information" (1988). At times, competent early childhood professionals may need to revise or work to eliminate the use of certain assessment or reporting techniques that are not developmentally appropriate. Additional methods of studying and documenting the behavior and development of children may need to be designed and used. The use of **portfolios,** which contain a variety of materials including child products which have dates written on them, can be helpful in documenting the on-going development of young children.

Early childhood professionals are very busy and not all teachers have an aide or teaching team. Consequently, they may need to be creative in devising ways that help them learn more about children in their own environment. There is no single correct way to study children. However, following are some guidelines for early childhood professionals to facilitate child study and observation:

Portfolio—a collection that contains child products, e.g., art, written work, and related materials, all of which are dated and used to document development and learning over a period of time.

1. In addition to ongoing assessment, try to identify times when observations might be conducted.
2. Try to identify how you can conduct observations. Parent volunteers, student teachers, or child development students can supervise young children occasionally, giving the classroom teacher the opportunity to do some observing.
3. Wear clothing with a pocket so that small note pads or cards and pencil are available for recording information as it occurs.
4. Keep all information confidential and do not talk about the young children in their presence.

Remember the quote at the beginning of this chapter? Take a look at it again. More than any other factor, your ability to study young children will be the key to understanding their behavior as well as your own. Child study is not to be looked upon lightly or grudgingly. Child study coupled with your knowledge of child development provides the foundation for your development into a competent early childhood professional.

> Observing children can be a key to understanding ourselves. People who develop observational skills notice human behavior more accurately. They become skilled at seeing small but important facets of human personality. They learn to differentiate between what is fact and what is inference. This increases an awareness of how one's biases affect the perceptions of children. The values and benefits of observations are long-lasting. Only by practicing observations—what it takes to look, to see, to become more sensitive—will teachers be able to record children's behavior fully and vividly, capturing the unique qualities and personality of each child. (Gordon & Browne, 1985, p. 138)

Key Terms

preservice
inservice
hypotheses
descriptive study
cross-sectional study
representative sample
longitudinal study
pre-primary
correlational study
experimental study
random
disabilities
least restrictive environment
mainstream
formal
informal
standardized test
achievement test

readiness test
developmental screening test
diagnostic test
intelligence test
narrative observation
running record
specimen record
anecdotal record
checklist
rating scale
time sampling
event sampling
interview
support staff
resource persons
peers
portfolio

Review Strategies/Activities

1. Interview early childhood professionals who work with young children of various ages, infants through the primary grades.
   a. Collect information about the methods of child study they feel are most effective.
   b. Analyze according to techniques used with varying ages of children.
2. Collect various evaluation forms used in early childhood settings from birth through age eight. After studying chapters 5 through 16,
   a. Analyze them. Do they attempt to document only certain aspects of development? Do they attempt to describe the whole development of the child?
   b. Evaluate them for developmental appropriateness. Do they attempt to measure the developmentally appropriate behaviors for children in that particular age group?
   (For more information regarding developmentally appropriate behaviors, read the NAEYC Position Statements on Developmentally Appropriate Practice (1987), Guidelines for Appropriate Curriculum Content and Assessment (1992), and Testing of Young Children (1988) as noted in the Further Readings section of this chapter.)
3. In several early childhood settings, try out a variety of child-study techniques: running records, specimen records, anecdotal records, checklists, rating scales, time sampling, event sampling, and interview.
   a. Discuss what you learned about children with students in your class.
   b. Discuss what you learned about these child study techniques with your class. What did you find difficult to do? What seemed easy? What are the drawbacks and benefits of certain techniques? When would it be most appropriate to use what technique?
4. Read a child development research study in one of the research journals.
   a. How would you categorize the research: descriptive, longitudinal, correlational, or experimental?
   b. Was the study conducted in an ethical manner?
   c. Were sociocultural factors taken into consideration in the study?
5. Interview early childhood professionals who have worked with young children for 10 years or more. Ask them what they continue to learn or discover about young children and working with them.
6. Choose one child to observe throughout an entire day. Note how the child's behavior changes depending upon the context of the setting, the people in the setting, and the time of day.
7. Read several articles in various professional journals. What did you learn about the development of young children that will help you?
8. Interview several early childhood professionals about the change in development and behavior that generally takes place in the children they work with over a year. What typical behaviors are they looking for? How do they identify atypical behaviors and what do they do about them?

Further Readings

Almy, M., & Genishi, C. (1979). *Ways of studying children* (rev. ed.). New York: Teachers College Press.

This "classic" in child study was first published in 1959. David Elkind states in the foreword that this book has both teacher sense and child sense. It is filled with interesting real-life examples.

Beaty, J. J. (1990). *Observing the development of the young child* (2nd ed.). Columbus, OH: Merrill.

This book begins with a very thorough discussion of the techniques of observation used in child study. It follows with chapters devoted to the study of the whole child, including self-identity, emotional development, social play, prosocial behavior, large and small motor development, cognitive development, spoken and written language, art skills, and imagination.

Cryan, J. R. (1986). Evaluation: Plague or promise. *Childhood Education, 62,* 344–350.

This article identifies the positive aspects of appropriate evaluation and the negative results of inappropriate evaluation of young children. The author describes formal and informal evaluation procedures which are most helpful to early childhood professionals.

Genishi, C., & Dyson, A. H. (1984). *Language assessment in the early years.* Norwood, NJ: Ablex.

This book provides information about the development and assessment of young children's oral and written language from birth through the primary years. Attention is given to children from different cultural and linguistic backgrounds. It is rich with examples of children using language and provides many ideas for early childhood professionals to use in studying children's language.

Kamii, C. (Ed.). (1990). *Achievement testing in the early grades: The games grown-ups play.* Washington, DC: National Association for the Education of Young Children.

This book emphasizes that well-intentioned but unknowing adults are playing games—the vote-getting game, the looking-good game, the keep-my-job game, and the buck-passing game—by advocating the standardized testing of young children. This higher test score solution is causing a great deal of damage, according to the contributors to this book, including teachers, state department officers, administrators, university researchers, and representatives from professional organizations. The authors suggest that standardized tests do not really provide the information that helps teachers facilitate appropriate learning experiences for young children. They call for a halt to standardized achievement testing through grade two and propose appropriate alternatives.

Meisels, S. J. (1987). Uses and abuses of developmental screening and school readiness testing. *Young Children, 42,* 68–73.

The difference between screening and readiness instruments is noted. Criticisms of the Gesell School Readiness Screening Test are discussed with response from the Gesell Institute staff.

Meisels, S. J. (1989). *Developmental screening in early childhood: A guide.* (3rd edition). Washington, DC: National Association for the Education of Young Children.

This publication provides a guide for developmentally appropriate screening of young children. This is an important resource, as some commercial and teacher-formulated developmental screening procedures are not always developmentally appropriate.

Morrow, L. M., & Smith, J. K. (Eds.). (1990). *Assessment for instruction in early literacy.* Englewood Cliffs, NJ: Prentice-Hall.

This book addresses the assessment of emergent literacy in children from ages two through seven. The authors stress that standardized testing of early reading remains virtually unchanged despite two decades of emergent literacy research that demonstrates the interrelationship of ongoing assessment and instruction. A large portion of this text is devoted to appropriate ways of assessing early literacy in the classroom.

Wortham, S. C. (1990). *Tests and measurement in early childhood education.* Columbus, OH: Merrill.

This is the first comprehensive book addressing measurement and evaluation of children under age 8. Because of the developmental variations between young children and older children, techniques used to evaluate young children must address these differences. This book includes information about standardized tests used with young children and also provides information about developmentally appropriate ways of evaluating and measuring young children.

Position Statements from Professional Organizations

Black, J. K., Puckett, M., Haws, A., Moberg, K., and Vernon, L. (1986). *Developmentally Appropriate Kindergarten Reading Programs.* The Texas Association for the Education of Young Children. Central Office, 8100 Bounty Trail, Austin, TX 78749–2813.

Developmentally appropriate assessment. The Southern Association on Children under Six, P. O. Box 5403 Brady Station, Little Rock, AR 72215, (501) 663–0353.

Developmentally appropriate practice in early childhood programs, serving children from birth through age 8. (1987). The National Association for the Education of Young Children, 1834 Connecticut Avenue N.W., Washington, DC 20009, (800) 424–2460.

Guidelines for appropriate curriculum content and assessment in programs serving children ages 3 through 8. (1992). The National Association for the Education of Young Children (see address above), and National Association of Early Childhood Specialists in State Departments of Education.

Perrone, V. (1991). *On standardized testing.* The Association for Childhood Education International, 11141 Georgia Avenue, Suite 200, Wheaton, MD, 20902, (800) 423–3563.

Quality child care. The Southern Association on Children under Six (see address above).

Quality programs for five year olds. The Southern Association on Children under Six (see address above).

Quality programs for four year olds. The Southern Association on Children under Six (see address above).

School readiness. (1990). The National Association for the Education of Young Children (see address above).

Testing of young children: Concerns and cautions. (1988). The National Association for the Education of Young Children (see address above).

These position statements serve the purpose of describing (1) young children's development, (2) developmentally appropriate education for young children, and (3) appropriate assessment of young children and programs for young children.

PART TWO

The Child's Life Begins

CHAPTER 3

A parent has the potential to gain what is without a doubt the highest satisfaction a human being can enjoy—the gratification of nurturing the development of a child into an emotionally stable and mature young man and woman. There is no greater reward for the adult; there is no greater gift to the child.

Richard A. Gardner

The Family Before Birth

After reading and studying this chapter, you will demonstrate comprehension by:

- Describing the importance of early childhood professionals in understanding the role of parents in the development of their children, prebirth through age 8.
- Outlining the possible implications of the presence or absence of choice for parenting.
- Identifying the impact of the sociocultural and economic factors in becoming parents.
- Identifying emotional and psychological aspects of preparing for parenting.
- Describing prenatal development.
- Describing quality prenatal care.
- Describing education for childbirth and parenting.
- Describing the importance of preparing siblings for birth.

Importance of Early Childhood Professionals in Understanding the Role of Parents

Throughout this text, there is much attention given to the role of parents in the development of young children. It is important for the early childhood professional to be aware of this information for several reasons. First, the behaviors and attitudes of parents directly influence the development of the young child even prior to birth. For example, as discussed later in this chapter, parents' use of chemical substances and the nutritional habits of the mother can affect the growth and development of the baby before it is born. These parental behaviors

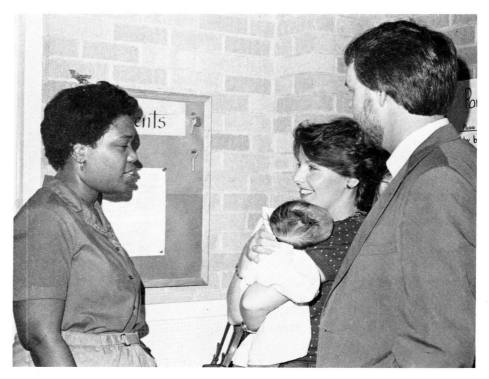

Parents and early childhood professionals must be partners if optimal learning and development are to occur in young children.

can have consequences upon the later development and learning of young children. Second, the behaviors and attitudes of the parents after birth and throughout the early childhood years continue to influence the development and learning of the young child. Third, parents' knowledge of their young child can be helpful to early childhood professionals. Thus, parents and early childhood professionals must be partners if optimal learning and development are to occur in young children. If this partnership is to be effective, it is vital that early childhood professionals have an empathetic understanding of the challenges and demands of parenting. For instance, third grade teacher Sharon Smith was upset with Joe's mother because she did not make him learn his multiplication tables. Through talking with the school counselor, Ms. Smith found out that Joe's mother was a single parent working two jobs, one of which was during the evening hours. There were five children in the family and they lived in a two-room apartment. An awareness of the demands upon Joe's mother helped Ms. Smith adopt a more empathetic attitude toward her. Tutoring by a sixth-grade boy during school and help from an older brother provided more support for Joe and his learning needs.

Early childhood professionals can also help parents understand the development of their young children and learn appropriate parenting techniques.

Remember in Chapter 2 how Mr. Hubbard helped Juan's parents become aware of the importance of their behavior in helping Juan adjust to the child care center? Mr. Hubbard encouraged Juan's parents to bring him to the center and stay with him for several short periods before he began to attend full time, and to bring Juan's favorite toy and blanket every day.

Finally, an increased understanding of parental roles not only facilitates the effectiveness of early childhood professionals in working with young children in their classrooms, but can also benefit early childhood professionals in their own parenting roles. Occasionally, students who are parents of older children wish they had had early childhood development information when their own children were young, but they may find it helpful in their role as grandparents. It is important to remember that all parents do the best they can and that many parents have never had a course in child development or parenting. Therefore, they may have some of the same attitudes and behaviors as parents described in the account of deMause's investigations as reported in Chapter 1. An awareness of the importance of the parental role and its impact upon the development and learning of young children is necessary if the early childhood professional is to effectively relate to young children and their families.

■ *Meet Jeremy*

Ann and Bill Johnson live in a large metropolitan area in the South. Ann is a technical illustrator for a publisher and Bill is an accountant. Bill grew up in a suburban area, where his father was an accountant and his mother was a child development specialist. Both parents were active in community affairs. Bill feels fortunate to have grown up with loving parents.

Ann's parents divorced when she was seven. While her relationship with her father was close, he was transferred to another company on the West Coast. As a result, she saw him only a few times each year. Ann's mother was a somewhat distant person and Ann never felt emotionally close to her.

After college graduation, Ann and Bill married. They worked hard to establish themselves in their respective careers. They traveled, saved their money, and eventually bought a home in the suburbs. When several of their friends began to start their families, Bill and Ann felt privileged to share in the discussions about pregnancy, childbirth, and what it was like to become parents. They began to talk about having children of their own. Bill wanted several children but Ann was not so sure. Her own unhappy childhood caused her concern about her ability to be a good parent. Eventually, Ann went to a counselor to work through her feelings. During this time she and Bill read many books about pregnancy, childbirth, and parenting. Eventually, Ann resolved her fears, deciding that she could provide a safe and secure childhood for her children.

Bill and Ann analyzed their family finances. Between the two of them, they had a comfortable income. Ann's company provided paid maternity leave and Bill's accounting firm would grant him parental leave. Ann and Bill began to investigate possible types of child care for infants. About this time, Bill's firm, along with several other businesses, decided to establish a child care center, which included an infant room.

Ann and Bill had always been health conscious. They exercised regularly and paid attention to their diets. Neither smoked or abused drugs or alcohol. Both had annual checkups. They consulted with their doctors and told them they would like to begin their family. The doctors asked for a brief family history and inquired about possible genetic defects. Ann and Bill requested the names of several obstetricians whose practice focused upon family-centered maternity care.

Bill and Ann had carefully considered whether to become parents. They assessed themselves emotionally and psychologically. They took care of themselves physically. They evaluated their finances and planned for the baby's care. They read about pregnancy, childbirth, and parenting. Bill and Ann felt that they were prepared to start their family.

Three months later, Ann missed her menstrual period. She made an appointment with one of the recommended obstetricians, Dr. Susan Windle. Bill went with Ann to see Dr. Windle. They were ecstatic when Dr. Windle confirmed that Ann was pregnant. Dr. Windle took a detailed medical history of both Bill and Ann, and shared information with them regarding the early stages of pregnancy. She described the care she would be providing for Ann and asked for questions. Dr. Windle also discussed various fees and hospital procedures, and encouraged Ann and Bill to visit the birthing center. She told them about two childbirth classes, the first on general information regarding pregnancy and the development of the baby, and the second on Lamaze prepared childbirth, to be taken near the end of Ann's pregnancy. As they left Dr. Windle's office, Ann and Bill were given a number of brochures and booklets to read. They celebrated at one of their favorite restaurants. Over a candlelit dinner, they decided to name the baby Jeremy if it was a boy. They were not quite sure about a girl's name. Bill liked Elizabeth, while Ann liked Julia, the name of a favorite aunt.

During the beginning of her pregnancy, Ann's moods varied from elation to mild depression. At times these mood swings were difficult for Bill to understand. At their first future parents' class, they found that other couples were experiencing similar problems. Jane, the instructor, explained that these mood swings were caused by the hormonal changes of pregnancy. Ann, like some of the other women, also reported increased fatigue and nausea. Jane told the class that usually by the end of the first three months, most of these normal but somewhat discomforting effects of pregnancy would subside.

Bill and Ann made regular trips to Dr. Windle throughout the pregnancy. Ann ate nutritious and well-balanced meals, increased her intake of dairy products and took no medication without the approval of Dr. Windle. Bill and Ann attended childbirth classes, visited the hospital, bought furniture and clothes for the baby, and compromised on a girl's name, Julia Elizabeth. They enjoyed talking with other new parents and reading books about parenting, finding that this helped relieve some of their normal feelings of anxiety. They followed the development of their baby with **ultrasound** tests, which indicated that the fetus was developing normally and would probably be a boy, Jeremy.

Ultrasound—a technique using sound frequencies which can detect structural disorders and the approximate week of pregnancy.

Bill and Ann finalized their plans for the baby's care after Ann returned to work. They discussed their parental leaves with their employers. Bill wanted to take at least a week off after the baby was born. Ann decided to return to work when the baby was 6 weeks old, but as the baby's birth drew near, Ann decided that she did not want to leave her young baby in a group care situation, even though Bill's firm had implemented an excellent program for infants and toddlers. Ann and Bill felt more comfortable having someone care for their baby in their home. Ann contacted an agency that provided trained nannies. After several interviews, Ann and Bill chose Phyllis. She was 23, had worked for several other families who provided excellent references, had a good knowledge of young children's development, and demonstrated a love of young children. Ann and Bill fixed up a bedroom and bath in another wing of their home for Phyllis. Since Phyllis was completing her position with another family, it would be possible for her to join the Johnsons about two weeks before Ann was to return to work.

Ann's mother wanted to come to help. Bill and Ann had learned from their parenting classes that each couple has to decide if they want family help with their new baby. Some people can be of great assistance to new parents, giving them information about the habits of babies as well as helping with household chores. However, some extended families are not very supportive and take control at a time when the new parents should be in charge. Ann finally decided that, given the somewhat tense relationship she had with her mother, it would be best to invite her mother for a visit after the new Johnson family had a week or two together. Bill and Ann had taken the time to prepare for the optimal development of their baby and to inform themselves about pregnancy and parenting. Now all they had to do was practice the exercises they had learned in the childbirth classes and wait.   ■

■ *Meet Angela*

Cheryl Monroe is 15 years old. She lives in an urban area with her mother and four brothers and sisters. Her grades are barely passing and she has considered dropping out of school but her mother tells her that it is important to get an education. Cheryl's mother takes the bus every afternoon downtown where she works until midnight cleaning corporate offices. Cheryl does not know who her father is.

Cheryl's dream is to be a movie star or a singer with a rock group. She, like most adolescent girls, is very interested in boys and has been seeing James for about seven months. They have been sexually active and spend their evenings watching TV, listening to music, and eating junk food.

It has been four months since Cheryl has had her menstrual period and her changing body is now reinforcing the idea that she is indeed pregnant. Finally, she shares her suspicions with several of her teenage friends. They generally respond that she is lucky because she will have a cute baby to love her. Eventually, Cheryl tells her mother that she is going to have a baby. Her mother knows that this will probably mean an end to Cheryl's high school education and is very disappointed. She shares her concern, anger, and disappointment with Cheryl. She doubts that James will be able to support Cheryl and feels that Cheryl's baby will be another mouth to feed in their already economically stressed household.

James is proud of his impending fatherhood and brags about it to his friends. He does care for Cheryl and intends to help support the baby from his occasional part-time work.

One day, Cheryl's mother shares her concern about her daughter with one of the women in their church, Linnie Hudson. Ms. Hudson tells Cheryl's mother that it is important for Cheryl to receive prenatal care as soon as possible. She tells her to talk to their minister about getting Cheryl into a clinic that provides care and service for unwed mothers. Ms. Monroe gets the information from Reverend Brown and helps her schedule an appointment for Cheryl.

During her first visit to the prenatal clinic, an examination reveals that Cheryl is 6 to 7 months pregnant. She is counseled on nutrition; told how to sign up for WIC (Women, Infants, and Children), a federally funded program that provides various dairy and food products for pregnant and nursing women and their young children; and is scheduled for follow-up visits.

Cheryl spends the last 2 to 3 months of her pregnancy working on her studies at home, watching TV, helping out around the apartment, seeing James and her other friends, and visiting the clinic for prenatal checkups. Medical personnel feel encouraged from their exams that the baby seems to be developing normally. Ultrasound tests indicate that they will probably have a girl. Cheryl convinces James to name their daughter Angela. Cheryl and James await Angela's birth.   ■

The two vignettes in this chapter describe two very different situations into which babies will be born. One is planned and optimal. The other is by chance and at-risk for a variety of reasons. This chapter discusses the importance of planning for a family, of good health in both parents, and of quality prenatal care throughout the pregnancy in promoting the optimal development of young children.

The Presence or Absence of Choice in Parenting

During the 1960s several events occurred that stimulated a great deal of research on the early years of life. The translation of Piaget's work (1952) indicated that the early years of life were critical in the development of intelligence. Benjamin Bloom's (1964) research on human intelligence revealed that the capacity for the development of intellectual potential is greatest during the first 3 years of life. The studies of J. McVicker Hunt (1961) documented the importance of environments and early experience in the development of intelligence.

This interest in the early years of life encompasses the study of the development and behavior of infants at birth and even before, and is demonstrated by the publication of many research articles on infants in journals such as *Infant Behavior and Development* and the *Infant and Mental Health Journal.* The research findings have caused increasing awareness about the importance of what happens before pregnancy, during pregnancy, and in the early years of life in relationship to long-term development. Consequently, many adults consider the choice of having a child as a serious decision, one that entails education and preparation before the baby is born and even before conception.

Increased recognition of the long-term emotional and financial commitment to child-rearing, the availability of natural and artificial methods of birth control, and the growing social acceptance of small, one-child, or no-children families have served to provide many options in terms of family planning. Ideally, the mother and father of a child will both decide that they want to become parents because they (1) enjoy children, (2) want to share their love and lives with children as they continue to grow and mature, and (3) are committed to providing opportunities for their children to become well-adjusted and productive members of society.

Unfortunately, many children are conceived under less than desirable circumstances. The relationship between the mother and father may be casual or unstable, rather than based upon a loving, supportive commitment. Many people may not realize the extent of responsibility involved in parenting. Others have children in an attempt to satisfy their own emotional needs, to please parents, or in response to pressure from friends. People who do not take parenting seriously or examine their motives for becoming parents are often frustrated and disappointed at the expense and the loss of flexibility, privacy, and freedom. If their lives are already stressful, a child adds to the frustration. The end result is unhappy parents whose children do not feel wanted or loved. Children in these families can become the victims of neglect or physical and emotional abuse. Overwhelmed parents often fail to introduce their children to the excitement of learning about the world as they grow and develop. These factors can set the stage for at-risk children, children who do not develop and learn in optimal ways.

Conversations with parents who are considered excellent mothers and fathers indicate that while they feel parenting brings many joys, it also is the most challenging and demanding job in the world. Becoming competent parents requires commitment and education. For the most part, good parents do not just happen, and the decision to have a child should not be made lightly—it is a long-term commitment requiring emotional maturity and financial resources.

Sociocultural and Economic Factors

There are a number of sociocultural and economic factors that affect the quality of life for newborn children and their families. Some of these include teenage pregnancy, the number and spacing of children in the family, cultural differences in prenatal care, and the income of the family. It should be noted that a number of these factors are common to a variety of cultural and economic groups. For example, teenage pregnancy transcends virtually all social and economic groups.

Teenage Parenting

Many children today are born to adolescents, some younger than 12 years of age. This epidemic of "children having children" has become one of the major concerns of a number of groups, including the Children's Defense Fund (1989). Children of teenage parents are often at risk for a number of reasons. Many teenagers do not eat a well-balanced diet, and good nutrition is absolutely necessary to the development of a healthy baby. Increased smoking and drug abuse of teenagers can also threaten the development of the **fetus.** Many teenagers, for a variety of reasons, do not receive **prenatal** care. Biological immaturity of the developing teenager can also contribute to the development of complications during pregnancy (Children's Defense Fund, 1989).

According to Children's Defense Fund data (1989), many teenage mothers do not marry the fathers of their babies. Teenagers often do not understand

Fetus—the developing human from 9 weeks after conception until birth.

Prenatal—the time from conception until birth, an average of 266 days or 38 weeks.

the reproductive process and lack reliable information about birth control. Some teenage girls want a baby to provide them with the love they feel they have never received from their parents—they do not understand that it is very difficult to be a single parent. At times, the father may want to be involved with his baby, but lack of job security may prevent the couple from marrying. Thus, many teenage mothers must rely upon their parents for social and economic support. Many times the parents of teenage girls resent having to sacrifice their time, financial resources, and jobs to help care for their grandchildren. These grandparents may also be caring for their own aging parents. The end result for many teenage mothers is that they and their children become dependent upon public assistance.

In order to reduce the rate of teenage pregnancy, the Children's Defense Fund (1989a) and other groups are helping to make teenagers aware of the risks and realities of teenage pregnancy. They are encouraging teenagers to postpone pregnancy through abstinence or the practice of safe sex. In the event of pregnancy, teenagers are being made aware of the importance of good pre-natal care. A number of programs have been implemented to encourage teenage girls to complete their high school education by providing on-site child care (Children's Defense Fund, 1989a, p. 96).

Size of Family

Another sociocultural factor to consider is the number of children already in the family, and their ages in relationship to the anticipated baby. Some child development experts suggest a spacing of three years between children as optimal for effective parenting and child rearing (Dunn, 1984; Dunn & Kendrick, 1982a). If there are several young children quite close in age, the addition of an infant can provide additional stress to the family, as caring for and nurturing young children is demanding and time-consuming. While some parents can handle a large family with children close in age, others cannot.

Attitudes of Extended Family

Another sociocultural factor affecting prospective parents is the attitudes of extended family and friends. The responses of family members toward the pregnancy also influence the perceptions and the feelings of the prospective father and mother. Unsolicited advice and "information" can serve to encourage and support or to create anxiety about approaching parenthood (Shapiro, 1987).

Economic Considerations in Having a Child

Many parents probably feel that they are not as financially secure as they would like, but the cost of adequately clothing and feeding a child should be consid-

Unsolicited advice and "information" from friends and family can support, encourage, or create anxiety about parenthood.

ered when making a decision about having a baby. Can the family's financial resources realistically support the child, or will the addition of a child create an undue economic hardship? Ideally, these questions should be considered in family planning. Families that are too large for the financial resources available can lead to stress and resentment in parents, and the children then feel that they are not wanted and are a burden to their parents (Garbarino, 1977).

In addition, lack of adequate economic resources can adversely impact the prenatal health care of the mother and the developing child. Unfortunately, within American society there are many families who do not have access to adequate nutrition and prenatal care. While there are some programs such as WIC (Women, Infants, and Children) that provide milk and other essential foods to low-income pregnant women and new mothers, their infants, and their young children, not all eligible people are served. People are often unaware of medical services, and if they are available, they may be underfunded and understaffed.

The consequences of poor nutrition and poor prenatal care are reflected in babies who have **low birth weight.** If these at-risk babies survive, the financial cost of possible extended hospital care and the social cost of long-term developmental problems are major concerns. Solutions to these problems include establishing a network of services that will provide appropriate education and health care to families during and after pregnancy.

Low birth weight—a weight at birth of less than 5½ pounds or 2500 grams.

Emotional and Psychological Aspects of Preparing for Parenthood

Ideally, the newborn child has a mother and father whose relationship is stable, mature, and based upon mutual love and support. Unfortunately, not all marriages are so fortunate, and the idea that a baby can help a troubled marriage is a myth. The demands of adjusting to another family member may only add to an already stressful situation. Couples who have an unstable relationship are wise to seek professional counseling before they decide to become parents.

Prospective parents react individually to pregnancy depending upon the choices and the social and economic factors which have been discussed. Some prospective parents feel elated and overjoyed; others fearful or resentful. It is not uncommon to have mixed emotions.

Reaction of the Prospective Mother

Trimester—the first, second, or third three months of pregnancy.

Anthony and Benedek (1975) propose that future mothers go through three emotional stages either at a conscious or unconscious level. During the first **trimester** or three months of pregnancy, the mother-to-be finds it difficult to accept the idea of a fetus within her body. She begins to think about the impending change in her lifestyle and family structure. These concerns, coupled with hormonal change, can create mood swings. During the second trimester, the future mother begins to think of the baby as a separate being, and in the third trimester, she comes to terms with the actual birth process and impending motherhood. Anthony and Benedek (1975) also indicate that developmental conflicts during the mother's life are often relived during pregnancy. These past events influence a woman's perspective of motherhood and her attitude toward her child. If these conflicts arise, they can best be resolved through professional counseling.

Reaction of the Prospective Father

In the past, attention has been focused primarily upon the prospective mother, but recently the emotional reactions and feelings of the prospective father have also been examined. It has been observed that prospective fathers are now more involved in preparing for the birth, helping with the birth, and sharing in the child care (Shapiro, 1987). However, their common feelings of anxiety, anger, sadness, and fear are often viewed as unacceptable. A study by Shapiro (1987) discovered that at least 40 percent of prospective fathers had some major fears and concerns, including: (1) queasiness about the actual birth process, (2) concern about increased financial responsibility, (3) feeling put down by obstetrical-gynecological staff, (4) questioning of paternity, (5) fear of loss of spouse and or child, (6) feeling left out as pregnant spouse begins turning inward and bonding with the growing fetus, and (7) an increased awareness of life and death in general. The study indicated that these concerns were not generally communicated with others, but when future fathers did share their concerns with their wives, the marriage relationship was strengthened and the couples felt closer. Shapiro (1987) suggests that these natural and normal feelings need to be recognized by the prospective father, his wife, the family, and society in general.

The prospective mother's emotional and psychological state affects the prospective father and vice versa. Thus, the emotional reactions of both the mother and father need to be acknowledged and accepted, and if special problems develop professional counseling is advised. As will be discussed in Chapter 6, it is the emotional climate created by the prospective parents' relationship that will be largely responsible for the psychological well-being of the newborn child.

Prenatal Development

You have probably noticed that all children are different from one another in the way they look and the way they act. These differences are due to the fact that everyone has a different set of inherited characteristics or **heredity**. In addition, everyone has a different **environment**, that is, different relationships, physical settings, and educational experiences. Even within the same family, everyone has a different set of inherited characteristics as well as different environmental experiences. Children are born in different order and as new family members are added, relationships change.

For many years people have debated the influence of heredity and environment on the development of an individual. In certain situations, the influence of heredity or environment may be obvious, but more often behavior is best explained by the combination or interaction of both heredity and environment. In any case, optimum development of an individual is dependent upon healthy genetic traits and also upon a healthy environment (Mange & Mange, 1990).

Chromosomes and Genes

At conception the sperm from the father penetrates the egg or ovum from the mother. The ovum can be fertilized by a sperm approximately every twenty-eight days during a period of about twenty-four hours. At the point of fertilization **chromosomes** of the mother and father unite. As seen in Figure 3.1, chromosomes are located in the nucleus of a cell and contain thousands of **genes**. This combination of genes from the mother and the father determines a person's genetic potential or **genotype**. Genotype also includes **recessive genes**. These genes are not evident if they are paired with dominant genes. Genes, composed of **DNA**, make the blueprint that codes the complex information that causes the development of tissues, organs, and physiological functions (Thompson & Thompson, 1986).

Heredity—*the inherited characteristics of humans carried by genes.*

Environment—*the experiences, conditions, objects, and people that directly or indirectly influence the development and behavior of a child.*

Chromosomes—*ordered groups of genes within the nucleus of a cell.*

Genes—*molecules of DNA that store and transmit the characteristics of past generations.*

Genotype—*the combination of genes inherited from both parents and their ancestors.*

Recessive gene—*a gene that carries a trait which may not appear unless a gene for the same trait is inherited from both parents.*

DNA—*deoxyribonucleic acid, the substance in genes that has the information that causes the formation of chains of protein that stimulate the development of tissue and organs, and affects other genes and physiological functions.*

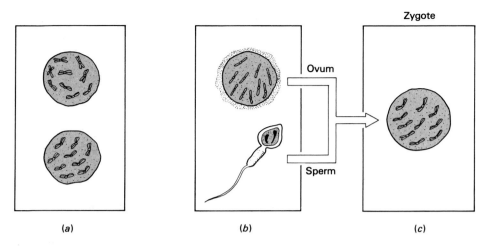

(a)   (b)   (c)

FIGURE 3.1
A fertilized egg (zygote) inherits a unique genetic code. (a) Each cell of the parents contains 46 chromosomes in 23 pairs with thousands of genes. (b) However, ovum and sperm each have only 23 chromosomes due to special cell division that divides the total number of chromosomes in half. (c) At fertilization, the 23 chromosomes from the sperm unite with the 23 chromosomes from the ovum, making a total of 46 chromosomes in 23 pairs.

Causes of Congenital Malformations

Abortion—the ending of a pregnancy, usually during the first trimester.

At times, numerical or structural abnormalities of chromosomes can result in incomplete or imperfect cell formation. Many of these abnormalities result in spontaneous **abortion** early in the pregnancy. If the baby is born, these defective chromosomes can result in **congenital malformations** and/or mental retardation. These physical abnormalities may be obvious at birth or they may be internal. Table 3.1 provides a brief overview of some of the more common congenital malformations.

Congenital malformations—skeletal or body system abnormalities that are caused by defective genes within the chromosomes and usually affect the developing embryo during the first 8 weeks of pregnancy.

One example of numerical chromosome abnormality would be Down's syndrome. Down's syndrome characteristics vary in degree but usually include mental retardation, certain physical characteristics, and congenital heart defects. Other disorders associated with abnormal genes include cystic fibrosis, Tay Sachs disease, thalassemia, dwarfing condition, and sickle cell anemia. These disorders can be evident when both parents' chromosomes carry the defective gene. Thus, the baby receives an abnormal gene from each parent.

Some congenital malformations result when two or more combinations of abnormal genes and environmental agents cause a defect. Spina bifida (opening in the spinal column), anencephaly (little or no brain development), cleft lip and palate, club feet, congenital heart disease, and dislocation of the hips are some of the disorders caused by genetic and environmental factors (Jones, 1988).

TABLE 3.1

Common genetic diseases and conditions (pp. 77–78)

Disease or Condition	Description	Mode of Transmission	Incidence	Prognosis	Prenatal Detection	Carrier Detection
Cleft palate, cleft lip (Hare lip)	The two sides of the upper lip or the palate are not joined	Causes include genetic defects, prenatal injury, drugs, and malnutrition	Unknown because not always reported; varies with ethnic group	Correctable by surgery	No	No
Cystic fibrosis	Lack of enzyme causes mucous obstruction, especially in the lungs and digestive tract	Recessive gene	1 in 21,000 live births in U.S.; most common in people of Northern European descent	Few victims survive to adulthood	No (possible in near future)	No
Diabetes melitus (juvenile form)	Deficient metabolism of sugar because body does not produce adequate insulin	Thought to be polygenic	1 in 25 to 40 of all diabetics	Fatal if untreated; controllable by insulin and a restricted diet	No	No
Down's syndrome	Physical and intellectual retardation; distinctive physical appearance	Chromosomal abnormality; extra chromosome 21	1 in 600 to 700 births	Moderate to severe mental retardation; eye, ear, and heart problems	Yes	Possible in cases of chromosomal rearrangement (only 5% of cases)
Hemophilia (bleeding disease)	Blood does not clot readily	X-linked gene; also spontaneous mutation	1 in 21,500 live births of males	Possible crippling and death from internal bleeding; transfusions are used to ameliorate effects	No	Yes
Huntington's chorea	Deterioration of the central nervous system and body in middle age	Dominant gene	Rare	Fatal	Yes	Yes
Klinefelter's syndrome	Affects males; failure to mature sexually at adolescence; sterility	Chromosomal abnormality; an extra X chromosome (XXY)	1 in 1,000 white males in U.S.	Emotional and social problems; treated by administering testosterone	Yes	No
Muscular dystrophy (Duchenne's type)	Weaking and wasting away of the muscles	X-linked gene	1 in 200,000 males under the age of 20	Crippling; often fatal by age of 20	Yes	Sometimes

TABLE 3.1
continued

Disease or Condition	Description	Mode of Transmission	Incidence	Prognosis	Prenatal Detection	Carrier Detection
Neural tube defects (anencephaly and spina bifida)	In anencephaly, part of the brain and skull is missing; in spina bifida, part of the spine is not closed over	Uncertain	1 in 1,000 live births in U.S.	Babies with anencephaly die shortly after birth. Those with spina bifida may survive with surgery; their prognosis depends on the defect's severity	Yes	No
Phenylketonuria (PKU)	Lack of enzyme causes abnormal digestion of certain proteins	Recessive gene	1 in 15,000 white births; lower in blacks and Ashkenazi Jews	Mental retardation and hyperactivity; controllable in many through diet	Yes	Often
Sickle-cell anemia	Abnormal red blood cells	Recessive gene	1 in 625 births among U.S. blacks	Possible heart and kidney failure; many survive into adulthood	Yes	Yes
Tay-Sachs disease	Lack of an enzyme causes waste build-up in the brain	Recessive gene	1 in 3,600 for Ashkenazi Jews in U.S.	Neurological degeneration leading to death before the age of 4	Yes	Yes
Thalassemia (Cooley's anemia)	Abnormal red blood cells	Recessive gene	1 in 100 births in populations from subtropical and tropical areas of Europe, Africa, and Asia	Listlessness, enlarged liver and spleen, occasionally death; treatable by blood transfusions	Yes	Yes
Turner's syndrome	Affects females; short stature, webbed neck, and broad chest; failure to produce the hormone estrogen; sterility	Chromosomal abnormality; single X chromosome (XO)	1 in 10,000 female births	Physical defect may lead to social and emotional problems; treated with hormone therapy	Yes	No

Source: *The Development of Children.* By Michael Cole and Sheila Cole. Copyright © 1989 by Michael Cole, Sheila R. Cole, and Judith Boies. Reprinted with permission by W. H. Freeman and Company.

Another condition which can cause congenital malformation and stillbirth is the Rh factor. The **Rh factor** (detected in the rhesus monkey after which this condition is named) is caused when the fetus of a mother who has Rh negative blood inherits Rh positive blood from the father. Usually this condition does not harm the first baby. At present there are two types of treatment for the Rh factor. One involves changing the blood of the fetus in the uterus before birth or immediately after. In the second type of treatment a serum, RhoGam, is administered to the mother during pregnancy or within several days after the delivery of her first Rh baby. This treatment prevents the formation of antibodies.

Rh factor—a treatable condition in the mother which produces antibodies that destroy the red blood cells of her second baby and subsequent babies.

Genetic Counseling and Testing

Genetic counseling can be helpful to couples whose background indicates possible genetic defects or whose fetus has been diagnosed as at risk. As indicated, problems can occur if a child is born to parents who both carry the same harmful trait.

While genetic counselors cannot accurately predict if a child will be born with a disorder, they can provide information to couples who can then decide whether they should have a child. In situations where conception has already occurred, various tests can provide information regarding the condition of the fetus. While this information cannot always predict the extent of the disorder, it may be helpful to parents in making the very difficult decision of whether to complete or terminate the pregnancy.

There are several techniques for determining genetic defects. Testing the blood of the prospective parents can be helpful in determining several possible problems. The gene for sickle cell anemia is present in 8 percent of African-Americans. Tay Sachs, an enzyme deficiency seen more commonly in Ashkenazi Jewish descendants, causes neurological degeneration and early death. Blood analysis can determine the presence of both sickle cell anemia and Tay Sachs. Another blood test, the **alphafetoprotein test** is used to determine if there are disorders in the brain or spinal column. Another procedure called **amniocentesis** can aid in identifying all chromosomal disorders and over 100 biochemical disorders. This procedure involves the analysis of the fetal cells in the amniotic fluid from the uterus. Amniocentesis is recommended when the mother is of advanced age or family history indicates that the fetus may be at risk. It is usually done approximately 14 to 16 weeks into the pregnancy, when there is sufficient amniotic fluid surrounding the fetus. Analysis takes about two weeks and the results are sometimes not available until the fifth month of pregnancy (Vogel & Motulsky, 1979).

A third method of determining chromosomal disorders is the **chorionic villus test (CVT)**. In CVT, a sample of cells is taken from the hair-like projections (villi) that are on tissue (chorion) in the placenta. The CVT has some advantages over amniocentesis, as it can be done as early as the ninth week of pregnancy and the results are usually available in several days.

A fourth technique helpful in determining possible problems with the fetus is ultrasound. Ultrasound exams are often used to confirm results of the tests

Genetic counseling—information provided to parents or prospective parents regarding the possibility and nature of genetic disorders in their offspring.

Alphafetoprotein test (AFP)—a blood test that can identify disorders in the brain or spinal column in the fetus.

Amniocentesis—a technique that involves extracting amniotic fluid from the uterus for the purpose of detecting all chromosomal and over 100 biomedical disorders.

Chorionic villus test (CVT)—a test that analyzes samples of the hair-like projections (chorionic villi) of tissue in the placenta for purposes determining chromosomal disorders (can be done earlier than amniocentesis).

Zygote—the first cell resulting from the fertilization of the ovum by the sperm.

Gender—the maleness or femaleness of the zygote as determined by the kind of sperm fertilizing the ovum (Y sperm—genetically male; X sperm—genetically female).

Placenta—the organ that is attached to the wall of the uterus, and transmits nutrients from the mother to the embryo/fetus and filters wastes from the embryo/fetus to the mother.

Identical twins—twins whose development began when the zygote split into two identical halves, thus ensuring that both twins have the identical genetic code.

Fraternal twins—twins whose development began by the fertilization of two ova (eggs) by two sperms causing both twins to have different genetic codes.

Embryonic stage—weeks three through eight of pregnancy during which the major organ systems are formed.

just described. Through scanning the uterus with high frequency sound waves, an outline of the fetus is created.

While these various techniques can be helpful in detecting problems, there still are a number of disorders that cannot be determined before birth. Nevertheless, recent medical advances provide new intervention procedures for some conditions. Blood transfusions, special diets, fetal surgery, and other kinds of treatment before and after birth can greatly reduce the severity of some conditions. Advances in genetics and genetic programming will continue to provide more information and improved treatments for these and other disorders. This discussion of prenatal development continues in the next section with information about the implantation stage.

Implantation Stage—Conception to 3 Weeks of Pregnancy. The fertilized cell of a developing human is called a **zygote**. The **gender** of the zygote is determined at conception by the sperm type. In simple terms, if the sperm cell carries an X chromosome, the zygote will develop into a female, and if the sperm cell carries a Y chromosome the zygote will develop into a male.

During the week after fertilization, the zygote has traveled to the Fallopian tube, where cell division begins. By about the fifth or sixth day, cell division has created two different parts. Inside is the cell mass which gradually develops into a human being. The complex outside cell mass becomes the **placenta**. The placenta is the organ that transmits nutrients from the mother's bloodstream to the developing embryo and fetus. The placenta also filters out waste from the fetus through the mother's bloodstream. By the end of the second week the zygote has moved through the Fallopian tube and become implanted in the uterus.

Twins

At times a zygote divides into two identical halves which develop separately, creating **identical twins**. These (monozygotic, or one zygote) twins will look alike, as they have the same genetic code. If there are two ova (eggs) fertilized by two sperm, the result is **fraternal** (dizygotic, or two zygotes) **twins**. These twins do not share the same genetic code.

Embryonic Stage—3 to 8 Weeks of Pregnancy. The **embryonic stage** is critical to the healthy development of the fetus. It is during the first 8 weeks that the major organ systems are developing. Exposure to **teratogens**, such as chemical substances, viruses, alcohol, drugs, or other environmental factors, can cause congenital malformations or birth defects.

Fetal Stage—Weeks 9 to the Conclusion of Pregnancy. By week 9, the embryo has a human-like appearance and is now a fetus. The **fetal stage** continues until birth. During the fetal stage, growth and differentiation in organs and tissues takes place. In addition, the weight and size of the fetus increase considerably. See Figure 3.2 for a general description of growth from fertilization to birth.

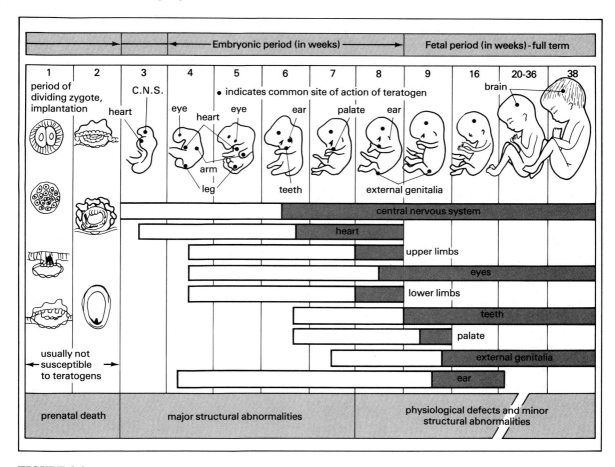

FIGURE 3.2
***There are critical periods during fetal growth for the development of each
major body part and system.*** (From *Before We Are Born*, 3rd ed., [p. 111] by K. L.
Moore, 1986. Philadelphia: Saunders. Reprinted by permission.)

Quality Prenatal Care

It is important that the expectant mother seeks prenatal care as soon as she
thinks she may be pregnant. Signs of pregnancy include one or several of the
following symptoms: a missed menstrual period, a need for more rest, nausea,
and swollen and sensitive breasts. As mentioned previously, the first 8 weeks
of pregnancy are critical to the developing fetus, as this is the time that all
major organ systems are developing. Early detection of problems is important
in ensuring the development of a healthy baby.

At the first prenatal visit, medical personnel will run one of several available
tests to determine pregnancy. An examination provides basic information about
the overall health of the mother-to-be. Blood tests are taken to determine if the

*Teratogens—envi-
ronmental factors
such as viruses
and chemical sub-
stances that can
cause abnormali-
ties in the develop-
ing embryo or
fetus.*

*Fetal stage—the
stage that begins
after the first eight
weeks of pregnancy
and continues until
birth.*

prospective mother is anemic, has syphilis, has had rubella, or if there could be Rh blood incompatibility. Questions about the prospective mother's and father's past medical history, family history, and personal health habits attempt to identify nutritional state, possible substance abuse, and the need for genetic screening. Prospective mothers are usually counseled about the importance of proper diet and avoiding drugs and X-rays, and are advised to check with the doctor before taking any medication. It is important that prospective mothers have medical checkups at regular intervals throughout pregnancy.

Nutrition

Research demonstrates (Wyden, 1971) that mothers-to-be at all economic levels may not eat proper diets to ensure the healthy development of a baby. Daily calorie intake from junk food and/or alcohol can endanger the healthy development of a baby. Likewise, excessive dieting and overuse of vitamins can also put the developing fetus at risk (Wyden, 1971). Balanced diets of proteins, complex carbohydrates, grains, fruits and vegetables, and dairy products should be a priority of every prospective mother. See Table 3.2 for information regarding nutrition from the four basic food groups.

Werner's investigation (1979) documented that undernutrition can interfere with the healthy development of the fetal central nervous system during two

TABLE 3.2
Four basic food groups and their major nutrients

Group	Example Foods	Significant Amounts of Major Nutrients	
		All Foods in Group	Some Foods in Group
Fruits & Vegetables	Apples, bananas, dates, grapefruit, tomatoes, broccoli, cabbage, beans, lettuce, potatoes	Carbohydrate, water	Vitamins (A, C, folacin), minerals (iron, calcium), fiber
Grain Products	Breads, rolls, tortillas, cereals, pasta, grains, flour, rice, oats, crackers, popcorn	Carbohydrate, protein, vitamins (thiamin, niacin), minerals (iron)	Water, fiber
Milk and Milk Products	Milk, yogurt, all types of cheeses, ice cream, ice milk, frozen yogurt	Protein, vitamins (A, riboflavin, B-12), minerals (calcium, phosphorus), water	Carbohydrate, vitamin D
Meats and Meat Alternatives	Fish, beef, pork, poultry, eggs, seeds, nuts, soybean products, legumes (beans and peas, all types)	Protein, vitamins (niacin, B-6), minerals (iron, zinc)	Carbohyrate, fat, vitamin B-12, fiber, water

critical periods of development. The first major period of brain growth occurs between the tenth and twentieth weeks of pregnancy. The second important period for brain growth takes place from the twentieth week of prenatal development to 4 to 6 months after birth (Winick, 1981).

Undernutrition during these times can cause impaired brain growth, which ultimately affects intellectual performance and physical development (Winick, 1976). If undernutrition occurs at these critical times, young children do not catch up with their peers, even if provided with nutritional diets later on. However, there is some evidence (Tanner, 1973) to suggest that children who were deprived during less-than-critical times can catch up on growth if they are fed proper diets. Dietary deficiencies can also cause anemia, poorly developed bones and teeth, physical abnormalities, low birth weight, and complications during pregnancy and labor. Nutritional and diet disorders such as **anorexia** and **bulimia**, which occur most often in teenage girls, can adversely affect the development of the fetus, particularly late in pregnancy.

Chemicals and Substances

For several decades, research has indicated that a mother-to-be's use and exposure to certain chemicals can influence the development of the fetus. Recent research indicates that there are also substances that can cause genetic abnormalities in sperm leading to permanent defects including heart abnormalities and mental retardation. Many researchers conjecture that environmental toxins may play a significant role in the 60–80 percent of birth defects of unknown cause. There is also some evidence that alterations in sperm may cause childhood cancer and learning disorders. Consequently, health and occupational safety officials are beginning to reevaluate safety regulations for the purposes of extending them to men whose jobs may be considered harmful to the sperm (Davis, 1989).

In general, use of chemicals or other substances should be avoided during pregnancy—any use of drugs or medication should first be cleared with a physician. However, certain medications prescribed by the physician may be necessary for the mother's well-being during pregnancy.

Use of chemicals during pregnancy can contribute to a number of abnormalities in the developing fetus. Several factors contribute to the degree of the abnormality, including (1) the amount of the chemical, (2) the stage of development of the embryo or fetus, and (3) the amount of time which the prospective mother was exposed to or used the chemical.

Various substances appear to have the potential to harm the developing embryo or fetus (Yaffee, 1980). These include: some drugs used in the treatment of cancer, thyroid malfunction, common cold (tetracycline), emotional stress (Valium, Librium, Miltown, phenobarbital), seizures (Dilantin, phenobarbital), and acne (Accutane). Caffeine (found in coffee, tea, cola drinks, chocolate, and certain medications), if taken in excess, may produce problems in the developing fetus, particularly if accompanied by cigarette smoking (Linn et al., 1982).

The Center for Chronic Disease Prevention and Health Promotion Office on Smoking and Health (DHHS, 1990) reported that there is no doubt that smoking

Critical period—a time of physiological and/or psychological sensitivity, during which the normal development of a major organ or structural system must take place or permanent damage to body structure and/or behavior will result.

Anorexia—a severe disorder usually seen in teenage girls, which is characterized by self-starvation.

Bulimia—a severe disorder usually seen in teenage girls, which is characterized by binging and then self-induced vomiting.

during pregnancy increases the risk of spontaneous abortion, fetal and newborn deaths, and smaller babies. There is some evidence (Evans, 1981) that smoking on the part of the father-to-be can produce abnormal sperm and increased death and birth defects when compared to nonsmoking fathers. Thus, the overwhelming evidence suggests that it is best for the healthy development of the baby if the prospective mother and father do not smoke.

Fetal alcohol syndrome (FAS)—the physical and mental abnormalities found in babies whose mothers consumed excessive amounts of alcohol during pregnancy.

Just as many physicians advise prospective mothers to stop smoking, they are also advising them not to consume alcoholic beverages. Studies indicate that alcohol abuse can contribute to **fetal alcohol syndrome (FAS)**. FAS can cause mental retardation, physical deformities of the limbs, muscle damage, heart disorders, dysfunction of the central nervous system, miscarriages, sleep disturbances in the newborn, and abnormalities of the face and head (Harlap & Shlono, 1980; Rosett et al., 1979). One study (Streissguth, Martin, Barr, & Sandman, 1984) examined 4-year-old children of moderate (one glass of wine or beer per day) drinkers and nondrinkers. Children of the moderate drinkers had longer response times and shorter attention spans than the children of the nondrinkers. At present, no safe level of alcohol consumption has been determined for pregnant women. Several drinks taken at a critical time may cause severe damage to an unborn baby. Therefore, it is best for all pregnant women to refrain from consuming alcohol.

Rubella—a virus that can cause birth disorders if the mother contracts during the first three months of pregnancy (also known as German measles).

Substance abuse is also dangerous to the developing fetus and can cause fetal death, premature birth, and retarded fetal growth. At birth, these children face severe withdrawal from the drug. Possible long-term effects include hyperactivity, brain damage, and other behavioral and physical abnormalities (Householder et al., 1982; Vorhees & Mollnow, 1987).

Other Teratogens

Toxoplasmosis—a microorganism that can be transmitted from cat droppings or raw meat to the mother and to the fetus or embryo via the placenta, causing birth disorders.

Physicians also usually caution mothers-to-be not to have X-rays during pregnancy and to be aware of possible environmental pollutants which may affect the developing fetus. Viruses can also cross the placenta and infect the fetus. If **rubella**, also known as German measles, is contracted during the first trimester, serious birth defects such as mental retardation, blindness, and deafness can result. A blood test can determine if the mother-to-be has had rubella. If she has, antibodies will prevent the fetus from being affected if she is exposed to rubella again. Rubella inoculation of children is required in all states.

Acquired Immune Deficiency Syndrome (AIDS)—a virus that can be transmitted from the mother to the fetus/embryo via the placenta and that attacks the immune system, causing death from illnesses that the immune system cannot prevent.

Physicians also may ask prospective mothers if they have cats as pets. **Toxoplasmosis** is a parasitic infection caused by contact with cat droppings or raw or undercooked meat. While this disease does not affect prospective mothers, it can cause serious damage to the central nervous system or eyes of the fetus. Pregnant women who have cats are advised not to change litter boxes, to seek inoculation, and to eat well-cooked meat.

Other infectious diseases which can affect pregnancy include mumps, rubeola (red measles), chicken pox, polio, syphilis, and **Acquired Immune Deficiency Syndrome (AIDS)**. Syphilis can be detected by a blood test, which is required in many states. This disease can be treated successfully, even during pregnancy. AIDS in babies seems to be caused by the presence of the virus in the uterus, with first indications usually appearing around 6 months of age. The symptoms are similar to a number of diseases, making accurate diagnosis difficult. Most babies live 5 to 8 months after the symptoms first appear (Minkoff et al., 1987). At present, there is no known cure for AIDS. Another disease which can be transmitted across the placenta and is not curable is genital herpes. Herpes infection is usually transferred to the newborn during the birth process and it can cause blindness, brain damage, and even death. Prospective mothers with active herpes are advised not to have vaginal deliveries.

Regular prenatal visits ensure that the mother-to-be will be monitored for **toxemia** of pregnancy and diabetes. Toxemia usually affects women in the last trimester of pregnancy, and the causes are unknown. Symptoms of this condition include high blood pressure, water retention as indicated by swelling of the legs and ankles, and protein in the urine. This disease can cause death in both mother and child, so early detection and treatment are important. Women with diabetes also need monitoring during pregnancy.

Toxemia—a disease for which the causes are unknown, occurring in the last trimester of pregnancy, which can cause death to both mother and child.

Education for Childbirth and Parenting

In the past, women were in control of where they gave birth and who assisted them. With the increased use of anesthetics to relieve pain, physicians began to play the dominant role directing the birth process, and fathers were usually relegated to the waiting room. Over a period of time, many parents became frustrated over their lack of involvement in one of the most important events in their lives. In addition, the increasing number of research studies documenting the negative effects of medication during labor and delivery caused increasing concern among many health care professionals (Sepkoski, 1985; Wilson, 1977). Over time, parents and health care professionals became advocates for educated childbirth and for more active involvement of the parents in the pregnancy, delivery, and care of the newborn in the hospital setting.

One of the better-known educated childbirth approaches is the **Lamaze method** (Karmel, 1959). The Lamaze technique instructs the mother-to-be and her coach, usually the father-to-be, in learning various breathing patterns that help to control the pain and discomfort during the different stages of labor. These techniques are practiced during the last months of pregnancy by the prospective mother and her coach.

Lamaze method— a method developed by Fernand Lamaze that involves the training of the prospective mother and a partner/ coach in breathing and relaxation techniques to be used during labor.

Prospective parents are given information about the various types of medication and their effects upon the fetus and the mother. They are encouraged to discuss their preferred medication with their physician in advance of delivery. Many Lamaze classes are preceded by a course dealing with general pregnancy and childbirth information. These classes usually occur earlier in the pregnancy and inform the prospective parents about physiological and psychological aspects of pregnancy, childbirth, and parenting.

Some parents-to-be are now opting to have their baby's birth at home with the assistance of a physician or midwife. While home births do provide the

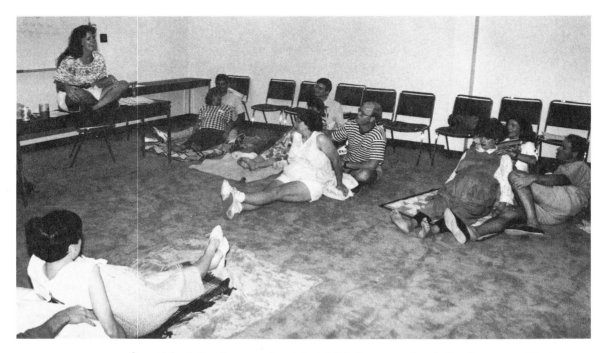

One of the better known educated childbirth approaches is the Lamaze method, which provides prospective parents with information and coping strategies concerning the labor and delivery of their baby.

prospective parents with more control over the birthing process and can involve family or friends, there are some risks involved. If complications arise, lack of hospital equipment and trained specialists can put mother and infant in danger. In response to consumer demand, many hospitals provide birthing rooms which allow the mother to remain in one room throughout labor and delivery with husband and family members often present. Birthing rooms usually are furnished in a home-like setting, yet provide all the necessary medical support services.

Ideally, prospective parents will take care in selecting their obstetrician and hospital. An obstetrician who is comfortable with the father's active involvement throughout the pregnancy and who recognizes the value of educated childbirth provides valuable support to the prospective parents. Likewise, a hospital that offers family-involved birthing experiences, allows the father, other children, and close relatives extended visitation privileges, permits the baby to "room in" with the mother, and has classes for new parents on the care and feeding of the newborn provides helpful services to new parents, giving needed support and information. Such experiences help parents to learn about their baby and get to know their baby, and provide them with opportunities to develop confidence in their parenting abilities.

Birthing rooms in hospitals are furnished like a home and allow the mother to remain in one room throughout labor and delivery with her husband, other family members, and friends, while providing emergency medical services if needed.

The Importance of Preparing Siblings for the Birth

Preparing brothers and sisters for the arrival of a new baby helps create positive sibling relationships from the beginning. Less jealousy and decreased sibling rivalry later on are the benefits of thoughtful attention to the needs of existing children within the family.

For children younger than three, parents need to plan some special activities or time spent alone with them after the birth of a new brother or sister. Thinking about how and when this will occur can prevent problems of feeling neglected. Buying a doll and various accessories used in the care of young babies can help during times when parents are busy with the newborn. Older brother and sister can feed, bathe, and change the baby just as mother or father does. Siblings can help in preparing the baby's room or bed, gathering clothes, and choosing the baby's name.

Some hospitals have special programs for siblings. Prospective brothers and sisters can visit the hospital to see where their mother and the new baby will stay. Hospital staff members talk to the children about what babies are like and what their care entails. Discussion of the range of feelings about being a brother or sister can also help children deal with their emotions.

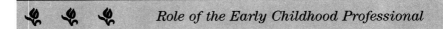

Role of the Early Childhood Professional

Working with Families with Young Children

1. Understand how parental behaviors and attitudes directly influence the development of the young child even before birth.
2. Understand that behaviors and attitudes of the parents influence the development and learning after birth and throughout the early childhood years.
3. Be aware of the challenges and demands of the parenting role.
4. Help parents understand the development of young children.
5. Assist young parents in developing appropriate parenting skills.
6. Understand that parents are valuable sources of information about their children and that early childhood professionals must work in partnership with parents if optimal learning and development are to occur in young children.

Careful thought needs to be given to who will care for the siblings during the mother's hospital stay. Those who care for the brothers and sisters need to be nurturant and understanding of their expression of distress of separation from their mother and other anxieties. Careful planning for siblings can reduce stress for the entire family and promote positive sibling relationships.

As indicated throughout this chapter, the decision of whether or not to become a parent needs to be given careful thought and consideration. Children who are not wanted do not develop positive self-concepts or grow into emotionally stable and mature young men or women.

Ideally, both prospective parents want a child for appropriate reasons. After deciding to become parents, the prospective mother and father need to evaluate finances and the social context of their family; become aware of the emotional and psychological factors in parenting; engage in quality prenatal care; become knowledgeable about prenatal development, child birth and parenting; and prepare siblings for the birth of a new brother or sister. Attention to these areas of parenting provides the opportunity for the family to have a positive adjustment to a major change in its structure, and helps ensure the optimal development of the new baby and promote quality family life.

Ann and Bill Johnson, like Cheryl Monroe and James, are awaiting the births of their babies. These babies will have been affected by very different sets of circumstances before their births. Chapter 4 will show how these circumstances influence the development of the babies and their family contexts, at birth and soon after.

Key Terms

ultrasound

fetus

prenatal

low birth weight

trimester

heredity

environment

chromosomes

gene

genotype

recessive gene

DNA

abortion

congenital malformation

Rh factor

genetic counseling

alphafetoprotein test

amniocentesis

chorionic villus test

zygote

gender

placenta

identical twins

fraternal twins

embryonic stage

teratogens

fetal stage

critical period

anorexia

bulimia

fetal alcohol syndrome

rubella

toxoplasmosis

AIDS

toxemia

Lamaze method

Review Strategies/Activities

1. Interview several parents of varying numbers of children: one, two, four or more. Ask them to:
   a. Describe a typical day in parenting.
   b. Discuss the joys and problems of being parents.
   c. Share how becoming a parent has changed their lives.
   d. Ask them to describe the kinds of care children require at various times: birth, beginning to walk, 2–8 years of age.
2. Interview several parents of newborns. Ask them to share with you:
   a. Their reactions at finding out they were going to be parents.
   b. Their feelings and reactions throughout pregnancy.
   c. The nature of prenatal care.
3. Check your local hospital to see what support services they provide to prospective parents.
   a. Gather brochures.
   b. Ask if you can visit some of the classes.
4. Read more about teenage pregnancy.
   a. Develop a list of possible solutions to this problem.
   b. Develop a list of strategies which can help the teenage mother, father, and baby.
5. Describe how you think heredity and environment has influenced your development. Share with your classmates in small groups.
6. Invite the following speakers to talk to your class:
   a. A genetic counselor on the importance of genetic counseling.
   b. A Lamaze instructor on the Lamaze method.
   c. A La Leche League representative on the advantages of breastfeeding.
   d. A pharmacist on the effects of drugs during pregnancy.
7. Make a list of practices that help ensure the birth of a healthy baby.

Further Readings

The local chapter of the March of Dimes provides pamphlets on genetic counseling, prenatal development, and ways to prevent birth defects.

Bettelheim, B. (1987). *A good enough parent.* New York: Vintage Books.

Child psychologist Bettelheim provides parents with ideas on how to develop their own insights to help them understand children's behavior and coping skills. He advises parents not to create the child they would like to have, but to help each child develop into the person he or she would like to be.

Nilsson, L., Sundberg, A., & Wirsen, C. (1981). *A child is born.* New York: Dell/Seymour Lawrence.

This book shows the development of a baby from conception through the first months of life through specialized microphotography. The vivid photographs and concise text provide the reader with a comprehensive understanding of prenatal development.

Queenhan, J., & Queenhan, C. (1987). *A new life.* Boston: Little, Brown and Company.

This book looks at the physiology and anatomy of the developing fetus and baby, and covers important information about the social, emotional, psychological, and physical aspects of parenting, including the father's role.

Spock, B. (1988). *Dr. Spock on parenting.* New York: Simon & Schuster.

This book deals with the new American family—single parent, two jobs, and lack of extended family. The effects of a new baby upon a marriage are thoroughly explored, along with other parenting concerns and questions.

CHAPTER 4

*To be a child is to know the fun of living. To have
a child is to know the beauty of life.*

(Author unknown)

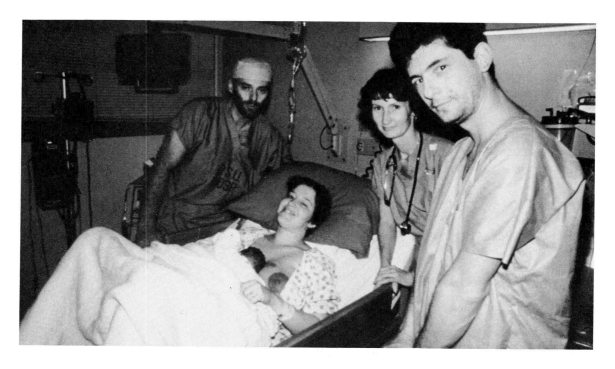

The Child and Family at Birth

After reading and studying this chapter, you will demonstrate comprehension by:

- Describing the stages of labor.
- Identifying the various types of deliveries.
- Describing the assessment and care of newborns.
- Outlining the change in family dynamics at birth: bonding; reactions of the newborn, parents, siblings, and extended family.
- Identifying sociocultural factors regarding the birth experience.
- Describing the needs and care of special infants and their families.

Stages of Labor

Labor is divided into three stages: dilation to delivery, the birth itself, and the expulsion of the placenta.

Stage 1—Dilation to Delivery

It is 6:25 in the morning. Ann Johnson feels a slight snap in her abdominal area. Amniotic fluid empties from her uterine cavity and soaks the bed linen. Ann quickly realizes that she is in **labor** and that Jeremy's birth will soon be a reality. **Dilation**, the first stage of labor actually began two days earlier. On Friday, Ann's checkup with Dr. Windle indicated that her **cervix** was dilated to 3 centimeters. By the time her baby is born, Ann's cervix will have dilated to 10 centimeters (4 inches). This space is usually wide enough to allow most babies to be born.

Labor—the three stages of the birth process: dilation, birth of the baby, and discharge of the placenta.

Dilation—the gradual opening of the cervix, which occurs in the first stage of labor.

Cervix—the opening of the uterus.

Bill and Ann have learned from their childbirth education classes that each labor and delivery is unique. Nevertheless, one or more of the following signs usually indicates that labor is in process: lower back ache, indigestion, diarrhea, abdominal cramps, the expulsion of the mucous plug, and the discharge of amniotic fluid. They have also learned that if the "water breaks" during the early part of labor, the fetus can be subject to infection.

Ann awakens Bill and tells him what has happened. He excitedly phones Dr. Windle. She tells Bill that since Ann's water has broken, it is best if they go to the hospital immediately. Dr. Windle says that she will meet them there in about 45 minutes. Ann and Bill dress; gather up their bags, which have been packed for several weeks; and drive to the hospital.

Contraction—the movement of the muscles of the uterus which forces the baby through the cervical opening and into the birth canal.

Ann's **contractions** have been relatively short, lasting about 30 to 45 seconds, and have occurred about every 15 to 20 minutes. She uses some of the Lamaze breathing exercises and records the time and duration of each contraction as Bill drives her to the hospital. Ann and Bill are greeted at the hospital by obstetrical nurse Maria Lopez. She helps Ann into a wheelchair and takes her to the birthing room while Bill checks Ann into the hospital. Maria is familiar with Lamaze techniques so she temporarily takes over as Ann's coach as the contractions occur.

The birthing room looks very much like a bedroom, attractively furnished in mauves and grays. In addition to the birthing bed, there is a sofa, several comfortable chairs and a table with four chairs. Unlike the traditional hospital setting where mothers are moved to the delivery room before the birth, Ann will remain in the birthing room for both labor and delivery. She is free to move about, eat, and drink. Friends and family can visit, according to Ann and Bill's wishes. Dr. Windle and Maria will be on hand to help Bill and Ann and to provide specialized medical assistance if it is needed.

The birthing bed is very different from the traditional delivery table where women lie down with their feet propped up in stirrups. It allows Ann to recline slightly, and there is a place to rest her legs to help in pushing during the final stage of labor. The position of the birthing bed will relieve pressure on Ann's back and allow the force of gravity to assist in the birth process.

Dr. Windle soon arrives. She checks Ann and determines that labor is progressing normally. Bill enters the birthing room and resumes coaching Ann and timing her contractions. During this first stage of labor, Ann's contractions become more frequent and intense. Ann adapts her Lamaze breathing patterns according to the types of contractions. She walks around the room or sits in the birthing bed, depending upon what feels more comfortable. Since she seems to be experiencing intense pain in her lower back, Bill rubs her back with a tennis ball to relieve the pressure. Throughout labor Dr. Windle and Maria check in on Bill and Ann. It is now 10:00 A.M. and Ann has been in labor at least four hours, possibly longer since she was asleep when her water broke. Jeremy is on his way into this world. Let's see what is happening to Cheryl Monroe and James.

It is four weeks before Cheryl Monroe's due date. She and James are watching TV. Cheryl does not feel well—she has indigestion and diarrhea. While she is

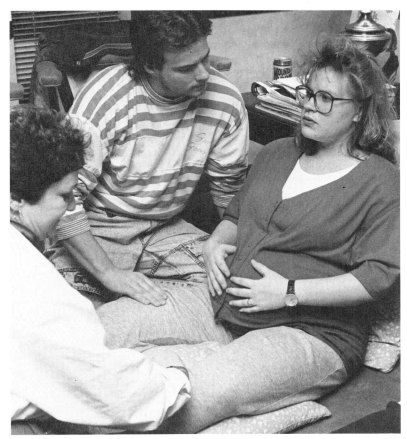

Supportive hospital environments and medical staff facilitate positive experiences for new parents.

in the bathroom, she notices that there is a mucus-like discharge tinged with blood on her undergarments. The social worker who has helped Cheryl has told her about the signs of labor. She walks to the living room and tells James and her sister that she thinks the baby is coming.

Cheryl's sister calls the emergency room to tell them of Cheryl's condition. Because it is a month before Cheryl's estimated due date, the emergency room nurse says Cheryl needs to come to the hospital as soon as possible. James goes to a neighbor who has a car to see if he will drive them to the hospital.

Shortly after midnight, Cheryl's mother arrives home from her evening job to find the house in an uproar. She quickly gathers clothes and cosmetics into a bag for Cheryl. Cheryl is afraid and her mother does her best to calm her while they walk to the neighbor's car for the short drive to the hospital. Cheryl's mother and James help her into the large hospital complex which also has a medical school. Preliminary paperwork about Cheryl has been forwarded by the social worker. It is pulled from the file and various forms are completed while Cheryl is placed in a wheelchair and taken to an examining room. The examination indicates that labor is well under way. Cheryl is then wheeled to a large room where she is prepared for labor and delivery. There are other women in the room, one in particular who is screaming with labor pains. This increases Cheryl's anxiety.

Electronic fetal monitor—a device used during labor which is attached to the abdomen of the pregnant woman or the scalp of the fetus to determine fetal heart rate.

Because of Cheryl's family's income level, she is not able to have access to a birthing room. Hospital and personal economics require that Cheryl share a room and medical personnel with a number of other pregnant women. Due to staff limitations, family and friends are not allowed in the labor or delivery room. Cheryl's mother, James, and the neighbor are asked to go to the waiting room. A nurse tells them that he will do his best to keep them informed of Cheryl's progress.

A specialist comes in to assess the condition of the fetus. He uses an **electronic fetal monitor** that places electrodes on the scalp of the fetus through Cheryl's cervix. Information indicates that the fetus is in stress. The specialist

Electronic fetal monitoring devices can provide information confirming that a fetus is in stress and that special medical attention may be needed at birth.

calls to the delivery room and asks that they prepare immediately for a **cesarean** delivery. Since Cheryl's baby will be **preterm** (born three weeks or more before due date), the doctor orders an **isolette** to be brought to the delivery room. Isolettes are small cribs that provide a controlled environment for the newborn. They monitor the physiological condition of the infant and provide nutrients to the newborn through a tube that runs from the infant's nose to the stomach.

Stage 2—Birth

Stage 2 of labor begins when the cervix has dilated to 10 centimeters and the head of the fetus pushes through the cervical opening into the vagina. After some time, Ann Johnson has the urge to push. However, Lamaze training has prepared Ann to know what to do during this part of labor. She begins a Lamaze breathing technique to help her control the urge to expel the baby. The pains from the contractions become intense, and Ann mentions to Bill that she would like some medication. In their Lamaze class, Bill and Ann learned that medication, at times, can be necessary and helpful in the birth process. However, it can also have some negative effects, the extent of which are determined by the type of medication, the amount given, and the stage of labor during which the drug is administered. Discussion with Dr. Windle and Maria reminds Ann that the most difficult part of labor is almost over and that the baby will soon be born. Along with Bill, they encourage her to continue without any medication because the fetal head has already numbed the vaginal opening. Medication at this point might prevent Ann from being as aware of the contractions and keep her from being as effective as she needs to be to help push during the final part of delivery. Bill also reminds her that if she could continue without medication that it would help the baby to be more alert not only at birth but also for some time after (Brackbill, 1979; Smolak, 1986). Buoyed by their encouragement, Ann decides to continue without medication.

Ann's last ultrasound had indicated that the baby could be large, 8 to 9 pounds. For this reason, Dr. Windle decides to do an **episiotomy**. An episiotomy is a small incision which helps prevent the opening of the vulva from tearing during the birth of a baby.

It is now close to 3:00 P.M. and it is time for Maria's nursing shift to end. She decides to stay longer since it is almost time for Ann to give birth. The intense contractions are about a minute apart and last for almost 60 seconds. Dr. Windle and Maria now tell Ann to push. As she squeezes Bill's hand, Ann pushes and the baby's head begins to appear. Shortly, with another push, the head emerges. Dr. Windle removes the mucous from the baby's nose and mouth. From the mirror above the birthing bed, Bill and Ann have their first look at Jeremy. With the next contraction, Ann gives another big push and Jeremy's full body appears. He begins to cry softly. (For an illustration of the first two stages of labor, see Figure 4.1.)

Cesarean—the surgical procedure during which an incision is made through abdominal and uterine walls of the mother to deliver the baby.

Preterm—infants born several weeks before the full term (38 weeks) of pregnancy.

Isolette—small cribs that provide a controlled environment for newborns who are considered at risk.

Episiotomy—an incision sometimes made in the opening of the vulva to prevent its tearing during birth.

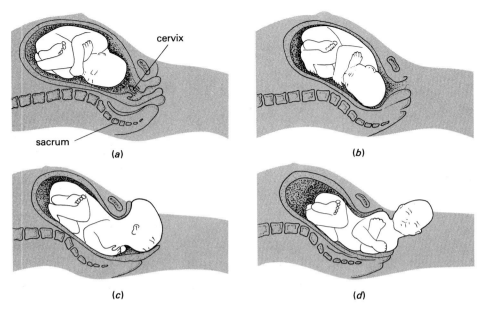

FIGURE 4.1
During the first stage of labor (a, b), the uterus contracts, causing the cervix to dilate. In Stage 2 (c, d), the baby moves down the birth canal and is pushed out. (From Berk, L. E. [1989]. *Child development* [2nd ed.]. Needham Heights, MA: Allyn & Bacon.)

Leboyer Method—a technique used during childbirth to help the baby in the transition from life inside to outside the uterus; characterized by warm delivery rooms, muted lighting, soothing music, a warm bath, etc.

The birthing room has been kept a comfortable 78 degrees, with relaxing music playing in the background. This provides a soothing setting for Jeremy's entrance into the world from the protective environment of the uterus. Dr. Windle and Maria quickly evaluate Jeremy for any signs of complications. He appears fine and is gently wiped off and placed on Ann's abdomen. Ann and Bill talk gently to Jeremy and begin cuddling him. He has dark hair like Ann's father. Jeremy stops his crying and looks directly into their eyes. Ann and Bill are truly in awe of the miracle of life. They examine his hands and feet. Bill decides he looks like one of his brothers. Ann places Jeremy at her breast and he begins to nurse. "You smart little thing," says Ann. After a while the blood in the blood vessels in the umbilical cord stops throbbing, and Dr. Windle cuts the umbilical cord. Bill then takes Jeremy and places him into a warm bath. This concept of "gentle birth" is the **Leboyer Method**, based upon the ideas of Frederick Leboyer (1975), a French obstetrician. Creating a calm, relaxed environment and placing the baby in warm water similar to the amniotic fluid are believed to help the baby adjust to life outside the uterus.

Stage 3—Expulsion of the Placenta

Afterbirth—the placenta, after it moves from the uterus and is expelled through the cervix.

The third stage of labor involves the expulsion of the placenta and cord, or **afterbirth**, through the cervix. Ann's afterbirth appears. Dr. Windle and Maria examine it to be sure everything has been completely discharged from the uterus.

Jeremy has been enjoying his first bath. A very calm and relaxed Jeremy is dried, then weighed and measured. He weighs 8 pounds, 14 ounces and is 21 inches long. Finally, an identification bracelet matching Ann's bracelet is placed around his wrist. Jeremy has arrived! What about Angela?

Cheryl is prepared for surgery. Because of her nervous state, the anesthesiologist administers medication to prevent her from observing Angela's birth. The doctor makes an incision and pulls away layers of skin and abdominal muscle. As Angela is lifted from the uterine cavity, the doctor discovers the umbilical cord is wrapped around her neck, depriving her of oxygen and creating a condition called **anoxia**. Angela does not begin breathing on her own. Quickly, a team of pediatric specialists is called. Angela is placed in the isolette and taken immediately to the neonatal care unit.

Anoxia—the condition caused by the lack of oxygen in the brain of an infant during labor and delivery; can cause brain damage.

Anoxia can also occur if the placenta detaches too soon during prenatal development, if the prospective mother smokes, is **anemic**, is Rh blood incompatible, or for other unknown reasons. Mild anoxia can destroy or damage some of the baby's brain cells. Oxygen deprivation can cause babies to cry more than normal and can lead to learning and behavior problems, but these problems usually decrease as the child grows older (Stechler & Halton, 1982). Severe anoxia can cause cerebral palsy, mental retardation, and death. Electronic fetal monitoring devices are frequently used during labor if there is concern about anoxia. Controversy has arisen about the overuse of fetal monitors in healthy pregnancies, their interference with the normal process of labor, and the mistaken identification of fetal stress that often precipitates cesarean deliveries (Samuels & Samuels, 1986).

Anemic—a condition caused by a lack of red blood cells.

In addition to fetal stress, another common reason for doing a cesarean delivery is **breech birth**. This complication occurs when another part of the body, usually the buttocks, feet, or umbilical cord, rather than the head is positioned to emerge first from the cervix. If the mother's pelvic bone structure is too small to accommodate the birth of a large baby, a cesarean delivery may also be performed.

Breech birth—a birth in which a body part other than the head presents itself for delivery first, usually the buttocks, feet, or in some cases the umbilical cord.

Some doctors and other interested persons (Rosen, 1981; United States Congress, Senate Committee on Human Resources Research, 1978) have questioned the increase in number of cesarean births. Explanations for this increase include possible lawsuits if the baby is at risk, fetal exposure to genital herpes, convenience for the obstetrician, and increased obstetrician earnings for cesarean deliveries. Since this procedure is considered major surgery and prolongs the recovery of the mother, it is important to use it only when necessary for the well-being of mother and child.

At times **forceps** are used to speed up delivery when there is danger to the fetus. In a forceps delivery, the doctor fits forceps, metal tongs, around the baby's head and pulls the fetus through the vagina. This procedure should only be used during the second stage of labor and with great caution, or brain damage can result.

Forceps—a surgical instrument similar to tongs, which is applied to the head of the fetus to speed delivery.

Assessment and Care of Newborns

*Apgar score—a
score that rates the
physical condition
of newborns in the
areas of appear-
ance, pulse, grim-
ace, activity, and
respiration.*

Dr. Virginia Apgar (1953) invented a process to evaluate the ability of newborns to cope with the stress of delivery and to adjust to breathing independently. The **Apgar score** is obtained usually by observing the newborn at 1, 5, and sometimes 15 minutes after birth. Five areas of appearance or performance are evaluated, the *a*ppearance (skin color), *p*ulse (heart rate), *g*rimace (reaction to slight pain), *a*ctivity (motor responsiveness and tone), and *r*espiration (breathing adequacy). These five categories spell APGAR, which helps to make them easy to remember. Each category receives 0, 1, or 2 points. Generally a score of 7 or above indicates that the newborn is doing well. If the newborn's score is between 5 and 7, there usually is a need for some type of additional care. Infants with a score of 4 or below require immediate medical attention, as the score indicates a life-threatening situation.

*Neonatal Behav-
ioral Assessment
Scale (NBAS
or Brazelton
Scale)—an assess-
ment of 16 reflexes,
responsiveness,
state changes, and
ability to calm self
in the newborn.*

A second evaluation procedure used to examine a variety of behaviors in newborns was developed by pediatrician T. Berry Brazelton in 1973. The **Brazelton Neonatal Behavioral Assessment Scale (NBAS)** assesses 26 behavioral items and 16 reflexes which newborns possess. This assessment technique requires training, as it tries to elicit the infant's highest level of performance and is most commonly used in research settings and on preterm or at-risk infants. The Brazelton Scale helps parents to become aware of the infant's competencies. Parents who have been trained to administer the Brazelton were, after 4 weeks, more knowledgeable about their infants, had more confidence in handling the infants, and had more satisfactory interactions with their infants than parents who had not learned the Brazelton (Myers, 1982). Fathers who learned how to administer the Brazelton also were more actively involved with their infants than fathers who had not received the training (Myers, 1982).

The Brazelton also helps identify infants who are not able to control or regulate the various states, ranging from deep sleep to crying. Ill or premature infants and those with immature central nervous systems may cry often, lack

TABLE 4.1
Apgar scale

Sign	Score		
	0	1	2
Heart Rate	Absent	Less than 100/min.	More than 100/min.
Skin Tone	Blue, Pale	Body pink, limbs blue	Completely pink
Muscle Tone	Limp	Some flexing of limbs	Active motion
Reflexes	No response	Grimace or cry	Startled, loud cry
Respiratory Effort (Breathing)	Absent	Slow, irregular	Strong, regular breath

Source: Apgar (1953) and Vaughn & Litt (1987).

the ability to settle themselves, and not want to be cuddled. Such behaviors can be upsetting and frustrating to new parents. These parents can be provided with continued medical assistance in coping with their infants.

■ Jeremy's Apgar scores were 9 and 9 with no third evaluation needed since he was doing well. Angela scored 3, 4, and 5 and required immediate attention due to her lack of ability to breathe independently. Dr. Jones, Angela's pediatrician, plans to return to the neonatal care unit later in the day to see if her condition has stabilized. That afternoon he reads her charts and examines her. After several days, Dr. Jones and the neonatal staff decide to conduct the NBAS, as he notes that Angela seems to have difficulty calming herself when she is in a fussy state. Dr. Jones thinks he may have to provide Cheryl with some techniques for helping Angela learn to comfort herself.   ■

Family Dynamics—A New Social System

The birth of a baby into a family unit establishes a new social system as different relationships and roles are created. According to Bronfenbrenner's ecological systems theory (1979, 1986), reactions on the part of all members of this new social system vary depending upon the nature of the pregnancy and birth experience, position in the family unit, various sociocultural factors, the state of health of various family members, and the nature of support from the medical profession and community health services.

Bonding

Marshall H. Klaus and John H. Kennell are two pediatricians who have conducted research on **bonding**. They define bonding as the establishment of a complex psychobiological connection from parent to infant (Klaus and Kennel, 1982). The connection from infant to parent is called attachment. Bonding and attachment will be discussed in greater detail in Chapter 6. Klaus and Kennell suggest (1976) that parents and child should have 30 to 60 minutes of time alone during the period after birth when the newborn is calm and alert. It is also recommended that parents and child have continued periods of togetherness during the hospital stay.

Bonding—a complex psychobiological connection between the parent and infant.

A number of research studies initially documented some immediate and long-term benefits of bonding. In one study (Klaus, Jerauld, Kreger, McAlpine, Steffa, & Kennell, 1972), a group of newborns were allowed to remain in their mothers' hospital rooms for a large portion of the day and night. The second group of mothers saw their babies briefly at birth and then during feeding times. Mothers who had extended contact with their infants soothed and fondled their infants more, had more eye contact, and stayed physically closer to their infants at 1 month of age. These same differences were in evidence when the babies were a year old. When the children were 2 years old, the mothers in the study had differing patterns of communication. Mothers with extended contact used fewer commands and more adjectives, and asked twice as many questions. Initial findings from bonding research prompted the American Hospital Association in 1978 to recommend parent touching and breastfeeding of newborns immediately after birth. Breastfeeding was viewed as an important part of the bonding process as well as stimulating the hormones which promote the contraction of the uterus and the production of milk.

Public awareness of the early bonding research tended to create guilt in parents who did not have the opportunity to be with their children immediately after birth. In the early 1980s, ideas regarding the bonding process began to be modified (Goldberg, 1983; Palkovitz, 1984). While there may be benefits to early bonding, it now appears that lack of parent-child contact immediately after birth does not permanently harm or prevent the establishment of good parent-child relationship.

■ Ann and Bill had the opportunity to be with Jeremy immediately after birth. Jeremy also "roomed in" with Ann in her hospital room, allowing continuous sustained contact. Bill was with them much of the time, as fathers had unrestricted visiting hours in their particular hospital.

Cheryl, however, was not able to see Angela immediately after birth because the anesthetic for her cesarean rendered her unconscious. Also, Angela's need for special attention in the neonatal care unit prevented Cheryl from sustained close contact with her after birth.   ■

In the past, at-risk infants have often been inaccessible to their parent's touch. Some of these infants remained in hospitals for months before they were brought home. Parents of at-risk infants often feel guilty for their babies' health problems. They can be frightened by the technology and tubes used to sustain their infant's life and feel cheated out of establishing a normal relationship with their baby. Fostering a positive parent-child relationship with an at-risk infant can be difficult, which may be reflected in statistics which show that abused children are twice as likely to have been preterm infants (Helfer, 1982). Much of the medical community is now encouraging parents to be with their at-risk infants as much as possible. Parents are taught early on how to caress, touch, and care for their babies.

Reactions of the Newborn

Reactions of newborns vary according to prenatal care, the labor and delivery experience, the nature of parental interactions, and the infant's own personal temperament. The uterus has provided consistent temperature and constant nourishment. After the arduous birth process, the infant must adjust to breathing independently and take an active role in the feeding process. Fortunately, most infants are resilient in nature and possess many capabilities that help

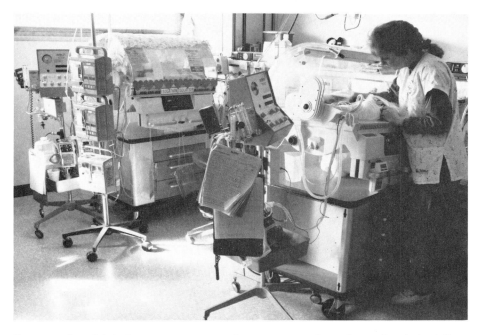

Parents of at-risk infants are encouraged to caress, touch, and care for their children as soon as possible.

them adjust. These competencies will be discussed in Part III. Nevertheless, good prenatal care, a normal labor and delivery process, positive interaction with parents, and quality care from the medical profession can promote optimal adjustment for the newborn.

Reactions of the Mother

Good prenatal care, educational preparation for childbirth and parenting, a normal labor and delivery, and a supportive husband and family all help the mother adjust to her new role. However, even new mothers who have optimal pregnancy and delivery conditions still feel overwhelmed, tired, and at times depressed.

In most instances giving birth is a very rigorous event demanding a great deal of physical and emotional energy. After delivery, the mother's body begins to undergo the tremendous hormonal adjustment to the non-pregnant state. These changes can create mood swings and depression. In addition, caring for a newborn who needs to be fed every few hours around the clock can be an exhausting experience.

The emotional high of anticipation of the baby's birth and then dealing with the realities and responsibilities of parenting can be overwhelming to some mothers. In addition, many mothers think that they should feel instant maternal love for their baby. If they do not, they feel guilty. Contrary to early research on bonding, human relationships take time to develop. One study (Robson, 1968) indicated that 59 percent of first-time mothers did not feel intense attachments to their infants at birth. Strong feelings began to develop between babies and their mothers between 4 and 6 weeks after birth.

New mothers often have many questions about their baby's behavior, particularly eating and crying. Books and advice from family, friends, and the medical profession can be helpful. However, at times, the mother's reading of her baby and her "instinct" may be the best way to handle situations.

■ Ann had been advised by the nurses at the hospital to bathe Jeremy when he awakened from his afternoon nap and then feed him after his bath. Hungry Jeremy cried more and more intensely during his bath. Ann became fearful that Jeremy would come to dislike bathtime. On her own, Ann decided to feed Jeremy first. She could see Jeremy relax as his tummy became full. After a time for burping and cuddling, Ann gave a relaxed and happy Jeremy his bath.

After several days in the neonatal care unit Angela seems to be breathing easier. Her skin tone has improved and the usual weight loss after birth has not been as great as the doctors feared. However, the doctors tell Cheryl that they want to keep Angela in the neonatal care unit for a week or two just to be sure that she is breathing independently.

Upon Dr. Jones's direction, Cheryl and James have been visiting Angela in the neonatal care unit several times a day. Angela cries frequently, which can be expected of preterm babies with anoxia. The nurses tell Cheryl that it is important to respond to Angela's cries as she is trying to communicate hunger, discomfort, or boredom. Cheryl replies that one of her hospital roommates told her that picking up crying babies can spoil them. The nurses reassure Cheryl that this is not the case. Cheryl feels confused. She has noticed that when she visits Angela and she has been crying that touching her and talking to her in a soothing voice do seem to calm her. Maybe the nurses are right.

Cheryl and James have felt extremely stressed by Angela's special needs. Visiting the neonatal care unit has been a frightening experience for them. Cheryl wonders if Angela will cry as much when she comes home. She feels glad that she will be at home without her for a while, but these thoughts make her feel guilty. The nurses tell her that she can visit Angela during the week or two that she needs to remain in the neonatal care unit. Cheryl wonders how she will get there, as her family has no car and little money for public transportation. Cheryl's minister talks with her social worker to try to work out some times when neighbors and friends in their church can take Cheryl and James to visit Angela. Cheryl notices that she, too, feels like crying much of the time. Her mother is concerned about her and wonders how they will manage when Angela leaves the neonatal care unit. ■

Postpartum depression—*a period of depression affecting most mothers for a few days and in some cases for weeks and months after childbirth.*

One study (Zaslow & Pedersen, 1981) indicated that 89 percent of mothers struggled with some degree of **postpartum depression**. As their bodies return to the prepregnancy state, their energy level increases, and they begin to develop confidence in their mothering abilities, most new mothers' depression disappears. A few mothers become severely depressed to the point where they cannot function in the mother role and may even be a danger to the well-being of the baby or themselves. Hormonal readjustment, lack of support from the father or other family members, and severe past emotional conflict in the mother are possible reasons for deep postpartum depression. Friends, relatives, and the medical profession need to be sensitive to severe postpartum depression and seek treatment for the new mother who may be incapable of obtaining help for herself (Hopkins et al., 1984).

Reaction of the Father

Recently, more attention has been given to the reactions of prospective fathers and to new fathers (see Chapter 3). New fathers worry about whether they will be good fathers, whether they will please their wives, added financial responsibility, changes in their relationship with their wives, and lack of freedom. If there are siblings, fathers wonder how they will react to the new brother or sister (Shapiro, 1987). A study by Zaslow and Pedersen (1981) indicated that 62 percent of the fathers who actively participated in childbirth classes and in the delivery of their children also experienced some degree of postpartum depression.

The women's movement, the need for two incomes to support a family, and family-centered maternity care have encouraged many fathers to become more involved in the birth and care of their children (Palkovitz, 1984). Studies indicate that a father's participation in the preparation for the birth, delivery and early care of the baby leads to later positive interaction patterns with his child (Klaus & Kennell, 1982; Parke & Sawin, 1981). The new mother, the medical profession, and friends and family need to be supportive of new fathers.

■ As Bill watches Ann breastfeed Jeremy in the hospital, he sometimes feels left out. In some ways he wishes that Ann had not decided to nurse Jeremy. He knows that breastfed babies have more immunity to illness and that a mother's milk is more nutritious than formula, but, if Jeremy were bottle fed, Bill could be a part of the feeding.

Bill mentions these feelings to Ann. She jokingly says that he will be glad that she is breastfeeding when he realizes that she has to get up to nurse Jeremy several times during the night. Ann thinks about Bill's comments. She asks Bill if he would like to help burp Jeremy and cuddle him after feeding.   ■

Reactions of Siblings

A study by Stewart et al. (1987) indicated that even though parents prepare children for the birth of a new brother or sister, there are many adjustments to be made. Stewart studied middle-class families with a first-born child of 2, 3, or 4 years of age over a 15-month period. Findings indicated that these firstborns spent much time trying to get their mother's full attention and that their strategies followed similar patterns regardless of age.

During the first 4 months after the birth of a brother or sister, the firstborns engaged in such behaviors as baby talk, using baby table manners, demanding a bottle or pacifier, and regression in toilet training. Another tactic included verbal and physical confrontations with the infant, parents, and even inanimate objects. At times, the firstborn children were whiny, withdrawn, clingy, and had a need for a security blanket or toy. By the fourth month after the birth of the baby, displays of imitation or confrontation usually disappeared. Anxiety behaviors continued, however. Four months later when new brother or sister was around 8 months old, the older siblings again used confrontational strategies. According to the researchers, these behaviors were explained by the baby brother's or sister's increasing mobility and responsiveness.

Parents can help their older children adjust to a new brother or sister by talking with them about the needs of the baby, pointing out the baby's interest in them, and planning time alone with the older children.

The brothers and sisters said that they helped care for the new baby. Ninety-five percent of the mothers confirmed this behavior. Over half said they liked to cuddle the new baby. During the last visit when the new baby was just over a year old, 63 percent of the firstborns said they were ready for a new baby.

Siblings of the same gender were reported to have a higher incidence of all types of behaviors. Fathers seemed to help out and give the firstborns needed attention. By the end of the study, the fathers were talking and playing with their firstborns as much as the mothers. This study (Stewart et al., 1987) indicates that at least in some middle-class families, the attention-getting behaviors of firstborns are normal, that fathers can help meet their need for attention, and that in spite of the obvious negative feelings of firstborns, there are also positive attitudes toward the new baby.

A study by Dunn and Kendrick (1982a) suggests that parents can help their older children adjust to a new brother or sister if they talk about the baby's needs and involve the older sibling in making decisions regarding the infant. Explaining the infant's behaviors and pointing out the infant's interest and attention in the older sibling can also facilitate positive interactions.

Reactions of Extended Family

Reactions of extended family can vary and also impact the immediate family of the newborn. Grandparents are usually thrilled. However, comments sometimes can suggest mixed or negative feelings about the birth of a grandchild. Grandparents often view the birth of grandchildren as a sign that they are getting older. Adjusting to the aging process can be difficult for some. At times, the feeling of failures or inadequacy that the grandparents had as parents can surface and create tension.

■ Ann's mother had not been successful at breastfeeding, and she kept telling Ann that her breasts were too small to feed Jeremy. Fortunately, Ann's childbirth classes had given her background information regarding the physiological process of nursing. She calmly responded to her mother's concerns explaining that the glands and not the size of the breasts stimulated milk production. Ann also volunteered that the sucking of the baby increased the supply of milk. This information seemed to relieve Ann's mother.   ■

Because a number of prospective parents today attend childbirth classes, they have new and up-to-date information. At times this may threaten some of the ideas about parenting held by grandparents. Grandparents may feel unsure about what they should do. This insecurity may be viewed as a lack of interest in the grandchild or new parents. In addition, some grandparents find it difficult to allow their children to become parents. The grandparents have been in control in their role as parents, and they feel a need to stay in control rather than allowing their children to take charge of their new family.

At times, the new parent's siblings may feel jealousy over all the attention that new parents are receiving. Becoming a new aunt or uncle also involves adjusting to a new role. If there has been a great deal of competition between the new parent and his or her siblings, old feelings of rivalry can surface and continue even when the sibling becomes a parent, and cousins can be pitted against one another.

Nevertheless, many extended family members can be helpful in providing information, needed support, and encouragement to the new parents. The reactions of the extended family add to the complexity of relationships surrounding the birth of a baby. An awareness of some of these feelings and their possible causes can help new parents better understand and cope with these behaviors and feelings.

Sociocultural Factors

Different cultural groups have different attitudes toward pregnancy, the birth process, and the care of newborns. An awareness of these differences and an understanding of the reasons for them can help early childhood professionals understand that there are many ways of behaving in the process of starting a family. Throughout this text, cultural differences in development will be presented to help the early childhood professional gain a better perspective about the variety of child and adult behaviors. Following are a few examples regarding varying cultural attitudes toward pregnancy, the birth process, and the care of newborns:

- Hispanic culture has a very negative view of pregnancy outside of marriage (Kirk, 1990).
- In the United States most babies are delivered in hospitals by physicians with mother and newborn being cared for by medical personnel for one to three days before returning home (Gordon & Haire, 1981). A few cultural groups, such as Alor Island people and Jarava Tribe in South America, look at childbirth as a part of everyday life (Mead & Newton, 1967). Mothers give birth and immediately resume their everyday routines.
- Freedman and Freedman (1969) found that Chinese-American newborns were more easily soothed and were better at self-calming than Caucasian-American infants. This information may help explain the perception that Chinese-American babies are "good" and that Chinese-American parents are better able to manage their infants when distressed.
- Another example of the influence of cultures on the care of newborns concerns the way African-American mothers handle their babies and keep them close to their bodies. This physical contact and stimulation of the changing environment as the babies are carried around has been suggested as the

 *Role of the Early Childhood Professional*

Working with Families with Newborns

1. Be aware of the possible relevance of special circumstances surrounding the pregnancy and birth of young children whose development appears atypical.
2. Help parents understand the reactions of siblings to a new baby.
3. Help parents with suggestions for preparing siblings for a new baby.
4. Be aware of possible changes in classroom behavior in young children during the weeks after the birth of a sibling.
5. Be aware of programs and services available to special-needs infants and their families.

reason for advanced physical and movement skills in African-American children (Ainsworth, 1967; Brazelton, Koslowski & Tronick, 1971; Geber, 1958).

Special Needs Infants and Their Families

Children born into families with limited economic resources may need additional assistance to ensure their continued growth and development. Infants with special physical or health needs and their families may need continued support from the medical profession and local community, state, or federal health services. Early identification and treatment of problems can reduce the cost of health care and increase human potential. These are two important reasons for providing private and public services for young children and their families.

The authors hope this chapter has made you more aware of the complex set of circumstances which affect newborns and their families. An awareness of these factors and dynamics can help facilitate a more complete understanding of young children and their families. A positive birth experience and adjustment of all family members to the newborn can help pave the way for a child to "know the joy of living" and for the parents to enjoy and celebrate "the beauty of life" (see the quote at the beginning of this chapter).

Bill, Ann, and Jeremy Johnson have had optimal circumstances for beginning their life as a family. Cheryl Monroe, James, and Angela have not been so fortunate. The following chapters will continue the story of the growth and development of Jeremy and Angela.

Key Terms

labor
dilation
cervix
contraction
electronic fetal monitor
cesarean
preterm
isolette
episiotomy
Leboyer method

afterbirth
anoxia
anemic
breech birth
forceps
Apgar Score
Neonatal Behavioral Assessment Scale
bonding
postpartum depression

Review Strategies/Activities

1. Interview several parents of newborns. Ask them to share with you:
   a. The delivery and hospital experience.
   b. Opportunities and experiences with bonding.
   c. The first two months after the baby's birth.
   d. Reactions of immediate and extended family to the baby's birth.
2. There is a saying that "all newborns look alike." Visit a hospital nursery and decide whether this statement is true or false. Support your position.
3. Invite an obstetrical or pediatric nurse to your class. Ask them to discuss:
   a. Use of the Apgar and Brazelton Scales.
   b. Important information parents need to have in caring for infants during the first few weeks of life.
   c. Care of at-risk infants and parent involvement.
4. Ask a group of parents from different cultures and backgrounds to visit your class. Have them share information on:
   a. Attitudes toward pregnancy and birth.
   b. Care of infants.

Further Readings

Galinsky, E. (1990). *The six stages of parenthood*. Reading, MA: Addison-Wesley.
   While many books for parents focus on how children develop, this one traces the stages of development that parents experience.

Lamb, M. E., & Sutton-Smith, B. (Eds.). (1982). *Sibling relationships: their nature across the lifespan.* Hillsdale, NJ: Earlbaum.

  This book describes sibling relationships from early in life and throughout the life-span. It provides interesting insights about the relationships we have with our siblings and the influence of various events upon these relationships.

Osfosky, H. J., & Osfosky, J. D. (1980). *Answers for new parents.* New York: Walker & Co.

  This book discusses the new roles and changes in relationships that occur in a family upon the birth of a baby. It provides sensible answers to common questions and provides support and reassurance to new parents.

PART THREE

Infancy

CHAPTER 5

Infancy conforms to nobody—all conform to it.
Ralph Waldo Emerson

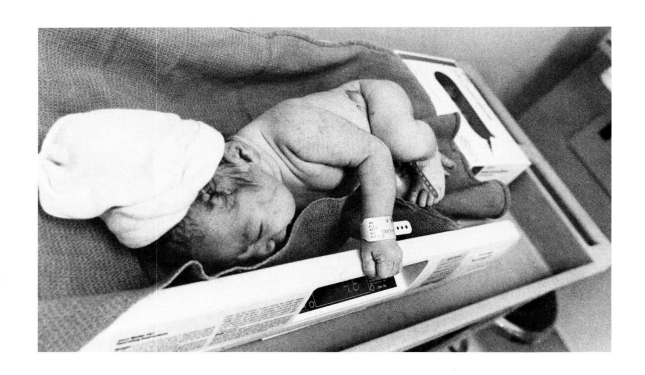

Physical/Motor Development
of the Infant

After reading and studying this chapter, you will demonstrate comprehension by:

- Outlining principles of development relating to the physical/motor development of infants from birth to the end of the first year.
- Describing major neonatal reflexes and their developmental implications.
- Outlining expected patterns of physical/motor development during the first year.
- Identifying major factors influencing physical/motor development.
- Suggesting strategies for promoting and enhancing physical/motor development during the first year.

Beginnings

The newborn enters the world with impressive abilities. From intrauterine to extrauterine living, the newborn must make a number of physiological adjustments, including breathing, taking in nourishment, and eliminating body wastes. The newborn makes adjustments from being surrounded by the warm amniotic fluid of the uterine environment, to being surrounded by air, which may fluctuate in temperature. The newborn has also adjusted from an environment of minimal sensory stimulation to an environment of varied stimuli which quicken all of the sensory mechanisms, including sight, sound, smell, touch, and taste. In spite of what might appear to be overwhelming demands on the previously totally dependent organism, the infant emerges as a remarkably competent individual. How might the newborn be described, and just what competencies are present in very young infants?

Physical Competence of the Newborn: Reflexes

Neonatal period—the first four weeks of life.

The **neonatal period** is usually defined as the first four weeks of life, and is a critical period in infant development. Many physiological adjustments required for extrauterine existence are taking place. During this period, all bodily functions and psychological states must be monitored to assure a healthy, hearty beginning.

Physically, the newborn may be a frightful sight, though individual parents may disagree with this generalization. The skin is wrinkled, red, and covered with cheese-like, greasy substance called **vernix caseosa,** which protects the skin during uterine development. In addition, the head is large in proportion to the rest of the body—the chest circumference is smaller than that of the infant's head. Sometimes the neonate's head has become temporarily misshapened during a lengthy delivery. Following the struggle to enter the world, the infant may fall into a deep sleep and for the first day or so may even have difficulty staying awake long enough to nurse.

Vernix caseosa—the oily covering that protects the skin of the fetus.

■ Jeremy, now 48 hours old, is cradled in his mother's arms and sleeping quite soundly. His neonatal face is scrunched into a tight expression—eyes closed very tightly, mouth puckered into an overbite position, chin almost buried in his chest. He is swaddled snugly under the soft baby wrap with arms folded comfortably against his chest, knees bent slightly upward and toes pointed inward.

His mother attempts to rouse her sleeping baby by gently rubbing her fingers across his soft cheek. He squirms slightly, stretching his legs and turning his head toward the touch; his mouth opens slightly, but he resists waking, and returns to his previous comfortable sleeping state. His mouth makes faint sucking movements briefly before lapsing into a fairly deep sleep.

Angela, 2 weeks old and now home from the neonatal care unit, is crying vigorously. Her legs stretch stiffly and her arms and hands seem to flail in the air. Her blanket is in disarray, and her mother is hurriedly preparing a bottle to feed her. As the nipple of the bottle brushes against her lips, Angela clumsily and almost frantically searches and struggles to grasp it. Her sucking response is somewhat weak, and she whimpers at first, until the hunger pains subside and the warmth and comfort of nourishment soothe her.   ■

These examples illustrate that there are individual differences in psychological states, responses to stimuli activity levels, and perhaps in these two cases, sleep and nourishment needs. Maybe Jeremy is still "recovering" from a strenuous labor and delivery. Maybe he simply is not hungry. Angela, two weeks older, has had time to recover from the complications surrounding her birth and is now alert. Angela may be demonstrating a heightened activity level.

The full term neonate is quite prepared for life and is equipped with a number of inborn movement patterns which help the infant adapt to new surroundings and new demands. These movement patterns, many of which are present prior to birth, are reflexes. **Reflexes** are unlearned, automatic responses to stimuli resulting from earliest neuromuscular development. Both Jeremy and Angela

Reflex—unlearned, involuntary response to stimuli.

display the infant reflexes of rooting and sucking. For the most part, these early reflexes are a function of **subcortical** (brain stem and spinal cord) mechanisms, though some cortical control is evident. The **cerebral cortex** is that part of the brain that is responsible for perception, memory, and thinking.

Some reflexes are called **survival reflexes** because they are necessary for the infant to survive. The obvious example is breathing. With the birth cry, which sometimes occurs before the infant is fully delivered, the respiratory mechanisms are set in motion, oxygenating the red blood cells and expelling carbon dioxide from the lungs.

Most subcortical, or **primitive reflexes,** gradually disappear as the cerebral cortex matures and begins to direct and control bodily movements and behaviors. Some reflexes such as breathing and bladder and bowel control may continue to have elements of both subcortical and cortical control. The developmental course of the individual reflexes varies—some disappear in the first few days, others within the first 12 to 18 months, and still others persist throughout life, becoming more precise and organized.

Subcortical—the portion of the brain just below the cerebral cortex that is responsible for controlling unlearned and reflexive behavior.

Cerebral cortex— the outer layer of the cerebral hemisphere made up of gray tissue that is mostly responsible for higher nervous functions.

Survival reflexes—reflexes that are essential to basic survival skills.

Primitive reflexes—reflexes controlled by subcortical structures in the brain that gradually disappear during the first year of life.

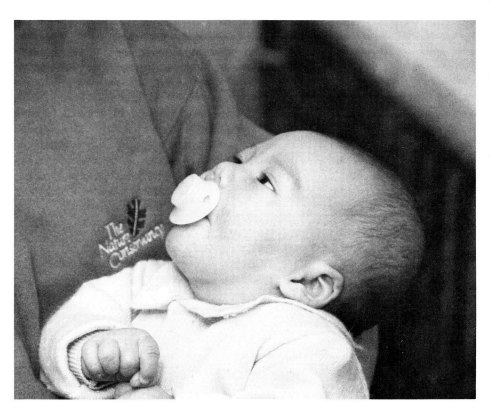

The full term infant exhibits an array of reflexes that sustain extrauterine life and assist the infant in adapting to new surroundings and demands

Frequently, in preterm infants, subcortical reflexes may not be evident at birth but will appear soon thereafter. Premature infants often exhibit weak rooting and sucking responses. Continued absence or weakness of these early reflexes suggests delayed development or dysfunction in the central nervous system. In premature infants, these early reflexes disappear somewhat more slowly than they do in full term infants. Table 5.1 lists the major reflexes observed in early infancy.

Gagging, sneezing, and hiccuping are also present before and after birth. In addition to an interesting array of reflexes, what are other beginnings which might be described? The answer falls into three additional categories: psychological states and activity levels; sensory capabilities; and expected growth and development patterns.

TABLE 5.1
Major reflexes present in infancy

Name	Description
Survival Reflexes	
Breathing reflex	Inhales/exhales, oxygenating the red blood cells and expelling carbon dioxide.
Rooting reflex	Turns in direction of touch on the cheek as though searching for a nipple. Serves to orient the infant to breast or bottle.
Sucking and swallowing reflex	Stimulated by nipple placed in mouth; allows the infant to take in nourishment.
Eyeblink and pupillary reflex	Eyes close or blink; pupils dilate or constrict to protect the eyes.
Primitive Reflexes	
Grasping reflex	Holds firmly to an object touching the palm of the hand. Disappearance around the fourth month signals advancing neurological development.
Moro reflex	Often referred to as the "startle reflex;" a loud noise or sudden jolt will cause the arms to throw outward, then return to an embracing-like position. Disappearance around the fifth or sixth month signals advancing neurological development.
Babinski reflex	Toes fan outward then curl when the bottom of the foot is stroked. Disappearance by end of first year signals advancing neurological development.
Tonic neck reflex	A "fencing pose," often assumed when sleeping—head turned to one side, arm extended on the same side, and opposite arm and leg flexed at the elbow and knee. Disappearance around 7 months signals advancing neurological development.

Psychological States, Activity Levels, and Temperament

Psychologists use the term **state** when describing the infant's relation to the world outside of himself. States are characterized in terms of the degree of arousal and alertness exhibited by the infant.

Psychological state—pertains to conditions of arousal and alertness in infancy.

An eagerly awaited milestone in infant development is that of "sleeping through the night." Sleeping patterns of infants are often the subject of proud (or perhaps, tired) parent discussions, and represent an interest in the characteristics and amount of sleep exhibited by the infant. Researchers, as well, are interested in infant sleep patterns. Patterns, characteristics, and problems of sleep in young children comprise a large body of literature and constitute a broad field of study.

Sleep patterns change as the infant matures. Newborn infants can be expected to sleep approximately 18 out of 24 hours (Berg, Adkinson, & Strock, 1973). The longest period of sleep may be 4 to $4\frac{1}{2}$ hours during the first days. By 4 to 6 weeks of age, the infant may be sleeping 12 to 14 hours a day, taking as many as seven different "naps" during a 24-hour period.

Some infants may sleep a 6-hour night by the fourth week after birth, but some will not sleep through the night until they are 7 or 8 months old. Some infants sleep more during the day, others at night, though most infants seem to sleep for longer periods at night. There is great variation in both the amount and type of sleep exhibited in infants. In his study of states of arousal in infancy, Wolff (1966) identified six states, as summarized in Table 5.2.

TABLE 5.2
Classification of infant states

State	Characteristics
Regular sleep	Little body movement; regular breathing; no response to mild stimulation.
Irregular sleep	Increased body movements; irregular breathing; more easily aroused by external stimuli.
Periodic sleep	Occurs between regular and irregular sleep and is accompanied by muscle movements and rapid breathing, then short periods of calm inactivity.
Drowsiness	Little motor activity, yet sensitive to external stimuli.
Alert inactivity	Visually and/or auditorially scans the environment; large motor activity (head, trunk, arms and legs), alert and relaxed.
Waking activity	More intense motor activity may signal physiological need.
Crying	Motor activity passes into a whimpering, crying state, becoming louder as distress increases. Thrashing; twisting of torso and kicking vigorously.

Note: Reprinted from *Psychological Issues*, "Causes, Controls and Organization of Behavior in the Neonate" by P. H. Wolff. By permission of International Universities Press, Inc. Copyright 1966 by International Universities Press.

■ Jeremy, now 4 months old, is usually quite content at bedtime. His mother usually holds him in her lap for a while after the evening feeding, while he drifts into drowsiness, and then into irregular sleep. Her soft voice hums to him while he languishes in her arms. Sensing his readiness for the crib, she carries him to his room. Placing him quietly in his crib, she continues to hum. She rubs his back softly and then leaves the room after knowing he has fallen soundly to sleep.

However, on this particular evening Jeremy resists sleep. His eyes are open and scanning his surroundings, though he appears tired and cries sporadically. Tonight, he is what most parents would call "cranky." His mother, also tired, wishes some magic formula would soothe him and help him rest. Nevertheless, after determining that Jeremy is not hungry, his diaper does not need changing, and his clothing is comfortable, she follows her established routine with him, sustaining each phase slightly longer. After being placed in his crib, he rouses somewhat and cries resistively while mother strokes his back gently. Though he has not fallen into sound sleep, she leaves the room.   ■

Predictable, unhurried bedtimes with regular routines help the reluctant infant to separate from the family and fall asleep more readily. Routines may include a relaxed bathtime during which the interaction between parent and child is satisfying to both, followed by being held in the parent's lap and rocked, and being sung to softly. Cuddling a soft stuffed toy while being held focuses attention away from other more stimulating activities occurring around the infant. This routine is followed by being placed in bed with a moment of slow back rubbing and a kiss on the cheek, a spoken "good night," and then departure from the room.

Such routines vary from family to family, however, the goal is to provide unhurried, yet interactive bedtime rituals that assure and comfort the infant. There is no need to insist that the household be abnormally quiet, as infants readily adjust to the typical and usual noises in their environments. Nor should siblings be expected to be particularly quiet—though rowdy play, of course, disturbs anyone's rest. It is possible that some infants are soothed by usual household noises, which may provide a sense of security and an auditory sense of the permanence of people.

Similar routines in out-of-home child care arrangements facilitate naptime for infants and reassure them of the support of their other caregivers. As with noise levels at home, rest times can be scheduled during periods of the day when noise levels are at a minimum; yet there is no need to expect that all noise can be curtailed during group-care naptimes.

Temperament—an individual's behavior style.

Temperament is defined as an individual's behavior style and helps us to describe the infant's responses (Chess, 1967; Thomas & Chess, 1977; Thomas, Chess, & Birch, 1968). While this dimension of infant development will be discussed in Chapter 6, it is mentioned here as one of the psychological states in infancy. In their research, Chess and Thomas (1987) identified several dimensions of temperament, including activity level, rhythms, approach and withdrawal behaviors, adaptability, responsiveness, intensity of reaction, quality of mood, distractibility, and attention span and persistence. Using these activity classifications, the researchers delineated three basic temperament patterns:

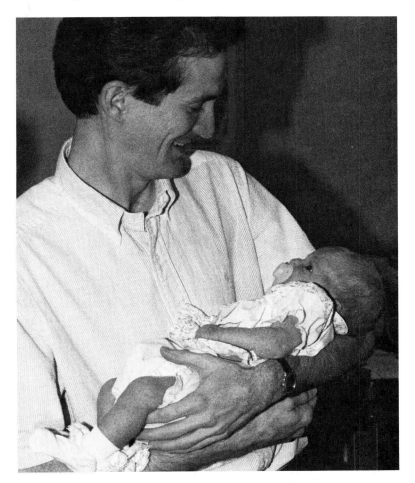

Infants' behavior styles influence reciprocal interactions between them and their caregivers.

easy, difficult, and slow-to-warm-up. These behavior styles influence the reciprocal interactions between infants and their caregivers.

Brazelton (1973) suggests that temperament can be evaluated along a continuum from quiet-alert to defensive and upset. There are wide variations in temperaments in infants—some are less soothable than others; some tend to be able to calm themselves or are easily comforted by their caregivers. As infants grow and mature and become accustomed to their individual environments, routines, and caregivers, their temperaments may change. However, in response-poor environments this change may not always be for the better.

■ Angela's temperament is less soothable than Jeremy's. At bedtime, she seems to be quite fretful and restless. Inferring from the usual afternoon and evening family routines that bedtime is drawing near, she begins to whine and cry and will not sustain her grasp on a soft toy offered to her. She resists being held and comforted.

Since birth, Angela has had a variety of caregivers, from hospital neonatal care nursing staff in her first two weeks to a home in which an extended family exists, including her grandmother and her own mother's siblings, some young children and some teenagers. All have been intrigued with Angela, each assuming responsibility for her care when needed. Angela's care has been neither predictable nor consistent.

Angela's grandmother, sensing a difficult bedtime, takes charge. She carries Angela on her shoulder as she walks about the house giving clean-up and bedtime instructions to her other children. Patting a fretful Angela, she continues to walk, talk, and hush the baby. Unsuccessful, she proceeds to a back bedroom where, separated from the rest of the family, she places Angela across her lap and begins to sing and talk softly to her. For a time Angela still wiggles, lifts her head and frets, and is easily distracted by the sound of children playing inside the house. Her grandmother continues to sing and talk or hum until at last Angela begins to rest and finally doze.   ■

Children seem to be born with distinctive temperaments and activity levels. The activity levels of neonates have been positively correlated with activity levels at ages four and eight (Korner, Zeanah, Linden, Berkowitz, Kraemer, & Agras, 1985). Activity levels have recently been associated with birth order (Eaton, Chipperfield, & Singbeil, 1989). In a study of 7,000 children ranging in age from 4 days to 7 years, including first- through sixth-born children, it was found that earlier-born children were more active than later-born children. Heredity seems to play a role in determining individual temperament, as does a child's environment. However, the relative influence of each has not been established.

Sensory Capabilities in Infancy

The newborn's sensory equipment is remarkably operative at birth. Neonates are capable of seeing, hearing, tasting, smelling, and responding to touch. The neonate takes in and processes information to a much greater extent than one suspects. **Perceptual** development begins as the infant seeks and receives information through the senses.

Perception—the physiological process by which sensory input is interpreted.

Touch

Scientists believe that the sense of touch emerges between $7\frac{1}{2}$ to 14 weeks of embryonic development (Hooker, 1952). Skin, muscular, and inner ear (vestibular) senses are more mature at birth than are the other senses (Gottfried, 1984). The sense of touch, particularly around the mouth area, is especially acute and facilitates infant nursing. Certain other parts of the body are sensitive to touch. These include the nose, skin of the forehead, soles of the feet, and cheeks. Most of the reflexes listed in Table 5.1 are stimulated by touch. In addition to touch, the skin is sensitive to temperature, pressure, and pain.

For obvious ethical reasons, there is little research on sensitivity to pain. Contrary to the previous notion that neonates do not experience great pain, we now know that they do. Recent studies of pain associated with infant circumcision procedures have helped to advance our knowledge. By analyzing the recorded vocalizations of newborn males during circumcision, researchers identified significant differences in vocalizations as each step of the procedure became more invasive (Porter, Miller, & Marshall, 1986). Some surgical procedures previously thought not to be painful to newborns are now accompanied by anesthesia whenever possible (American Academy of Pediatrics, 1987).

The importance of touch and the infant's need for it have been of interest to researchers for years. Lack of soothing tactile sensations during infancy has been associated with delays in cognitive and affective development (Ainsworth, 1962; Yarrow, 1961). So in addition to the sheer pleasure experienced by both infant and caregiver when hugging, rocking, caressing, patting, and so on, these experiences provide the infant with tactile stimulation essential to perceptual and sensory development.

Vision

The neonate's vision functions well at birth, though visual acuity is imperfect with a tendency toward farsightedness. Neonates can follow a moving light and fixate on an object at a distance of about 9 inches. In his pioneering studies of infant visual preferences, Fantz (1961) found that infants prefer human faces and enjoy bold patterns such as checkerboards or bullseye patterns, but do not attend well to solid colors. Infants tended to look at the edges of the designs or at the point where two contrasts come together. Other researchers have found that infants watch more intently a face that is active, smiling, talking, blinking, or laughing (Haith, 1966; Samuels, 1985). Others have found that infants attend longer to a face that imitates their own facial movements and expressions (Winnicott, 1971). Bornstein (1984, 1985) found that infants respond to differences in colors and suggested that later ability to categorize by color, thought to be a result of cognitive development, has its origins in earliest visual perceptual processes. Whereas vision improves rapidly over the first few months of life, mature 20/20 vision is not achieved until about age 5 (Bornstein, 1988).

Hearing

Though the passages of the ear (Eustachian tubes and external canal) may still have amniotic fluids in them for the first few days after birth, the newborn hears fairly well. After the fluids are absorbed, the neonate responds vigorously to varying sounds in the environment. The infant will be startled by loud noises and soothed by soft sounds. It has been suggested that neonates can discrim-

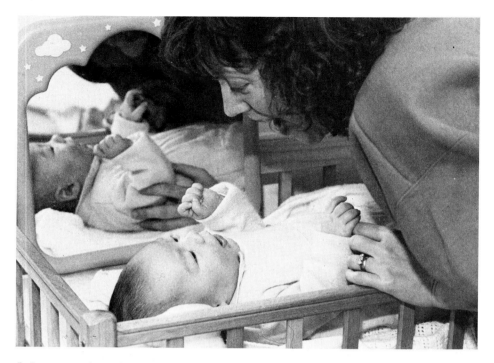

Infants gaze intently at a human face, particularly an active, smiling, talking face.

inate between loud and soft sounds but do not respond to variations in pitch (Bench, 1978). Researchers have also demonstrated that neonates are capable of discriminating between sounds that differ in duration, direction, and frequency, as well as loudness (Bower, 1982).

Neonates seem particularly responsive to the human voice (Caron, Caron, & MacLean, 1988). The neonate will often stop crying when spoken to, visually scan when voices are heard, and attempt to vocalize (Rosenthal, 1982). Could it be that human infants are genetically "programmed" to react to human speech?

Taste

The taste of milk seems to elicit a reaction of satisfaction in infants. Infants prefer sweet tastes, and will usually react negatively to sour, bitter or salty tastes (Steiner, 1979).

Smell

Infants sense a variety of odors and will turn away from noxious odors such as vinegar or alcohol. Interestingly, they seem to be able to recognize the smell of their mothers within the first few days of life (MacFarlane, 1977; Makin & Porter, 1989). Musick and Householder (1986) suggest that the early bonding process might be facilitated if the mother were to leave her breast pad or other small article of her clothing in the bassinet to reinforce the infant's sensory attachment to her.

Overview of Physical/Motor Development in the First Year

It is helpful to describe expected patterns of development during the first year in the context of known principles of growth and development.

Principles of Growth and Development

1. *Growth and development follow a* **cephalocaudal** *and* **proximodistal** *direction.* That is, growth and development proceed from the head downward and from the central axis of the body outward. This is evident in the bodily proportions of the newborn. The newborn is quite top-heavy with the head comprising $\frac{1}{4}$ of the total body length. At birth the newborn's head is 70 percent of its eventual adult size. These proportions are illustrated in Figure 5.1.

    This law of developmental direction applies not only to body proportions, but also to other forms of development. It is most significant in the development and coordination of large and small muscles. Coordination of the large muscles of the upper body, including the neck, shoulders, upper trunk, and upper arms precedes the coordination of smaller muscles in those body

Cephalocaudal—refers to the head to tail or long axis of the body.

Proximodistal—refers to the direction from body's center outward to the extremities.

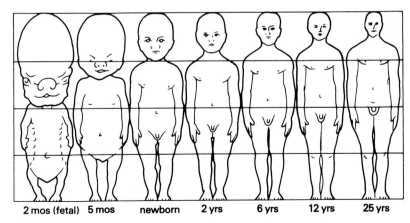

2 mos (fetal)   5 mos   newborn   2 yrs   6 yrs   12 yrs   25 yrs

FIGURE 5.1
At birth, the newborn's head is 70 percent of its eventual adult size. (From *Biology* by William A. Jensen, Bernd Heinrich, David B. Wake, and Marvalee H. Wake © 1979 by Wadsworth, Inc. All rights reserved. Reprinted by permission of the publisher.)

regions. Also, throughout infancy and early childhood, the upper body muscles will be more mature and coordinated than those of the lower, with the large muscles of the hips and upper legs developing before the smaller muscles of the lower legs, ankles, and feet.

2. *Most children follow a similar developmental pattern.* As a rule, one stage of the pattern lays the foundation for the next. In motor development, for instance, there is a predictable sequence of developments that precedes walking. The infant lifts and turns his head before he can turn over, and is able to move his arms and legs before grasping an object. Figure 5.2 depicts posture and locomotion in infants.

3. *Growth and development proceed from general to specific.* In motor development, the infant first makes very generalized, undirected movements, waving arms or kicking before reaching or creeping toward a desired object. The infant will be able to grasp an object with the whole hand before using only the thumb and forefinger.

4. *There are individual rates of growth and development.* While the patterns or sequences for growth and development usually remain the same, the rates at which individual children reach specific developmental milestones will vary. For example, one child may begin walking unassisted at 9 months; another may begin walking at 15 months. It should also be noted that most children grow in spurts, but some grow in what appear to be steady increments.

   Likewise, rates of development are not uniform within an individual child. For instance, a child's intellectual development may outpace his emotional or social development. Another child may show precocious language development, but be less motorically coordinated than many of his age-mates. As a rule, girls precede boys in the progression toward maturation.

5. *Development results from a combination of maturation, learning, and environmental influences.* Maturational patterns are innate—they are genetically programmed. Learning occurs as a result of experiences, and the environment sets the stage for maximizing or perhaps impeding optimal growth and development.

   Rates of physical and motor development are primarily the result of heredity. However, opportunities to explore the world when crawling, along with the provision of a rich and varied environment in which to explore, enhance both physical/motor skills and cognitive development in infancy. By contrast, an infant in the crawling stage who is confined to a playpen has limited opportunities to practice motor skills and limited environmental stimulation for learning. Fullest realization of inherited growth and development potential may be thwarted in such instances.

Expected Growth and Development Patterns

Having briefly discussed some basic principles of growth and development, it is now possible to outline some of the expected patterns for physical and motor

FIGURE 5.2
During the first 15 months of life, the cephalocaudal and proximodistal
pattern of development is obvious. (Mary M. Shirley, *The First Two Years.*
Institute of Child Welfare Monograph No. 7. Minneapolis: University of Minnesota
Press. Copyright © 1933, renewed 1961 by the University of Minnesota Press.
Reprinted by permission.)

development during the first year. Growth and development during this first
year is both dramatic and significant. According to Sandra Anselmo (1987,
p. 148), "In no other one-year period until puberty are there so many physical
changes. The changes in infancy are measured in terms of days and weeks
rather than in terms of months and years."

Physical Development

Birth weight and birth length are always of interest to parents, grandparents, and health-care professionals. While answering questions about birth weight and length often makes for proud conversation, physical measurements are quite significant in the larger context of infant health and development. Low birth weight, for instance, has serious implications for survival and for subsequent normal development.

The average birth weight for full term infants is $7\frac{1}{2}$ pounds, with a range from $5\frac{1}{2}$ to 10 pounds. Boys usually are slightly heavier than girls at birth. Birth length ranges from 18 to 22 inches, with an average of 20 inches. The neonate frequently loses weight in the first few days, due to loss of body fluids and the inability to adequately take in nourishment, but will gain at a rate of 6 to 8 ounces per week, and by 5 to 6 months may have doubled the birth weight. The infant's length also will have increased by 6 to 7 inches.

During the second half of the first year, gains in pounds and inches will decelerate some, though growth continues at a rapid pace. Weight may increase by 4 to 6 ounces weekly, and height by 3 to 4 inches. By the first birthday, infants may have tripled in weight and have grown 10 to 12 inches since birth. If growth were to proceed at such pace, an 18-year-old would measure more than 15 feet tall and weigh several tons! Fortunately, growth slows appreciably after the first 2 years.

Weight and height are observable characteristics. However, as this outward growth is observed, there is significant internal growth taking place as the central nervous system matures and bones and muscles increase in weight, length, and coordination.

Ossify—*to convert cartilage or membrane to bone.*

The soft bones of early infancy gradually **ossify** as calcium and other minerals harden them. The bones are soft and pliable and are difficult to break. They do not support the infant's weight in sitting or standing positions. The skull bones are separated by **fontanelles** (or "soft spots," as they are often called), which may compress to facilitate passage through the birth canal. These fontanelles tend to diminish after 6 months and may close between 9 and 18 months.

Fontanelles—*membranous space between cranial bones of the fetus and infant.*

Interestingly, the bones of the skull and wrists ossify earliest, with the wrists and ankles developing more bones as the child matures. Girls may be several weeks ahead of boys in bone development at birth. Physicians may utilize x-rays of the wrists to determine **"skeletal age"** of individual children. Such x-rays reveal the number of bones in the wrist along with the extent of ossification. This information assists in the assessment of expected growth progress and in diagnosing growth disorders and disease.

Skeletal age—*a measure of physical development based on examination of skeletal x-rays.*

Though infants are born with all the muscle cells they will ever have (Tanner, 1978), there is a large amount of water in muscle tissue. Gradually, as protein and other nutrients replace this cellular fluid, the strength of the muscles increases.

Neurological development experiences a growth spurt in the last trimester of prenatal development and during the first two years of life. During this period, more than half of the brain's mature weight is added. As is true of other organs, not all parts of the brain develop at the same rate—at birth, the brain stem and the midbrain are the most highly developed. These are the areas of the brain which control consciousness, inborn reflexes, digestion, respiration, and elimination.

The cerebrum and the cerebral cortex surround the midbrain and are significant in the development of primary motor and sensory responses. Following the law of developmental direction, the nerve cells that control the upper trunk and arms mature before those that control the lower trunk and legs. Observation of infant motor activity reveals a growing number of skills that utilize the muscles of the neck, arms, and hands, skills that precede ability to turn over, sit up, or crawl. By 6 months of age, the cerebral cortex has matured sufficiently to control most of the infant's physical activity. At this point in growth and development, many of the reflexes of early infancy should be disappearing, signaling the maturation of the neurological system.

Special Needs Infants

One must be cautious in applying the ages for specific developmental achievements such as those listed in Table 5.3. Any one child may exhibit developmental differences on a number of the items listed, with certain skills occurring sooner or later than the chart suggests. Individual differences in rates of development make such charts useful only for approximations or estimates of individual performances.

If individual performance deviates appreciably from the developmental charts, there may be cause to seek pediatric consultation. Minor deviations may be the result of lack of experience, a stimulus-poor environment, or a passive temperament. Individual differences in motor development do not necessarily indicate advanced or delayed neuromuscular development, nor do these differences predict potential for later motor skills.

Nevertheless, motor development is one of a number of observable behaviors that can indicate underlying neurological development and maturity. Significant deviations from the norms in motor development may occur from a variety of causes: bone and muscle abnormalities; mental retardation; prolonged and/or traumatic illness; minimal brain dysfunction; blindness; deafness; and problems relating to muscle tone, balance, and strength associated with prematurity or poor nutrition.

While discussion of each of these causes is beyond the scope or purpose of this text, some points need to be made. Routine examinations by a pediatrician can detect bone or muscle abnormality early, and, in most cases, response to treatment is enhanced with early detection. The pediatrician is the expert of preference in these instances. Where further assessment and treatment is needed, the pediatrician may refer the child to another specialist.

Children with mental retardation progress through the expected sequences of motor development, but do so at a slower rate (Melyn & White, 1973). However, the assumption should never be made that children progressing through

TABLE 5.3
Developmental milestones in motor control during the first year

Age	Motor Development
Birth to 3 months	Supports head when in prone position Lifts head Supports weight on elbows Hands relaxing from the grasping reflex Visually follows a moving person Pushes with feet against examiner's hands Turns from side to back Sits with support Head self-supported when held at shoulder
3 to 6 months	Slaps at bath water Kicks feet when prone Plays with toes Reaches but misses dangling object Shakes and stares at toy placed in hand Head self-supported when held at shoulder Turns from back to side Sits with props Makes effort to sit alone Crawling behaviors Rocking on all fours Drawing up knees and falling forward
6 to 9 months	Rolls from back to stomach Crawls using both hands and feet Sits alone steadily Pulls to standing position in crib Raises self to sitting posture Successfully reaches and grasps toy Transfers object from one hand to the other Stands up by furniture Cruises along crib rail Stepping movements around furniture
9 to 12 months	"Mature" crawling Cruises holding on to furniture Walks with two hands held Sits without falling Stands alone May walk alone Attempts to crawl up stairway Grasps object with thumb and forefinger

the motor control sequence slowly have mental retardation. Delays in motor skills can be attributed to a variety of factors.

Because prehension involves eye-hand coordination, infants with visual impairments are slow to develop this ability. Infants with normal vision bring their hands into their visual field at around 15 weeks of age. In the absence of vision, hand play is not sustained. Likewise, crawling and walking are delayed sometimes by several months. These infants need a variety of sound, tactile, and movement cues to assist their motor development (Fraiberg, 1976).

Relation of Physical/Motor Development to Cognition

Motor experiences in infancy form the basis of meaning in earliest cognitive development as physical movements emerge. At first the movements are unintentional (as with many reflexes), and later most of them become purposeful. As will be discussed in Chapter 7, Piaget's (1952) stages of cognitive development begin with what he termed the "sensorimotor" stage, which occurs from birth to age two. According to Piaget, the sensorimotor stage of cognitive development follows a pattern from random, involuntary reflex activity in which cognition is dominated by sensory input, to anticipatory and intentional behaviors facilitated by increasing mobility and large and fine motor controls.

An environment rich with sensory input—sights, sounds, tastes, aromas, textures, and movement enhances cognitive development in infants. In addition, talking, singing, and interacting with the infant provide necessary input for a rapidly developing mind. An environment that encourages interactions and freedom of movement, then, is essential to a well-integrated cognitive system.

Factors Influencing Physical/Motor Development

Regardless of the rate of progress in physical/motor skill development, or presence of developmental delays or disease, the infant's environment plays an important role in influencing the child's health and vitality. Environments that facilitate optimum growth and development are those providing proper nutrition, interactive and supportive relationships, healthy feeding schedules, safe surroundings, and regular health and medical assessments.

Nutrition

The role of nutrition in assuring optimal outcomes is a critical one during prenatal development and infancy. During prenatal development and the first 2 years, brain growth is particularly dramatic. Studies have linked impaired functioning of the central nervous system to poor nutrition in the early months of life (Dobbing, 1984; Galler, Ramsey, & Solimano, 1984, 1985). Appropriate nutrition helps to prevent illnesses (Guthrie, 1986) and assures the developmental integrity of the individual.

One of the first decisions regarding feeding the newborn is whether to breast or bottle feed. This decision is a personal one and best determined after weighing the advantages and disadvantages of each. Consultation with the obstetrician and the pediatrician assists in determining which method best suits both infant and mother.

The choice will be related to such factors as personal preference of the parents; the health status of the mother and any medications she may be taking that can be transmitted through breast milk to the infant; adequacy of her milk supply to meet the infant's demands; and the anticipation that her diet will contain sufficient proteins and vitamins to enrich her milk. In addition the health status and individual nutritional needs of the infant will be considered, as will practical considerations of costs, availability, preparation, storage, and protection of milk from contamination.

Since commercial formulas today attempt to meet standards of composition closely approximating that of human milk (American Academy of Pediatrics, 1976), infants thrive on it quite well when it is prepared according to recommended proportions of water to formula. Interestingly, since 1966, there has been an increase in the incidence of breastfeeding (Pipes, 1989). Breast milk is considered the most ideally suited food for infants, although supplements of vitamin D, iron, and fluoride are often recommended. Vitamin C supplements may also be recommended in cases where the mother's diet is deficient in it.

Breast milk contains a number of substances uniquely suited to the infant's needs. **Colostrum**, a substance that precedes the breast milk in the first days of breastfeeding, provides immunity to a number of infections when the mother carries the immunities. In addition to its immunological benefits, colostrum is high in protein and carotene and has less sugar and less fat than mature milk, making it particularly compatible with the neonate's digestive capacities (Worthington-Roberts & Williams, 1989). Mature breast milk is secreted between the third and sixth day after childbirth. For most babies, breast milk is best suited to their immature digestive systems and is least likely to trigger allergic reactions or gastrointestinal distress.

Colostrum—first liquid secreted by the mammary glands soon after childbirth.

Colic is abdominal discomfort which occurs in young infants, usually under 3 months of age. It can be quite painful for the infant and distressing to parents. Some possible causes of colic are: swallowed air, high-carbohydrate foods, intestinal allergy, stressful environment, or impending illness (Barness, 1983). Some infants seem to be more prone than others to colic, and there seems to be no universal treatment, since the causes vary. Physical examination by a pediatrician may be needed to detect possibly serious problems.

Some preventive measures can be taken to reduce the incidence of colic. Careful attention should be given to feeding in an unhurried and calm atmosphere, burping at regular intervals during feeding, avoiding either overfeeding or underfeeding, and identifying any possible food allergies. When colic occurs, holding the baby upright or lying the baby prone across the lap may be helpful (Barness, 1983). Sometimes changing caregivers helps. A tired and frustrated parent or caregiver whose attempts to soothe the infant have led to crying may, in their continued efforts, actually exacerbate the problem.

Bottle-fed infants should always be held during feeding. The infant's bottle should never be propped. Lacking motor controls necessary to move the bottle, the infant could choke on the formula. Propping the bottle has other risks, as well. Tooth decay is caused when formula stays in the mouth too long, coating the teeth with sugars. Also, when the infant is lying down to drink from a bottle, bacteria grow in pooled liquid in the mouth and cheeks, which then makes its way to the eustachian tubes, resulting in painful ear infections.

The psychological needs of infants to be held when being fed are also important. Whether breast-fed or bottle-fed, infants experience bonding and attachment during the feeding process. Feeding time should be a time of close physical and emotional contact between infant and parent or caregiver. When the routine is calm and unhurried, both the infant and the adult find tremendous satisfaction in the encounter. Infants develop a sense of trust and security when they are allowed to determine when they are hungry and when they are allowed to determine the amount of food they need at feeding time. Overfeeding or underfeeding result when adults are not sensitive to infant cues of satiety or continued hunger.

When allowed to do so, infants soon settle into individualized rhythms of eating and sleeping, adjusting to their own metabolic needs. For most healthy full term infants, this schedule breaks into 4-hour intervals. Some infants may need to be fed every 3 hours; smaller infants will need food every 2 hours. Caregivers soon learn to adjust to these rhythms, knowing that as the infant grows and matures, the schedule will become more comfortable for everyone.

Solid foods are usually introduced sometime beween the third and fourth months, on the advice of the pediatrician. There does seem to be a trend today toward introducing solid foods as early as 6 to 8 weeks (Burton & Foster, 1988), though this does not seem to be generally advised. Contrary to an often-held belief, however, early introduction of solid foods does not always assist the infant in sleeping through the night. Hunger does awaken infants in the night, but nutritionists advise that the decision to introduce solid foods must be based on the infant's need for the nutrients provided by solid foods and on the infant's physiological readiness to handle solid foods (Christian & Gregor, 1988). Efforts to feed an infant solids through the use of a "feeder" (special syringe-type container) is dangerous and inappropriate. It ignores infant physiological and biological readiness, and is a form of force feeding (Endres & Rockwell, 1985).

The introduction of solid foods usually begins with iron-fortified cereals. Individual infant needs and pediatric guidance determine just when solid foods should be given. New foods are introduced one at a time, and usually once a week, in order to accustom the infant to this new experience and to detect any allergic reaction to specific foods. As the intake of solid foods increases, the need for milk or formula decreases. Neither sugar nor salt should be added to foods given to infants—their immature digestive systems do not handle added seasonings well.

As the infant grows and learns to eat a variety of foods, care must be given to providing a balanced diet in which foods are selected from vegetable, fruit, meat, grain, and cereal food groups. Foods selected for youngest eaters should appeal in color, flavor, texture, and shape. Self-feeding foods which can be held in the hand or grasped from a tray must be easy to chew and swallow. Mealtimes should be unhurried and pleasant.

When providing solid foods to an infant, several precautions must be taken, and foremost among those precautions is avoiding food contamination. Foods should be fresh and properly stored. Adults must observe scrupulously clean procedures for preparing and serving baby meals: washed hands, clean utensils, foods kept at appropriate hot or cold temperatures, and covered, sanitary, and refrigerated storage of unused portions. It is best not to reheat leftover baby food, as illness can be caused by microorganisms that grow in foods at room temperature.

In addition to contamination concerns, precautions should be taken in the selection of finger foods for infants. Taking in solid foods is a different developmental task from sucking and swallowing liquids. Now the infant must mouth or chew the food to soften it, experience the texture as well as the taste of it, move it to the back of the mouth and successfully swallow it. This task is not always well coordinated, as demonstrated by the infant's need for a bib.

Infants develop a variety of motor skills during the first year of life that include the ability to grasp objects, such as small finger foods.

There are some foods that present particular problems for infants and young children. For instance, honey and corn syrup have been found to contain **clostridium botulinum**, the organism responsible for **botulism**. In infants under a year old, the immature gastrointestinal tract allows this organism to become active and potentially lethal (Christian & Gregor, 1988). Foods that have caused choking include hot dogs, candy, peanuts, grapes, large chunks of meat, hard or chewy cookies, carrots, popcorn, and chewing gum. Selection of nutritional substitutes for these foods and close supervision as the infant learns to handle new foods is imperative. Infants and small children should not be given foods to eat in a moving vehicle or as they are toddling about, as this increases the risk of choking.

Clostridium botulinum—bacteria that causes botulism.

Botulism—an often fatal food poisoning.

Any discussion of nutrition would be incomplete without a word about under- and overnutrition. **Undernutrition** is defined as inadequate intake of necessary nutrients for growth and health maintenance. **Overnutrition** is defined as the overconsumption of nutrients necessary for growth and health maintenance. Since nutrition deficiencies during earliest growth and development may not be reversible with later improved diets (Alford & Bogle, 1982), assuring adequate amounts of all necessary nutrients is crucial during infancy and early childhood.

Undernutrition— inadequate intake of nutrients essential for growth.

Overnutrition— overconsumption of nutrients needed for growth.

Contemporary concerns about obesity, cholesterol, and other diet-related health problems have led some parents to mistakenly believe that reducing fat and calories in the infant's diet is necessary. Body size, proportions, and composition are in a period of very rapid change. The infant's calorie needs per unit of body weight far exceed that of older children and adults to maintain this growth. In the absence of teeth, infants are dependent upon consuming sufficient amounts of breast milk or formula to meet their increased caloric needs. In addition, during the last trimester of prenatal development and during the first few years of postnatal development, rapid **myelination** of the nervous system is taking place. Fat is a major component of myelin (the tissue which surrounds the nerves as they mature) and, as such, is an essential part of the infant's diet if optimum neurological integrity is to be obtained (Eichorn, 1979). The American Academy of Pediatrics, Committee on Nutrition (1986) advises against practices that limit the diets of infants.

Myelination—the process of covering the nerve cells within the central nervous system with fatty tissue (myelin), which promotes efficient transmission impulses along the neurons.

On the other hand, overfeeding infants leads to an inability in infants and young children to recognize and respond to their own **satiation** (fullness) cues. Obesity can result with excessive intake of food. Adults must learn to recognize and accept infant cues: turning the head away from the nipple, facial expressions of distaste, and other bodily attempts to refuse food. Allowing infants to eat what they need, without insisting on further intake, helps infants recognize their own feelings of hunger or fullness. Adults must also avoid giving food indiscriminately in an attempt to curtail crying. Not all crying is hunger-related—to provide food or drink every time the child cries establishes a pattern of satisfying one's discomforts, regardless of what they are, by eating. The obvious outcome to this psychological behavior is obesity and poor physical and psychosocial health.

Satiation—feeling of fullness or adequate intake of food.

Optimal physical, mental, and emotional health at all ages, then, depends upon adequate nutrition, especially during the earliest growth years. A large body of research on this critical issue continues to emerge. Parents, caregivers, and health-care experts have a responsibility to assure the nutritional well-being of children.

General Health

General health refers to the qualities of total physical, mental, and social well-being. The infant's physical well-being is affected by and affects his mental and social well-being. These dimensions of health are interrelated. For instance, stressful environments can lead to restlessness, fretfulness, and symptoms of illness such as colic. On the other hand, infants who are healthy generally exhibit robust energy, appetite, and for the most part, contentment. Good general health during the first year of life depends on a number of factors:

- medically supervised prenatal, neonatal, and infant care,
- appropriate and adequate nutrition,
- feeding schedules and procedures that are sensitive to the infant's cues,
- balance between play and resting times,
- early dental care,
- safe and sanitary surroundings,
- supportive and interactive adults,
- predictable routines and consistency in daily living, and
- limited stress.

Immunizations

Some immunity to infectious diseases is transferred to infants from their mothers during prenatal development; thus, most infants are born with some immunity. However, this immunity is temporary, making immunizations essential within a few weeks. The American Academy of Pediatrics (1986) recommends the following schedule:

2 months	Diphtheria, pertussis, tetanus (DPT), and trivalent oral polio vaccine (TOPV)
4 months	DPT and TOPV
6 months	DPT and TOPV (In certain cases, this dose of TOPV may be optional)
15 months	Measles, mumps and rubella (MMR)
18 months	DPT and TOPV
24 months	HBPV (influenza)
4 to 6 years	DPT and TOPV
14 to 16 years	DT (Diphtheria and Tetanus)
Every 8 to 10 years	DT

Because of potentially serious complications resulting from common childhood infectious diseases, adults have a responsibility to protect children. Conscientiously following the immunization schedule recommended by the child's pediatrician assures the infant immunity to some of the most dangerous diseases. There are additional vaccines that can be administered for other diseases such as hepatitis. These additional immunizations are administered on an individual basis.

Sociocultural Influences in Development

There are cultural differences in physical development among children. Research comparing Ugandan children with European children indicated ethnic differences in these two groups. The Ugandan children tended to be well ahead of their European counterparts in motor skill development in the earliest years (Geber, 1958). Further, Geber's studies revealed that Ugandan infants support their heads as early as the first day after birth. At 4 months these babies are able to sit alone, at 8 months they may stand alone, and at 10 months they are able to walk. These differences become less dramatic as the children get older.

Social class differences in physical/motor development are more often associated with height, weight, and general health conditions. According to Ausubel and Sullivan (1970), there are no social class differences in the development of motor skills. There are, however, differences in growth rates. Perhaps the differences are related to differences in nutrition, health care, and growth supporting environments. Contemporary growth charts seem to support the observation that children today are taller and weigh more than their parents or grandparents did.

Dental Health

A child's first teeth begin to erupt between 5 and 9 months. The first teeth to erupt are usually the two lower middle incisors, followed in a few months by four upper middle incisors. By the end of the first year, most infants have these six teeth. The complete set of 20 teeth do not erupt until around $2\frac{1}{2}$ years of age.

Pain associated with the eruption of teeth varies from infant to infant. Some cry, are sleepy and fretful, seem to want to chew on anything, and drool considerably. Others do not appear to feel any pain or discomfort and suddenly smile a "toothed" smile to a surprised parent.

Care of teeth during the first year involves relieving the discomfort accompanying eruptions of new teeth and providing adequate diet of protein and minerals, particularly calcium and fluoride. Fluoride is frequently available in adequate amounts in community water supplies. Now is the time to begin a lifelong habit of limiting refined carbohydrates such as cookies, candies, soft drinks, and sweetened dry cereals. Also to be curtailed is the indiscriminate use of the baby bottle as a pacifier. "Nursing bottle" caries, or decay, occurs when sweetened water and juices are consumed from baby bottles taken to bed or provided to the infant as a "constant companion" (Nizel, 1977).

Infant Mortality

*Infant mortal-
ity—deaths during
the first year of life.*

Infant mortality rates (deaths during the first year of life) in the United States are alarmingly high for a modern industrialized and technologically advanced nation. In spite of great strides over the years in medical and child health protection, the 1985 infant mortality rate for all races in the United States was 10.6 per 1,000 live births, or 40,000 infant deaths a year. In the United States, an African-American infant is more than twice as likely to die during the first year as an Anglo infant (Children's Defense Fund, 1989b). The causes of neonatal and infant deaths among all races relate to poor prenatal and newborn care, low birth weight, congenital malformations and diseases, factors associated with fetal alcohol **syndrome**, chemical withdrawal syndrome, and sudden infant death syndrome (SIDS).

*Syndrome—a
group of combined
symptoms that
characterize a
physiological or
psychological dis-
order.*

Sudden infant death syndrome is the sudden and unexpected death of an apparently healthy infant during the first year. An estimated 12.6 percent of infant deaths are attributed to this mysterious syndrome (Colon & Colon, 1989). In the past, it was thought that infants who died in their cribs had smothered in their covers (thus the term "crib death"). However, since its identification as a "syndrome" in the 1960s, this perplexing phenomenon has commanded considerable research, and its actual cause or causes are still difficult to pinpoint.

In their vigorous, yet elusive search for causes over the past three decades, scientists have identified a number of factors associated with SIDS. While these factors are not in themselves causes, they assist researchers in identifying high-risk populations. The following factors have been associated with SIDS: prematurity, **apnea**, low birth weight, multiple births, cold weather, young mothers who have had poor prenatal care, low socioeconomic status, maternal history of smoking, anemia, or drug abuse (particularly methadone), and siblings with SIDS.

*Apnea—absence of
breathing for a
period of up to 20
seconds.*

A number of theories have attempted to explain the syndrome. Some have implicated heredity; others, upper respiratory viruses or bacterium such as botulism; still others have proposed **metabolic** disorders, allergies, hyper- and hypothermia, and central nervous system abnormalities. One popular explanation relates to the infant's cardiovascular system. Studies have found, in a number of cases, an abnormality in the way the brain regulates breathing and heart rate (Hunt and Brouillette, 1987). However, not all infants studied exhibited this abnormality, so this theory needs additional research. SIDS probably has multiple causes (Kelly & Shannon, 1982).

*Metabolic—per-
tains to the body's
complex chemical
conversion of food
into substances
and energy neces-
sary for mainte-
nance of life.*

Physicians today attempt to identify those infants who may be at risk. For some of these infants, monitoring their respiration and heart rate during sleep is recommended. Monitoring machines which can alert adults should apnea (suspended breathing) occur are available; however, these are quite expensive and complicated and may cause more anxiety than relief. There is no evidence to date that these machines help to prevent SIDS deaths (Hunt & Brouillette, 1987). Further, undue stress and worry surrounding an infant can interfere with positive and enjoyable parent-infant interactions.

Parents who have experienced this tragedy may benefit from support groups such as those sponsored by the National Foundation for Sudden Infant Death and the Guild for Infant Survival. They will need accurate information and supportive friends and professionals to help them cope effectively and avoid undue feelings of guilt, which often accompany such a loss.

Fortunately, most infants are born healthy and robust. Most illnesses during the first year are of short duration, lasting only a few days, but the importance of education, quality prenatal care, and medical supervision during the infant's earliest development is crucial.

Safety

Environments for infants must always be kept sanitary and safe. Awareness of the infant's growing mobility and inclination to put things in his mouth is a critical factor in providing a clean and safe environment. The infant's surroundings must be examined for potential dangers—objects on the floor that could scratch, cut, or go into the mouth; electrical outlets and wires that are pulled or mouthed; furnishings that topple easily; poisonous substances in easy reach; swimming pools and bathtubs of water; hot water faucets, unsanitary toilet bowls, etc.

By childproofing the environment, adults and infants alike can relax and enjoy themselves. As infants become more and more mobile, they can exercise growing movement abilities in surroundings free of impending dangers and constant adult restraints. Large motor and cognitive development is enhanced for infants who can move freely and safely in a protected but enriched and comfortable environment.

Infant safety must also be considered when riding in motor vehicles. Proper use of infant safety seats helps to prevent death and injury. Federal Motor Vehicle Safety Standard Act 213 mandates that passenger safety seats manufactured after January of 1981 must meet certain standards for design and use. However, this law did not forbid the sale of infant passenger seats manufactured before this date. Consequently, some unsafe infant passenger seats may still exist on the market or be loaned by a well-meaning friend or relative. Such equipment should not be used. Rather, adults must be certain that the infant passenger safety seat meets the federal standards. Proper use of the infant passenger seat is imperative if the safest child transportation is to be provided.

Neglect and Abuse

Neglect and abuse of young children are associated with failure to grow and develop adequately. It is reported that more than 1200 children died from abuse and neglect in the United States in 1986 (Children's Defense Fund, 1989a). Data from the National Center on Child Abuse and Neglect estimated that 2.3 million children and adolescents were abused, neglected, or both in 1987 (cited by Colon & Colon, 1989). Legally, abuse and neglect are defined as "the physical

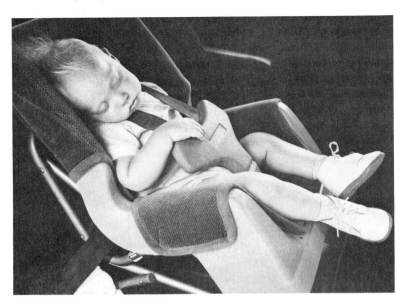

Proper use of approved infant safety seats helps to prevent death or serious injuries.

Failure to thrive—a condition in which apparently healthy infants fail to grow normally.

or mental injury, sexual abuse, negligent treatment, or maltreatment of a child under the age of eighteen by a person who is responsible for the child's welfare under circumstances which indicate that the child's health or welfare is harmed or threatened thereby" (Child Abuse Prevention and Treatment Act of 1975, 42 U.S. Code 5101).

Failure to thrive in infancy due to maternal deprivation or neglect has been documented. Studies have shown that children who are raised in impoverished and neglectful conditions during the first year of life show signs of severe developmental retardation (Province & Lipton, 1962). These infants exhibit delayed physical growth and skeletal development resulting in heights and weights far below that expected for their ages (Barbero & Shaheen, 1967). Neglected children are more susceptible to disease, have more gastrointestinal upsets, and are particularly emotionally vulnerable.

Neglect may take different forms, such as inadequate dietary practices, which impede growth, and failure to provide other necessities—clothing, shelter, supervision, and protection. Sometimes neglect includes denial of medical attention. Intellectual stimulation and emotional support may also be absent. Some infants are simply abandoned.

Abuse also takes many forms: physical, in which bodily injury is inflicted; psychological, in which a child is cursed, berated, ignored, or rejected; and sexual abuse, which ranges from exposure and fondling to incest and rape. The victims of sexual abuse are sometimes infants. Infants and children under 3 are particularly susceptible to child abuse (Mayhall & Norgard, 1983). Frustrations over infant crying, colic, diaper soiling, eating, sleeping, and other stresses related to early child development may provoke an abusive adult.

Role of the Early Childhood Professional

Facilitating Physical/Motor Development in Infants

1. Provide adequate food, clothing, shelter, and medical attention.
2. Provide safe and secure surroundings for a growing and curious infant.
3. Provide sensorimotor stimulation through enriching interactions, sensory-rich environments, and movement opportunities.
4. Provide an encouraging, supportive, and predictable atmosphere of love, acceptance, and satisfying human interactions.
5. Provide guidance that is positive and facilitative, helping the increasingly mobile infant to discover his capabilities in an atmosphere of both physical and psychological protection and safety.
6. Establish cooperative and supportive relationships with parents of infants.

Abuse and neglect are found in all socioeconomic levels, all ethnic groups, and all types of families—one-parent, two-parent, extended, large, and small. The incidence of abuse and neglect in families can be cyclical. Children who have been abused may become abusive adults (Gelles & Edfeldt, 1990), though intervention, which includes counseling and therapy, education, support groups for families, and subsequent positive life experiences, may break such a cycle. In some cases, children may need to be removed from neglective and/or abusive situations. All states today have child abuse reporting laws, under which suspected child abuse must be reported to appropriate authorities. The individual reporting suspected child abuse in good faith is provided confidentiality protections under these laws.

Key Terms

neonatal period
vernix caseosa
reflex
subcortical
cerebral cortex
survival reflexes
primitive reflexes
psychological state
temperament
perception
cephalocaudal
proximodistal
ossify
fontanelles

skeletal age
colostrum
clostridium botulinum
botulism
undernutrition
overnutrition
myelination
satiation
infant mortality
syndrome
apnea
metabolic
failure to thrive

Review Strategies/Activities

1. With the class, visit a neonatal intensive care unit of a children's hospital in your area or invite a neonatal care nurse to talk to the class. What types of developmental difficulties are demonstrated by the infants in this setting? How does the hospital staff relate to at-risk infants? What kinds of care is required for them? How does the medical team include the parents in the care and nurturing of their infant?

2. Compare infant formulas available at your local supermarket. What nutrients are listed on the individual labels? How do the formulas differ? How are they alike? What considerations are essential in the selection of a formula for individual infants?

3. Invite a Child Protective Services professional from your state or regional Human Resources Department to talk to the class about child abuse and neglect. What is the responsibility of the early childhood profession in dealing with abuse and neglect of young children?

4. Visit an infant care center or a family day home that cares primarily for infants. Make a list of health and safety precautions practiced by the child caregivers and staff in these settings.

5. Invite a pediatrician or a neonatologist to discuss health management and care of the newborn with the class.

Further Readings

Chase, R. A., & Rubin, R. R. (Eds.). (1979). *You and your baby: the first wondrous year.* New York: Collier Books. (Johnson & Johnson Child Development Publication).

This highly readable book is written primarily for parents. It provides thorough coverage of developmental milestones during the first year.

Dittmann, L. L. (1984). *The infants we care for* (rev. ed.). Washington, DC: National Association for the Education of Young Children.

This brief book addresses "outcome goals" for the first two years of life, with emphasis on healthy, supportive, and nurturing experiences for infants, regardless of type of care settings in which they are found.

Godwin, A., & Schrag, L. (1988). *Setting up for infants: Guidelines for centers and family day care homes.* Washington, DC: National Association for the Education of Young Children.

The growing need in our country for quality group care for infants and toddlers was the impetus for this timely and comprehensive guide. The book covers critical issues in child care including growth and development, health and safety, interactions between parents and caregivers, selection of caregivers, and considerations for both center and family day-care homes.

Harrison, H., & Kositsky, A. (1983). *The premature baby book.* New York: St. Martin's Press.

This book traces the development of the premature infant starting with the prenatal period. It covers such topics as medical complications and intensive care, assessment of development, parent-infant interactions, attachment, breast-feeding, and many others.

Krauss, M., & Castle, S. (1988). *Your newborn baby.* New York: Warner.

Based on guidelines set by the American Academy of Pediatrics, this is a particularly helpful book for new parents. It provides both medical and practical guidance and covers a wide range of topics typically of concern to new parents.

Mount Vernon Hospital Epidemiology Department. (1987). *A reference guide for the control and prevention of communicable disease in child care centers.*

Intended for professionals in child care settings, this reference includes critical information on protecting the health of children in group care and preventing the spread of disease among children and adults who work in these settings.

Pipes, P. L. (1989). *Nutrition in infancy and childhood* (4th ed.). St. Louis: Times Mirror/Mosby College Publishing.

This is a very comprehensive textbook on nutrition in infancy and childhood. While its coverage is often technical, it is quite readable and provides significant and up-to-date information about nutrition in earliest growth and development.

CHAPTER 6

*The first cry of a newborn baby in Chicago or Zamboango, in
Amsterdam or Rangoon, has the same pitch and key, each saying, I
am! I have come through! I belong! I am a member of the Family!*
Carl Sandburg

Psychosocial Development of the Infant

After reading and studying this chapter, you will demonstrate comprehension by:

- Describing the psychosocial development of the infant during the first year.
- Identifying major social and emotional milestones in infancy.
- Identifying factors that influence earliest psychosocial development.
- Describing the role of adults in healthy psychosocial development of the infant.

Listen to the musings of parents as they attempt to ascribe personality characteristics to their newborns:

"He has such a peaceful look on his face."

"She is really very squirmy."

"When he cries, he really wants to be heard!"

"She is such an easy baby."

"He is much more alert than his sister was."

What do such early observations foretell of infant personality, emotions, and possible social interactions? What are the influences of heredity and environment on psychosocial development? How do infants respond to their experiences and their interactions? In short, what do we know about psychosocial development during the first year of postnatal life?

Freud's Theory of Psychosexual Development

Recall that Freud (1933) was the first to propose a theory of personality based on underlying psychological structures and needs. His theory focused on psy-

chosexual development. In it, he proposed that there are inborn psychosexual instincts that change over the years from infancy to maturity. The focus of psychosexual energy relating to these instincts shifts from one part of the body to another as the individual matures. Development is characterized as a series of five stages revealing the shift in psychic energy (see Table 6.1).

Erikson's Theory of Psychosocial Development

The psychosexual stages of development suggested by Freud provide a backdrop for our understanding of Erik Erikson's theory of personality development. Erikson's psychosocial theory derives from, but enlarges upon, Freud's theory. Like Freud, Erikson explored crucial interactions between children and their caregivers and emphasized the importance of early experiences to later personality development. But Erikson was interested in the larger societal and cultural milieu in which psychosocial development occurs. By expanding on Freudian theory, Erikson identified eight stages of life, which amplify our understanding of the significant encounters between the children and their social world.

TABLE 6.1
Freud's psychosexual stages of development

Oral stage (1st year)	Primary focus of stimulation is the mouth and oral cavity and the primary source of gratification is eating, sucking, and biting. Mother (or primary caregiver) is the source of satisfaction of the basic needs of this period.
Anal stage (2nd to 4th year)	Elimination and retention of fecal material become the focus of the child's attentions and energies. The child must learn appropriate time and place for elimination. It is the time when the child first learns to conform to social expectations.
Phallic stage (4th to 6th year)	Psychic energy is focused on the genital organs and pleasure received through organ manipulation. The realization that one is biologically and psychologically separate from others occurs, and the resolution of conflicts relating to appropriate sex roles becomes an issue. Children are said to develop incestuous desires for the parent of the other sex.
Latency stage (middle childhood)	Energy formerly directed toward sexual concerns becomes channeled to other directions, mainly that of forming affectional and social relationships with parents and other children (usually same-sex friends).
Genital stage (adolescence)	Physical sexual changes and development become the center of attention. Sex-role identity becomes a serious issue.

Source: Freud (1933).

The eight stages of personality development proposed by Erikson are characterized by basic life conflicts to be resolved. These conflicts result from both biological maturation and societal expectations. Erikson suggests that there are critical periods, or developmental crises, associated with each stage of healthy personality development.

According to Erikson, the first year of life seems to be a critical period for the development of a sense of trust. The conflict for the infant involves striking a balance between trust and mistrust. This primary psychosocial task of infancy provides a developmental foundation from which later stages of personality development can emerge. It is represented in Figure 6.1 as the first step in an 8-step diagram of Erikson's theory.

Infants learn to trust when their caregiving is characterized by nurturance, warmth, and predictability. Needs for food, comfort, and satisfying interactions with others are dependent upon a responsive and protective environment. The infant's first experiences of being fed when hungry, held and stroked soothingly when fretful, dried when wet, and played with when bored establish the basis for a developing sense of trust. Infants must be able to depend upon their caregivers to come when beckoned; to interact with them in warm, supportive and affectionate ways; and to respond appropriately to their various physiological and psychological needs. When caregiving is responsive to infant cues,

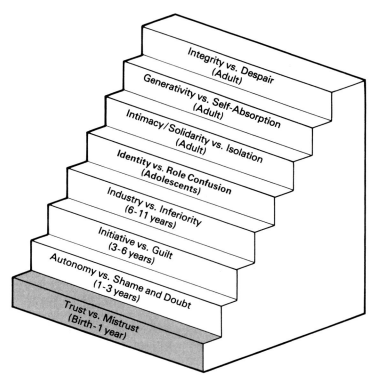

FIGURE 6.1
Erikson divided human development into psychosocial stages.

infants learn to trust their own ability to signal needs and to get a response from caregivers. This helps to establish not only a trust in others but a trust in oneself (Brazelton & Yogman, 1986).

Mistrust arises when the infant's caregivers do not adequately respond to cues of hunger, discomfort, boredom, and other needs, or do so in inconsistent and unpredictable ways. The infant subjected to neglect, rejection, or inappropriate expectations, or infants who are repeatedly left to "cry it out," learn that other people cannot be trusted. Equally detrimental is the failure to learn to trust oneself and to gain a sense of self from positive and responsive interactions with others caused by one's own efforts.

It is during this first year that the infant comes to realize that persons and objects exist even though they may not be present. Piaget (1952) considered this a major milestone in cognitive development, and termed it "object permanence." It is discussed in greater detail in Chapter 7 as it relates to cognitive development. The infant's appreciation of object permanence helps her to realize that parents or caregivers exist even when they cannot be seen and that they can be trusted to return.

Parents and adults who care for infants will want to help them develop a healthy ratio of trust to mistrust, with trust outweighing mistrust, which is the goal of this first stage of psychosocial development. The infant who has established a hearty sense of trust is better equipped for the next stage—developing a sense of autonomy, which emerges during the second and third years. This topic is covered in Chapter 9.

Attachment

Attachment—a strong emotional relationship between two persons, characterized by mutual affection and a desire to maintain proximity.

The subject of infant bonding and **attachment** has received considerable attention in both the professional and the popular press in recent years. Recall from Chapter 4 that bonding refers to the strong emotional tie from the mother or father (or caregiver) to the infant, usually thought to occur in the early days or weeks after delivery. Attachment, which emerges gradually during the first year and may be an outgrowth of the parent/infant bond, is a strong emotional relationship directed from the infant to the parent or some other significant person. It is based on the quality of the interactions between the child and the parent or caregiver.

During the 1950s and early 1960s John Bowlby, a psychiatrist and pioneer in the study of attachment, published a series of papers based on extensive research on mother-child attachments and separations. These papers, later enlarged and refined, were published in three volumes (Bowlby, 1969/1982, 1973, 1980) and have provided the impetus for much scholarly research and discussion.

Studying children who had been raised in institutions, Bowlby focused on their inability to form lasting relationships with others. Bowlby attributed this inability to the lack of opportunity to form an attachment to a mother or mother-figure during infancy. He also studied children who, after experiencing strong infant-mother attachments, were separated thereafter, for long periods of time. He observed that these children also developed resistance to close human ties. Bowlby was convinced that to understand these behaviors, one should examine infant-mother attachments.

In the institutions in which the subjects of Bowlby's studies lived, staff members tended adequately to custodial responsibilities of feeding, clothing, bathing, and overseeing their safety. They did not necessarily respond to the infants in affectionate and nurturing ways. Staff members did not respond to infants' cries or return their smiles, nor did they coo and babble with them or carry them about. In spite of the fact that their physical needs were being met, infants in these settings failed or were severely impaired in their ability to relate to caregivers. Studies of attachment highlight the critical need to form these attachments during the early months and years and suggest that failure to do so may have a life-long effect on healthy personality development. (Ainsworth, 1973; Bowlby, 1973; Bretherton & Walters, 1985).

Bowlby (1969/1982, pp. 265–330) proposed a sequence for the development of attachment between the infant and others. The sequence is divided into four phases: indiscriminate responsiveness to humans, focusing on familiar people, active proximity seeking, and partnership behavior.

Phase I (Birth to 8–12 weeks): Indiscriminate Responsiveness to Humans.   During this phase infants orient to persons in their environment, visually tracking them, grasping and reaching for them and smiling and babbling. The infant will often cease to cry upon seeing a face or hearing a voice. These behaviors sustain the attentions of others and thus their proximity to the infant, which is the infant's goal.

Phase II (3 to 6 months): Focusing on Familiar People.   The infant's behavior toward others remains virtually the same except that these behaviors are more marked in relation to the mother, or perhaps the father. Social responses begin to become more selective however, with the social smile reserved for familiar people. Strangers receive a long intent stare. Cooing, babbling, and gurgling occur with familiar people. A principal attachment figure begins to emerge, usually the mother.

Phase III (6 months to 3 years): Active Proximity Seeking.   Infants show greater discrimination in their interactions with people. They become deeply concerned for the attachment-figure's presence and cry when that person starts to leave. Infants will monitor the attachment-figure's movements, calling out to them or using whatever means of locomotion are available to maintain proximity to them. The attachment-figure serves as a base from which to explore and is to be followed when departing and greeted warmly upon return. Certain other people may become subsidiary attachment-figures; however, strangers are now treated with caution and will soon evoke alarm and withdrawal.

It is during Phase III that two rather disconcerting fears emerge. **Separation anxiety** occurs as the relationship between the infant and the attachment-figure becomes more intense and exclusive. The infant will cry, sometimes quite vo-

Separation anxiety—*fear of being separated from the attachment figure.*

ciferously, upon the departure of the attachment figure and exhibit intense joy upon their reunion. Figure 6.2 offers suggestions for adults during this difficult phase.

Stranger anxiety is another fear characteristic of Phase III. Occurring around 7 to 8 months, the infant's stranger anxiety is characterized by lengthy stares and subsequent crying at the sight of an unfamiliar person. Alarmed, the infant will cling tightly to the attachment-figure and resist letting go. Figure 6.3 includes suggestions for dealing with stranger anxiety.

Phase IV (3 years to the end of childhood): Partnership Behavior.   Prior to this phase, the child is unable to consider the attachment-figure's intentions. For instance, the suggestion that "I will be right back" is meaningless to the child who will insist on going along anyway. By age 3, the child has developed greater understanding of parental intent and plans and can envision the parent's behavior while separated. The child is now more willing and able to let go and can be more flexible.

Differences in attachment behaviors have been studied by Mary Ainsworth (1967; 1973; Ainsworth, Blehar, Waters, & Wall, 1978; Ainsworth & Wittig, 1969).

FIGURE 6.2
A sensitive response is most appropriate when dealing with separation anxiety.

- Recognize that new experiences present new challenges for the infant; some of these challenges can be quite unsettling, maybe even alarming.
- Provide predictable, unhurried schedules, particularly when introducing the infant to new experiences.
- Begin to accustom the infant to short separations at home by:
  - maintaining visual and auditory contact by leaving the infant's door open at nap and bedtimes;
  - maintaining voice contact across rooms, and when departing the room of a protesting infant, providing softly spoken verbal assurances.
- Ritualize bedtimes and naptimes; e.g., provide slower pace, softened volume on TV, bath and change of clothing, brush teeth, read a story, rock and sing, kiss good-night, and tuck in bed.
- Provide prior opportunities for the infant to become familiar with a new babysitter or child care arrangement.
- Select caregivers on the basis of their ability to respond to the unique rhythms and temperament of the infant.
- Familiarize the caregiver with the infant's routines and preferences.
- Have available for the infant any special blanket, stuffed toy or other object from which the infant gains comfort.
- Ritualize departure time: hug, kiss, spoken good-byes, wave, and so on. Never slip away when the child is not looking; rather, let confidence in the arrangement be felt by the infant.
- Anticipate the new experience with pleasure.
- Be dependable. First separations should be brief in duration, and reunions unwaveringly predictable.

FIGURE 6.3
Stranger anxiety is another normal part of development that calls for a sensitive response.

Learning to distinguish mother and father from others is an important task in infancy, and for many of today's infants, adapting to a nonparental caregiver may be an added task. The parent or caregiver must recognize that fears in the first year relate to new learnings and inadequate experiences.

- Discourage the unfamiliar person from attempting to hold the baby.
- Provide ample time for the infant to assess the stranger and sense your reaction to the stranger.
- When introducing the infant to a new caregiver, invite the new person to visit. Spend time together, allowing the infant time to accept this new person into her world.
- During this session, the mother or caregiver serves as the secure base from which the infant can venture forth to make friendly overtures with the new acquaintance.
- Allow the infant to "control" the encounter, deciding when to approach and when to retreat.
- Provide the infant familiar and comforting objects to hold.
- The confidence of older siblings, already familiar with this "stranger," may encourage the infant's comfort and acceptance.

Using her Strange Situation test, Ainsworth and her colleagues attempted to delineate individual differences in the quality of attachments that infants form. She devised a series of eight episodes (Table 6.2) designed to induce increasing anxiety in the infant. She recorded and analyzed exploratory behaviors, reaction to strangers, reaction to separation, and infant behaviors upon reuniting with mother after separation.

From her studies, Ainsworth identified three categories of attachment: (1) insecure attachment—anxious and avoidant; (2) secure attachment; and (3) insecure attachment—anxious and resistant. Securely attached infants were found to be visibly upset upon separation from the mother; greeted her heartily and sought close physical contact with her upon reunion. In her presence, these infants more willingly explored their environments; and in her presence, they were friendly with the stranger.

Insecurely attached, anxious/resistant infants, on the other hand, were less likely to explore when their mothers were present and were distressed when she departed. The reunion was strained as the infant maintained proximity but resisted the mother's efforts at physical contact, displaying apparent anger at her absence. These infants were quite wary of strangers, even with the mother present.

Insecurely attached, anxious/avoidant infants showed little distress when mother departed and no great joy upon her return, generally avoiding contact with her. With strangers, the behavior was similar, tending to avoid or ignore the stranger.

Differences in parenting behaviors which influence the development of attachment have also been cited (Ainsworth, Bell, & Stayton, 1974; Grossmann,

TABLE 6.2
Eight episodes that make up the strange-situations test

Episode Number	Persons Present	Duration	Brief Description of Action
1	Mother, baby, and observer	30 seconds	Observer introduces mother and baby to experimental room, then leaves. (Room contains many appealing toys scattered about.)
2	Mother and baby	3 minutes	Mother is nonparticipant while baby explores; if necessary, play is stimulated after 2 minutes.
3	Stranger, mother and baby	3 minutes	Stranger enters. First minute; stranger silent. Second minute; stranger converses with mother. Third minute; stranger approaches baby. After 3 minutes mother leaves unobtrusively.
4	Stranger and baby	3 minutes or less	First separation episode. Stranger's behavior is geared to that of baby.
5	Mother and baby	3 minutes or more	First reunion episode. Mother greets and/or comforts baby, then tries to settle him again in play. Mother then leaves saying "bye-bye."
6	Baby alone	3 minutes or less	Second separation episode.
7	Stranger and baby	3 minutes or less	Continuation of second separation. Stranger enters and gears her behavior to that of the baby.
8	Mother and baby	3 minutes	Second reunion episode. Mother enters, greets baby, then picks him up. Meanwhile stranger leaves unobtrusively.

Source: Ainsworth, M. D. S., Blehar, M. C., Waters, E., & Wall, S. (1978). *Patterns of attachment: a psychological study of the strange situation* (p. 413). Hillsdale, NJ: Lawrence Erlbaum Associates, Inc. Copyright 1978 by Lawrence Erlbaum Associates, Inc. Reprinted with permission.

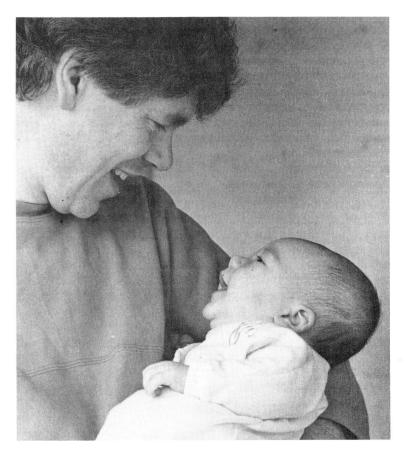

Social responses become more selective as infants get older.

Grossmann, Spangler, Suess, & Unzner, 1985). Mothers of securely attached infants were found to be sensitive to their infants' signals; they enjoyed close contact with their infants and were affectionate. These mothers were accessible and encouraged infant exploratory behaviors. In contrast, mothers of insecurely attached infants were insensitive, inconsistent, or ill-timed in their responses to infant cues; some were simply negligent. Overstimulating and intrusive caregiving has also been associated with avoidant type attachments (Isabella, Belsky, & von Eye, 1989).

Numerous studies over the past decade have explored topics relating to father attachments, effects of non-parental caregivers on parent attachments, relationships between attachment and later behavior problems, abuse and attachments, attachments and self-esteem and social competence, infant temperaments and attachment, and later adult behaviors of securely and insecurely attached infants (reviewed in Bretherton & Waters, 1985). Longitudinal studies have documented the long-term results of secure and insecure attachments. Many have found that personality development is either positively or negatively affected by these early secure or insecure attachments. This expanding area of research has been enormously helpful to the early childhood professional by:

- emphasizing the importance of the first year for the development of parent-child bonds;
- affirming the ameliorative potential for subsidiary attachment when other attachments are insecure;
- affirming the importance of the non-parental caregiver in complementing and supporting parent-child attachments; and
- supporting the need for professional intervention where parent-child relationships are dysfunctional.

Other Infant Emotions

In addition to attachment and the early fears of separation and strangers, other emotions of infancy are worth noting. The infant displays an array of emotions including affection, joy, surprise, anger, fear, disgust, interest, and even sadness (Campos, Barrett, Lamb, Goldsmith, & Stenberg, 1983). The newborn shows interest and surprise when something catches her attention (Field, 1982). The newborn smiles at a pleasing sound or when hunger has been satisfied. A sudden jolt or loud noise may evoke fear. The infant may show anger or even rage at being restrained or uncomfortable.

Earliest emotions are thought to be mostly reflexive, perhaps of a survival nature, assisting the infant in communicating needs and sustaining adult response. Later emotional responses are caused by external stimuli such as frustration with a toy or fear of an animal. Sequences for the emergence of discrete emotions have been suggested by a number of scholars (Greenspan & Greenspan, 1985; Izard & Buechler, 1986; Stroufe, 1979). For instance, it is believed that distress, disgust, and surprise are expressed by newborns, while anger and joy emerge during the first 4 months; fear and shyness emerge between 6 months and a year.

While most emotions seem to be present from birth (Campos, Barrett, Lamb, Goldsmith, & Stenberg, 1983), differences in infant emotional responses occur as the infant gets older. The most significant changes in emotional and social responses in infants occur during the period from 6 to 12 months, due primarily to the dramatic cognitive development taking place during that period. The ability to recall the past, to sense discrepancies, and to attend to facial expressions of emotion in caregivers contribute to these differences (Lamb, Morrison, & Malkin, 1987). It is during this period that both stranger and separation anxiety occur.

Crying

Infants communicate their needs through crying. At first the cries are reflex reactions to physiological needs for nourishment, warmth, movement, touch, or relief from other discomforts. The infant has no control over her crying and will not be able to stop crying until a need has been met, or the infant has become exhausted. As the infant gets older, the causes of crying change from internal to external stimuli and may be provoked by such things as loud noises, physical restraint, frustration with clothing or toys, and, as mentioned, fear of strangers and of separation.

Infant crying frequently has different tones, rhythms, and intensities. Parents soon learn the nature and the "message" of their infant's various cries and respond accordingly to various acoustical differences (Green, Jones, & Gustafson, 1987). Shaffer (1971) identified three distinct patterns of crying: the basic cry that is usually associated with hunger, an angry cry, and a pain cry.

Crying can be quite unsettling to parents and caregivers, particularly when they are unable to determine the infant's needs. Learning to respond appropriately to crying is one of the tasks of parenting and infant caregiving. Bell and Ainsworth (1972) found that infants whose parent responded promptly to their cries and other signals cried less often. When the infants did cry, it was of shorter duration. Further, infants who cried and fussed the most after 3 months of age were the ones whose parents did not respond readily to their cries. Another study found that infants who were held and carried about during the day cried less during the night (Hunziker & Barr, 1986).

Parents and caregivers who are cognizant of the infant's various means of communicating, such as whimpering, facial expressions, wiggling, and vocalizing are better able to respond before the infant begins to cry. Infants whose caregivers respond to these noncrying signals soon learn to communicate without crying, unless, of course, there is urgent pain, fear, frustration, or exhaustion. These infants will grow in the sense of trust in their caregivers and in themselves as communicators.

Caregivers must also recognize that infants, like anyone else, experience loneliness and a need for personal contact. Some crying may simply signal a need for companionship, for the sound of a familiar voice, and the sensation of a familiar touch or smell. Infants also experience boredom and may cry for a change of position or place, or for the nearness and interaction of others. Rocking the infant, holding the infant to one's shoulder to provide opportunities for visual scanning, talking in soft soothing tones, and gentle caresses are usually successful ways to calm the infant.

Crying has its positive developmental effects. Demos (1986) suggests that one of the developmental tasks of infancy is to learn to modulate emotions. Others suggest that caregivers need not feel that they must extinguish all crying. Snow (1989, p. 240) suggests that "crying is necessary for infant behavioral organization and normal physiological functioning." Persistent and unmodulated crying, however, calls for caregiver response.

■ Cheryl's mother, finding it difficult to work as a domestic and help care for her grandchild, Angela, while Cheryl goes to school, feels pressed to find other child care arrangements for her daughter's infant. The older siblings in the family have been called upon to help with babysitting, but that has not always worked out, because they forget or have other activities they want to pursue.

Securely attached infants more willingly explore their environments.

James has tried to be helpful but his visits to his infant daughter are becoming less and less frequent. His own need to work and his desire to stay in school devour his time and his energies. His feelings for both Cheryl and their baby are becoming ambivalent and confused, and sometimes he feels depressed. He isn't sure what his role should be.

Cheryl has experienced mixed feelings, as the realities and constancy of meeting an infant's needs become more apparent to her. She isn't sure of James anymore, and anticipates that they will probably be splitting up soon. She feels sad, though she does not blame him. She is tired most of the time, for she has returned to school and her lessons have become quite demanding. Sometimes she feels like a failure at school and at mothering, and her baby seems cranky much of the time.

Cheryl's mother shares her frustrations with a friend at her church. She frequently shares with her friend the trials and tribulations of making a living and raising a two-generation family. Her friend was aware that some high schools in the area provide on-site child care for teenage mothers. Through a number of inquiries, Cheryl's mother is able to identify one such high school. It isn't the high school in which Cheryl is currently enrolled, and will necessitate a family move if Cheryl is to take advantage of the child care program.

After several weeks of searching, Cheryl's family locates a small home within walking distance of the new high school. Cheryl doesn't want to leave, yet she feels she has no choice. She will miss James and her other friends. James offers to help—he will borrow his brother's pickup truck and will help them clean the new house. Cheryl is pleased at this show of caring and experiences some hope that her relationship with James will continue.

Angela, meanwhile, has experienced continual change in caregivers. Now 8 months old, her sleeping patterns are irregular and unpredictable. She is hungry at odd hours and is a finicky eater. She cries easily and often, seems to demand the company of others, and vigorously resists being put to bed. She can be quite playful and enjoys the attentions of her school-age aunts and uncles. She responds readily to Cheryl, but her relationship with her grandmother seems stronger and more comforting. She watches the comings and goings of all the family members and frets or cries when left in her playpen as others depart the room. ■

■ Jeremy's experiences have been quite different. His psychosocial world has included his mother; father; Phyllis, his nanny; an occasional visit from grandparents; and not-too-frequent visits to the church nursery. Except for occasional bouts with colic, Jeremy's routines of sleeping and eating are generally without incident. Bathing, dressing, playing, and interacting with Phyllis and his parents are, for the most part, relaxed, predictable, and enjoyable.

Ann, now back at work, is making every effort to maintain a sense of order in their lives, though meeting Jeremy's needs has, at times, become overwhelming to her. Ann and Bill talk frequently and frankly about the dramatic change in their lifestyle, their daily schedules, their social life, and certainly, their physical stamina.

Bill feels a need and desire to nurture Jeremy, and misses him when he is at work. Jeremy has become his "buddy," and Bill cherishes the smiles, the reaching toward Daddy's face when being held, and the pounding with uncoordinated hands at his legs to get attention or to be held. Dinner times are not always serene, nor is bedtime, yet Bill and Ann both seem to savor the changes they are observing in their growing baby. Indeed, Jeremy has a distinct personality. Does he take after Bill's side of the family or Ann's? They anticipate together Jeremy's changing looks, behaviors, and interactions with each of them.

Since Jeremy's routines have been, for the most part, predictable and pleasurable, with the adults in his world responding to his cues in caring and nurturing ways, his sense of trust is emerging and he has learned which cues result in which responses from others. At 8 months, however, he is beginning to fret upon separation from his parents, and sometimes from Phyllis. He is especially wary of strangers and seems to need more close physical contact than usual. He seems to cry more frequently than he used to and is especially difficult in the mornings when Ann and Bill are scurrying to dress and leave for work. ■

Interactions with Others

In the first few weeks of life, the infant's interaction patterns relate primarily to survival needs, signalling these needs to parents and caregivers through crying, squirming, and fretting. As the infant becomes more alert and begins to study the faces and responses of her parents and to discriminate mother and father from others, the infant's responsiveness increases. As experiences with others increase during the first year to include not only parents, but siblings, grandparents, nonparental caregivers, and in some cases other infants and young children, psychosocial development proceeds.

Infants' efforts to interact are characterized by gazing for some time at a face, reaching toward it, imitating facial expressions, and visually and auditorially tracking a person. Socially, the infant enjoys being gently tickled and jostled while cooing, gurgling, babbling, kicking, and wiggling. Such behaviors elicit playfulness, attention, and encouragement from others.

Around 5 months, interest in other children and siblings increases. The infant engages in prolonged onlooker behavior when placed in the same room with other children. This is considered by some to be an early stage of social/play development. Observing others is entertaining in and of itself, and infants derive considerable pleasure from simply being near the action.

Interest in siblings is particularly profound during the latter half of the first year. It is generally thought that playful and responsive siblings increase infant sociability; however, some scholars feel that the infant's sociability, itself, influences the amount of attention received from siblings (Lamb, 1978). At any rate, infants can be extremely interested in their siblings, following them around, imitating them, actively seeking their attentions, and exploring their toys and other belongings. Siblings can be taught to respond to the infant in gentle and playful ways. Around 6 to 8 months, the infant will participate in and enjoy games such as "peek-a-boo" and "pat-a-cake" and infant-initiated reciprocal activities, such as repeatedly dropping a toy to be retrieved, handed back to the infant, and dropped again.

How infants respond to other infants has been the focus of a number of studies (Adamson & Bakeman, 1985; Field, 1979; Fogel, 1979; Hay, Nash, & Petersen, 1983). Infants will react to the sound of another's cry and show an awareness of the presence of another infant. At 6 months of age, the infant will reach toward another infant, watch intently, and perhaps smile and make friendly sounds. At this age, infants have been shown to respond positively to one another in groups of two and to generally find other infants interesting. Infants, intrigued by another infant, may crawl into or fall on another in clumsy efforts to interact; yet, infant-infant interaction is seen to be positive, in spite of its awkwardness.

Social Smiling

While smiling is observed in the neonate, such smiles are thought to be triggered by internal stimuli associated with the immature central nervous system. There seems to be a developmental pattern for smiling (Campos & Stenberg, 1981; Emde & Harmon, 1972) that proceeds from internal to external elicitations.

At first, infants smile at faces regardless of facial expression. Then from 3 to 7 months, the infant begins to notice and respond to differences in facial expressions. In the latter part of the first year, the infant not only can discrim-

The frequency of smiling in infancy increases with age.

inate differences in facial expressions, but may respond to each in different emotional ways (Campos & Stenberg, 1981).

True social smiling is thought to occur at approximately 6 to 8 weeks. It is believed that when the infant can remember and recognize the face and perhaps the voice of her primary caregiver, smiling becomes more social (Wolff, 1963; Kagan, 1971). As infants get older, they become more discerning in their smiling behavior, choosing to smile at familiar faces over unfamiliar ones. Yet, the frequency of smiling increases with age. Cognition seems to play a major role in the emergence of smiling that is triggered by external stimuli.

Social Cognition

Social cognition is defined as the ability to understand the thoughts, intentions, and behaviors of oneself and others. As infants are developing a basic sense of trust when caregivers are nurturing and responsive, they learn to associate certain behaviors with certain responses from caregivers. This marks

Social cognition— the ability to understand the thoughts, intentions, and behaviors of oneself and of others.

the beginning of social cognition. Scholars believe that by the end of the first year, the infant's social understanding is fairly sophisticated (Lamb, 1981).

From experiences during the first year of life, infants become aware of the rhythms, sights, and sounds of the household; feel the warmth of a parent's arms around them; anticipate certain responses to their various cues; recognize the unique aromas of their mothers, fathers, and caregivers; and perhaps, sense the moods of these individuals by the manner in which they respond to them. The infants' responses to facial expressions indicate that they look to others, usually attachment-figures, for clues in understanding the sights and sounds around them (Tronick, Cohn, & Shea, 1986).

In adult-infant interactions, the adult typically imitates the infant's facial expressions and vocalizations. In turn, as the infant experiences these pleasant interactions, the imitation becomes reciprocal with the infant imitating the gestures, facial expressions, and vocalizations of the parent or caregiver.

Imitations, then, become a means of interpersonal communication. Imitations seen in games of "pat-a-cake," "peek-a-boo," and in learning to kiss or wave are behaviors indicative of emerging social cognition. As the infant experiences these social events and finds them pleasurable, the desire to repeat them emerges. These earliest interpersonal communications contribute to social cognition and have far-reaching implications for later language and cognitive development (Clyman, Emde, Kempe, & Harmon, 1986).

Factors Influencing Psychosocial Development

Many factors influence psychosocial development—the infant's personality, the quality and consistency of care, and the type of nonparental care the infant receives.

Infant Personality

Infants, themselves, influence the way others respond to them. Certain personality characteristics seem to affect the quality and the quantity of interactions with others. Some researchers believe that the primary caregiver's interactions with the infant and subsequent attachments result from infant behaviors (Stroufe, 1985). It seems that the child's own temperament and personality affect the development of attachment behaviors, how caregivers respond to her needs, and how the infant will later interact with others. This suggests an interactionist view of psychosocial development that holds that parent or caregiver and infant reciprocally affect the personalities of one another.

In studying individuality in children and identifying the components of temperament, Stella Chess and Alexander Thomas (1987) have illustrated the effects of certain temperaments of children on their responses to the demands of the environment and their interactions with others. These researchers found that components of temperament (including activity level, rhythmicity, approach and withdrawal behaviors, adaptability, sensory threshold, intensity of response, quality of mood, distractability, and persistence and attention span) tended to cluster around three categories of temperament. The three temperament types are:

1. The easy child is one who is usually easygoing, even-tempered, more tolerant of change, playful, responsive, and adaptable; eats and sleeps with some regularity; is easily comforted when upset; and generally displays a positive mood.
2. The difficult child is one who is slower to develop regular eating and sleeping routines; is more irritable; derives less pleasure from playtime activities; has difficulty adjusting to changes in routines; and tends to cry louder and longer than more soothable children.
3. The slow-to-warm-up child displays only mild positive or negative reactions; resists new situations and people; and is moody and slower to adapt. Interactions such as cuddling may be resisted.

The easy child's behaviors provide positive feedback and reinforcement to caregivers and, in so doing, influence the kinds and amounts of attentions that she will receive throughout early development. These children, more often than not, experience what Chess and Thomas (1987) have called a "goodness of fit" between themselves and the personalities and expectations of their caregivers. Goodness of fit is defined as a principle of interaction in which

> the organism's capacities, motivations and styles of behaving and the demands and expectations of the environment are in accord. Such consonance between organism and environment potentiates optimal positive development. Should there be dissonance between the capacities and characteristics of the organism on the one hand and the environment opportunities and demands on the other hand, there is poorness of fit, which leads to maladaptive functioning and distorted development. (Chess & Thomas, 1987, pp. 20–21)

Infants described as temperamentally difficult may fail to elicit nurturing and support from their caregivers. Adults who find this temperament hard to respond to may become overly demanding or, conversely, appeasing in their interactions. They may feel helpless and confused, be inconsistent in their responses and expectations, or engage in power struggles for control. One can readily see the "poorness of fit" in this situation and its potential for ineffective and negative adult-child relationships and childhood behavior disorders that may persist into adulthood.

The slow-to-warm-up child generally does not present substantial difficulties in the adult-child relationship. However, this child, slower to adapt and reticent with new acquaintances and situations, may not receive persistent effort on the part of caregivers to maintain positive interactions.

While not all children fall neatly into these categories, easy children are not always easy, difficult children are not always difficult, and slow-to-warm-up children are not always reticent. These descriptions help us to appreciate wide variations in infant and child behaviors. Recognizing and appreciating individual differences help adults respond appropriately to these behaviors. Adults must

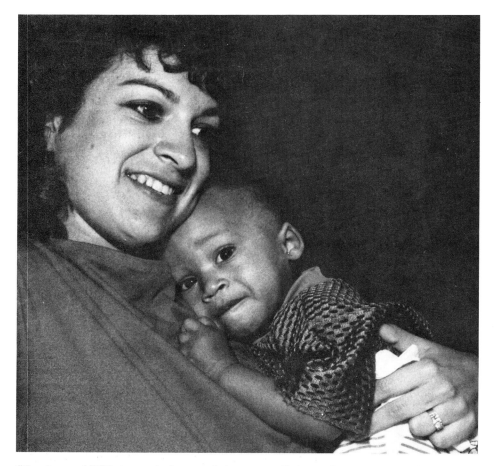

"Goodness of fit" between infants and the personalities and expectations of their care-givers promotes optimum psychosocial development.

be cautious in the use of these categories, however. Self-fulfilling prophesies may occur, in which the child behaves according to adult expectations. If adults ascribe labels and misunderstand the cues of infants, they may fail to support the infant's needs for positive and nurturing interactions, regardless of temperament or personality type.

Quality and Consistency of Care

Whether an infant is cared for by a parent at home or by other arrangements, among the most important qualities of infant care in terms of healthy psychosocial development are consistency, predictability, and continuity of care. Though personalities and adult responses to infants vary greatly, infants need their different caregivers (mother, father, siblings, nonparent caregivers) to respond to their cues in relatively similar and nurturing ways. As well, the infant needs to trust that certain events will occur in reasonable order and with some predictability. The more predictable the infant's routines and caregiver behaviors can be, the greater the likelihood of developing a healthy sense of trust in one's world and in one's self.

Continuity of care refers to caregivers' developmental expectations of the infant, knowledge and acceptance of the infant's individual temperament, rhythms, interaction patterns, and all those characteristics that make the infant unique. Continuity is maintained when the infant experiences a minimum number of caregivers during the course of a day or a week. Many child care centers today provide a "primary caregiver" to infants in an effort to reduce the number of adults to whom the infant must adapt. This practice enhances the infant's sense of order and facilitates opportunities to form positive relationships and, perhaps, healthy attachments between infant and nonparental caregivers. Infants need continuity in their daily interactions.

The vignettes on Angela and Jeremy earlier in this chapter reveal two very different situations in the quality and consistency of care each infant is receiving. Angela's routines are less predictable, as are her caregivers, as they change from moment to moment and from day to day. The quality of care that she is receiving is not optimal, nor is the opportunity for her to develop stable, trusting relationships.

On the other hand, Jeremy is being provided daily schedules and routines which, while not rigid or inflexible, are nevertheless predictable to him. His caregivers are limited in number, and each responds effectively to his cues for attention and other needs. In both cases, the infants are being provided nonparental care while their parents are away at school or work. What is the relationship of **nonparental care** to optimal psychosocial development in infants?

Nonparental care—child care provided by someone other than the child's parent.

Nonparental Child Care

Research on nonparental infant care prior to the 1980s examined issues such as the long-term effects of **nonmaternal** infant care; forms or types of available infant care; what happens to the infant in various infant care situations; and if nonmaternal infant care can provide effective short-term or long-term intervention functions. Today, researchers are concerned with issues relating to distinguishing between low- and high-quality child care programs and the effects of length of day, amount of time in child care, and age at entry. As well, researchers are interested in the relationship between families, family needs, and various child care arrangements.

Nonmaternal care—child care provided by someone other than the child's mother.

In a scholarly and comprehensive summary of research, the Volume 3, Numbers 3 and 4 (1988) issues of *Early Childhood Research Quarterly* are devoted entirely to the topic of Infant Day Care. In this work Belsky (1988) extensively reviewed the literature relating to the impact of early nonmaternal care on infant socioemotional development. While not all of the authors agree with Belsky, he states the following conclusion:

> There are too many findings linking more than 20 hours per week of nonmaternal care experience in the first year with increased avoidance of mother following separation, heightened insecurity, and subsequent aggression and noncompliance not to draw attention to the findings and raise concerns about their meaning. These developmental correlates, it must be acknowledged, are seen almost exclusively among children with extensive nonmaternal care experience, appear more probable in the case of boys and ... may have as much to do with the child's experiences at home as with any in the child care setting itself. (Belsky, 1988, p. 265)

Belsky's words give us pause when we consider the number of infants who are in need of day care, and whose families are seeking nonparental care in greater and greater numbers, and for younger and younger infants. So what about parents who must seek nonparental child care arrangements for their infants?

In terms of psychosocial development, Stroufe (1988) suggests that infant day care need not inevitably have negative consequences if:

Working model—
mental construct or
image of an event
or set of circum-
stances.

- the infant can develop a **working model** of basic expectations concerning the availability of others;
- the infant can develop a "working model" of herself as capable of impacting on the environment;
- the infant has repeated experiences with predictably terminated separations;
- the infant's caregivers are emotionally available;
- the infant's caregivers remain emotionally close and accepting despite efforts on the part of the infant at distancing (Stroufe, 1988, p. 288)

Stroufe further emphasizes the need for parents and caregivers to be aware of earliest development and how one phase of development builds upon another; how infant-caregiver relationships evolve; and the link between extensive nonparental child care and anxious attachment. The need for wise selection of child care arrangements with emphasis on stability and emotional closeness to the infant during periods of difficulty is also stressed. Stroufe suggests that until we know more about the long-term developmental effects of infant day care, it should be delayed until the child's second year (Stroufe, 1988, p. 190).

The fact still remains that many families are in need of nonparental infant care. Research on age at child care entry may be helpful, particularly for parents who can project their expected infant care needs and plan ahead for them. Parental leaves of absence from the workplace can be considered in tandem with the infant's developmental needs. Recent studies of the age during which parental attachments are forming suggest that nonmaternal care begin either before the age of 6 months or after the age of 12 months (Benn, 1985; Braun, 1985; Farber & Egeland, 1982).

For parents who work outside the home or who for other reasons require supplemental care for their infants and children, professional debate over the appropriateness of such care could cause considerable anxiety and guilt. It seems, then, that professionals should assist parents in seeking the type of care that best suits their individual infant's and current family needs. Parents should become informed about child care options available in their communities. They should visit, ask questions, and pursue only those persons or programs that meet quality standards (see Chapter I on NAEYC Accreditation Standards) or whose references are well known and reliable.

In addition, parents have a responsibility to assess their infant's responses on an ongoing basis. Are positive and nurturing relationships developing among all who share in the care and nurturing of the infant? Does the infant need the routine at home to be more like that of the infant care program, or vice versa? Is the infant over-tired or over-stimulated from the day's experiences? What is the parent doing to ensure consistency, predictability, and continuity in the infant's life at home? Is the infant's health and safety paramount to all caregivers? Is the infant developing basic trust, secure attachments, healthy emotional tone, and enjoyment in parents and other caregivers?

Employers are beginning to recognize the increased productivity and longevity of employees who feel comfortable about their child care arrangements and who are supported in their efforts to provide sound parenting. Some employers provide parental leave opportunities for both mothers and fathers during the earliest weeks and months of their infant's development. Some provide leave opportunities without penalty for parents whose infants or children are ill. Employers of the future may well find other ways to encourage and support effective child-rearing practices. Employer policies that support child and family development go a long way in facilitating healthy psychosocial development in children, and should be encouraged for the long-term impact such healthy personality beginnings may have on society in general.

Qualities to assess in seeking appropriate infant care are listed in Figure 6.4. Parents will want to make studied and wise choices for themselves and their infants, choosing according to the infant's unique developmental needs and the caregiver's ability to adequately and appropriately meet those needs.

FIGURE 6.4
Looking for these characteristics will help a parent select quality child care.

1. Trained, knowledgeable, and nurturing caregivers.
2. Safe, sanitary, healthy environment for infants and children.
3. Low adult-child ratios, with emphasis on providing primary caregivers to individual infants.
4. Cognitively and linguistically enriching, socially stimulating, emotionally supportive environment and caregivers.
5. Sensitivity to parental needs, goals, and concerns.
6. Exceeds local and/or state licensing standards.
7. Accredited through the National Association for the Education of Young Children.

Sociocultural Factors Influencing
Psychosocial Development

Parents who have knowledge of child growth and development tend to relate to their children with a greater sense of confidence, are more positive and nurturing, and exhibit more developmentally appropriate expectations. In doing so, they facilitate the healthy psychosocial development of their children. This is particularly critical during infancy, as the antecedents of healthy personality development are occurring.

However, in some families of low socioeconomic status (SES), survival needs supersede social and emotional needs of children and often the physiological needs for food and medication. In such situations, opportunities to learn about children and child development are limited, or not realized. Surviving may be so overwhelming that it interferes with healthy parent-child interactions. Children in such families may be hungry, cold, suffer more illnesses, and may even be neglected or abused. Parental efforts to provide food, clothing, shelter, and transportation for the family may be extremely difficult, or thwarted. Providing psychosocial nurturance to the children is superseded by fatigue, frustration, anxiety, and sometimes resentment or a sense of futility. Infants in these situations, then, can be at risk for development of healthy personalities.

For such families, high-quality child care is imperative. The professionals involved may provide access to needed social and health-care services, job counseling, and parenting education. Along with a full day of quality nurturing and psychosocially sound interactions, the infant is given a better chance at healthy development. The relief from the stress associated with child-rearing and the assurance that the infant is well cared for during a number of hours of the day (or night) should provide some relief for the parents in this potentially unhealthy situation.

Cultural differences among families also influence psychosocial development. Expressions of emotions, expectations and encouragement of infant responses, tolerance for infant behaviors, and perceived parental roles vary among families and among cultures. Attitudes toward feeding, crying, holding, and clothing may vary. Families differ in the nature and amount of language to which the infant is exposed. Each of these factors within the family influences the psychosocial development of the infant. Yet, in spite of the infinite ways in which parents pursue their roles, most infants thrive and become competent and happy toddlers.

Health of Infant as an Influence
on Psychosocial Development

Certainly, the assumption can be made that healthy, hearty infants are better equipped to deal emotionally and socially with their environments. Obstetric and pediatric supervision during prenatal development and infancy provides preventive and corrective measures to facilitate healthy, hearty development.

Role of the Early Childhood Professional

Promoting Psychosocial Development in Infants

1. Provide predictable, consistent, and continuous care.
2. Respond readily to the infant's cues for food, comfort, rest, exercise, and social interaction.
3. Recognize that crying is the infant's way of communicating her needs.
4. Be aware of sensitive periods relating to attachment behaviors, separation and stranger anxiety, and respond in supportive and empathic ways.
5. Provide stimulating and satisfying social and emotional interactions.
6. Recognize and accept the infant's unique ways of interacting with others.
7. Recognize and accept the infant's various emotional responses as another way in which she communicates.

Proper amounts of rest, nutrition, exercise, and socially and emotionally satisfying interactions are essential to this health.

Infants who suffer chronic illnesses, birth defects, injury, violence, emotionally unstable caregivers, or inconsistent or contradictory child-rearing practices are most likely to develop psychosocial problems. As we have seen throughout this chapter, manifestation of these problems in infants depends upon factors such as age, temperament, past experiences, and bonding and attachment success. Factors relating to the intensity and the duration of the problems the infant is encountering, including the temperament and coping abilities of various family members, and the willingness and/or ability of the family to seek and benefit from professional help, also influence the infant's response.

Infants tend to exhibit signs of stress through physiological functions, such as changes in sleeping and waking patterns, feeding disturbances, heightened emotionality, frantic crying, depressive behaviors, withdrawing, and avoidant behaviors. When these behaviors are evident, parents and professionals might examine the family or child caregiving situation to determine causes and look for solutions. Again, professional counseling may be needed to help the family respond appropriately to their troubles and to the infant.

Key Terms

attachment
separation anxiety
stranger anxiety
social cognition

nonparental care
nonmaternal care
working model

Review Strategies/Activities

1. Discuss in class the differences in the early lives of Angela and Jeremy. In terms of psychosocial development, what kinds of experiences are these infants having? What environmental influences on optimal psychosocial development are evident? What suggestions can you make to enhance the psychosocial development of each child?
2. Review the qualities of a good infant care center. Visit an NAEYC accredited child care center in which infants are enrolled.
   a. What were the outstanding qualities of this center?
   b. Would you feel comfortable obtaining the professional services of this center?
   c. Observe the interactions between adults and infants, and between infants and other infants.
   d. How did the infants respond to you as a stranger? What was the response? How old were the infants whose responses you observed?
3. Interview a working parent. Ascertain how they juggle work and parenting. Do they feel generally positive about their lifestyles? What have they found to be most frustrating and most rewarding?
4. List some ways siblings might support and enhance an infant's psychosocial development.
5. How might parents and/or primary caregivers assure that the infants develop a healthy sense of basic trust? Develop a list of "dos and don'ts."

Further Readings

Brazelton, T. B. (1984). *To listen to a child*. Menlo Park, CA: Addison-Wesley.
   Dr. Brazelton, a well-known pediatrician, discusses a number of common early childhood problems that often result in parental concerns or anxieties. Problems such as fears, feeding, sleep-related issues, and thumbsucking are placed into a developmental perspective. This book provides a resource for parents and should increase their sense of self-confidence in responding to their very young children.

Brazelton, T. B. (1987). *Working and caring*. Menlo Park, CA: Addison-Wesley.
   This book is most helpful to working parents who seek guidance in healthy, wholesome parenting.

Greenspan, S., & Greenspan, N. T. (1985). *First feelings*. New York: Penguin Books.
   This small, concise book charts the emotional development of children from infancy to age 4.

Phillips, D. (Ed.). (1987). *Quality in child care: what does research tell us?* Washington, DC: National Association for the Education of Young Children.
   This small volume takes discussion of child care beyond the "whether" debates and into a thorough exploration of how to make child care better. The researchers each have attempted to identify key ingredients of quality child care.

CHAPTER 7

The goal of infant and early education should not be to increase the quantity of knowledge, but to help the child—through guiding her experience and creating possibilities—to construct, invent, and discover.

Judith S. Musick and Joanne Householder

Cognitive/Language/Literacy Development of the Infant

After reading and studying this chapter, you will demonstrate comprehension by:

- Describing cognitive development during the infant's first year.
- Outlining language development during the infant's first year.
- Relating cognitive, language, and literacy development to other developmental areas.
- Identifying major factors influencing cognitive, language, and literacy development during the infant's first year.
- Suggesting strategies for promoting and enhancing cognitive, language, and literacy development in infancy.

Cognitive Development

Studies in recent years have heightened our awareness of the tremendous potential for learning that exists from the moment of birth. In an effort to understand **cognitive development,** researchers are studying how and what newborns sense and to which stimuli they respond. Research areas include reflexive activities as indicators of sound neurological development; motor behaviors as indicators of maturing cognitive development; imitative behaviors; potential for memory; the social/emotional context in which learning occurs; emerging language; and the genesis of literacy.

Cognitive development—the aspect of development that deals with thinking, problem-solving, intelligence, and language.

Cognitive development is an ever-changing process that proceeds from infancy throughout life. It is that area of development in which the child acquires information, expands and modifies it, stores, retrieves, and uses it. Such mental activities may be evident to observers through the nonverbal or verbal, social, emotional, and physical/motor behaviors and activities of the infant.

Piaget's Theory of Cognitive Development

The most familiar theory of cognitive development is that of Jean Piaget (1952). Piaget's studies of cognitive development have dominated the fields of child study, psychology, philosophy, pediatrics, and education since the 1920s. He is perhaps the best-known and most widely quoted of contemporary learning theorists. While, as we will see later in the chapter, other theorists may differ with or modify Piaget's theory, he nevertheless has made an astounding impact upon knowledge and practice in early childhood education.

Foremost among Piaget's contributions to early childhood education is the recognition that the thinking processes and problem-solving abilities of infants and young children are quite different from those of older children and adults. As you read through the stages that follow, think about the implications of these differences for caregiving and teaching or learning experiences during the infant's first year.

Four Stages of Cognitive Development.

In Piaget's theory, four major stages of cognitive development are proposed—the sensorimotor period (birth to age 2), the preoperational period (age 2 to 7), the concrete operations period (age 7 to 11), and the period of formal operations (age 11 and beyond).

According to Piaget, all children proceed through these stages, with each stage benefiting from the accomplishments of the previous stage. Piaget viewed these stages as invariant, that is, one stage always follows the other in a predictable sequence. All individuals proceed through the invariant sequence, but they do so at their own rates of development. These differences in rates of entering and exiting the stages are attributed to differences in individual genetic timetables and differences in cultural and environmental influences.

Sensorimotor—learning that occurs through the senses and motor activities.

The **sensorimotor** period extends from birth to the onset of gestures and language at around age 2. During this period the infant's cognitive development depends upon direct sensory experiences and motor actions, hence the term sensorimotor. Recall the reflex activities of the newborn as described in Chapter 5. These genetically programmed reflexes provide a basis for later cognitive development. Piaget believed that all mental processes are rooted in and are a continuation of earliest reflex and motor activities. As the infant gains control over his reflexes, movement (motor) behaviors become more purposeful. Purposeful motor activities facilitate the infant's explorations and, hence, the infant's awareness of and interactions with people and objects in the environment.

From birth on, through interactions with the environment the infant begins to form mental structures, which Piaget termed *schemata*. These schemata help the infant organize and interpret his experiences. Each additional experience brings new schemata, or perhaps a modification of old schemata. The infant grows in knowledge of the environment through direct actions on objects and experiences with others. Piaget describes the infant at this stage as egocentric, or able only to perceive from his own perspective, not from that of others.

Adaptation—the process by which one adjusts to changes in the environment.

Assimilation/Accommodation/Equilibration.

According to Piaget, **adaptation** to environmental demands involves two complementary processes, assimilation and accommodation. As infants attempt to fit new ideas and concepts into existing ones, they are assimilating additional schemata. At first, the infant visually gazes and tracks, and the infant's hands and arms respond to environmental stimuli by reflex. Later these activities become integrated into "whole" activities of looking and grasping simultaneously, or coordinated eye-hand movements. This higher order of functioning increases the infant's interaction with the world, which in turn increases his schemata, building new learning upon previous actions, events, or experiences.

Accommodation is a process by which a previous schema (or experience) is modified in order to include or adapt to a new experience. The breastfed infant who is changed from breast-feeding (existing schema) to bottle-feeding (new experience) must alter sucking behaviors in order to "succeed" with the bottle. This alteration of sucking behavior is accommodation to a new environmental demand. Each assimilation of an experience is complemented by accommodation to that experience, and this leads to adaptation. Adaptation to an event or experience brings about equilibrium between the individual and his environment.

Equilibrium is said to occur when assimilation and accommodation are in balance with one another, that is, the infant has adapted to the demands of the environment. However, this state is usually a short-lived one, as the infant is constantly acquiring and incorporating new information that requires additional assimilations and additional accommodations.

Development During the Sensorimotor Stage.

The sensorimotor period of cognitive development is divided into six substages. Development through these substages is both rapid and dramatic. During the first year, the infant will proceed through the first four of these substages:

1. ***Reflexive stage*** *(birth to 1 month).* During this period, **reflexes** dominant since birth modify over time as the infant experiences various sensory stimuli and interacts with the environment. Piaget believed that the infant constructs schemata from the numerous sensory and reflexive experiences of these first weeks. The human face or voice, the positioning in mother's arms prior to breastfeeding, or the sounds and rhythms of the household are examples of possible early schemata.

    Reflexes—unlearned, involuntary responses to stimuli.

2. ***Primary circular reactions*** *(1 to 4 months).* At this time, infant reactions center upon bodily responses. For example, the infant can now purposefully bring the thumb to the mouth to suck. Previous thumb-sucking occurred as a result of accidental and uncoordinated reflex activity. During this stage, the infant will engage in other purposeful motoric activity. This period is called primary because of its focus on bodily responses; it is called circular because the infant repeats the activities over and over again. This repetition may be the first indication of infant memory.

    Primary circular reactions—simple, pleasurable, repetitive acts that are centered on the infant's body.

3. ***Secondary circular reactions*** *(4 to 8 months).* This period is characterized by the infant's enlarging focus on objects and events in the environment. It is called secondary circular because it involves that infant's growing awareness of objects and events outside his own body. Through chance events,

    Secondary circular reactions—simple, pleasurable, repetitive acts centered on external objects.

Emerging coordination of motor skills facilitates exploring and discovery.

the infant learns that he can make things happen to external objects. For example, the infant hits his bath water and a big splash occurs. This novel experience generates a desire to repeat it; and repeat it the infant does, presumably just for the pleasure such activity evokes. These behaviors represent early experimentation and may become means/ends behaviors. During this substage, the infant imitates sounds and actions that he has previously produced and currently holds in his own repertoire. The infant will now search for a hidden object, which in previous stages was not pursued if not within the infant's visual field. Piaget believed that, for the infant, an object not seen did not exist.

4. ***Coordination of secondary schemata*** *(8 to 12 months).* This is the period in which the infant's behaviors are clearly evident. Imitative behaviors are emerging, signaling the infant's growing ability to learn from observing the behavior of others. Play becomes more clearly differentiated from other means/end activities, and is enjoyed for its own sake. **Object permanence,** the realization that an object may exist even though it cannot be touched or seen, is beginning. As is illustrated in Table 7.1, object permanence is not fully achieved until substage VI.

Object perma-nence—the realiza-tion that objects and people con-tinue to exist even though they may not be visible or de-tected through other senses.

TABLE 7.1
Bower's stages of development of object permanence

Stage	Age (Months)*	Success	Fail
I	0–2	No particular behavior shown in response to hiding event.	
II	2–4	Infant will track a moving object that goes behind a screen. Infant can learn to track an object from place to place.	Infant continues to track a moving object after it has stopped. Infant will look for an object in its familiar place even when the infant sees the object moving to new place.
III	4–6	Infant no longer makes tracking errors of Stage II. Infant recovers an object that has been partially covered by a cloth.	Infant cannot recover an object that has been fully covered by a cloth.
IV	6–12	Infant can now recover an object that has been completely hidden under a cloth.	Infant searches for an object in the place where it was previously found, ignoring the place where it was seen to be hidden.
V	12–15	Infant no longer makes place error of Stage IV.	Infant cannot cope with invisible displacements of an object.
VI	15–18	Complete success—infant can find object no matter where or how hidden.	

Note: *These ages are approximate; there may be considerable individual differences.

From *Development in Infancy 2/e.* By T. G. R. Bower. Copyright © 1974, 1982 by W. H. Freeman and Company. Reprinted with permission.

Views That Differ from Piaget's

Some researchers have challenged Piaget's assumptions regarding cognitive development. Object permanence, for example, has been called into question by contemporary scholars using more sophisticated research strategies than those used by Piaget (Bower, 1982; Wishart & Bower, 1985). Recall that Piaget relied primarily upon naturalistic observations of infant behaviors (often his own children) for the collection of his data. Today, through the use of such research tools as videotape analysis and heart-rate monitoring, scientists have been able to subject Piaget's theories to further analysis.

Through such experimentation, Bower has taken a further look at object permanence in the infant at 6 to 8 months. Whereas Piaget proposed that an object hidden behind a screen is not searched for because the infant believes that the object no longer exists, Bower believes that immature space perception may explain the infant's failure to search. He suggests that, for the infant, the screen has replaced the hidden object—two objects, therefore, cannot occupy the same space. It is suggested that Piaget underestimated what infants come to know about objects, and that their failure to search for or locate a hidden object may represent lack of spatial knowledge rather than lack of knowledge of object permanence.

Bower proposed that if, as Piaget suggested, an object no longer exists if it is out of sight, then the infant should not be surprised if it does not reappear when the screen is removed. On the other hand, if the infant exhibits surprise when it does not reappear when the screen is removed, this quite likely implies that the infant had maintained a consistent mental image of the object. Bower suggests that infants as young as 5 months old will not only anticipate the reappearance of an object that has been moved to a position behind the screen, but will attempt to look for it when a different object or no object appears.

Other theories of cognitive development differ somewhat from the constructivist/developmentalist approach of Piaget. Behaviorists (Bijou & Baer, 1961; Skinner, 1938) place little emphasis on developmental stages, emphasizing instead that cognition is shaped primarily by the individual's experiences. Greater importance is given to external factors such as reward and punishment in influencing learning than to innate abilities or biological processes. Since behavior is thought to be a result of its consequences, the consequences of trial and error behaviors are considered critical to thinking and learning.

Social learning theory (Bandura, 1977), a relative of behaviorist philosophy, emphasizes the role of imitation in cognitive development. Many behaviors are learned simply by watching others, and much learning occurs in social situations. It is believed that very young infants can imitate the facial expressions of others (Meltzoff & Moore, 1983) and that infants may have an innate ability to compare information received through two different modalities—vision and their own body movements. This information is then used to coordinate imitative behaviors based on actions observed in others. This behavior is evident when a model remains in the infant's visual field; however, true imitation of remembered events does not usually occur until the end of the first year (Kaye & Marcus, 1981).

The information processing theory of cognitive development (Rebok, 1987) likens it to the modern-day computer's "inputs," "throughputs," and "outputs." Input refers to the individual's gathering of information from sensory stimuli: vision, hearing, tasting, smelling, and tactile sensations. Input information is then acknowledged, compared to other "data" already stored in memory, categorized, and stored for future use. This process represents "throughput." Subsequent verbal and/or nonverbal responses represent "output." Studies of information processing with older children will be described in Chapters 10, 13, and 16.

Contextualistic theories (Bronfenbrenner, 1977, 1986), are among the most contemporary. They describe cognitive development as an integral part of the social and cultural context in which an individual grows and develops. Cognitive development is viewed as an interactive process between the individual and a variety of social and cultural contexts. Cognition continually changes, as does the context in which it occurs. It is determined by many factors, including direct instruction, exploration, discovery, observation, and imitation. From this perspective, cognition is also viewed as developing in many and varied directions simultaneously; for instance, motor, language, and social learning may all be proceeding at the same time. As you will see in the vignettes below, the child both influences and is influenced by the context in which he exists. Thus the context and the infant each play a role in shaping cognitive development.

■ Jeremy, in his crib, is intently watching a yellow soft-sculpture airplane dangle from the mobile above him. He kicks and squeals with glee, then stops and stares at the object bouncing above his crib. Lying still, he seems to notice that the object stopped swinging; kicking some more, the object begins to swing again. The entertainment is quite exhilarating, and is repeated several times.

Phyllis, Jeremy's nanny, noticing his playfulness and his interest in the mobile, recognizes as well that Jeremy has discovered the joy of his own bodily movements and the subsequent jiggling of the colorful airplane. She approaches, detaches the soft-sculpture airplane from the mobile, holds it within Jeremy's reach while saying to him, "Do you want to hold the airplane? "I think you like this bright toy, Jeremy."

Jeremy's kicking subsides when he is distracted from his previous activity. He stares at the soft toy, looks at Phyllis (a bit puzzled), then back again at the soft toy. His eyes then travel to the mobile above where the airplane had been, then back to Phyllis and the toy in her hand. He reaches for the soft toy, grasps it and brings it to his mouth momentarily, then drops it, only to return to the original activity of kicking and watching the mobile. Somehow it isn't the same, and he immediately tires of the effort and begins to fret to be held.   ■

Which of Piaget's sensorimotor substages does Jeremy's behavior exhibit? Approximately how old is Jeremy? If your answer is substage III, secondary circular reactions, you are correct. If you recalled the approximate age range for this substage, you guessed Jeremy's age to be somewhere between 4 and 8 months. Jeremy is now 6 months old. His own motor activity and the resulting movements of the mobile were, in and of themselves, entertaining. Possibly Jeremy was discovering that his actions could make the airplane wiggle.

However, playful infants attract their caregivers' attention. Phyllis could not resist getting in on the "action," but when she did, Jeremy was presented with a choice perhaps difficult for him to make—reach for and hold the toy airplane, interact with Phyllis, or continue the pleasurable activity of kicking and watching the mobile move.

While her timing might have been a little out of synchronization with his, Phyllis was supporting Jeremy's cognitive development by noticing what held his attention, namely the object, and bringing it within touching reach. Observant adults soon learn to synchronize their interactions with the infant's, recognizing when to enter an activity and when to leave the infant to his own explorations.

■ Angela, now 8 months old, is in her high chair. She still has some difficulty sitting alone and slides under the tray only to be restrained by the high chair safety strap between her legs. Cracker crumbs are in her hair, on her eyebrows, between her fingers, clinging to her clothing, and sprinkled about on the floor on both sides of her. James and Cheryl, seated at the table nearby, have just finished their take-out fast food burgers and are arguing over James' dating activities. It seems that James is seeing some other girls now, and Cheryl is angry.

Angela slides under the high chair tray and frets in discomfort. James off-handedly pulls her back into a seated position and continues his argument with Cheryl. Angela begins to cry intermittently. Cheryl places another cracker on her high chair tray, still arguing with James. Quieted momentarily, Angela bangs the cracker on the tray, holds what is left of it over the floor, then releases her grasp and watches the cracker fall to the floor. Sliding under her tray again, she begins to cry, this time more forcefully. She is pulled back to a seated position by Cheryl, but this does not comfort or quiet her. James, tired of arguing, and a bit distracted by the baby's crying, decides to leave.

Frustrated and angry, Cheryl picks up Angela, scolds about the mess; takes her to the sink to wash her face and hands, then puts her in her playpen even though Angela is fretful. Unable to respond to Angela's needs—her own are more overwhelming at this time—Cheryl turns on a television soap opera, props her feet up on the coffee table and lapses into self-pity.

Unable to elicit her mother's attention, Angela cries a while longer. Defeated and tired, she picks up her blanket, puts her thumb in her mouth, watches her mother, and listens to the sounds of the television set until she finally falls asleep.   ■

Angela's predicament involves psychosocial, physical motor, and cognitive aspects. At 8 months old, what are Angela's cognitive needs? Is the manner in which her physical motor and psychosocial needs are being handled conducive to optimal development? What constraints to furthering her cognitive development seem apparent in this vignette? What does her inability to sit comfortably in the high chair tell about her development? Still in the sensorimotor stage, what strategies are needed to promote her cognitive development? Let's continue to explore these and other facets of cognitive development.

Sensory and Perceptual Abilities in Infancy

Recall from Chapter 5 the sensory capabilities of infants. Vision is reasonably acute, with an ability to visually track an object or person moving within the visual field. Infants (sometimes within the first few weeks) recognize and respond to the sight, sound, and odor of their mothers. Hearing, taste, and touch are also quite functional. Infants may distinguish their own mother's voice from other female voices (DeCasper & Fifer, 1980). Breastfed infants within the first two weeks may also recognize the odor of their mothers (MacFarlane, 1977). Tactile and kinesthetic sensations complete the sensorial repertoire. Thus the infant is prepared, at least physiologically, to receive environmental stimuli from which perceptions may form. Perceptions dominate learning in the earliest stages of cognition.

Specific perceptions such as size, shape, weight, distance, and depth, if present at all in early infancy, are imperfect. In efforts to determine specific perceptual abilities of infants, researchers have studied infant responses to facial patterns, geometric patterns, targets that approach and recede from their visual field, looming objects, and depth awareness when placed on an elevated platform. Generally, these perceptions develop over the course of the first year and remain dependent upon the maturation of imprecise vision and experience. One can imagine the potential for accidents and mishaps during infancy due to faulty perceptions.

While perceptions dominate infant learning in the first months, infant responses to the same stimuli become less noticeable over time as the events repeatedly occur and become familiar to the infant. Vaughn and Litt (1987) refer to the infant's "orienting response" in which the infant is observed to suppress body movements, exhibit alertness, and turn head toward the stimulus. (Recall Jeremy and the yellow soft-sculpture mobile.) Heartbeat is accelerated during this orienting response, and as the stimulus becomes repetitive and familiar, the orienting response habituates—that is, the infant's response is less dramatic. Additional stimuli or events elicit this orienting response.

During the first year, infants become aware of their own bodies and body parts, noticing and gazing at their hands, clasping them together, sucking on fists and fingers, and playing with feet, toes, and genitalia. Emerging coordination of motor skills leads the infant to use his body and abilities to explore, experience, and discover, thus opening infinite avenues for learning. The ability to grasp and let go leads to handling, mouthing, and experimenting with a variety of playthings. As the infant manipulates a variety of objects, knowledge is being constructed. The ability to sit, pull to a standing position, cruise, and return to a seated position provides variety to the infant's visual fields and sources of knowledge. Mobility through crawling and walking further extends the infant's sources for new explorations, discoveries, and experiences.

During the first year, infants also develop self-awareness, the awareness that certain actions on their part result in certain responses from caregivers. Thus, infants learn that they can have some control over events and others. Recall from Chapter 6 that positive responses to the infant's cues result in positive feelings about oneself and feelings of security and trust—qualities that lead to confidence and eagerness to explore the environment and its many possibilities. Success in obtaining caregivers' attentions to their needs provides infants with a sense of self and support for a growing sense of competence.

Language Development

One of the most remarkable cognitive achievements of early childhood is the acquisition of language. From beginnings characterized by communication through crying, to a variety of interpretable vocal utterances, the infant begins to cognitively construct a very complex communicative system. This system includes focusing attention on another person, gazing and gesturing at sources of sounds, associating certain sounds and voices with certain events and people, developing reciprocity in verbal interactions (as when adult and infant coo back and forth with one another), and learning to use communicative systems to convey needs, feelings, and new learnings.

From the moment of birth, infants seem to be "preprogrammed" to communicate. Infants respond readily to the sound of the human voice, and have been shown to distinguish the voice of their mothers from other female voices (Mehler, 1985). Infant crying communicates a variety of messages—hunger, discomfort, distress, anger, and boredom—and does so through different intonations and patterns, which become recognizable to the infant's mother and caregivers.

As with cognitive development, a number of theoretical approaches have attempted to explain language development. Some theorists have proposed an inborn capacity for learning language (Chomsky, 1968, 1980; McNeill, 1970) called the **language acquisition device** (LAD). The LAD is a set of innate skills that enable the child to infer phoneme patterns, word meanings, and syntax from the language they hear. This skill facilitates the child's own attempts to communicate. This theory represents a nativistic point of view about how language develops; that is, heredity is believed to play a major role.

A behavioristic point of view, in contrast, holds that infants gradually learn languages through imitation of the sounds and speech that they hear. When the infant spontaneously and often accidentally creates or repeats a sound and the parents respond with glee and encouragement, vocal productions become plea-

Language acqui-sition device (LAD)—an innate mental mechanism believed by some linguists to make language develop-ment possible.

Adults and infants learn to use communication systems to convey needs, feelings, and new learning.

surable experiences worth repeating (Skinner, 1957). Language is believed to be taught through reinforcement in the form of attention and approval.

The social interactionist point of view emphasizes the importance of the infant's interactions with caregivers in which vocal exchanges occur (Bruner, 1975, 1983; Clark-Stewart, 1973; Golinkoff, 1983). These researchers recognize the communicative aspects of these early vocal exchanges and the emotional satisfaction that accrues from successful exchanges between caregiver and child.

Language Development in the First Year

The development of speech in the first year of life varies from child to child, with a few children speaking in sentences by the end of the first year. Others may use only one-word "sentences" which can only be understood by those who participate consistently in the infant's everyday world. Piaget (1923/1926) thought that cognition influenced language. Since he viewed infants and young children as egocentric, Piaget therefore concluded that earliest speech was egocentric. He observed that the speech of infants and young children appeared to be addressed to no one in particular.

Vygotsky (1934/1962) suggested that language influenced cognition and that the speech of infants and young children was not egocentric but was communication with the self. These ideas will be explored more in depth in Chapters 10, 13, and 16.

Under normal circumstances, infants follow similar, predictable sequences in the development of language. This is true regardless of culture. As is true with other areas of development, most children follow a predictable pattern, but not all children proceed through the sequences at the same rate. The sequence for language development during the first year is illustrated in Table 7.2.

As noted earlier, crying conveys a variety of messages and caregivers soon learn to interpet the sounds and intensities of the infant's cries and respond appropriately. Around 4 weeks, infants make small, throaty noises which are perhaps precursors to the vowel sounds that will begin to appear around 8 weeks. Infants discover their own voices around 12 weeks and enjoy gurgling and cooing, repeating the same vowel sound over and over, with perhaps some variation in its tone. The infant is content to play with his voice alone or in "concert" with a very entertained mother or father. It is about this time that laughing aloud also occurs. Infants are thought to view this exchange as a noisemaking activity in which infant and others "speak" at the same time (Rosenthal, 1982).

Around 6 months, babbling begins to occur in which the vowel sounds are combined with some consonants: m, p, b, k, g. Babbles such as "baba" are repeated over and over in succession, producing **echolalia.** It is believed that regardless of culture or locale, children all over the world produce similar babbles (Olney & Scholnick, 1976). As infants get older, linguists are able, through the use of tape-recorded infant vocalizations, to distinguish subtle dif-

Echolalia—the infant's babbling of one sound repeated over and over.

TABLE 7.2
Milestones in language development

Age	Phonology	Morphology and Semantics	Syntax	Pragmatics
Birth	Crying			
1 Month	Attends and responds to speaking voice			
2 Months	Cooing, Distinguishes phoneme features			
3 Months	Vocalizes to social stimulus			
4 Months	Chuckles			Pointing and gestures
6 Months	Babbling			
9 Months	Echolalia	Understands a few words		Understands gestures: responds to "bye-bye"
12 Months	Repeated syllables, Jabbers expressively	First word		Waves "bye-bye"
18 Months		Comprehends simple questions, points to nose, eyes, and hair, Vocabulary of 22 words	Two-word utterances, Telegraphic speech	Uses words to make wants known
24 Months		Vocabulary of 272 words	Uses pronouns and prepositions; uses simple sentences and phrases	Conversational turn-taking

Source: From the Manual of the Bayley Scales of Infant Development. Copyright © 1969 by The Psychological Corporation. Reproduced by permission. All rights reserved.

ferences in the babbles of children in different environments (DeBoysson-Bardies, Sagart, & Durand, 1984). This is possible at around 6 to 7 months, when babbling becomes more varied in intonation, loudness, and rhythm, and additional consonants are produced. At this age infants begin to take turns in their vocalizations with a parent or caregiver (Rosenthal, 1982).

Around 8 to 10 months, the infant may vocalize with toys, as though talking to them. Streams of babbles that sound like a conversation occur, yet there are no meaningful words in this rich array of sounds. The infant may use sounds that approximate words or which are his own creation to represent objects or events. These are called **vocables** (Ferguson, 1977). In the later weeks of this period, the infant may have learned a few isolated words. These words may or may not have true meaning for the infant, and probably are not associated with actual objects or people. Sometimes the streams of babbles include the interjection of an occasional word, creating a kind of pseudolanguage.

Vocables—early sound patterns, used by infants, which approximate words.

By the end of the first year, the infant may use one or two words correctly and comprehend simple commands and phrases, such as "no-no" and "bye-bye," and some nonverbal language in the form of gestures, like "come to Daddy" and "peek-a-boo." The infant responds to his own name and knows the names of a few objects, though he may not speak these names. **Holophrasic** words may emerge, in which one word or syllable represents a whole sentence, "baba," means "I want my bottle."

Holophrasic—refers to the infant's use of one word to convey a phrase or sentence.

Of interest to scholars and parents alike is the emergence of first words. Katherine Nelson (1973, 1979, 1980), whose research in the area of child language has enhanced our understanding, refers to the infant's growing awareness of two different worlds—objects and people. During the latter half of the first year, infants begin to realize that these different entities provide different experiences. Nelson argues that coordination of these two worlds is essential for the development of language. First words, **overgeneralized speech,** represent one or the other category; for instance, "ball" may come to represent all toys, not just the child's ball. "Mama," on the other hand, may come to imply a full message to someone about the infant's need. Nelson places some emphasis on the interactive experiences infants have with adults who are aware of and "in tune" with the child's emerging language. Adults who provide names of objects and events promote optimal language development during this first word acquisition period.

Overgeneralized speech—the use of a single word or label to represent an entire category of objects similar in use or appearance.

Early Print Experiences

Based on the belief that the origins of literacy are in infancy, researchers in language and literacy development are now suggesting that infants benefit from and enjoy the interaction of sharing chants, songs, and books with their parents and caregivers. Hearing softly spoken language with the rich intonations that accompany stories and songs is an enriching and enjoyable experience for infants.

Linda Lamme (1980) suggests five categories of literature for infants: musical literature; point-and-say books; touch-and-smell books; cardboard, cloth, and

The origins of literacy can be seen in infancy.

plastic books; and early stories. Establishing routines in the infant's day that include shared time with such literature enhances parent-child relationships, facilitates language development, and lays the foundation for later reading abilities.

Factors that Influence Cognition, Language, and Literacy Development

Think again about Jeremy and Angela. From the descriptions of their lives so far, several factors influencing development in all areas are beginning to become evident. Compare the lives of Jeremy and Angela to these factors that influence cognition, language, and literacy.

1. Full-term infants get off to a healthier, less vulnerable start in life. Optimal health from the beginning facilitates all of development including cognition, language, and literacy.
2. Proper nutrition is essential to good health and supports optimal brain and neurological development. There is some evidence that good nutrition in the

Role of the Early Childhood Professional

Promoting Cognitive/Language/Literacy Development in Infants

1. Convey confidence, enjoyment, and curiosity to the infant.
2. Provide a safe, supportive and nurturing environment, one in which exploration beyond the crib or playpen is facilitated.
3. Provide a sensory rich environment, including vocal and verbal interactions with the infant, soft singing, story reading, bright and cheerful surroundings, visual access to windows, simple uncluttered pictures on the wall, and other visual interests.
4. Provide appropriate auditory stimuli, including sharing talk and laughter, reading aloud, or playing taped music or voices or pleasing household sounds, wind chimes, and other sources of interesting sounds.
5. Vary the tactile stimuli with appropriate stuffed toys and soft sculptured items made from a variety of textures.
6. Provide rich interactive environments that include opportunities for the infant to watch, interact with, and feel and be a part of the family or child-care group.
7. Alter the child's "scenery" periodically: move crib to other side of room, move high chair to other side of the table, and occasionally change the visuals on the wall around the crib or play areas.
8. Provide simple, satisfying, age-appropriate toys and crib items and rotate them when the infant no longer uses them.
9. Explore the surroundings with the infant, carrying him about looking in the mirror, pointing to the photograph on the wall, looking out the window, finding the lowest kitchen drawer, and so on.
10. Take older infants on brief outings with you. Talk about where you are going, what you are doing, what you are seeing. Name objects and places and people as you go.
11. Place the older infant's toys on low, open shelves for easy access and clean-up.
12. Recognize the infant's attempts to initiate playfulness and interaction. Respond with enthusiasm.

---

earliest months is particularly important to brain growth, and in severe cases of malnutrition during the first 6 months, the deleterious effects can be irreversible.

3. Environments that support the cognitive needs and motivations of the infant with enriching sensory stimuli, opportunities for motoric explorations, appropriate toys, and enlarging and enriching experiences promote optimal development.
4. Interactions with others who are responsive, supportive, and stimulating enhance not only the psychosocial development of the infant, but cognition, language, and literacy development as well.

There are a number of ways in which adults may facilitate and enhance infant cognition, language development, and emerging literacy. Development cannot be hurried, and any efforts should first take cues from the behaviors of the infant. Bombarding the infant with too much stimuli, inappropriate toys, visually and auditorially overstimulating environments, and developmentally inappropriate expectations can be disconcerting to the infant and can result in a frustrated and unhappy baby. Infants in this stressful state do not eat, sleep, or play well; instead, they become fretful and distracted. An appreciation of the infant's own developmental timetable should guide parents and caregivers.

Key Terms

cognitive development	object permanence
sensorimotor	language acquisition device (LAD)
adaptation	echolalia
reflexes	vocables
primary circular reactions	holophrasic
secondary circular reactions	overgeneralized speech

Review Strategies/Activities

1. In this book, you have been introduced to a variety of theories of child growth and development and sequences of development in the first year. Angela and Jeremy have provided examples of development during the first year. Reread the stories of Angela and Jeremy. Based on what you have learned so far about child development, make a list of your observations about Angela's and Jeremy's development and their potential. Discuss and compare your lists with those of your classmates.
2. Describe a child-care program that offers optimal opportunities for cognitive, language, and literacy development.
3. Tape-record the vocalizations of an infant between the ages of 5 and 12 months. With pencil in hand, listen to the various sounds the infant makes and record the vowels and consonants that you think you hear. Which ones occur most often? Describe the tonal quality of the vocalizations. How long did each last? What events stimulated and/or prolonged the vocalizations? Compare your findings with the descriptions in this chapter.

Further Readings

Fisher, John J. (Ed.). (1988). *From baby to toddler.* New York: Pergee Books.
   Written for Johnson & Johnson Baby Products, this is a straightforward guide for parents that answers many common questions about child development. A short section describes book experiences with infants.

Forman, G. E., & Kuschner, D. S. (1983). *The child's construction of knowledge: Piaget for teaching children.* Washington, DC: National Association for the Education of Young Children.

This book is written for the student of Piaget and is a thorough explanation of Piagetian theories of cognitive development.

Healy, J. M. (1987). *Your child's growing mind.* Garden City, NY: Doubleday.

The author of this book translates neurophysiology and psychology research into practical applications for parents and teachers. She provides descriptions of the developing mind from birth and suggests activities to promote thinking skills.

Lamme, L. L., Cox, V., Matanzo, J., and Olson, M. (1980). *Raising readers: A guide to sharing literature with young children.* New York: Walker and Company.

Practical suggestions for enhancing the enjoyment of reading are presented in this book. Descriptions of appropriate literature for youngest readers are included.

Oppenheim, J. F. (1987). *Buy me, buy me! The Bank Street guide to choosing toys for children.* New York: Pantheon.

The title is self-explanatory. A very helpful guide for parents and early childhood educators.

PART FOUR

The Young Child
Ages 1 Through 3

CHAPTER 8

Little children are not logical—they are motor.
To give a child joy, give him something to do.

Lucy Gage

Physical/Motor Development of the Young Child Ages 1 Through 3

After reading and studying this chapter, you will demonstrate comprehension by:

- Outlining expected patterns of physical/motor development from age 1 through age 3.
- Identifying developmental landmarks in large and small muscle development.
- Identifying developmental landmarks in perceptual motor development.
- Describing the beginnings of body and gender awareness.
- Delineating major factors influencing physical/motor development.
- Suggesting strategies for enhancing physical/motor and perceptual motor development from age 1 through age 3.

Stages and Patterns of Development

By the end of the first year, the infant has made dramatic developmental strides in all areas of development—physical, social/emotional, cognitive, and language. Of special interest to parents and child development observers is the physical growth that proceeds quite readily, and the accompanying repertoire of motor skills. Indeed, some of the first large motor skills of pulling up, standing alone, and taking the first steps are often cause for celebration. These developments signal the beginnings of a new period in child development, typically referred to as the toddler period. This period extends from age 1 through age 2 and into the third year. Let us explore the distinguishing physical characteristics and patterns of growth during this toddler period.

General Physical Characteristics

The growth rate, quite rapid during infancy, decelerates somewhat during the second year. For example, while the infant's birth weight typically tripled during the first year, the toddler's weight gain will be around 5 to 6 pounds over the course of the second year. Likewise, the infant's length, which increased by about 10 to 12 inches during the first year, is followed by growth of about 5 inches during the second year.

Body proportions begin to change from the round, short, plump characteristics of the 1 year old to a more lean and muscular configuration by age 3. However the head, which is still large in proportion to the rest of the body (comprising $\frac{1}{5}$ of the total body length at age 1), still gives a top-heavy appearance to the toddler (see Figure 5.1, page 125). The toddler's early attempts to walk result in a posture characterized by a protruding abdomen, arms held upward and feet spread wide apart to balance (not always successfully), and a "leading" forehead. Awkward and unsure locomotion, body proportions, and characteristic posture make the term "toddler" quite appropriate for this period in child growth and development. By age 3, the changes in body build and proportions lower the center of gravity from the upper regions of the body to the midsection, facilitating more coordinated locomotion and a more lean and upright body profile.

It is estimated that by the end of the first year, the brain is $\frac{2}{3}$ of its adult size; and by the end of the second year it will be about $\frac{4}{5}$ of its adult size (Restak, 1984). Pediatricians, when examining infants and toddlers, often measure the circumference of the child's head, though this is not done routinely after age 3. Head circumference during these first 3 years is significant in physical examinations because it assists the physician in the assessment of the ossification of the cranial bones as fontanelles begin to close, and of brain growth, which is most rapid during the period from birth to 3. Whereas the head circumference at birth was greater than that of the chest, it is about equal to the chest circumference when the child is about a year old.

Facial proportions are also changing. The infant or young child has a rather high, rounded and prominent forehead, resulting from early and rapid brain and cranial growth. Due to this early growth pattern, facial features comprise a smaller portion of the facial area than they will as the child gets older. The face is round with a small jaw and a small, flat nose. Eyes are set close together, and the lips are thin. Over the course of the next few years, facial proportions will change, and the child will lose the "baby face" appearance.

Deciduous teeth—the first set of teeth, which erupts during infancy; often called temporary or baby teeth. Will later be replaced by a set of 36 permanent teeth.

The eruption of teeth contribute to changes in facial proportions. By age 1, six to eight teeth may have appeared, though for some children teeth appear at a much slower rate, with some children having no more than 3 or 4 teeth by their first birthday. By age $2\frac{1}{2}$, most children have all 20 of their **deciduous** ("baby") **teeth** (McDonald & Avery, 1983). Deciduous teeth tend to appear sooner in boys than in girls. However, girls, generally thought to progress toward maturity more rapidly than boys in most areas of development, will be slightly ahead of boys in the eruption of permanent teeth.

Other body proportions can also be observed. Look again at Figure 5.1, and notice the changes in body proportions from fetal development to adulthood. Notice that the arms of the newborn seem too long and the legs quite short in proportion to the trunk. Then compare the arm and leg lengths with those of the 2 year old—as the legs grow longer, the arms appear shorter, and the head comprises a much smaller proportion of the body length.

Skeletal development is characterized not only by an increase in size, but also in the number and composition of bones. Beginning in fetal development with soft, pliable cartilage, which begins to ossify around the fifth prenatal month, bones gradually become hardened as calcium and other minerals are absorbed. Not all bones of the body grow and develop at the same rate. The cranial bones and long bones of the arms and spine exhibit earliest ossification. Bones of the hands and wrist tend to mature early and serve as valuable indicators of general growth progress in the child (Tanner, 1978).

The amount of **adipose** (fatty tissue) that children have depends on a number of factors, including heredity, body type, eating habits, activity levels, and exercise opportunities. During infancy, adipose develops more rapidly than muscle. However, there is a tendency for children to lose adipose tissue toward the end of the first year and to continue to do so in the next few years as they become upright and more mobile. The decrease will continue until about age $5\frac{1}{2}$, when increases in weight will be the result of skeletal and muscle growth.

Adipose—the name for tissue in which there is an accumulation of connective tissue cells, each containing a relatively large deposit of fat.

Locomotor development refers to the growing ability to move independently from place to place. As in other areas of development, motor development follows the "law of developmental direction," that is, a head-to-foot direction with control over muscles of the upper regions of the body preceding control over muscles in the lower regions. This development parallels neural development, which also proceeds in a head-downward pattern. Brain development, particularly of the cerebellum, which is involved with posture and balance, grows rather rapidly between 6 and 18 months of age. Thus, neural and muscular development in tandem with changing body proportions facilitate locomotion, and do so in a fairly predictable pattern (Gesell, 1954).

Locomotor—the ability to move independently from place to place.

Large Motor Development

By the end of the first year, the child has mastered such motor skills as rolling over, sitting alone, crawling, pulling up, and perhaps standing alone. Between the ages of 10 to 15 months, the child may walk when being held by one hand or may pull to a standing position and "cruise" by holding on to furniture. These activities are referred to as large motor activities because they enlist the use and coordination of the large muscles of the arms, trunk, and legs. Because these muscles mature earliest, children will master large motor skills much sooner than small muscle skills such as handling a spoon, crayon, or buttons.

There are predictable patterns in large motor development. Table 8.1 identifies **developmental milestones** of the period from 1 to 3. Review Table 5.3 (p. 135), and notice the progression as motor development proceeds from birth

Developmental milestones— significant events during the course of growth and development.

Children master large motor skills, such as maneuvering wheeled toys, before small motor skills.

to 1, and from 1 through 3. Is the law of developmental direction evident? Notice the stunning array of large motor coordinations and skills that emerge during this first 36 months. This sequence does not include all possible motor coordinations, but illustrates the drama of motor development during its earliest stages. Keep in mind that there are individual differences in rates of development in all aspects of child growth and development. Any such sequence of developmental events can only provide approximations with which to observe and understand emerging abilities. Understanding of the sequence is generally more helpful to us than any attempt to apply strict age/stage placements.

Small Motor Development

Equally dramatic, but probably not always as obvious, is the emergence of small motor development. Small muscle development and motor skills also follow the law of developmental direction proceeding from the head downward and from the central axis outward. This means that the coordination of the smaller muscles of the wrists, hands, and fingers is preceded by, and for the most part dependent upon, the coordinations of the large muscles of the upper trunk, shoulders, and upper arms.

The ability to reach, grasp, manipulate, and let go of an object becomes more precise during the second year. Coordination of eyes and hands improves rap-

TABLE 8.1

Developmental milestones in large motor controls during the period from age 1 through age 3

Age	Motor Development
12 to 14 months	Pulls to standing position holding onto furniture Throws objects from crib Cruises while holding onto furniture Walks with one hand held Crawls up steps Rolls a large ball, nondirected, using both hands and arms Attempts to slide from lap or high chair Beginning to make shift from crawling to walking
14 to 18 months	Stands alone Climbs onto a chair Takes two or three steps without support, clumsily, with legs widespread and arms held upward for balance Gets into a standing position unassisted Squats to pick up an object Reverts to crawling when in a hurry rather than attempting to walk Cannot yet make sudden stops or turns "Dances" in place to music
18 to 24 months	Bends to pick up objects Walks without falling Pulls, drags toys Seats self in a child's chair Walks up and down stairs assisted Walks backward Move-about "dancing" to music Mimics household activities: bathing baby, sweeping, dusting, talking on telephone
24 to 36 months	Runs Walks on toes Jumps in place Kicks a large ball Imitates rhythms and animal movements; e.g., gallops like a horse, waddles like a duck Throws a ball, nondirected Catches ball rolled to her Jumps in place Rides a tricycle Walks stairs one step at a time Jumps from lowest step Attempts to balance standing on one foot
36 to 48 months	Balances on one foot Hops, gallops, runs with ease Avoids obstacles Stops readily Walks on a line Jumps over low objects Throws a ball, directed Enjoys simple dances and rhythms

Prehension—*the coordination of fingers and thumb to grasp.*

Flexors—*muscles that act to bend a joint.*

Extensors—*muscles that act to stretch or extend a limb.*

idly during the toddler period, and with ever-increasing locomotor skills, new and intriguing vistas for exploration become more accessible. Locomotion, coupled with improving eye-hand coordination becomes a primary vehicle for learning. Successful exploration is facilitated by the coordination of large muscles, small muscles, vision, and hearing.

By age 1, **prehension**, the ability to use the thumb and fingers in opposition to one another, has become reasonably efficient. Recall that during the first year of development, the grasping muscles (**flexors**) are stronger than are the releasing muscles (**extensors**). During this toddler period, grasping and letting go become quite refined. Indeed, the activities of pouring objects from a container and then, one by one, putting them back into the container can be an absorbing activity, requiring both abilities, grasping and releasing. Emerging small motor coordinations and skills are illustrated in Table 8.2. As with large motor coordinations, notice again the principles of development illustrated by this progression in the development of small motor skills.

Perceptual Motor Development

Perception is a neurological process by which sensory input is organized. Researchers study various perceptual abilities relating most often to visual, auditory, and tactile-kinesthetic perceptions. For instance, visual perception involves the ability to recognize and discriminate faces, patterns, sizes, shapes, depth, distance, and so on. Auditory perception involves abilities to use auditory clues to identify people, objects and events, and to discern distance, speed, space, and so on. Tactile-kinesthetic perception provides information relating to touch, textures, temperature, weight, pressure, and one's own body position, presence, or movements. One can readily see that perception plays a critical role in learning.

Perceptual motor—*interrelationship between perception and motor abilities.*

Perceptual motor development refers to the interrelationship between the child's perceptions and her emerging motor abilities. Since perceptions are derived from the senses and underlie awareness and understanding, motor development and perception are interdependent. Development and learning are impaired or enhanced by the integrity of each.

Such abilities as space perception, depth perception, and weight perception depend to a great extent on locomotor experiences for their development. Thus, child development observers are interested in the effective integration of perceptual and motor development. When perceptual and motor cues are integrated, the child uses her visual, auditory, tactile, or other sensory data to plan and carry out motor activities. Imitating the scribbles of another is an example of visual-motor integration. Responding to the rhythms of music from the television set is an example of audio-motor integration. Curling into one's own cubbyhole at the child care center is an example of kinesthetic-motor integration.

■ Jeremy is now 13 months old. He is aware of his parents' delight in watching him attempt his first steps. Feet widespread, arms bent at the elbows, reaching upward

TABLE 8.2
Developmental milestones in small motor development during the period from age 1 through age 3

Age	Motor Development
12 to 14 months	Picks up small object with pincer movement Drops and picks up toys Releases toy into a container Knocks over tower with wave of hand Throws objects to the floor Finger feeds efficiently Uses a spoon awkwardly Stacks 2 cubes after demonstration
14 to 18 months	Pours objects from container Builds tower of 3 or 4 cubes Holds 2 cubes in one hand Takes off shoes, socks Points to things Uses cup for drinking Feeds self efficiently
18 to 24 months	Manages spoon/cup awkwardly Turns pages of book, 2 or 3 pages at a time Places large pegs in peg board Holds crayon in fist Scribbles Squeezes a soft squeak toy
24 to 36 months	Eye dominance becoming established Builds tower of 5 to 7 cubes Strings 3 or 4 large beads Turns pages one page at a time Imitates demonstrated vertical and circular scribbles Manages spoon/cup with increasing efficiency Lines up object in "train" fashion
36 to 48 months	Builds tower of 8 to 10 cubes Imitates variety of shapes in drawings Feeds self with minimum spills Unbuttons front clothing Zips, handles velcro fasteners Works puzzles of 3 to 6 pieces Handles books efficiently Exhibits hand preference Spreads butter/jam on toast Dresses/undresses with assistance

to balance, he lifts heavily one foot to step, loses his balance and tumbles sideways. Another attempt, and he is able to toddle two or three steps before falling. His new skill is a thrill, but also somewhat frightening. His parents clap, laugh, coax, and praise profusely with every attempt. Tiring, he reverts to a more expedient mode of locomotion and crawls easily to his mother's outstretched arms.

Jeremy's parents have attempted to provide space for Jeremy's increasing mobility. Furnishings are arranged to provide obstacle-free movement and to eliminate sharp edges or items over which he might trip. Jeremy especially enjoys climbing the three steps at the front door when he has been on an excursion, and now that he is learning to walk, his mother "experiments" with his stair climbing skills.

Holding both hands from behind him, Mother and Jeremy walk toward the three steps to descend. Jeremy at first throws one foot forward into the air, bringing it back to the same level of the first step, as though he were walking on a level plane. Consequently, his mother must "rescue" him, or he will tumble into space. Not too happy with this effort, Jeremy returns to a crawling position and proceeds to back his way down the steps.   ■

This vignette illustrates some aspects of perceptual motor development. Jeremy's parents are aware that his space and speed perceptions are faulty, so they have arranged their living spaces to accommodate his poorly coordinated movements. Also, in Jeremy's mother's "experiment," lack of depth perception seems evident. Perhaps Jeremy's visual, kinesthetic, and/or depth perceptions are still immature, or the integration of these perceptions with existing motor capabilities has not yet occurred. In such cases, one would assert that Jeremy, at 13 months, needs more time for visual-motor abilities to become integrated. While this integration is occurring along with other developments during these toddler years, it will be some time before descending steps (in an upright/ forward position) will be mastered. Typically, children do not descend stairs smoothly and unassisted, until around age 4.

Visual-motor development is enhanced through opportunities to use developing locomotor abilities and small motor skills. Body awareness, balance, rhythm, and space and temporal awareness are increasing as the toddler explores her surroundings and experiences her own body movements and abilities.

■ Angela is also 13 months old. Her motor controls are somewhat, though not dramatically, delayed. (Recall that Angela was a premature delivery, complicated by anoxia.) Measured against the usual age ranges for emergence of motor skills, Angela has performed approximately 4 to 6 weeks behind her full-term counterparts. Nevertheless, her development appears to be quite normal, though she exhibits more excitability, restlessness, and frustration, which is not unusual for preterm babies. Her excursions about the house are far-reaching when allowed to explore beyond the playpen or crib.

Her mother, Cheryl, now 16 years old, has had a happy and successful year in her new school. With help from the child care center on her high school campus, Cheryl is learning to juggle mothering and education. She is taking a child development course and is thrilled to learn about the different stages and abilities Angela is exhibiting. She has learned to provide a safe environment at home, in which Angela can explore. Cheryl's siblings' activities tend to create a less-than-safe environment, so Angela is often relegated to the playpen, sometimes for lengthy periods of time. She cruises around the parameters of the playpen, watches the other children, hears the television, cuddles her soft toys, and drops small blocks into a bucket, dumps them out, and enjoys repeating this activity. The older children bring her other items to play with, and when she gets fussy, they increase their verbal interactions with her, playing games like peek-a-boo, or "which hand is the toy in?" Angela's environment is verbally rich.

The limited visual, tactile-kinesthetic environment of the playpen, however, has further delayed Angela's perceptual-motor integration. Delayed perceptual-motor integration could place Angela at risk for learning difficulties later on. What needs to happen in Angela's daily living to enhance her perceptual-motor development?   ■

Body and Gender Awareness

Toddler **body awareness** emerges with the acquisition and repetition of each new motoric activity. Motor behaviors, once discovered, are repeated over and over again. Throwing an object from the crib, pulling to a standing position beside furniture and dropping back to a seated one, dumping toys from a container, climbing the staircase, and opening a drawer all become activities to be repeated and mastered. Such activities provide the toddler with a sense of power and control over herself and the environment. For the toddler it is exhilarating. It is also a time for close adult supervision!

With these activities, toddlers form physical images and concepts of themselves as they become aware of their increasing physical/motor abilities. During this same period, children learn to identify themselves according to gender. They will begin to name their body parts: eyes, nose, mouth, feet, tummy, and so on. Naming body parts often becomes a game, with the adult asking for identities and delighting in the toddler's answers.

The toddler may demonstrate emerging body awareness through curiosities about anatomy of themselves and others. The toddler may touch mother's breasts, watch intently as father urinates, become intrigued with the body parts of siblings, and explore their own genitalia. These behaviors reflect normal curiosity, are harmless, and represent the child's growing body awareness. Parents should respond in a manner that does not convey shock or embarrassment. Simply naming the body parts is all that is required at this stage. It is appropriate to use anatomical terms such as "urinate," "bowel movement," "breasts," and so on, as this assists the toddler in understanding and helps prevent the development of misconceptions.

Questions often accompany the toddler's gender curiosity—why are girls and boys different, why do they use the toilet in different ways, how do babies get here, how do babies get in a Mommy's tummy, why don't girls have a penis, and a variety of such questions. Parents and caregivers must be matter-of-fact in answering these questions—factual, yet simplistic enough for the young child to understand. It should be psychologically safe for the child to ask anatomical questions. Adults need to be approachable on topics relating to gender and human anatomy, yet, there is little need at this age for elaborate anatomical or value-laden discussion. Answering questions as they arise is always favored over postponement to a later time (or age), deferring to the other parent or another adult, or preplanning a selected time for a formal discussion about gender and

Body aware-ness—the individual's cognizance of one's own body and its parts, and one's internal and external controls over its capabilities.

*Gender identity —
one's understand-
ing that one is
(biologically) male
or female.*

reproduction. Such strategies convey confusing messages to children who have asked what are, to them, reasonable and logical questions.

Discriminations between male and female emerge during the first year (Brooks-Gunn & Lewis, 1982). Children's awareness of their own gender (**gender identity**) is usually established by the age of $2\frac{1}{2}$ to 3 years.

Toilet Learning

In infancy, the elimination of body wastes occurs involuntarily as a reflexive activity when bladder or bowels need emptying. During the first year or so, the infant must develop a conscious awareness of the feelings of bowel and bladder fullness and develop some control over anal and urethral sphincters. Such control cannot occur until certain nerve pathways have developed and matured. The infant must have developed some language and locomotor skills to signal her need to others, get to the toilet in due time, manage clothing, and then manage toileting itself. This is not a small order.

*Toilet learning — a
gradual matura-
tional process from
which the child can
gain control over
elimination.*

Toilet learning is a gradual maturational process that extends over a period of several years. It is not, as the term "toilet training" implies, something which can be taught at some predetermined age. Parents and caregivers must learn to respond to readiness clues from the child. Efforts to impose toilet schedules are usually unsuccessful and can result in undue stress for parents and unnecessary strain on the toddler/parent relationship.

Between 18 and 20 months, the toddler begins to indicate toileting needs to caregivers. Usually bowel control precedes bladder control. The toddler may have a toileting expression, such as "poo poo" or "potty," to signal a need for assistance. Verbally expressing the need indicates the child's growing mental awareness of discomfort prior to toileting. For some children, this is only the beginning, since the other skills of voluntarily controlling the sphincters, getting to the toilet in time, managing clothing, and so on are imperfect. The child will need the adult's patience and assistance as this process of toilet learning begins.

Some children may have control over their toileting needs by age 2, others may not have such control until age 3, and still others may go beyond age 3. Once control seems to be established, children will have relapses for a variety of reasons: impending illness, diarrhea, bladder infections, sound sleep, too busy to notice the need, excitement, anxiety, or psychological trauma, to mention a few. Toddlers sometime revert to precontrol stages when family life is altered in some manner: a family move, a new baby in the family, a family member going to the hospital, death or divorce in the family, or maybe an unusually exciting and happy event such as a birthday party. Adults should expect uneven development in toilet learning, and should not show disappointment when the toddler is sometimes unsuccessful; nor should the adult punish the toddler for relapses, as this can only serve to prolong the process of developing control. The positive and supportive manner in which adults handle toilet learning will be instrumental in assuring continued control and healthy attitudes about the human body and about elimination.

Theorists have related healthy gender awareness experiences and toilet learning to psychosocial development. Erikson, for instance, has related toileting to the child's developing sense of autonomy during the toddler period, and suggests that its healthy management is critical to this stage of healthy personality development. This topic is covered in greater detail in Chapter 9.

Special Needs Children

It is estimated that of the 3.4 million infants born each year, about 7 percent have congenital abnormalities (Haring & McCormick, 1990). The most severely impaired infants are more easily identified at birth or soon thereafter; however, many remain to be identified during the preschool years. Another large number of children are born into families who are unable to provide care and nurturing for them. Many of this latter group suffer poor health care, poor nutrition, unhealthy living environments, disease, or neglect and abuse. Often these children are **developmentally delayed**. It is estimated that over 4 million children under age 6 live under such circumstances (Haring & McCormick, 1990).

Developmentally delayed—a course of development that is significantly slower than is typical.

Since the earliest months and years of life are critical for growth and development in all areas—physical/motor, psychosocial, cognitive—it is crucial for parents and caregivers to watch for early signs of growth and development problems. Knowledge of expected trends in growth and development helps adults to recognize the **atypical**. Ongoing health care and observations of individual growth and development trends can signal needs for formalized assessments, special treatments, or perhaps, intervention.

Atypical—not typical.

For instance, in cases of preterm and low birth weight infants, developmental trends will differ somewhat from other infants. Because preterm and low birth weight infants are at risk for neurological difficulties, learning disabilities, and physical/motor and language delays, supervision of their care during these first 3 to 4 years is imperative (Desmond, Wilson, Alt, & Fisher, 1980; Hall, 1985; Kopp & Parmelee, 1979). Parents will be advised of the expected differences in rates and patterns of growth, and will need to closely follow the advice of their health care professionals and strive to provide optimal environmental and experiential opportunities for healthy growth and development. Provided a nurturing and supportive infancy and toddler period, most premature infants catch up within the first 2 to 4 years and present no visible differences with their age-mates.

Observation of large motor development, when coupled with observations of other sensory and perceptual abilities, alerts us to potential developmental delays or other signs of neurological difficulties. Tactile sensations, visual and auditory acuity, and other sensorial perceptions contribute to or impede the coordination of motor activities. When sensory input is insufficient, the child has difficulty interpreting various events or stimuli, resulting in poor perceptual motor development. Poor perceptual motor development has been associated with prematurity and low birth weight children, infants and children suffering from fetal alcohol syndrome, prescription and nonprescription drugs taken during pregnancy, birth complications, and accidents and disease. It is often observed in emotionally disturbed children, children with minimal brain dysfunction, and children with other learning disabilities (Haring & McCormick, 1990).

Many disabling conditions, recognized and identified early in the child's development, can be treated and often ameliorated. Regular physical examinations and ongoing observations of growth and development trends in individual children can go a long way in assuring that any unusual deviations from expected patterns and rates of development are not overlooked and are responded to in an appropriate and timely way.

Factors Influencing Physical/Motor Development

Physical/motor development is influenced by several important factors: genetics, sociocultural background, the family's socioeconomic status, nutrition, and safety.

Genetic Makeup

Studies of twins have yielded a large body of literature on the relative influences of genetic makeup and environment. Similarities observed between identical twins support the hypothesis that there is in each individual a genetic blueprint for growth potential and for individual rates of growth and development. Identical twins tend to be more similar in stature and age of eruption of teeth, and they tend to reach menarche within a few weeks of one another (Tanner, 1978). Twin studies have established a strong case for the genetic influence on the emergence of motor controls. There is greater similarity between identical twins in motor performance than among fraternal twins (Gesell, 1954). Such studies suggest a genetic predisposition toward the capacity to acquire motor skills. However, the attainment of motor skills will also depend upon the environment and the opportunities it affords for use and practice of emerging motor skills (Malina, 1982).

Sociocultural Differences

While charts exist that depict expected normal growth patterns in children, there is no universal standard for all children. Differences among children are related to such factors as genetics, ethnicity, socioeconomic level, absence or presence of disease, and nutritional status. Physicians use reference standards to determine relative height and/or weight for age to evaluate the health status of individual children. These standards represent a cross-section of ethnic and economic groups of children in the United States.

Ethnicity plays a role in differences in physical development among children. Cross-cultural studies reveal that people from different ethnic groups may vary appreciably in their expected physical heights, weights, and motor skills development. Children from some cultures will be tall and lean; others may be short and stocky. Some groups exhibit earlier advances in motor skills than others.

For instance a number of studies suggest that African-American children are precocious in the area of motor development, perhaps having more physical energy than their Anglo peers (Morgan, 1976; Werner, 1979; Malina, 1982). Some Asian and Central American Indian groups show earlier motor development than Anglo children (Lester & Brazelton, 1982). Cratty (1986) suggests that differences may be a result of early training—in some African cultures, special effort is made to teach children specific motor skills of sitting, standing and walking. Contemporary studies suggest that developmental differences among minority groups, while biologically influenced, may result from differences in parental goals and interactions (Coll-Garcia, 1990).

Socioeconomic Factors

In addition to differences among ethnic groups in physical/motor growth and development, there are a number of environmental influences that impact upon optimal growth and development. Health, safety, nutrition, parental expectations, and the provision of opportunities to enhance emerging motor abilities are influenced by the child's environment.

Socioeconomic factors are among the environmental influences to which differences in physical development among children are attributed. The risks to optimal development are particularly profound among children in low SES families. According to statistics gathered by the Children's Defense Fund (1988), the following data command our attention:

- One of every four preschool children lives in poverty.
- Poor children are twice as likely as non-poor children to be born at low birth weight.
- Low birth weight infants are 20 times more likely to die in the first year of life than those of normal weights.
- Low birth weight infants are at significantly greater risk of disabilities such as autism, retardation, cerebral palsy, visual and hearing impairments, and learning disabilities.
- Many children in the United States are not receiving needed immunizations against measles, mumps, rubella, diphtheria, pertussis, polio, and tetanus.
- Malnutrition affects almost 500,000 American children.
- Members of families with children represent more than one-third of the homeless population nationwide.
- One in five poor teens (all races) with lower than average basic skills is a mother.

Children from lower socioeconomic levels often trail their age-mates in physical development, due to improper or inadequate prenatal and postnatal health care, nutrition, and exercise. Home environments are often lacking in knowl-

Optimal growth and development are often compromised in children of poverty.

edge of and opportunities for optimal physical, sensory, and motor development. The need for intervention programs that provide education and work opportunities for adults in these families, and early health, nutrition, and child development programs for the infants and toddlers seems particularly imperative.

Nutrition

Nutrition is perhaps the most critical environmental factor relating to optimal growth and development. The visible effects of prolonged malnutrition on young children are seen almost daily on television newscasts and in magazine and newspaper advertisements soliciting help for children in underdeveloped countries. Yet, as we have seen in the statements above, malnutrition affects alarming numbers of American children as well.

Hollow eyes, protruding abdomens, and skeletal bodies are frightening characteristics of severely malnourished children. In addition to impaired growth, prolonged malnutrition has been associated with retarded brain growth (Chase, 1976; Tanner, 1978), impaired intellectual development (Winick, 1976), anemias, susceptibility to illnesses, and vulnerability to environmental poisons. Malnutrition is among the leading causes worldwide of childhood mortality (Children's

Defense Fund, 1989). The effects of both under- and over-nutrition command the attention of parents, health care professionals, and child caregivers. Children who are poorly nourished in the earliest months and years grow more slowly, suffer more illnesses, and are at risk for learning disabilities.

Short-term malnutrition usually is not as devastating. Some researchers are unwilling to attribute all of the developmental problems listed above to malnutrition alone. Ricciuti (1980) suggests that inadequate housing, sanitation, medical care, and child care practices; limited educational opportunities; and increased exposure to disease all contribute to growth and development **anomalies**.

When children in less than optimal circumstances are provided the essentials for healthy growth and development, many of the effects of poor nutrition may be reversed. A "catch-up" phenomenon has been described by Tanner (1978), in which poorly nourished children who have been provided adequate diets experience a faster than normal growth rate for a time. This catch-up growth seems to be the body's innate attempt to follow its own genetically programmed growth schedule. Catch-up growth may also follow certain lengthy illnesses. Once back on schedule, the growth rate returns to its expected pace. Permanent physical and intellectual damage seems to result from malnutrition when (1) it occurs early in life; (2) it has been prolonged; and (3) it is left untreated (Ricciuti, 1980). Figure 8.1 summarizes the characteristics of healthy home and child care environments.

Anomaly — a deviation from the norm.

FIGURE 8.1
Healthy environments for young children

Healthy home and child care environments for young children are characterized by:

1. **Adequate space.** Toddlers need sufficient space in which to try out their emerging and uncoordinated motor controls. Tumbles, falls, and running into furniture are kept at a minimum when adequate space is provided.
2. **Clean, sanitary surroundings.** Toddlers put their hands, toys, and other objects in their mouths. All necessary precautions must be taken to protect toddlers from infections and disease.
3. **Safe space and play materials.** Reaching, grasping, and mobility skills facilitate the natural curiosity of the toddler, and vice versa. The toddler's environment must be free from obstacles, poisons, sharp edges, small objects, unstable furnishings and play equipment, exposed electrical cords and outlets, and so on.
4. **Developmentally appropriate play items and equipment.** Developmentally appropriate play items ensure safety and provide satisfying and engaging experiences that facilitate and enhance physical, motor, and perceptual development, and enrich play activities.
5. **Unrelenting supervision.** While toddler mobility and curiosity enhance physical, motor and perceptual growth, and cognitive development, constant vigilance is essential. Safety concerns are paramount at this age.
6. **Supervised health care.** To maintain healthy bodies, health care needs must be supervised by appropriate medical and dental professionals. Diets, immunizations, rest and exercise, and specialized medical attention as needed enhance chances for optimal growth and development.

Safety

The safety concerns of the toddler period need special attention. Increased mobility and growing curiosity catapult the child into a world of exploration, experimentation, and discovery. Lacking intellectual judgment and a background of experience to temper impulses, the toddler needs constant supervision. Yet an overprotective, confining environment may preclude optimal physical, motor, and perceptual development. What constitutes a good balance between overprotection and freedom to explore?

Opportunities to repeat and practice newly discovered skills are essential to continued progress in the areas of physical, motor, and perceptual development. Keep in mind that growth and development cannot be hurried. Toddlers prepare for each subsequent stage in motor development by mastering what they can do in their present stage (Gonzalez-Mena & Eyer, 1980). Yet motor development can be facilitated by allowing toddlers the freedom to explore and to manipulate safe and developmentally appropriate objects and toys within the environment and with the security of watchful adults to protect them from unsafe situations.

Stress and Physical/Motor Development

Deprivation dwarfism—a retardation in physical growth thought to be triggered by insufficient emotional support.

There is a phenomenon known as **deprivation dwarfism** that results from emotional factors such as lack of affection and excessive stress. A most interesting study is that of Lytt Gardner (1972), whose research focused on children whose daily lives were severely lacking in affectional interactions with their caregivers. The children Gardner studied were healthy, had not been physically abused, and their physical needs were adequately met. The growth and development of these children, however, was severely retarded. This phenomenon is also referred to as the failure to thrive syndrome.

It is estimated that as many as 3 percent of the preschool children in the United States may suffer from this failure to thrive syndrome (Lipsitt, 1979). This syndrome is seen more often in infants, but it does occur in older children. It is characterized by failure to gain weight, or loss of weight, sometimes due to an inability to digest and absorb food, and sometimes due to food having been withheld from the child. Failure to thrive is associated with neglect and abuse, physical handicaps such as cleft palate, behavioral disturbances, and disease.

When growth rates are considerably slower than expected, a physical examination by a pediatrician will help to determine if the cause is environmental or related to heredity, disease, or other factors, and may suggest an appropriate treatment procedure. Most children, when provided satisfying interactions with parents and caregivers, adequate and nutritious diets, and relief from severe environmental stressors, return to normal growth patterns and achieve physical development within the normal ranges (Barbero & McKay, 1983; Smith & Berenberg, 1970).

The return to thriving however, does not alleviate all the effects of earlier deprivation. Many of these children will suffer learning disabilities and language delays, and some will exhibit neurotic or antisocial behaviors later (Barbero & McKay, 1983). These are, of course, extreme examples of the effects of stress on infants and young children. All homes and all environments are subject to stress from time to time. If the adults in the home cope adequately and in productive, constructive ways with their stressors, the children will also learn to cope. Toddlers need assurances of their protection, affection, and acceptance. They also need reasonably predictable schedules for eating, sleeping, playing, and interacting with others. Supportive and predictable schedules, environments, and people enhance all development—physical, motor, and perceptual.

Opportunities to Enhance Physical/Motor Development

Keeping in mind that each child has her own inherent timetable for growth and development, the relative influence of teaching and practice is called into question. To what extent do teaching and practice speed the process of large or small motor development? How are emerging large and small motor skills enhanced?

Toddlers need assurance of protection, affection, and acceptance.

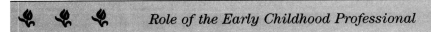

❦ ❦ ❦   *Role of the Early Childhood Professional*

Promoting Physical/Motor Development in Children Ages 1 Through 3

1. Create and maintain a safe and healthy environment.
2. Provide for nutrition and for ongoing health care.
3. Provide a reasonably accepting and stress-free environment.
4. Encourage exploration, discovery, and independence.
5. Provide positive, supportive, and protective guidance.
6. Encourage positive body and gender awareness.
7. Provide a variety of materials to manipulate.

To a great extent, physical growth and maturation determine the course of motor development. In a very early study of growth and maturation (Gesell & Thompson, 1929), identical twins were given different opportunities to practice a variety of motor tasks. One twin was provided opportunities to practice, and the other was not. The twin who did not practice and had been provided no special instructions actually made more progress within 3 weeks after instructions ceased. The researchers concluded that practice would make no difference unless a child is biologically mature enough for a particular skill.

Most developmentalists today believe in the importance of both maturation and experience. The abilities to sit, crawl, walk, climb steps, and manage eating utensils and clothing are skills that grow in proficiency as they are practiced. Toddlers need environments that provide opportunities and supportive encouragement for practicing motor skills. They also need an array of developmentally appropriate toys and household items to explore, manipulate, and enjoy.

But caution is also necessary. Inappropriate motor performance expectations place young children at risk for injury and psychological damage. The concept of "miseducation of young children" has been advanced by David Elkind (1987), wherein adults are warned of a growing number of misguided notions about what and when children learn. For instance, attempts to teach infants and toddlers to swim reveal adult expectations that are developmentally inappropriate. According to Elkind, swimming lessons for infants and toddlers places them at risk for middle ear infections and possible hearing loss, for asphyxiation from swallowing water, and for diarrhea from urine-contaminated water, since young children being taught in the swimming pool may not have bladder control yet. Elkind also admonishes that the added risk of false security that the adult acquires and then comes to trust—that the swimming lessons will protect the child from drowning—is a serious misapplication of adult responsibility.

Expecting small children to use writing tools or scissors or to "color within the lines" is equally inappropriate and damaging. Following the developmental cues provided by the interests and emerging capabilities of individual children assures that the opportunities and practice provided them will serve fruitful purposes.

Key Terms

deciduous teeth	body awareness
adipose	gender identity
locomotor	toilet learning
developmental milestones	developmentally delayed
prehension	atypical
flexors	anomaly
extensors	deprivation dwarfism
perceptual motor	

Review Strategies/Activities

1. Observe two children in a child care setting for approximately 1 hour during outdoor and indoor activity times. Using the physical/motor milestones lists in this chapter, record all motor behaviors observed. Record both gross and fine motor observations. Compare your lists with those of a classmate. How are the children the same? How are they different? To what might the differences in motor abilities be attributed?
2. Invite a nutritionist to talk with your class. What dietary plan would she recommend for a 1 year old? 2 year old? 3 year old? How do these diets change as the child gets older?
3. Discuss with a classmate safe ways to encourage toddler exploration, discovery, and independence. List your suggestions. What physical/motor or perceptual development will your suggestions enhance?
4. Visit a nursery school in which toddlers (ages 1 to 3) are enrolled. How is child health and physical well-being protected or enhanced? What precautions are taken to prevent the spread of infection or disease?

Further Readings

Endres, J. B., & Rockwell, R. E. (1985). *Food, nutrition and the young child* (2nd ed.). St. Louis: Times Mirror/Mosby College Publishing.

A very readable, informative, and comprehensive text for students who want to know more about nutrition and young children. One need not have advanced knowledge of nutrition in order to benefit from the basic information provided by this book.

Kendrick, A. S., Kaufmann, R., & Messenger, K. P. (Eds.). (1991). *Healthy young children: A manual for programs*. Washington, DC: National Association for the Education of Young Children.

This book, designed to be a reference and resource for professionals who work with young children, reflects current research and recommendations for health and safety protection of young children of leading health and early childhood education authorities.

Metzger, M., & Whittaker, C. P. (1988). *The childproofing checklist: A parent's guide to accident prevention.* New York: Doubleday.

An excellent resource for parents and caregivers who wish to assess the safety of the young child's surroundings.

Snow, C. W. (1989). *Infant development.* Englewood Cliffs, NJ: Prentice Hall.

Designed as an introductory text for courses in infant development, this book provides a comprehensive overview of growth and development during the first 3 years.

CHAPTER 9

Our words should be like a magic camera upon which a child cannot help but paint a positive picture of himself.

Haim G. Ginott

Psychosocial Development of the Young Child Ages 1 Through 3

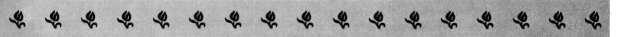

After reading and studying this chapter, you will demonstrate comprehension by:

- Describing the psychosocial development of the young child ages 1 through 3.
- Relating selected theories of psychosocial development to the study of the toddler period of development.
- Identifying factors that influence psychosocial development ages 1 through 3.
- Outlining the role of adults in healthy psychosocial development of the young child ages 1 through 3.

The toddler period in child growth and development presents new challenges for parents and caregivers. The formerly dependent, compliant infant now exhibits a striving for independence and for ever-widening opportunities to interact, explore, and learn. Increasingly refined motor capabilities and communication skills are emerging and lead to new and unexpected behaviors. These new behaviors can, at the same time, thrill, perplex, frustrate, and intrigue parents and caregivers.

Attachments

From about 6 months to age 3, the toddler is passing through phase III, "active **proximity seeking**," of Bowlby's attachment sequence (Bowlby, 1969, 1980). During this phase, the child becomes quite aware of and monitors the presence or absence of his attachment figure, usually the mother. The child actively seeks to be near and to be held, and cries upon separation. When the attachment

Proximity seeking — the child's attempts to maintain nearness and contact with the attachment figure.

figure is present, the toddler will, at first, remain quite close, perhaps in the lap of the adult, then will tenuously venture forth and away, but will return periodically to the attachment figure for assurance and interaction. As a sense of trust and self-confidence grows, these ventures will be sustained over longer periods of time.

The success of these ventures is thought to relate to the quality of infant-caregiver attachments. Studies have suggested that secure attachments in infancy can lead to more enthusiastic, affectively positive, and persistent behaviors at age 2 (Matas, Arend, & Stroufe, 1978). Other studies have found securely attached infants to be more sociable (Pastor, 1981), compliant, independent, and empathic, and to show greater self-esteem as toddlers (Stroufe, 1983).

Studies of insecurely attached infants have revealed less promising results. Some researchers believe that insecurely attached infants, particularly anxious avoidant infants, are at heightened risk for noncompliant and uncooperative behaviors, particularly with adults, and for aggression and difficulties in social interactions at later ages (Ainsworth, 1973, 1982; Bowlby, 1969; Erickson, Stroufe, & Egeland, 1985). These researchers believe that the quality of attachment at 12 and 18 months is a strong predictor of behavior at age $4\frac{1}{2}$ and 5. These predictions are based on assumptions that the kinds of care and support systems that children experience are consistent over time and that changes in existing patterns of care can alter the child's behavior in positive or negative ways.

The ability to visually and auditorally remain "attached," even though the attachment figure may not be near, occurs as the toddler gets older. The toddler learns to "feel attached" from a distance, through looking, listening, and vocally communicating (Greenspan & Greenspan, 1985). The child becomes more exploratory as feelings of security with the attachment figure and with the environment increase. The toddler begins to rely upon self-comforting behaviors such as thumbsucking or fondling a soft toy or blanket, and may begin to find comfort through interactions with persons other than the attachment figure.

Extrafamilial relationships—those relationships that include people outside the immediate or extended family.

Primary child caregiver—the person from whom the child receives nonparental care, and with whom a warm relationship can form.

Familial and Extrafamilial Attachments

Forming secure attachments and trusting relationships with parents and family members is among the first and the most important psychosocial tasks of the infant/toddler period. As the toddler gets older, successfully forming attachments to others beyond the family becomes another important psychosocial task. **Extrafamilial relationships** are those that include people outside the immediate or extended family, e.g., a neighbor, family friend, or **primary child caregiver**. Infants and toddlers can, and do, develop strong feelings for and attachments to others outside the family. Positive interactions and successful experiences with extrafamilial relationships enhance the child's psychosocial development.

Positive interactions and successful experiences with extrafamilial relationships enhance the child's psychosocial development.

■ Angela's high school based child care center is, by most standards, "state of the art." Situated in its own separate building on the high school campus, it is readily accessible to the young mothers whose children are enrolled. Its program and management is guided by a director with skills and knowledge in early child care and education. The center exceeds local and state licensing requirements and is accredited by the National Association for the Education of Young Children. Child caregivers are educated in child development and early education and are warm, nurturing, and effective teachers. The setting is aesthetically appealing and is rich with developmentally appropriate materials and activities. The daily pace is unhurried, comfortable, yet appropriately stimulating.

Two-year-old Angela is active, alert, and eager to explore, and has become reasonably secure in her child care center. She has developed a strong attachment to her primary child caregiver, Ms. Ruiz, whose feelings for Angela are equally strong.

Upon arrival today, Angela visually and auditorily scans the playroom for the sight and sound of Ms. Ruiz. Her facial expression shows anticipation, anxiety, and expectation. Locating Ms. Ruiz, she runs eagerly toward her, reaching up for Ms. Ruiz to acknowledge her presence with a hug. Ms. Ruiz greets Angela with a wide smile and obliges with a hug, then offers to help Angela with her coat. Angela resists, however, wanting to do this herself. Ms. Ruiz reminds Angela to say "Good-bye" to her departing mother, as Cheryl must leave to attend her algebra class. While removing her wraps, Angela stops and watches tentatively as Cheryl leaves. Rushing to the door, she calls to her mother, who returns, kisses her good-bye, tells her to have a good time, and then goes on to class. Perhaps Angela still feels some separation anxiety, for her facial expression shows signs of impending tears.

However, Ms. Ruiz, sensitive and assuring, directs Angela's attention to the large classroom aquarium, points to the fish and begins to name the items in the aquarium: "gravel," "light," "water." She talks with Angela about the fish: "Yes, that is a fish, Angela. This one is an angelfish. Let's put some food in the aquarium for the fish." This interaction has become somewhat routine each morning, and though quite brief, it serves to help Angela make the transition from home to center, and from mother to child caregiver.

Once at ease, Angela asserts "No more fish," and proceeds to another part of the room to play. Very soon she will be seen approaching her friend Leah, and a different interaction ensues as the girls proceed to the sand table. ■

■ The child care center in which Jeremy is enrolled is also judged to be of high quality, not unlike the high school child care center. Jeremy's parents visited a number of child care centers and preschool programs, asked many questions, and discussed their options before making their final selection.

Jeremy enjoys attending the child care center. However, in recent weeks separation has become a particular problem for him and for his parents and caregivers. The parent's inquiry with the center director reveals an unusual amount of staff turnover in recent months, and as a consequence, Jeremy has encountered three different primary child caregivers in less than 6 months.

Unable to comprehend where the child caregivers go and why they are not present, Jeremy demonstrates his confusion and anxiety by clinging to his mother and crying loudly. On this particular day, he has created quite a scene with an angry and fearful tantrum. He resists the attempts of Ms. Bell to comfort him, shrugging her away.

Presently, his special friend Josh arrives and, noticing Jeremy crying, makes his way to where Jeremy and his detained and perplexed mother are standing. Josh stares with some concern, as though he understands, but isn't sure what is happening. Ann coaxes Jeremy: "Hi, Josh. Jeremy, here is Josh. Josh wants to play with you." Reluctantly and slowly, Jeremy reaches toward his mother in a gesture seeking to be hugged. Thus, he signals that he will kiss her good-bye. Mother and child hug and kiss, and Ann begins to lead Jeremy and Josh toward the block center. Once the two are involved, Jeremy's mother says a firm, yet assuring "good-bye," and departs without further incident. ■

These examples tell us that attachments can be formed with individuals, both adults and children, beyond the home and family. These attachments can be quite strong and can provide another source of security for the toddler. It is clear that both children have found a sense of security and well-being in their child care center friends. For Angela, the adult child caregiver has become a reliable and trusted source of security in the absence of her mother. For Jeremy, his young friend and playmate Josh has become a trusted friend, helpful in the absence of a continuous relationship with a child caregiver.

Child care arrangements, wisely selected, afford an expanded circle of friends and healthy, supportive relationships for young children. However, if we take Jeremy's situation, we can see that staff changes create temporary stress for some children, returning them to earlier and less mature forms of coping. Howes (1987b) cautions that continuity of caregiving is related to the development of secure attachments in out-of-home settings. This continuity helps the child make a smooth transition between the home and the child care setting. Howes also asserts that the child who experiences many different caregivers may not become attached to any of them.

Toddler/Toddler Friendships

Past studies of toddler friendships and play behaviors characterized the toddler as engaging in onlooker and/or **parallel play** (Parten, 1933). In parallel play, the toddler enjoys being near and playing beside other children, but pursuing his own play interest. In parallel play there is little, if any, interaction between children. It was thought that onlooker and parallel play represented least mature levels of social interaction. More recent studies of toddler interactions suggest that while parallel play occurs frequently during the toddler period, it is not limited to the toddler period and changes in form as cognition changes and interaction skills emerge. Thus, parallel play has been described as "parallel-functional," "parallel-constructive," "parallel-dramatic," and "parallel-games," each representing different forms and purposes (Rubin, 1982; Rubin, Watson, & Jambor, 1978).

Parallel play—activities in which two or more children play near one another while engaged in independent activities.

Young children today spend more time in out-of-home child care situations than did children of past generations. Therefore, infants and toddlers have encountered other children from a very early age. Recent studies have demonstrated that genuine friendships can develop between children in toddler play groups (Greenspan & Greenspan, 1985; Vandell & Mueller, 1980). While first attempts at interaction are clumsy and perhaps antagonistic, they nevertheless can be quite pleasurable for the toddler.

As described by Greenspan and Greenspan (1985), a sequence of attempts at interaction begins with the toddler first noticing something about another toddler that seems to attract him—the color of clothing, long curly hair, or a pretty ribbon, for example. This is followed by mutual explorations between the two children in which the child touches or pulls at the attraction—the ribbon, pretty hair, or whatever it may be. The other child in this interaction usually passively allows the explorations to take place—the ribbon to be pulled, for instance. Following this level of interaction, the toddlers may seek a nearby adult, who then becomes an assistant to the interaction. The toddler hands an object to the adult, and the adult in turn hands it to the other toddler, who hands it back to the adult to begin the sequence again. Greenspan calls these interactions "collaborative interactions," as the toddlers use the adult as a conduit for the sharing of objects, toys, or food. He further describes toddlers as exhibiting humor in these encounters, laughing together as a block tower falls or another playful event ensues. Then the toddlers go off to play together, during which time they will continue to interact through facial expressions and gestures.

Toddler friends will imitate one another, laugh with and at one another, and share activities such as looking at books together or filling and dumping objects from a container (Press & Greenspan, 1985). These friendships may be transitory and short-lived, yet their importance to early extrafamilial attachment behaviors and to emerging social development should not be underestimated. One study of separation of nursery school infants and toddlers when they were being "promoted" to new classrooms found that when infants and toddlers were moved to new classrooms with a close friend, they adapted more comfortably (Field, Vega-Lahr, & Jagadish, 1984).

The types and availability of toys also influence the quality and success of toddler interactions. Developmentally appropriate toys assure reasonable successes for toddler play. A truck with a missing wheel cannot be successfully rolled back and forth. One pull-toy, instead of two, creates frustration and tears, whereas pulling toys together about the room can be a joyous social encounter.

Fears and Anxieties of Toddlers

In addition to describing attachments and friendships, the vignettes above demonstrate the continuing presence of stranger and separation anxieties, which continue from infancy into the toddler period. The occurrence of these anxieties, as we discussed earlier, parallels the development of attachments, influencing and being influenced by the quality of the attachment relationships. These anxieties begin to wane around age $2\frac{1}{2}$ to 3 years.

Around 18 months, however, additional fears begin to emerge. This indicates increasing social/emotional and cognitive development. Because all development is interrelated, the discussion of fears must recognize the interrelated role of cognition. As the child can manipulate mental images and mentally elaborate upon past events and experiences, new understandings—and misunderstandings, concepts and misconceptions—can bring about new fears. As the toddler begins to imagine, fantasy and reality become difficult to separate.

Fears are normal. Fears are quite real to the child, can be very disturbing, and can be difficult to allay. In addition to separation and stranger fears, common fears of the toddler include the dark, the bathtub drain, animals, some storybook or media characters, monsters and ghosts, loud noises, lightning and thunder, and vacuum cleaners or other noisy equipment.

Toddlers may acquire some of their fears through social learning. Parents who become fearful during a thunderstorm, or who discuss frightening or painful experiences relating to accidents or illnesses, visits to the physician or hospital, or other adult fears, may inadvertently instill these fears in their young children. When fear tactics are used to discipline, unhealthy and inappropriate fears are imposed on the child. Imploring the toddler, for instance, to "be quiet, or Aunt Marti will get you," creates an unfortunate wariness of Aunt Marti and extends no favor to Aunt Marti's efforts to establish her own positive relationship with the toddler.

Helping the toddler to understand and cope with fears requires sensitivity and patience. Because fears can be quite real to the child, adults should neither laugh, ridicule, nor minimize them. Very young children will not understand logical explanations—instead, toddlers need adults to help them find ways to deal with their fears. A child who is afraid of the bathtub drain, for instance, can be given "control" over it by being the one who opens or closes the drain or by getting out of the tub before the drain is opened.

Fears are necessary for survival, as they signal dangers to be avoided. However, the toddler may not yet have necessary survival fears for most potentially dangerous situations. The toddler neither has the judgment nor the backlog of experiences and understanding to avoid such things as the street, "friendly" strangers, fire, poisons, heights, and a host of other perils. Toddlers do not have adequate space, speed, depth, or other perceptions to perceive risks accurately. Toddlers need to be protected from dangers through close supervision and must be taught about dangers in ways that provide knowledge, caution, and skills, but do not frighten them unnecessarily. Adults cannot assume that toddlers are aware of dangerous situations. In the event of the child's self-endangerment, adults should not react with physical punishment for the child's lack of experience and knowledge. It is the adult's responsibility to monitor and maintain the child's safety and well-being.

Thumbsucking

Most infants sooner or later find their fists and thumbs and derive pleasure and solace from sucking on them. Brazelton (1984) suggests that parents should expect their infants to suck their thumbs, fingers, or fists, and attribute little consequence to this behavior. Thumbsucking can be the child's source of self-comfort when tense or frightened, or when simply trying to relax or fall asleep. Brazelton advises adults to expect a great deal of thumb- or fingersucking in the first year, somewhat less in the active second year, and even less after the third and fourth years.

While pacifiers are sometimes given to infants to satisfy the sucking need, most often they are provided in an attempt to quiet or calm a fussy child. For some infants and toddlers, the pacifier is satisfying; others reject it or find little pleasure in it. Whether thumb or pacifier have provided the source of self-comfort to the child, either is usually given up at about the same age. Children may fall back on one or the other of these self-comforting modes of behavior during periods of stress or fear.

Attachment to an object such as a soft toy or blanket is a common behavior, beginning in the latter part of the first year and frequently extending into the primary years and beyond, particularly in times of stress.

Transitional Objects

Transitional object—an object, usually a soft, cuddly item, to which a child becomes attached.

Another self-comforting strategy employed by the toddler is the use of the **transitional object**, so named because it assists the child in making the transition from the dependency and protection of infancy to the independence and uncertainty of the toddler period. Attachment to an object such as a teddy bear, special blanket, swatch of soft fabric, doll, or favorite piece of clothing is common and begins in the latter part of the first year, usually around 8 or 9 months. Because these objects have been invested with certain meanings and comforting associations, the child forms an emotional tie to them (Winnicott, 1953, 1971, 1977). The child's attachment to the object can last to age 7 or 8.

Adults often provide "soft name" labels for these objects, such as "loveys" or "cuddlies"; the child also provides a name, for example, "banky" or "bear-bear." These attachments are usually quite strong and extremely important to the child.

Transitional objects serve a variety of comforting roles. Some believe the soft, familiar objects provide a kind of security link with the home, mother, or other attachment figure during times of separation. In this sense, it serves to ease separation anxiety. The transitional object provides a sense of security in new or strange settings, or frightening or stressful situations. Children often treat their transitional object with love and caring, exhibiting their own abilities to express affection. Sometimes these objects are the child's substitution for the thumb or pacifier and replace these earlier forms of self-comfort. Other children use the transitional object and the thumb or pacifier in combination as a self-comforting strategy.

How should parents and caregivers respond to these transitional objects? Most authorities agree that these objects fulfill some natural need and provide the child a source of security. Interference with these attachments is strongly discouraged; rather, adults are encouraged to expect, accept, acknowledge, and appreciate the child's new attachment. Brazelton (1984, p. 65) writes:

> If a thumb or a beloved object can help a child to grow up, it seems obvious to me that we should treasure them. As children mature, other loves and interests will replace these, but the inner sense of competence they will have learned early from such self-reliant patterns will serve them well.*

Autonomy Versus Shame and Doubt

The toddler's efforts to buckle a seat belt, turn the light switch on or off, open a door, and take off his socks, shoes, or other clothing are intensely and personally important at the moment and can result in tears and tantrums when thwarted by an unsuspecting or impatient adult. Previously dependent behaviors are now being overshadowed by the toddler's efforts to be independent. Locomotion encourages this independence, as the toddler gains confidence in walking, climbing, running, moving, and manipulating. Language reveals a striving for independence as the toddler asserts, "Me do it!" and "No." and "Mine." The toddler adamantly wants to do things for himself. While it is true that these behaviors tax adult patience and understanding, they can be viewed as indicative of positive and healthy psychosocial development.

---

*T. B. Brazelton, *To Listen to a Child*, © 1984 by T. Berry Brazelton, M.D. Reprinted by permission of Addison-Wesley.

Autonomy—
a sense of
independence or
self-government.

According to Erik Erikson's (1963) stage theory of psychosocial development, the toddler is entering a period in which the psychological "conflict" to be resolved is that of autonomy versus shame and doubt. **Autonomy** means self-government or independence. Its development extends over a period from about 15 months to age 3 (see Figure 9.1).

During infancy, from birth to about 18 months, developing a sense of trust (versus mistrust) was the critical psychosocial task. A healthy sense of trust, derived from consistent and predictable nurturing, is perhaps the most important stage in psychosocial development. Its healthy development paves the way for the successful resolution of subsequent stages.

The development of a sense of autonomy in the toddler is facilitated and enhanced by a sturdy sense of trust developed during infancy. The psychosocial opposite of autonomy is shame or doubt. Adults assist toddlers in their strivings for autonomy when they recognize that the toddler needs to feel independent, self-sufficient, and capable. When this does not occur, shame and doubt may override the sense of autonomy. When shame and doubt exceed the sense of autonomy, children may exhibit an array of unhealthy feelings and inappropriate behaviors, including feelings of guilt and apology, self-consciousness, reluctance to try new things, and overdependence upon adults.

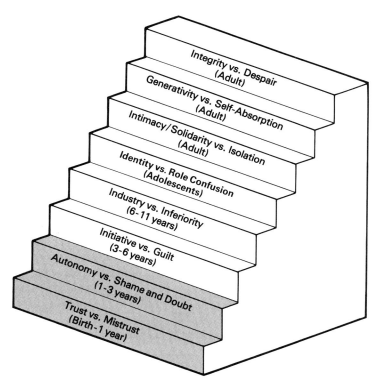

FIGURE 9.1
Development of a healthy sense of trust paves the way for successful resolution of the next stage of psychosocial development, that of autonomy.

*Adults assist toddlers in their striving for autonomy when they recognize toddlers'
needs to feel independent, self-sufficient, and capable.*

The challenge for adults who provide care for the toddler is to find that
important balance between meeting the toddler's needs for both dependence
and independence and for freedom and control. The toddler, on the one hand,
needs and wants to do things for himself. On the other hand, the toddler also
wants and needs the security-building presence, protection, and guidance of a
nurturing and supportive adult. Successes with locomotion and other motoric
efforts, the feeding process, toileting, play, choice-making, imitations of more
mature behaviors and activities, interactions with others, and so on enhance
the toddler's sense of autonomy.

As with other areas of development, adult responses to the toddler's efforts
to be autonomous that are overrestrictive, overprotective, or too permissive, or
that expect behavior or performance beyond the toddler's developmental capacities interfere with the developing sense of autonomy. When autonomy exceeds feelings of shame and doubt, the child develops a sense of adequacy,
competence, security, worthiness, and healthy self-acceptance.

Because toilet learning is a developmental milestone during this period, Erikson has related the developing sense of autonomy to it. The toddler soon
learns to utilize emerging physical skills of "holding" and "letting go" in bowel
and bladder control. For the toddler, there is a good sense of self-government

in this ability. However, recall that bowel and bladder control are not sufficiently developed for the toddler to always be successful. Yet, there is a genuine desire on the part of the toddler to please his caregivers. Adults who shame or exhibit frustration or anger at the child's inabilities or relapses will undermine the developing sense of autonomy. Instead, adults should encourage, praise, and take cues from the child.

Temperament

As we saw in Chapter 6, each child has his own unique way of feeling, thinking, and interacting with others. Temperament is the term generally used to reflect this uniqueness. Temperament is probably genetically determined, though certainly it influences and is influenced by the environment (Thomas, Chess, & Korn, 1982). Think of your own brothers, sisters, cousins or other relatives. What are the similarities and differences in their temperaments? Differences in temperament of individual children within the family are often noted with surprise, as parents marvel at how different one child is from his siblings. Mothers and fathers themselves exhibit unique temperaments.

Parents and other family members represent an amalgam of differing temperaments. Each member brings to the family different age-stage needs and reactions that influence the manner in which individual members respond to the unique temperaments of the toddler in the family.

Earlier chapters describe the backgrounds of experience that the parents of Angela and Jeremy bring to the parent-child relationship. The quality of their own childhood experiences, the relationships with their parents and other family members, and the role models that were available to them influence the perceptions they have of themselves and of their roles as parents. Knowledge of child growth and development plays a critical role in this regard. The interplay of all of these factors influences the individual temperaments and responses of the parents and the child.

■ Cheryl—young, single, and still an adolescent—has her own set of developmental needs typical of most adolescent girls. In addition to her needs relating to obtaining and maintaining support networks to assist her in nurturing Angela, she has needs relating to learning about and gaining satisfaction in the role of mother and single parent, completing her education, participating in the social life of her age mates, and working through Erikson's fifth psychosocial stage, that of developing a sense of identity versus role confusion (Erikson, 1963). Participating in an extended family and projecting a future beyond high school are also tasks before her.

Jeremy's family also creates its own needs milieu. His parents, now in their thirties, are striving for success in individual and demanding careers. They seek social and economic upward mobility, which has become demanding in terms of time, energy, and allocation of family resources. Their needs at this age-stage relate to maintaining an intellectually, emotionally, and physically satisfying relationship with one another; meshing career, civic, religious, and social desires and responsibilities; relating to extended family members; providing for an economically stable existence; and integrating all of this with their plans for Jeremy and possibly additional children.

James, low-key and affectionate, enjoys holding Angela on his lap and looking at and reading books with her. His manner has an enjoyably calming effect upon Angela, and she responds by seeking to be held by him the moment he arrives for his visits. Knowing that he enjoys reading to her, Angela scurries off to obtain a book—any book—to offer to him. Sometimes, James greets her with, "Go get a book," whereupon she promptly and happily obliges.

Angela is outgoing, affectionate, observant, and quite verbal, as she names many objects and people in her environment. Though unable to sustain attention for more than a few minutes, she seems to need and enjoy the sustained interaction with James and with the books they share. In anticipating her interest, James encourages Angela's autonomy by sending her to fetch a book. Angela, on the other hand, has learned how to seek and hold James' attention. Thus, her developing sense of autonomy, along with her own temperament, is becoming enmeshed with the temperament and personality of her father.

Cheryl, on the other hand, is more inclined to engage in physically active interactions with Angela. She may chase Angela about the house, play hide and seek, take her on outings, walk about the neighborhood with her, and dance and sing with her to music from the television. They especially enjoy playing pantomime "copycat" games with one another. Angela has learned when and how to engage her mother in these playful moments, which can be quite emotionally satisfying to both of them. James and Cheryl each relate to Angela in different ways, each bringing to the interactions their unique personalities and skills. Yet, while quite different in their interactions with Angela, they are complementary. ■

Egocentrism

The toddler's behavior is punctuated with assumptions, faulty though they may be, that others feel, see, and hear the same things he does. Inability to share is related to this thinking and is expected behavior at this stage. A coveted toy possessed by another may be proclaimed "Mine!" The toddler who says to his mother, when observing her nursing a younger sibling, "Does her have a mommy?" is demonstrating a lack of perspective beyond his own experiences. The 3-year-old who attempts to console a crying nursery school friend with his own fuzzy blanket assumes his friend can be comforted as he is by this particular transitional object.

Egocentrism characterizes both the cognitive abilities of toddlers (Piaget, 1952) and their psychosocial development (Erikson, 1963). Piaget theorized that, during the preoperational period of cognitive development, the child can only view the world from his own perspective and is unable to appreciate another's point of view. While it is true that egocentrism characterizes the toddler's way of thinking, a growing body of evidence now suggests that young

Egocentrism—the tendency to view the world from one's own perspective; the inability to see another point of view.

children may not be as egocentric as was once believed. Studies of prosocial behaviors and empathy in young children have begun to modify our thinking about egocentrism.

Prosocial Behaviors

Prosocial behavior—behavior that benefits others—helping, sharing, comforting, and defending.

Kindness, sympathy, generosity, helpfulness, and distress at injustice or cruelty are behaviors not atypical in young children. Psychologists refer to these as **prosocial behaviors**, for they are intended to benefit or help others without expectation of reward.

Children before the age of 3 have been observed demonstrating prosocial behaviors through sharing, helping, and cooperating (Leung & Rheingold, 1981; Zahn-Waxler, Radke-Yarrow, & King, 1979). Researchers have studied comforting, defending, and protective behaviors in preschool children (Zahn-Waxler et al., 1979). These studies and others have led psychologists to believe that very young children are not as egocentric as Piaget's theory suggests.

Prosocial behaviors in toddlers are most likely to occur during pretend play (Bar-Tal, Raviv, & Goldberg, 1982) and occur with greater frequency as the child's opportunities for interactions with others increases (Rubin & Everett, 1982). Growing cognitive abilities contribute to the child's abilities to view situations from the perspective of others. More mature levels of thinking enhance **perspective-taking** abilities and **empathy**.

Perspective-taking—the ability to understand another's point of view.

Empathy—involves experiencing the feelings or emotions that someone else is experiencing.

Prosocial behaviors are also influenced by behaviors that are modeled by others. Parents and caregivers who demonstrate helpfulness, altruism, cooperation, sympathy, and other prosocial attributes are providing powerful examples for the toddler. Guidance and discipline strategies with young children also affect the development of prosocial behaviors. Guidance that is empathic, supportive, reasonable, and explained assists the toddler in his understanding of social interactions.

■ Jeremy's teacher had asked him to sit by her and talk about the unfortunate encounter he just had with a playmate over the use of a puzzle. Both children wanted to work the puzzle, but not together. Jeremy was asked how he thought his friend felt when he hit her. He was also asked to think about what he might do about the situation now that she was crying and hurt. His response was not exactly what the teacher sought, but revealing nevertheless, when he replied, "I think you better watch me, 'cause I think I'm going to hit her again." ■

Like Jeremy, toddlers need adults to help them control their impulses. Adults who say, "I can't let you hit Shannon; hitting hurts people," are helping the still egocentric toddler to think about the other person. This guidance should be supportive of each child in the encounter. Blaming and punishing only serve to reinforce negative behaviors and do not provide the child with alternative prosocial options.

Toddlers' spontaneous attempts to share, help, or cooperate should be reinforced through positive recognition and responses. "Shannon feels better now that you are friends again." "That was kind of you to get Shannon a puzzle like yours." "That was very helpful for you to put the blocks away with Josh." Such verbal responses, while providing positive feedback and reinforcement, also provide labels for expected and prosocial behaviors. With these labels, the child grows in understanding and appreciation of the views and needs of others.

Development of Self-Concept and Self-Esteem

The idea of self-concept is derived from the theories of Carl Rogers (1961), Abraham Maslow (1970), and other humanistic personality theorists. The **self-concept** is the summary definition the child devises of himself; it represents an awareness of oneself as a separate and unique individual. The self-concept is derived from interactions with others, the child's interpretation of those interactions, and the child's ability to accept or negate positive or negative feedback from those interactions. For the most part, the manner in which others respond to and relate to the child determines the self-concept that the child will devise.

Self-concept— one's sense of oneself as separate and uniquely different from others.

The self-concept is dynamic, in that it changes over time and through additional experiences and understandings. Generally, the development of the self-concept is comprised of four accomplishments: (1) self-awareness, (2) self-recognition, (3) self-definition, and (4) self-esteem.

Self-awareness occurs as infants begin to realize that they are distinct and separate from others and that objects are not extensions of themselves. Margaret Mahler (1968), a Freudian psychologist, refers to the emerging independence of the infant and toddler as "separation and individuation." This process takes place around the fourth and fifth month and continues to age 3. Its first stages reflect the infant's growing awareness of separateness, and the latter stages are characterized by the toddler's ambivalence over dependence and a desire for independence. Mahler proposes that mother-child interactions during this process are critical to the self-concept that will emerge.

Self-awareness— refers to infants' perceptions of themselves as distinct and separate from other people and objects.

Self-recognition refers to the infant's ability to recognize himself in a mirror, photograph, or other form (Lewis & Brooks, 1978). This ability seems to parallel the cognitive achievement of object permanence, when the child can form and hold mental images. It is usually evident by the age of 18 months, and by age 2, most children can distinguish their own from someone else's picture (Lewis & Brooks-Gunn, 1979).

Self-recognition— the infant's ability to recognize his or her image in a mirror, photograph, or other representation.

Self-definition occurs as children begin to use language to describe themselves. The toddler's growing awareness of his age, size, gender, and skills assist the child in this definition. This development is observed when young children take pride in telling you how old they are. Holding up 2, 3, or 4 fingers and exclaiming, "I am 3" is an attempt to define oneself. As well, when children invite attention with "Watch me!" they are demonstrating the skills by which they are defining themselves. "I can reach it"; "Watch me jump"; "I am big"; and so on, are verbal clues to the emerging self-concept.

Self-definition— refers to the criteria by which the self is defined; e.g., age, size, and physical and mental abilities.

Toddlers develop positive self-concepts when adults respond to them in affirmative ways. When efforts at independence, self-help, and social interactions are facilitated by sensitive adults, the toddler's self-concept is enhanced. Adult words and interactions that convey acceptance and respect for the developing person encourage a positive sense of self.

Children who perceive themselves as loved, valued, worthy, and competent develop healthy **self-esteem**. As children's interactional opportunities expand, self-evaluations naturally occur. Healthy self-esteem assures that these evaluations weigh more heavily on the positive than on the negative side.

Self-esteem—one's positive or negative self-evaluation.

Gender Identity

Most children are able to proclaim that they are a boy or a girl by age $2\frac{1}{2}$ to 3. This represents gender identity. Gender identity has both biological and environmental origins. Biological determinants at conception predetermine whether the child will be male or female. Environmentally, the hopes and aspirations of mothers, fathers, and other relatives set the stage for gender identity and for gender role expectations.

Environmental influences on gender identity often begin during prenatal development, when sonogram examinations reveal the sex of the fetus. Parents begin to "think pink or blue" and anticipate and prepare for the expected boy or girl baby. Name, clothes, toys, crib, nursery, and other arrangements suggest the baby's gender. Conversations reveal anticipated behaviors and **gender role** expectations as parents project their roles as parents of a boy or a girl.

Gender role—the public expression of one's gender identity.

The newborn is thus subjected to pre-existing gender related expectations, but despite all the gender-specific planning on the part of parents, there is very little difference in the behaviors of girls and boys during the first year (Fagot & Kronsberg, 1982). During the second year, play behaviors begin to reveal differences between boys and girls, much of which is stereotypical and perhaps derived from gender-specific experiences provided by the parents. Perhaps parents tend to be more gentle and cuddling with girls and more "rough and tumble" with boys; parents may talk more softly and gently to girls and more directly to boys. Toy preferences are particularly indicative, as boys tend to play with transportation toys, blocks, and manipulatives. Girls choose soft toys and dolls and enjoy dressing up and dancing (Fagot, 1974, 1978). Perhaps these play choices reflect the types of toys parents have provided for their boys or girls.

Gender constancy—the realization that one's gender remains the same regardless of age or changes in clothing, hairstyles, or wishes.

It is not unusual for toddlers to assume that their biological sex can change; that is, that boys can grow up to become mothers and girls can grow up to be fathers. This thinking demonstrates a lack of gender constancy. **Gender constancy** is the realization that one's sex does not change over time or as a result of changes in hairstyle, clothing, or other outward characteristics. Gender constancy is not expected to occur until age 5 to 7 (Kohlberg, 1966).

While gender itself is biologically determined, both gender identity and gender role are influenced to a great extent by important people in the child's life.

Parents, siblings, child caregivers, and others impose certain gender standards and expectations upon young children. Parents seem to impose more stringent gender role expectations upon boys than upon girls (Forman, Hatznecker, & Dunn, 1983). Toddlers tend to imitate the parent of the same sex, and when gender role behaviors are deemed appropriate, parents provide positive feedback. On the other hand, when the behavior is deemed gender inappropriate, parents tend to intervene. Many a preschool teacher has been approached by an anxious father wanting to know why his young son is playing with dolls in the dramatic play center. Yet, few, if any, mothers inquire about their daughters play with trucks in the block center. From a developmental perspective, either play choice is sound and in no way threatens the gender identity of the child.

The fact that boys are often allowed to be more active and aggressive than girls has both environmental and possibly biological antecedents. Are boys just naturally more active and aggressive than girls? Or do standards for and expectations of certain behaviors vary between boys and girls, resulting in boys and girls simply being treated differently? Again, studies (Fagot, 1982; Fagot & Kronsberg, 1982) suggest that there are gender differences in responding to aggressive behaviors of boys and of girls. At the same time the difference in assertiveness and aggressiveness in boys and girls at age 2 to $2\frac{1}{2}$ may well be related to constitutional and temperamental differences in boys and girls at that age (Forman, Hetznecker, & Dunn, 1983).

Psychologists and educators are encouraging less gender stereotyping in the child's early experiences with children's books, toys, television programming, and adult expectations. Boys can certainly be allowed to show feelings, to nurture and be nurtured, and to participate in a range of activities both "gentle" and "rough." Girls can be encouraged to pursue physical activities and to assert themselves in constructive and positive ways. Neither of these efforts need be viewed as endangering gender role behaviors at later ages. Congruence, though never absolute between gender identity and gender role expectations, occurs as children experience a broad range of both feminine and masculine situations and as role models provide healthy and satisfying gender acceptance.

Racial Awareness

There are a number of processes to be examined in the study of childhood responses to racial differences. Ramsey (1987) delineates these processes as perceptual awareness, valuative concepts, racial identification, racial preferences, behaviors toward other races, and knowledge of racial differences.

Ramsey's categories illustrate that the development of racial awareness, understanding, and acceptance is complex. Researchers have attempted to address racial awareness from these various perspectives, though research on infant and toddler racial awareness seems limited. There is evidence that racial awareness has its origins before age 3 (Katz, 1976, 1982). There is further evidence that earliest experiences and learnings about race result in attitudes that persist into later years (Katz, 1982).

During the toddler period, racial awareness is dominated by perception of superficial features. Children begin to make distinctions between darker skins and lighter ones as early as age 3, though labeling is often inaccurate (Williams & Moreland, 1976). By age 3 to 4, children apply conventional labels of black and white to pictures, dolls, and people (Katz, 1976). Young children also attend to facial features, hair colors, textures and styles, clothing and voice and speech patterns. However, racial-group referenced identities do not develop until between age 3 and 8 (Ramsey, 1987). Mature forms of racial awareness, which do not rely upon superficial features, but depend upon deeper understandings of ethnicity, do not emerge until age 9 or 10 (Aboud, 1988).

The toddler's primary source of information about race is the family. Within the family racial pride is fostered, and racial attitudes are transmitted. Children learn about race when their child care arrangements provide experiences with children and adults of other races and cultural groups. Toys, books, and television, as well, impart knowledge and attitudes toward race. While recent years have seen improvements in the accuracy with which diverse races and cultural groups are portrayed in children's books, toys, and the media, there is still a need to monitor these sources of information to assure accurate and positive portrayals. The toddler's own racial identity and valuative and preferential behaviors depend upon accurate information and sensitive guidance.

Moral Development

Moral behavior—the ability to consider the needs and welfare of others and exhibit appropriate behaviors consistent with a set of standards or value orientation.

Moral behavior is most often described as the ability to consider the needs and welfare of others. People who are thought to be "moral" exhibit such behaviors as honesty, dependability, helpfulness, and fairness. These individuals do not steal from others or physically hurt or emotionally abuse others. They do not betray trusts and are loyal to their family, friends, and commitments. In short, these people have a personal morality that guides their behaviors. These behaviors represent moral values, reasoning, judgments, and actions.

Cognitive and social development and experiences are necessary for the development of moral reasoning and judgment. The conscience also plays a role in moral development. Moral values, reasoning, judgment, and conscience rely upon certain levels of maturity and experience for their realization.

Piaget (1965) and Kohlberg (1968) have each proposed developmental sequences for moral reasoning and judgment. These theorists based their conclusions on studies of children beyond the infant/toddler ages, but their theories can offer insight into the infant/toddler period. These theories are described more fully in Chapters 12 and 15.

Moral development has origins in infant (1) intellectual development; (2) social cognition—the manner in which children perceive the behaviors of others and their own interactions with others; (3) adult socialization efforts—whereby adult values, standards and expectations are imposed upon the child; and (4) the pleasant results of prosocial behaviors. Piaget (1965) emphasized both cognitive development and social experiences as precursors to moral thinking, reasoning and judgments. Piaget associates moral development in children with emerging abilities to interpret rules.

For very young children, notions of right or wrong are just being formulated, and most "rules" are just being introduced. Since moral values are learned, infants and toddlers are thought to be **premoral**. The premoral child is guided by external rules and expectations of obedience, rather than an internal system of values, beliefs, or understandings. The premoral child comes to think of good or bad in terms of doing what one is told to do. "Moral behaviors" (obedience) are motivated by the expectation of rewards (praise and attention) or the avoidance of punishment (having a toy or privilege taken away).

Premoral—that period in early childhood when the child is unaware of moral rules or values.

Unlike the better-known theories of Piaget and Kohlberg, Hoffman (1988) has advanced a theory that provides further insights into the beginnings of moral behavior. Hoffman projects an "empathy scheme" in which motivation to behave in moral ways is prompted by empathic feelings, particularly "empathic distress" (Hoffman, 1988, p. 509).

Empathy is defined by Hoffman as "a vicarious affective response that is more appropriate to someone else's situation than to one's own" (Hoffman, 1988, p. 509). Empathy includes both affective and cognitive aspects, with the level of empathy depending to some extent upon the child's level of cognition. Toddlers, for instance, may respond empathically to another's distress, but lack sufficient knowledge and experience to fully grasp the whole situation.

Hoffman describes four developmental levels of empathic distress: global empathy, egocentric empathy, empathy for another's feelings, and empathy for another's life condition. The first three levels have implications for the study of infant/toddler behaviors. The following description of these stages has been adapted from Hoffman (1988, pp. 497–548).

Global empathic distress is observed in infants during the first year. Because of the infant's inadequate self-other distinction, the child will respond to distress cues from others, such as another child's crying, as though the discomfort were his own. Self-comforting strategies such as seeking mother or thumbsucking are employed; such behaviors would have been employed anyway, had the distress truly been his.

Egocentric empathy occurs in the second year during which a sense of the other emerges as distinct from the self. At this level, the toddler is aware that the other person is in distress, but is not capable of understanding the internal states of the person in distress. The toddler then, inaccurately, assumes that the distressed person's feelings and needs are his own. Hoffman cites an 18-month-old boy who fetched his own mother to comfort a crying friend although the friend's mother was present.

Around age 2 or 3, the child becomes aware that other's feelings are different from his own and thus exhibits the third level of Hoffman's scheme, that of empathy for another's feelings. The fourth level, empathy for another's life condition, does not occur until later in childhood. At this level, the child can appreciate the larger life contexts in which distress occurs.

This sequence seems particularly helpful in understanding psychosocial origins of moral development. The adult's role in the socialization process should be to recognize the egocentric perspective of the toddler as he attempts

Toddlers often exhibit an awareness of the feelings of others, though they may lack sufficient knowledge and experience to fully understand those feelings.

to address the "welfare of others," not an easy task with limited cognitive abilities and social experience.

Development of Self-Control

Self-control—*the ability to govern one's own behavior.*

An important goal in child growth and development is that of **self-control**. This is a long-term goal, for self-control develops over a period of many years. For the most part, self-control is learned behavior. It is dependent upon external controls at first, then gradually the individual assumes more and more responsibility for his own behaviors. In very young children, this process is not a smooth one—self-control emerges haltingly. Marion (1991) lists the following as indicators of self-control in children: (1) control of impulses, (2) tolerance of frustration, (3) the ability to postpone immediate gratification, and (4) the initiation of a plan that is carried out over a period of time.

As with other areas of psychosocial development, cognition and social experiences both play a role in the development of self-control. Marion (1991, pp. 198–199) provides a sequence for the development of self-control. A summary of that sequence follows:

Birth to approximately 12 months: Voluntary motor acts evolve from earlier reflex activity. This activity can be modulated, but not always consciously.

12 months to about 24 months: Control of walking, running, and other motor activities makes it possible for the child to respond to the demands of adults ("Come here." "Stop running." "Take this to Mommy.") More sophisticated communication skills facilitate the child's understandings of adult instructions and modeling. Children at this age are "susceptible" to control by others.

Approximately 24 months: Actual beginnings of self-control due to the ability to recall instructions and behaviors; however, self-control is quite limited at this age.

Approximately 36 months: With age, the ability to delay gratification begins to emerge. This is one of the characteristics of self-control.

Toddlers can be assisted in their development of self-control if adults use developmentally appropriate teaching and guidance techniques. The following are suggestions for maximizing self-control in very young children:

1. Provide an environment in which the child's growing sense of autonomy can flourish with:
   - play items and experiences that are engaging and enriching
   - low open shelves for personal and play items
   - adequate space for the use, storage, and retrieval of personal and play items
   - safe and sturdy furnishings and toys
   - dangerous and off-limit items out of sight and reach.
2. Provide an atmosphere in which the toddler is encouraged to explore and discover, but one that is in keeping with the child's developmental capacities and free of inappropriate expectations and pressures to perform.
3. Provide a daily schedule that is predictable so that the toddler can sense its rhythms and anticipate and respond appropriately to regular events: mealtime, bathtime, naptime, storytime, etc.
4. Set limits for behavior that are consistent, reasonable, and fair and are enforced in supportive, yet predictable ways.
5. Meet the toddler's needs for food, clothing, rest, and attention expeditiously. Adults who impose undue delays on toddlers fail to recognize their inability to delay gratifications and to tolerate frustrations.

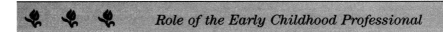

Enhancing Psychosocial Development in Children Ages 1 Through 3

1. Recognize the role of the adult model in directing the course of psychosocial development in young children.
2. Understand toddler egocentrism.
3. Facilitate autonomy by providing safe surroundings and reasonable limits.
4. Provide positive, predictable, supportive discipline.
5. Understand the toddler's continuing dependency and need for security and protection.
6. Encourage and facilitate play opportunities with other children.
7. Promote self-esteem through sensitive and accurate responses to questions about race and gender.
8. Provide developmentally appropriate books, toys, and media events to enhance understandings of self and others.

Factors Influencing Psychosocial Development

It is clear that a number of factors influence psychosocial development in children. The child's unique temperament and personality affects and is affected by others. The quality and quantity of these early interactions affirm or discredit the child's emerging sense of self and self-esteem.

The manner in which parents and caregivers respond to the toddler's need for autonomy is critical to healthy psychosocial development. Guidance and discipline techniques should be consistent, predictable, logical, and supportive. Toddlers need the security of a guidance system that nurtures their growing independence, while recognizing their continuing needs for rules, limits, and protection.

Interactions with siblings and age-mates provide social experiences that lead to social understandings and a grasp of the feelings and intentions of others. Age-mate friendships between toddlers are transitory and short-lived, yet they provide experiences for the development of self-other distinctions.

Television and other media can be powerful tools in the development of race and gender attitudes and gender roles. Media events should be carefully monitored for their positive and appropriate role models and for the prosocial and moral values portrayed, for very young toddlers learn from the media and will imitate it.

Play interactions with adults or children and with developmentally appropriate toys enhance psychosocial development in toddlers. Through play, the toddler tries out a variety of social roles and emerging social skills. Language and cognition are enhanced, thus furthering the quality and quantity of social interactions. Through play, toddlers grow in a sense of competence and can resolve a number of fears and anxieties. In play, toddlers are also introduced to rules from which later behaviors may be self-regulated.

There are sociocultural factors in psychosocial development wherein children learn to appreciate their own and others' uniqueness. Racial awareness has its origins in these very early years. Feelings of self-esteem, family pride, acceptance, and respect for others are fostered in the home and in sensitive child care programs.

Children with delayed development, chronic disease, or handicapping conditions are especially in need of sound and supportive emotional or social interactions. Because these children can be more vulnerable to prolonged attachment behaviors, fears, anxieties, frustrations, and disappointments, self-concept development and healthy self-esteem can be at risk. Adults will need to be particularly sensitive to needs for assistance and encouragement in social situations and to the child's needs for opportunities to develop autonomy.

Key Terms

proximity seeking	self-concept
extrafamilial relationships	self-awareness
primary child caregiver	self-recognition
parallel play	self-definition
transitional object	self-esteem
autonomy	gender role
egocentrism	gender constancy
prosocial behavior	moral behavior
perspective-taking	premoral
empathy	self-control

Review Strategies/Activities

1. Take a survey of your classmates. How many recall ever having a transitional object? What was the object? For how long did they persist in their attachment to the transitional object? What does this survey illustrate about transitional objects?
2. Volunteer to assist in a program for toddlers for at least one day. In a journal, describe instances of prosocial behaviors. What preceded the response? How did the recipient respond? What followed the encounter?
3. Engage a 3-year-old in conversation. What clues does the child give about his or her self-perceptions regarding age, size, abilities, gender, race, friends, family, and so on. Be careful not to prompt or suggest expected answers.
4. In small groups, discuss how play enhances psychosocial development in toddlers. Share these discussions with the class.
5. Observe arrival and departure times at a childcare center. How do toddlers respond to their parents when they drop them off and arrive to take them home? How do parents respond? Ask the instructor to discuss what these behaviors mean in terms of attachments and separation anxieties.

Further Readings

Brazelton, T. B. (1984). *To listen to a child*. Understanding the normal problems of growing up. Menlo Park, CA: Addison-Wesley Publishing Company.

> Dr. Brazelton, a well-known pediatrician, discusses a number of common early childhood problems which often result in parental concerns. Topics such as fears and anxieties, loves, thumbsucking, independence, discipline, and many others are placed into a developmental perspective, providing a source of understanding for parents.

Marion, Marian (1991). *Guidance of Young Children* (3rd Ed.). Columbus, OH: Merrill.

> Written for both parents and teachers, this superb book reflects current research and thinking about guidance and discipline; social, moral, and prosocial development; and aggression in children, with very logical and practical guides for facilitating healthy psychosocial development in young children.

Powell, G. J., Yammamoto, J., Romero, A., & Morales, A. (Eds.). (1983). *The psychosocial development of minority group children*. New York: Brunner/Mazel.

> A scholarly and research-based reference, this book provides a comprehensive overview of psychosocial development of minority children. African-Americans, Hispanic-Americans, Asian-Americans, and Native-Americans are represented, along with some cultural subgroups, including Mexican-Americans, Puerto Ricans, Filipino-Americans, and Korean-Americans.

Lickona, T. (1983). *Raising good children: Helping your children through the stages of moral development—from birth through the teenage years*. New York: Bantam.

> This book covers many topics relating to moral development in children. The author's discussion of child development from birth through age 3 as a period in which foundations for moral development occur is particularly germane to the topics of this chapter.

CHAPTER 10

*Piaget's system requires that a child **act** in the environment if cognitive development is to proceed.*

Barry Wadsworth

*The major concepts applied to oral language development appear to apply to written language development as well. Children **actively** develop their own models of how written language works by purposely **interacting** with people and objects in their environment.*

Celia Genishi and Anne Dyson

Cognitive/Language/Literacy Development of the Young Child Ages 1 Through 3

After reading and studying this chapter, you will demonstrate comprehension by:

- Describing the cognitive development of children ages 1 through 3.
- Describing the oral language development of children ages 1 through 3.
- Describing the development of literacy of children ages 1 through 3.
- Identifying the factors influencing the cognitive/language/literacy development of children ages 1 through 3.
- Describing the role of the early childhood professional in promoting the cognitive/language/literacy development in children ages 1 through 3.

Between the ages of 1 and 3, there is a tremendous change in the development of young children. Children learn to walk and therefore can more readily explore the environment. This active exploration promotes the development of the young child's knowledge of the world. Simultaneously, this active exploration often involves interacting with others, who talk with young children about their actions, behaviors, and observations. Repeated actions associated with repeated verbalizations by others in the environment promote the development of cognition and language in the young child.

Reread the quotes at the beginning of this chapter. You will notice that the words *act*, *actively*, and *interacting* are highlighted. The themes of acting upon objects in the environment and interacting with others will be addressed throughout this chapter. Acting upon objects in the environment and interacting with others are the two prerequisites for cognitive/language/literacy development in the young child.

Piaget's Stages/Patterns of Cognitive Development

Young children ages 1 and 2 are still in the sensorimotor period of cognitive development. Around the end of the second year, young children move into what Piaget called the stage of preoperational intelligence. This section provides a discussion of the last two substages in the sensorimotor period and the beginnings of preoperational thought (see Table 10.1).

Sensorimotor Substages 5 and 6

Substage 5 usually occurs when young children are 12 to 18 months of age (Piaget & Inhelder, 1969). This substage is characterized by toddlers' use of **tertiary circular reactions**, or experimentation, more systematic imitation, and further development of object permanence.

Tertiary circular reactions—reactions in children between 12 and 18 months of age that indicate that the toddlers are experimenting in order to develop knowledge of the environment around them (Piaget's Substage 5 in the sensorimotor period).

■ Over a period of time, Jeremy has experimented with stacking foam blocks. Through trial and error and related experimentation, he has learned how to balance four of the blocks. Such activity provides Jeremy with the opportunity to learn about cause and effect. He can now begin to use trial and error to help him accomplish his goal.

Eventually, Jeremy's attempts at imitation become more accurate. On Friday evening, Bill and Ann decide to go out to eat while Phyllis has the weekend off. While they are waiting for their food, Bill claps his hands and says, "Jeremy, do this." Then Bill shakes his head and says, "Jeremy, do this." Their game continues with Bill and Ann noting that Jeremy's imitative responses were quicker and more accurate than they were the last time they played this game.

One evening when James visits, he brings Angela a ball that he has purchased from his earnings working part time in a fast-food restaurant. Angela, now eighteen months old, is delighted with the ball. James covers the ball with Angela's favorite blanket. Angela lifts the blanket and screams with delight when she sees the ball. When Angela is not looking, James hides the ball. She cannot find it. This behavior

TABLE 10.1
Piaget's sensorimotor stage during the second year of life

Substage	Age	Accomplishments
5: Tertiary Circular Reactions	12–18 months	Experiments with objects. Imitates accurately, needing little "trial and error." Thinks of objects as having permanence and searches for them where last seen.
6: Object Permanence	18–24 months	Works out solutions to problems mentally. Defers imitation. Comprehends object permanence and can even imagine movements of unseen objects.

is typical for toddlers of this age. While their understanding of object permanence allows them to search for an object, they still must observe the actual hiding of the object. They cannot find an object without seeing it hidden.   ■

Substage 6 usually occurs between 18 months and 2 years of age. This substage is characterized by the development of true object permanence, which also includes person permanence and representational intelligence.

True object permanence indicates that toddlers can search for objects that they did not see hidden. Following is a frequently cited example of true object permanence as demonstrated by Piaget's daughter, Jacqueline:

> Observation 64.—AT 1;7(20) Jacqueline watches me when I put a coin in my hand, then put my hand under a coverlet. I withdraw my hand closed; Jacqueline opens it, then searches under the coverlet until she finds the object. I take back the coin at once, put it in my hand and slip my closed hand under a cushion situation at the other side (on her left and no longer on her right); Jacqueline immediately searches for the object under the cushion. I repeat the experiment by hiding the coin under a jacket; Jacqueline finds it without hesitation.
>
> II. I complicate the test as follows: I place the coin in my hand, then my hand under the cushion. I bring it forth closed and immediately hide it under the coverlet. Finally, I withdraw it and hold it out, closed, to Jacqueline. Jacqueline then pushes my hand aside without opening it (she guesses that there is nothing in it, which is new), she looks under the cushion, then directly under the coverlet where she finds the object. . . .
>
> I then try a series of three displacements: I put the coin in my hand and move my closed hand sequentially from A to B and from B to C: Jacqueline sets my hand aside, then searches in A, in B and finally in C.*

Thus, according to Piaget, children in this stage of development now realize that objects and people have an identity of their own and continue to exist even when the toddler is not present. As mentioned in Chapter 7, Bower (1982) suggests that it is maturing spatial perception that causes children in this age range to search for objects, rather than the development of object permanence. In any event, most young children around 2 years of age develop the ability to think about events, physical objects, and people that are not immediately in their presence. This ability sets the stage for rapid cognitive development and language development, which will be described later in this chapter.

Young children in this substage can now solve problems in their minds (representational intelligence) without the aid of sensorimotor trial and error. The following vignette indicates that Jeremy does not always have to experiment to find a solution.

■ Jeremy tries to place a triangular shape into the appropriate opening in a three-dimensional puzzle. The puzzle slips and Jeremy misses the opening. He immediately uprights the puzzle and holds it with one hand while using the other hand to insert

---

*From *The Construction of Reality in the Child*, by Jean Piaget, translated by Margaret Cook. Copyright 1954 by Basic Books, Inc. Reprinted by permission of Basic Books, Inc., Publishers, New York.

Young children's participation in games such as "peek-a-boo" indicates that object permanence is developing.

Deferred imitation—the child's ability to imitate behaviors observed at an earlier time or another place—occurs near the end of the sensorimotor stage.

the piece into the appropriate opening. Jeremy's ability to upright the puzzle and secure it with one hand indicates that through his action on objects during the sensorimotor stage, he internalized information about what to do in various situations. He uses this representational intelligence to help him complete his goal of putting the shape through the opening. ■

Children at this stage of development are also able to imitate behavior they have observed at another time. Piaget called this **deferred imitation** (Piaget, 1952, 1962). For example, Angela picks up the remote control for the TV and pretends she is talking on the phone. She does this when no one has been talking on the phone for several hours.

Transition to Preoperational Stage

Children at the end of the sensorimotor period generally understand that objects have certain basic characteristics and that these objects continue to exist even when the object is out of sight. Children at this point are able to carry a mental image of the object. This development sets the stage for learning further concepts about the social and physical world. These abilities, coupled with the increasing use of symbols through language and play, facilitate the child's transition into Piaget's next period of cognitive development, the preoperational stage.

Preoperational Stage

The **preoperational stage** of cognitive development extends from 2 to approximately 8 years of age. This section focuses upon 2- and 3-year-olds at the beginning of this stage. Part V of this text will address later preoperational behaviors.

Preoperational— the second of Piaget's stages of cognitive development, in which children from the ages of 2 to approximately 8 develop the ability to internally represent sensorimotor actions, but cannot engage in the operational or logical thinking of older children and adults.

People do not move from one cognitive developmental stage to another at any definite time. Rather, behaviors in and out of various stages are common throughout life. For example, driving a car is essentially a sensorimotor experience. Similarly, adults often find it necessary to engage in some sort of trial and error behaviors of substage 5 when tending to automobile and household repairs.

According to Piaget (1952), preoperational children are not capable of operational or logical thinking. Logical operational thinking involves the ability to reverse a mental action. For example, the process of addition is reversible through subtraction. While most older children and adults understand this process, preoperational children do not. However, this inability to reverse thought should not suggest that young children are deficient in their thinking. They are not. They are *different* in their thinking from older children and adults. Learning about this difference in young children's thinking is a fascinating process. Adults who understand and appreciate this stage in cognitive development in young children are likely to relate to young children in more appropriate ways than adults who do not. Knowledge of preoperational thought helps explain young children's behaviors. Viewing preoperational behavior as normal helps teachers and parents use developmentally appropriate learning and management strategies with young children.

Piaget's studies have demonstrated that young children's thinking cannot be simply explained as immature or based on lack of experience. Rather the young child's thought patterns or cognitive processes are uniquely different from those of older children and adults. Remember how Piaget became intrigued with young children's answers while he was helping Binet norm his intelligence test? Piaget noticed that young children gave amazingly similar incorrect answers to the questions. This behavior motivated Piaget to research the idea that young children's thinking is not just immature adult thinking, but is qualitatively different. His research and the research of others has substantiated his hypothesis.

The realization that young children's thinking is different from older children and adult thinking has provided a basis for the field of early childhood education. This awareness is reflected in the increasing number of states that require adults who want to work with children to take specialized courses in the development and learning of young children if they are to be certified to teach young children. Early childhood professionals must know and understand young children's thought processes if they are to be effective in helping young children develop and learn.

Mental symbols— the behaviors that occur at the beginning of the preoperational stage, including speech, imitation of others, and using one object to represent another.

Young preoperational children continue to develop the ability to use **mental symbols** such as language, play, and dreams (Piaget, 1962). Language and the use of words to represent objects will be discussed later in this chapter. The imitation of adult roles and the creation and use of mental symbols through play is indicated in the following vignette.

■ Jeremy has had the opportunity to observe the city sanitation workers collecting the trash around his neighborhood on his walks with Phyllis. After observing this process for several weeks, he one day begins to dump all his toys on his bunk bed. Between loads, he presses the bolts at the end of his bed to "grind up the trash." Through Jeremy's play, he imitates the adult behaviors of the sanitation workers and uses the bolts on his bed to represent the buttons the sanitation workers use on their truck. ■

As mentioned earlier, Piaget's studies indicate that the thinking of children in the early preoperational stage is different from that of older children and adults. These differences are reflected in the young child's reasoning, idiosyncratic concepts, and egocentric behaviors (Piaget, 1952).

Transductive reasoning—according to Piaget, reasoning that occurs in the preoperational stage and involves the young child's attention to the specifics of the immediate situation rather than all aspects of an event.

Maybe you can think of some comments that young children have made that are indicative of their unique reasoning. Often these remarks are described as "cute," "humorous," or "off the wall." Their **transductive reasoning** can be described as attending to only one of a number of aspects in a situation, or confusing general and specific events. Transductive reasoning can, at times, lead to appropriate conclusions. However, much of the transductive reasoning of the young preoperational child leads to inappropriate conclusions, as indicated in the following vignette about Jeremy.

■ Jeremy and his parents visit Bill's relatives for the holidays. Bill's brother's family is also there. After dinner, Great Aunt Sarah gives the children their gifts. Jeremy's 3-year-old cousin Matthew receives several presents, while Jeremy is given only one present. Aunt Sarah has spent approximately equal amounts of money on both children, thinking that she was being careful to show no partiality to either child. As is typical of the young preoperational child, Jeremy attends to the specifics—the number of presents—because the more overall or general thinking of the cost is not within his range of conceptual development. Jeremy becomes upset because cousin Matthew "gots more presents." Aunt Sarah tells Bill and Ann that next year she will get the boys the same number of presents and make them the same or very similar. An awareness of young children's thought processes can prevent such situations from occurring.

Idiosyncratic concepts are concepts relating to personal experience that are often overgeneralized to other contexts. Jeremy was awakening at night with dreams of ghosts and monsters. In her training to become a nanny, Phyllis had learned that young children blend fantasy with reality. She knew that Jeremy's dreams were real to him. For this reason, she did *not* say, "Jeremy, there are no ghosts or monsters. They are pretend." Instead, she comforted him and reassured him that she and his parents were there at night to keep him safe. Phyllis told Jeremy that they would not let the ghosts and monsters hurt him. After these disturbing dreams continued for several more weeks, Phyllis had another idea, which she thought might help Jeremy. She asked him what he thought could be done to keep the ghosts and monsters out of his room. Jeremy thought for a moment and then said, "Get a sign that says 'Stop. All ghosts and monsters keep out.'" Phyllis got some paper and crayons and drew a sign with that message. She and Jeremy then posted the sign on his door.

Idiosyncratic concepts—ideas of the preoperational child that are based on personal experience and overgeneralized to other situations.

Jeremy used his past experience with signs in other contexts and overgeneralized its use to meet his personal experiences. Phyllis did not impose adult problem solving and reasoning upon Jeremy but allowed him to problem solve at his cognitive level. As Jeremy prepares for sleep, Bill, Ann, and Phyllis remind him that they are there to keep him safe and that there is a sign on his door telling the monsters and ghosts to "keep out." During the next few weeks, Jeremy's sleep seems more peaceful and less filled with nightmares.   ■

Egocentrism means "centered on self." Piaget (1952, 1962, 1969) found that young children view situations from their perspective and do not seem to be able to consider the thoughts and feelings of others. He suggested that through interactions with other children and adults, egocentric thought becomes more socialized. Piaget also thought that conflict was beneficial, as confrontations could force children to see another's point of view.

■ Angela's teacher takes the 3-year-olds outside to play. Angela and two other children begin to play in the sand pile. Angela grabs a sifter from one of the children. This child stares at Angela and then leaves the sand area. After several minutes, Angela tries to take a large bucket from another child named Cedrick. He firmly grasps the bucket and refuses to let her have it. Angela then begins hitting Cedrick, and he runs crying to the teacher. The teacher calmly asks Cedrick what happened. He takes her hand and leads her to the sand box, telling her that Angela took his bucket and hit him. Angela's teacher asks Cedrick to tell Angela why he was crying and the teacher repeats what Cedrick tells her. Calmly and objectively, the teacher describes the consequences of Angela's behavior. "Angela hit Cedrick. Hitting hurts. Cedrick feels bad and is crying. He said he had the bucket first. Here is another big bucket for you, Angela. We have lots of big buckets in our sand pile."

Angela's teacher understands that egocentric behavior is normal for 3-year-olds. Therefore, she does not convey to Angela that she is "a bad girl" for hitting Cedrick. Rather, she repeats what Cedrick says, describing her behavior and the consequences of her actions. The teachers have organized the environment so that there are many duplicate materials, including several big buckets in the sand pile.

Duplicate items, such as several buckets in the sand pile, provide opportunities for children to continue their activities without interruption by other children who want or need similar materials.

They know that children at this age can become easily frustrated if they see and want something that another child has. Multiple materials can prevent the interruption in children's concrete activity and can promote problem-solving skills. When it is not possible to duplicate materials, teachers can promote more socialized behavior by reinforcing children's concerns. "Cedrick said he had the big bucket first. He still wants to use it. When he is done Cedrick will give it to you." The teacher then observes carefully to make sure Cedrick eventually shares the bucket with Angela. ■

Beyond Piaget's Theory

■ Angela is playing in the sociodramatic center of her childcare center classroom. She dumps plastic fruit out of a wooden bowl. As she turns the bowl over, its

inverted shape seems to suggest that it could become a hat. Angela takes the bowl
and with considerable force places it on Maria's head, causing Maria to cry. Angela
looks very surprised at Maria's reaction. She pats Maria and tries to comfort her.
Angela's teacher observes this interaction and tells Maria that Angela did not mean
to hurt her. Ms. Ruiz puts Maria on her lap and attempts to calm her. Angela
observes Maria and then goes to her cubbyhole, pulls out her "blanky" and gives it
to Maria.   ■

Similar behaviors by other young preoperational children have caused observant teachers, parents, and researchers to question Piaget's notion of egocentrism. Angela's behavior appears to indicate that she empathized with Maria.
She tried to comfort her through her gentle pats and by bringing her the blanket.

A number of studies have documented that under certain conditions, young
children have demonstrated that they are not completely egocentric. As indicated in Chapter 8, one of the earliest studies examining Piaget's notion of
egocentrism in very young children was by Yarrow and Zahn-Waxler (1977).
After examining 1500 incidents, they determined that children as young as 1
year old demonstrate compassion and other types of prosocial behavior. Other
researchers have modified Piaget's well-known mountain experiment (Piaget &
Inhelder, 1967) as a basis for demonstrating that young children are not completely egocentric. In Piaget's experiment, a three-dimensional model of three
mountains was used. These three mountains were different in appearance. One
had snow on it, the second had a house on it, and the third had a red cross on
it. Children were seated at a table in front of the model of the mountains. The
experimenter then positioned a doll at various locations on the mountains.
Children were then asked to select a picture that showed the doll's perspective.
Most children usually selected a card that showed their own perspective rather
than that of the doll. Piaget reasoned that these behaviors indicated that young
children were egocentric because they could not take on the perspective of
someone else.

In several experiments, Hughes and Donaldson (Borke, 1983; Donaldson,
1979; Donaldson, 1983; Hughes & Donaldson, 1983) determined that if tasks
were more appropriate and familiar to young children, they were capable of
taking the perspective of other people. Using such props as a toy policeman,
"Grover" from Sesame Street, a car, boats, and animals, the children were able
to take the viewpoint of another. Eighty-eight percent of the 3-year-olds
(Hughes & Donaldson, 1983) and 80 percent of three- and four-year-olds
(Borke, 1983) were able to see another's point of view.

Gelman and Gallistel (1983), in a study involving a "magic task," explored
young children's conservation of number. Piaget's experiments indicated that
if there are two rows with the same number of objects and one row is length-
ened, the preoperational child will say that there are more objects in the longer
row. In the "magic task," children were not asked to distinguish between more
and less, which are very abstract terms for young children. Rather, the children
were asked to choose a winner or loser in a number of conservation experi-

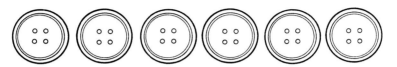

FIGURE 10.1
*Piaget's experiments indicated that the preoperational child will say that
there are more objects in the longer array. Recent research using more
relevant questions and tasks suggests that many 3-year-olds can conserve.*
(Gelman & Gallistel, 1983).

ments (see Figure 10.1). Ninety-one percent of the 3-year-olds were able to
conserve when presented with various arrays.

Hughes and Grieve (1983) also suggest that the nature of children's answers
to bizarre questions often asked in Piaget's experiments demonstrates their
attempt to make sense of all situations. They suggest that researchers need to
reexamine the underlying assumptions for children's responses when asked
these questions. Thus, if experiments are made more relevant to the real-life
experiences of young children, it appears that they are not as egocentric as
Piaget indicated.

Sociocultural Differences in Piaget's Theory

Are there sociocultural differences in Piaget's theory? Research on various cultures that engage in planting, harvesting, and cooking of grain suggests that
children in these groups may acquire the ability to conserve earlier than children
who are not a part of such cultures (Ginsburg & Opper, 1979). In a number of
cross-cultural studies, Kagan (1982) found that 2-year-olds begin to demonstrate empathetic behavior and the ability to understand the emotions of those
around them. Kagan's comprehensive research indicated that very young preoperational children are not completely egocentric, but have the ability to consider the perspective of another person.

After considering the discussion above, you may be wondering about the
relevance of Piaget's theory. Remember the discussion of theory from Chapter

1. Over time, most theories are modified and some are discarded. As more research is conducted and refined, new or different information and interpretations arise.

Piaget made a major contribution in the understanding of young children's thinking. More recent research indicates that in some contexts, if children are given appropriate materials with which they can identify, if the tasks involve basic human purposes to which children can relate, and if the questions asked take into account young children's understanding of language and their motivations in answering questions, they can and do demonstrate that they are not totally egocentric (Black, 1981). These ideas will be discussed further in Chapter 13. In addition, alternative explanations as proposed by the information process theorists will be explored.

Language Development

> The young child acquires his linguistic and thinking habits only through communication with other human beings. It is only this association that makes a human being out of him, that is a speaking and thinking being. (Chukovsky, 1971, p. 9)

The translated quote above was written in 1925 by Kornei Chukovsky. Chukovsky was a Russian scholar of adult literature, a poet who wrote for young children, and "an observer of children, of their speech, and their patterns of learning, as was the Swiss scientist, psychologist, and educator, Jean Piaget" (Chukovsky, 1971, p. viii). Chukovsky's perceptive observations of young children's language development reflect the conclusions of recent research on language acquisition—that young children learn about language and how to use it through communication and interaction with others (see Figure 10.2). Understanding this process requires a "comprehensive view that incorporates the child and his capabilities to think, to feel and act; what his genes have provided; and what his physical and social environment contribute" (Genishi & Dyson, 1984, p. 9).

Parents do not formally teach young children how to talk. For example, Bill and Ann do not say, "This is the week we are going to teach Jeremy nouns." Rather, young children learn about the nature of language as they participate with significant others in meaningful situations. First and foremost, young children learn that language is used to communicate, to express needs, and to evoke behaviors in others that help accomplish their goals.

■ Angela awakens from her nap at her child care center. She sits up, rubs her eyes and says, "Waa-waa." Ms. Ruiz, her caregiver, fills a glass of water and brings it to a thirsty Angela. She quickly empties the glass. Ms. Ruiz then allows Angela to play with the empty cup as she changes her diaper and says, "Water all gone, water all gone. Angela drank it all up. Is Angela still thirsty?" ■

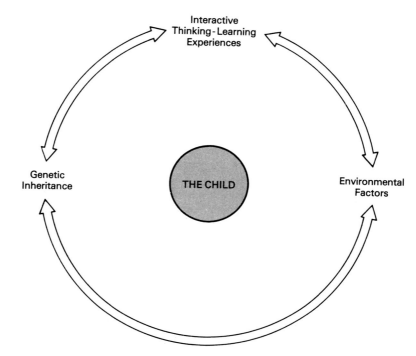

FIGURE 10.2
A number of factors interact to influence language development in young children.

Semantics—the meaning of language.

This vignette demonstrates that Angela is learning about the **semantics** or meaning of language. She indicates that she knows that language is used to communicate—to mean something. She vocalizes to Ms. Ruiz that she wants "Waa-waa." Ms. Ruiz responds, reinforcing to Angela the notion that she is a meaning-maker, that she can control and influence others to meet her needs through language. Ms. Ruiz facilitates this idea with Angela as she changes her diaper and talks with Angela about the cup, water, and being thirsty.

Phonology—the speech sounds of a particular language system.

As children attend to the language used in these meaningful interactions, they absorb the speech sounds or **phonology** of the language system. Jeremy and Angela internalize the basic sounds of the English language system used within the United States, just as French children learn the sounds of the French language. As Jeremy continues his phonological development, he will begin to produce the sounds of language typical of his community and geographic region. Angela will also produce sounds that are typical of her sociocultural context.

Syntax—the grammar or structure of a particular language system.

As Angela and Jeremy begin to form their first sentences, they demonstrate that they are learning the **syntax** or structure of the language system. It is Saturday and Bill takes Jeremy with him to run errands. When they return Ann asks Jeremy, "Where did you eat lunch?" Jeremy replies, "We eated at Mc-Donalds." Jeremy's response indicates that he has learned how to put words together in a sentence to convey meaning. In addition, his use of "eated" reflects that he had processed the rule of grammar indicating that past tense words end in "-ed." This ability to form such generalizations is an example of young children's amazing cognitive ability. As Jeremy matures and learns more about the language system, he will come to realize that there are some exceptions to the general patterns of language and will begin to use "ate" instead of "eated."

Thus, young children in the first few years of life learn (1) that language conveys meaning, (2) the sound system of the language, and (3) the structure of the language system. In addition to this linguistic or grammatic competence, they begin to learn a repertoire of behaviors which are often called "interactional competence" (Cicourel, 1972) (see Figure 10.3).

Young children acquire **interactional competence** just as they acquire linguistic competence, by participating with significant others in meaningful situations. Young children learn appropriate nonverbal behaviors; conversational techniques, such as turn-taking; and strategies for drawing attention to their talk. Grammatic and interactional competence interact and create the child's communicative competence (Hymes, 1971).

Interactional competence—the repertoire of behaviors that helps young children communicate effectively with others.

■ Angela's grandmother has given Angela some juice to drink. She finishes it and walks to her mother who is watching TV. Angela thrusts her cup toward Cheryl and says, "More." Cheryl continues to watch TV. Angela repeats her behavior. Cheryl does not respond. Angela then begins to tug at Cheryl's knee simultaneously raising the volume and pitch of her "More!" Finally, Cheryl acknowledges her and says, "Go get juice from Grandma." Angela turns and finds her grandmother in her

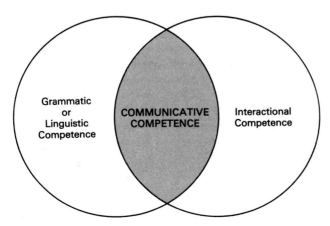

FIGURE 10.3
Grammatic and interactional competence interact to create the child's communicative competence.

bedroom. She thrusts her cup and says, "More." Grandma walks to the kitchen and pours Angela some more juice.   ■

Angela demonstrates that she has internalized a range of interactional behaviors that accompany her request for more juice. She knows to repeat her request. Angela uses nonverbal gestures, such as tugging at Cheryl's knee. She also raises the pitch and volume of her voice. These three interactional techniques helped Angela get more juice. Angela is learning much about becoming communicatively competent.

Interaction Between Thought and Language

As presented in Chapter 7, Piaget believed that young children's thought influenced their language (1926). He observed that many children under the age of 7 frequently talked to themselves. This behavior was interpreted by Piaget as indicative of young children's egocentric thought. Because Piaget felt that young children could not take the perspective of others, he believed that their speech was speech for the self. In addition, he attributed this behavior as the child's way of verbalizing random thinking. Piaget thought that as children matured in their cognitive development, egocentric speech eventually disappeared and socialized speech developed.

As mentioned earlier, some of Piaget's ideas are now being reevaluated. The major deviation from Piaget's idea regarding the relationship between thought and language has come from Vygotsky (1962, 1978). Vygotsky noted that young children's talking to themselves occurred most often when they were confused or encountered problems. Vygotsky hypothesized that young children talked to themselves for the purpose of solving problems or guiding behavior. He felt that talking to one's self was communication with the self.

It is interesting to note that adults, at certain times, also make comments addressed to themselves. Such behavior is usually viewed with humor. However, research (Berk, 1986b) indicates that adults and older children talk to themselves for the same reasons that young children do: to clarify situations, guide behavior, solve problems, or internalize information. Vygotsky (1962) felt that talk to oneself became internalized in older children and adults as "inner speech." This inner speech helps guide behavior in our daily lives. However, if problems arise, adults and older children often verbalize this "inner speech."

Scaffolding—according to Vygotsky, the process by which adults or more skilled children facilitate concept development or classification in young children by providing verbal information.

It was Vygotsky's theory that language and talking to oneself originated in the child's early interactions with others. In fact, Vygotsky (1978) thought that all cognitive functioning first evolved in social contexts with others. He believed that adults and other more cognitively aware children help less intellectually mature children learn by providing verbal suggestions or information. Without this assistance or **scaffolding**, children would be unable to accomplish the task or learn the concept. Children then incorporate these suggestions and information into inner speech to aid them in problem solving, guiding behavior, internalizing new information, or clarifying existing concepts. Vygotsky called

Scaffolding, according to Vygotsky, is an important process during which adults or more skilled children help other children learn by providing verbal suggestions or information.

the level of concept development at which the child could not accomplish tasks or understand concepts alone but could do so with assistance from adults or more cognitively aware children the **zone of proximal development** (Berk, 1986b; Berk, 1989; Vygotsky, 1978).

While Piaget (1927) emphasized the idea that children learn or invent primarily through their interaction with objects in the environment, he acknowledged that interaction with other children or peers stimulates children to become more aware of the perspectives of others. Vygotsky, however, points out that social interaction through language with both adults and more astute children facilitates cognitive development. As indicated by Berk (1989), recent research supports the importance of young children's interaction with both adults and other children in the development of cognition (Brown, Bransford, Ferrara, & Campione, 1983; Kerwin & Day, 1985).

The studies conducted over the past several decades tend to support Vygotsky's ideas regarding the relationship between thought and language. As a result of these findings, what Piaget called "egocentric speech" and what Vygotsky called "inner speech" are now referred to as **private speech**. Berk (1989) indicates that, contrary to Piaget's ideas, very young children who use private speech have higher rates of social participation and are more socially competent than children who do less "talking to themselves" (Berk, 1984, 1985; Kohlberg, Yaeger, & Hjertholm, 1968). In addition, research suggests that cognitively ma-

Zone of proximal development—according to Vygotsky, the level of concept development that is too difficult for the child to accomplish alone, but can be achieved with the help of adults or more skilled children.

Private speech—speech to oneself that helps direct one's own behavior or communication with oneself.

ture children used private speech at earlier ages (Berk, 1986a; Berner, 1971; Kleiman, 1974; Kohlberg, Yaeger, & Hjertholm, 1968). These two findings demonstrate the importance of social interaction and communication in the development of language and cognition in young children. This information provides one of the most important implications for promoting the cognitive development of young children, that is, providing opportunities for children and adults to interact and communicate with each other.

Vocabulary Development

***Fast mapping**— term used to describe children's rapid learning of language by relating a word to an internalized concept and remembering it after only one encounter with that word.*

Young children's rapid vocabulary development is explained by a process called **fast mapping** (Carey, 1978). Fast mapping refers to the way young children learn and remember an average of nine words a day from the onset of speech until age 6 (Clark, 1983). By this time young children have acquired approximately 14,000 words (Templin, 1957).

Children's initial understanding of a word during the fast mapping process is often expanded and refined as children continue to learn about the world. The following vignette demonstrates this clarification of vocabulary.

■ One of Jeremy's favorite early books is Eric Carle's *The Very Hungry Caterpillar.* Jeremy's first referent for a caterpillar was the tube-shaped animal that crawls. He was somewhat puzzled later on when he had his first encounter with another type of caterpillar, a toy replica of the earth moving machine. As children refine and extend their vocabulary, they discover that there are words that sound the same but have different meanings. ■

First Sentences

***Telegraphic speech**—children's early speech which, like a telegram, only includes words necessary to understanding meaning.*

***Rich interpretation**—acknowledging that young children know more than they can verbally express and that they use nonverbal behaviors to communicate.*

When children are around 18 to 20 months of age, they usually have a vocabulary of about 40 to 50 words. At this time, they usually begin to form their first sentences consisting of two words. Two-word sentences are often called **telegraphic speech**, which means that only the most meaningful words are used (Brown & Fraser, 1963). Usually prepositions, articles, auxiliary verbs, conjunctions, plurals, possessives, and past endings are left out of telegraphic speech. An analysis called **rich interpretation** acknowledges that children know more than they can express and are capable of using nonverbal behaviors to facilitate their meaning. Bloom's (1970) classic example of "Mommy, sock" indicated that these two words could convey a variety of meanings: "Mommy's sock," "Mommy, put on my sock," or "Mommy, give me my sock." Thus, context becomes essential to understanding the child's true meaning in these earliest sentences.

Early sentences usually involve questions, descriptions, recurrence, possession, location, agent-action, and negation and wish. Bloom (1970) found that children's first use of "no" conveys nonexistence, for example, "no juice." Next, "no" is used as a negative, as in "no go home." Then, "no" is used to convey what the child believes to be not true.

Between the ages of 2 and 3, simple sentences begin to appear. Cross-cultural research indicates that children begin to incorporate the word order of their particular linguistic community (Maratsos, 1983). Gradually, children between $1\frac{1}{2}$ and $3\frac{1}{2}$ years of age begin to acquire grammatical **morphemes**, which expand the mean length utterance (MLU) or "sentence." Brown's (1973) research demonstrates that English speaking children in these age groups acquire grammatical morphemes in a regular order (see Table 10.2).

Morpheme—the smallest unit of meaning in oral or written language.

Young Children's Oral Language Approximations

Approximations— children's attempts at conventional oral or written language which, when produced, are not quite conventional.

Most parents and teachers delight in young children's attempts to acquire language. Their **approximations** or attempts at conventional adult language are often viewed as cute, charmimg, or creative. The majority of adults seem to

TABLE 10.2
Order of acquisition of English grammatical morphemes

Morpheme	Example
1. Verb present progressive ending (-ing)	"She swinging."
2. Preposition "on"	"On Daddy's shoulders."
3. Preposition "in"	"In my car."
4. Noun plural "-s"	"Books."
5. Verb irregular past tense	"Kitty ran." "Chair broke."
6. Noun possessive	"Mommy's shoe."
7. Verb uncontractible "be" form used with adjective, preposition, or noun phrase	"Are cookies hot?"
8. Articles "a" and "the"	"A book." "The spoon."
9. Verb regular past tense ending (-ed)	"Jessica fixed it."
10. Verb present tense, third person singular regular ending (-s)	"Justin hates it."
11. Verb present tense, third person singular irregular ending (-s)	"He has (from have) a hose." "Daddy does (from do) make pizza."
12. Auxiliary verb uncontractible "be" forms	"Are you sleeping?"
13. Verb contractible "be" forms used with adjective, preposition, or noun phrase	"He's outside." "They're happy."
14. Auxiliary verb contractible "be" forms	"Mommy's coming." "Caitlin's crying."

Source: Adapted from Brown (1973, p. 274).

know that, given a supportive language environment and time to develop, children's approximations eventually become more conventional (Snow & Ferguson, 1977).

At times, some adults misinterpret young children's developmentally appropriate language behaviors as incorrect and feel it is their duty to correct the language. However, this is not the case. Appropriate teacher and parent responses to young children's language behavior will be described later in the chapter. The purpose of this discussion is to provide an understanding of some of the more common oral language approximations that young children exhibit.

Overextension— when young children use a word to refer to a similar but different object, situation, or category.

Overextension involves young children's use of a word to refer to a similar but different object, situation, or category. Do you remember the example of Jonathan, who pointed to the Goodyear blimp and said, "Truck, truck." Jonathan's use of "truck" indicates that he was overextending the word to refer to other objects. Young children's efforts at cognitive processing are evident in their use of overextensions. Overextensions always apply to a class of similar referents (Clark, 1983). Blimps look similar in shape to trucks.

Interestingly, some researchers suggest that overextension may be a strategy that young children use because they have had no opportunity to learn the appropriate word or because they cannot remember the appropriate word. For example, Jonathan had never seen a blimp before, so he attached the label "truck" to the blimp. He had no knowledge of the word "blimp" and to what it referred (Clark, 1978).

In addition, there is considerable evidence that given the correct names in a comprehension task, children can point out specific objects even though they overextend. This may be another example of comprehension of language preceding the production of language (Clark, 1978; Rescorla, 1980).

Creative vocabulary—when young children create new words to meet the need for words they have not learned, have forgotten, or for which there is no word in the language system.

Creative vocabulary is used when young children create new words in order to meet the need for a word they have not learned, they cannot remember, or for which there is no actual word in the language system. For example one young child referred to a calculator as a "countulator." Another example occurred when several children in an early childhood classroom were playing "restaurant." They decided that Justin would be the "cooker."

Overgeneralization, as discussed in Chapter 7, also occurs when young children generalize a grammatical rule to apply to all situations. Interestingly, early in the language acquisition process, very young children seem to use the irregular forms of frequently used words conventionally (Menyuk, 1964). Later as children begin to unconsciously internalize the general rules for making plurals or past tense, they overgeneralize the rules. For example, the general rule for making past tense is to add "ed" to a word. Children apply this principle and they create "goed," "runned," "breaked," and so on. Remember when Jeremy told his mother that they had "eated at McDonalds"?

The discussion indicates that young children's efforts at language development reflect great abilities of cognitive processing. The acquisition of oral language and the relatively short time in which it takes place is one of the most amazing accomplishments in human development.

Sociocultural Aspects of Language

As teachers in multicultural schools, our work is to educate children in our care, but not transform them. We must have the courage of our convictions to open up avenues leading into the English language and culture, so that the children of other traditions may enter and move forward in our society, but we must never lose the integrity which enables us to recognize and respect those individual qualities which should remain untouched and unchanged—the rightful heritage of each nationality. (Brown, 1979, p. 167)

People who plan to work with young children and who come from mainstream America need to examine their own belief systems regarding possible prejudices and negative attitudes toward children who may come from families of different cultural, linguistic, and economic backgrounds. "The long American tradition of negative attitudes toward childhood bilingualism has been fueled by racial and ethnic prejudices, for bilingualism in the United States is strongly associated with low income and minority status" (Berk, 1989, p. 401).

Teachers of young children need to accept all children and their languages. According to linguists, dialects are not inferior forms of language, but are different forms of language.

Unless you are Native American (American Indian), your roots are in another country, culture, and language system. Reflect on what it must have been like for your forebears to leave their native land and extended or immediate family to come to this country. Think about their struggle to find shelter, to make a living, and to learn a new language, new laws, and new ways of doing. Consider what it would be like if your family decided to move far away to a new country where the food, housing, clothing, customs, and language were different. Perhaps some reflection in this area will encourage a more empathetic reaction on your part to children and families who come from a background that is different from yours.

Dialects

Linguists say that there are many dialects all over the United States. Consider the variations of sounds and pronunciations of the New England area, the South, and the Midwest. The state of Texas is said to have five regional dialects.

Dialects—different forms of language used by various ethnic groups or by people who live in certain geographic regions.

Linguists define **dialects** as speech differences that are unique to various ethnic populations or geographic regions. Dialects vary in pronunciation of words, verb tenses and sound omission. According to linguists, dialects are *not* inferior forms of language, but are simply *different* forms of language. Dialects are rule-governed just as standard English is rule-governed. *All* young children learn the dialect of the home and community in which they live.

Bilingualism and Multilingualism

Increasing numbers of children in the United States come from homes where English is not the first language. Many young children will be in home and school environments where different languages are spoken. Some important background information about learning two or more languages follows:

- Children who do not yet speak English are often very quiet. This lack of verbalization should not be equated with a lack of cognitive ability. Reluctance to speak may indicate that these children are still internalizing the sounds of the new language system, just as infants and toddlers do. If you have no knowledge of the German language, but were expected to speak it, write it, and take tests in it, you would not perform well. Your performance would not indicate that you are lacking in intelligence; rather, you would simply be in a language environment that differs from your specific language. Therefore, you cannot express your thoughts so that they can be understood by others. The same is true for children who are learning a second language.
- There are great differences in the rates and strategies used to acquire second language just as there are in first language acquisition (Strong, 1982; Wong Fillmore, 1976).

- Oral language development is not affected in the first language because the child is learning a new language. There does appear to be a slight delay around age 2 or 3, as children learn to separate the phonological and grammar systems. By age 4, children demonstrate normal native ability and good to normal ability in the second language, depending upon the amount of exposure (Reich, 1986).
- Second language acquisition facilitates both cognitive and linguistic skills (Ben Zeev, 1977; Bialystok, 1986; Diaz, 1985). Children who are bilingual, when matched with children who are monolingual, have outperformed them in areas of verbal and nonverbal intellectual measures, analytic reasoning, concept formation, and metalinguistic awareness.
- The patterns of second language development parallel those of first language development. Second language acquisition, like first language acquisition as described earlier in this chapter, is creative (MacLaughlin, 1978; Wong Fillmore, 1981).
- Input or social interaction with other children and adults is necessary to second language acquisition, just as it is to first language acquisition (Krashen, 1981).

Socioeconomic Differences in Language Acquisition

Just as children who speak in dialects or have a different first language possess differences in language, not deficits, linguists and sociolinguists suggest the same is true for children who come from varying socioeconomic backgrounds (Bernstein, 1972; Heath, 1983). Children from the lower socioeconomic classes have a language system that is useful within their culture and community. Thus, children who have language differences based upon cultural and economic differences need to be respected for possessing viable language systems. They should not be perceived as deficient either in intelligence or language.

Our language and our culture are of vital importance to each of us because they help to define who we are and give us our identity. If teachers or other adults who work with young children convey disapproval or do not accept children with cultural and linguistic differences, these children's self-esteem and self-concepts will be severely diminished. A feeling of self-worth is necessary if young children are to feel they are competent learners. Early childhood professionals need to accept young children's dialects and respond to the meaning of their language, rather than correcting them. The following provides an example of how a teacher accepts a child's dialect and responds to the meaning of the child's language.

Angela: I be gettin' new shoes.
Teacher: You'll be getting new shoes? Great! What kind do you want?
Angela: Daddy done got me sneakers!
Teacher: Your daddy got you sneakers! What color are they?
Angela: He got me red ones.

Literacy Development

■ Cheryl had been doing her homework in front of the TV. She takes a break and walks to the kitchen to get something to eat. As she walks back to the living room, she discovers Angela (now 26 months of age) writing on her notebook. "Angela, that's my homework," shouts Cheryl. Angela looks up at Cheryl and says, "Angela, homework."

It is Saturday. Ann's father has come to visit them and they decide to go to the mall. As they drive into the mall, 2-year-old Jeremy says, "There's Sears." Ann's father cannot believe his ears. "Jeremy is only two and he can read 'Sears,'" the proud grandfather remarks. ■

The above vignettes demonstrate that very young children are not only learning about oral language but are also learning about written language. The idea that very young children learn about literacy is relatively recent.

Interaction Between Thought, Language, and Literacy

In the past, it was thought that children needed to spend approximately the first five years of their lives developing a good foundation in oral language before learning to read. When children reached the age of $6\frac{1}{2}$, they were perceived as generally possessing the maturity and perceptual development required to learn how to read (Morphett & Washburn, 1931). After learning the basic rudiments of reading, children were then ready to begin to learn how to write—to communicate with others via written symbols. This writing for the purpose of communicating with others, as opposed to the perceptual motor task of handwriting, usually received attention somewhere around the end of the first grade or the beginning of the second. Once introduced to writing, young children were expected to produce interesting stories, with conventional spelling, appropriate grammar, good handwriting, and correct punctuation on their first attempt. If they were not successful, their papers and stories were returned with numerous red corrections. With such unrealistic expectations, it is no wonder many adults do not like to write.

In the 1960s and 1970s, a number of researchers began to question this sequential idea of the development of literacy. Their questions, research, and findings have provided some new and fascinating information about how young children develop literacy.

As the oral language researchers (Ninio & Bruner, 1978; Snow, 1983) analyzed the tapes of young children's verbalizations, they noticed that many young children talked about and were very much interested in print. The vignettes throughout this chapter about Jeremy and Angela have indicated their awareness and interest in print.

Reading researchers also recognized that some young children came to first grade already knowing how to read. While there were those who suspected that

Involving young children in real-life, purposeful events helps them understand that reading and writing are used to communicate their ideas with others.

these children's parents had formally taught them to read, Delores Durkin (1966) undertook a study of early readers and their families to determine exactly how these young children had actually learned to read. The results of this well-known investigation have now been substantiated by other researchers (Clark, 1976; Hall, Moretz, & Statom, 1976; Wells, 1981).

The findings of these studies indicate that the parents did not formally teach their young children how to read. However, these parents displayed a number of other behaviors that seemed to facilitate early reading behaviors. Specifically, these parents (1) read to their children on a consistent and regular basis when they were quite young; (2) provided their children with access to a wide range of print materials in the home; (3) themselves read and interacted with print; (4) responded to their children's questions about print; and (5) made writing and drawing tools and paper available to their children.

Observing and participating in meaningful print contexts with parents and the availability of paper and writing tools provided the opportunity for the children to express themselves symbolically, to explore print, and to develop concepts about the nature of print. One of the most interesting findings of Durkin's research was that the parents reported that their children did a great deal of writing just before they began to read, or that writing and reading seemed to emerge at the same time.

This notion that very young children were interested in writing was a rather startling idea, given that the prevailing thought was that children were not expected to write communicatively until somewhere around the end of the first grade. Consequently, Durkin's research raised some important questions: Do opportunities to write facilitate learning to read? Should young children be encouraged to write? If the answer is "Yes," exactly how should adults encourage writing in young children? These questions prompted a flurry of early literacy research, which continues to the present.

Much of the literacy research had focused upon the process by which young children develop literacy. Specific details of this development will be discussed in Part 5 of this text. However, there are several general ideas that describe current thinking about the development of literacy in young children:

- Young children learn about literacy (reading and writing) by interacting with significant others in meaningful print situations (Teale, 1986).
- Learning about print begins quite early in life, certainly during the first year of life (Ninio & Bruner, 1978; Teale, 1984).
- Young children's learning about print is different from the knowledge that older children and adults have about print (Ferrerio & Teberosky, 1982; Read, 1971).
- Young children develop an awareness of oral and written language in a holistic and interrelated way, rather than a sequential stage process. In other words, very young children develop simultaneous notions about oral and written language while they are involved with significant others in meaningful situations (Goodman, 1986).
- Virtually all children, regardless of socioeconomic background, learn about literacy early in life (Heath, 1983). Only in those few cultural groups where written language is not used do children not have an awareness of print.

The interaction of meaningful experiences with oral and written language is a very important factor in the development of literacy. Such an awareness suggests that it is important for young children to have active meaningful experiences with others involving both oral and written language. These experiences facilitate the child's competence in the development of thought and oral and written communication.

Developing an Awareness of Print as a Form of Communication

A major concept that all children in literate societies must acquire is the awareness that print conveys meaning. Many young children begin to develop this idea as their parents read stories to them (Ninio & Bruner, 1978; Snow & Ninio, 1986; Wells, 1981). There are other contexts that also seem to help children from a variety of socioeconomic backgrounds develop the idea that print gives us messages. Situations that demand attention to environmental print—religious ceremonies, written directions, writing checks, using the TV guide to select programs—and children's TV programs like Sesame Street also serve to help children develop the understanding that print communicates (Anderson & Smith, 1984; Taylor 1986; Teale, 1986). The two primary sources of young children's learning about the communicative nature of print are environmental print and book print.

Environmental Print

Remember the vignette about Jeremy and Sears? How did Jeremy come to associate that large building at the mall with the large letters S-E-A-R-S on the facade with his verbalization, "There's Sears." The answer is, through a variety of meaningful experiences that involved both oral and written language. Jeremy had been in the Sears store on numerous occasions. He was with Bill and Ann when they purchased a new washer and dryer. He watched as the Sears truck arrived and the washer and dryer were delivered and installed. Almost every time Bill and Ann are in Sears, they take Jeremy to the toy department to look around. Jeremy has also heard and seen advertisements for Sears on TV. Participating in these meaningful experiences with the accompanying oral and written language had helped Jeremy internalize the nature of printed symbols that represent Sears.

As children use and/or observe objects in meaningful contexts, they pay attention to what they look like. Seeing the box of Cheerios every morning on the breakfast table, or the tube of Crest toothpaste on the sink—as well as at the grocery store or on TV—helps children become familiar with and internalize certain features about print encountered in the environment. Studies indicate that while young children around the age of 2 recognize environmental print such as, "Coke," "McDonalds," and "K Mart," they attend to this print in a very global manner (Goodman, 1980). That is, they pay attention to the whole context and not just the print. For example, very young children attend to the shape of the object, its color, and the design of the print and logo. As they develop in their print awareness, they will begin to focus more directly on the print. Thus, experiences with environmental print are important in facilitating beginning print awareness.

Book Print

For the most part, book print is different from environmental print in that it usually consists of more than just one or two words, and it is organized into a line or many lines. Its purpose is somewhat different from environmental print and it requires a more extended focus. Knowledge of book print and how it works is critical for success in the school context (Teale, 1984).

Learning about book print begins at home when parents share books with their children. Many parents introduce their children to books during the first year of life; some even before! Often these experiences involve the naming of

Rereading children's favorite books over and over is very important in helping them become literate.

pictures or talking about the pictures. Usually during the second or third year, parents begin to read the book text or story to their children. As children hear these stories, they begin to develop the idea that books can bring them information, pleasure, and comfort. This idea seems to foster a love of books and independent reading in children.

Family book reading provides many opportunities for young children to learn a number of important concepts (Schickedanz, 1986). Specifically, they learn:

- New information about the world around them.
- New vocabulary.
- Turn taking (when parents ask questions and children respond).
- Information about book handling knowledge and the features of print.
- The concept of "story."

An important factor in an awareness of book print is the parents' behavior. Parents serve as "scaffolders." Remember Vygotsky's zone of proximal development? By responding to the children's behaviors, asking them questions, and making comments, parents facilitate young children's understanding and challenge their thinking. Talking with children about the stories encourages reflective thinking, as the stories are often related to their past experiences. Talking about stories also helps children develop **metalanguage**, or the ability to talk about language.

Metalanguage— talk about language itself.

Finally, intimate encounters with books provide time for parent-child communication. Time spent with books not only facilitates literacy development but can promote positive parent-child interaction. Parental behaviors in the acquisition of literacy provide important implications for the role of early childhood professionals in promoting literacy in their classrooms.

Sociocultural Differences

This chapter has emphasized the need for interaction in young children's development of oral and written language. A review of Heath's (1983) study presented in Chapter 2 provides information about apparent variations in this social interaction, which occurs in differing sociocultural contexts. She examined story-reading events in a middle-class, an Anglo working-class, and an African-American working-class community in the Piedmont Carolinas. She found distinctive sociocultural differences in the way children were involved in literacy events. Heath then documented the effects of these differences upon children's success in school.

The middle-class children in the Piedmont area did well in school. Their socialization into literacy events included parents asking questions about books, relating book events to the children's experiences, and encouraging children to tell their own stories based on both reality and fantasy.

Working-class Anglo children were also introduced to books by their parents. Parents centered upon children's retelling of factual events rather than thinking about the books in a way that encouraged reflective thinking. These children did well in responding to literal recall questions. However, they had difficulty in the higher grades with analyzing, predicting, and evaluating.

The working-class African-American children had few book-reading interactions with their parents. Questions asked by adults were different from those asked in the other two communities. Children were asked to compare rather than name or describe. The parents told stories to their children rather than reading them stories. The stories were fictional in nature while often using familiar events as the basis for the story. These children did not do well in school, even though they had advanced skills in fictional narration and analogical reasoning.

In studying African-American, Anglo, and Mexican-American families of low income, Teale, Estrada, and Anderson (1981) found many differences among these families regarding literacy interactions and events. This research suggests that there are many variations even within cultural and socioeconomic groups. Therefore, it is important to know children as unique individuals and accept variations in their home literacy experiences and emerging development.

Factors Influencing Cognitive/Language/ Literacy Development

We have alluded to some of the factors that influence the early development of young children in the areas of cognition, language, and literacy. This section specifically addresses these factors.

Genetic, Nutrition, and Health Factors

While there are general patterns of cognitive, language, and literacy development, it should be emphasized that each child has unique genetic characteristics. Research by Gardner (1983) indicates that there are six forms of intelligence based upon the child's genetic predisposition. These include linguistic, musical, spatial, personal, bodily-kinesthetic, and logical-mathematical. Individuals may possess more than one of these "frames of mind." Nelson (1981) has identified differences in young children in the early stages of oral language development that may be a function of brain hemisphere dominance as well as environmental factors. Referential speakers rely mostly upon nouns, a few verbs, proper nouns, and adjectives, and they frequently label objects. Expressive speakers use varying forms of speech combinations, and frequently use pronouns and compressed one- or two-word sentences. Dyson's (1981) research in the area of young children's writing also documents variation in writing strategies. These differences could be related to individual genetic predisposition, as well as environmental influences.

It is important that young children between the ages of 1 and 3 continue to have proper nutrition and health care. Two-year-olds have developed 70 percent of their adult brain weight, with complete brain weight achieved by age 6 (Kunjufu, 1980). Thus, it is critical that young children continue to eat well-balanced diets, if their learning potential is to be realized.

Children who do not have regular medical checkups also may have various health needs that are not identified, but that ultimately can impact cognitive, language, and literacy development. Vision and hearing problems can adversely affect young children's development in these areas.

The Nature of Adult-Child Interactions

Motherese—*modification in the mother's speech when talking with young children.*

Fatherese—*modification in the father's speech when talking with young children. Can differ from motherese.*

Another factor influencing cognitive, language, and literacy development in children between the ages of 1 and 3 is the nature of adult-child interaction. Throughout this chapter you have seen the importance of interaction with adults.

As summarized by Genishi and Dyson (1984), research suggests that behaviors of both mothers and fathers influence the nature of young children's language acquisition (Gleason, 1975; Lamb, 1977; Nelson, 1973; Snow & Ferguson, 1977; Wells, 1981). The modifications adults make in their speech to communicate with very young children is called **motherese** and **fatherese**. "Motherese" in mothers of children whose language developed more rapidly than others involved asking more questions than most, accepting the child's comments, and responding as if the child's talk was meaningful (White, 1985). These mothers also used fewer commands and less directive speech to their young children. Fatherese has not been examined to the extent of motherese. Nevertheless, unique language behaviors on the part of fathers serve to elicit different language responses and behaviors from children than those of mothers. Fatherese has been identified as being more playful (Lamb, 1977), using more direct commands (Gleason, 1975), and eliciting more sophisticated language from young children (Masur & Gleason, 1980) when compared with motherese. The importance of parental responsiveness to the meaning of young children's talk was documented by Cross (1978) and Wells (1981).

In a longitudinal study, Wells found that the nature of adult responsiveness to 3-year-old children's speech was associated with rapid oral language development and with reading achievement at age 7. Specifically, the children who did well in language development and reading achievement had parents who made "developing responses" to their children's verbalizations. These parents added new information to the topic the child was discussing and they encouraged the child to continue talking about the topic, often by asking questions. In addition to the behaviors mentioned, research (Snow & Ferguson, 1977) indicates that when talking to young children, adults use speech that is short and grammatically simple, repeat their speech, and raise and vary the tone and pitch of their speech. Adults have also been observed to "scaffold," that is provide the support necessary for children to advance in their language development (Teale, 1981).

Adults also facilitate the language development of young children through **extensions** and **expansions**. Extensions are responses that include the essence of children's verbalizations and extend the meaning while expansions provide children the opportunity to hear the conventional forms of language. Jeremy said, "Get ball." Bill replied, "Oh, you need me to help you get your ball. It rolled under the table." Through this extension Bill conveys to Jeremy that he understood what Jeremy was verbalizing. Bill also adds more information about the context through his verbalization. Expansions are used by adults to provide feedback to young children regarding their use of overgeneralizations. Jeremy tells Ann, "We eated at McDonalds." She replies, "Oh, you ate at McDonalds. What did you have to eat?" She does not directly correct Jeremy's "eated" but uses the appropriate form in a conversational context and also extends by asking what Jeremy had to eat. There is evidence to suggest that adults who use these techniques help children to progress more rapidly in their language development and produce more complex sentences than children who are around adults who do not use extensions and expansions (Cross, 1978; Nelson, Carskaddon, & Bonvillian, 1973; White, 1985).

The effect of varying parental behaviors on the development of literacy was discussed earlier in this chapter. Research by Durkin (1966) and others documents the importance of parent interaction with children in print situations. Parent responses to children's questions about print also document the "scaffolding" that parents can provide to help children's literacy development.

Extensions—*responses to children's language that extend the meaning of their language.*

Expansion—*responses to young children's use of overgeneralizations by using the conventional form in the conversational context.*

Variety of Print Contexts

The nature of the child's interaction in a variety of print contexts influences the child's awareness of various literacy contexts. Children whose parents actively involve them in reading environmental print and book print, provide them with writing tools so they can explore print, and respond to the children's concerns and questions about print facilitate greater awareness of print than parents who do not respond to children's interests (Bissex, 1980; Durkin, 1966; Heath, 1983).

Background of Experiences

Scripts—the knowledge of a social procedure or event, which includes sequence of events and of roles, often observed in young children in play contexts.

The kinds of experiences young children have, the frequency, the nature of the scaffolding role of adults, and the opportunities for young children to play out these experiences all influence the young child's cognitive, language, and literacy development. Children around the age of 3 begin to demonstrate that they know certain procedures, events, or **scripts**. Scripts are events that are organized in a sequential manner (Schank & Abelson, 1977). Knowledge of scripts is demonstrated through verbal and nonverbal behaviors. Once children have internalized a script, they can organize their behavior and language. Jeremy's experiences in observing and participating in the collection of refuse around his neighborhood have provided him with the script about what happens during this event. His knowledge of this script is reflected in his play when he collects his toys, dumps them in his bunk bed (garbage truck) and presses the bolts (buttons) to grind up the "trash." Children whose parents can provide a variety of experiences and the opportunity for their children to re-experience these various events have an opportunity to develop a greater number of scripts and more elaborate and detailed scripts than those parents who do not (Fivush, 1984; Nelson, 1986).

Children also internalize scripts when hearing or telling stories. Studies indicate that young children can remember more details from stories based upon familiar events (Hudson & Nelson, 1983). This information suggests that background of experience is a critical factor when young children are involved in literacy or print settings.

Background experiences and subsequent script formation appear to facilitate "category of concept" formation (Lucariello & Nelson, 1985). It appears that after children have developed a number of scripts involving similar objects, sequences, and functions, they can combine elements of these scripts into larger categories, thus promoting cognitive development.

Play/Concrete Activity

Opportunities for play or concrete activity and the quality of this play are perceived by most child development experts as important factors in facilitating the young child's cognitive, language, and literacy development.

Opportunities for children to engage in sociodramatic play help them internalize scripts, which organize their language and behavior around concepts.

Most experts on play suggest that sensorimotor play with oneself and with objects facilitates the young child's beginning cognitive development (Piaget, 1962; Smilansky, 1968; Sutton-Smith, 1967). Garvey (1977) indicates that object play often involves a four-step sequence: exploration, manipulation, practice, and repetition. Repetitive play with objects facilitates the development of **physical knowledge** and the eventual development of **logico-mathematical knowledge** (Piaget, 1969).

Young children's play with language also encourages language development. Children between the ages of 1 and 3 often play with sounds, syllables, and

Physical knowledge—*knowledge of physical characteristics of objects and events gained through sensorimotor interaction.*

Logico-mathematical knowledge—*knowledge that is primarily constructed from children's actions on and interpretations of objects.*

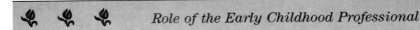

Role of the Early Childhood Professional

**Promoting Cognitive/Language/Literacy Development
in Children Ages 1 Through 3**

1. Remember that in many instances, young children think differently from older children and adults.
2. Provide safe environments so young children can explore freely.
3. Provide a variety of interesting materials to promote thinking, talking, reading, and writing.
4. Provide opportunities for young children to interact, talk, read, and write with other children and adults.
5. Demonstrate interest and curiosity about the world.
6. Use oral and written language in meaningful contexts.
7. Provide scaffolding to help young children stretch their cognitive, language, and literacy development while making sure that all experiences are developmentally appropriate.
8. Remember that each child is unique.
9. Respect sociocultural, linguistic, and socioeconomic differences in young children and their families.
10. Identify cognitive, language, and literacy needs in young children that may require special attention, services, or programs.

words. This play with language can occur when the child is alone, often at bedtime (Garvey, 1977; Weir, 1962).

During the child's third year, play with social materials and others begins. Sociodramatic play of 3-year-olds usually has no organized theme or plot. Their enactments of play roles are often one-dimensional and change frequently due to the lack of a general theme. Play at this age often involves collecting of objects, hauling, carrying, and dumping. Children tend to repeat play over and over. Jeremy's garbage play is such an example. Opportunities for play provide children at this age to act out the basics or essentials of certain scripts, eating a meal, visiting the doctor, or picking up the trash.

Opportunities for play, the nature of the play, materials available, and adult behaviors during children's play all influence cognitive, language, and literacy development.

Sociocultural and Special Needs

Throughout this chapter attention has been given to the differences in children's development in the areas of cognition, language, and literacy. Awareness and an understanding of these differences are essential in promoting the development of young children in these three interrelated areas. It is important that children develop a sense of worth and pride in their identity. This can be difficult to achieve if adults view children who are culturally and economically different as deficient. Understanding young children's differences can help those who work with young children to emphasize their strengths and provide appropriate experiences for young children.

An awareness of children's appropriate cognitive, language, and literacy development can help educators provide programmatic assistance to children who have special developmental needs. Regular medical checkups can also help teachers and parents become aware of atypical development. Various health professionals can serve as resources in obtaining needed special services and developing intervention strategies for young children.

In 1986 Congress passed Public Law 99–457, which established a state grant program for children with disabilities from birth through 2 years of age who have been identified as developmentally delayed. By 1992, participating states must make services available to all infants and toddlers with disabilities. By 1992, states applying for funds from the federal government for P.L. 99–457 or P.L. 101–476 (reauthorization of P.L. 91–142, the Education for All Handicapped Children Act of 1975) will be required to provide documentation that they are providing "free and appropriate education" to all children with disabilities between the ages of 3 and 5. In addition to the child's Individual Educational Plan (IEP), an Individualized Family Service Plan (IFSP) must be written. P.L. 99–457 must contain provisions for providing a variety of program options and services to special needs children and their families in the IFSP.

Key Terms

tertiary circular reactions
deferred imitation
preoperational
mental symbols
transductive reasoning
idiosyncratic concepts
semantics
phonology
syntax
interactional competence
scaffolding
zone of proximal development
private speech
fast mapping
telegraphic speech

rich interpretation
morpheme
approximations
overextension
creative vocabulary
dialects
metalanguage
motherese
fatherese
extension
expansion
scripts
physical knowledge
logico-mathematical knowledge

Review Strategies/Activities

1. Observe parents interacting with their child or children ages 1 through 3. Tape record the language, then analyze it for evidence of scaffolding.
2. Do the same in an early childhood classroom. Look for evidence of scaffolding behaviors on the part of the teachers of children ages 1 through 3.
3. Observe in a classroom of 2- or 3-year-olds. List examples of whole language (interaction of thought, experience, oral and written language).
4. Observe the classrooms of 1-, 2-, and 3-year-olds.
   a. Describe how the environment is organized to promote cognitive, language, and literacy development.
   b. List the materials available and how they promote cognitive, language, and literacy development.
   c. Describe how the day is organized. Is there evidence of scheduling to promote cognitive, language, and literacy development? List and describe.
   d. Observe teacher role. What behaviors facilitate cognitive, language, and literacy development? List and describe.

Further Readings

See references listed in Chapter 1 under cognitive theory.

Genishi, C., & Dyson, A. H. (1984). *Language assessment in the early years.* Norwood, NJ: Ablex.

> This book provides information about the development and assessment of young children's oral and written language from birth through the primary years. Attention is given to children from different cultural and linguistic backgrounds. The book is rich with examples of children's language and provides many ideas for early childhood professionals to use in assessing and facilitating young children's language development.

Johnson, J., Christie, J., & Yawkey, T. (1987). *Play and early childhood development.* Glenview, Il: Scott, Foresman.

> This book provides a clear discussion of current play research and theory. It includes interesting and relevant anecdotes. Many practical ideas and suggestions should prove helpful to most parents and early childhood teachers.

Pflaum, S. (1986). *The development of language and literacy in young children* (3rd ed.). Columbus, OH: Merrill.

> This book provides an excellent overview of the development of oral language and literacy in young children. It provides many examples of children's development and ideas for parents and teachers. Chapter 4 provides important information on "Variations in Language and Literacy Development."

Smith, B., & Strain, P. (1988). *Does early intervention help?* (Report No. R188062207). Reston, VA: Clearinghouse on Handicapped and Gifted Children (ERIC Digest #455).

> This resource provides background information about the importance of early intervention.

PART FIVE

The Young Child Ages 4 Through 5

CHAPTER 11

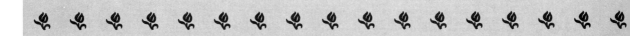

*The first and foremost thing you can expect
of a child is that he is a child.*

Armin Grams

Physical/Motor Development of the Young Child Ages 4 Through 5

After reading and studying this chapter, you will demonstrate comprehension by:

- Outlining expected patterns of physical/motor development during the years from 4 through 5.
- Describing developmental landmarks in large and small muscle development.
- Describing perceptual motor development in children ages 4 through 5.
- Describing body and gender awareness in children ages 4 through 5.
- Identifying major factors influencing physical/motor development.
- Suggesting strategies for enhancing physical/motor and perceptual motor development in children ages 4 through 5.

General Physical Characteristics of 4- and 5-Year-Olds

Physical growth in children seems to follow four periods. From conception to 6 months, growth is dramatically rapid; during the toddler/preschool period, the growth rate tends to level off and proceed at a steady pace until puberty. Then the growth rate increases dramatically for a period and slows again until adult growth is achieved. The growth rate for children ages 4 through 5 is steady, with children gaining $2\frac{1}{2}$ to $3\frac{1}{2}$ inches in height and 4 to 5 pounds in weight each year until around age 6. Each child will grow at his own rate, although the patterns for growth are fairly predictable. How tall, heavy, or well-coordinated a child is depends on the child's heredity, general health, health history, nutrition, emotional well-being, and opportunities for physical/motor activity.

Body proportions change from the chunky, top-heavy look of the toddler to a more lean and upright figure. The child's head, which at age 2 is one quarter

of the total body length, is now by age 5 to $5\frac{1}{2}$ about one sixth of the total body length. The brain reaches 90 percent of its adult weight by age 5, and myelination of the brain is fairly complete, making more complex motor abilities possible (Tanner, 1970).

Boys and girls during this age period have similar physiques, both losing the baby fat of earlier years and gaining more bone and muscle. However, boys tend to have more muscle at this age, while girls tend to have more fat. Changing body proportions include larger chest circumference and a flatter stomach, longer arms and legs, and feet that have lost the characteristic fatty arch pad of baby feet.

General health assessment of children during their growing years requires monitoring their height and weight gains. Measurements of height and weight obtained on a regular basis provide a preliminary indication of health and nutritional status. Growth charts developed by the National Center for Health Statistics, commonly used by health care professionals, provide a **percentile** measure for children at each age. For instance, a 4-year-old girl who is 41 inches tall and weighs 39 pounds would be found at the 75th percentile point on the chart. This percentile tells us how her height and weight compare with other girls the same age. The 75th percentile means that 75 percent of girls her age will be smaller than she is, and 25 percent will be larger.

Percentile—a statistical measure that ranks subjects from lowest to highest based on a common characteristic or results of an assessment.

Large Muscle Development

By age 4 through 5 children are quite motoric. Having mastered walking and running, their movements are expansive and include coordinations required in climbing, hopping, jumping, sliding, running, and so on. Their large motor skills generally include the following:

Age 4	*Age 5*
Rides tricycle	Rides bicycle
Climbs stairs alternating feet	Descends stairs alternating feet
Balances for short period on one foot	Balances on one foot to count of 5 to 10
Climbs playground equipment with agility	Experiments with abilities on playground climbing equipment
Enjoys creative responses to music	Enjoys learning simple rhythms and movement routines
One-footed skip	Two-footed skip
Jumps easily in place	Hops on one foot in place
Throws ball	Catches ball
Likes to chase	Enjoys follow-the-leader
Walks a straight taped line on floor	Walks a low, wide kindergarten balance beam

Facility in large motor development enhances the total development of the child. Overall health and vitality depend on it, and autonomy and self-sufficiency are encouraged by it. Cognitive development is furthered through an ever-enlarging world in which to explore and discover. When a child feels mastery over his movements, the self-concept is enhanced, as are a sense of competence and self-confidence. Self-confidence generally leads to enhanced social interactions.

Opportunities to use, expand, and refine large motor coordinations should comprise a significant portion of the child's day. Sufficient large motor activities lead to what Gallahue (1982) described as **physical fitness** and **motor fitness**. Physical fitness refers to muscular strength, muscular endurance, flexibility, and circulatory-respiratory endurance. Motor fitness refers to speed, coordination, agility, power, and balance. In considering children's needs for healthy, sturdy, well-coordinated bodies, it helps to be aware of these different aspects of physical/motor development (see Figure 11.1).

Physical fitness — a physical state in which muscular strength, endurance, flexibility, and the circulatory-respiratory systems are all in optimal condition.

In a study of children enrolled in day care centers and nursery schools, Poest, Williams, Witt, and Atwood (1989) provided some insights into physical fitness characteristics of preschool-age children. Through questionnaires of parents and teachers, these researchers revealed that (1) preschool children were not engaged in physical activity on a year-round basis—they showed more physical activity in spring and summer; (2) boys were more physically active than girls; (3) parents who were involved in year-round physical activity were more likely to have children also involved in physical activity; and (4) children in nursery schools were more physically active than children in day care.

Motor fitness — a physical state in which motor coordination facilitates speed, agility, power, and balance.

From their findings, these scholars expressed a number of concerns. The fact that child care programs often emphasize fine motor skills, academics, and social development, while limiting the opportunities for large motor activities, raises concern about the general health of these children, as well as their later abilities to participate fully in physical education opportunities. From patterns of year-round physical/motor activities, health benefits accrue; however, these benefits are not realized if physical activities are forsaken due to seasonal and weather conditions. Teacher training seems to be a factor in recognizing and providing for large motor activity in preschool experiences. The need for teacher training to include emphasis in motor development and physical fitness was identified, as was the need for parents to be better informed of their child's physical/motor status. Physical health and fitness are viewed as prerequisites to quality development in other domains—cognitive, social, and emotional.

Large motor fitness and physical fitness are enhanced through a variety of opportunities to engage in physically active exploits. Environments that allow children to run, jump, climb, skip, and dance facilitate this development. Environments for young children must be safe yet free of undue restrictions. Wise selection of toys and equipment to enhance motor development is also critical— wheeled toys, large balls, bean bags, musical instruments, and music to encourage marching and dancing all encourage the use of large muscles.

COORDINATION

The rhythmical integration of motor and sensory systems into a harmonious working together of the body parts.

SPEED

The ability to move from one point to another in the shortest time possible over a short distance.

AGILITY

The ability to move from point to point as rapidly as possible while making successive movements in different directions.

POWER

The ability to perform one maximum explosive force.

BALANCE

The ability to maintain one's equilibrium in relationship to the force of gravity in both static and dynamic movement situations.

FIGURE 11.1

Opportunities to use, expand, and refine motor coordinations enhance motor fitness. (Reprinted with permission from Macmillan Publishing Company from *Developmental Movement Experiences for Children* by David L. Gallahue. Copyright © 1982 by Macmillan Publishing Company.)

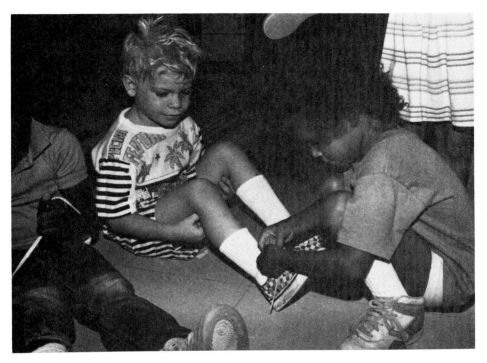

As large motor controls become refined and coordinated, fine motor abilities, such as lacing and tying shoes, emerge.

Fine Motor Development

Because motor development follows a head-downward direction, fine motor development will lag behind large motor controls and coordinations. As large motor controls become refined and coordinated, the muscles of the extremities come into more precise control, and children are generally equipped to perform a variety of tasks such as the following:

Age 4	Age 5
Self-help skills of dressing: some difficulty with zippers, small buttons, tying shoes	Dresses with ease
	Ties shoes
Pours from a pitcher	
Works puzzle of several pieces	Enjoys puzzles with many pieces
Right- or left-handedness evident; occasional ambidextrous behaviors.	Right- or left-handedness is evident
Enjoys crayons, paint, clay	Enjoys drawing, painting, and using a variety of writing tools
Uses beads/strings, snap blocks, and various manipulative toys	Uses Tinker Toys, pegs, and various manipulative toys

Perceptual Motor Development

■ Angela has just awakened from her afternoon nap. Hearing the voice of her grandmother visiting with her teacher across the room, she is further aroused. She sits up, rubs her sleepy eyes, clumsily retrieves her shoes, and makes her way toward the area from which grandmother's voice was heard. There she is greeted with hugs of affection and conversation about her day in the childcare center. ■

Angela has just demonstrated a simple perceptual motor sequence that involved hearing a sound (auditory sensation), recognizing and identifying the sound as that of grandmother's voice (perception), and making a decision to walk to the source of the sound (locomotion).

Individuals come into the world equipped with an array of sensory abilities: touch, vision, hearing, smell, and taste. The sense organs provide information about what is going on around us and within us. The ability to make sense of these sensations—to interpret them—is called perception.

Kinesthetic—the *sensation of body.*

Perception is not an ability present at birth. It is dependent upon adequate functioning of the sense organs, and **kinesthetic** sensitivity (the sensation of body presence, position, and movement), along with cognitive development and experience. Once a sensation is perceived, one must cognitively decide what to do with that information. Actions that follow are often motoric, e.g., turning toward a sound, placing hands over eyes to shield them from a bright light, reaching for an object, and so on. Perceptual motor skills enhance cognitive abilities, body awareness, spatial and directional awareness, and effective time-space orientation (Gallahue, 1982).

Perceptual motor skills are fostered through activities that encourage the child to explore, experiment, and manipulate. Early childhood classrooms, for instance, include a variety of sensory activities: fragrance containers to match (olfactory); mixing and matching fabric patterns (visual) or textures (tactile), and cooking (taste). Musical and rhythmic activities integrate auditory and motor abilities, as children respond to such elements as tempo and pitch (kinesthetic).

Children who do not master early sensory/perceptual/motor skills will have difficulty with more sophisticated cognitive tasks in later school years. Perceiving shapes necessary for forming letters and numbers later on; attending to context clues in picture books; responding adequately to tone of voice as clue to another's message; or perhaps, interpreting facial and body language cues of others are tasks that rely on sensory/motor/perceptual abilities.

Body Awareness, Movement, and Simple Games

Children at age 4 through 5 have mastered the basic locomotor skills of crawling, walking, running, jumping, rolling, sliding, and climbing. These skills evolve rapidly from earlier infant reflex activity, and do so without specific training. Through these unfolding abilities, the child's body awareness also emerges.

Body awareness involves how the child perceives and feels about his body and what it can be willed to do. Body awareness is furthered through the child's visual, auditory, tactile, and kinesthetic perceptions. Particularly important to body awareness are the child's kinesthetic perceptual abilities, that is, the awareness of the body as a whole that occupies space, and how one's body "fits" the available space, functions within it, and adjusts to it. This awareness includes **directionality, left/right dominance**, and **balance**. The ability to move from place to place without running into people or stumbling over objects includes kinesthetic perception, along with vision, hearing, and touch.

Directionality—pertains to the perceptual awareness of direction.

Body awareness becomes a powerful and driving force in all areas of the child's development—psychomotor, psychosocial, and cognitive. Body awareness is incorporated into the child's emerging sense of self and of competence. Body awareness, which involves a sense of control, motivates the child to attempt increasingly complex physical motor activities and simple games.

Left/right dominance—occurs when one or the other side of the body takes the lead in motor coordination activities such as eating or writing.

Movement activities and simple games help to coordinate and refine fundamental body movements; establish directionality, balance, and left-right orientation; and enhance the development of more complex motor abilities. Movement activities and simple games are especially enjoyed by 4- and 5-year-olds as they continue to discover what they can do. They enjoy responding to music in spontaneous and creative ways, pantomiming, playing follow-the-leader, and throwing and catching balls and bean bags. Balancing on one foot, jumping over obstacles, reaching the "highest" point, walking the balance beam forward, sideways, and backwards, touching one's toes to one's nose, and so on, become challenging and self-affirming activities.

Balance—a body awareness component in which postural adjustments prevent one from falling.

Physically active games at this age are simple, noncompetitive, and often child-created, with spontaneously established rules. Some games were played by earlier generations of children, such as "ring around the rosy." Games serve important psychosocial functions in child development (as described in Chapters 9 and 12), as well as encouraging and enhancing the physical and motor well-being of the child.

Gender Awareness

By age 3, children accurately label themselves as boys or girls. However, gender constancy, the realization that one's gender remains the same regardless of changes in appearance, age, clothing, hairstyles, individual wishes, or other factors, does not begin to emerge until around age 5. In Kohlberg's (1966) theory, this development occurs between the ages of 5 and 7. Some scholars have associated this development with the ability to cognitively classify and conserve (Leahy & Shirk, 1984; Marcus & Overton, 1978), an ability that begins to emerge around age 6 or 7 (Piaget, 1952). There seems to be a pattern in the development of gender constancy, with children attributing gender constancy to themselves before others (Eaton & Von Bargen, 1981). The suggested pattern is: (1) gender constancy for self; (2) gender constancy for same-sex others; and (3) gender constancy for members of the opposite sex.

Emerging gender constancy brings with it the awareness that boys and girls, men and women, differ in a number of ways, not the least of which is anatomy. As children begin to realize that anatomy, rather than other factors, defines gender, they become interested in the human body. They are curious about the physiological differences between boys and girls, and men and women. They observe and compare the anatomy and behaviors of each, forming ideas, some stereotypical, about male and female roles and behaviors. They imitate male/female behaviors in their sociodramatic play, experimenting with "being" either male or female. Some of their behaviors evoke chagrin or consternation on the part of adults: peeking up the skirt of a female; asking direct questions about body parts and their functions; giggling about and teasing or ridiculing members of the opposite sex; engaging in "bathroom talk;" and playing "doctor." These normal behaviors are indicative of a growing awareness and need to find acceptance and satisfaction in one's own gender identity.

Adult responses to these behaviors influence the outcomes of positive or negative gender identity and gender role acquisition. A frank and matter-of-fact approach is certainly preferable to shock, embarrassment, or avoidance. Children need adults to help them learn about the differences between boys and girls, and to do so with honest and straightforward answers to their questions. Providing accurate labels, discussing gender roles and behaviors, setting examples, and modeling healthy gender identity and self-acceptance are necessary to building accurate and healthy concepts in children. Children must feel comfortable and safe in asking questions as they arise. Adults must keep in mind that as children establish gender constancy, they are intensely interested in gender role behaviors and are particularly interested in and observant of gender role models.

Special Needs Children

There are many types of disabling conditions affecting young children, and varying degrees of severity. Early diagnosis is critical to efforts to intervene and to prevent complications and serious developmental problems. With the reauthorization of public laws such as P.L. 94–142 (P.L. 101–476) and (P.L. 99–457), which mandate early screening and identification of children with disabilities, this need for early diagnosis has become a matter of widespread knowledge and practice. Children who were previously not served or poorly served by existing programs are now being provided stimulating and enriching educational opportunities, with ongoing growth and development assessments to assure each child provision of needed medical, nutritional, psychological, or other health care services. This, along with sound and enriching educational and psychosocial experiences, ensures each child's chance for optimal growth and development.

As screening for at-risk children has become widespread, its potential for abuse has emerged. Professionals in child development and early education stress the importance of standards in the selection of screening instruments

Adults who are aware of individual differences among children are more accurate in their developmental observations and assessments.

and in the qualifications of those who screen and diagnose (Meisels, 1989). Programs to which children are assigned must meet professional standards of quality and developmental appropriateness.

Sociocultural Differences

Cross-cultural studies have revealed that people from different ethnic groups vary in their expected physical height, weight, and motor skills development. While there are always exceptions, children of North American and European ancestry are generally shorter than children of African ancestry. Children of Asian ancestry are usually shorter than North American and European children. Differences in body proportions also reflect cultural differences between groups. For instance, children of African descent will develop relatively long legs and arms and narrow hips. In contrast, the Asian children usually develop shorter legs and arms and broader hips (Eveleth, 1976).

Higher activity levels and precocious motor abilities are attributed to African-American children (Morgan, 1976). In preschool, this higher activity level is often misperceived as "hyperactivity," and can result in inappropriate adult responses. Precocious motor abilities are evident in the numbers of successful African-American athletes (Hale-Benson, 1982).

Adults who are aware of individual differences among children are more accurate in their developmental observations and assessments. Opportunities for enhanced growth and development can be provided when adults are aware of the attributes that children bring with them to the learning situation.

Factors Influencing Physical/Motor Development

A number of factors, both genetic and environmental, influence physical/motor development. The following factors serve to enhance or perhaps interfere with optimal physical and motor growth and development: genetic makeup of the child, healthy caregiving environments, nutrition, medical and dental care and supervision, opportunities for physical activity, diagnosis and treatment of special needs, and parenting styles and expectations.

Genetic Makeup of the Child

Genes control the child's rate of development, dictating when motor abilities will emerge, growth spurts will occur, teeth will erupt, and adult growth will be achieved. Each individual has inherited a genetic blueprint from his parents. This blueprint determines such characteristics as gender, blood type, skin color, hair color and texture, eye color, stature, intellectual potential, temperament, sociability, certain psychoses, and a host of other characteristics that make each person unique and explain the enormous array of differences among people. Optimal development depends on healthy genetic traits and supportive, healthy environments.

Because each child grows at his own pace, comparisons with siblings or age-mates can be very misleading. Each child's growth occurs according to his own biological blueprint. Adults should be cognizant of their expectations and their reactions to individual developmental accomplishments. For instance, a parent or teacher who conveys disappointment to a 4-year-old child who fails to achieve mastery over the use of scissors is exerting unfair expectations upon the child, who simply does not have the requisite biological maturity for such mastery. On the other hand, undue pride for developmental accomplishments over which the child has no control is equally misleading; the child is simply exhibiting observable manifestations of an inner developmental plan.

In the emergence of attributes and skills, the interactions of heredity and environment undoubtedly play a role. Height and weight, for instance, depend on nutrition and other health factors. Motor coordinations rely on opportunities to move about, explore, discover, and practice emerging abilities. Certain personality characteristics such as activity level, fearfulness, and sociability, which seem to be inheritable traits, are influenced by the environment. Environmental factors can impede or support and enhance growth and development. Health care, nutrition, freedom from accidents and stress, appropriate expectations, and sociocultural factors all contribute to the full realization of a person's genetic potential. So while individuals bring blueprints for development with them when they are born, the development that occurs is intertwined with and dependent on environmental influences.

Healthy Environments

Many elements in the child's environment influence the successful journey toward optimal growth and development. Which ones enhance or impede optimal physical growth and development? Healthy environments for children support their physical growth needs through proper nutrition; immunizations and other protections from disease; medical and dental supervision and care; adequate rest and sleep; play and exercise in safe, sanitary, and protected surroundings; availability of developmentally appropriate and engaging toys and equipment; and satisfying and healthy psychosocial interactions. Some guidelines for selecting appropriate toys and play equipment are given in Figure 11.2.

Nutrition

As with the infant and toddler, the nutritional needs of the 4- through 5-year-old continue to be a critical area of concern, if optimal growth is to occur. Appetites begin to wane as children get older, and food preferences and aversions begin to emerge. Parents and adults, anxious to provide adequate and nutritious meals and snacks for preschool children, are often perplexed when children show little interest in or even distaste for some foods. There are logical explanations for these behaviors.

The eating behaviors of young children reflect their changing growth patterns and physiological and psychological needs. Children at 4 and 5 are growing less rapidly than in previous years and now require less nourishment to support their growth needs. At the same time, food preferences are emerging that reflect the child's growing sense of self and the accompanying desire to make choices. The ability to help oneself to available foods and snacks at age 4 and 5 provides a sense of independence and control.

Food preferences may show a change as children experience a variety of mealtime and other food events outside the home. Changes in food preferences may reflect the influence of older siblings, or perhaps playmates who share

FIGURE 11.2
Selecting appropriate toys and play equipment for young children

1. What age group does the manufacturer recommend for a specific toy?
2. Is the toy safe for young children?
   - Does it have sharp edges?
   - Is it poorly constructed?
   - Does it come apart easily?
   - Can the child choke on it or parts of it?
   - Is the weight of the toy appropriate for its size?
   - Is the toy made of non-toxic materials?
   - Is the toy flame resistant?
3. Is the toy responsibly manufactured?
   - Is it appropriately priced?
   - Is the toy color-fast?
   - Is it appealing on a long-term basis?
   - Is it overly packaged?
   - Is it easy to care for and store?
   - Does the toy have essential parts that could be lost?
   - Is it strong enough to withstand normal use?
4. What areas of growth are enhanced by the toy?
   - Cognitive/intellectual development
     a. Does it promote problem-solving?
     b. Does it elicit dramatic play?
     c. Does it invite multiple uses?
   - Communication skills (speaking/listening)
     a. Can the toy be used by two or more children?
     b. Does the toy elicit discussion and creative language?
   - Large/fine motor skills
     a. Does the toy elicit action and movement from children?
     b. Does the toy encourage movements, both large/dynamic movements and fine/small motions?
   - Self-concept development
     a. Are children intellectually and physically challenged by the toy in a developmentally appropriate manner?
     b. Are the toys non-stereotypical, not gender-biased, and adaptable to the special needs of exceptional children?
   - Socialization
     a. Does the toy *require* more than one participant?
     b. Will children want to share the toy and related activities with siblings and friends?
5. Is the toy adaptable to children's needs and wishes?
   - Can the toy be used in various ways?
   - Is the toy appropriately ambiguous? (Does the toy allow children to use their imaginations? Is it overly specific to a singular use?)

mealtimes in preschool settings. Television advertising also influences the child's food preferences. A previous illness may become associated with a certain food, making it aversive for a time. Adults should recognize that fluctuations in appetite and in food preferences are normal and should expect them to occur from time to time. As with most adults, there may also be certain foods that a child may never like.

Mealtimes need not become a battleground between adult and child. The amount of food a child consumes is not necessarily as important as the quality of the foods consumed and the attitudes and habits that children come to associate with foods and mealtimes. Regular and predictable mealtimes provide the child who is hungry an opportunity to meet his food needs. Nutritious meals and snacks supply the necessary requirements for growth and energy. Selecting and offering nutritious foods that have "child-appeal" in color, texture, aroma, and manageability increase the likelihood that they will be eaten. Pleasant conversation and social interactions at mealtime provide associations conducive to positive attitudes toward food.

Children's diets must supply sufficient nutrients to meet the needs of growing bones and muscles, healthy formation and eruption of permanent teeth, and continued growth and development of all body tissues and organs. Much energy is needed to sustain the high activity levels typical of young children. We should point out that activity levels in children also vary; more active children may need more food than a less active friend of the same age and size.

A number of issues relating to foods and children have surfaced in recent years: the relationship between certain foods and behaviors of children (e.g., sugar and food additives with hyperactivity); cholesterol and later heart disease; obesity in children and its causes and prevention; fast-food diets; and insecticides and cancer. While deserving research and attention, many of these issues have been exaggerated through the media, creating diets and food fads of questionable value for the American child.

While some hyperactive children may benefit from altered diets (Lipton & Mayo, 1983), well-controlled scientific studies have not been able to substantiate a strong association between sugar consumption and unusual behaviors or mental performance in children (Kruesi & Rapoport, 1986; NIH, 1982). The relationship between cholesterol levels in the blood and later heart disease and concern over obesity in children has prompted a number of diets low in necessary nutrients for growing children. While these are legitimate issues, their treatment should be based on sound information, thorough physical examinations to determine individual needs, and sensible provisions of nutritious meals and snacks, along with adequate amounts of rest and exercise.

Recommended nutrient intakes for children are shown in Figure 11.3. Adults should responsibly provide nutritious and adequate diets for children. On the other hand, since hunger can only be felt by the child, the child should exercise control over how much he will eat. Helping children to establish regular eating times; avoiding unnecessary snacks high in calories but low in nutrients; and encouraging adequate amounts of exercise and activity assist children in developing sound nutritional habits and preferences that will support their growth and ensure health and well-being.

FIGURE 11.3
Recommended nutrient intake for young children

Meat group. Meat, poultry, fish, organ meats, or meat substitutes

Age 1–3	4–6	7–10
2 servings	2 servings	2 servings
(1 oz. ea.)	(1$\frac{1}{2}$ oz. ea.)	(1$\frac{1}{2}$–2 oz. ea.)

Substitutes for the protein of 1 oz. meat: 1 egg, 1 oz. cheese, $\frac{1}{4}$ c. cottage cheese, $\frac{1}{4}$ c. peanuts, $\frac{1}{3}$ c. other nuts, $\frac{1}{2}$ c. cooked dry peas or beans, 2 T. peanut butter

Milk group. Milk (whole, skim, dry, evaporated), buttermilk, yogurt, cottage cheese, and other dairy products

Age 1–3	4–6	7–10
2 cups	2 cups	2 cups

Substitutes for the calcium of 1 cup milk: 1 c. yogurt, 1$\frac{1}{3}$ c. cottage cheese, 1$\frac{1}{2}$ c. ice cream, 1$\frac{1}{4}$ oz. ($\frac{1}{3}$ c. grated) natural cheese, 1$\frac{3}{4}$ oz. processed cheese

Vegetable/fruit group. For vitamin A: deep yellow-orange or very dark green; For vitamin C: citrus fruit, melon, strawberries, broccoli, tomatoes, raw cabbage

Age 1–3	4–6	7–10
4 servings or more	4 servings or more	4 servings or more
(3 T. ea.)	($\frac{1}{4}$ c. ea.)	($\frac{1}{4}$ c. ea.)

One vitamin C source daily and one high vitamin A source at least every other day should be eaten. Other fruits and vegetables fill out this food group.

Bread/cereal group. Whole-grain or enriched bread, cereal, rice, pasta

Age 1–3	4–6	7–10
3 servings	4 servings	4 servings or more

Calorie needs

Age 1–3	4–6	7–10
1,300	1,800	2,400

Source: Reprinted from *Meal Time! Happy Time!* by the American Dietetic Association, 1975. Chicago: Author. Copyright 1975 by the American Dietetic Association. Used with permission.

Dental Care

Diet, dental hygiene, and heredity determine the dental health of each individual. Children need guidance in setting good dental hygiene habits. Four- and 5-year-olds can be taught proper brushing technique and the importance of regular tooth brushing. They can be responsible for brushing their own teeth after meals, if this routine has been established from earlier years. Regular visits to the dentist for examinations and cleaning prevent dental problems and promote healthy attitudes toward caring for one's teeth, mouth, and gums. Children can also be taught the destructive effects of candies, gum, and other

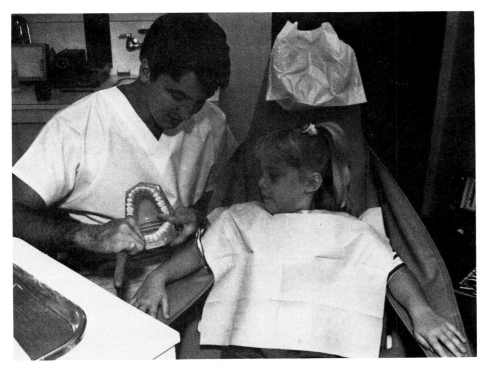

Children need guidance in developing good habits of dental hygiene.

sugars on their teeth and be provided with low-sugar and fresh fruit snacks instead. Habits of dental hygiene begun early in life continue into adulthood.

Opportunities for Physical Activity

Children have a natural impulse to be active—to run, climb, jump, hop, skip, shout, and ride wheeled toys. Opportunities to develop and use these abilities occur when children are provided the space and developmentally appropriate equipment to do so. The development of large motor controls and abilities enhances self-concept, self-confidence, social interactions, and emerging fine motor controls.

Because children need to be physically active, efforts to restrain and keep them quiet for long periods of time are unhealthy and usually futile. Preschool and kindergarten programs that require children to work at tables or desks or expect children to listen to teacher-directed lessons for extended periods of time are obviously developmentally inappropriate and curtail opportunities for more active and beneficial pursuits. The need for movement, for manipulations of real objects and concrete materials, and for verbal interactions must be acknowledged by adults who work with young children. Each child's day must

   *Role of the Early Childhood Professional*

Enhancing Physical/Motor Development in Children Ages 4 Through 5

1. Provide safe and healthy surroundings for children.
2. Provide for the child's nutritional needs.
3. Oversee provision of health care through immunizations and other protections from disease.
4. Provide regular dental examinations.
5. Establish healthy routines for rest, sleep, play, and activity.
6. Control the stress-producing events in the child's life.
7. Provide encouragement for emerging large and small motor abilities and body awareness.
8. Provide age and developmentally appropriate toys and equipment for the child to manipulate, explore, and use.
9. Assure the child's safety through adequate supervision and removal of environmental temptations and hazards.
10. Provide opportunities for satisfying and supportive psychosocial interactions with parents, other adults, and other children.
11. Facilitate the child's awareness of health and safety practices.
12. Encourage a sense of responsibility for one's own health maintenance and safety.

include opportunities for movement about the classroom and the learning centers, for singing and dancing and creative movement, and for use of equipment that requires large motor coordinations. Outdoor play should be a daily event in every child's life, where running, jumping, skipping, and other large motor activities and games can occur in safe and protected surroundings.

Lack of adequate physical activity impedes physical growth and development and motor coordinations. Perceptual motor abilities are adversely affected, which in turn affect later academic success. Psychological development is affected through reduced self-esteem and decreased social interactions. Both the amount and the quality of social interactions are affected when children do not participate in active play opportunities. Physical fitness—including strength, endurance, balance, and flexibility—is adversely affected. Lack of activity contributes to obesity, poor resting and sleeping habits, poor appetite, and other health problems. One can readily see the importance of opportunities for physical activities to the overall health and well-being of children.

Special Needs

It can be said that all children share the same basic needs for nourishment, medical and dental care, protection from disease and accidents, adequate rest and sleep, play and exercise, and satisfying interpersonal relationships. Specific handicapping conditions affect the course of a child's development in specific ways. The extent to which these basic needs are met, or are modified to meet individual handicapping conditions, influences the ultimate growth and development for the child, as well as his ongoing health and well-being.

Sociocultural Differences

Cultural differences in child-rearing practices influence the types of activities that are valued and encouraged. There are cultural differences in the amount of freedom that children have and the amount of physical activity that is tolerated. There are differences in the kinds of activities for which coaching and, perhaps, lessons are provided and the extent to which an individual child's interests and capabilities are supported through the provision of toys and equipment. There are also cultural differences in attitudes toward medicine and medical supervision.

Food preferences and methods of preparation are also unique to cultural groups, as are food-related traditions. Ethnic food traditions influence the food intake and preferences of children. When these diets are adequate in all of the four food groups, good nutrition occurs. Diets deficient in certain food groups may need to be supplemented or enhanced to meet the growth needs of children.

Key Terms

percentile   directionality
physical fitness   left/right dominance
motor fitness   balance
kinesthetic

Review Strategies/Activities

1. Visit a school playground during recess for kindergarten and also for second or third grade. Compare the types of activities and games of the children in each group. How do the activities differ? How do the children's large motor abilities in the older and younger groups compare?
2. Plan a week of nutritious snacks for young children. Using a calorie and nutrient guide, what nutrients will children derive from these snacks, and how many calories will be supplied?
3. Visit a toy store. Using the checklist in Figure 11.2, make a list of acceptable and unacceptable toys or equipment for 4- and 5-year-olds.

4. Interview a pediatrician. Ask about his or her perceptions of the health status of today's child. What are his or her greatest concerns about child health today? How might parents promote optimal growth and development for their children? Compare your findings with other classmates.

5. Develop a home safety checklist. Inspect your own home for health and safety hazards to children.

Further Readings

Endres, J. B., & Rockwell, R. E. (1985). *Food, nutrition and the young child* (2nd ed.). St. Louis: Times Mirror/Mosby College Publishing.
> Written for students of child development and early education, this book provides basic concepts of food and nutrition for young children. Techniques for integrating food and nutrition insights into meal planning and into the curriculum for young children are provided.

Froschl, M., Colon, L., Rubin, E., & Sprung, B. (1984). *Including all of us: An early childhood curriculum about disability*. New York: Equity Concepts, Inc.
> This helpful book is a guide for creating early childhood curricula that are nonsexist, multicultural, and disability sensitive.

Gallahue, D. L. (1982). *Developmental movement experiences for children*. New York: John Wiley & Sons.

Gallahue, D. L. (1982). *Understanding motor development in children*. New York: John Wiley & Sons.
> These companion texts provide both theoretical and practical information on the motor development and needs of young children. Although written for physical education teachers, they provide extensive information and guidance for early childhood educators as well.

Kendrick, A. S., Kaufmann, R., & Messenger, K. P. (Eds.). (1988). *Healthy young children: A manual for programs*. Washington, DC: National Association for the Education of Young Children.
> A comprehensive manual for those who work with children in group settings. This book reflects current research and recommendations of experts in the fields of health and early childhood education. An excellent reference document.

Meisels, S. J. (1989). *Developmental screening in early childhood: A guide* (3rd ed.). Washington, DC: National Association for the Education of Young Children.
> A guide to the laws behind and purposes of developmental screening, selection of appropriate screening instruments for the identification of at-risk children, and setting up screening programs in early childhood settings.

CHAPTER 12

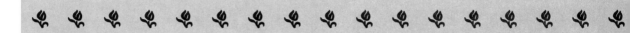

*And the first step, as you know, is always what matters most,
particularly when we are dealing with those who are young and
tender. That is the time when they are taking shape and when any
impression we choose to make leaves a permanent mark.*

Plato

Psychosocial Development of the Young Child Ages 4 Through 5

After reading and studying this chapter, you will demonstrate comprehension by:

- Describing the psychosocial development of the 4- through 5-year-old child.
- Listing major social and emotional milestones in psychosocial development during this period.
- Identifying factors that influence earliest psychosocial development.
- Describing the role of adults in healthy psychosocial development of 4- and 5-year-olds.

In contrast to the turbulent toddler period, 4- and 5-year-olds are composed. Refinements of physical/motor abilities have enhanced self-help and autonomy. Advances in cognitive development have sharpened the child's perceptions and increased understandings. Language development has opened new and more effective communications. An increased ability to delay gratification of needs and desires has led to more patient and negotiable interactions with others. The desire for and enjoyment of age-mates has expanded the child's social circle beyond attachment persons. These developments result in a period during which the child is more amiable, compliant and socialized.

Effects of Earlier Experiences on 4- and 5-Year-Olds

For centuries, as the Plato quotation suggests, philosophers and psychologists have hypothesized that events in the earliest years of a child's life influence

later development, sometimes in critical ways. Centuries since Plato's admonitions, scholars continue to speculate on the relationship between early and later experience. Sigmund Freud's (1905/1930) psychoanalytic theory, for instance, proposed that experiences and conflicts occurring during early psychosexual stages of development can have lasting effects on later personality development. Freud placed considerable importance upon the mother-infant relationship in influencing the child's interpersonal relationships.

Stanford University psychologist Robert Sears, known for overseeing the now-famous Terman longitudinal studies of gifted children (Terman, 1959), has asserted that many adult behavioral patterns are acquired in childhood. Through his various studies of childhood dependency, aggression, and child-rearing practices, Sears, a behaviorist, viewed early life experience and the "rewards" of the socialization process as significant to the child's later behaviors. For instance, in an early study he and his colleagues found high levels of dependency in normal preschool children who had experienced abrupt and severe weaning (Sears & Whiting, 1953). Another study related hostile and aggressive behaviors in parents to later disobedient, aggressive, and delinquent behaviors in their children (Sears, Maccoby, & Levin, 1957).

Erikson's Theory of Psychosocial Development

Influenced by and building upon Freud's works, Erik Erikson's theory of psychosocial development (1963) supports an early experience/later development hypothesis. Successful outcomes at each of Erikson's eight stages of personality development are thought to prepare the child for subsequent stages.

Studies by Bowlby, Ainsworth, and other ethological theorists have examined the effects of early attachments on later psychosocial development. Securely attached infants have been shown to be more socially competent upon entering preschool and more responsive to their age-mates in kindergarten (Stroufe, 1983; Stroufe, Schork, Motti, Lawroski, & LaFreniere, 1984). In other studies, securely attached children were found to be less dependent on adults and more curious than were children who had been insecurely attached (Arend, Gove, & Stroufe, 1979; Stroufe, Fox, & Pancake, 1983).

In contrast to the early experience/later development hypotheses, a life-span view of growth and development assures us that single events in early child growth and development do not result in behaviors that are not or cannot be modified as a result of later growth and development or subsequent life experiences. Indeed, throughout life, the potential for both positive and negative influences on growth and development exists. Family interaction patterns influence the course that psychosocial development takes. Guidance and discipline techniques, adult expectations, unusual or stressful events, individual or family life joys and successes, disappointments and traumas, and various role models are all influencing factors. Keep these factors in mind as we explore the very complex subject of psychosocial development in 4- through 5-year-old children.

Initiative versus Guilt

The 4- to 5-year-old has entered Erikson's third stage of psychosocial development (see Figure 12.1). Building upon the previous stages of trust and autonomy, the child is now struggling between a sense of **initiative** and a sense of guilt. Of this stage, Erikson says:

Initiative—The third of Erikson's psychosocial stages, in which the child pursues ideas, individual interests, and activities; when thwarted the child becomes self-critical and experiences guilt.

> There is in every child at every stage a new miracle of vigorous unfolding, which constitutes a new hope and a new responsibility for all. Such is the sense and the pervading quality of initiative. The criteria for all of these senses and qualities are the same: a crisis, more or less beset with fumbling and fear, is resolved in that the child suddenly seems to "grow together," both in his person and in his body. He appears "more himself," more loving, relaxed and brighter in his judgment, more activated and activating. He is in free possession of a surplus of energy which permits him to forget failures quickly and to approach what seems desirable (even if it also seems uncertain and even dangerous) with undiminished and more accurate direction. Initiative adds to autonomy the quality of undertaking, planning, and "attacking" a task for the sake of being active and on the move, where before self-will more often than not, inspired acts of defiance or, at any rate, protested independence. (1963, p. 255)

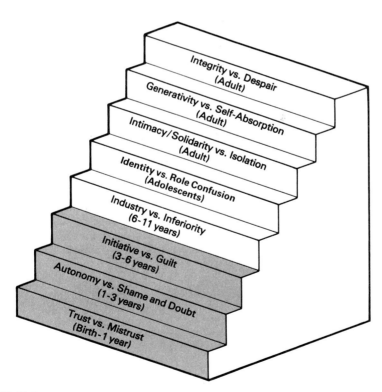

FIGURE 12.1
The child whose sense of initiative is emerging is eager to master new skills.

The child whose sense of initiative is emerging is eager to master new skills, use language to ask questions to seek new meanings, and enlist others in work and play interactions. The child's social circle is expanding rapidly beyond the attachment persons of earlier years, and interactions with others are vigorously sought. Mastery of motor skills frees the child to try new feats, e.g., climbing with greater agility on playground structures or riding the bicycle without its training wheels. The child is eager to learn and genuinely enjoys those events that enlarge and enrich understandings of an ever-widening world. The child enjoys planning and cooperating with others and anticipating coming events or activities. Activities like planning a family outing or cleaning the house or classroom for a special visitor are pursued with exhilaration and shared purpose.

Initiative is used to engage others in conversation and to enlist playmates. Play becomes more social and elaborated. Imitation, imagination, and fantasy thrust play into complex and fluid sociodramatic enacting. Extended sociodramatic scenarios, alone or with playmates, evolve. Sociodramatic scenarios extend, digress, and diverge with new fantasies as playmates enter and exit the play group.

The developing sense of initiative is not always characterized by positive behaviors, however. Sometimes initiative gets out-of-bounds. Misdirected energy and enthusiasm can lead children to use physical or verbal aggression. Pushing a playmate aside in order to be "next" on the balance beam is an example of coercive and negative interactions in which the child attempts to control others. Coercion such as "I won't be your best friend" or "you can't come to my birthday party" are examples of misdirected initiative. In addition, growing facility with language increases the child's use of language to shock, or perhaps to deceive, another form of misdirected initiative.

Out-of-bounds initiative can produce feelings of anxiety, embarrassment, and guilt as the child becomes aware that her behaviors are unacceptable to others. Unsure and socially unskilled, the child's sense of initiative is placed at risk, unless appropriate alternative behaviors are suggested. Adult guidance is needed to redirect initiative toward positive, more constructive outcomes. Guidance, however, must balance control and freedom for the child. Failure to guide (undercontrol), or the opposite, overcontrolling, undermines the child's opportunities to succeed with initiating behaviors.

When a sense of guilt exceeds a sense of initiative, children tend to seek undue assurances and permission from adults and peers. They are reluctant to take personal risks, try new activities, or reach out to others for interactions, and often fail to fully enjoy their own emerging capabilities. Both under- and overcontrolling guidance techniques contribute to the development of a sense of guilt. Thwarted in efforts to initiate ideas, interests, and activities, or teased, ridiculed, or treated as though their many questions are annoying or their pretend play silly, children may develop a lack of self-confidence that persists through later ages.

Initiative is fostered through opportunities to explore and engage in new and challenging activities. Four- and five-year-old children must have expanded opportunities for social interactions, cooperative endeavors, and mind-engaging projects. They need raw materials from which to create, and space and props for fantasy and imaginative play. Children in this stage of psychosocial development need adults who answer their numerous questions with respect and focused interest. They need adults to encourage and support their unique interests and abilities. At the same time, children need protection from their impulses and help in developing effective social interaction skills. Child guidance must set reasonable limits on behavior, yet encourage the child to trust her own ideas.

Fear and Anxiety

Early studies of fear attributed its evolution to maturation and increasing cognitive development (Gesell, 1930; Jersild & Holmes, 1935a, 1935b; Jones & Jones, 1928). In one of the earliest studies of childhood fears, Jones and Jones wrote, "Fear arises when we know enough to recognize the potential danger in the situation but have not advanced to the point of complete comprehension and control of the changing situation" (p. 143).

Maturation and learning contribute to changes in fear behaviors from the infant/toddler period to ages 4 through 5. A variety of fears are experienced by the 4- through 5-year-old child, due to insufficient experience, incomplete information or knowledge, and a variety of misconceptions.

> After the divorce of her parents, Josie feared her own impulses and behaviors, lest she "cause" the other parent to leave her.

Some fears are due to the child's inability to separate fantasy and reality:

> In role playing the *Three Billy Goats Gruff*, Angela became so immersed in the drama that she began to cry and cling to the teacher in fear that the troll would harm her. For a time thereafter, she had nightmares, feared the dark, and resisted the retelling of the fairy tale.

Still other fears are learned through observation of fears modeled by parents, siblings, relatives and friends:

> Franky's mother always referred to rain, regardless of amount of precipitation or accompanying elements as a "storm." Her own childhood experience in a tornado had left a lingering fear of storms and a generalization of all rains as potential storms. Thus, she modeled fear of all rainy weather.

Fears are also learned through one's own experience: bitten by a dog, a child may fear all dogs, or perhaps all small animals, for a time.

The sources of fear and anxiety are numerous. All children experience fear and anxiety from time to time and in varying degrees of intensity. Yet, not all childhood fears are the same. Some children fear the dark, others do not. As well, there are individual differences in the way children respond to fear stimuli. One child may quietly withdraw, or hover unobtrusively near a trusted adult; another may cry loudly, cling desperately, and resist being consoled.

Many fears or anxieties serve important adaptive or "self-preservation" functions and, as such, are considered "healthy" fears. Fear of traffic, strange animals, motorized tools and equipment, fires, dangerous elevations, and firearms are healthy because they prompt appropriate avoidance behaviors. Some children do not develop a healthy fear of danger and require guidance and supervision to protect them from avoidable mishaps. Such guidance should be informative without arousing curiosity, which can lead the child into dangerous explorations; explanations should not exaggerate the danger or alarm the child.

Helping young children understand and cope with their fears is a matter of providing appropriate experiences, explanations, and encouragement. Children need age-appropriate dialogue and explanations that provide labels and insights. When adults are calm, encouraging, and knowledgeable, children are assured. In time, some fears subside and disappear, new fears emerge, and new coping strategies become a part of the child's behavior repertoire.

Transitional Objects

Though the role and the importance of transitional objects varies from child to child, transitional objects continue to represent an important part of the psychosocial development of children ages 4 through 5. The duration of attachments to transitional objects varies from child to child. For some, the attachment is long-lived; for others, the attachment may be brief, perhaps even transitory from one object to another for varying periods of time. Affection for the transitional objects can be quite deep and openly expressed. At the same time, the objects can become the target of aggressive and serious mistreatment, as children fantasize or work through emotional and social understandings.

The need for the transitional object recedes as children shift their energies and attentions from themselves to others, and from fantasy to real-life tasks. The child may then choose to carry the object in the car en route to school, but leave it there for "reunion" when the school day is over. Or the child may wish to carry it into the classroom, only to stuff it into a cubbyhole to be "visited" on occasion during the day. Sometimes symbolic substitutes signal a more mature approach. A symbolic substitute can take the form of a photograph of the child with the transitional object, or perhaps a family photograph carried in the child's backpack or lunch box. Often classroom teachers provide bulletin board space for children's photographs of themselves and their families.

The child herself must make the decision to forego the transitional object. Coercion, disparaging remarks, ridicule, or other attempts to separate the child from the transitional object only serve to intensify the child's resolve to cling to it (Jalongo, 1987). Adults must accept the child's right to refuse to share the transitional object with others. Sometimes maturity in other areas leads adults to believe that the child should have outgrown the need for the transitional object, but it does not necessarily signal a readiness to abandon the transitional object.

Transitional objects continue to represent an important part of the psychosocial development of children ages 4 through 5.

■ Jeremy's interest in astronomy has found support in books provided for him by his parents and teachers. Though beyond the expected reading abilities for his years, Jeremy reads his astronomy books with some facility. Each morning his backpack is carefully prepared for school with one or two of his current favorite astronomy books *and* his well-worn teddy bear. For the duration of kindergarten, Jeremy carries his teddy bear to school with him, carefully tucked into his backpack. Wisely, neither his parents nor his teachers discourage this practice. ■

Egocentric Behavior

Few kindergarten teachers would disagree that 4- and 5-year-old children exhibit egocentric behaviors. Fifteen 4- or 5-year-olds in a group often present 15 or more competing requests for the teachers's attention:

- In the middle of a finger-play, Jeremy discovers a hangnail on one of his fingers, leaves his seated position and climbs and oversteps through the group to show his injured finger to the teacher.
- Upon arrival at kindergarten, Angela tempts her teacher with, "Do you want to see what I brought in my lunch today?"
- During the school nurse's demonstration of handwashing, Kari interjects, "You know what? My daddy washed his new car last night."
- Lawanda shouts from across the room, "Teacher, Shannon is sitting in *my* chair."

Egocentrism in 4- and 5-year-olds is characterized by the belief that others are experiencing the world as they are. However, through social interactions in preschool groups, children experience the needs and wishes of others and are exposed to a variety of points of view. Peer group interactions provided by preschools and kindergartens offer unlimited opportunities for children to experience the perspective of others. Perspective-taking is a skill that emerges through social interactions and assists children in becoming less egocentric.

During sociodramatic play, pretending promotes perspective-taking. As the child engages in a variety of role-taking experiences ("You be the nurse, and I'll be sick"), awareness of others' roles emerges. In attempting to play out a sociodramatic scenario, the child becomes aware of discrepancies between her own intentions and those of playmates. In adjusting the sociodrama to the wishes of others, the child's perspective-taking abilities are enhanced.

In their review of research on social perspective-taking in young children, Rubin and Everett (1982) identified three forms of perspective-taking: (1) cognitive perspective-taking, which includes the ability to consider others' thoughts and intentions; (2) affective perspective-taking, the ability to take into account the feelings and emotions of others; and (3) spatial perspective-taking, the ability to consider the other person's physical view of the world. A child who attempts to organize a game may be exhibiting cognitive perspective-taking. A child who attempts to comfort a crying playmate may be exhibiting an awareness of the child's distress or its cause. A child who removes an obstacle from the path of another, preventing an accident, is demonstrating spatial perspective-taking.

Prosocial Development

Altruism — intentions to help others without the expectation of reward.

Prosocial behaviors include empathy and **altruism**. Empathy is the ability to recognize the feelings of others and to vicariously experience those feelings — feelings such as distress, anxiety, or delight. Altruism is defined as behavior intended to help another without expectation of reward. In young children, prosocial behaviors are influenced by a number of factors. Among these factors are age, level of cognitive functioning, perspective-taking abilities, individual personality, family interactions, discipline strategies, and role models.

Studies have shown that when children observe prosocial models, they generally become more prosocial themselves (Bandura, 1977; Radke-Yarrow, Zahn-Waxler, & Chapman, 1983). This is particularly true when the child and the model have had a warm relationship and when children have experienced warmth and nurturing from the model (Hoffman, 1975; Sears, Maccoby, & Levin, 1957; Yarrow, Scott & Waxler, 1973).

■ Jeremy's friend Shaun has just recovered from chicken pox and is finally available for a visit. Ann greets Shaun upon his arrival and hustles the two children off to Jeremy's room to play. Jeremy's delight in seeing his absent friend is somewhat overshadowed by his observation of his mother's greeting. He, nevertheless, leads Shaun to his room and the two become involved with a new and rather difficult puzzle. Stumped in putting the puzzle together, Jeremy runs to another room to summon his mother's assistance. Walking back to his room together, Jeremy engages his mother in his concern, "You didn't tell Shaun you were sorry." Confused, his mother inquires, Sorry? About what, Jeremy?" "About he's been sick," Jeremy responds.

Jeremy's own previous experiences with being sick had been accompanied by expressions of concern such as, "I am so sorry you are not feeling well." "I am really glad you feel better today." As well, he had observed his parents convey similar concern with others. Thus, through observation, Jeremy had learned to verbally express concern for others and felt some incongruence when such concern didn't occur on this happy occasion with Shaun—an unintentional oversight on his mother's part.   ■

Studies of discipline maintain that when **inductive discipline** strategies are employed, prosocial behaviors are more likely to emerge (Baumrind, 1972; Hoffman, 1975; Moore & Eisenberg, 1984). Inductive discipline is characterized by respect, reason, warmth, affection, and clear expectations.

Inductive discipline—a positive, nonpunitive form of discipline that relies on reasons and rationales to help children control their behaviors.

In addition to role models and disciplinary techniques, prosocial development is fostered by:

1. Experiences that promote positive self-concepts. There is some evidence that positive feelings about oneself are related to higher frequencies of cooperative behaviors among 4- and 5-year-old children (Cauley & Tyler, 1989).
2. Assignment of age-appropriate responsibilities whereby children come to feel a contributing part of the family, class, or other group (Whiting & Whiting, 1975).
3. Opportunities to interact with other children, to engage in sociodramatic play in which role-taking and perspective-taking are enhanced (Rubin & Everett, 1982).
4. Opportunities to participate in noncompetitive, cooperative games (Orlick, 1981).

5. Exposure to literature, television programs, and electronic games and toys that project prosocial themes (Coates, Pusser, & Goodman, 1976; Moore & Eisenberg, 1984).

Self-Concept

According to Erikson (1963), autonomy facilitates new discoveries and the acquisition of new skills and leads to an activity-based self-concept appropriate to the emergence of a sense of initiative. With autonomy in place, the 4- to 5-year-old describes herself according to skills that are being mastered. The self-concept is based mostly on the child's perceptions of her physical attributes and possessions (Damon & Hart, 1982). A self-description based on perceptions of physical attributes is evident in statements such as, "I am bigger"; "I can tie my shoes"; and "Watch me skip." Self-descriptions related to age and possessions are also utilized by the child to affirm the sense of self, for example, "I'm going to be four on my birthday," or "I have a new bicycle with training wheels."

Some children have difficulty forming positive self-concepts due to a variety of reasons, including parental and child caring methods that militate against the development of a positive self-concept. Limited opportunities to use and enhance emerging physical/motor abilities, lack of affection and appropriate attention, harsh and punitive discipline, family stress, or excessive negative responses to the child are examples of factors that preclude effective development of self-awareness, self-concept, and self-esteem.

Gender Identity and Gender Role Development

Related to the sense of self is the awareness of one's gender. Since parents and caregivers tend to respond differently to males and females from birth, socialization and the gender-role expectations placed upon the child during early development influence both gender identity and development of gender role behaviors. Parents often provide gender-typed toys for their children, including dolls for girls and trucks for boys (Huston, 1983). From the time they are infants, boys are encouraged to be more physically active than girls (Frisch, 1977; Smith & Loyd, 1978). Parents are more inclined to encourage boys to explore and learn about the environment, while girls are encouraged to remain dependent and helpless (Fagot, 1978). Parental treatment seems to favor boys with regard to freedom and independence (Block, 1983; Saegert & Hart, 1976).

There is some evidence that parents interact quantitatively differently with boys and girls, providing more attention to girls (Fagot, 1978). As a rule, boys receive more pressure than girls to assume gender-typical behaviors. Mothers do not seem to get as disturbed over gender "inappropriate" play behaviors as do fathers (Langlois & Down, 1980). Some of this anxiety on the part of parents stems from confusion about how gender identity and gender role development occur.

Kohlberg (1966) proposed a cognitive stage sequence for the development of gender roles. The sequence he proposed follows:

1. Gender identity, wherein the child can provide a label for himself or herself as either a boy or a girl. This is usually achieved by age 3.
2. Gender stability, wherein the child realizes that boys grow up to be men and girls grow up to be women.
3. Gender constancy, wherein the child realizes that changes in hairstyle or clothing do not alter a person's sex. Gender constancy emerges between ages 5 and 7.

Prior to gender stability, children's pretend play is quite androgenous—boys can be mothers, and girls can be fathers. Scholars in child development find little cause for concern for these play behaviors in young children, for they represent opportunities for children to affirm their own gender identities and gender roles. Honig (1983) asserts that children need role models who encourage a wide spectrum of expressions of feelings and behaviors. Role models who are comfortable with their own gender assist children in developing healthy gender identity and gender role behaviors.

Race Awareness

As noted above, self-concept emerges as children become aware of their distinguishing physical characteristics, gender, and abilities. Also related to the emerging sense of self is the child's awareness of race. Between the ages of 3 and 5, children are becoming aware of differences between people. When a young child discovers racial differences, the disturbance in her own tenuous self-identification may cause her to respond with rejection or hostility toward others whose racial characteristics are different (Stevenson, 1967). Children at this phase are not forming generalized negative attitudes toward other races, but are dealing with their own self-concepts and racial identity. There are now discrepancies between self-perceptions and what the child is seeing in others.

With this discovery, young children behave in a variety of curious, prosocial, and sometimes negative ways toward one another. They feel each other's hair, compare skin colors while holding arms side by side, and ask questions about their differences. They may verbally experiment with names of racial groups. There is some evidence that children from minority groups develop racial awareness earlier than other children (Katz, 1982). Further, young children seem particularly vulnerable to racial stereotyping (Thurman & Lewis, 1979). Sensitive and positive support of these early encounters among young children provides the scaffolding for positive relationships that generally emerge among young children.

Child-rearing, from birth onward, occurs in a cultural context that inculcates in the child concepts and attitudes about race, cultural identities, values, and expectations. Cultural contexts include the language spoken in the home, modes of expression, celebrations, holidays, family traditions, family cohesion, discipline techniques and authority relationships, food and clothing preferences, family goals and values, achievement orientations, and choices and opportunities in education, work, and recreation. The child's concepts, understandings, and attitudes about race—her own and that of others—are derived at first from the cultural contexts of home and family.

Early child care, preschool, and kindergarten experiences support and extend the child's growing sense of membership in a particular cultural or racial group. Early childhood programs support multicultural perspectives in the following ways (Ramsey, 1982):

- Enhancing self-concept development and cultural identity.
- Helping children develop social skills of perspective-taking, communicating, cooperating, and conflict resolution.
- Broadening children's awareness of other lifestyles, languages, points of view, and ways of doing things through enriched multicultural curriculums.

Self-Esteem

The journey from self-awareness and self-recognition in infancy, to a reasonably accurate and positive self-concept in early childhood, to hearty self-esteem is punctuated with evaluative events in which the child assesses herself against the responses of others. Along the way, the child takes in and processes information about her own physical attributes, gender, race, family, friends, and cognitive and social abilities. From this information, the child draws conclusions about her worthiness, thus forming impressions that may or may not be accurate and that may or may not be positive or self-affirming. When the child has experienced positive and self-affirming relationships with parents, caregivers, siblings, and peers, she feels competent, worthy, accepted, loved, and valued. This self-evaluative information provides the underpinnings for hearty self-esteem and enhanced interactions with others.

Interactions with the child need to be supportive, positive, and nurturing and must convey acceptance of the child's uniqueness, age, stage, and capabilities. Expectations must be age and developmentally appropriate to assure a cumulative history of successes. As children get older, peer reactions become important and, for a time, may surpass those of adults in influencing the child's self-evaluations.

Self-Control, Compliance, and Discipline

Studies of child-rearing practices have provided insights into the kinds of adult-child interactions that are most likely to result in child behaviors that are cooperative, self-controlled, and compliant. Infant attachment studies emphasize the importance of the infant-mother attachment in later development of compliance (Matas, Arend, & Stroufe, 1978). When infants and toddlers have developed a warm, mutually affectionate relationship with their caregivers, they are more inclined to obey requests. Toddlers whose mothers are affectionate, verbally stimulating and responsive, and use positive methods of control are more compliant (Olson, Bates, & Bayles, 1984).

Conversely, children whose parents have used arbitrary commands, physical control, or coercive strategies to bring children into compliance are less inclined to cooperate or comply with other adults, regardless of how gentle or friendly the other adult may be (Londerville & Main, 1981; Main & Weston, 1981). The implications for these children as they enter preschools and kindergartens are clear. Caregivers and early childhood teachers may encounter challenges with such children in establishing rapport and in engendering a spirit of cooperation and compliance within the group.

Guidance and discipline techniques are often classified into three types: inductive, power assertive, and permissive. Inductive discipline utilizes a teaching mode in which children are provided reasons and rationales for expectations imposed upon them. Inductive discipline sets logical limits for behavior and includes reasonable and logical consequences for noncompliance.

Power assertive strategies, on the other hand, use coercion in the form of unreasonable and illogical threats (e.g., withdrawal of love), deprivation of material objects and privileges, belittling remarks, and physical force or punishment. Permissive strategies tend to ignore inappropriate behaviors and generally fail to teach appropriate ones.

The consequences of these styles of discipline have been the subject of numerous studies. Inductive discipline results in more cooperative, compliant, and self-controlled behaviors and has been associated with more positive relationships and popularity with peers (Hart, DeWolf, Royston, Burts, & Thomas, 1990; Hart, Ladd, & Burleson, 1990; Maccoby & Martin, 1983). It has also been associated with advanced moral development (Hoffman, 1975). See Figure 12.2 for a comparison of discipline and punishment.

Diana Baumrind (1967, 1971, 1972) contrasted the behaviors of three groups of nursery school children and the child-rearing practices of their parents. She later observed these same children and their parents when the children were 8 to 9 years old. Baumrind identified three patterns of parental control, each with corresponding patterns of child behaviors.

1. **Authoritative** parents combined control with positive encouragement of autonomy and independence in children. These parents directed their child's activities, but in a rational, reasoned manner. They valued verbal give-and-take and self-expression in their children and respected the child's interests and individual capabilities. Children of authoritative parents were self-reliant, self-controlled, explorative, and content. They tended to be more responsible, friendly, cooperative, and achievement-oriented. In addition, they appeared more curious, cheerful, and better able to handle stress.

2. **Authoritarian** parents, by comparison, were detached, controlling, and less warm toward their children. These parents attempted to shape and control child behavior and attitudes according to a set standard of conduct, often

Power assertive discipline—a form of discipline in which the power of the adult is used to coerce, deprive of privileges or material goods, or use physical punishment to modify a child's behavior.

Authoritative discipline—a child-rearing style in which child behavior is directed through rational and reasoned guidance from the adult.

Authoritarian discipline—a child-rearing style in which parents apply rigid standards of conduct and expect unquestioning obedience from the child.

FIGURE 12.2
Discipline or punishment?

Children are disciplined when . . .	*Children are punished when . . .*
they are shown positive alternatives rather than just told "no";	their behavior is controlled through fear;
they see how their actions affect others;	their feelings are not respected;
good behavior is rewarded;	they behave to avoid a penalty or get a bribe;
adults establish fair, simple rules and enforce them consistently.	the adult only tells the child what not to do.
Children who are disciplined . . .	*Children who are punished . . .*
learn to share and cooperate;	feel humiliated;
are better able to handle their own anger;	tend to be angry and aggressive;
are more self-disciplined;	fail to develop control of themselves.
feel successful and in control of themselves.	

Source: Miller, C. S. (1984). Building Self-Control: Discipline for Young Children. *Young Children, 40*, 15–19. Reprinted with permission from the National Association for the Education of Young Children.

absolute, and often theologically motivated. Obedience, respect for authority, respect for work and for the preservation of order and tradition were valued. Verbal give-and-take was not encouraged and children were expected to accept the parent's word as right. Often, punitive and forceful methods of discipline were used. Children of authoritarian parents tended to be distrustful, discontent, and withdrawn. These children exhibited more moody, unhappy, easily annoyed behaviors, and were inclined to be passively hostile, vulnerable to stress, aimless, and unfriendly.

Permissive discipline—a noncontrolling, nondemanding form of discipline in which the child, for the most part, is allowed to regulate his or her own behavior.

3. **Permissive** parents were noncontrolling and nondemanding, though relatively warm. While these parents were accepting and affirming in their behaviors, they made few demands for responsibility and orderly behavior. The child was allowed to regulate her own behaviors and was expected to use the parent as a resource to be sought as the child wished. Children of permissive parents were found to be the least self-reliant, explorative, and self-controlled of the three groups. They exhibited more impulsive, aggressive, and rebellious behaviors, were less self-reliant and self-controlled, were often aimless, and were lower achievers.

Young children gain self-control from their interactions with the environment and other children. Figure 12.3 provides suggestions for helping children gain self-control through their use of time, space, materials, and interactions with other children.

FIGURE 12.3
Supporting compliance and self-control in 4- and 5-year-olds

1. Provide an environment in which the child's growing sense of initiative can flourish. Such an environment includes:
   • adequate space for the child to use and pursue toys, equipment, creative materials and realia;
   • developmentally appropriate play items and activities through which children can experience success and enhanced self-confidence and self-esteem;
   • low, open shelves for personal work and play materials;
   • engaging, enriching play items that encourage decision-making, sharing, and co-operating; and
   • safe and sturdy furnishing, play items, and surroundings.
2. Provide an atmosphere in which it is not only physically, but psychologically safe to explore, experiment, and ask questions. Such an atmosphere includes:
   • rich interactional opportunities, wherein dialogue and discourse are encouraged and enjoyed for the intellectual initiative these represent; and
   • answers to questions and encouragement of further curiosities.
3. Provide opportunities to interact with other children and to participate in peer groups. This allows children to:
   • share and problem-solve with age-mates; and
   • engage in sustained sociodramatic play with other children.
4. Establish a predictable daily schedule from which a sense of time might emerge and the child can anticipate and respond appropriately to regular events. Such a schedule:
   • meets the child's physiological needs for food, water, rest, and exercise;
   • adjusts activities and expectations to the child's short, but expanding attention span;
   • provides advance notice of a need to change from one event to another;
   • allows time for the completion of tasks, once they are started; and
   • avoids long waiting times.
5. Involve children in the setting of rules, limits, and standards for behavior:
   • Set simple rules that are few in number, truly necessary, and focused on the most crucial behaviors first. Perhaps the three D's of discipline is a good starting point: set rules that help children recognize that which is dangerous, destructive, and/or disturbing or hurtful to others. However, rules should always be stated in a positive way, telling children what to do, rather than what not to do.
   • Explain the reasons behind rules and engage children in conversations about logical consequences and the need for reciprocity.
   • Assign age-appropriate chores and responsibilities with adult assistance if needed. Chores can include returning personal items to assigned places, tidying room or toy shelves, watering certain house plants, or caring for a pet.

Moral Development

Piaget's (1932/1965) studies of moral development focused on how children develop a respect for rules and a sense of justice. He studied the former by quizzing children about rules as he engaged them in marble play. To assess childhood conceptions of social justice, he used moral dilemma stories with children, followed by questions of guilt, punishment, or appropriateness of certain behaviors. From these studies Piaget proposed a stage/sequence of moral development consisting of (1) a premoral stage; (2) a stage of **moral realism;** and (3) a stage of **moral relativism.**

Moral realism—a morality that focuses on rules and the seriousness of the consequences of an act, rather than the intentions behind the act.

Children below age 6 are thought to be in a premoral stage of morality, because of an absent or limited concern for rules. For instance, play groups seem to exhibit an assortment of rules and behavior expectations, making rules up as play proceeds and altering them arbitrarily and unilaterally. Awareness of the use of or the reasons for rules is minimal.

Moral relativism—a morality that focuses on the judgment of situations and intentions underlying individual behavior, rather than focusing solely on the consequences of an act.

Toward the end of this stage, around age 6, children begin to exhibit characteristics of Piaget's second stage, moral realism. During this stage, children become quite rule-bound, believing that rules are unalterable, set forth by "all-knowing" authority figures (God, parent, teacher). They believe that one's behavior is judged to be "right" or "wrong" based on having followed the rules or on the seriousness of the consequences. This stage is often referred to as a **heteronomous** stage of morality, in that the child's behaviors are governed by others, rather than by herself, as would be true of autonomous behaviors.

Heteronomous morality—a morality that is governed by others rather than self.

Due to characteristic egocentrism of this age, the child believes that others are subject to the same rules and that others perceive rules in the same way. As well, the magnitude of the consequences of a deed determines for the child whether it is right or wrong. For instance, the breaking of a large but very inexpensive item would be judged more serious than the breaking of a small but expensive one. Moreover, any deed that is punished is viewed as wrong.

At this stage of morality, children perceive punishment as it relates to breaking the rule, usually without regard for the rule-breaker's intentions. For these young moralists, punishment should be quickly forthcoming when rules are broken; their suggestions for punishment do not necessarily relate to the misdeed. Some children at this stage may believe that injury or misfortune following their own misdeeds is deserved punishment for having broken a rule. Sometimes, unable to control the rule conformity of playmates, older preschoolers often seek the assistance of an adult through "tattling." One should view this behavior as a natural part of the child's emerging sense of rules and rule infringement and not necessarily as an attempt on the child's part to be unkind to a playmate. In this regard, tattling might be viewed as a positive aspect of psychosocial development.

Kohlberg's Developmental Sequence of Moral Thinking

Lawrence Kohlberg (1968, 1984) expanded and modified Piaget's theory by proposing an invariant developmental sequence, consisting of three levels of moral thinking: premoral (or preconventional), conventional, and postconventional, the end product of which is a sense of justice. Children are believed to pass through each of the stages, though perhaps at different speeds. Each stage incorporates the developments of the preceding stage and builds upon them. The premoral and conventional levels are summarized here.

Premoral Level

Stage 1: Punishment and obedience orientation—The child's moral behaviors are oriented toward punishment and exhibit unquestioning deference to superior power. The physical consequences of action, regardless of their human meaning or value, determine goodness or badness.

Stage 2: Naive instrumental hedonism—The child views right actions as those which instrumentally satisfy her own needs and occasionally the needs of others. Elements of fairness, reciprocity, and equal sharing are present, but they are always interpreted in a physical, pragmatic way. Reciprocity is a matter of "you scratch my back and I'll scratch yours," not of loyalty, gratitude, or justice.

Conventional Level

Stage 3: Morality of conventional role conformity—At this level, we see a "good boy/good girl" orientation. Good behavior is that which pleases or helps others and is approved by them. There is much conformity to stereotypical images of what is majority or "natural" behavior. Behavior is often judged by intention; "He means well" becomes important for the first time and is often overused. One seeks approval by being "nice."

Stage 4: Authority-maintaining morality—The child's behaviors are oriented toward authority, fixed rules, and the maintenance of the social order. Right behavior consists of doing one's duty, showing respect for authority and maintaining the social order for its own sake. One earns respect by performing dutifully.

Kohlberg's third level, that of postconventional moral thinking, is characterized by "a major thrust toward autonomous moral principles which have validity and application apart from authority of the groups or persons who hold them and apart from the individual's identification with those persons or groups" (Kohlberg, 1968, p. 63).*

Four and 5-year-old children exhibit Kohlberg's Stages 2 and 3. As children are better able to ascertain intentions, to take another person's perspective, and to understand reciprocity, they make the transition from premoral thinking and behaviors to the conventional level of thinking and behaving.

Contemporary research continues to examine various aspects of moral development. Topics such as the child's abilities to understand intentions; moral emotions; notions of negligence, responsibility, and restitution; and role-taking are elaborating upon the theories of Piaget and Kohlberg and increasing our knowledge of moral development in children (Hoffman, 1988; Krebs & Gillmore, 1982; Nunner-Winkler & Sodian, 1988; Shultz, Wright, & Schliefer, 1986; Surber, 1982).

---

*Excerpts from *The Psychology of Moral Development* by Lawrence Kohlberg. Copyright © 1984 by Lawrence Kohlberg. Reprinted by permission of Harper & Row, Publishers, Inc.

Young children at ages 4 and 5 believe that others perceive rules in the same way.

Social Competence and Friendships

In Miriam Cohen's (1967) sensitive children's book entitled *Will I Have a Friend?*, Jim asks his father on the way to his first day at preschool, "Will I have a friend?" His father answers, "I think you will." This worried question is not atypical for children entering preschool or new play groups. It signals a very important aspect of psychosocial development, that of developing social competence and establishing and maintaining friendships.

Social knowledge and skills emerge from early experiences in the home (Damon, 1988; Hart, Ladd, & Burleson, 1990) and are often enhanced through sibling interactions (Dunn & Munn, 1986; Lamb, 1978a, 1978b); however, the peer group is a particularly significant contributor to childhood social development (Hartup, 1977, 1983; Howes, 1987a).

Some studies have contrasted the effects of home care and preschool experiences on the development of social competence in young children. These studies suggest that children who have been enrolled in regular play groups, preschool, or day care programs exhibit more social competence with peers than do their age-mates who have been cared for at home with fewer opportunities to interact with other children. (Harper & Huie, 1985; Roopnarine, 1985).

In a recent study, maternal and paternal disciplinary styles were explored as they related to the young child's competence with peers in childcare playground settings (Hart, Ladd, & Burlson, 1990). This study revealed a strong relationship between inductive disciplinary strategies—particularly on the part of the mother—and competence in peer groups. Other studies have explored parental involvement in initiating and monitoring their children's peer experiences in nonschool settings. Ladd and Golter (1988) suggest that children whose parents initiated a high proportion of peer contacts had children who enjoyed more play partners. These researchers were also able to associate higher levels of parent-initiated peer contacts with later peer acceptance in school, particularly for boys. However, parents who were too directive and monitoring in these nonschool peer interactions hindered later social adjustment.

Social competence is an important goal for early childhood. Becoming socially competent with peers involves the development of certain social skills (Asher, Renshaw, & Hymel, 1982): (1) initiating interactions; (2) maintaining ongoing relations; and (3) resolving interpersonal conflicts.

Some children are more adept than others at initiating interactions, such as a newcomer finding a way into the kindergarten class or joining a group of children already at play. According to Asher et al. (1982), children who tend to be popular with their peers initiate interactions by suggesting a joint activity or engaging others in talk. These children seemed to have a better sense of timing, waiting for an opportunity to join in, perhaps during a natural break in an ongoing activity. These children are also less obtrusive and create less disruption of the play behaviors in progress. In contrast, unpopular children are more uncertain about how to initiate interactions and use vague strategies such as smiling or tactics that call attention to themselves rather than integrating themselves into the ongoing activity.

Friendships in 4- and 5-year-old children have their own characteristics, indicative of increasing cognitive and social development. Friendships in early childhood tend to be transient. That is, today's "best friend" may not be so tomorrow—or perhaps even this afternoon! As children reach ages 4 and 5, friendships become more durable. Yet, during play sequences conflict may arise over the use of a toy or just how a shared activity should proceed, and a friendship can be promptly terminated, only to be reinstated quickly.

As a rule, friendships at this age are dependent upon proximity, shared activities or toys, and physical attributes (Selman, 1981). This differs from friendships of a later age, which are more often based on shared values, perceived virtues, and common interests. In young children, bartering for friendships is not uncommon: "I'll be your friend if you'll let me hold your doll"; neither is threatening uncommon: "If you don't give me one of those trucks, I won't ever, ever be your friend!"

Once successfully initiated, social interactions teeter precariously on the edge of conflict. Young children do not have social behavior strategies, facility with language, or social knowledge sufficient to manage friendships well. Conflicts are frequent and can be quite intense.

In order for skills of friendship maintenance and conflict resolution to emerge, young children need to experience peers in a variety of contexts—as visitors in their homes, in preschool settings, neighborhood play groups, family gatherings, and so on. Charlesworth and Hartup (1967) suggested that children need opportunities to interact with a minimum of adult interference in order to experience peer feedback and reinforcement for their developing social skills. Through such experiences, children may experiment with various strategies for interacting and may come to re-use successful ones and modify or discard less successful attempts.

Children also need good role models. Parents and teachers, child caregivers, and friends are role models in whom children observe methods of interacting with others. Adults can help children acquire social knowledge and skills by coaching children in the art of taking turns, negotiating, perspective-taking, and positive verbal strategies to use when interacting with others.

Friendships and Play

Associative play—*a loosely organized form of social play characterized by overt social behaviors indicating common activities, shared interests, and interpersonal associations.*

Cooperative play—*a well-organized form of social play characterized by well-defined social roles within play groups, influential peer leaders, and shared materials and equipment in order to pursue a well-understood group play theme.*

Play provides an essential medium for the development of social knowledge, skills, and competence, and for the establishment of friendships. According to Parten's (1932) descriptions of play patterns, 4- and 5-year-olds exhibit **associative** and/or **cooperative** play behaviors. The onlooker, solitary, and parallel play of previous ages continues to be observed in older children, however. In associative play, children may share and converse about materials and activities, but each will explore and use the materials in individual ways. Associative play may involve following another child around or imitating the play behaviors of others, yet one's own play preferences supersede those of the other child or children.

Cooperative play, on the other hand, signals the child's growing ability to acknowledge the ideas of others and to incorporate those ideas into her own play behaviors. This play is characterized by planning, sharing, and organizing play scenarios around goals or themes. Group membership is decided by certain members of the group and can be inclusive or quite restrictive.

Recall the social skills necessary for developing social competence—initiating interactions, maintaining relations, and resolving interpersonal conflicts. Could it be that associative play is a form of experimentation with initiating interactions? William Corsaro (1985) suggests that friendship is a device that children use to gain access into play groups and to initiate social interactions during free play. Further, he describes social interactions during play activities as a way young children protect not only their toys or their play equipment, but also the ecological area in which the social exchanges occur (p. 125). Could it be that through associative play, some friendships effectively "connect" through subtle verbal negotiations and physical posturing? Cooperative play allows children to experience the interests and wishes of others and counterbalance those with their own to prevent or resolve conflict. The value of play in friendships, peer relationships, and social competence cannot be overstated.

Factors Influencing Psychosocial Development

A number of factors can be attributed to healthy psychosocial development. Among these are the child's own personality; the nature of adult interactions and caregiving strategies; sibling and peer relationships; television and other media; handicapping conditions; and sociocultural differences in interactions and expectations. Let's look briefly at each of these.

Child's Personality

In previous chapters, we explored the role of individual temperaments, which children seem to innately possess, and the effects of the "goodness-of-fit" relationships proposed by Chess and Thomas (1987). Additional studies of the reciprocal relationship between the personalities of children and their caregivers expand upon these theories.

In their studies, Bell and Chapman (1986) proposed a "control system model" of how parents and children regulate each other's behaviors. The model suggests that both parent and child have behavioral repertoires that elicit predictable responses in one another. Both parent and child are said to have upper and lower limits of tolerance for the intensity, frequency, and situational appropriateness of behaviors exhibited by the other.

In addition to temperament and control systems, there are other characteristics of children that influence the types of responses they get from others. Physical appearance, notions of attractiveness or unattractiveness, health, vitality, cleanliness, and grooming produce behaviors that can be either positive and prosocial or negative and difficult. A study by Langlois and Down (1979) found that social behaviors of attractive and unattractive children at age 3 did not differ appreciably; but by age 5, unattractive children exhibited more aggression toward their peers, suggesting a behavior response to being perceived as unattractive. The manner in which others respond to a child determines, to a great extent, the child's reciprocal responses.

It is apparent that the child both influences and is influenced by the behaviors and responses of others. Recognizing this, adults should be aware of their own behaviors and expectations and assess the possible effects those behaviors are having on the child. It is the adult who manages the "equilibrium/disequilibrium" dimensions in the adult-child relationships. The supportive adult both accepts the uniqueness of the child's personality and capabilities and adapts her own responses to that uniqueness. The adult's goal is to help the child learn to manage relationships in positive and mutually accepting and respecting ways.

Nature of Adult Care and Interactions

Though 4- through 5-year-olds are becoming more independent, self-sufficient, and eager for social interactions with their peers, they continue to depend on adults for support and guidance as they explore an ever-widening social world.

As was true during infancy and the toddler period, 4- through 5-year-old children continue to seek intimacy and affection, communication and companionship, encouragement and assistance, and assurances and affirmation from those who care for them. Children also look to adults to protect them from harm, provide reasoned guidance and leadership, and teach them or help them discover acceptable and effective social behaviors and emotional outlets. As children attempt to understand their own feelings and desires and strive to govern their behaviors and interactions, they take many of their cues from the behaviors of those around them.

■ Angela is setting the table in the home-living center at kindergarten. Her friend Jason joins her and proceeds to pour water in the cups for "hot chocolate." The two seat themselves and begin to sip, when Angela interrupts and reprimands Jason: "You have to put your napkin in your lap first." To which Jason queries, "Why?" Angela responds, "Because that's the way my Mama does it."   ■

Young children carefully observe the interactions and responses, both verbal and nonverbal, of adults who care for them. Young children are particularly cognizant of the words and actions of those with whom they have close and warm relationships (Bandura, 1977; Grusec & Abramovitch, 1982). These observations often become incorporated into the child's behavior and have the potential for becoming internalized and lasting.

In addition to the impact of the adult model on psychosocial development, adults (parents, caregivers, preschool teachers) influence psychosocial development through the quality of the support system they provide for the emerging sense of self, self-esteem, and self-confidence. The nurturing dimensions of their relationships with children are critical. Guidance and disciplinary strategies, developmentally appropriate (or inappropriate) expectations, and the degree to which adults attempt to coach children in social skills are determinants of positive or negative outcomes for psychosocial development.

Sibling Relationships

Siblings influence, in reciprocal ways, the psychosocial development of one another. Though the quality of sibling relationships varies from family to family and is related to a variety of factors, including the number and ages of siblings in the family, children learn from interactions with their siblings. Children learn family rules and values, and how to play with others of a different age, from their siblings. They learn to share family time, space, and resources. They learn about the other sex and gender role behaviors. They learn to communicate their needs and to respond to the needs of others. They learn to disagree and to resolve disagreements. They learn about individual differences and individual rights, and they learn about loyalty and mutual caring.

Older siblings may be called upon to care for younger ones. In this role, the older sibling becomes playmate, teacher, and disciplinarian. Children sometimes form attachment relationships with their older siblings (Stewart, 1983).

While older siblings may focus on the parent as the role model, younger ones focus on the older sibling (Baskett, 1984). In time of family grief or trauma, siblings may rely upon one another for support and comfort (Bank & Kahn, 1982b; Chess & Thomas, 1987), or they may suffer a deteriorated peer relationship (Hetherington, Cox, & Cox, 1982).

Sibling rivalry, a common occurrence in families, receives considerable attention in both popular and scholarly literature. Yet studies are beginning to show that kindness and affection are more common in sibling relationships than are the antagonistic and rivalrous behaviors so often discussed (Abramovitch, Corter, Pepler, & Stanhope, 1986; Baskett & Johnson, 1982).

Sibling rivalry is generally a response to feelings of jealousy or loss of attention or nurturing. Changes in family structure due to divorce, remarriage, blended or reconstituted families, a new baby, or the illness of a family member may give rise to these feelings. Rivalry can occur when there is perceived favoritism, inconsistent child-rearing practices, or sex stereotyping within the family, such that the allocation of affection, assignment of chores, and the expectations of certain behaviors and achievements differ according to the sex of the child.

Teachers and child caregivers must recognize the positive and supportive nature of sibling relationships for children. Four- and 5-year-olds want to talk about their younger and older siblings. They also enjoy having a sibling visit their classroom, showing them around, and introducing them to friends. In school and child care settings where siblings may be attending in other classrooms, sensitive adults allow brothers and sisters to visit with one another when possible. It is particularly comforting for younger siblings to locate the older one's classroom, so as to have a mental picture of where a brother or sister is while they are separated. This may often be just as true for the older sibling. In times of illness or distress at school, siblings can provide a measure of security until parents can be summoned.

Peer Relationships

Young children enjoy the company of their peers. There is wide variation among children in our society in the amount and types of peer interactions they may have experienced by 4 or 5 years of age. Some children have experienced age-mates from infancy through child care arrangements; others may have had few peer group interactions before enrollment in kindergarten at age 5.

From peers, children learn both appropriate and inappropriate behaviors. As models, peers often serve as frames of reference for self-evaluation. Experience with prosocial peer models may encourage prosocial imitative behaviors. Aggressive models encourage experimentation with aggressive forms of behavior. Peer groups may be viewed as a testing ground for the child to explore and experience social interactions. While peers serve to enhance and enlarge the child's social awareness at ages 4 and 5, adults remain the source of greatest influence. At a later age, peers will become more and more influential in the social lives of children.

Television and Other Media

Today's child is privileged to enjoy the products of a changing and expanding electronics industry. Television, the most common and readily available electronic medium, has been a topic of concern and research for decades. Much of the literature relating to television's influence on the minds and behaviors of children has addressed violence and aggression, inadequate and inappropriate gender and cultural role models, and the effects of advertising directed to young consumers. Other studies have attempted to identify the positive influences of television on such developments as language, literacy, cognition, and prosocial behaviors. The more recent technologies of computers, video equipment, and video games are finding their way into more and more American homes, and like television, they are coming under the scrutiny of child development and early education researchers.

The effects of television and newer electronic devices on psychosocial development depends upon a number of factors, including the amount of time used and taken from other healthy and productive activities; the content and quality of the programs and games; and the attitudes and values surrounding the use of these technologies.

The amount of time that children devote to television has been and continues to be of concern to psychologists, educators, and health care experts. By some estimates, young children view 28 hours of television per week, and will have watched 22,000 hours of television by age 18. Time spent with a television set

A child's limited ability to separate fantasy and reality makes the content of television shows and video games confusing and misleading.

precludes physical activities needed to enhance psychomotor development. The reduced opportunities to engage in focused attention with playmates, parents, or other human beings interferes with healthy psychological development.

It is believed that children learn best through interactive processes. Because children seek feedback from manipulated objects, and from events and people to help them make sense of their experiences, excessive television viewing is considered disruptive to this process. Moreover, the child's limited abilities to separate fantasy from reality and the emerging sense of rules and their applications often make the content of television and video games confusing and misleading.

Concern over violence, aggression, vulgarity, and explicit sex in television programs has prompted numerous studies on long-term effects and child advocacy efforts through state legislatures and congress to curtail programming known to result in imitative and desensitized behaviors. One study in 1972 revealed that 98 percent of all cartoons contained violent episodes; and the frequency of violent acts were found to be six times greater than that in adult programs (Gerbner, 1972). Another study estimated that by the time children graduate from high school, they will have seen 13,000 violent deaths on television (Gerbner & Gross, 1980). The number of violent acts per hour a decade ago was estimated to be 18.6; today, the estimate is 26.4 violent acts per hour (Gerbner & Signorielli, 1990). Responding to increasing concern over violence in the media, the Governing Board of the National Association for the Education of Young Children has published a position statement (NAEYC, 1990) condemning violent television programming, movies, videotapes, computer games, and other forms of media to which young children are exposed.

Bronfrenbrenner (1970, 1986) expressed concern about the effects of television on family interactions when he suggested that "[it is] not so much in the behavior it produces as the behavior it prevents" (1970, p. 170). Family interactions including talking, arguing, playing games, and taking part in family festivities are among the circumvented opportunities Bronfrenbrenner sees as essential for learning and the formation of character.

Because a number of programs do promote prosocial behaviors and understandings, child and family viewing can be guided toward them. Regular exposure to such programming has been shown to positively influence the behaviors of children (Coates, Pusser, & Goodman, 1976; Friedrich & Stein, 1975). However, viewing alone does not presuppose such behaviors. Children need adults to discuss and help them verbalize their understanding (and misunderstanding) of program topics and role models, and to encourage them to role play and utilize prosocial behaviors of admired characters in their own daily interactions. David England describes his concern over television's potential influence on his daughter Jessica's life:

> From the beginning, there is television. Though she did not know it immediately, TV was a conspicuous part of the world our youngest daughter first entered five years ago. Jessica's home was not unlike most of the others around it. An entire room, appropriately referred to as 'The TV Room,' was dominated by a gray-faced deceptive piece of furniture around which other furniture was arranged. Within hours of Jessica's first coming into our home, that box clamored for someone's

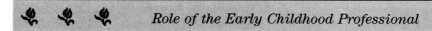

❧ ❧ ❧   Role of the Early Childhood Professional

Enhancing Psychosocial Development of Children Ages 4 Through 5

1. Support the child's continuing need for nurturance and security.
2. Support the child's emerging sense of self and provide experience and interactions that enhance self-esteem.
3. Model prosocial behaviors.
4. Facilitate initiative while providing safe, reasonable limits.
5. Help children understand and cope with their fears.
6. Understand the young child's moral development and egocentric behaviors.
7. Provide inductive, authoritative discipline.
8. Encourage interaction with other children.
9. Facilitate positive sibling relationships.
10. Respond to the child's questions about gender, race, and family with focused interest and helpful and forthright answers.
11. Provide media experiences that focus on prosocial themes.

attention, beguiling us with a colorful and noisy life of its own. Very early on, then, my wife and I had to decide whether TV would raise Jessica, be her best friend, broaden her experience, or steal her youth. (England, 1984, p. 7)

Children with Special Needs

Children with special needs are at heightened risk for socialization problems. Self-concept, self-esteem, prosocial behaviors, and the development of friendships may be particularly vulnerable areas. Some examples of socialization problems that children with delayed development, chronic diseases, or handicapping conditions may experience include problems in learning how to initiate friendships and activities (Bryan, Sonnefeld, & Greenberg, 1981); and shyness and withdrawal, and the accompanying difficulty with reciprocal interactions. Hearing-impaired children are inclined to have difficulties in this area and are often misinterpreted by others as unfriendly (Lerner, 1985). A lack of social comprehension skills is not uncommon in learning disabled children (Weiss, 1984), who frequently misread the social cues of others and consequently use inappropriate means of initiating contacts and making friends. These children may also have difficulty in perspective-taking, preventing them from taking into consideration the feelings and views of others (Bryan & Bryan, 1986). Visually impaired children may fail to provide facial cues of friendliness and other non-verbal cues that encourage interactions with others (Van Hasselt, 1983).

Special needs children may benefit from direct instruction on the social skills they need to interact successfully with others. Lerner, Mardell-Czudnowski, & Goldenberg (1987) suggest that role playing, peer assistance, and the adult model can be employed to teach needed social skills. These events can readily occur in well-planned, developmentally appropriate early childhood classrooms in which teachers are sensitive and supportive to the needs of individuals.

Helping children accept and interact with special needs children provides them with learning experiences. Because young children are curious and often quite frank, teachers will want to provide reassuring and accurate information about the special needs child, but should avoid labeling or otherwise embarrassing the special needs child. The teacher should provide opportunities for all children to interact, with as little adult interference as possible. Teachers can assist all children in learning how to initiate activities and friendships and provide playmates who model social competence for the children who need help in this area.

Sociocultural Factors

Each person brings to interactions with others a unique repertoire of culturally derived behaviors. These behaviors influence the manner in which members of different cultures seek and maintain friends, respond to authority, use language to communicate, respond to gender roles, and so on. The extent to which one takes pride in her culture and enjoys positive self-acceptance and self-esteem determines to a great extent her acceptance of others.

Key Terms

initiative	permissive discipline
altruism	moral realism
inductive discipline	moral relativism
power assertive discipline	heteronomous morality
authoritative discipline	associative play
authoritarian discipline	cooperative play

Review Strategies/Activities

1. Visit a prekindergarten or kindergarten classroom in your local public schools.
   a. Observe and record teacher behaviors that model social skills for children: empathy and altruism, initiating conversations and friendships, accepting and understanding others, and perspective-taking.
   b. Observe and record attempts to teach social skills to children.
2. At another time in this same classroom, observe and record anecdotal accounts of associative and cooperative play behaviors among the children. What types of activities promote cooperative play behaviors?
3. Interview several parents of 4- and 5-year-old children. Ask what kinds of limits they set for their children. Which ones do they emphasize more often? Why? How do they enforce these limits at home? What did you learn about behavior priorities of parents? Are you able to identify authoritative, authoritarian, or permissive styles in their answers?
4. Now interview several prekindergarten or kindergarten teachers. What kinds of limits do they set for children in the classroom? Why? How do they enforce these limits at

school? What did you learn about behavior priorities of teachers? In what ways are teachers and parents the same or different?

5. Watch three popular children's television shows several times over a period of three weeks. Record the prosocial events that take place in each. Compare the different programs. Were there differences in the specific prosocial behaviors emphasized by the different programs? Were you aware of any violent or aggressive models? How did the commercials communicate with young viewers?

6. With your classmates, develop a list of television programs that might be considered developmentally appropriate for 4- and 5-year-olds.

7. Discuss with your classmates the role of adults in helping children use modern technology to enhance psychosocial development.

Further Readings

Bank, S. P., & Kahn, M. D. (1982). *The sibling bond.* New York: Basic Books.
A comprehensive study of sibling relationships, including insights into early sibling influences on personality development, struggles for individual identity, sibling rivalry, and gender influences of siblings.

Damon, W. (1988). *The moral child: Nurturing children's natural moral growth.* New York: The Free Press.
Provides current information on the moral development of children from birth through adolescence. The author stresses authoritative rather than authoritarian parenting to foster ethical thinking and behaving.

Elkind, D. (1987). *Miseducation: Preschoolers at risk.* New York: Alfred A. Knopf.
This book effectively relates the education choices families make for their children to sound psychosocial development. Erik Erikson's theory of psychosocial development is interfaced with these choices, and the possible consequences of inappropriate expectations are explored. The author makes a strong statement for developmentally appropriate goals and expectations in child-rearing and early education.

Essa, E. (1983). *Practical guide to solving preschool behavior problems.* New York: Delmar Publishers, Inc.
A how-to book for solving typical behavior problems in children—aggressive and antisocial behaviors, disruptive behaviors, dependency behaviors, social behaviors in school activities. Suggestions are sensitive, supportive, and cognizant of child growth and development principles.

Paley, V. G. (1984). *Boys and girls: Superheroes in the doll corner.* Chicago: University of Chicago Press.
Explores the play of kindergarten children as observed by this author/kindergarten teacher, who sought to dispel notions about sex role adoptions and stereotypes in young children, often precipitated by adult directions and play prompts.

Piers, M. W. & Landau, G. M. (1980). *The gift of play and why young children cannot thrive without it.* New York: Walker.
This book summarizes current thinking on play as a critical issue in the child's cognitive, emotional, and social development. The author describes play behaviors of children that often trouble adults and practical suggestions for handling them. The book covers a multitude of subjects relating to play, including the disruptive influence of television on opportunities to learn through play.

Rubin, Z. (1980). *Children's friendships* Cambridge, MA: Harvard University Press.

The author explores the development and the consequences of various kinds of children's friendships. The book stresses the importance of peer interactions to the development of social skills and the role of adults in facilitating social skill development in children.

Walsh, H. M. (1980). *Introducing the young child to the social world.* New York: Macmillan.

Walsh stresses the importance of social development of the young child and provides practical suggestions for facilitating the emergence of social competence in young children.

CHAPTER 13

Was it not then that I acquired all that now sustains me? And I gained so much and so quickly that during the rest of my life I did not acquire a hundredth part of it. From myself as a five-year-old to myself as I now am there is only one step. The distance between myself as an infant and myself at five years is tremendous.

Leo Tolstoy

Cognitive/Language/Literacy Development of the Young Child Ages 4 Through 5

After reading and studying this chapter, you will demonstrate comprehension by:

- Describing the cognitive development of children ages 4 and 5.
- Describing the oral language development of children ages 4 and 5.
- Describing literacy development of children ages 4 and 5.
- Identifying special needs and sociocultural concerns relating to the cognitive/language/literacy development of children ages 4 and 5.
- Defining the role of adults in promoting the cognitive/language/literacy development of children ages 4 and 5.

Chapter 10 discussed the dramatic changes in cognitive/language/literacy development through age 3. As indicated by the quote at the beginning of this chapter, development through age 5 is "tremendous." You may remember that sometime around age 2, Piaget says that young children move from the sensorimotor stage into the preoperational stage of intelligence. Chapter 10 discussed the child in the early preoperational stage. The first part of this chapter will discuss the continuing cognitive development of the young child. The evolving development of young children's thought during the preoperational stage and new ideas concerning the intellectual processing of young children will be presented. Language and literacy development will be discussed later in the chapter.

More on Piaget's Preoperational Stage

Piaget's research indicated that children under age 6 or 7 were not capable of mental operations, hence the term "preoperational." From Piaget's perspective,

this means that children cannot yet form accurate internal representations of action because thought is still dependent upon the young child's perception (Piaget & Inhelder, 1969).

Piaget came to his conclusions about children's thinking during the preoperational stage after conducting a number of conservation experiments. **Conservation** is the ability to understand that the physical attributes of an object or substance remain the same even if the appearance changes. Figure 13.1 depicts some of Piaget's conservation tasks. Most of the results of these experiments suggest that children generally do not conserve until they are in the stage of concrete operations (Piaget, 1963).

Piaget's explanation of this lack of ability to conserve was based upon young children's behaviors in a number of his experiments. For example, he noted that preoperational children tended to focus their attention on specific events of a situation rather than on the process of **transformation**; that is, attending to all states or stages of an event from the beginning to the end. For example, preoperational children had difficulty representing the in-between successive stages of a pencil falling. According to Piaget, young children's thought is transductive in that it is centered on specific events of a situation rather than a perception of the relationship of all the parts of that situation. Piaget indicated that young children lack the ability to reason inductively—to proceed in their thinking from the specific to the general. Conversely, they cannot reason deductively—move from the general to the specifics of a situation (Flavell, 1963).

Piaget also explained preoperational thought as occurring because children between ages 2 and 7 were **perceptually bound**. In other words, their explanation of certain phenomena is largely dependent upon their perceptions. This behavior is most often documented by Piaget's experiment with water poured from a tall, narrow container into a short, wide container (Inhelder, 1960). Preoperational children state that there is less water in the short wide container than the tall narrow container because it "looks" that way according to their perceptions.

A third characteristic of preoperational thinking is **centration**. In centration, young children center on one aspect of a situation. According to Piaget, if young children are asked to compare two rows, with one containing a lesser number of objects but spread further apart, they usually state that this row has "more" objects. In other words, young children center upon the length of the row and do not attend to the number of objects in each row (Inhelder, 1960).

Irreversibility, according to Piaget (1963), is the most distinguishing difference between the thinking of preoperational children and the thinking of older children and adults. Irreversibility refers to the inability of very young children to reverse their thinking and return to the beginning of their thought. This characteristic of preoperational thinking can be explained in a variation of the row experiment described earlier. This time, the same number of objects are placed in each row and the rows are the same length. Then as children watch, the objects in one row are spread so they appear in a wider array than the other row. When asked which row has more objects, preoperational children point to the longer row. Children's inability to reverse their thinking to the beginning of the experiment where there were two rows with the same number

Conservation—*the ability to understand that physical attributes (e.g., mass and weight) stay the same even if appearance changes.*

Transformation—*attending to all the states of an event from the beginning to the final stage.*

Perceptually bound—*young, preoperational children's explanations for certain phenomena because it "looks" that way.*

Centration—*the preoperational child's inclination to attend to one aspect of a situation.*

Irreversibility—*the inability of preoperational children to reverse their thinking and to return to their original point of thought.*

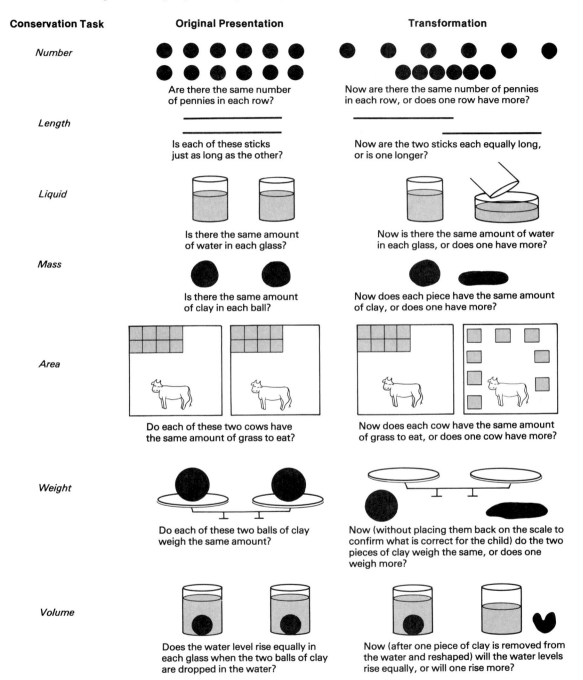

FIGURE 13.1
*Piaget's conservation experiments indicated that preoperational children
had difficulty with these tasks.* (From *Child Development* by L. E. Berk. Copyright
© 1989 by Allyn & Bacon, Inc. Reprinted by permission.)

Block play and other active experiences promote cognitive development in young children. These young children are learning underlying geometry and physics principles regarding spatial relationships, weight, mass, and balance.

of objects of the same length prevents them from understanding that both rows contain the same number of objects.

Changes from Early in the Preoperational Stage

If children ages 2 to 3 are asked to group objects that belong together, they are generally unable to do so. Sometime between the ages of 4 and 6, children can classify objects on the basis of their attributes. However, their efforts are not systematic and they often forget the attribute to which they were originally attending. Late in the preoperational period, children can systematically classify objects based upon attributes. However, they cannot deal with **class inclusion** or the hierarchies of classification. This behavior is most often explained by the flower experiment (Flavell, 1985). Children are presented with an array of flowers, most of which are red, with a few white ones. The children are asked whether there are "more red flowers or more flowers." The usual response of the preoperational child is that there are more red flowers. This experiment illustrates the preoperational child's inability to focus upon the whole class — flowers — and his tendency to center on certain aspects of a situation.

Another distinguishing feature between the thought of early and later preoperational children appears in **transivity** or the ability to seriate or order according to size. Children of ages two to three generally cannot arrange a series of objects from shortest to longest. Older preoperational children can arrange objects in order. However, they cannot seriate representationally. This ability to order mentally, without the use of concrete objects, appears later in the development of thought (Piaget & Inhelder, 1956).

A third example of the evolution of thought that develops during the preoperational stage is **identity constancy**. Identity constancy is the understanding that the characteristics of a person or species remain the same even though their appearance can be altered through the use of masks or costumes. Younger preoperational children do not demonstrate identity constancy. Children around the ages of 5 and 6 seem to understand that identity remains constant even though physical appearance is changed (DeVries, 1969; Harris, Donnelly, Guz, & Pitt-Watson, 1986). A change in identity constancy can be observed in the following vignette about Jeremy.

Class inclusion — understanding the relationship between class and sub-class, which occurs during the period of concrete operational thought.

Transivity — the ability to representationally seriate or order according to size, which usually occurs in the period of concrete operational thought.

Identity constancy — the understanding that a person or species remains the same, even though appearance is changed through masks or costumes, which occurs during the late preoperational stage.

■ Shortly after Jeremy turned 3, Ann's mother came to visit for several weeks. It was close to Halloween and Grandma wanted to help make Jeremy's costume. Jeremy decided that he wanted to be a ghost. Ann found an old white sheet and Grandma began to make Jeremy's costume. At first, Jeremy seemed quite enthusiastic about being a ghost for Halloween. However, as time went on he seemed increasingly reluctant to be fitted for his costume. When Ann and her mother picked up Jeremy at school on the day of the Halloween party, they asked Jeremy's teacher if he had worn his costume during the parade. Ms. Buckley said that he had. Ann then described the change in Jeremy's behavior while the costume was being made. Jeremy's teacher then explained that at this age, the understanding of reality and fantasy are not clearly defined in the young child's mind. Jeremy was probably fearful that he might actually become a ghost if he wore the costume. The ghost costume was put in a toy box and Jeremy did not play with it. Shortly after Jeremy's fourth birthday, he was taking all the toys out of his large toy box. He discovered the ghost costume, put it on and ran around the house shouting, "Boo!" From then on Jeremy would play "ghost" occasionally. Ann thought about what Ms. Buckley had said. She also noted that when they were reading, Jeremy was beginning to talk about whether the story could "really happen." These behaviors seemed to indicate that Jeremy was achieving identity constancy and that he was increasingly able to differentiate between reality and fantasy. ■

Beyond Piaget's Theory

Chapter 10 indicated that currently there is a great deal of new research regarding Piaget's theory. This new information indicates that even children early in the preoperational stage are more competent in their cognitive development than Piaget suggested. Similarly, research with older preoperational children also concludes that Piaget's ideas probably need some modification. Following is an overview of some of this research as summarized by Berk (1989).

Gelman and Shatz (1978) found that children at 4 years of age use simpler speech when talking to 2-year-olds than when talking with adults. Gelman (1979) also found that 4-year-olds indicated through their speech behaviors that they were aware that adults knew more than they did. Gelman says that this adjusting of speech to younger children and adults could not take place if preoperational children were truly egocentric.

Additional research also suggests that both 3- and 4-year-olds are capable of attending to transformations and can reverse their thought (Bullock & Gelman, 1979; Gelman, Bullock, & Meck, 1980). Other studies indicate that when the number of items in conservation of number tasks is reduced from six or

Research indicates that preoperational children use simplified language when talking to younger children, suggesting that 4-, 5-, and 6-year-olds are not as egocentric as Piaget theorized.

seven to three, children of ages 3, 4, and 5 are able to conserve (Fuson, Secada, & Hall, 1983; Gelman, 1972). Other researchers, however, argue that true conservation should occur without reducing the number of items. In addition, these researchers believe that true conservation only occurs when children can reverse a transformation internally without actual counting or matching (Halford & Boyle, 1985).

In summary, there appears to be a growing trend of thought that suggests that younger preoperational children may be perceptually bound in their approach to conservation problems. However, as children move through the preoperational stage, their reliance upon perceptual strategies to solve problems decreases. Gradually, they begin to solve conservation problems through counting and pairing. They learn to solve problems containing a large number of items, and later in the elementary school years they do not have to rely upon concrete experiences to solve conservation problems (Siegler, 1981; Siegler & Robinson, 1982).

Based on studies within the past two decades, there appears to be an accumulation of evidence that suggests that young children's thought is more sophisticated and evolving than Piaget indicated. However, Piaget's notion that true understanding of conservation of number, length, liquid, and mass is probably not possible until age 6 and after is probably accurate (Flavell, 1985). In addition, the effects of training of the development of logical operations in the preoperational child appear to be influenced by age (Beilin, 1980). Older preoperational children seem much more likely to be able to generalize to situations outside the training context (Field, 1981; Siegler, 1981).

Researchers who have modified Piaget's ideas are called **neo-Piagetians**. One group of neo-Piagetians believes that researchers may eventually be able to identify global stages that can be applied to all areas related to cognitive development, such as language, the arts, and mathematics (Case, 1985; Case, Marini, McKeough, Dennis, & Goldberg, 1986). These researchers feel that as research methodology is refined and appropriately designed, Piaget's idea of global stages will be verified. Another group of neo-Piagetian researchers is suggesting that there are not well-defined stages in the development of cognition (Feldman, 1980; Gelman & Baillargeon, 1983; Karmiloff-Smith, 1986). These investigators think that there is little carryover from what a child learns in one situation to another. They believe that children do learn through assimilation and accommodation. However, they suggest that each domain or area of learning has its own stages and that there are no global stages that apply to all domains. Thus, stages in learning language differ from the stages in learning about drawing or mathematics.

Neo-Piagetians— researchers who support Piaget's ideas, but are updating his theory according to recent findings about cognitive development.

Information Processing/Levels of Processing

As mentioned in Chapter 7, another approach to explaining the cognitive development in young children is the information processing model. This approach is often compared to the way a computer works (Shriffin & Atkinson,

1969). Figure 13.2 demonstrates a simplified version of this way of thinking about young children's cognitive development. One explanation for the limitations of young children's cognitive processing is their lack of sustained attention (Vurpillot, 1968; Zinchenko, Chzhi-Tsin, & Tarakanov, 1963). In addition, limited ability to store information in long-term and short-term memory and to apply it is viewed as a second problem for young children (Case & Khanna, 1981; Chi & Klahr, 1975; Siegler, 1986). However, many parents and early childhood professionals have observed that young children hold information in long-term memory and at times can demonstrate considerable attention spans. Consider the number of 4- and 5-year-olds with long-term memory and long attention spans when dealing with the subject of dinosaurs. Indeed, investigation has demonstrated that short-term memory appears to vary more widely than previously thought (Siegler, 1983). Consequently, some researchers have abandoned the memory-store information processing approach for a **levels of processing theory**. This idea suggests that the attention is not limited by memory constraints. As indicated in this chapter and Chapters 7 and 10, recent studies suggest that cognitive performance is influenced by young children's increasingly effective use of strategies and needs to be examined in local, meaningful circumstances, rather than in global or general situations.

Levels of processing theory—an information processing model that focuses upon the depth of attention rather than aspects of memory in explaining levels of cognitive performance.

In other words, when young children are interested, when they have background knowledge, when there is some degree of routine to free them to combine and consolidate previous ideas or generate new ones, and when information is presented appropriately, levels of attention and cognitive performance are increased (Case, 1977, 1978; Craik & Lockhart, 1972; Craik & Tulving, 1975; Vygotsky, 1987). Information that is processed meaningfully and linked with

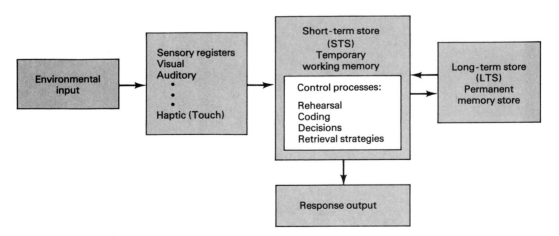

FIGURE 13.2
The information-processing approach compares cognitive development to the way a computer works. (From *The Development of Children* [p. 322] by Michael Cole and Sheila R. Cole. Copyright © 1989 by Michael Cole, Sheila R. Cole, and Judith Boies. Reprinted with permission by W. H. Freeman and Company.)

other background information is retained and can be demonstrated by the young child. Information presented in a superficial way is soon forgotten and cannot be used by the child. These ideas are reflected in the concept of developmentally appropriate practice for young children (Bredekamp, 1987). Early childhood professionals should assist young children in developing an awareness of daily routines and provide interesting and meaningful experiences that develop background information. Detailed information/levels of processing models for very young children are still being formulated, with some researchers believing that development is a continuous process. Other theorists, like Piaget, are stage-oriented in their thinking.

Other Explanations for Cognitive Differences in Young Children

Another explanation for the differences in young children's thinking when compared with the thought of older children and adults is addressed in the **biological model**, which focuses upon the processes of growth and development in the brain. The **sociocultural model** takes into account the child's experiences in the various layers of the ecosystem (Bronfenbrenner, 1979), which promote cognitive development through scripts. This section of the chapter provides information regarding biological influences on cognitive development in young children.

Biological model—the explanation of cognitive development as influenced by biological processes of growth and development in the brain.

In Chapter 8, the rapid brain growth of young children was discussed. You will remember that by age 6, the brain has developed about 90 percent of its adult weight (Tanner, 1978). Along with this weight gain myelinization occurs. During myelinization, fatty tissue covers the nerve cells, facilitating the sending of impulses along the neurons (see Figure 13.3). Rapid growth and myelinization in the brain coincide with the development of the auditory system, rapid language development, and increased processing of visual, spatial, and temporal (or time) information. Simultaneously, these increased connections promote better processing of information, and their presence in the speech center of the brain facilitates the development of symbolization and communication. Gains in short-term memory and small motor skills are also attributed to the rapid myelinization occurring during the ages of 4 and 5 (Cole & Cole, 1989).

Sociocultural model—the explanation of cognitive development as influenced by various sociocultural experiences within the family, community, and society.

Another explanation for children's differences in cognitive development concerns the influence of the sociocultural experiences within the family, community, and society upon the formation of scripts. Recall from Chapter 10 that as young children repeatedly participate in routine events with adults over a period of time they develop ideas about the roles people play in certain situations, the objects or materials used, and the order of events in the situation. This information is called a script. As children experience certain contexts over a period of time, they develop more complete scripts.

Children at 4 and 5 years of age demonstrate generally more knowledge of certain scripts than do most 3-year-olds (Nelson, 1986; Nelson & Gruendel, 1981). When playing restaurant, they take time to decide the roles—who will

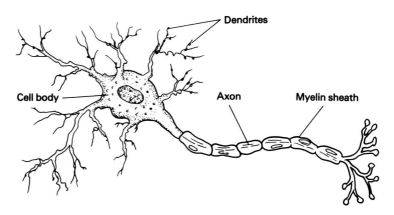

FIGURE 13.3
The growth of myelin, or fatty tissue, around the nerve cells of the brain coincides with development of the auditory system, rapid language development and increased processing of visual, spatial, and temporal information.

be the "cooker," the waiter, and the people eating in the restaurant. Then, children enact these various roles, demonstrating knowledge of behaviors and sequences of events such as entering restaurants, ordering, eating, paying for the food, and leaving the restaurant. Four and 5-year-old children often use appropriate materials to facilitate script enactment. They may use menus, ordering pads, pencils, dishes, pots and pans, tables, chairs, and cash registers. They may wear aprons and chefs' hats. Thus, as children mature, increased cognitive awareness of the culture is reflected in their scripts.

The idea of scripts can also be used to help explain some of the differences in cultural behaviors of young children (Childs & Greenfield, 1980). For example, children from some Asian cultures become very skilled at eating with chopsticks, origami (the art of paper folding), and other fine motor tasks because adults in the culture provide many opportunities to practice these skills. These skills may not be important to the scripts or contexts of other cultures. Therefore, children from other cultures do not have the opportunity to repeatedly practice the same fine motor tasks and thus are not as proficient in their fine motor development as children from some Asian cultures.

These various attempts to explain young children's cognitive development are not complete when considered alone. Until a more complete theory is developed, the suggestions of Piaget, the neo-Piagetians, the information processing model, the biological model, and the sociocultural model should be considered as possible pieces to the puzzle of cognitive development. Cole and Cole (1989, pp. 333–338) provide an interesting example of how all these approaches can be used to facilitate the understanding of a cognitive behavior such as drawing. This example is partially summarized in the following section.

The Development of Drawing

Stage Perspective

Cross cultural research suggests that children all over the world move through similar stages in the development of their drawing (Gardner, 1980; Kellogg, 1969). This information supports Piaget's notion that development proceeds in stages. The first stage is that of scribbling.

■ Angela had seen her mother write while doing her homework. Cheryl would give her paper and pencil, and Angela would then scribble. Angela makes no attempt to label these spontaneous scribbles. Rather, her scribbling is uncontrolled and she engages in this activity for the pleasure of movement and to observe the marks made by her movement. ■

Around the age of 3, children develop more fine motor control. They also begin to realize that lines can be used to make representations of objects that interest them. The month after Angela turns 3, she brings home her first representational picture. It is October and Angela's class in the childcare center has been talking about Halloween. Her interest in this special day is reflected in her picture of a witch (see Figure 13.4).

Gradually, Angela's drawings become stereotyped repetitions with radiating suns, rainbows, and square houses with triangular roofs. She then begins to draw pictures with both people and objects reflecting a variety of experiences and interests. At around age 6, Angela, like other children of this age, will begin to become more realistic in her drawing.

Information-Processing Perspective

Cole and Cole (1989, p. 335) use the child's gradual ability to draw a three-dimensional house as an example of how the information processing perspective relates to the development of drawing. Over a period of time, children gradually learn the drawing rules for creating objects in the third dimension. They remember that all three spatial coordinates—length, width, and depth— must be in their drawing (see Figure 13.5).

Biological Perspective

This perspective views the mind as having the ability to focus on particular kinds of environmental information. While most children seem to develop drawing ability in the stages previously described, there appear to be some interesting deviations from these patterns. A well-known exception to the typical stages of drawing was described by Selfe (1977). An autistic child named Nadia began to exhibit well-developed perspective and coordination in her drawings

FIGURE 13.4
Angela's first representational picture of a witch with face, hair, eyes, and two legs protruding from the head is an example of the stage perspective in the development of drawing.

at age $3\frac{1}{2}$. In other situations, her hand movement was uncontrolled. Selfe (1977) and Gardner (1980) suggest that a few individuals must possess mental modules or mental computational devices, which cause advanced development in certain isolated areas. Nadia had very coordinated movements in her drawing but not in other areas of fine motor behavior.

Sociocultural Perspective

The sociocultural perspective takes the view that the traditions of the culture will be reflected in the content of the child's drawings. In addition, children

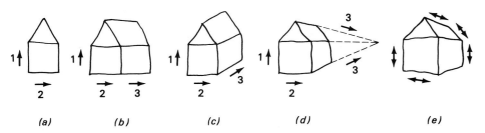

(a)   (b)   (c)   (d)   (e)

FIGURE 13.5
The increasing ability of school-age children to remember to represent all three spatial coordinates of length, width, and depth in three-dimensional drawing is an example of the application of the information processing model to the development of drawing. (From *The Development of Children* [p. 335] by Michael Cole and Sheila R. Cole. Copyright © 1989 by Michael Cole, Sheila R. Cole, and Judith Boies. Reprinted with permission by W. H. Freeman and Company.)

FIGURE 13.6
Jeremy names this picture "a cricket," indicating that he has become aware of sociocultural expectations to name and label pictures.

generally absorb adult and cultural expectations about what it means to draw a picture.

■ Shortly after Jeremy turned 3, Ann asked Jeremy to tell her about his drawing, seen in Figure 13.6. Jeremy said that it was a cricket. Jeremy's scribbled picture is not at all representational of a cricket. He probably did not plan to draw a cricket and did not have the motor control to draw an identifiable cricket. Yet, he is beginning to understand that marks he makes can be named, that he is expected to produce in his drawings objects that can be named. Children at 4 and 5 years of age gradually come to understand adult requests to "draw a picture." ■

The above examples adapted from Cole and Cole (1989) should help you understand that differing theories or ideas should not necessarily be viewed as competing. Rather, different perspectives considered together can present a more complete picture of development, including typical patterns and explanations for exceptions to the patterns.

Language Development

By the age of 4, young children's communication skills appear to be adult-like. However, research indicates that children continue to develop in the area of language into the elementary school years (Menyuk, 1988; Pflaum, 1986).

Interaction Between Thought and Language

As mentioned previously, the child's developing cognitive ability to remember more information seems to facilitate language development. In addition, as children have more experiences, they internalize more scripts and language that is appropriate to those scripts. This common knowledge of scripts and sequencing of events results in a new event in the development of language, that of sustained dialogue between children (Nelson & Gruendel, 1981). This sustained dialogue is often observed as children play out the scripts with which they have become familiar, such as "going to the doctor," "eating out," or "grocery shopping."

In spite of this developing competence, young children at 4 and 5 years of age still have a great deal to sort out in terms of language and exactly what it means. For example, one evening as Ann helped Jeremy out of the tub and was drying his feet, she noticed how much his feet were shaped like Bill's. She said, "Jeremy, you sure have your daddy's feet." Jeremy replied, "I do not have Daddy's feet. These are my feet!" Ann's **indirect speech act**, or speech that actually infers more than the actual utterance, was not comprehended by Jeremy.

Understanding indirect speech begins to take place around the ages of 4 and 5. At first, all young children take others' speech literally. Humor and lying are

Indirect speech act—speech that infers more than the actual uttered words.

two indirect speech acts that appear during the early childhood years. Children around 5 years of age begin to be interested in riddles and jokes. They often create "jokes" that have no humorous element to older children and adults. Yet when young children provide the punch line, they laugh uproariously. They have the notion of the form of jokes or riddles and they know it is appropriate to laugh. However, most young children around age 5 have yet to internalize the idea that words can have double meanings (Sutton-Smith, 1975). Young children also gradually become aware of lying. They are usually not very proficient at lying because they cannot take into account all the attributes of the addressee, the relationship between the addressor and the addressee, and the context (Menyuk, 1988).

As was discussed in Chapter 10, the scaffolding of adults and older children can help younger children develop in their thought and language. In addition, adults need to provide many experiences for children to develop meaning. Thus, the ideas of activity and interaction continue to be important for the language development of 4- and 5-year-olds, just as they were for children through 3 years of age.

Development of Syntax

As children enter the fourth year, conjunctions with "and" begin to appear. "I want cookies *and* milk." Later connectives such as "then," "because," "so," "if," "or," and "but," appear. Use of "when," "then," "before," and "after" develop later (Bowerman, 1979, p. 287). Embedded sentences, tag questions, indirect object/direct object constructions, and passive sentence forms also begin to appear during ages 4 and 5. For examples of these forms of language, see Figure 13.7. By the end of the fifth year, most children also have a broader understanding of pronouns. For example, they know that a pronoun does not always refer to the name of another person in the sentence, as in *"She* said Sally was sick." During the fifth and beginning into the sixth year, children begin to incorporate irregular inflections into their speech (Menyuk, 1964). At this time, they may include both the irregular forms and the overgeneralization within the same sentence: "We goed, we went, we wented to my grandma's house last night." These behaviors indicate that children are becoming aware that there are some exceptions to the regularities of inflectional endings and are trying to incorporate these irregularities into their speech.

Sound Production

Many children become considerably more proficient in the production of various sounds between the ages of 4 and 5. However, a number of children are still learning to produce some sounds even into the elementary school years. Table 13.1 (pp. 342–343) provides information about the approximate ages at which sounds are learned. Ingram (1986) indicates that some children can hear

FIGURE 13.7
The emergence of grammatical forms and usage during ages 4, 5, and 6

I. Conjunctions
   1. Using "and" to connect whole sentences:
      "My daddy picked me up at school *and* we went to the store."
      "We ate breakfast *and* we ate doughnuts, too!"
   2. Later expressing relations between clauses, using "because" and "if":
      "I can't hold my cup, because I'm just little."
      "I'll play with my new truck, if my daddy will bring it."

II. Embedded Sentences
   "*I want to hold it* myself!"
   "*I want to go to sleep* in my big boy bed."
   "My mommy said *she could fix it.*"

III. Tag Questions
   "I can do it myself, can't I?"
   "Caitlin is crying, isn't she Mommy?"
   "Mommy this shoe is too small, isn't it Daddy?"

IV. Indirect Object-Direct Object Constructions
   "My Mommy showed Daddy her new briefcase."
   "I gave Nikki my new toy . . . just to share."
   "Ms. Gray called me on her telephone!"

V. Passive Sentence Forms
   "The car was chased by the dog."
   "My toy was broken by the hammer."
   "The page was ripped by a ghost, Daddy!"

contrasting sounds but cannot produce them. Teachers of 4- and 5-year-olds need to be aware of the relative ages for the development of various sounds so that they can detect delays. In addition, this knowledge can help alleviate fears of parents who are concerned that their children may need speech therapy.

■ Ann was concerned about Jeremy's inability to pronounce the *th* sound. Ann asked about Jeremy's speech at the spring conference with Ms. Buckley. Ms. Buckley showed Bill and Ann a chart (similar to Table 13.1) indicating that the production of *th* is expected to develop in the seventh year. Ms. Buckley reassured Bill and Ann that at this stage of Jeremy's language development, there was no need to be concerned.   ■

Development of Communicative Competence

As discussed in Chapter 10, while young children are expanding their vocabularies and learning how to express their thoughts through oral language, they are also gaining interactional competence. Interactional competence refers to the child's knowledge of the uses of language, appropriate nonverbal behavior, and awareness of conversational conditions and constraints. Grammatic and interactional competence interact to create the child's communicative competence.

Halliday (1975) studied the development of the child's understanding of how language can be used to achieve goals or purposes. Halliday found that children between $2\frac{1}{2}$ and approximately 4 years of age demonstrate an awareness of the uses or **functions of language**. In other words, children increasingly use language for a variety of communication purposes, such as:

1. *instrumental:* language used to satisfy personal goals and needs;
2. *regulatory:* language used to control others;
3. *personal:* language used to share information about self;
4. *interactional:* language used to interact with someone else;
5. *heuristic:* language used to learn;
6. *imaginative:* language used to pretend and fantasize; and
7. *informative:* language used to share information (Halliday, 1975, pp. 19–21).

Functions of language—the various uses of language, which accomplish a variety of communication purposes.

Tough (1977) also looked at the functions of speech in young children and developed different categories:

1. *directive:* directing self and others;
2. *interpretive:* telling present and past experiences;
3. *projective:* predicting, imagining, and empathizing with others; and
4. *relational:* relating to others and maintaining self-control (Tough, 1977, pp. 68–69).

Halliday (1975) and Tough (1977) documented that by the ages of 4 and 5, young children know how to use language to accomplish their needs or purposes. However, children will continue to learn more about the functions of language as they mature. Language acquisition is a "long and complicated process" (Clark & Clark, 1979, p. 373).

Young children also provide evidence of an awareness of using appropriate nonverbal behaviors such as gestures, facial expressions, body movement, and vocal intonation and stress (Black, 1979). Children at age 5 also demonstrate the ability to adapt to changes in the conversation and use normal **conversational conditions and constraints**, such as knowing when to speak first or next, how to terminate a conversation, and how to use the techniques of repairing, recycling, or repeating conversation (Black, 1979). As has been discussed, young children's increased knowledge of scripts also contributes to their interactional competence.

Conversational conditions and constraints—appropriate behaviors and procedures used during communication, such as taking turns speaking and terminating conversations.

Literacy Development

As indicated in Chapter 10, virtually all young children have the opportunity to interact with a variety of forms of print, including business logos, print on familiar products used in the home or seen in stores, and environmental signs. However, young children need more than environmental print experiences to learn about reading and writing. They need to understand that reading and

TABLE 13.1
Phonologic development

Age*	Behavior
Birth	Crying
1 week	92% of front vowels present—/i/, /ɪ/, /e/, /ɛ/, /æ/
	7% of middle vowels present—/ɝ/, /ɚ/, /ʌ/, /ə/
	No back vowels present—/u/, /ʊ/, /o/, /ɔ/, /a/
1 month	Reflexive vocalization (undifferentiated vocalizations)
	One half of the vowels and a few consonants present—/æ/, /ɛ/, /ʌ/, /ɪ/, /e/, /u/, /l/, /h/, /k/, /g/, /m/, /n/
2 months	Vocal play and babbling (differentiated vocalizations)
	Perceptual development begins
	Behaviors up to and including this level are derivative of chewing, sucking, and swallowing movements
	Vowel distribution—front vowels, 73%; middle vowels, 25%; back vowels, 2%
	Consonants present—/m/, /b/, /g/, /p/, /j/, /w/, /l/, /r/
	Occasional diphthongs are heard
3 months	Sounds added—/ə/, /j/, /ŋ/
	Increased vocal play and babbling
4 months	Sounds added—/t/, /v/, /z/, /θ/, /ɔ/, /o/
	Vowel distribution—front vowels, 60%; middle vowels, 26%; back vowels, 14%
5 months	Syllable repetition
	Sixty-three variations of sounds present
6 months	Lalling begins
	Imitation of sounds
	Vowel distribution—front vowels, 62%; middle vowels, 24%; back vowels, 14%
7 months	Syllables and diphthongs continue to develop
8 months	Marked gain in back vowels and front consonants
	Babbling peaks
9 months	Echolalia appears
	Continued imitation of sounds
	Jargon (jabber)
	More back vowels, central vowels, and consonants appear
10 months	Invention of words
	Continued imitation of sounds and words
11 months	First true word may appear
12 months	Vowel distribution—front vowels, 62%; middle vowels, 16%; back vowels, 22%
	Consonants begin to develop faster than vowels

writing are tools that can help children (1) achieve goals and needs, (2) communicate with others, and (3) increase their knowledge and understanding.

Interaction Between Thought, Language, and Literacy

Children at 4 and 5 are very observant and demonstrate increased awareness that drawing and writing communicate thought (Dyson, 1982, 1983, 1985; Teale

TABLE 13.1
continued

Age*	Behavior
12 months (continued)	Diphthongs continue to develop
	Word simplification begins
	Reduplication occurs
16–24 months	Intelligibility is 25%
	Deletion of unstressed syllables
	Word combinations begin to develop
	Use of holophrastic words
	Diphthongs continue to develop
	Better production of some sounds now than later
24–30 months	90% of all vowels and diphthongs are learned
	Mean length of utterance—three and one half words
	Articulation is intelligible 60% of the time
	Front consonants continue to develop
30–36 months	All vowels are learned except /ɜ˞/ and /ə˞/
	All rising diphthongs—/aɪ/, /aʊ/, /oʊ/, /eɪ/—are learned except /ju/
	Consonants /p/, /b/, /m/, /w/ are learned
	Articulation is intelligible 75% of the time
	Mean length of utterance—five words
36–54 months	Centering diphthongs develop /iə˞/, /ɛə˞/, /aə˞/, /ɔə˞/, /uə˞/
	Some stops are substituted for fricatives
	Consonants /n/, /ŋ/, /j/, /t/, /d/, /k/, /g/ are learned
	Mean length of utterance—six words
54–66 months	Consonants /f/, /v/, /j/, /θ/, /ð/, /l/ are learned
66–78 months	Consonants /r/, /s/, /z/, /tʃ/, /dʒ/, /ʃ/, /ʒ/ are learned
	The remaining middle vowels /ɜ˞/ and /ə˞/ are learned as well as all centering diphthongs
84 months	All consonant clusters are learned, and articulation is completely normal; morphophonemic rules continue developing to age 12 years

*It should be noted that whereas many vowels and consonants are used by the infant in the first weeks or months of life, they are not actually "learned" or used consistently and meaningfully, not usually for the purpose of communication, but are random vocalizations and babbling. These sounds are gradually refined (learned) and assume semantic significance. It is interesting that a number of consonants, which are relatively late to be "learned," such as /l/, /r/, /t/, /v/, /z/, and /θ/, are used very early by the infant but often do not reappear until the child is ready to learn them and use them for purposeful communication.

& Sulzby, 1986). As 4- and 5-year-olds encounter more drawing and print contexts, they become increasingly aware that the thoughts they have and share with others can be drawn or written down and read by others. This notion evolves over a period of time and in a variety of contexts. In addition, the development of fine motor skills encourages these drawing and writing behaviors. If children of 4 and 5 are provided with paper and drawing or writing tools, they usually begin to draw about experiences that are meaningful to them. As they think about these experiences and represent them through drawing, they often talk to themselves or with others who are nearby about their thoughts and drawings (Dyson, 1990). These thoughts are often incorporated into the drawings via print. An adult may say, "Tell me about your picture," or "Let me write down what you said." As children observe adults writing down their thoughts and verbalizations, they begin to understand that thoughts can be expressed not only through words and pictures but also through print. They may then begin to incorporate print into their drawings or produce "written" products themselves.

■ James, Cheryl, and Angela decided to celebrate James's pay raise by going out to eat. Some friends join the celebration. Angela becomes restless while waiting for their food. One of Cheryl's friends gives Angela a pencil, and she begins to write lines imitating adult cursive on her paper placemat. Suddenly she tugs at Cheryl's arm, points to her writing and says, "This says double cheeseburger. This says coke. This says fries." Angela's behavior indicates an awareness of how print is used to make a request. She has observed and been part of thinking and deciding what she and others want to eat. These decisions were discussed and then given to the waitress, who wrote down what was thought and said regarding the food they wanted to eat. Thought, oral language, and written language were all used in an interactive way to get what was wanted—food. ■

■ Ann and Jeremy are in the mall at the card store. Five-year-old Jeremy knows it is close to Ann's birthday and tells her that he wants to get her a card. Ann asks Jeremy how much money he has in his Mickey Mouse billfold. He tells her, "four dollars." Ann shows Jeremy how the price is marked on the back of the card and helps him decide whether he has enough money. Jeremy begins looking at cards and selects one that has pretty flowers on it. Ann looks at it and tells him that it is a get-well card. She then directs Jeremy to the birthday cards for mothers. Jeremy finds one he likes and checks with Ann to see if he has enough money. Having enough money, he takes it to the cash register and pays for it. As soon as they get home, Jeremy goes to a basket on his toy shelf which has pencils and felt pens. He selects a red pen and writes "4 U" on the envelope. Inside the card he writes, "I ♡ U ⌐EREMY." Jeremy's behavior indicates that he knows about cards and how thoughts are written on cards to help celebrate birthdays. He uses thought, drawing, and written language to convey his birthday greeting to his mother. ■

Awareness of Print as a Form of Communication

The two vignettes indicate the varied contexts in which young children continue to learn about how their thoughts can be talked about and written down. These examples also demonstrate how adults continue to serve as scaffolders in promoting literacy development. Adults help children write their thoughts down, provide experiences for them to participate in literacy events, help them become aware of appropriate literacy behaviors, and provide the tools for them to practice their developing literacy awareness. Thus, there are four major behaviors on the part of adults that ensure the continuation of print awareness

Adults serve as scaffolders in young children's literacy development by answering their questions about print, taking advantage of literacy opportunities, and providing writing tools and print materials.

in young children. The first is to be sensitive to the opportunities for literacy development in the home, school, and community (Schickedanz, 1986). Appropriate scaffolding and providing answers to children's questions also help children become more aware of print. Adults can also provide time and the tools for children to engage in the act of writing. Finally, adults need to continue to provide opportunities for children to experience books and literature. Just as children need to hear oral language to learn to talk, hearing written language helps them learn how to write. Following is a discussion of how early writing and reading behaviors emerge and of the importance of the interrelationship between reading and writing experiences in promoting literacy development.

Early Writing Behavior

It appears that young children first consider drawing and writing as the same. At some point during the fourth or fifth year, most children begin to realize that drawings usually represent objects and persons within the environment and that writing represents the words for objects, persons, or thoughts. However, some young children in the primary grades continue to incorporate drawings into their writing if it helps them convey meaning (Davis, 1990; Dyson, 1990). Jeremy's "I ❤ U," is such an example. Occasionally, letters and numerals are also combined to express thought, for example, "I 8 ic krem" ("I ate ice cream").

Children's first attempts at writing may include imitation adult cursive, letter-like shapes, their name or various configurations of the letters in their name, and other letters of the alphabet that they recognize and can reproduce (Clay, 1975). Just as young children experiment with blocks and paint, they play with letters and experiment with them (see Figure 13.8). Through this experimentation and opportunity to explore writing, children begin to learn about the organization of written language (Ferreiro & Teberosky, 1982). This is a complex process that takes time and support from adults. Adults often forget that developmental tasks such as learning to walk and talk take place over a period of months and years. Likewise, literacy develops over a period of years. However, parents and teachers are not always patient and encouraging. Adults often convey to young children that they expect conventional or mature reading and writing behaviors within a relatively short time. Pressuring young children to conform to adult conventions of writing and reading can be the beginning of problems in reading and writing that could have long-term impact (Holdaway, 1979). Thus, emerging literacy researchers caution adults to be patient, supportive, and aware of developmentally appropriate experiences.

At first, children's use of print is not always horizontal. Gradually, they internalize the notion that print should proceed from left to right (Clay, 1975). At times letters are inverted, sideways, or not in the conventional position. One of the major concepts that young children have to learn about print is **constancy of position in space**. For example, a shoe is a shoe regardless of what position it is in. The same is true for a hamburger, a glass, a towel and most other objects in the environment. This is not so for letters of our alphabet. Change the position of *b* and it is no longer a *b*. It can become a *d*, a *p*, or a *q*.

In addition, young children may reverse certain letters, words or phrases. These **reversals**, or backward printing of letters, often cause parents to become concerned that their child has **dyslexia**, a general term for reading disorders. Teachers of 4- and 5-year-olds need to reassure parents that these reversals are a normal developmental behavior. Only if the behavior is still frequent by the end of first grade, or if there are other developmental concerns, should teachers refer a child for evaluation based upon reversals of letters.

Constancy of position in space—*the notion that letters of the alphabet must have fixed positions if they are to maintain their identity.*

Reversals—*printing letters or words in reverse.*

Dyslexia—*a general term for the condition affecting the auditory and visual processes so that print cannot be perceived without distortion.*

FIGURE 13.8
*Four-year-old Jon has "labeled" the rocks in his drawing. He has used
various letter-like shapes and configurations of the letters in his name, such
as O's and inverted or partial J's and N's.*

One explanation for these reversals or "mirror writing" is based upon the nature of various letters of the alphabet. Certain letters, for example, "J" and "S" end in a right to left orientation. Thus, it probably is somewhat natural for children who have names beginning with these letters to continue writing right to left rather than left to right. As children use these letters in their writing and work to understand the principles of directionality, reversals of these letters also appear. Jeremy signed his name on Ann's card by reversing the "J." This behavior suggests that he is working on the left to right principle of print, but has not yet sorted out letters that end in the opposite direction. Sorting out these irregularities of written language can be compared to young children's sorting out irregularities in oral language, "We goed to Grandma's," rather than "We went to Grandma's."

In addition, it is difficult for children to attend to spacing concerns. They may run out of space and finish part of a word by starting another line of print below the first. Or, a picture may take up most of the space, so the word is written in a vertical or other unconventional position. Another common writing behavior is that young children often do not leave spaces between words. Explanations for this behavior include lack of knowledge about the concept that a word is a group of letters printed in close proximity. Children may also not be aware that in our language system, there are spaces between words. There are language systems where there is no spacing between words. Laotian print has spacing between sentences, not between words. A third explanation is that children may not think about the needs of the reader of their writing—that using spaces between words is a convention that makes it easier for others to read their writing. Finally, since writing is a complex task, it is difficult for young children to think about what they want to write, how to make the letters to represent the sounds in the words, and to remember at the same time to leave spaces between words. Some children may use their own markers, such as a dash between words, when they realize a need to separate words.

At some point, most children realize that each letter represents a sound or phoneme in our language system. If children are encouraged by supportive adults, it is often at this point that they will begin to invent their own forms of spelling. This **invented spelling** (bs for bus, mi for my, snac for snake) may cause concern to adults who long ago learned conventional spelling and most of its idiosyncracies. In reality, close examination of these spellings often reveals very logical processing of speech in terms of articulation features on the part of young children. In fact, the more adults examine these invented spellings, the more respect they often have for the young language learner. Read (1971) did an extensive investigation of young children's spellings. His research documents that these invented spellings are reasonable based upon similarity in articulation features and the substitution of one short vowel for another. Usually young children's invented spelling first contains consonant sounds, perhaps only the initial consonant sound, such a "b" for bus. Later, final and medial sounds may appear with long vowel sounds, such as "bs" for bus, and "lik" for like. Short vowel sounds usually appear later and are often substituted for one another, for example, "git" for "get."

Invented spelling—*spelling that young children create based upon their own knowledge of sound-symbol relationships and that over a period of time evolves into conventional spelling behaviors.*

Adults should not insist that young children spell conventionally. Encouraging them to use their private spelling facilitates their active involvement in the writing process. Young children can be told that there is **public spelling**, the spelling that everyone learns over a long time. There is also **private spelling**, which is their own way of spelling words. Adults can remind children that learning to spell conventionally takes time, just like learning to walk, talk, play soccer, or play the piano.

A print rich environment based upon use and meaning in young children's lives helps them gradually become aware of conventional spellings. Interaction with the print in favorite books, environmental print, print in the classroom such as signs, labels, charts, stories accompanying artwork, and the placing of relevant print in various learning centers all encourage young children's gradual awareness of conventional spelling (Fields, Spangler, & Lee, 1991).

As young children encounter various print situations, their knowledge of various forms of print is reflected in their writing. Recipes are in list order, newspaper have columns, letters take letter-like form, while stories appear in connected print format.

Public spelling—conventional spelling that children learn over a period of time during the schooling process.

Private spelling—invented spelling or spelling that young children create to meet their personal communication needs before they learn public or conventional spelling.

Early Reading Behavior

As mentioned in Chapters 7 and 10, adults need to begin reading to children very early. This early reading on a consistent basis is the most reliable factor in successful literacy development (Clark, 1976; Doake, 1981; Durkin, 1966; Wells, 1981).

Young children who have many story-reading experiences learn **book handling knowledge**, or how to use a book. They learn that there is a front and back to the book, and that the story does not begin on the title page. They learn about reading one page and then going to the next, page turning, and the general left-to-right progression of pages. While young children often indicate that the illustrations tell the story, the scaffolding behavior of adults can help young children realize that it is actually the print that tells the story. Discussions about the title of the book, the names of the author and illustrator, telling and showing the child, "This is where the words are that tell me what to read to you," and casually pointing to the words can help young children get the notion that print conveys information about the book, the title, and the author, as well as the story (Clay, 1979).

Using **predictable books**—books with repeated patterns and predictable text—facilitates print awareness (Rhodes, 1981). Repeated readings of these books encourage children to internalize the story line. Because the illustrations in a good predictable book support the text on that page, young children often become aware of the text and how it works on that particular page. Early on, many children think that each letter represents a word. Attempts to match the predictable text with the letters in a word may not work out. Children eventually figure out that each cluster of letters represents a word. Or, adult behaviors can help young children scaffold to the relationship of words to story line. An

Book handling knowledge—knowledge of front and back of books, where the story begins, left-to-right progressions of the pages, and differences between print and illustrations.

Predictable books—books that have repeated patterns and predictable text.

Young children acquire book handling knowledge through story-reading experiences.

adult pointing to the text, or using of a pointer when reading a predictable book, also helps children understand the relationship between speech and print. In this early stage of literacy development, pointing with the fingers is helpful in establishing the one-to-one relationship between speech and text (Holdaway, 1979).

Continued reading to 4- and 5-year-olds helps develop other important ideas that facilitate literacy development. Just as young children need to hear oral language so they can learn to talk, they need to hear written language so they can develop ideas about how to read and write. Oral language differs from written language. Spoken language often relies upon the immediate context of the situation to provide needed meaning, while written language must be more formal and complete so that the reader can comprehend the meaning. In addition, as children interact with books, they see the meaning that stories in books can have for them in their own lives. They can see that in one book, Alexander has "terrible, horrible, no good, very bad days," just like they do. They find it interesting to learn that a triceratops has three horns. They discover that books can provide information, comfort, and joy in their lives.

Studies indicate that interaction in the form of interruptions, questions, and comments between adults and children while stories are being read facilitates children's comprehension of the story and also of school dialogue patterns (Heath, 1983; Mehan, 1982). For example, the questions that adults ask very young children about the story are similar to the kinds of questions teachers ask children in the more formal learning of the elementary school years.

Relationship Between Reading and Writing

Chapter 10 indicated that in the past it was thought that reading developed first, followed by learning to write. It is now widely accepted that children can learn about reading and writing at the same time and at earlier stages than previously thought. However, this does not suggest that children at age 4 and 5 should be expected to read and write like older children and adults. Even though it is now recognized that children learn about reading and writing earlier than previously thought, this process takes time. Furthermore, early reading and writing behaviors differ in many ways from those of older children and adults. Invented spelling and the use of fingers to match the text with verbal language are two such examples.

An awareness of the apparent interrelationship between reading and writing is important in facilitating literacy development. In the previous discussion about the importance of books and reading to young children, information was provided about how young children can gradually become aware that words, not letters, match with the oral text of the story. If young children are also

Opportunities to write about meaningful and interesting experiences help young children learn how to read because they want to read what they have written.

provided with opportunities to write or to have their thoughts written down, they can also begin to develop concepts about what a word is. Learning to write their names, developing their own vocabulary cards, and having adults who talk about what letters are in words and what words say, all help children learn to read as well as write. In addition, if children have thoughts that they want to write about, this motivates them to read what they have written. Thus, experiences in writing help provide the young children with information about reading, and vice versa.

Role of Play in Promoting Cognitive/ Language/Literacy Development

Piaget (1962) suggests that children follow a developmental pattern of stages that is a unique interplay between innate human characteristic and the environment. Typically, 4 and 5-year-old children's play activities correspond to their level of cognitive development. Preschoolers frequently engage in sociodramatic and fantasy play activities. Sociodramatic play activities are characterized by a group of children assuming roles and performing loosely coordinated "performances." These sociodramatic "plays" represent common daily events in children's lives; e.g., going to the store, playing house, firefighters, or hospital. The play scripts are based on reality, and as children more frequently engage in social play they expect their peers to be knowledgeable about the details of particular roles or social contexts. Early in the preoperational stage these enactments are one-dimensional, easily understood, and generally simplistic by adult standards. However, these early attempts to integrate a body of social knowledge and to allow these ideas to dictate their role play is rather remarkable for an egocentric, preoperational child. As children's cognitive abilities develop, their sociodramatic play incorporates more detailed information and more peer participants. However, children are less reliant on play objects to facilitate their activities. During the latter period of the preoperational stage, children begin to engage in fantasy play activities. Fantasy play is characterized by multifaceted characterizations by the children and dynamic, intense physical activities. Surprisingly, with more abstract social information, more peer participants, and a heightened level of activity, older preschool children perform the task of coordinating fantasy play. Concrete objects that were used in sociodramatic play are no longer a necessity. Fantasy roles are constantly shifting, changing focus, and adding new characteristics at the whim of the participants. Fantasy play activities incorporate new themes and new participants to suit the desires of the entire play group or the play group leader (Bell, 1989).

According to Johnson and Yawkey (1988) the development of language, shared meaning, and basic literacy are greatly influenced by the development of decentralization; that is, the ability to comprehend a peer's point of view in social situations. The integration of social knowledge into a common, consistent, and unified body of information is essential to the development of social relationships among young children. Johnson, Christie, and Yawkey (1987) suggest that a close relationship between group sociodramatic play and perspective-taking exists. During the initiation and development of group play activities, an understanding of others' perspectives among participants is essential. Further, they suggest that during dramatic play two styles of communication occur. First, pretend communication takes place and is acted out "in character" in a way that is generally consistent with the social parameters of the dramatic activity. Second, metacommunications occur when children break the play script and comment on the play activity as a matter of theme management. Both Garvey (1977) and Rubin (1980) suggest that these shifts between fantasy and reality are responsible for the positive effects of sociodramatic and fantasy play on young children's cognitive, language, literacy, and social development.

Special Needs in the Development of Cognition/Language/Literacy

Earlier chapters have emphasized the importance of early identification of special learning needs of young children. If these needs can be identified early and appropriate programming planned, any negative, long-term impact can be eliminated or reduced.

Identification of special learning needs in young children usually involves **primary disabilities** involving attention, memory, and perception, and **secondary disabilities**, which focus on thinking and oral language (Kirk & Chalfant, 1984). These disabilities can create the need for special learning environments for young children. It is critical for the early childhood professional to be aware of normal development in young children. As has been previously discussed, adults lacking in knowledge of how young children develop can interpret the common reversal of letters as an indication of dyslexia. Similarly, some adults who are not knowledgeable about the development of young children may label a young child as "hyperactive" when in reality the child is demonstrating the curiosity and motor behaviors demonstrated by normal, active young children. As discussed previously, early childhood professionals realize that attention span is dependent upon the child's interest in an activity, the appropriateness of the activity, and the child's background of experience for the activity. Two- and 3-year-old children have been observed to attend to interesting activities for periods of 30 to 45 minutes. Therefore, adults need to make sure that they provide children with interesting and appropriate activities in which to participate.

At times, special needs identification results in labeling the young child. These labels can remain when they are no longer appropriate or can create erroneous ideas about young children. Language-delayed children can be viewed as lacking in intellect simply because they do not have the ability to express thought verbally. There has been some attempt on the part of professional organizations to reword some of the labels into more positive terms such as "learning challenged," "physically challenged," and "developmentally challenged." Table 13.2 provides some general characteristics of learning-disabled children younger than 5. It is important to remember that behaviors need to be

Primary disabilities—learning disabilities involving attention, memory, and predictable text.

Secondary disabilities—learning disabilities involving thinking and oral language.

TABLE 13.2
Characteristics of children with learning disabilities

Characteristics	Description
Attention	Difficulty attending to a stimuli or task for a developmentally appropriate period of time.
Memory	Problems storing and retrieving information visually and auditorily (e.g., experiences, stories, pictures, colors, numbers).
Language	Developmentally inappropriate deficits in receptive and expressive language. May exhibit problems in vocabulary development, listening, spatial orientation, following directions, and concept formation.
Cognitive functioning	Developmentally inappropriate progress in cognitive functioning. Difficulties in problem solving and acquiring prerequisite skills necessary for academic learning.
Motor coordination	Delayed development of appropriate gross and fine motor skills. May exhibit gross motor difficulties with coordination, balance, walking, running, catching, and climbing. Fine motor problems may include poor eye–hand coordination and difficulty manipulating tools such as pencils, scissors, etc.
Perceptual disorders	Delayed development in visual, auditory, tactile, and kinesthetic perception. May result in developmentally inappropriate abilities to recognize, discriminate, and interpret stimuli. These difficulties may manifest in developmentally inappropriate problems copying letters (e.g., reversing letters); perceiving differences between shapes, letters, or words, and discriminating differences between sounds.
Hyperactivity/Impulsivity	Developmentally and situationally inappropriate excessive movement or activity. (Hypoactivity may also be seen in some students with learning disabilities.)

Source: Contributed by Dr. Bertina Hildreth, Department of Educational Foundations, Research, and Special Education, University of North Texas, Denton, Texas.

demonstrated over a period of months and that assessments of learning needs should be done by knowledgeable professionals using a variety of evaluation procedures involving parents.

Public Law 101–476 and Public Law 99–457 provide support services to children ages 3 to 5 with special learning needs. States must provide services for special needs children if they are to receive federal funding. Wherever appropriate, the law requires that instruction for parents must be included in the IFSP.

Head Start is a well-known program that attempts to meet the special learning needs of children ages 2 through 5 who come from families with low income levels. It was begun in 1965 and provides a program based upon the cognitive and social development of young children. Parent involvement, health services, and community participation are also important components of Head Start programming. Head Start funding requires that at least 10 percent of the enrollment slots be set aside for children with disabilities, with an additional 10 percent enrollment for children who are above the income level required for admission to Head Start.

Many early childhood programs such as Head Start mainstream or incorporate children with disabilities into the regular classroom as the least restrictive environment. In the least restrictive environment, children with disabilities will be provided with programming that is as normal as is possible. Head Start funding can only provide services to about 50 percent of all children who qualify for this program. Consequently, over half of the states now have programming available for 4-year-olds and some 3-year-olds who come from low-income backgrounds or from homes where English is not spoken.

The term "special needs" usually brings to mind children who are identified as at risk because they come from families with low incomes. It is important to caution against stereotyping children who come from these environments as always having learning problems. Low income 4- and 5-year-old children who have had limited or different home literacy experiences from middle-income children demonstrate continued literacy learning if they are in supportive literacy environments in the school setting (Taylor & Dorsey-Gaines, 1988; Teale, 1986). Thus, attitudes of early childhood professionals and the learning environments they create are critical in facilitating the development of young children's concepts about literacy and about themselves as learners.

Another special needs area that has begun to receive more attention concerns gifted young children. Wolfle states, "Every child deserves a developmentally appropriate education, not just 'average' children and children who are 'behind' " (1989, p. 42). The **gifted** are identified as "children who give evidence of high performance capability in areas such as intellectual, creative, artistic, leadership capacity, or academic fields who require services or activities not ordinarily provided by the school in order to fully develop such capabilities" (Education Consolidation and Improvement Act, 1981, Sec. 582). Identification of young gifted children can be difficult. It is important to use multiple means of identifying and to use parents as important sources of information.

Gifted—children who give evidence of high performance in various areas of development.

Teachers need to remember that the development of gifted young children may be quite uneven. One child may demonstrate advanced abilities in the area of math, yet his motor development could be quite typical for a 4-year-old. At times, he could become frustrated with other children because he can't understand that they do not know all that he does in the area of math. Teachers need to remember that a gifted young child should be treated as a *young* child, not as an older child or miniature adult (Wolfle, 1989). Early childhood professionals also need to be aware of gifted young children with disabilities and those who come from low-income or culturally different backgrounds. Karnes and Johnson (1989) caution that attention to this population is virtually nonexistent.

Providing a variety of activities in learning areas from which children can self-select is one approach that can help the early childhood teacher serve gifted children as well as children with other learning and developmental needs. Identifying the areas that children are interested in and providing materials and experiences in these areas can help support the learning needs of gifted 4- and 5-year-olds. Using parents, the community, and older child volunteers to engage in special activities and projects with gifted young children is another approach (Wolfle, 1989). Using community resources both inside and outside the classroom is a further suggestion. Finally, just as teachers of young children need

Role of the Early Childhood Professional

Enhancing Cognitive/Language/Literacy Development in Children Ages 4 Through 5

1. Provide opportunities for *child-initiated activity*. Child-initiated activity can best be described by the following statements taken from *Developmentally Appropriate Practice* (NAEYC, 1987).
   - Much of young children's learning takes place when they direct their own play activities (p. 6).
   - Learning takes place as children touch, manipulate, and experiment with things and interact with people (p. 7).
   - Adults provide opportunities for children to choose from among a variety of activities, materials, and equipment; and time to explore through active involvement (p. 10).
   - Children select many of their own activities from among a variety of learning areas the teacher prepares (p. 23).
2. Provide opportunities for literacy development (Black, 1984).
   - Read to young children, encouraging their comments about books and relating books to them personally.
   - Write to and with children.
   - Provide opportunities for children to engage in meaningful literacy experiences that are used for real-life purposes (greeting cards, letters, shopping lists, labels, signs, pen pals, vocabulary banks, language experience stories, environmental print).
   - Provide a variety of drawing/writing materials (unlined paper, blank books, construction paper folded like greeting cards, pencils, markers, chalk and chalkboards, paint and paint brushes, plastic magnetic letters).
   - Provide print and writing materials in all learning areas and respond to children's evolving needs for different print materials.
   - Provide a wide range of print materials (picture books, wordless picture books, magazines, newspapers, catalogs, menus, junk mail, class-made books, individually made books, big books, predictable and pattern books, cookbooks, telephone books).
   - Draw attention to letters, words and conventions of print in situations which are meaningful to children.
   - Accept children's approximations (reversals, invented spellings, etc.) as developmentally appropriate.
   - Involve parents in literacy experiences at home and school.
3. Share with parents, administrators/program directors, and other teachers developmentally appropriate practice position statements from your professional resources.
   - A Joint Statement of Concerns About Present Practices in Pre-First Grade Reading Instruction and Recommendations for Improvement (Association for Supervision and Curriculum Development, International Reading Association, National Association for the Education of Young

Children, National Association of Elementary School Principals, National Council of Teachers of English), available as a brochure from the International Reading Association, 800 Barksdale Road, PO Box 8139, Newark, DE 19714–8139. Single copies are free with a self-addressed stamped envelope, and quantities of 100 cost $5.00 prepaid.

- "Helping Children Learn About Reading," by Judith Schickedanz is available as a brochure from the National Association for the Education of Young Children, 1834 Connecticut Avenue, N.W., Washington, DC 20009–5786. Single copies are free with a self-addressed stamped envelope; 2–49 copies are 25 cents each; 50–99 copies are 15 cents each; 100 or more copies are 10 cents each.
- Developmentally Appropriate Kindergarten Reading Programs: A Position Statement. Texas Association for the Education of Young Children, TAEYC Central Office, 8100 Bounty Trail, Austin, TX 78749–2813. Individual copies are free with a stamped self-addressed envelope. Additional copies are 15 cents each.
- Various articles on literacy from professional journals and magazines.

4. Encourage young children's oral language.
   - Provide opportunities for children to use oral language in learning areas, sharing times, finger plays, poems, songs, and sociodramatic play.
   - Analyze the classroom and the organization of the daily schedule to make sure there are opportunities for children to use the various functions of language and to develop communicative competence and the knowledge of scripts.
   - Analyze the classroom to determine if there are opportunities for children to use language to think, imagine, and problem-solve.
   - Use the techniques of expansion and extension to facilitate more mature language development in young children.
   - Listen to young children.
   - Use behaviors that encourage children to continue talking: smiling, nodding, commenting about what the child just shared, avoiding questions which only require a "yes" or "no" response, and using indirect questions such as "I wonder . . ." and "What makes you think that?" (Tough, 1973).
   - Use puppets with children who seem hesitant to verbalize.

5. Provide developmentally appropriate cognitive/language/literacy experiences for all young children on the learning continuum, including at-risk and gifted children.

6. Provide for appropriate multicultural education for young children.

7. Involve parents in the cognitive/language/literacy experiences for young children ages 4 and 5.

to be aware of possible negative attitudes toward children who are at risk, they need to be conscious of possible prejudices toward gifted young children. Wolfle comments, "There is a great deal of teacher prejudice against gifted children. Is it fair? Is it professional?" (Wolfle, 1989, p. 48).

Sociocultural Factors in Promoting Cognitive/ Language/Literacy Development

Multicultural education—learning experiences that help young children become more aware of and appreciate the commonalities as well as the diversity of various cultural and ethnic groups.

Chapter 10 provided information regarding children who come from bilingual or multilingual homes. The recommendations for 1- to 3-year-olds can be used for 4- and 5-year-olds. In addition, it is important that early childhood teachers create classrooms in which all children and parents feel accepted. **Multicultural education** helps children become more aware of the commonalities among all groups of people and to appreciate the differences between cultural groups.

Key Terms

conservation	conversational conditions and constraints
transformation	constancy of position in space
perceptually bound	reversals
centration	dyslexia
irreversibility	invented spelling
class inclusion	public spelling
transivity	private spelling
identity constancy	book handling knowledge
neo-Piagetians	predictable books
levels of processing theory	primary disabilities
biological model	secondary disabilities
sociocultural model	gifted
indirect speech act	multicultural education
functions of language	

Review Strategies/Activities

1. Reread the quote at the beginning of the chapter. Do you agree with Tolstoy? Make a list of the cognitive/language/literacy development that occurs during the fourth and fifth years of life.
2. Conduct traditional Piagetian conservation experiments with young children. Write up your results. Next conduct modified conservation experiments using more appropriate oral language, more appropriate materials, and experimental settings. Write up your results and compare your findings from both sets of experiments. Were your results the same or different? Why?

3. Observe children in the sociodramatic area of the classroom or in learning areas. Document the following areas of communicative competence:
   a. knowledge of scripts
   b. appropriate nonverbal behavior
   c. knowledge of conversational conditions and constraints
   d. use of language functions according to Halliday's or Tough's classification
4. Collect samples of young children's writing. Analyze them for the child's concepts about print:
   a. meaning
   b. use of space
   c. knowledge of directionality
   d. concept of word
   e. invented spelling
5. Visit special programs for young children
   a. Head Start or prekindergarten programs
   b. programs for gifted children
   c. a program based on P.L. 101–476 or P.L. 99–457
   How are they like regular programs for young children? How are they different?
6. Interview early childhood professionals who mainstream young children in their programs. Ask them to describe how they provide for the range of learning differences and developmental needs in their classes.
7. Describe how you would provide an ongoing multicultural program for young children. Interviewing early childhood professionals, visiting classrooms where multicultural education is emphasized, or reading the suggested reference may provide some background material.

Further Readings

Cognitive Development

Copple, C., Sigel, I., & Saunders, R. (1979). *Educating the young thinker: Classroom strategies for cognitive growth.* New York: Van Nostrand.

This book provides developmental information on cognition. It emphasizes the role of the teacher as the decision maker in educating the young thinker. Art and construction, music and movement, science, the social-affective domain, and the imaginative domain are all discussed in relation to their role in promoting young children's thinking.

Kamii, C. (1982). *Number in preschool and kindergarten.* Washington, DC: National Association for the Education of Young Children.

This book describes learning about number from the Piagetian perspective. Kamii provides concrete ideas for the teacher to use in the preschool and kindergarten classroom to help children learn about number.

Kamii, C., & DeVries, R. (1978). *Physical knowledge in preschool education.* Englewood Cliffs, NJ: Prentice Hall.

Kamii and DeVries explain how physical knowledge is learned by young children based upon Piagetian ideas. They provide ideas for the use of materials and constructing various types of simple equipment in the early childhood classroom, which will help children's development of physical knowledge.

Language Development

Paley, V. (1988). *Bad guys don't have birthdays: Fantasy play at four.* Chicago: University of Chicago Press.

> This is one of a number of Paley's books about young children's language. Paley's books are filled with delightful vignettes of child-child and child-teacher language. They provide ideas on how the early childhood professional can promote development through oral language.

For excellent sources describing language development of 4- and 5-year-olds, see references to Genishi and Dyson (1984) and Pflaum (1986) in the Further Readings section in Chapter 10.

Literacy Development

Dyson, A. H. (1990). Symbol makers, symbol weavers: How children link play, pictures, and print. *Young Children, 45*(2), 50–57.

> This article reviews the research demonstrating the interrelationship of oral and written language, play, and art, in the representation of young children's knowledge of the world.

Fields, M., Spangler, K. & Lee, D. (1991). *Let's begin reading right: Developmentally appropriate beginning literacy.* (2nd ed.). Columbus: Merrill.

> This book emphasizes how children learn about reading and writing through developmentally appropriate settings. Real-life vignettes of families and classrooms add to the understanding of appropriate literacy environments at home and through the primary grades.

Loughlin, C., & Martin, M. (1987). *Supporting literacy: Developing effective learning environments.* New York: Teachers College Press.

> This book draws on current literacy research and describes environments that promote literacy development. The authors provide a detailed description of the components that support a functioning literacy environment. Effective literacy environments involve much more than simply bringing print into the classroom. The authors emphasize the importance of the teacher in providing authentic purposes and opportunities for reading and writing.

Schickedanz, J. (1986). *More than the abc's: The early stages of reading and writing.* Washington, DC: National Association for the Education of Young Children.

> This book provides a description of the stages of reading and writing from birth through the kindergarten year. The importance of story books and opportunities to write are discussed in the context of young children's learning about reading and writing. Specific ideas on how to organize the early childhood environment and parent involvement are also included.

Teale, W., & Sulzby, E. (Eds.). (1986). *Emergent literacy: Writing and Reading.* Norwood, NJ: Ablex.

> This book contains articles by leading researchers in the field of literacy, and addresses important implications for practice.

Special Learning Needs

Karnes, M. B., & Johnson, L. J. (1989). Training for staff, parents and volunteers working with gifted young children, especially those with disabilities from low-income homes. *Young children, 44*(3), 49–56.

Kitano, M. (1989). The K–3 teacher's role in recognition and supporting young gifted children. *Young children, 44*(3), 57–63.

Wolfle, J. (1989). The gifted preschooler: Developmentally different but still 3 or 4 years old. *Young Children, 44*(3), 42–48.

These three articles present needed information about gifted young children. Identification, parent involvement, and programming strategies are presented in each article.

Kendall, F. (1983). *Diversity in the classroom: A multicultural approach to the education of young children.* New York: Teachers College Press.

This short book provides excellent information on organizing the early childhood classroom for multicultural education. Parent involvement, ideas for each curricular area, developmental concepts, ideas for developing multicultural units, and resources are included.

Involving Parents

Berger, E. (1991). *Parents as partners in education: The school and home working together.* Columbus: Merrill.

This book provides information about how to involve parents in the school. The need for parent involvement, effective home/school/community relationships, and examples of school- and home-based parent involvement programs are included. Helpful features address working with parents of exceptional children, the abused child, and resources on parent involvement.

Trelease, J. (1982). *The read aloud handbook.* New York: Penguin.

This book is a must for any early childhood professional's library. Although intended for parents, it is a detailed guide of more than 300 read-aloud books that can also be used by teachers of young children. It provides information about the stages of read aloud, explains how to read aloud, and discusses home and public libraries and the effects of television on reading.

PART SIX

The Young Child Ages 6 Through 8

CHAPTER 14

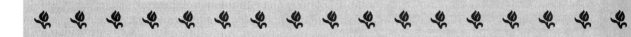

*Children are, after all, growing organisms whose development shows
an organization, pattern, and direction that is characteristic of
the species.*

David Elkind

Physical/Motor Development of the Young Child Ages 6 Through 8

After reading and studying this chapter, you will demonstrate comprehension by:

- Outlining expected patterns of physical/motor development during the years from 6 through 8.
- Describing developmental landmarks in large and small muscle development.
- Describing perceptual motor development in children ages 6 through 8.
- Describing body and gender awareness in children ages 6 through 8.
- Identifying major factors influencing physical/motor development.
- Suggesting strategies for enhancing physical/motor and perceptual motor development in children ages 6 through 8.

General Physical Characteristics of the 6- Through 8-Year-Old

Physical growth proceeds at a slow but steady pace during the years from 6 through 8. The rate of growth will continue to be slow, perhaps declining, until around age 11 or 12, when a growth spurt will occur. The expected height for a 6-year-old is about 45 inches. Over the next 2 or 3 years, increases in height will average 2 to 3 inches each year. Individual heights can range 2 to $2\frac{1}{2}$ inches on either side of the average of 45 inches. Children's heights are closely related to the heights of their parents, though children today seem to "top out" at an average of 1 to 2 inches taller than their parents. This is thought to be due to improved nutrition and health care for children over the past 50 years.

Gross deviations from the average may be cause for concern. Unusual variations in height and growth rates could be a result of illness, malnutrition, thyroid or pituitary gland dysfunction, or some inherited defect. As well, the failure to thrive syndrome mentioned in Chapter 8, associated with severe lack of emotional security, may be a contributing factor. Once the cause or causes are identified, appropriate treatment may set the growth rate back on course. However, keep in mind that each individual is genetically programmed for her own growth patterns.

Weights of boys and girls reveal similar trends. While boys are heavier than girls at birth, girls catch up with them and by age 8, boys and girls weigh about the same. The weight of 6-year-old boys at the 50th percentile on the growth chart is around 45.5 pounds. Boys will gain an average of about 5 pounds per year over the next 3 years. The weight of girls at the 50th percentile position on the growth chart shows them to weigh slightly less than boys at 6 years old (42.9 pounds), but by age 8 there is little difference in their weights, with girls weighing around 54.6 pounds, and surpassing the boys in weight by age 10 to 12.

Variations in weight are due to many of the same factors as those associated with variations in height. Differences may be attributed simply to differences in body build, but may also be attributed to over- and undernutrition. Activity levels and metabolic disorders are often related to weight deviations in children. Efforts to remedy weight problems in children should always be guided by a physician familiar with the individual child's health history and current health status.

Body proportions change with increases in height, as slender legs and arms continue to grow longer in proportion to the trunk. Muscles of arms and legs are small and thin; the hands and feet continue to grow more slowly than arms and legs. The abdomen becomes flatter, the shoulders more square, and the chest more broad and flat. The trunk is slimmer and more elongated, and posture is more erect. The head is still proportionally large, but the top-heavy look is diminishing. Facial features are also changing. The forehead is more proportionate to the rest of the face, and the nose is growing larger. The most dramatic change to facial features during this period will be changes brought on by the shedding of deciduous (baby) teeth and the eruption of permanent teeth (see Figure 14.1).

Large Muscle Development

Fundamental movements — *coordinations that are basic to all other movement abilities.*

Healthy psychomotor development affects all facets of a child's life. The importance of coordinated large muscle abilities has been stressed in earlier chapters. Well-coordinated large muscles facilitate **fundamental movements** of running, walking, jumping, climbing, kicking, and reaching. Facility with fundamental movements paves the way for the acquisition of more complex

(a) Primary Teeth

Upper Teeth	Erupt	Shed
Central incisor	8-12 mos.	6-7 yrs.
Lateral incisor	9-13 mos.	7-8 yrs.
Canine (cuspid)	16-22 mos.	10-12 yrs.
First molar	13-19 mos.	9-11 yrs.
Second molar	25-33 mos.	10-12 yrs.

Lower Teeth	Erupt	Shed
Second molar	23-31 mos.	10-12yrs.
First molar	14-18 mos.	9-11 yrs.
Canine (cuspid)	17-23 mos.	9-12 yrs.
Lateral incisor	10-16 mos.	7-8 yrs.
Central incisor	6-10 mos.	6-7 yrs.

(b) Permanent Teeth

Upper Teeth	Erupt
Central incisor	7-8 yrs.
Lateral incisor	8-9 yrs.
Canine (cuspid)	11-12 yrs.
First premolar (first bicuspid)	10-11 yrs.
Second premolar (second bicuspid)	10-12 yrs.
First molar	6-7 yrs.
Second molar	12-13 yrs.
Third molar (wisdom tooth)	17-21 yrs.

Lower Teeth	Erupt
Third molar (wisdom tooth)	17-21 yrs.
Second molar	11-13 yrs.
First molar	6-7 yrs.
Second premolar (second bicuspid)	11-12 yrs.
First premolar (first bicuspid)	10-12 yrs.
Canine (cuspid)	9-10 yrs.
Lateral incisor	7-8 yrs.
Central incisor	6-7 yrs.

FIGURE 14.1
Facial features change dramatically during the period from age 6 to 8 with the shedding of (a) deciduous teeth and the eruption of (b) permanent teeth.
(Copyright by the American Dental Association. Reprinted by permission.)

coordinations and movements involved in typical games and sports of the 6- through 8-year-old—chasing, dodgeball, catching, and throwing.

Phases of motor development are outlined by Gallahue (1982) in Figure 14.2, which shows the progression in motor development from reflexive movements of prenatal and infant development, to rudimentary movements of the toddler, to fundamental movements during the 3- through 7-year-old period, and then to the sport-related movement abilities of the 7- to 14-year-old. The latter two phases are important to our discussion of the 6- through 8-year-old, as there are a number of implications to be drawn about developmentally appropriate and inappropriate physical activities and expectations for this age group.

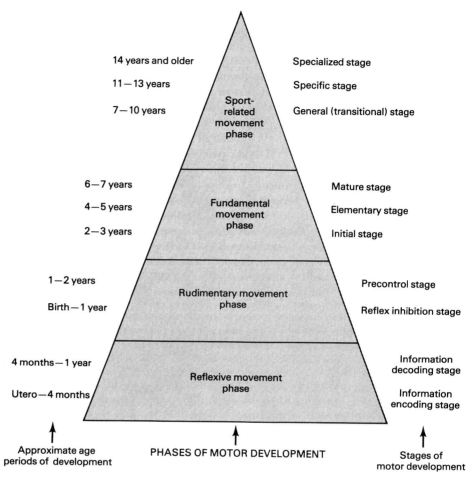

14 years and older — Specialized stage

11 — 13 years — Specific stage

7 — 10 years — General (transitional) stage

Sport-related movement phase

6 — 7 years — Mature stage

4 — 5 years — Elementary stage

2 — 3 years — Initial stage

Fundamental movement phase

1 — 2 years — Precontrol stage

Birth — 1 year — Reflex inhibition stage

Rudimentary movement phase

4 months — 1 year — Information decoding stage

Utero — 4 months — Information encoding stage

Reflexive movement phase

Approximate age periods of development   PHASES OF MOTOR DEVELOPMENT   Stages of motor development

FIGURE 14.2
Gallahue (1982) outlines the progression of motor development from prebirth to adolescence. (Reprinted with permission of Macmillan Publishing Company from *Development Movement Experiences for Children* by David L. Gallahue. Copyright © 1982 by Macmillan Publishing Company.)

Organized Games and Sports

Motor skills advance with increasing age and are enhanced by opportunities to use emerging abilities in active, unstructured play and child-initiated games. What about specific skill areas? Should children be given instruction in specific skill areas, such as dance, gymnastics, or swimming? If so, is there an optimal time to begin such instruction? Is there a period in development when such instruction could impede further development or interest?

It can be seen in Figure 14.2 that there may be optimal periods for instruction in specific skill areas. Gallahue (1982, p. 23) asserts that fundamental movement abilities must not only be present, but must also be refined before the introduction of specific skill training. The following fundamental abilities are identified by Gallahue as prerequisite to such training:

Basic locomotion: walking, running, leaping, jumping, hopping

Locomotion combinations: galloping, sliding, skipping, climbing

Propulsive manipulation: throwing, kicking, punting, striking, volleying, bouncing, rolling

Absorptive manipulations: catching, trapping

Axial stability: bending, stretching, twisting, turning, swinging

Static and dynamic postures: upright balances, inverted balances, rolling, starting, stopping, dodging, floating

According to Gallahue, these skills do not automatically emerge with maturation, but rely upon some guidance and planned opportunities for their development. However, not until these coordinations are refined will children benefit from instruction and participation in such formalized activities as baseball, hockey, tumbling, track, swimming, wrestling, racket games, dance, and so on. Preschool and primary grade children are in the process of developing and refining these fundamental movements. Opportunities to use these abilities should be provided in both informal and guided ways through rhythm and movement activities, well-designed and well-constructed outdoor play equipment, simple games, and guided practice. Children can be assisted with such activities as aiming for a target when throwing a ball or bean bag, jumping specified distances, hopping on one foot and then the other for a specified count, catching balls thrown from various distances, kicking a ball to a target, balancing on balance beams, and walking with facility on the balance beam forward, backward, and sideways.

Based on the foregoing information, organized sports training and competition may not be desirable for children 6 and 7 or younger, whose fundamental coordinations are not sufficiently refined. For the 8-year-old, such organized activities must be pursued with understanding of the specific motoric capabilities and interests of the individual child. Consideration must be given not only to the physiological ramifications of early specific skill training, but also to social, emotional, and cognitive aspects. Individual children bring to formal instruction of any kind their own interests, aptitudes, motivations, and perceptual/motor and cognitive abilities. In addition, as children enter the school years, peer group acceptance becomes a critical goal in their lives. Success with a particular sport confers status upon the child, while failure can be embarrassing and sometimes socially ostracizing. Parental expectations and disappointments strain the child's efforts to achieve and tax the child's sense of autonomy, initiative, industry, and self-esteem. To prematurely impose formal training and competition on young children places them at risk for injury, diminished interest in participating, lowered self-esteem and self-confidence, and unnecessary social/emotional pressures.

Fine Motor Development

Fine motor development refers to the coordinated movements of the extremities—using the hands and fingers with precision and in concert with other sensory modalities, usually vision and touch. Two major categories of fine motor development are prehension and **dexterity** (Harrow, 1972). Prehension combines a number of motoric actions to grasp or grip an object or to let go of it. Dexterity refers to quick and precise movement and coordination of the hands and fingers.

Children from ages 6 to 8 are developing and refining fundamental movements and complex motor coordination.

Prehension involves the ability to handle crayons, paintbrushes, small beads and strings, pegs and peg boards, and other small manipulatives. By ages 6, 7, and 8, prehension includes the ability to hold a pencil or other writing implement, select and pick up the small pieces of a jigsaw puzzle, squeeze glue from a plastic bottle, and use scissors. Dexterity in fine motor efforts is revealed in assembling models and other small constructions, playing jacks with facility, shuffling and sorting playing cards, and using household tools such as a hammer or screwdriver with reasonable efficiency. Managing clothes and food packaging, unlocking a door with a key, turning the pages of a book, and folding paper along straight lines all require dexterity and are generally exhibited by the early primary grades.

As children enter the primary grades, handwriting becomes an important expectation of the school curriculum. Since fine motor coordinations are de-

Children need varied opportunities to use emerging handwriting skills in both guided and unguided endeavors.

pendent upon fairly well-established large motor coordinations, most first-graders do not exhibit skilled drawing and handwriting abilities. Children who have difficulty with handwriting may be given additional opportunities to refine their large motor skills. Additional large motor activities, along with a variety of manipulative games and activities, enhance small muscle development and eye-hand coordinations.

Mastery of drawing and handwriting skills are dependent on both large motor and fine motor development and coordination. Adults who are cognizant of the emerging fine motor skills needed for handwriting will provide opportunities for children to use these skills in both guided and unguided endeavors. Lamme (1979) lists the following prerequisites to skilled handwriting:

1. small-muscle development,
2. eye-hand coordination,
3. ability to hold a writing tool,
4. ability to make basic strokes,
5. letter perception, and
6. orientation to printed language.

In addition to continued large motor activities and a variety of manipulative games and activities, opportunities to use the tools of reading and writing assist children in eye-hand coordination and visual/perceptual refinements. An assortment of writing implements such as felt markers, pencils, ballpoint pens, and a variety of papers encourage children to use their emerging handwriting skills. Experiences with print, story reading, noticing and reading environmental print, and opportunities to write notes, lists, and stories serve to enhance the visual/perceptual abilties necessary for later skilled drawing and handwriting.

Perceptual Motor Development

Children at ages 6, 7, and 8 have fairly well-organized perceptual capabilities (Bornstein, 1988). These abilities continue to be refined as children combine sensory and motor activities with cognitively challenging endeavors. Perceptual motor development is dependent upon both maturation and experience.

Recall that the components of perceptual motor development include both sensory abilities and kinesthetic sensitivity. The sensory components of perceptual motor abilities include visual (depth, form, and figure perception), auditory (discrimination and memory), and tactile (discrimination and memory) perception. Kinesthetic abilities include body, spatial, and directional awareness, and temporal awareness relating to rhythm, sequence, and synchrony (Gallahue, 1982).

Some important perceptual abilties during this period include recognizing and adjusting to personal space and the personal space of others and spatial and directional awareness needed for effective participation in games. Following directions in school (e.g., "Please walk in a single line on the right side of the hallway.") requires perceptual abilities, as does developing **figure-ground discrimination** (the ability to focus on the dominant figure in a picture without being distracted by elements in the background). Figure-ground discrimination is dependent on size, shape, and form perceptions, which are helpful in forming letters and numbers. Visual memory assists the child when attempting to follow written instructions, and auditory memory facilitates carrying out verbal instructions delivered by the teacher or parent.

Figure-ground discrimination—the ability to focus on the dominant figure in a picture without being distracted by elements in its background.

Perceptual motor abilities at this age are fostered through both large and small motor activities. Games and activities that require visual-motor coordinations, such as tossing a beanbag to a target (large motor) and manipulating puzzle pieces (small motor) foster visual-perceptual development. Auditory-motor coordinations are fostered through rhythm and dance activities (large motor) and listening in order to match pairs of tone bells (small motor). Tactile discriminations occur when children attempt to tear, rather than cut, shapes from art paper. Kinesthetic awareness is fostered by playing games such as walking through a maze or traversing an obstacle course.

The relationship between these abilities and school success has been of interest to scholars, particularly in reading (Gibson & Levin, 1975; Kavale, 1982). There is no question that refined perceptual motor abilities enhance the child's ability to meet the expectations of the school experience. Keen visual, auditory, tactile, and kinesthetic perceptions, integrated with refined motoric coordinations, enhance all types of learning.

Gender Awareness

When we relate gender identity and gender role behaviors to physical/motor development in children, we must look at the choices children make for play and leisure activities. From the study of psychosocial development we learned that, from a very early age, parents influence the play behaviors of children through the selection and purchase of gender-typed toys (dolls for girls; trains for boys) (Brooks-Gunn & Matthews, 1979). Through the kinds of behaviors condoned or expected, boys may be encouraged to be independent, aggressive, and exploratory, while girls may be protected, cuddled, and hugged (Fagot, 1982; Fagot & Kronsberg, 1982).

These early gender-typed experiences influence the perceptions children form about themselves and their gender, and about gender role expectations held by persons important to them. In turn, choices of play themes, physical activities, and friends emerge during the years from 6 through 8 that reflect these perceptions. In a study of children's toy requests in letters to Santa Claus, Richardson and Simpson (1982) found that toy preferences for children ages 5 to 9 were quite stereotypical. Boys requested such items as race cars, sports equipment, construction sets, bicycles, and so on, while girls requested dolls, domestic accessories, and stuffed animals. Girls requested "opposite sex" items more often than boys.

Such experiences, coupled with the child's increased attention to role models, influence the child's gender awareness and gender role preferences. Gender awareness and role preferences influence play choices and can encourage or impede physical activity essential to health and motor development. As role models within the family become more androgynous and as educators become aware of and alleviate gender stereotyping in curriculums and expectations, girls and boys may be less constrained to participate in gender-typed activities.

Another issue relating to gender awareness and gender role models is the child's emerging interests in topics relating to sex and procreation. Six- and 7-year-olds whose earlier questions about anatomy and "where babies come from" have been answered frankly for them are more likely to continue such dialogue with their parents as they get older. However, television, books, and peers will augment the child's knowledge in this area. Sometimes the information derived from these other sources is accurate and helpful. Often, however, television depicts human sexuality and reproduction in sensational, distorted, and perhaps sordid and frightening ways. As well, information shared with friends can be inaccurate and misleading.

As children get older, sexual curiosity becomes more disguised. The frank and open questions and unrestrained curiosities of an earlier age are less forthcoming. Interests tend to focus on pregnancies and babies, e.g., how long the baby will be in mother's tummy, how the baby will get out, and the role the father plays in reproduction. The 6- to 8-year-old does not, however, seek as much information as one might think. Children need simple and accurate information from adults who are cognizant of what the child is really asking and sensitive to the child's developmental abilities to understand. At times, asking the child what she thinks about a question that she asked can provide the adults with background information regarding what the child is really asking, reveal possible misinformation, and give clues on how to respond to the child's question.

During this age period, self-consciousness occurs as sexual modesty begins to emerge. Dressing and undressing in the presence of others, or toileting in the presence of others, is fiercely avoided. Bathroom talk of earlier ages decreases, though occasionally it is used to shock or insult others. Adults who provide an atmosphere of rapport and respect with children are better able to maintain open communications in which the child feels comfortable asking questions and talking about human sexuality and reproduction. As with earlier ages, the amount of information must be based on an awareness of the child's age, stage, and ability to understand.

Special Needs Children

As children with disabilities enter the primary grades, opportunities for physical/motor development are expanded. Through specialized physical education programs for children with disabilities, and through experiences in regular classrooms, psychomotor development can be enhanced. The nature of the child's disability will determine the most appropriate types of activities and the extent to which the child can participate. Ongoing assessment by trained professionals provides guidance for planning for their physical and psychomotor needs. Figure 14.3 lists some children's books about various mental and physical disabilities.

Children with special needs benefit from opportunities to learn about nutrition, health, and safety. Self-care, to the extent possible, and the individual's responsibilities to take a part in assuring her own well-being through proper diet, exercise, rest, and appropriate medications or therapy are attainable goals.

FIGURE 14.3
Children's books about disabilities

Books read to or by children can facilitate their understanding of disabling conditions. Ideally, these books show children with special needs as being active participants, not observers. Some excellent children's books about disabilities are listed below.

Introduction to Differences
Simon, N. (1976). *Why am I different?* Chicago: Whitman.

Hearing Impaired
Glazzard, M. (1978). *Meet Camille and Danille. They're special persons.* Lawrence, KS: H & H Enterprises.
Peterson, J. W. (1977). *I have a sister—My sister is deaf.* New York: Harper.

Cerebral Palsy
Mack, N. (1976). *Tracy.* Milwaukee, WI: Raintree Editions. (205 W. Highland Ave., Milwaukee, WI 53203)

Physically Challenged
Fanshawe, E. (1977). *Rachel.* Scarsdale, NY: Bradbury.
Fassler, J. (1975). *Howie helps himself.* Chicago: Whitman.
Lasker, J. (1980). *Nick joins in.* Chicago: Whitman.

Mentally Disabled
Brightman, A. (1976). *Like me.* Boston: Little, Brown.
Glazzard, M. (1978). *Meet Lance. He's a special person.* Lawrence, KS: H & H Enterprises.

Learning Disabled
Glazzard, M. (1978). *Meet Scott. He's a special person.* Lawrence, KS: H & H Enterprises.

Multiply Disabled
Glazzard, M. (1978). *Meet Danny. He's a special person.* Lawrence, KS: H & H Enterprises.

Source: Adapted from "Teaching Children about Differences. Resources for Teaching" by M. Sapon-Shevin, 1983. *Young Children, 38,* pp. 24–31. Copyright 1983 by the National Association for the Education of Young Children. Adapted by permission.

Sociocultural Differences

As we have learned from earlier chapters, there are differences in physical development among cultures. Cultural differences are most often found in measures of height and in rates of motor skill development. Though physical differences among cultures are, for the most part, genetically derived, genetic effects do not occur independent of the environments in which the cultures exist.

Comparisons of physical development among socioeconomic groups also reveal differences. Children from lower socioeconomic groups may be smaller than children from higher socioeconomic groups. Such differences are usually attributed to nutritional factors and health care provided during the growing years.

Factors Influencing Physical/Motor Development

A major and overriding goal of early childhood development is that the general health and well-being of children be promoted and protected. A number of factors contribute to this goal. Certainly, the genetic makeup of the child sets limits on growth and development and determines the presence or absence of certain disabilities. Genetic makeup has been addressed in previous chapters.

In addition to genetic attributes and limitations, environmental factors influence the extent to which optimal growth and development can be achieved. Proper nutrition; medical and dental care (including timely immunizations and other protections from disease); adequate rest, sleep, and physical/motor activity; protection from accidents and injury; and emotional/social support are necessary for optimal growth and development. Because many of these factors have been discussed in previous chapters, this chapter will address only certain factors as they apply to the 6- through 8-year-old.

Nutrition

Generally, American children are more likely to be overnourished than undernourished (Christian & Greger, 1988). Having outlined previously the nutritional needs of young children, let's turn our attention to some of the issues commonly associated with nutrition in school-age children.

Overnourishment (Obesity).   There is evidence that the number of obese children in the United States is increasing (Kolata, 1986). Some reports suggest an increase of 54 percent among 6- to 11-year-olds over the past 15 to 20 years. It has been estimated that 30 percent of males and 25 percent of females in the 6- to 10-year-old age group are obese (Dietz, 1986). Of children who are obese at age 7, 40 percent will be obese as adults (Kolata, 1986).

For the obese child, there are physiological and psychological penalties. Adults hoping to prevent these adverse effects of obesity look for causes. Obesity has many possible causes, including:

1. Inactivity and poor habits of physical exercise;
2. Television viewing, which interferes with other more active pursuits, and may also encourage snacking;
3. Overeating, associated with boredom and psychological needs for self-comfort or self-reward;
4. Parenting styles that use food for rewards, or to relieve parental anxiety or guilt; or parents who judge their success as parents on how well their children are fed; and
5. Inherited body types may predispose some children to obesity (Pipes, 1989).

Children prone to obesity should be under a physician's supervision. With the guidance of the physician, parents and teachers will need to monitor growth rates, nutrient and calorie intake, exercise and physical activity, and psychosocial health. The family may need nutrition counseling, and may need to modify food and exercise habits. Responses of those who care for the child must be sensible and sensitive. Only medically approved diets should be embarked upon, for the child's nutrient needs remain basically the same as for all children the same age. Failure to adequately meet the child's nutrient needs places the child at risk for complications associated with malnutrition, decreased resistance to disease, and failure to grow in height (Lloyd-Still, 1976).

Sensitivity to the child's emotional and social needs is particularly important. Care must be taken to affirm the child's dignity and worth. The child may need help finding acceptance within the peer group and realizing her own special attributes. The child's need for acceptance and belonging, self-esteem, initiative, and industry must be supported and encouraged.

Nutrition and School Performance. Does skipping breakfast affect a student's performance in school? There is some evidence that it does. Late morning problem-solving ability was shown in one study to be impaired for those children who skipped breakfast (Pollitt, Leibel, & Greenfield, 1981). Poor performance on arithmetic tasks on days when breakfast was skipped was shown in another study (Kruesi & Rapoport, 1986). When children do not eat breakfast they do not attend well. The energy required for learning is diminished for these weakened children.

School Lunch Programs. The National School Lunch Program provides meals intended to meet one-third of the daily dietary requirements for protein, vitamins, minerals, and energy. While in the past school lunches were high in carbohydrates, many schools today are including more options, such as salad bars, fresh fruit and vegetable choices, and some ethnic foods. In addition, food selection and service takes into consideration child appeal and appetite-enhancing presentation of meals.

Role of the Early Childhood Professional

Enhancing Physical/Motor Development of Young Children Ages 6 Through 8

1. Provide safe and healthy surroundings for children.
2. Provide for the child's nutritional needs.
3. Oversee health care through immunizations and other protections from exposure to disease.
4. Provide regular dental examinations.
5. Establish healthy routines for rest, sleep, play, and activity.
6. Control the stress-producing events in the child's life.
7. Provide opportunities to refine perceptual motor abilities.
8. Provide age and developmentally appropriate games, play equipment, and sports activities.
9. Assure the child's safety through adequate planning, rules, supervision, and education.
10. Facilitate satisfying and supportive psychosocial interactions with peers, family, and others.
11. Encourage a sense of responsibility for one's own health maintenance and safety.

TABLE 14.1
Family characteristics that affect children's use of drugs

Drug abuse is more likely in these families	Drug abuse is less likely in these families
Family members feel lonely, isolated, frustrated.	Family members have warm, positive relationships.
Parents and children communicate poorly, particularly fathers and sons.	Parents are committed to education.
Parents demonstrate little sense of ethics.	Parents believe in society's general values.
Parents and children lack self-esteem.	Family attends religious services.
Parents drink heavily.	Household tasks are distributed among all family members.
Children feel rejected.	Families have high aspirations for children's success.
Parents have low expectations for children.	
Family follows rigid, stereotyped sex roles.	Strong kinship networks exist in the family.
Family management is inadequate.	The family is proud of children's accomplishments.
Parents excessively dominate and control their children.	Affectionate, supportive parent-child relationships meet the children's emotional needs.
Parents use negative discipline measures (either extremely strict or too permissive).	Children derive a great deal of satisfaction from their families.
Adults fight about discipline and other issues.	Parents use a reasoned, democratic discipline style.

Source: From "Drug Abuse Prevention Begins in Early Childhood" by U. J. Oyemade and V. Washington, 1989, *Young Children*, 44, p. 11. Copyright 1989 by NAEYC. Reprinted by permission.

The Roots of Drug Abuse

There is some evidence that the roots of drug abuse are found in early childhood (Oyemade & Washington, 1989). Child-rearing practices, family life patterns and trauma, and role model attitudes and behaviors contribute to later propensities toward drug abuse. See Table 14.1 for a description of family characteristics that could increase the likelihood of drug abuse in children.

Safety and the School-Age Child

Children at 6 to 8 are subject to many of the same hazards as younger children, with some increased risk as they begin to expand their activities beyond the home or classroom. Their ability to explore the neighborhood, visit with friends, and play in groups or playgrounds; their interest in physically active, "rough-and-tumble" play; and their use of bicycles and other wheeled toys all subject them to additional hazards. They may be away from home more and have less direct supervision by adults. They are eager to do things for themselves and are often willing to try anything to "go along" with their friends. Common hazards for this age group are: traffic, swimming pools (and other bodies of water), tools, home appliances, poisons, playground equipment, firearms, and agents that burn. Accident and injury prevention includes the following:

1. Selecting developmentally appropriate toys, play equipment, and leisure-time activities. Some play items require adult assistance and supervision in their use.
2. Speaking with children about potential dangers and the kinds of activities, play materials, and equipment considered appropriate (safe) and inappropriate (unsafe). Adults must help children recognize potential hazards and teach them how to deal with emergencies; examples and role playing are helpful in conveying safety concepts to children.

Key Terms

fundamental movements
dexterity
figure-ground discrimination

Review Strategies/Activities

1. Take a survey of as many children as you can find in the 6 to 8 age range. Ask them what three gifts they would like for their birthdays. Compare the boys' and the girls' preferences. How many of the items are gender stereotypical? How many are not gender-specific? How many were opposite-gender items? Compare your survey with a classmate. What trends do you see in gender-related toys or gift preferences of boys and girls?

2. Visit a physical education class for children with disabilities. What kinds of activities are planned for these children? What physical motor benefits can be realized from these activities? How do these activities differ from regular physical education requirements?

3. Attend an organized sports event for children in the 6 to 8 age range. Are the expectations developmentally appropriate? Does each child have an opportunity to participate? Is the coach sensitive to individual differences? Are children's needs for rest and refreshments recognized? Which is apparently more stressed—winning or participation and fun?

4. Collect a month's supply of public school menus. Compare them for child appeal, nutrients, variety, and estimated calorie content.

Further Readings

Bergstrom, J. M. (1984). *School's out—now what?: Creative choices for your children.* Berkeley, CA: Ten Speed Press.

A guide for parents in planning for the best use of time for children when out of school. It is based upon sound principles of child growth and development, and stresses the need for children to have ample opportunity to simply play.

Glover, B., & Shepherd, J. (1980). *The family fitness handbook.* New York: Penguin USA.

A guide to physical fitness activities for the whole family.

Thain, W. S., Casto, G., & Peterson, A. (1980). *Normal and handicapped children: A growth and development primer for parents and professionals.* Littleton, MA: PSG Publishing.

A concise and easy-to-read synopsis of child growth and development in both normal and disabled children. Suggestions for sources of help and approaches to the prevention of defects are provided.

CHAPTER 15

If you see a child without a smile, give him yours.
Talmud

Psychosocial Development of the Young Child Ages 6 Through 8

After reading and studying this chapter, you will demonstrate comprehension by:

- Describing the psychosocial development of the 6- through 8-year-old child.
- Listing major social and emotional milestones in psychosocial development through this period.
- Identifying factors that influence psychosocial development during this period.
- Describing the role of adults in healthy psychosocial development of 6- through 8-year-olds.

In a popular United States Children's Bureau booklet from the 1960s, the 6- to 8-year-old is described as a "commuter to the wonderful outside world of middle childhood," traveling "back and forth between the outside world and the smaller more personal one of [the] family." The child's travels are said to start with short trips at age 6, becoming longer trips away from the family's "home station" with increasing age (Chilman, 1966, p. 5).

As this metaphor implies, the psychosocial world of the 6- through 8-year-old is expanding rapidly beyond the home and family. By age 6, children are growing less dependent upon their parents and are now encountering an ever-widening array of extrafamilial influences. New psychosocial challenges ensue, along with some fairly predictable developmental changes.

During the first part of this age period, the child is characterized as highly active, boisterous, sometimes verbally aggressive, and teasing. Boys enjoy "rough-and-tumble" play; and both boys and girls enjoy creative projects and playing games with rules. Children at this age are inclined to dawdle and are talkative, boastful, impatient, and competitive. They are sensitive, affectionate,

and enjoy playful interactions that employ humor, jokes, and riddles. Giggling is also characteristic.

Around age 7, children exhibit more brooding behaviors and become sensitive, private, and moody. The child is growing more reflective and more conscious of the reactions of others. Expressions of self-confidence are not quite as verbose as before, and the child is as inclined to listen as to talk. While the 6-year-old is described as quite active and talkative, the 7-year-old is more introspective and contemplative. Helpfulness and consideration of others are evident, as is the enjoyment of friends, often over family.

By the end of this age period, we see once again behaviors that are outgoing and interactive. Interests are outward bound and spurred by curiosity. The child is self-confident and self-aware, yet self-critical and self-conscious. The child reacts with both interest and hostility toward the opposite sex; is peer-oriented, independent, and for the most part, dependable. Interest in the adult world is marked by listening to adult conversations and seeking to be included in more "adult-like" activities.

What do these behavioral descriptions tell us about the processes of psychosocial development? In this chapter, we will explore major areas of psychosocial development and explain how 6- through 8-year-olds acquire these characteristics.

Erikson's Theory of Psychosocial Development: Industry Versus Inferiority

Industry—Erikson's psychosocial stage during which the child is mastering social and academic skills sufficient to feel self-assured. The opposite result of this "nuclear crisis" is a sense of inferiority.

Between the ages of 6 and 11, the child is in Erikson's fourth stage of psychosocial development, that of developing a sense of **industry.** The fantasy and make-believe of earlier years begin to defer to more reality-based perceptions. Children at this stage are eager to learn how things work and want to master "real" tasks. Whereas process characterized the efforts of previous stages, products are now important as children begin to take pride in their abilities to create and to produce. Art projects, block and other constructions, cooking, and participating in household chores become sources of pride and accomplishment. The child's activities are, in a word, industrious.

At this time, formal schooling takes on new importance to the child, setting goals and expectations, imposing limits on behaviors and activities, and multiplying social interactions. Eager to learn the "real" skills that school can teach, the child's sense of competence becomes vulnerable to the influences of classmates, teachers, curriculums, and grades. Success with school tasks fosters a sense of competence, self-worth, and industry. However, the child who experiences too many failures in school, academic or social, develops a sense of inferiority. As a result, confidence and self-worth suffer.

It is during the industry/inferiority stage of psychosocial development that individual skills and interests become evident. Aspirations emerge, though levels of aspirations often out-pace capabilities. Children find their skill areas as they explore a variety of interests and enjoy the products of their own labors, which emerge from these explorations. The fifth stage of psychosocial development, developing a sense of identity (versus role confusion), has its origins in these early skill discoveries.

Theoretical Perspectives on Psychosocial Development

Different theoretical perspectives attempt to explain psychosocial development during this period. Freud's psychoanalytic theory places the 6- to 8-year-old in the latency period, the fourth of his 5-stage psychosexual sequence which includes the oral, anal, phallic, latency, and genital stages. To Freud, this is a period of expanding relationships that go beyond the family and focus primarily on same-sex peers. The psychosexual conflicts of earlier stages are channeled into a variety of activities including school, sports, and social development (Freud, 1930).

Arnold Gesell

Arnold Gesell's maturationist theory (Gesell & Ilg, 1949) highlights developmental principles mentioned in the child characterizations at the beginning of this chapter. Periods of equilibrium and disequilibrium are illustrated in these characterizations by the alternatingly easy and difficult behaviors exhibited in children as they progress toward maturity. Gesell would stress that these behaviors are predictable and biologically driven. **Periods of disequilibrium** seem to occur around 15 months, $2\frac{1}{2}$ years, $3\frac{1}{2}$ years, $5\frac{1}{2}$ years, and at puberty. During these periods, the child seems less focused, less well adjusted, and less compliant. For the most part, the early school years represent a **period of equilibrium,** in which the child is focused and reasonably well adjusted. Individual rates of development, however, can result in earlier or later passage through these alternating states.

Abraham Maslow

Abraham Maslow's (1968, 1970) humanistic theories suggest that each individual is striving to attain uniqueness and to reach his fullest potential in terms of capabilities and talents. Success results in the self-actualized person. To reach the goal of becoming a self-actualized person, there are certain basic needs to be fulfilled. These needs occur in a hierarchical order, proceeding from the most basic (physiological needs) to the more advanced human needs (self-esteem and self-actualization). Maslow's theory is important to our discussions of school-age children because school and other extrafamilial experiences play significant roles in the child's sense of self, self-evaluations, and self-esteem. This theory will be discussed more fully later in this chapter.

Period of disequilibrium—a phase in development during which the child seems less well-adjusted and exhibits tensions and uncertainties (Gesell).

Period of equilibrium—a phase in development during which the child appears to be well adjusted and reasonably content (Gesell).

Carl Rogers

Carl Rogers (1961), another humanistic psychologist, also stressed the importance of self-concept and self-esteem. His theories, like Maslow's, suggest that each individual has the capacity for positive growth. Central to this positive growth is a sturdy sense of self. Rogers asserts that the self-concept is derived from the general background of all the person's growth and experiences. Educators find in Rogers' theories the importance of positive self-concepts to motivations to learn in school. This theory will also be explored when we discuss the developing self-concept.

Effects of Earlier Attachments

As children move into ages 6, 7, and 8, attachment behaviors of earlier ages change dramatically. Children seek greater and greater independence and pursue relationships that reach well beyond the attachment figures and immediate family. An expanding social world tests the child's sense of self, autonomy, initiative, and social competence. Elements of these attributes are traced to the quality of early attachments occurring in infancy, toddlerhood, and the pre-primary years.

At 6, 7, and 8, the relationships with parents are still dependent and affectionate; however, these relationships are often punctuated with oppositional behaviors and challenges to parental authority. Attention-getting behaviors, perhaps a form of proximity seeking, appear. The child employs behaviors known to irritate, in an apparent attempt to sustain parental attentions (arguing, teasing, shocking, bragging, and name-calling). Such behaviors reveal the child's ambivalence about his emerging independence and, to some extent, the child's growing recognition of the inequality of the adult-child relationship (Elkind, 1974).

The parent's role is shifting from protector to facilitator, and to "program director," as the child's itinerary begins to include out-of-home activities. Moreover, the parent becomes the child's cheerleader and sometime go-between, preventing problems in an expanding and often demanding interactional world. Other shifts in the parent role are from being an "all-knowing" source of information and authority, to knowing "less and less" as teachers become the source of "all knowledge." In spite of these role changes, children still need their parents to be nurturing, predictable, and supportive, and to provide parameters for often out-of-bounds behaviors. Table 15.1 illustrates findings of a recent study by Main and Cassidy (1988), in which the relationship between early attachment and later behaviors is shown.

Fears

The close relationship between fears and cognitive development is evidenced by the changes in causes of and responses to fears as children get older. Cog-

TABLE 15.1
Four forms of attachment organization observed at 12 months and at 6 years of age

Attachment organization/age	Description
Insecure-avoidant 12 months[a]	Actively avoids and ignores parent on reunion, looking away, and remaining occupied with toys. At extremes, moves away from parent and ignores parent's efforts to communicate.
6 years	Minimizes and restricts opportunities for interaction with parent on reunion, looking and speaking only briefly and minimally as required and remaining occupied with toys or activities. At extremes, moves away but subtly, with rationale such as retrieving a toy.
Secure 12 months	Seeks interaction, proximity, physical contact or any combination therefore, with the parent on reunion, often actively attempts to maintain physical contact. Readily soothed after distress by parent and returns to exploration and play.
6 years	Initiates conversation and pleasant interaction with the parent on reunion or is highly responsive to parent's own initiations. May subtly move into proximity or physical contact with parent, usually with rationale such as seeking a toy. Remains calm throughout episode.
Insecure-ambivalent 12 months	Distress because of separation is not effectively soothed by parent, although infant seems to want proximity and contact. Overt to subtle signs of anger toward the parent are often present (e.g., child may seek proximity and contact, then resist it).
6 years	In movements, posture, and tones of voice child appears to attempt to exaggerate intimacy, with the parent as well as dependency on the parent. May seek proximity or contact, but shows some resistance or ambivalance (e.g., lying on parent's lap while wriggling uncomfortably). Moderately avoidant, often subtle signs of hostility are sometimes present.
Insecure-controlling[b] 12 months	Child shows one or several signs of disorganization (e.g., crying for parent at door, then moving sharply away when door opens; approaching parent with head averted) or disorientation (e.g., stilling or freezing movement for a few seconds) during the Strange Situation.
6 years	Seems partially to assume a parental role toward parent. Attempts to control and direct the parent's behavior, either through punitive behavior (directing, embarrassing, or humiliating the parent) or through overbright/caregiving behavior (exhibiting extreme enthusiasm for reunion, solicitious behavior to parent, or careful attempts to guide and direct parent).

[a]Descriptions of reunion behavior used to classify infant attachment organization at 12 months are taken from Ainsworth, Blehar, Waters, and Wall, 1978.
[b]Sixth-year classification title is used for general title. There is no controlling category for infancy; in infancy these children were identified as disorganized/disoriented.
Source: Main, M., & Cassidy, J. (1988). Categories of response to reunion with a parent at age 6. *Developmental Psychology, 24*, 420. Copyright © 1988 by the American Psychological Association. Reprinted by permission.

nitive development results in increasing abilities to perceive meanings not previously perceived and to relate those meanings to one's self. With increasing experiences and understandings during the 6- to 8-year period, fear is less specific (fear of dogs, fear of the dark) and more general (fear of not being liked at school). The ability to imagine, to empathize, and to take the perspectives of others changes the nature of children's fears. Table 15.2 summarizes the way children's fears change as they get older.

Unlike the toddler, whose fear responses were often vociferous, the older child responds in less intense or overt ways when frightened. Older children may repress or mask their fears. Their behaviors bespeak their discomfort—nailbiting, inattention or distractibility, changed eating or sleeping patterns, heightened emotionality, increased dependency, or feigned illness. They may deny that they are afraid or boast of their bravery.

Previous experiences and life circumstances influence what children fear and how they respond: family life trauma, accidents and illnesses, loss of a parent to death or divorce, severe punishments, frightening movies or television programs, adult conversations not fully comprehended, and so on. School-age children typically fear being different from their peers, and in school they fear teacher rejection. Physical and psychological well-being also influence fear responses. As with adults, conditions of hunger, fatigue, illness, and stress cause one to exaggerate events, real or imagined, and respond in disproportionate ways.

Peers influence children's fears. Playmates may share frightening experiences, fabricate or exaggerate scary stories, or perhaps spread unsubstantiated rumors among other children. Peers who say that a certain teacher "never lets you go to the bathroom," that the principal "locks those who misbehave in a closet," that there is a "volcano under the school building," and so on, are exhibiting fabrications that, even when unbelievable, leave a measure of doubt. By the same token, peers often serve as models in which coping with a fear is demonstrated, thus influencing in positive and sometimes negative ways childhood response to fear (Bandura, Grusek, & Menlove, 1967).

Gender differences in fear responses are sometimes noted. Girls are often allowed to be more fearful; they may squeal at crawling things and run away from pretend monsters. These real and pretend fear responses are socially permissible for girls, but often ridiculed in boys. Boys are expected to be stoic in the face of fearful events and are often discouraged from overtly expressing fears.

As with fears of earlier years, children at this stage need adults to talk with them about their fears and to help them find ways to cope with and control the feared situation. Adults should allow children to bring up subjects that concern them and explore with them, in an authoritative and unemotional way, the topics of concern. In addition, adults should provide accurate information on topics such as nuclear war, weather, volcanos, and other fearful subjects; talk about what individuals can do to protect themselves; and deal with the subject of death forthrightly and honestly, yet with gentle understanding of the anxiety this topic evokes. It is important to accept children's fears and worries as real and show respect for the child's concerns, even though they may seem unrealistic.

TABLE 15.2
Changes in children's fears as they get older

Infants	Toddlers	4–5	6–8
Loud noises	Heights	Noises	Dark
Loss of support	Separation	Imaginary creatures	Being left alone
	Strangers	Punishment	Scoldings
	Sudden surprise; e.g.,	Dogs/Small animals	Physical injury/sickness
	Jack in the Box toy	Storms	Ridicule/failure
		Supernatural	Criticism
		(ghosts/witches)	Being different in clothes/hairstyles, etc.
			Worries (what could be): nuclear war, hurricane, family safety, death of family member
			Parental/teacher rejection

Transitional Objects

Attachment to transitional objects of earlier years may well persist into the period from ages 6 through 8. By age 7, a child who still clings to the transitional object may do so in more private and subtle ways, perhaps preferring its comfort only at bedtime, or seeking it during times of stress or illness. Soon, other sentimental objects will compete for the child's attentions, and the need for the original transitional object may wane. For some children, however, discarding the transitional object altogether is out of the question. The teddy bear may remain on the shelf well into adolescence; the worn and thin special blanket may find a home safely tucked in a drawer to remain there indefinitely. No attempt should be made to dispose of transitional objects, as they represent the child's continuing need to find self-comforting strategies. The affection for the object continues, and only the child should decide what to do with the transitional object when it is no longer in use.

Collections

During their early school years, children find enjoyment and interest in objects to collect: baseball and football cards, rocks, seashells, matchbox cars, insects, postcards, jewelry, doll clothes and accessories, stuffed toys, candy wrappers, bits of foil rolled into an ever-enlarging ball, comic books, and so on. Sometimes, trading and bartering go along with these collections, with some children becoming avid collectors through this process. Children also enjoy perusing toy and electronics catalogs and thumbing through junk mail for hidden "treasures." Making lists is another form of collecting: "What I want for Christmas," telephone numbers, addresses, and birthdays.

Collections and hobbies enhance the child's sense of self.

Collections and hobbies enhance the child's sense of self and his abilities, interests, and aspirations and expand the child's knowledge of certain objects or topics. Collections and hobbies engage the child in identifying, sorting, ordering, classifying, and researching endeavors; they expand the child's knowledge and awareness and enhance cognitive development. They provide focus and entertainment during moments of self-imposed privacy. They provide a medium for initiating contacts with others. To adults, some childhood collections may seem valueless and trivial. However, these collections—and others yet to come—may spark an interest that will be sustained and grow into other related interests. Some may represent the origins of what may someday become an avocation or occupation.

Gender Identity and Gender Role Development

As children reach ages 6 through 8, gender identity and gender role behaviors are evident in their mannerisms, occasional sexist language, play choices, and friendships. Having formed gender role stereotypes, children now have rather inflexible ideas about girl/boy expectations, attributing to gender certain behaviors, clothing, hairstyles, play and school activities, home chores, and adult occupations.

Children's stereotypes are learned from those around them and are sometimes imposed upon them by their families and cultures. School experiences comprise a particularly significant area of influence in gender identity and gender role development. There is some evidence of gender bias on the part of classroom teachers. A study by Myra and David Sadker (1985) showed that teachers engage in more conversations, assistance, and praise of boys than they do of girls and respond to boy's questions with more precision. Girls' questions are more often answered with bland or diffused responses. The following is an example from their research (Sadker & Sadker, 1985, p. 166):

TEACHER: "What is the capital of Maryland? Joel?
JOEL: "Baltimore."
TEACHER: "What's the largest city in Maryland, Joel?"
JOEL: "Baltimore."
TEACHER: "That's good. But Baltimore isn't the capital. The capital is also the location of the U.S. Naval Academy. Joel, do you want to try again?"
JOEL: "Annapolis."
TEACHER: "Excellent. Anne, what's the capital of Maine?"
ANNE: "Portland."
TEACHER: "Judy, do you want to try?"
JUDY: "Augusta."
TEACHER: "Ok." (Reprinted with permission from Psychology Today Magazine. Copyright © 1985 [P. T. Partners, L. P.]).

This teacher was probably not aware of the different responses given to male and female students. Such stereotyping is often unconscious and subtle, though its potential for perpetuating stereotyped attitudes in children should not be overlooked. Stereotypes imposed upon girls and boys, such as attributing aggression, independence, and mathematical skills to boys and verbal, dependent, and passive behaviors to girls, may persist well into adult life (Richardson, 1981).

Scholars are encouraging an increasingly androgynous view of gender identity and gender roles. Androgyny suggests that an individual may possess characteristics that are both masculine and feminine (Ruble, 1988). Some studies suggest that androgynous individuals show greater self-esteem and enjoy more enhanced psychological health than do the more gender-typed individuals (Whitley, 1985).

According to Kohlberg (1966), once the child has established gender role constancy between ages 5 and 7, he becomes increasingly interested in observing and imitating the gender role behaviors of others. Parents and teachers become powerful role models, as do other individuals admired by the child, such as siblings, relatives, friends, media personalities, athletes, or other celebrities.

Recent research on gender role development emphasizes gender schema in which young children organize and internalize information about what is typical or appropriate for males and females in their particular sociocultural contexts (Levy & Carter, 1989; Martin & Halverson, 1981, 1987). According to these scholars, such schemas do not necessarily wait for the development of gender constancy to emerge, but are being derived from a variety of developmental and experiential sources from infancy onward. While Kohlberg's stage descriptions emphasize the importance of the child's notion of gender constancy as a point at which children become more cognizant of gender-related attributes, these recent theories emphasize an information-processing perspective. This point of view proposes that there may be within each person internal motivations (schemas) to conform to sociocultural gender role expectations and stereotypes.

Racial Awareness

Sociocentric — the opposite of egocentric; a state in which interests and concerns are focused on others and the person is generally sociable.

As cognitive development moves from preoperational thinking to concrete operational thinking (Piaget, 1952), there are differences in the way children view race. As children begin to decenter (focus on more than one attribute) and become less egocentric and more **sociocentric**—they focus on their family, friends, and culture group rather than primarily on themselves. They now begin to focus on various aspects of individual differences. In this process, children establish a race and culture group identity in which they seek to feel pride and a sense of belonging and security. Good feelings about one's race or culture group identity are tested when children experience diverse groups of people, some of whom may harbor feelings of prejudice.

Aboud (1988) believes that prejudice has origins in cognitive changes. Taking a social-cognitive developmental point of view, Aboud believes that ethnic attitudes have their origins in two overlapping sequences of development. The first sequence relates to developmental processes that flow from affect (feelings) to perceptions and then to cognition. The other sequence flows from one's self-concerns, to awareness of and attentions to cultural groups, to individuals within groups. A child's responses to ethnic groups is determined by the child's developmental placement in these sequences and is most influenced by information and guidance that fit the child's level of racial awareness development (p. 23). The following is a summary of Aboud's descriptions of the affect/perception/cognition sequence.

Step 1
- Wariness of strangers
- Wariness of strangers who are different and unpredictable
- Happiest with people who supply their wants and meet their needs

Step 2
- Perceptions rather than cognition dominate
- Perceptions are relative to oneself
- Aware of similar/dissimilar people
- Dominated by observable qualities; e.g., language, skin color, clothing, etc.
- Ethnic self-identification
- Modifies preferences to bring them into line with self-perceptions

Step 3
- Cognitive understandings

- Begins to understand that ethnicity is based on ancestry, not observable identifiers
- Decentering helps child to accept another's preferences and perceptions

In Aboud's theory, children at Step 3 should be most susceptible to information and interventions that build positive relationships with others. At this point, children can appreciate the fact that ethnicity doesn't change, that there are individual internal qualities to be appreciated, and that differences between groups are reconcilable (p. 24). Aboud called this development the focus of attentions sequence and noted the following progression:

Step 1
- Egocentrism

Step 2
- Preoccupation with groups and the differences between one's own and other groups
- Exaggerates contrasts between groups which may lead to pro-anti dichotomies
- Later, becomes aware of similarities as well as differences between one's own and other groups

Step 3
- Focuses on individuals and unique personalities
- Persons are liked or disliked on the basis of personal rather than ethnic group qualities
- Some ethnic group stereotypes continue

As is true in the development of self-concept (Yammamoto, 1972) and gender identity (Block, 1973), the child's growing acceptance and appreciation of his own ethnicity pave the way for acceptance of the uniqueness of others. Individuals comfortable with their ethnicity have little difficulty building relationships with members of other groups, and do so without feelings of conflict or insecurity (Aboud, 1988).

Self-Concept

The self-concept is more stable at ages 6 to 8, due at least in part to gender constancy and to realizations about the permanence of racial and cultural group memberships. The self-concept of this period begins to include not only what the child himself thinks, but what the child believes others think about him. It is a self-comparing, self-critical period. Home, school, peers, and organized groups all provide experiences that engender self-appraisals.

Carl Rogers is a clinical psychotherapist whose theories (1961) have appreciably influenced our understanding of the self-concept. Through his work in counseling and psychotherapy, Rogers became interested in how the unique self evolves and what it means to be a "fully functioning person." Rogers' self-theory proposes that each individual is responding to countless events in his ever-changing world. Perceptions of each experience are subjective and private, holding special meanings for the individual. The self-concept emerges as a result of these subjective interactions.

Rogers asserted that each individual is striving to become a fully functioning person. Such a person is self-accepting, governed by his own expectations rather than the expectations of others, and open to new experiences. He has no need to mask or repress unpleasant thoughts, feelings, or memories. The fully functioning person accepts others as separate and different individuals and can tolerate those behaviors not preferred for himself.

Adults help children become fully functioning persons when they:

1. Recognize and accept their own feelings, and recognize the role these feelings and attitudes play in their relationships with children;
2. Establish relationships with individual children characterized by acceptance, rapport, mutual support, and recognition;
3. Recognize and accept the child's feelings (both positive and negative), and help the child to find constructive emotional outlets;
4. Enlist a helping process through which genuine understanding and empathy are effectively communicated to the child; and
5. Support the child's growing sense of self, by helping the child recognize and build upon his strengths and capabilities.

Research on the self-concept consistently reports a relationship between the self-concept and achievement. Since the development of a sense of industry is a major psychosocial task of this period, and feelings of competence and self-confidence are necessary for the development of a sense of industry, we should not overlook the critical role school plays in the child's sense of competence or incompetence. The child who perceives himself as capable shows little hesitance in trying new tasks and often succeeds with them. On the other hand, children who feel they are incapable often experience reduced success in new tasks. Successes at this stage, then, are paramount; failures are damaging and can lead the child to a self-perception of inadequacy and inferiority, the polar opposite of Erikson's sense of industry.

Defense mechanism—a psychological response to ego threat, frustration, or failure.

When children feel inadequate, they often employ coping strategies known to psychologists as **defense mechanisms**. There are a variety of types of defense mechanisms. Defense mechanisms begin to emerge during the school years. Freud was among the first to suggest that during these years, defense mechanisms occur to protect the ego from frustration and failure. Defense mechanisms serve to relieve anxiety when a person anticipates or experiences failures, mistakes, or mishaps. Their positive functions lie in their ability to at least temporarily relieve distress or embarrassment.

However, when defense mechanisms are relied upon excessively, or with increasing insistence, the individual is unduly attempting to escape reality. In such cases, parents and teachers must assess the expectations and stresses being placed on the child to ascertain the causes of the child's defense mechanisms. Failure to respond to this behavioral cue places the child at risk for social and emotional problems. Perhaps the child is subjected to too much

TABLE 15.3
Common defense mechanisms

Defense Mechanism	Description	Example
Regression	Returning to earlier, less mature behaviors	Bedwetting; thumbsucking; wanting to be carried in arms
Repression	Inhibiting uncomfortable, frightening memories and storing them in the unconscious	Child abuse victim's inability to name abuser
Projection	Attributing to others one's own thoughts, motives, and traits	A child seeks for himself a cookie, asserting that a playmate needs it
Reaction formation	Behavior opposite from true feelings	Jealous sibling's exaggerated show of affection for newborn brother or sister
Displacement	Shifting feelings or emotions from something that is threatening to a substitute	Premature weaning and adult disapproval of thumbsucking leads to child's nailbiting or chewing on a toy
Rationalizing	Attempting to provide a logical excuse for one's own disappointments, failures, or shortcomings	Person uninvited to party says, "I didn't want to go to her birthday party, anyway—parties are boring."
Denial	Refusing to accept or acknowledge the reality of a situation	Clinging to Santa Claus myth after learning the truth
Fixation	Serious (or severe) conflicts or trauma at one age or stage that arrests further development	Prolonged separation anxiety resulting from traumatic event associated with an earlier separation
Sublimation	Channeling of psychological energies (e.g., aggression) into other outlets	Overachiever in school, sports, and hobbies
Escape/Withdrawal	Avoiding a situation by physically or psychologically removing oneself from it	Nonparticipation in classroom dialogue; avoiding eye contact with others lest they intrude
Compensation	Finding a satisfying substitute for inadequate abilities	Pursuing hobbies or collections when social interactions are difficult

teasing or ridiculing from an older sibling; perhaps the child's school experience involves too much competition or developmentally inappropriate expectations; perhaps the child fears parental disappointment or redress at his inadequacies or failures; or perhaps the child is fearful and wants to be in control. These are but a few examples of underlying reasons for defense mechanisms. Table 15.3 lists a number of common defense mechanisms.

Self-Esteem

Maslow (1968, 1970) described a hierarchy of human needs leading to self-esteem and self-actualization. Individuals are said to progress from lower needs to higher needs on the way to becoming self-actualized. Lower and higher needs differ in the degree to which they are "species-specific"; that is, the lower physiological needs for food and water are common to all living things. The need for love might be shared with higher apes of the animal kingdom, but the needs for self-esteem and self-actualization are uniquely human and shared with no other animals. Figure 15.1 illustrates Maslow's hierarchy.

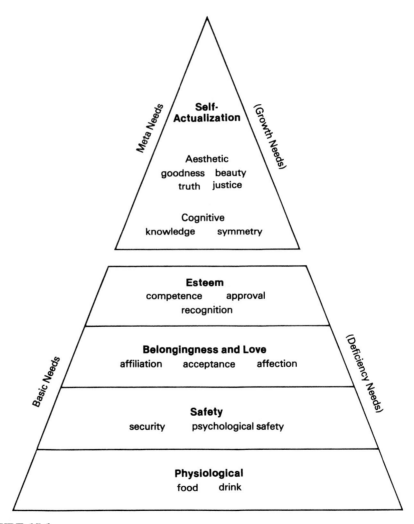

FIGURE 15.1
In Maslow's hierarchy of needs, the needs at the lowest level have the most potency—they must be fulfilled before a person is motivated to try to fulfill higher needs. (From *Psychology For Teaching: A Bear Always Usually Sometimes Faces the Front*, 3/e by Guy R. LeFrancois. ©1979 by Wadsworth Publishing Co., Inc. Reprinted by permission of the publisher.)

The lowest and first of the five levels in Maslow's hierarchy of needs is the one with the greatest "potency" (to use his term), the level of physiological needs such as hunger and thirst. All other needs are superseded by this one. Classroom teachers are quite aware that children who come to school hungry are not motivated to learn. According to Maslow, their energies and innermost thoughts are directed toward this physiological need.

At level 2, safety needs include security, stability, dependency, freedom from fear, anxiety and chaos; and need for structure, order, law, limits, protection, and strength in a protector (Maslow, 1970). Predictable routines, as mentioned frequently throughout this text, help children feel safe. Unpredictable adults and routines are unsettling to children. Chaotic and uncontrolled classroom behaviors elicit fear and a wish that the teacher (protector) were more in control. Children need adults to provide safe, secure surroundings and enough structure to assure them of their boundaries, both physical and psychological.

At level 3, belongingness and love needs are evident when the person feels the need for others. Hungering for love, affection, and acceptance, the individual seeks a place in the family, play or school group, or other social entity. Parents and teachers must seek to assure children of their place within the family or school and their value to the group.

Level 4 represents the level at which esteem needs emerge. According to Maslow, a need for a stable and firmly based positive self-evaluation is prevalent in all individuals. The need for self-respect and the esteem of others is central to healthy personality development. Self-esteem includes feelings of self-confidence, self-worth, and capability, and feelings of being wanted and needed. Individuals who lack self-esteem feel helpless, weak, discouraged, and unneeded. These feelings can lead to compensatory behaviors such as the defense mechanisms described above and possibly to neurotic tendencies.

Maslow cautions that true self-esteem is derived from authentic accomplishments or deserved respect, not from contrived or trivial praise, popularity, or fame. An individual must come to base his self-esteem on real competence and adequacy to a task, rather than on the opinions of others. This raises the question about the often overused classroom management technique in which the teacher praises inane events or inconsequential behaviors with "I like the way Maria is sitting" "... holding her pencil" or "... using a soft voice" (Curry & Johnson, 1990)

Of level 5, Maslow says, "What a man can be, he must be." (1970, p. 46). The self-actualized person is seeking to meet his potential. The individual has interests, talent, and abilities to be pursued, fostered, and mastered. The desire to be the best one can be, to be self-fulfilled, is the dominant theme of this level. It can only be achieved when the preceding lower-level needs have been satisfied.

During the 6 through 8 age period and beyond, self-appraisals find their verification in both home and school. Frequent successes, positive results from efforts, and teachers and peers who respond in helpful and accepting ways further the child's good feelings about himself. On the other hand, frequent failures or repeated negative responses undermine the development of self-esteem and impede the child's progress in becoming a self-actualized person.

Moral Development

Recall that Piaget's stage-sequence theory of moral development cited three stages: (1) premoral, (2) moral realism, and (3) moral relativism. Earlier chapters discussed Stage 1 in describing the moral behaviors of children under 6. Children in the 6 through 8 age group exhibit characteristics of Piaget's Stage 2 level of moral development, that of moral realism. Moral realism is characterized by rule-bound thinking and behaving. Children at this stage of moral development believe:

1. Rules are rules, regardless of intentions;
2. Rules are unalterable;
3. Rules have been set by an all-knowing and powerful authority figure (God, parent, teacher);
4. The importance of the rule is in direct proportion to the severity of the punishment;
5. Obedience to rules means one is good; disobedience means one is bad; and
6. Punishment is a necessary result of breaking a rule.

The term heteronomy describes this stage, for it implies that individuals are other-governed, rather than autonomous or self-governed. Parents, teachers, and other authoritative adults impose a variety of rules and expectations to which children must comply. Many children comply with adult rules without question, believing in the absolute authority of the adult. With the emergence of autonomy, initiative, and curiosity, the child begins to challenge adult rules.

With these developments, children begin to encounter and distinguish different kinds of rules—social conventional rules and moral rules (Turiel, 1980). Social conventional rules are social regulations such as modes of dress for certain occasions, which side of the street to drive on, how to address the classroom teacher, and so on. Such rules are arbitrary in that they do not generalize to all situations, places or cultures—they are not universal. Moral rules, on the other hand, are rules relating to generalized values such as honesty, fairness, justice, and so on. According to Turiel, children as young as age 6 are able to distinguish between conventional rules and rules of morality and justice.

Children imitate the social conventions and moral values of those adults who are important to them. Through these imitations during their own social interactions, children become increasingly aware of moral rules and values. However, adults can be misled by some of these behaviors, believing that verbalized values and imitated social conventions indicate understanding and internalized behaviors. Quite the contrary, children are in the process of understanding, and such behaviors must be practiced and the consequences observed or experienced before internalized moral behavior can occur.

At this age, sociodramatic play continues to be a powerful source for moral understandings. Imitations of adult moral and social conventions and transgressions can be explored in the safe context of pretend play. Moreover, role-taking abilities increase through sociodramatic play, as does experiencing competing points of view. These experiences are necessary precursors to solving moral dilemmas later on.

As children move from preoperational thinking to concrete operations during this period, they can compare, classify, and draw logical conclusions. These abilities assist the child in making the shift from rule-bound morality to the realization that there are many sources of rules (parents, teachers, and laws). As well, children have decentered and become less egocentric and are becoming aware that others have needs, intentions, feelings, and expectations and that others' needs may from time to time be more important than their own. This represents Stage 3 of Kohlberg's sequence of moral development.

This stage is referred to by Kohlberg as the "good boy/good girl" stage, wherein children seek approval. They are more inclined to conform in order to be perceived as "good." The desire to please peer groups as well as adults is evident in this phase. Often children find themselves in situations where they choose between family and peer group rules. They may go along with the peer group in spite of known prohibitions. These behaviors are not necessarily deliberate, nor resistive of established rules or authority; they simply preempt previous constraints. Parents who respond to these transgressions with reason and an attempt to understand the child's motivations, help children develop a conscience and further the development of inner controls, which can guide behaviors in the absence of authority figures.

Development of Conscience

Conscience generally emerges out of the child's identification with his parents (Mussen, 1979; Snyder, Snyder, & Snyder, 1980). Love-oriented discipline that maintains supportive and affectionate relationships is more readily associated with the development of a conscience than are other forms of discipline. Apparently, fear of loss of love from a loving parent underlies this development. Inductive discipline techniques, which elicit perspective-taking, empathy, altruism, and other prosocial thought and behaviors, are closely associated with the development of a conscience. Power assertive strategies, on the other hand, provide little impetus for the development of a conscience.

Children who have internalized standards of right and wrong from their earlier family experiences fall back on these standards when confronted with discrepancies and temptations outside the family. While self-control may not always be present in these situations, the conscience is. The conscience becomes a "stand-in" for the parent and attempts to guide behaviors along internalized family expectations.

Friendships

The peer group emerges as a powerful socializing force in the child's life during the early school years. The child has shifted from seeking interactions with adults more than children, to seeking interactions with children more than adults. Peer group acceptance gains primary importance to the child.

Friendships begin to segregate along gender lines during the 6- through 8-year age period. The beginnings of this segregation are seen in the preprimary years, but by the time children are 7 or 8 years old, the preference for same-sex peer groups becomes the rule, not the exception. In another year or so, same-sex peer group preference will reach its peak.

Friendships are now less transient than they were in previous years. It has become somewhat more difficult to make friends, and dissolved friendships can be quite emotionally unsettling. The circle of friends is smaller than in previous years. As children become somewhat choosy, not only gender, but also race and economic background influence friendship choices (Hartup, 1983). Choices become based on attributes ("He is real nice"), rather than possessions or situation factors, as with younger children ("I like him because he has a Lego game to play with") (Boggiano, Klinger, & Main, 1986). One can see that the social competence skills of initiating, maintaining, and resolving conflicts become important skills to have mastered by early school age.

Participation in games and activities involving rules brings children into frequent conflicts, as rules become debatable and as children discover that each player may perceive the rules differently. Through conflict encounters such as these, children's points of view compete and their negotiating skills are tested. Lever (1976) found a difference in the amount of conflict engaged in by boys and girls. Boys' games tended to result in more conflict, while girls were more inclined to engage in turn-taking behaviors. Girls were also found to be more inclined to try to diffuse conflict situations. Boys were more likely to use heavy-handed persuasion to get what they wanted. Boys were shown to use these tactics whether in conflict with boys or with girls. Interestingly, girls were inclined to use heavy-handed tactics with boys, but seldom with girls (Miller, Danaher, & Forbes, 1986). Some of these differences may be explained by the expectation that boys will behave more aggressively than girls (Maccoby & Jacklin, 1974/1980). There is also the expectation that social harmony is preferred by girls, and therefore they provoke less conflict (Gilligan, 1982).

Cooperation emerges through these early friendships and sustains them (Hartup, 1989). Through friendships children derive companionship, emotional security and support, enhanced feelings of self-worth, interpersonal relationship skills, and knowledge about cultures and social conventions.

Special Needs Children

Children with special needs face greater psychosocial challenges as they begin to move through the elementary grades. Their needs for acceptance, belonging, and self-esteem are shared with their age-mates. The extent to which they have developed social skills for initiating and maintaining friendships and for resolving conflicts will influence their successes with interpersonal relationships and peer acceptance. By the same token, the extent to which other children have learned to understand and relate to those with disabilities also influences the climate for acceptance and participation in peer group activities.

A common challenge for special needs children regardless of disability is that of feeling different from other children. The self-concept of many children with disabilities may center too heavily on their disabling conditions. Teachers seeking positive and successful psychosocial experiences for children with special needs will find effective ways to promote group understandings and acceptance. The teacher will structure both the physical and the psychosocial environments to encourage social interactions among all children.

Teachers should be aware that any emphasis on competition among children can be particularly detrimental to the psychosocial development of children with special needs. Instead, arranging for more cooperative group endeavors assists all children in the development of social skills and social competence (see Figure 15.2).

FIGURE 15.2
Cooperation versus competition

Compared with competitive and individualistic learning situations, working cooperatively with peers:

1. Will create a pattern of promotive interaction, in which there is
   a. more direct face-to-face interaction among students;
   b. an expectation that one's peers will facilitate one's learning;
   c. more peer pressure toward achievement and appropriate classroom behavior;
   d. more reciprocal communication and fewer difficulties in communicating with each other;
   e. more actual helping, tutoring, assisting, and general facilitation of each other's learning;
   f. more open-mindedness to peers and willingness to be influenced by their ideas and information;
   g. more positive feedback to and reinforcement of each other;
   h. less hostility, both verbal and physical, expressed towards peers.
2. Will create perceptions and feelings of
   a. higher trust in other students;
   b. more mutual concern and friendliness for other students, more attentiveness to peers, more feelings of obligation to and responsibility for classmates, and desire to win the respect of other students;
   c. stronger beliefs that one is liked, supported, and accepted by other students, and that other students care about how much one learns and want to help one learn;
   d. lower fear of failure and higher psychological safety;
   e. higher valuing of classmates;
   f. greater feelings of success.

Source: D. Johnson and R. Johnson, "Classroom Learning Structure and Attitudes toward Handicapped Students in Mainstream Settings: A Theoretical Model and Research Evidence," in R. L. Jones (Ed.), *Attitudes and Attitude Change in Special Education: Theory and Practice* (Reston, Va.: The Council for Exceptional Children, 1984). Reprinted with permission.

Sociocultural Differences

Regardless of race or cultural group membership, parents play a major role in helping children establish racial identities and in building pride in their racial and cultural backgrounds. Through the family, children experience the traditions, religion, values, and goals of their culture. Through the family, children are socialized into unique cultural patterns that include dress, food preferences, celebrations, language, intrafamilial relationships, and social behaviors and expectations. The psychosocial development of children will differ from culture to culture along these various dimensions.

As children enter school, concerns for healthy cultural experiences emerge. Often teachers are from different cultural groups than those of their students. Classroom populations often include children from several different cultures. Adults who have knowledge of differences among and within cultural groups are better equipped to provide positive multicultural experiences and productive and satisfying social interactions among classmates. Teachers understanding of differences in parenting styles and of differing expectations and goals parents have for their children are able to provide positive and supportive home-school relationships. Andrews (1981) lists four basic cultural needs of young children and their families: (1) self-esteem, (2) belonging, (3) achievement, and (4) dignity. According to Andrews, all children, regardless of ethnic or racial background, have these same basic cultural needs.

Factors Influencing Psychosocial Development

Among the factors contributing to healthy psychosocial development in the 6- to 8-year-old are the child's own personality; the nature and quality of adult/child relationships; experiences beyond school in before- and after-school child care settings; sibling relationships; increasing social interactions; television; and the child's sociocultural context.

Child's Personality

From previous chapters, we have learned that children have distinctive temperamental characteristics that are probably genetically derived but are also influenced in a variety of ways by the child's environment. The concept of temperament refers to a number of behavioral aspects: activity level; regularity of behavior; distractibility; approach and withdrawal in new experiences; adaptability to change; attention span/persistence; intensity of reaction to stimuli; response threshold (amount of stimulation needed to evoke a response); and mood (Chess & Thomas, 1987; Thomas, Chess, Birch, Hertzig, & Korn, 1963).

The social context in which these variable temperament qualities are exhibited determines the effect they may have on others and how others will respond to the child. For instance, a child with a very high activity level could be viewed in positive terms ("energetic" and "lively") or negative terms ("jumpy" and "restless"). Such views influence the person's responses and interactions with the child. The child, then, is subjected to a variety of responses of others based on how others perceive his temperament.

Differences in personality at ages 6 through 8 have their roots in these early and continuing perceptions and interactions. Recent studies have attempted to ascertain the relation of early personality traits and later psychosocial adjustment. Some traits are found to persist. For instance, highly aggressive children have been found to remain relatively more aggressive than others as they get older (Huesmann, Eron, Lefkowitz, & Walder, 1984). Other studies have suggested that negative emotional behavior such as aggressiveness, being hard to please, undercompliance, and having difficulty with peers are fairly stable over the course of childhood and affect later adjustment. Children who have been socially rejected during their earliest elementary years may be more at risk for social difficulties in adolescence and early adulthood (Hymel, Rubin, Rowden, & LeMare, 1990).

The complex social interactions of children ages 6 through 8 encompass the family, school, peer groups, organized activity groups, and a plethora of incidental social encounters. This complex network of interactions expands the child's insights into the personalities of others and into his own developing personality. Though self-awareness has been emerging since infancy, the self-perceptions of this age period are becoming more acute. Maturing social perceptions also help children to appreciate the needs of others and engage in cooperative activities.

Nature of Adult/Child Relationships

As previously discussed, qualities of early experiences such as attachment, parenting styles, and nonparental child care have been associated with various psychosocial outcomes. Certain aspects of the relationship between the parent and the child have also been related to the child's psychosocial development. A recent study observed playful mother-child and father-child interactions and correlated them with the child's adaptation to peers (MacDonald & Parke, 1984). The findings suggest that boys who were competent with their peers had fathers who were physically playful and affectionate. The fathers of competent girls engaged their daughters in stimulating verbal exchanges. Certain maternal behaviors have been found to influence social acceptance with peers. Maternal use of positive verbal interactions, such as polite requests and suggestions and maternal behaviors that were less demanding and disagreeable with their children, led to children who were also less abrasive and positive in their peer interactions (Putallaz, 1987).

It is generally believed that social skills necessary for later successful peer group interactions are learned through early experiences in the family (Petit, Dodge, & Brown, 1988). But the quality of parent-child interactions is not the only influence on psychosocial development. By providing opportunities for peer group interaction, encouraging and facilitating friendships, and monitoring their children's relationships for positive outcomes, parents provide the scaffolding essential to the development of social competence.

Before- and After-School Care

In recent years the need for child care has increased appreciably. As well, the availability and utilization of before- and after-school care arrangements has increased. The experiences children have in these programs influence psychosocial development. The need for adults in these settings to be good role models—to be nurturing and supportive of growth and development—is crucial. The expectations placed on children in child care situations must be scrutinized. As with developmentally appropriate schooling experiences discussed in previous chapters, child care programs must meet the physical/motor and social/emotional needs of children, along with cognitive needs.

For some school children, the out-of-home day may be as long as 10 to 13 hours. Long days are tiring and stressful. The daily before school/school/after school routine may involve two or more different settings, perhaps in two or more locations; different sets of adult authorities with different levels of education and training; different teaching and discipline styles; different behavior and performance expectations; and different modes of interacting with individual children. There may be different peer groups with different group configurations and interactional dynamics. Clearly, children in these situations are being called upon to be flexible, resilient, and adaptable, not to mention physically hearty!

For some children, these demands present no problems. For others, adapting to multiple authority figures and different peer groups can be stressful and difficult. Parents, caregivers, and classroom teachers must be sensitive to the physical and psychological demands of these routines. When there is a balanced schedule that includes rest, relaxation, play, self-directed activities, outdoor and indoor activities, and group and solitary moments, along with structured and adult-directed activities, the day can be a healthy and quite tolerable one. However, emphasis on group participation, school work, and academic endeavors before, during, and after school would tax any child.

Teachers and caregivers will want to provide space (both physical and psychological) for children to distance themselves from the group from time to time. Schedules in both the school and the child care program need to be sensitive to the physiological needs for nourishment, physical exercise, recess, spontaneous play, and informal interactions with friends and siblings. After-school programs need to resist the urge to "help" with schooling by insisting on additional school work activities. Likewise, schools and teachers must resist the temptation to defer practice and reinforcement activities to after-school times. This, of course, opens the debate on whether or not homework should be regularly assigned. This topic, while a critical one, is beyond the intent of this discussion. The points to be made are:

1. Long days with repeated structured activities may impede school learning through fatigue, frustration, and burnout.

2. The physical-motor needs (addressed in Chapters 11 and 14) must not be circumvented if children are to be motorically and neurologically healthy.
3. Sound psychosocial development relies upon warm, nurturing, supportive, and meaningful adult-child relationships.
4. Social competence, including social problem-solving skills, perspective-taking, and prosocial abilities depends upon opportunities to interact with friends in meaningful ways and being reasonably free from adult interference.

Before- and after-school child care can play a positive and supportive role in psychosocial development. When children are allowed to experience autonomy and control in the use of their time and energies, and are provided activities over which they can have a sense of mastery, adaptability of the routines of child care and school are eased (Bryant, 1985).

Programs that provide for the safety and nurturing needs of children offer a valuable support system for families. When parents feel secure and confident about the experiences their children are having during their work days, family relationships are enhanced. Relieved of the worry and stress associated with unpredictable or latchkey arrangements, parents are able to pursue their work days in a more productive manner. Emerging paradigms for child care will include more family/school/child care coordinations and more efforts to meet a variety of family support service needs (Kagan, 1989; NASBE, 1988).

Sibling Relationships

The positive and constructive relationships among siblings have not received as much attention in popular press, media, and research as has sibling rivalry and jealousy. Yet studies reveal that siblings are nurturing, protective, and cooperative with one another, and are more likely to be so with one another than with unrelated children (Dunn & Kendrick, 1982b).

The sense of self is in part derived from the relationships a child has with his siblings. Yet, siblings are faced with a variety of self-concept issues relating to their close or distant relationships with brothers and sisters, their feelings of acceptance or rejection of one another, and their feelings of being similar or different from one another (Bank & Kahn, 1982b). These relationships and the perceptions that accompany them play a complex role in the child's developing sense of self as a unique and separate individual, yet part of a larger identity that includes brothers and sisters.

Rivalrous behavior at 6 through 8 is often an indication of the child's emerging sense of identity. Children at this age compare themselves with others in an attempt to affirm their self-worth. In families, brothers and sisters become objects for comparison as children seek to distinguish similarities and differences between themselves and others. At the same time, siblings begin to identify with one or more of their siblings, who are often powerful role models.

It is difficult to establish a comfortable and separate identity when parents dress siblings alike; provide the same enrichment opportunities (lessons in swimming, piano, ballet, or tennis) or group memberships (Little League, Scout

Siblings typically move in and out of their close relationships with one another.

troops); or adopt an "if it is done for one, must be done for the other" approach to child-rearing. Each child's unique needs, interests, and capabilities need nurturing and support. Self-confidence and self-esteem emerge from finding one's own attributes, separate and apart from those of others, particularly those of siblings.

Parents who project their own unfulfilled ambitions (to play baseball, master the violin, or be the top of the class) on one or more of the siblings—perceived by the parent to have these skills and interests—place the child and his siblings at risk on several fronts. The full realization of one's own interests and capabilities are thwarted in the child on whom these projections are imposed. The child grows to believe that success in the parent-selected pursuit will bring favor to him over others; and failure will bring serious disappointment to the parent and perhaps lead to retribution. The sibling excluded from these particular expectations perceives himself as less important to the parent, or perhaps less capable, even in the absence of interest in the activities in question. The sibling relationship is undermined by feelings of rejection, envy, competition, and other negative responses to the parent's insensitive expectations. The parent-child relationship in both cases is undermined.

Classroom teachers and other adults with whom the child interacts often compare, both favorably and unfavorably, one sibling to another. This, as well, impedes self-concept development and aggravates sibling relationships. Where sibling relationships are at-risk or already strained, differential treatment by parents, teachers, or others can exacerbate the situation for the siblings.

Increased Social Interactions

As children get older, an expanding social circle, from parents and family to individuals and groups outside of the family, brings with it additional influences on the child's psychosocial development. Social interactions include incidental encounters (sharing the "sights" of the toy aisle at the supermarket with an acquaintance); informal interactions with individuals (riding bicycles with a special friend) and with loosely formed groups (the neighborhood play groups); and formal or organized activities (Pee-Wee and Little League sports).

At this age, children establish and maintain close friendships with one or more age-mates and enjoy visiting in one another's homes, sometimes overnight. Such friendships help children to grow in independence and social interaction skills. Through these friendships, children learn the importance of "give and take" and gain a sense of loyalty.

Children enlarge their friendship circles through loosely formed social groups. As a rule, these groups simply "play around" with one another; yet, their organization may take on the elements of a club or gang, with leaders and followers, membership preferences, rules, and sometimes a name. Adults can harness the energy and enthusiasm that emerges from these friendship groups.

■ Jeremy is a member of the "Walla Street Club." The group to which he belongs includes the 7-year-old boy next door, the two brothers (8 and 9) who live across the street, a 7-year-old from several doors down the street, and another 6-year-old from a block away. Girls are not admitted to the "club," though two of the members have younger sisters who on a few rare occasions are allowed to participate in their games. They spend as much time together after school or on weekends as they can. These boys seem to have an insatiable desire to be together and boundless energy when engaged in play.

Jeremy's dad has instigated a weekend project for the boys, that of building a clubhouse in the backyard. The design, collection of building materials and tools (some borrowed from other members' households), and the construction of the house has been an ongoing project for about 2 months. The boys plan each step with energy and enthusiasm. Their wills clash as perceptions differ as to which board should go where, where the door will be, and who is going to bring more nails. At home the boys draw pictures of their clubhouse, gather items with which to furnish it, and brag to their siblings about their own private place. They may talk about the fun or complain about the conflicts with their parents.

They anticipate with one another their meetings and what they will do, who will come, and who can never come into the clubhouse. It is a dynamic and ongoing "avocation" in their current lives. ■

What do children gain from experiences like these? What about a child excluded from the play group? In these loosely formed groups, children experience leading and following, negotiating and compromising, rule setting, rule changing, and rule constraints. They become aware of the needs and wishes of others, and they practice perspective-taking and diplomacy. They experience loyalty and disloyalty, democracy and autocracy. Their sense of industry is tapped, and their sense of belonging is reinforced. Their confidence and self-esteem are enhanced.

In spite of all the positive influences of these social groupings, there can be difficulties associated with membership. Children from 6 through 8 are measuring themselves against their perceptions of others, and in so doing are self-critical and critical of others. When group expectations are at odds with the child's abilities and desires, conflicts occur and group membership may become detrimental. Treating others unkindly, expecting members to engage in mischief or forbidden activities, setting standards for dress, imposing undesired rivalry and competition, excluding a valued friend, and devaluing one's other activities (e.g., piano lessons, participation in scouting or a family picnic) are influences that can strain the child's abilities to negotiate. Adults need to be cognizant of these occurences and sensitive the child's dilemma. Guidance and support are needed, and in some instances, intervention and coaching, will be necessary.

These informal groups, often based on proximity and accessibility, can also define their memberships arbitrarily along age, gender, socioeconomic, racial, cultural, or religious lines. While there are positive effects for children in these groups, children who are excluded may suffer negative outcomes. Children excluded on such bases suffer some of their first lessons in prejudice. Sensitive adults will need to be open to discussion about the prejudice the child has experienced and provide positive guidance for handling these situations when they arise. Here again, adults serve as positive social role models for children. Adult intervention may be necessary to guide the group toward more prosocial goals and behaviors.

In addition to informally structured social groupings, the child from 6 through 8 is exposed to a variety of other extrafamilial social interactions. Older now, and more predictable and dependable, children are included in various celebrations and recreational events—weddings, graduation ceremonies, football games, and concerts. Children often join their parents in religious services on a more regular basis than in previous years. These opportunities enlarge the child's social awareness and provide additional role models. The developmental appropriateness of special lessons or sports training for a particular child should be of concern. Athletic training can be physically risky and should be pursued upon the advice and counsel of the child's physician. Participation in athletic teams should be viewed with this same caution, as these activities can place the child at risk for physical injury, and can be emotionally and socially taxing for the child.

Stress

Children, like adults, experience stress from time to time. Unlike adults, young children do not have sufficient knowledge and experience to understand their stressors, nor do they have a repertoire of coping strategies for dealing with stress.

The causes of stress in young children are many and varied. Honig (1986) categorized stressor variables as (1) personal, including prematurity, sex, temperament, neurological sturdiness, age of child, and intellectual capacity; (2) ecological, including characteristics of living environments such as neighborhood crime, antisocial role models, unesthetic surroundings, household density, individual privacy requirements, or inadequate play space; (3) socioeconomic status; (4) catastrophes and terrors, including hospitalization, societal disasters, threat of nuclear war and terrorism; and (5) family events, including birth of siblings, death of parent or sibling, separation and divorce, and blended families.

Pressures to perform tasks or to achieve beyond one's years and developmental capacities, changes in school or child care arrangements, and childhood social events, such as birthday parties and school field trips, may also be stressful. Obviously, there are a great number of potential stressors for young children. Certainly, not all of these events cause anxiety or stress in all children. Responses to stress are as varied as the stressors themselves and may be physiological (headache, stomachache, loss of appetite, sleep disturbances) or psychological (crying, nightmares, regression, irritability, increased dependency).

Responses to stress are related to temperament, cognitive styles, and social support networks (Owens-Stively, 1987). Characteristics often associated with stress-related personalities, such as competiveness, impatience, aggressiveness, low frustration tolerance, hostility, and high achievement orientation, have been found in very young children. The child's ability to appraise a stressful situation influences the extent to which the child will cope. Children need adults to help them identify their stressors and to evaluate them with a goal toward either eliminating the stressors when possible or finding constructive ways to deal with stress.

■ Jeremy's second-grade teacher has invited his parents to a conference. His usual classroom performance has deteriorated since the beginning of the school year, and she is concerned. Jeremy's behaviors in school are off-task and disruptive. He teases his classmates, antagonizes his project partners, and resorts to name-calling when they protest. When the teacher intervenes, he withdraws, becomes sullen, and often cries.

In conference, Ann and Bill reveal that similar behaviors occur at home, and they are at a loss to know what to do. Their individual work commitments, church work, and social life are consuming larger and larger amounts of their time and energies. In addition, Ann's mother has recently undergone surgery and has needed Ann's assistance during her recovery.

The teacher asks them to focus on Jeremy's routines. What does he do before and after school and on the weekends? Jeremy's schedule includes regular before- and after-school care at a childcare center near the school. In addition, he takes piano lessons early each Monday morning, karate lessons on Wednesday afternoon, and has Pee-Wee league baseball on Saturday mornings.

Clearly, all members of the family have become overcommitted and overprogrammed. The stress of such scheduling, the logistics of transportation and attendance, and the reduced opportunities for family interaction and mutual support are beginning to take their toll on each member. Jeremy's behavior in school is a clue to the stress he is encountering.

A reassessment of their commitments, goals, and priorities led Bill and Ann to conclude that each member of the family would benefit from a change. Jeremy was encouraged to talk about the extracurricular activities in which he was enrolled, and was allowed to decide which one or ones were most important to him and most enjoyable. Ann and Bill did the same assessment of their own activities. From this exercise, each family member eliminated all but the most pressing and important activities. Jeremy chose to drop the piano and the karate lessons. Maybe later he will want to pursue those lessons; for now, he feels relieved. With commitments and extracurricular activities returned to a manageable level, Jeremy and his parents have more time and energy to respond to one another and to interact with focused attention. ■

Television

The amount of time school-age children spend viewing television is a major concern to parents, educators, child advocacy groups, and government officials. The following research statements alert us to this concern:

> More time is spent watching television in the first 15 years of life than going to school; in fact, by the time a child reaches age 18, more time will have been spent watching television than any other single activity besides sleeping. (Liebert, Sprafkin, & Davidson, 1982 p. ix)
>
> The average high school graduate will have spent 22,000 hours in front of a television set, and will have been exposed to 350,000 commercials. (Adler, Lesser, Meringoff, Robertson, Rossiter, & Ward, 1980, p. 1)

It is clear that television plays a major role in the socialization and culturalization of children. Children learn from television, and their behaviors are influenced by what they learn. Studies of violence and aggression on television have overwhelmingly concluded that there is a measurable impact on behavior. Concern continues over this issue. Studies of gender and of racial and cultural groups on television have pointed out misrepresentations in television programming and the potential deleterious effects of stereotyping. Studies of commercials have likewise suggested that childhood values and attitudes may be distorted and that commercials exploit children for financial gains.

Programs with prosocial themes and role models have been shown to influence behavior, though the strength of the impact of these programs is thought to be less potent than that of violence and aggression (Radke-Yarrow, Zahn-Waxler, & Chapman, 1983). Contemporary studies of the impact of television on children's lives are attempting to determine to what extent children actually attend to television when the set is on; what types of program events or program attributes attract and hold the child's attention (e.g., other children, puppets, peculiar voices, animation, rhyming, laughing, and repetition); and to what extent children comprehend what they view on television.

Large amounts of time viewing television interfere with psychosocial development in the following ways:

1. Physical activity and outdoor play are curtailed. Lack of exercise impedes physical motor development and sound physical and mental health.
2. Interaction with other children is reduced. As we have seen, children at this age need the social experiences that peer group interaction affords. Without these experiences, children are deprived of opportunities to gain social knowledge and social competence.
3. Children unskilled in social interaction with peers, or unpopular and rejected by playmates, find escape in television viewing, further reducing their interactions with others and further impeding their psychosocial development.
4. Parent-child conversations and interactions are interrupted. Both children and parents forego dialogue and in-depth conversations when television viewing dominates their free time. Opportunities to address issues of concern to the child and to provide needed emotional/social guidance are often lost and cannot be readily retrieved.
5. Opportunities to discover one's own interests and unique capabilities or talents are encroached upon. Children this age who are developing initiative, industry, self-concept, and self-esteem need to explore and experience a variety of endeavors and interests on the way to self-discovery.

Based on the assumption that school-age children can be taught to use critical viewing skills, scholars are developing programs and strategies to be used in classrooms and perhaps at home (Dorr, Graves, & Phelps, 1980). The objectives of these programs include:

1. Decreasing the belief that TV programs are real;
2. Increasing the child's tendency to compare what is seen on TV with other sources of information;
3. Decreasing television's credibility by teaching children about the economic and production aspects of it; and
4. Teaching children to evaluate television's content.

At home, critical viewing skills can be practiced with children by pointing out how television provides both worthwhile and objectionable programs; family values can be conveyed in these comparisons. Role playing and pantomime illustrate that characters on television are actors playing a particular role. Adults can help children compare these roles with individuals in similar roles in real life, perhaps with individuals the child knows personally. Adults can watch and listen with children for special effects such as laugh tracks, sounds, lighting, and fast sequenced photos; listen to background music for familiar tunes or specific instruments; dialogue about the story just viewed; retell the story with a "better" ending; answer questions about the story while they are fresh in the child's mind; critique a program for both its good qualities and its shortcomings; or help children identify implied messages by pointing out how commercials

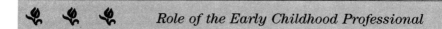

❧ ❧ ❧   *Role of the Early Childhood Professional*

Enhancing Psychosocial Development in Children Ages 6 Through 8

1. Support the child's continuing need for nurturance and security.
2. Enhance the child's self-esteem through positive and supportive interactions.
3. Model prosocial and moral behaviors; help children understand the need and rationales for rules.
4. Support the child's sense of industry through opportunities to participate in meaningful activities.
5. Understand the child's increasing needs for social interactions, and encourage and facilitate a variety of social interactions.
6. Provide positive, inductive, authoritative discipline.
7. Recognize the child's continuing need for boundaries and guidance.
8. Respond to the child's changing interests in gender with acceptance and respect.
9. Assist the child in accepting and appreciating others.
10. Provide appropriate media experiences and help the child to become a critical evaluator of media programs.

use loud, fast talk, and flashy colors and music to obtain the viewer's attention. Together, parents and children can make a list of famous people who make commercials to illustrate how these people are used by the industry to promote products; compare products advertised with the ones the family already prefers; and when shopping, make price and quality comparisons, helping children draw conclusions about the feasibility of purchasing an advertised product.

Parents and teachers have important roles to play in facilitating the positive effects of television for children. The amount of time children spend viewing television can be curtailed in favor of more physically and mentally challenging activities and increased social interactions with others. Wise program choices can evolve when children are taught to evaluate the offerings. As well, children need adults to talk with them about the content of programs they see and to help them become discerning viewers.

Sociocultural Factors

People in different sociocultural backgrounds have different social priorities for their children relative to discipline and authority, independence, school achievement, responsibilities to family, and gender role behaviors. Meeting families and learning about their goals and priorities for their children assists the teacher in working effectively with the children in the classroom.

Teachers must strive to provide opportunities for positive social interactions and to incorporate a multicultural perspective into the curriculum. Instructional materials should reflect a variety of racial and cultural backgrounds and should be particularly sensitive to the racial and cultural make-up of the class. Instructional groupings should include diverse memberships to maximize opportunities to interact, build friendships, and expand sociocultural understandings.

Key Terms

industry   sociocentric
period of equilibrium   defense mechanism
period of disequilibrium

Review Strategies/Activities

1. Develop an annotated bibliography of children's books that address the issues children confront in making and maintaining friendships.
2. Observe a third-grade classroom. How is social interaction encouraged? Are informal social groups evident? Observe these friendship groups on the playground at recess. What are the compositions of the groups? How do they interact with one another? Is there a leader? What rules seem to be evident? How do the children respond to non-group members?
3. Visit the home of a friend of a different race. Discuss differences in your child-rearing with regard to school achievement, respect for authority, independence, responsibilities to family, choice of friends, gender role, and racial identity.
4. With a partner, brainstorm ways to promote and facilitate the developing sense of industry in young school-age children.

Further Readings

Aboud, F. (1988). *Children and prejudice.* New York: Basil Blackwell, Inc.
   This book addresses the issue of prejudice in children, its developmental course and what forms of prejudice emerge over the childhood years relative to cognitive changes taking place. The environmental influences of prejudice and the role of parents and other authorities are discussed. This book provides a guide to understanding and combating prejudice in children.

Carlson-Paige, N., & Levin, D. E. (1985). *Helping children understand peace, war, and the nuclear threat.* Washington DC: National Association for the Education of Young Children.
   This brief book offers suggestions to parents and teachers for helping children understand the nuclear age in which they live. Today, children hear about a variety of threats through television, radio, and adult conversations. Helping children make sense of what they hear, and helping them feel that their ideas and actions can make a difference, is the goal of the book.

Curry, N., & Johnson, C. (1990). *Beyond self-esteem: Developing a genuine sense of human value.* Washington, DC: National Association for the Education of Young Children.
   This book emphasizes that self-esteem cannot be achieved merely by giving children

empty praise, extra pats, or cheers of support. Self-esteem is presented as a dynamic multidimensional phenomenon that must be considered in the context of the child's total development.

Derman-Sparks, L. (1989). *Anti-bias curriculum: Tools for empowering young children.* Washington, DC: National Association for the Education of Young Children.
This book sets forth principles and methodologies for creating anti-bias curriculums. It addresses issues relating to race, culture, gender, and disabilities. It discusses ways to assist children in their own development of positive identities and attitudes.

Hale-Benson, J. (1986). *Black children: their roots, culture, and learning styles* (rev. ed.). Baltimore: The Johns Hopkins University Press.
This very readable book provides valuable insights into the effects of African-American culture on the intellectual and psychosocial development of African-American children.

Lickona, T. (1983). *Raising good children: Helping your child through the stages of moral development.* New York: Bantam.
Handling ethical problems is placed in the context of the child's developmental capabilities. Suggestions are provided about how to help children through the stages of moral development.

Liebert, R. M., Sprafkin, J. N., & Davidson, E. S. (1982). *The early window: Effects of television on children and youth* (2nd ed.). New York: Pergamon Press, Inc.
This book is a fascinating account of the social, political and economic factors that have surrounded network child-related programming decisions over the years. An extensive review of the research on television's effects on children is included.

Riley, S. S. (1984). *How to generate values in young children: Integrity, honesty, individuality, self-confidence, and wisdom.* Washington, DC: National Association for the Education of Young Children.
The title of this booklet speaks for itself. Containing examples and guidance for parents and teachers, the book helps adults to focus on characteristics we want children to develop.

Newsletter: School Age Notes
This is a bimonthly newsletter for teachers and directors of programs for school-age children. Provides many developmentally sound and practical suggestions. Available from: P.O. Box 120674, Nashville, TN 37212.

CHAPTER 16

Continual interaction with materials in the classroom supports the construction of knowledge and meaning for the learner. No cut off age of six exists for such interaction.... During all the early childhood years the search for meaning is facilitated or impeded by the nature of the environment: opportunities for exploration, discovery, and the integration of learnings are essential.

Evelyn Weber

Cognitive/Language/Literacy Development of the Young Child Ages 6 Through 8

After reading and studying this chapter, you will demonstrate comprehension by:

- Describing the continuum in development and learning throughout *all* the early childhood years.
- Describing the cognitive development of children ages 6 through 8.
- Describing the oral language development of children ages 6 through 8.
- Describing the literacy development of children ages 6 through 8.
- Identifying special needs and sociocultural information relating to the cognitive/language/literacy development of children ages 6 through 8.
- Defining the role of adults in promoting the cognitive/language/literacy development in young children ages 6 through 8.

Continuity in Development and Learning Through All the Early Childhood Years

- It is in the spring of Jeremy's kindergarten year. Ms. Buckley, Jeremy's teacher, has sent several letters about the first grade year to the parents of the children in her class. One letter tells of a first grade open house in the evening for kindergarten children and their parents. As Ann, Bill, and Jeremy discuss their upcoming visit, Jeremy indicates that he already knows much about the first grade in his school. Throughout the year, there have been many opportunities for the kindergarten children to interact with the first grade children and their teachers. Class books have been exchanged. Informal plays of nursery rhymes and fairy tales have been shared at both grades. Visits to see special displays have occurred. The kindergarten and first grade classes have gone together to the park for nature scavenger hunts.

Both classes have worked cooperatively cleaning up the playground once a month. They have eaten popcorn and sung songs together. Thus, Jeremy has been in the first grade classrooms, he knows the teachers, and he has interacted with first-graders. He feels comfortable about going to first grade for these reasons and also because he knows that he will continue to see his kindergarten teacher and from time to time will be in his "old room."

After returning from the visit of the first grade classes, Bill remarks that these classrooms sure look different from his first grade classroom. The desks are clustered in fours so that the children can interact while they are learning. There are learning centers throughout the room. Bill also notes that there was much of the children's writing displayed around the room. The writing contained invented spellings and was not corrected by the first grade teachers. Bill thinks that times sure have changed. Because of Jeremy's involvement and of the teacher's orientation explaining the importance of the transition between kindergarten and first grade, Bill feels relatively comfortable with these changes.

The principal and the kindergarten and first grade teachers were aware that many parents, based upon their own experience, would think that first graders only learn in quiet classrooms where the desks are arranged in rows, with the teacher conducting reading groups and other learning from the front of the classroom. In order to help the parents understand the need for continuity in learning experiences between the kindergarten and first grade years, the professionals at Jeremy's school provide written information, plan meetings and open houses for the parents of future first-graders. ■

In reality, the unification of kindergarten and the primary grades is not a new idea. Weber (1984) says,

> Early specialists of kindergarten education worked not just for more kindergartens, but also for the extension into the primary grades of the principles and the philosophy of the education they espoused so heartily. Those staunch reformers believed their "new" educational design to ensure a more child-centered curriculum employing different methods and procedures for early learning. They also believed that the nature of children of five, six, and seven years of age was similar; in social, emotional, and intellectual characteristics they were much alike. So adult leaders strove toward the unification of kindergarten-primary education. (pp. 198–199)

Currently, there is much renewed interest in the importance of providing continuity between programs for children in the early years. Bredekamp (1987) indicates that when young children move from one early childhood program to another, adjustments must be made. Teachers, administrators, and parents can work cooperatively to promote successful adjustment in the transition from one early childhood environment to another.

In October of 1988, the National Association of State Boards of Education (NASBE) Task Force on Early Childhood Education issued a report entitled *Right From the Start*. This report calls for a restructuring of the early years of the elementary school based upon child development knowledge and curriculum from successful pre-primary programs, that is, programs for children before first grade. The recommendations include the creation of early childhood units for children ages 4 through 8 in elementary schools. In addition, increased cooperation between schools, parents, and other programs and services is proposed. Thus, continuity from one early childhood program to another is important throughout all the early years, including the primary grade years. Mixed-age grouping is an attempt to promote continuity of learning in the early years of schooling (Friedman & Koeppel, 1990; Katz, Evangelou, & Hartman, 1990; Nachbor, 1989).

While this chapter will discuss the differences and changes in development that occur during the primary grade years, it is important to remember that the years from 6 through 8 are still part of the early childhood years. Therefore, many of the same experiences that facilitate cognitive, language, and literacy development earlier also contribute to these areas of development in 6-, 7- and 8-year-olds. Before you read the next section, reread the quote at the beginning of this chapter. This quote will set the stage for the final discussion of how young children develop cognition, language, and literacy in the primary grades. Notice how the word "interaction" is used in the quotation. Where have you read about this before?

Cognitive Development

Piaget's research indicated that young children develop concepts about the world through active, physical, and sensorimotor interaction with the environment. This is in contrast to the quiet, more passive learning of older children and adults. Piaget's research also suggested that young children cannot be directly taught a body of knowledge as can older children and adults, but learn rather by constructing their own knowledge. For example, a young child who is playing with sand may pour sand from one container to another, feel the sand in his hands, or put the sand in his mouth. Through actions like these, young children discover and construct their knowledge of sand: what it does, how it feels, and how it tastes. The child cannot construct accurate knowledge about sand unless he acts upon the sand. Adults cannot simply tell a child that sand feels gritty. This process is how young children develop physical knowledge (Wadsworth, 1984, pp. 22–23).

The second type of knowledge Piaget identified was what he called logical-mathematical knowledge. In this type of knowledge, the child thinks about, constructs, or invents knowledge from his actions upon objects. However, in this type of learning the objects serve merely as a means of permitting the construction of knowledge to occur. For example, a little girl plays with a set of six buttons. She puts them in a row and counts them. Then she puts them in a circle and counts them. Next, she puts them in a stack and counts them. Through active experiences like these, children eventually construct the concept that the number of objects in a set remains the same regardless of the arrangement of the individual elements. As experiences are repeated in different settings with different materials, the concepts become more refined. Like physical knowledge, logical-mathematical knowledge is *not* acquired from reading or listening to teachers talk. It is constructed or invented in the child's mind (Wadsworth, 1984, pp. 23–24).

This section will first discuss the transition from the preoperational stage to the stage of concrete operations. Next, Piaget's ideas regarding cognitive processing during concrete operations will be presented. Finally, more recent thought regarding cognitive development in children ages 6 through 8 will be introduced.

Transition from Preoperational to Concrete Operational Stage

Concrete operational stage—according to Piaget, the stage when children, approximately 7–11 years of age, can use logical reasoning (rather than relying upon perceptions) in situations that are concrete, that is, involve objects and events in the child's immediate environment.

Chapter 10 indicated that there are some researchers who think that children in the preoperational stage give evidence of some concrete operational behaviors (Fuson, Secada, & Hall, 1983; Gelman, 1979; Gelman, Bullock, & Meck, 1980; Gelman & Shatz, 1978). As mentioned previously, some of these investigations are suggesting that there may not be stages of cognitive development. However, Piaget's (Piaget & Inhelder, 1956) viewpoint is that between the ages of 5 and 7, most young children undergo dramatic changes in their cognitive processing, indicating a new stage of development, the **concrete operational stage**. Some children begin to move into more concrete operational stage behaviors at age 5. Other children do not provide much evidence of concrete operational behavior until around age 7 (Gardner, 1978). The wide age range involved in this transition is an important reason for maintaining a continuum of experiences between the pre-primary and the primary grades.

Piaget's Stage of Concrete Operations

Piaget viewed the shift from the preoperational stage to the stage of concrete operations as a major milestone in the development of cognition. Children in this stage are no longer perceptually bound in their thinking. They can now perform mental operations if the physical objects are present. According to Piaget, the ability to perform mental operations without concrete objects, to think abstractly, and to reflect develops in adolescence during the stage of **formal operations** (Inhelder & Piaget, 1958; Piaget & Inhelder, 1956; Piaget & Inhelder, 1969).

Formal operations—according to Piaget, the fourth and final stage of cognitive development, which occurs during adolescence, when mental operations can be performed without concrete objects and abstract thinking begins.

Children in the stage of concrete operations gradually master a variety of conservation tasks. Refer to Chapter 13 for a review of these tasks. Piaget and others have determined that conservation of number occurs first, followed by conservation of length, mass and liquid, and finally weight and volume (Brainerd, 1978; Brainerd & Brainerd, 1972; Gruen & Vore, 1972). This increasing ability to conserve helps children's thinking become more logical and flexible. Children can now return to their original point in thought and can think about alternative ways to solve problems. Elkind (1978b) noted that children in the stage of concrete operations gradually become aware of more aspects to a problem.

This ability to see more aspects of a situation appears to promote the gradual awareness of views of other children and adults (Krauss & Glucksberg, 1969; Rubin, 1973; Shatz, 1983). The decline of egocentric behavior also causes chil-

The improved cognitive ability of 6- to 8-year-olds to see the viewpoints of others results in increased proficiency in playing games with rules and team sports.

dren to think about how others perceive their behavior (Selman, 1976, 1980). This improved ability to see the viewpoints of others results in increased proficiency at games with rules and team sports.

■ Jeremy gradually has changed in his behaviors at his soccer games. At age 6, when playing goalie, he easily became distracted, often looking at the ground or hunting bugs in the grass. But at age 8, he consistently focuses on the game and actively positions himself to block the soccer ball.

   Jeremy also likes baseball. He has become an avid collector of baseball cards. From time to time he classifies the cards in various ways: teams, player positions, leagues, batting averages, and other statistics.   ■

Jeremy's ability to create multiple classifications is also reflective of the differences in cognitive processing between preoperational children and concrete operational children. Thus, the changes in intellectual processing described above in Piaget's viewpoint are substantially different from those of preoperational children and warrant the designation of another stage—the stage of concrete operations. However, Chapter 10 indicated that there are theorists and researchers who think that the development of cognition occurs over a period of time in varying domains rather than in separate stages. Following is a discussion regarding cognitive development during ages 6 through 8 from this perspective.

Beyond Piaget: Recent Ideas in Cognitive Development in 6- to 8-Year-Olds

Some researchers suggest that children around the ages of 6, 7, and 8 begin to develop the ability to hold information in short-term memory (White & Pillemer, 1979). Changes in children's intellectual functioning at these ages are thought to be the result of more efficient mental processing (Case, 1985). Rehearsal techniques and improved memory organization appear to increase children's ability to store and retrieve information in an organized and systematic manner (Kail, 1984; Weissburg & Paris, 1986). Another suggested reason for improved cognitive abilities during this time is that children of 6, 7, and 8 years of age simply have had more time than pre-primary aged children to establish a knowledge base or a background of information to apply in new contexts (Chi, 1978; Chi & Koeske, 1983).

Meta memory— an awareness or knowledge about how one's memory processes work.

Finally, 7- and 8-year-olds demonstrate that they have increased knowledge about the process of remembering, or **meta memory** and **metacognition**, the understanding of their own cognitive processes (Flavell, Friederichs, & Hoyt, 1970; Leonard & Flavell, 1975). This increased awareness of their own memory processes appears to facilitate more sophisticated cognitive processing. Some of these new ideas are reflected in current thinking regarding the development of mathematical concepts in young children.

Metacognition— an awareness or knowledge of how one processes information and thought.

New Ideas on the Development of Mathematical Concepts—Information Processing/Cognitive Science

Price (1989) reports that researchers and theorists in the area of mathematical development are currently revising Piaget's ideas in relation to information processing theory and the cognitive science perspective. According to Price's (1989) review of research, the information processing theory suggests that the limitations on short-term memory can create problems for young children as they attempt basic mathematical tasks such as counting and simple mental addition. Moreover, unfamiliarity can put an additional load on short-term memory. Implications from research suggest that it is important for teachers to provide opportunities for young children to develop ways to cope with the simultaneous demands of short-term memory when counting (Baroody, 1984). In addition, it is important for teachers to create situations where young children can gain familiarity at counting or recognizing numbers through practice in meaningful and socially natural situations without "even remotely resembling drill" (Price, 1989).

Cognitive science—the investigation of the knowledge and strategies used in the cognitive process that distinguish expert cognitive processes from novice cognitive processes.

Cognitive science is a second perspective on explaining the development of math in young children. **Cognitive science** examines the strategies and knowledge that separate experts from novices. According to Price (1989), experts possess knowledge special to a particular domain, and it appears that expertise in a particular domain, such as counting, can be taught. Skill in counting involves (1) tagging or touching each object, (2) learning that tagging must occur in order, and (3) making the connection between the process of counting and the concept of number.

A second area of expertise in young children involves addition and subtraction in word problems. According to Price (1989), research in this area has revealed some differences between types of word problems in terms of difficulty for young children. While these differences may seem minor to adults, they are very real to young children. The four basic kinds of addition and subtraction problems are Join Problems, Separate Problems, Combine Problems, and Compare Problems. Join Problems and Separate Problems involve action. The action of *adding* or *joining* elements to the set with which one started is representative of Join Problems. The action in Separate Problems requires *subtracting* elements from the set with which one started. In both Join and Separate Problems, three quantities are involved: (1) the *start*, or the amount before the action; (2) the *change*, or the amount involved in the action; and (3) the *result*, or the amount after the action. Price says, "Teachers and curriculum designers unfamiliar with this research are likely to favor one of these types—typically, Result Unknown Join Problems—and omit others" (Price, 1989, p. 56). Within some of these categories of problems, there are several types. Awareness of the differences between these categories of problems has enabled some first grade teachers to create more developmentally appropriate instructional strategies (Carpenter, Carey, & Kouba, 1990; Carpenter, Fennema, Peterson, & Carey, 1988; Carpenter, Fennema, Peterson, Chiang, & Loef, 1989; Fennema, Carpenter, & Peterson, 1990).

The concept of place value and learning the appropriate notation of place value are difficult for young children. One reason they are so difficult is that the procedures for writing numbers vary from the procedures for writing print. For example, children of 6 and 7 years of age often write "23" as "203," thinking that "20" represents twenty (Ginsburg, 1977). Children are used to the left-right orientation in reading and writing and therefore find it difficult to remember that in math, place value dictates an orientation from right to left. Such processing produces approximations such as:

$$\begin{array}{r} 1\ 1 \\ +\ \ 1 \\ \hline 2\ 1 \end{array}$$

Close examination of children's math approximations usually reveals that they are applying knowledge in a logical way based upon their prior experience (Kamii, 1985, 1989). Comprehending place value and its accurate representation are tasks that usually take several years to master, from the primary grade years and beyond.

Price (1989) does not make specific recommendations for teachers in order to help children develop their cognition in the area of math. However, he suggests that teachers should (1) "not put math down," (2) "take pains to not make math seem difficult," and (3) "not discourage child invented problem solving techniques that work and 'feel right'—such as counting on one's fingers" (Price, 1989, p. 57).

Counting experiences with concrete objects, including children's use of their fingers, continue to help children ages 6 to 8 develop the concept of number.

In conclusion, whether viewing children's cognitive development from a Piagetian stage perspective or from the information processing perspective, children ages 6 through 8 differ from pre-primary age children and from adolescents and adults. However, primary age children still need continued interaction with materials and people. The availability of concrete experiences continues to promote cognitive development.

Oral Language Development

Children at 6, 7, and 8 demonstrate many competencies in the area of language development. In fact, they appear very "adult-like" in many oral language contexts. However, studies indicate that there are still some aspects of language development that children continue to acquire through the elementary school years, into adolescence, and throughout life (Clark & Clark, 1977). The following section will discuss the relationship between thought and language and the continuing development of syntax, vocabulary, and interactional competence during the primary grade years.

Interaction Between Thought and Oral Language Development

The shift in children's cognitive development during the ages of 6, 7, and 8 is reflected in their oral language in several ways. Children gradually become aware of the meanings of metaphors. For example, the metaphor, "She eats like a bird," is no longer interpreted literally as a girl eating worms or pecking at food in a bird-like manner. Rather, this metaphor is gradually understood as meaning that a person eats sparingly. Children understand metaphors before they actually produce them (Green, 1985; Winner, Rosenstiel, & Gardner, 1977).

Children of primary grade age also demonstrate increasing awareness of puns and jokes because of their ability to think about the multiple meaning of words, the relationships between words, and the structure of narratives (Menyuk, 1988). They also become more proficient liars, both because they can now think about events simultaneously and because of their broader knowledge base. The use of "white lies" and of lying to prevent hurting another's feelings also appears due to children's increased social and cognitive awareness (Menyuk, 1988).

Another area of increased understanding of language is reflected in the comprehension and use of sarcasm. Ackerman (1982) determined that first-graders were able to interpret sarcasm if the context was evident before the sarcastic remark was made. However, third-graders were able to detect sarcastic remarks under an increasing variety of situations.

Metalinguistic awareness, or the ability to consciously think about the meanings and forms of language, becomes more evident as children mature. Researchers have determined that around age 7, children begin to separate words from phrases (Tunmer, Bowey, & Grieve, 1983). Around 8, children can identify the phonemes in words that are spoken aloud (Tunmer & Nesdale, 1982). Menyuk (1976, 1985, 1988) suggests that metalinguistic abilities do not develop suddenly. Rather, the awareness of various aspects of language develops at different times for different categories and relationships in language. However, the process in which metalinguistic awareness develops appears to have a definite pattern. First, children incorporate new structures on an unconscious level. Then they develop the ability to recognize appropriate or inappropriate uses of the structure. Finally, children become able to talk about the structure (Bialystok, 1986; Menyuk, 1983).

Metalinguistic awareness—the ability to think about the forms and meanings of language.

As young children continue to develop in their cognitive abilities, language increasingly becomes an independent symbol system. That is, children gradually begin to talk more about topics that are not in their immediate context. Bloom says, "This transition from maximum dependence in contextual support to speech which is independent of the states of affairs in which it occurs is the major accomplishment in the school years" (1975, pp. 283–284).

Another area that demonstrates the interrelationship between language and thought is primary grade children's use of pronouns. The understanding of pronominal references appears to increase with age. Children 7 years of age use more referenced pronouns in their stories than children of 5 and 6 years of age (Solan, 1983).

Development of Syntax

Development of syntax also continues through the primary grade years. One grammatical development that occurs during the elementary school years is the ability to understand infinitive phrases. At age 5, children do not relate the grammatical subject with the agent role. For example, when presented with a blindfolded doll and asked, "Is the doll easy or hard to see?" their response is "Hard to see." By age 10, the response changes to "Easy to see" (Chomsky, 1969; Karmiloff-Smith, 1979). Understanding the passive voice ("The ball was hit by Joe," rather than "Joe hit the ball") also takes place over an extended period of time and is not achieved until the end of the elementary school years (Bever, 1970; Sudhalter & Braine, 1985). According to Menyuk (1971), virtually all morphological indicators of plurals, possession, and past tense are acquired between the ages of 6 and 8. Menyuk (1964, 1983) suggests that children first become "aware" of a new structure and use it in an unconscious manner. Their knowledge is tentative at this point. Children use both old and new forms from time to time and may use both forms within the same utterance. In time, the earlier form disappears and is replaced by the conventional form.

Vocabulary Development

Vocabulary development continues to expand with increased cognitive development, experience, and formal education (Carey, 1986). Children of 6, 7, and 8 years of age use their vocabularies in more accurate and conventional ways. Lindfors (1980, 1987) describes how new experiences influence the school age child's vocabulary: "Overextensions continue to disappear as six, seven, and eight year olds develop new vocabulary to accommodate new cognitive structures" (Lindfors, 1980, p. 151). For example, a child may not just use the word "doggie" anymore, but may talk about "poodles," "German shepherds," "mutts," and "puppies," indicating her increased cognitive awareness of the various categorical labels under the general class of dogs. Menyuk (1988) states that "continued development of the meaning of words can take place over a lifetime, since meanings change as a function of wide experiences" (Menyuk, 1988, p. 153).

Interactional Competence

Children at 6, 7, and 8 have an increasing number of experiences in new environments and with different people. Upon entering first grade, children not only learn about their teacher and classroom but also about other teachers; about expected behaviors in the lunchroom, the library, and on the playground; and about special classes such as art, physical education, and music. In addition, many school-aged children visit friends' homes, join Scouts, take lessons, and participate in religious activities. Based upon their interactions with other chil-

As children ages 6 to 8 interact with peers and older children, their communicative competence increases.

dren and adults who serve as scaffolders, they gradually learn the scripts, or behaviors and language appropriate to each context. Participation in these varied contexts promotes increased interactional competence in 6-, 7-, and 8-year-old children. For example, Dorval and Eckerman (1984) noted that second-graders took turns in their conversation. Other researchers (Wanska & Bedrosian, 1985) have observed that children between the ages of 5 and 9 increasingly use the technique of **shading** to change topics of conversation. Younger children usually change topics of conversation abruptly, while older children change topics of discussion gradually.

Primary grade children also demonstrate an increasing awareness of the intent of many utterances. A second-grader knows that when her mother says, "This room is a disaster area," she had better get her room cleaned up right away. In addition, children of 6, 7, and 8 years of age indicate an increasing awareness of **registers**, or the speech variations needed in different social situations. For example, Ervin-Tripp, O'Connor, and Rosenberg (1984) found

Shading—*gradually changing the topic of conversation.*

Registers—*variations in the style of speech according to varying social settings.*

that children of primary grade age indicate deference when making requests of adults who appear busy and preoccupied.

In conclusion, language development of 6-, 7-, and 8-year-olds continues to mature and expand due to their increasing cognitive development and increasing interaction with people in new and varied contexts. Children enter first grade knowing much about oral language and how it works. This knowledge can be extended by helping the child engage in experiences that add to this knowledge. Activities that encourage the child to plan, remember, and learn promote further language development (Vygotsky, 1962).

Nevertheless, some investigators have noted that language used in the home can be quite different from language used in the school setting (Heath, 1983; Wells, 1981). Frequently, children who enter the primary grades are expected to listen and engage in little verbal interaction with other children and teachers. Much of the verbal interaction with teachers consists of children responding with a "yes" or a "no" and a single-word answer to teacher questions. These

Meaningful opportunities for young children ages 6 to 8 to talk with other children in a variety of settings within the classroom promote oral language development.

contexts may be outside the zone of proximal development for some children. Thus, it is important for teachers in the primary grades to continue oral language experiences from the prekindergarten and kindergarten years: opportunities to talk with other children in a variety of settings, including learning centers; discussing stories and tapes; giving dictation; interviewing; sharing information in group sharing times; role playing; storytelling; and improvisation (Flood & Salus, 1984). Teachers need to be aware of the linguistic backgrounds of their children and gradually introduce children to other means of communicating and more formal ways of acquiring knowledge (Wells, 1981). In addition, as children of 6, 7, and 8 years of age develop their metalinguistic awareness, teachers can help them bring their intuitive knowledge into conscious awareness. Such scaffolding helps primary grade children to strengthen and extend their knowledge of oral language. Such experiences can play a role in the acquisition of written language. The following section on the development of literacy will address this important relationship.

Literacy Development

Our discussion of literacy development in the primary grades will focus upon three themes: the holistic nature of the development of literacy, the continuity of literacy experiences between the pre-primary and primary grades, and the necessity of opportunities for interaction with adults and children in meaningful print contexts.

Interaction Between Thought, Language, and Literacy Development

Chapters 10 and 13 have provided background information on current thinking regarding the development of literacy in young children. In review, recent information suggests that: (1) young children learn about reading and writing in the early years of life, certainly well before first grade; (2) in many ways, young children's reading and writing is different from the reading and writing of older children and adults; and (3) meaningful experiences seem to facilitate learning about reading and writing in young children.

In many primary grade classrooms, literacy learning is very different from the prekindergarten and kindergarten classroom experiences (Kamii, 1985a). First graders are often asked to focus on parts of words, memorize phonics rules and sound out words. Writing experiences may consist of copying teacher-printed material from the chalkboard, with emphasis on making letters properly and staying on the lines. This concentration on the form of written language rather than the meaning can create several problems for young children (Holdaway, 1979).

First, if children cannot make sense out of learning experiences, they begin to doubt themselves as learners. Their self-concepts and self-esteem can be affected in negative ways. Second, children can develop distorted concepts about the processes of reading and writing. If young children are in the first grade classrooms, where reading is done mainly in reading groups emphasizing sounding out words and oral reading without mistakes, they probably do not perceive reading as a meaningful experience (Holdaway, 1979).

Both the Piagetian and information processing perspectives note the 5 to 7 age shift in cognitive development. As previously discussed, Piaget (Piaget & Inhelder, 1956) suggests that many children are not yet able to focus on more than one part of a situation. The information processing theorists suggest that short-term memory is still developing (White & Pillemer, 1979). For these reasons, asking first graders to remember phonics rules, read without error, and sound out words—all at the same time—makes it very difficult for children to also think about the meaning of the story or text.

Likewise, copying teacher writing from the chalkboard does not provide children with the opportunity to develop the concept that writing is communication. Rather, children may tend to view writing at school as lacking in meaning and even as a painful, laborious process (Black & Martin, 1982). Thus, the teaching of reading and writing from the perspective of form is usually not related to thought or meaning.

Recent literacy research suggests that young children learn about reading and writing best in a holistic manner in which thought, oral language, and written language are interrelated (Goodman, 1986). The following vignette demonstrates the holistic nature of literacy development.

■ Five-year-old Joanie was playing with several neighborhood children in her garage. One of the children discovered a tarantula crawling across the cement floor. The children discussed what they should do and whether tarantulas were really dangerous. Finally, one of the children suggested killing the tarantula with "bug spray." The tarantula was sprayed and sprayed. Finally, it died. The children used a garden tool to turn the tarantula over, and then closely examined it. Next, they scooped it up, put it in a plastic container, and went on a tour of the neighborhood, showing the tarantula to children who had not been in the garage. The tarantula episode was the main topic at Joanie's family dinner table that evening.

The next day Joanie went to her mixed-age classroom comprising 4-, 5-, and 6-year-olds. She painted a picture and then dictated the story (see Figure 16.1) to one of the teachers in her classroom. The spelling of the word "tarantula" was checked by using the dictionary. Joanie's picture and story (consisting of 23 words) was hung on the classroom wall at children's eye level. One of the teachers found some books about tarantulas to read to interested children. They discovered, among other things, that tarantulas are really not all that dangerous. Several days later, a teacher and Joanie were looking at her picture/story and talking about her experience with the tarantula. The teacher asked Joanie if she could find the word "tarantula." Without any hesitation, Joanie pointed to the exact location of the word.   ■

The vignette above demonstrates the powerful relationships between thought, experience, oral language, and literacy. Joanie had a very meaningful experience. It was talked about and read about with others in several contexts— in the neighborhood, at the family dinner table, and at school. The experience

We had a big tarantula
We killed it by bug-spray
We had a black wasp in
   our house.

We were scared to death.

FIGURE 16.1
*Long words with meaning, such as "tarantula," are easier for young
children to identify than shorter words without meaning, such as "the" and
"what."*

was shared symbolically, through her painting; through oral language; and was translated into written language, which was read by Joanie, her teacher, and other children. The interaction of thought, oral language, and written language in this experience demonstrates how the wholeness of language can promote the development of literacy. Joanie knew where the long word "tarantula" was located among an array of 23 other words! Figure 16.2 provides a definition of whole language.

Relationship Between Reading and Writing

Chapter 13 discussed the relationship between reading and writing. As the vignette about Joanie and the tarantula indicated, reading and writing appear to be interrelated and to facilitate the development of literacy. Children learn to read by reading what they write or by reading print that is important to them. They learn to write if they feel they have thoughts and messages that are important enough to be shared with others in a written context (Chomsky, 1971; Goodman & Goodman, 1983).

■ Both Jeremy's and Angela's first grade teachers see the teaching of reading and writing as inseparable. They do not isolate the teaching of reading and writing into separate time slots during the day. Rather, both reading and writing are taught throughout the day in many contexts and in interrelated ways. Both teachers

FIGURE 16.2
Whole language

What is whole language?	What is not whole language?
It's real and natural.	It's artificial.
It's whole.	It's broken into bits and pieces.
It's sensible.	It's nonsense.
It's interesting.	It's boring.
It's relevant.	It's irrelevant.
It belongs to the learner.	It belongs to somebody else.
It has social utility.	It has no social value.
It has purpose for the learner.	It has no discernible purpose.
The learner chooses to use it.	It's imposed by someone else.
It's accessible to the learner.	It's inaccessible to the learner.
The learner has the power to use it.	The learner is powerless.
THIS IS EASY!	THIS IS HARD!

Whole language programs get it all together: the language, the culture, the community, the learner, and the teacher.

When schools break language into bits and pieces, sense becomes nonsense, and it's always hard for kids to make sense out of nonsense.

Source: *What's Whole in Whole Language?* by Ken Goodman. Heinemann Educational Books, 1986, p. 8.

continue many of the literacy experiences that Angela and Jeremy experienced in
their pre-primary classrooms.

Jeremy's and Angela's primary grade classrooms are organized to promote
interaction with materials and with other children. There are many print materials
located throughout the classroom and in learning centers. These materials include:
calendars; several kinds of charts—helper charts, charts with pen pal names, charts
written by the children with spelling strategies, strategies for figuring out words,
strategies listing the steps in the writing process, and charts of science experiment
results; recipes for apple sauce and pancakes; the Pledge of Allegiance; the
weekly schedule; a story about the author of the week, Leo Lionni; children's
artwork and written reports; learning center signs describing the learning that takes
place in the center; books; and magazines. Paper and writing tools are located in
each center. The class library is stocked with a wide variety of books: class-made
books, individually made books, big books, and many patterned or predictable
books. There are a variety of centers in the classrooms: art, publishing/writing,
computer, math, science, listening, and a display area. There are animals and
plants to observe and to draw and write about. Both teachers display children's
writing on attractive bulletin boards. Desks are clustered in groups of four to
promote interaction. Children are encouraged to talk as they engage in their
learning activities, and they do so for much of the day.

The schedule in Jeremy's room reflects the teacher's plan to emphasize
the interaction and integration of reading and writing in all learning activities.
Basal readers are used when it seems appropriate and not on a daily basis
or in a sequential order. See Figure 16.3 for a typical daily schedule in
Jeremy's classroom.   ■

The above descriptions of materials, organization of the classroom environment, and daily schedule should provide information about how reading and
writing develop in an interrelated and holistic manner. The following two sections discuss the teaching of reading and writing separately for the purpose of
documenting how children learn about the form or skills of reading and writing,
even though the emphasis is on meaning.

Writing in Children Ages 6, 7, and 8

■ Ms. Wood continues many of the writing and print experiences of Jeremy's
kindergarten in her first grade classroom. She models writing for the children and
facilitates purposeful opportunities for the children to write in a variety of
situations, from thank-you notes to stories to lists of needed classroom supplies.
Ms. Wood allows children to freely explore their writing. She provides ample time
for the rehearsal stage of writing, in which the children can draw or talk about
their writing. This talking and drawing helps to organize children's thoughts so they
can write.

Ms. Wood also continues to read to the children. Hearing the written language
helps children learn about writing. They learn how to write fairy tales, dialogue,
narratives, and other forms of literature. Ms. Wood also carefully observes children
and acts as a scaffolder to move them into new awareness of the processes of
reading and writing.

FIGURE 16.3
Daily schedule for Jeremy's first grade class

8:15–8:30 Opening   Children do calendar, weather, and lunch count. The class shares information and announcements.

8:30–9:00 Music   The class goes to the music classroom.

9:00–9:30 Journal writing   When children return from the music classroom, they write in their journals. Ms. Wood and the classroom assistant write in their own personal journals as well.

9:30–10:15 Reading and writing   The children read the story, *Case of Clyde Monster*. In the story specific words are missing. Each cluster of children works on this together and decides what word needs to go in the blank. They work together or write out some answers to questions after they have read the story.

10:15–10:30 Outdoor activity

10:30–11:15 Learning centers   Children go to learning centers to work on various projects.

11:15–11:45 Sharing time   Children share books they have produced or favorite books from the library, information about special projects and upcoming events.

11:45–12:15 Lunch

12:15–12:30 Sustained silent reading   Children and Ms. Wood read books of their choice.

12:30–1:00 Math   Lesson is on coupons. The children use real coupons and work on assignments together in their clusters.

1:00–1:30 Science   Each cluster works or experiments to determine if air is matter. Their conclusions are written on a chart.

1:30–2:00 Physical education

2:00–2:30 Teacher reading   Ms. Wood reads a chapter from *Charlotte's Web*.

2:30–2:45 Closing   Announcements and reminders for the children.

Early in the school year, the PTA at Jeremy's school invites a children's book author to visit for a day. Through this experience, children learn about the editing process and what it means to be an author. Approximately once a month, Jeremy's class publishes a class book. Ms. Wood serves as the editor and helps the children with revisions. Suggested revisions are made in pencil and then the children recopy their stories for the published book. The final edition is read to other classes and then is placed in the school library for a period of time before becoming part of the classroom library. This experience introduces Jeremy and the other first grade children to the editing process. Ms. Wood does no other correcting of the children's writing in her first grade classroom. She wants the children to feel competent about their writing, and she knows that invented spellings, reversals, inattention to spacing, and lack of punctuation are developmentally appropriate behaviors. Figure 16.4 shows a typical first-grade attempt at writing.

A Six-Year-Old's Letter to His Grandparents during Holiday Time

Just as it takes time for infants and toddlers to learn to walk and talk, it takes time for young children to learn to read and write. Early childhood professionals are patient with young readers and young writers and appreciate their approximations in spacing, spelling, handwriting, and punctuation. Analysis of this letter written by a 6 year old demonstrates developmentally appropriate writing behaviors.

Spacing	Some words run together (niespesnts = nice presents). Sometimes it is difficult to write in a linear fashion (icsiting = exciting).
Spelling	Sometimes it is conventional ("you," "and," "love"). Sometimes it is invented (HIO = hello, hv = have, icsiting = exciting, gbl = gobble, git = get, sam = some, nys = nice, pesnt = presents, em = am, giting = getting, abowt = about, ckaming = coming; note that both "c" and "k" are used here, indicating the child's awareness that "c" and "k" can represent the same sound).
Handwriting	Reversals: "dring" for "bring."
Punctuation	Used sometimes. Question mark at end of question, "Have you been doing anything exciting?" Periods appear in various places.
Editing	Evidence of beginning attempts at editing are seen in the "g" which was "Xed" out before the question mark and also after "abowt."

Translation: "Hello. Have you been doing anything exciting? Gobble, gobble, gobble. Get some nice presents. I am getting (excited) about you coming. Bring some nice presents and — for us. Love Jon XOXOX"

FIGURE 16.4
A six-year-old wrote this letter to his grandparents during holiday time.

Ms. Wood shares her reasons for not correcting children's papers at the parent orientation sessions and conferences. Showing examples of how writing develops throughout the first grade year also enables parents to see that children will make progress in their written language without those red corrections. If parents need further information about young children's writing, Ms. Wood shares articles from professional journals and books concerning the development of young children's writing. She also helps parents to understand that they can help their children to write at home by providing writing materials, taking advantage of opportunities to write, and being supportive of children's efforts to write at home.

The children's ability to write varies greatly in Ms. Wood's first grade class. The children want to write and have others read their writing. Mail boxes, pen pals, and message boards facilitate this communication process. Through writing that is of interest to the children, they gradually learn about the forms of writing, including spelling and punctuation. They discover that the spelling of some words makes sense. However, there are a number of words that are spelled in ways that do not make sense. Jeremy says that "egg" should have an "a" in it, not an "e." First-graders struggle with the silent "e," and try to understand how the same letter can be used for different sounds, such as the "g" in "giant" and "gate." ■

Phonics — the sound-symbol relationship of a language system.

Invented spelling provides a meaningful way for children to learn about sound-symbol relationships, or **phonics**, and other word recognition skills (Willert & Kamii, 1985). Through children's observation of print in many contexts, their own reading, discussions with classmates about how to spell, and teacher-peer scaffolding, children gradually become more aware of conventional spellings during the course of the primary grades.

As children communicate through their writing, they not only become more aware of conventional spelling but also learn about other forms of written language: handwriting, the spacing between words, and punctuation. It is not unusual to see young children's writing with no spaces between words, filled with repeated exclamation marks and periods inserted here and there as children try to learn what a sentence really is and where it ends.

■ By the end of the first grade year, the children in Ms. Wood's room have learned much about writing. The environment has been supportive, meaningful, and rich with print experiences. Jeremy's story about dinosaurs reveals that he is most confident in himself as a writer (see Figure 16.5). He organizes and presents his thoughts in a logical manner. He demonstrates no hesitancy in spelling long dinosaur names. He indicates that he has learned much about handwriting, spacing, and punctuation, and he gives evidence of moving into conventional spelling. ■

As children progress through the primary grades, many changes appear in their written language (Lamme, 1984). Their spelling becomes more conventional. Maturing fine motor development makes handwriting more readable, and eventually children move into cursive writing. Reversals decline and only appear occasionally. Children also become more adept at writing in a variety of forms: jokes and riddles, newspaper, plays, and reports. Second- and third-graders can learn the process of writing from the modeling of their teachers.

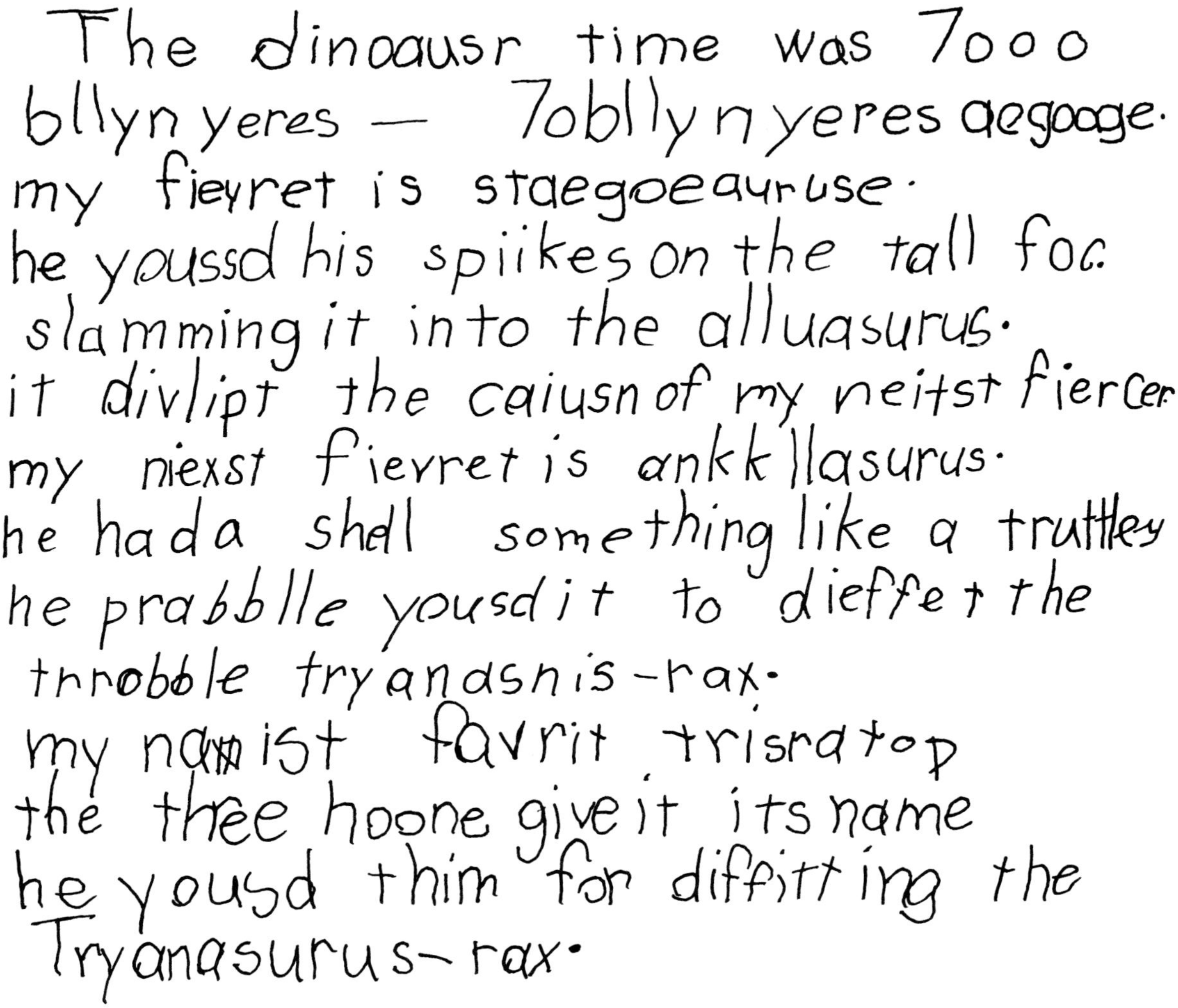

The dinoausr time was 7ooo bllyn yeres — 7obllyn yeres aegooge. my fievret is staegoeauruse. he youssd his spiikes on the tall foc. slamming it into the alluasurus. it divlipt the caiusn of my neitst fiercer my niexst fievret is ankkllasurus. he had a shdl something like a truttley he prabblle yousd it to dieffet the tnrobble tryanasnis-rax. my nawist favrit trisratop the tree hoone give it its name he yousd thim for diffitting the Tryanasurus-rax.

FIGURE 16.5

Jeremy's story about dinosaurs, written in first grade, reveals that he is most confident in himself as a writer. He organizes and presents his thoughts in a logical manner. He demonstrates no hesitancy in spelling long dinosaur names. He indicates that he has learned much about handwriting, spelling, spacing, and punctuation, and gives evidence of moving into conventional spelling.

■ Mr. Rodriguez is Angela's third grade teacher. Angela and the other children use the computer to write lengthy stories and reports. Before the children begin to write, they engage in prewriting activities. Talking, drawing, and making lists about what they want to write helps them prepare the "fast write" or first draft. Angela shares her writing with other children who help her edit her writing, first for meaning and then for spelling, grammar, punctuation, and paragraphs. Reading aloud what she has written helps Angela and her peers decide whether pauses require commas, or whether inflections of the voice indicate a need for exclamation marks. After the editing process, Angela returns to the word processor and revises her writing and prints it out. If the computer is not available, Angela tries to be very neat and uses her best handwriting for her final copy. Mr. Rodriguez helps the children understand that the editing process is only used when writing for an intended audience. Journal writing, list making and other forms of writing for individual use generally do not require editing. As Angela has become more aware of the viewpoints of others, her ability to take her audience into account in the writing process has increased. ■

Given supportive environments, children in the primary years can develop positive attitudes about writing as well as knowledge about the functions of writing. These experiences in writing also facilitate competence in reading. Following is a discussion about reading during the years from 6 through 8.

Reading in Children Ages 6, 7, and 8

Sight words— words that young children recognize immediately.

When children read for meaning, they gradually internalize the skills related to reading. However, if young readers are encouraged to focus on skills before meaning, it can be difficult for them to develop comprehension. Consider the following example in the discussion of **sight words**. Sight words, or words that young children recognize immediately, are helpful to young readers. Knowledge of sight words helps children feel successful as they begin to read and provides them with a basis for learning about phonics and word analysis skills.

■ Angela's first grade teacher, Mr. Bray, does not use word lists that have been developed commercially. Isolated words in a list have no meaning. It is only through words in context that children can really focus on the real purpose of reading: getting meaning from print. Therefore, Mr. Bray uses a variety of meaningful experiences to help children build their own banks of sight words written on 3 × 5 cards and stored in recipe file boxes.

The most important sight word to young children is their name. Mr. Bray has all the children's names displayed on the helper's board. He also has poster board strips with each child's name on them in the writing center. Mr. Bray is amazed at how fast first graders learn each other's names. One day Angela saw a drawing with Charles's name on it. She commented that it was Charlotte's drawing. Charlotte quickly told Angela that it was not her drawing. "My name is longer than Charles's," she said. She took Angela to the writing center, found the name cards with her name and Charles's name on them, and showed them to Angela.

Through dictations, signs, labels, class and individual books, predictable books, and reading their own writing, the children begin to recognize frequently used words and can point them out to Mr. Bray and their classmates. Mr. Bray also has the children select words that are important to them from their journal writing to go into the children's individual word banks. These special words are frequently used and referred to by the children in their writing. Mr. Bray scaffolds by calling attention to words that he knows the children are repeatedly encountering. Mr.

Bray uses the children's interests and writing rather than workbooks or ditto papers because he knows that children learn better when they are interested. In many instances, word lists in workbooks or on worksheets have little or no meaning to young children. ■

Mr. Bray knows that it is frequently the larger words with specific meaning that are easier for young children to learn. Remember Joanie and "tarantula"? Often the short, simple words used in pre-primers and primers—the beginning books of the basal reading series—are more difficult to remember. Some of these short words are **service words**, or words that hold sentences together. They may not have specific meanings to which young children can relate. Many of these service words look like other words and are confusing to young children, for example, "the," "then," "they," "there," "them," and "those." If children are in learning environments where they want to share their thoughts with others through writing, they will use these words in their own dictation and writing. Actual use of these words in their own stories and writing encourages children to notice or pay attention to the subtle differences in these words (Holdaway, 1979). These kinds of experiences help children learn not only sight words but also phonics (Graves, 1983). Recent literacy research suggests that young children learn about phonics from meaningful reading and writing experiences, rather than learning reading and writing from phonics (Graves, 1983; Teale & Sulzby, 1986).

Service words— words that help hold a sentence together, e.g., "the" and "to."

■ Mr. Bray explains this global-to-specific or whole-to-part learning of young children to their parents. Parents often think that phonics is the way to learn to read. Mr. Bray helps parents understand that phonics is a part of reading, but that it should not be the primary focus. He reassures parents that children do not have to know all the sounds in a word to learn to read. Actually, children need to understand the concept of "word" before they can understand phonics. Early in their literacy development, young children often think that each letter in a word represents a separate word. Using word banks, taking dictation so that children can see their own words, pointing to words in big books, and drawing children's attention to spacing between words help them develop the notion that words are composed of clusters of letters that represent the sounds of that word.

Mr. Bray knows that his first-graders will find the regular consonants at the beginning and ends of words the easiest to recognize. Later they recognize the consonants in the middle of words. Long vowel sounds are easy for children to detect. Short vowel sounds are more difficult. Mr. Bray knows that most first graders often substitute one short vowel sound for another, for example, *git* for *get*. As children progress through the primary grades, their development in the area of phonics moves from the global to the specific. They begin to become more aware of phonics in general, of short vowels, and of various consonant combinations. In addition, their increasing physiological maturity enables them to more accurately hear and reproduce the sounds. Remember the chart of sound production from Chapter 13? Take another look at it. Do you notice that it indicates that some sounds do not develop in young children until they are 6 or 7 years of age? Jeremy still substitutes "f" for "th" during most of the first grade. He makes a book entitled *The Wndrfl Fgin A dat Burds (The Wonderful Things About Birds)*. He also spells "birthday" as "brfday," as he cannot hear or articulate "th" (see Figure 16.6). Yet he is progressing normally as a young reader. In short, children do not have to know all the sounds in a word in order to learn how to read. Formal phonics instruction is not necessary for a child to be a successful reader in first grade.

As children of 6, 7 and 8 years of age write rhyming poems, they often discover similar word patterns. Children delight in finding relationships in words. Questions by Mr. Bray also help children develop **word analysis skills**. Looking for words that have similar patterns on charts, lists, recipes, familiar songs, and poems help children learn about the parts of words. Angela's first grade teacher has a flip chart full of favorite finger plays, poems, and songs, and a big book of nursery rhymes. As the children recite these charts and songs, Mr. Bray or one of the children points to the words. While the children engage in the various activities in the first grade classroom, they often stop and read these poems and chants to themselves or with a classmate, using a yardstick to point at each word. In this process, they discover similarities in many of the words. Mr. Bray made small versions of these poems and chants with cards of the individual words so the children can

Word analysis skills—*the ability to analyze words using a variety of strategies, e.g., rhyming words.*

FIGURE 16.6
"The Wndrfl Fgin A dat burds." Children ages 6 to 8 are still developing their physiological ability to hear and reproduce sounds. Jeremy substitutes "f" for "th," says "fings" for "things" and "birfday" for "birthday." This auditory processing and verbal production of sound is reflected in his spelling. Teachers in the early primary grades should not expect all children to be able to produce all sounds conventionally in oral or written language.

match the similar words with the actual text of the poem, finger play, or nursery rhymes.

Mr. Bray also helps the children develop strategies for reading by encouraging them to look at the **configuration** or overall shape of the word. Joanie's teacher's comment about the length of the word "tarantula" probably helped her remember that word.

Configuration—the general shape or outline of a word.

Mr. Bray helps Angela become an independent reader by encouraging her to read silently. He does not have large reading groups on a regular basis, but has individual or small groups of children read to him from a variety of materials, both commercial or child-made, at various times throughout the day. He encourages children to read in pairs or in their desk clusters. Children are encouraged to incorporate a number of strategies if they do not know a word, such as rereading the sentence, looking at the illustrations, asking a friend, or substituting a word that makes sense. Rather than always asking the children to sound it out, Mr. Bray helps them use a variety of strategies to focus on the meaning of what they are reading. If the children are reading with him, he allows them about 7 seconds to respond. This allows the children time to explore various strategies for selecting an appropriate word that relates the meaning of the text to the form of the word. ■

Both Jeremy's and Angela's first grade teachers know that if children in their classes are to become truly literate, **comprehension** or understanding of the text is essential. Fields, Spangler, and Lee (1991) say that literacy development is "a process in which reading involves *interacting* with the thoughts someone else has expressed in writing, in which writing is perceived as recording one's own thoughts, and in which thinking is basic" (p. 133).

Comprehension—understanding the meaning of print.

As children continue to develop in their reading ability in second and third grades, it is important to keep the focus on the meaning of print and the wholeness of language. Third grade is usually the year in which children are expected to deal with more content knowledge in the areas of science, health, and social studies. Specific textbooks are often introduced during this grade level and children are expected to read for meaning and be accountable for the material through tests. If literacy experiences during the first and second grades have been meaning based, children have the critical mindset that print has a message for them. This concept will help them as they continue to learn throughout their school years. On the other hand, if young children view reading as an isolated performance activity, comprehending content material and reading independently could be a problem as they progress through the elementary school grades.

If primary grade teachers have students who do not seem to be comprehending or thinking about what they are reading, they may want to do an analysis of children's concepts about reading (see Figure 16.7). If the results indicate that children have distorted concepts about the reading act and limited strategies for reading, primary grade teachers need to help children learn that (1) reading is getting meaning from print; (2) good readers sometimes read quickly and sometimes read slowly, depending upon the purpose for reading; and (3) good readers make mistakes in reading, but they have a number of strategies they can use to help them identify and correct their mistakes.

FIGURE 16.7
Primary grade teachers can use this questionnaire to determine whether children view reading as a meaning and comprehension experience or a recitation and performance activity.

Name _____ Age _____ Date _____

Occupation _____ Education Level _____

Sex _____ Interview Setting _____

1. When you are reading and you come to something you don't know, what do you do?
   Do you ever do anything else?

2. Do you think that (ask teacher's name) is a good reader?
   or Who is a good reader that you know?

3. What makes her/him a good reader?

4. Do you think that she/he ever comes to something she/he doesn't know when she's/he's reading?

5. Yes   When she/he does come to something she/he doesn't know, what do you think she/he does about it?

   No   Suppose or pretend that she/he does come to something that she/he doesn't know. What do you think she/he does about it?

6. If you knew that someone was having difficulty reading how would you help them?

7. What would a/your teacher do to help that person?

8. How did you learn to read?
   What did (they/you) do to help you learn?

9. What would you like to do better as a reader?

10. Do you think that you are a good reader?   Yes   No   Why?

Additional Notes

Source: Contributed by Dr. Carolyn Burke, Department of Language Education, School of Education, Indiana University, Bloomington, IN.

In conclusion, children of 6, 7, and 8 years of age learn most effectively about reading and writing if the emphasis is on meaning. Through meaningful opportunities in which they can engage in reading and writing, they will also learn about the skills used in reading and writing.

Special Needs and Sociocultural Influences

It is important to remind the reader that while there may be overall patterns to development, there are also individual differences and variations in development. Dyson (1987) notes this in her research on young children's writing. If teachers of 6-, 7-, and 8-year-old children do not take into account individual differences and the need for continuity of learning environments through the primary grades, young children may not develop positive attitudes about themselves as learners. It is essential for teachers of young children not to misinterpret differences in cognition, language, and literacy behaviors as deficits. For example, research on story schemata, or knowledge of the structure of stories, indicates that some minority children do not lack story schemata, but rather have different story schemata (Michaels, 1981).

It is also important for teachers of young children to be aware of possible stereotypical attitudes about young children in their classrooms and the effects of these attitudes upon young children's cognitive, language, and literacy development. At times, teachers may consider a particular income level, race, or ethnicity an indicator of inability to learn, read, and write. Taylor and Dorsey-Gaines (1988) refute this notion in their in-depth study of African-American children from urban low-income homes who were growing up literate. In addition, Rhodes and Dudley-Marling (1988) challenge the assumption that learning-disabled students can become literate only through a skills-based approach. They indicate that whole language strategies facilitate language and literacy development with young children in special education settings.

Finally, it is important for teachers of young children to be aware of how school curriculum expectations and timetables for achievement may put young children at risk. Increasingly common practices of retention, transition classes, and earlier entrance age cutoffs are the result of inappropriate downward extension of the curriculum into earlier and earlier grades. However, research does not indicate that retention helps children to achieve more later or at the same time with less stress (Shepard & Smith, 1986, 1987). All teachers of young children, including primary grade teachers, need to be aware of developmentally appropriate learning and work to maintain curricula that support it. All teachers of young children need to "take young children where they are, move them along as far as they can and then communicate clearly to the next grade teacher the child's strengths and needs" (Bredekamp & Shepard, 1989, p. 22).

Media and Technology

Two other influences on the cognitive, language, and literacy development in young children are television and computers. The effects of these media upon young children and recommendations regarding their appropriate use will be discussed in this section.

Television

Television literacy—understanding the specialized symbolic code conveyed through the medium of television.

Anderson and Smith (1984) suggest that young children must develop **television literacy**, or the understanding of the special symbolic way in which television conveys information. They indicate that it takes time for children to develop an understanding of the medium of television.

In order to become television literate, young children must understand the distinction between reality and fantasy. Research by Dorr (1983) indicates that even 7- and 8-year-old children are still confused regarding the television and real-life relationships and behaviors of actors and actresses. In addition, studies indicate that many television production techniques are not grasped by young children before the age of 8. Because young children have difficulty inferring and relating past events to the present and future, they often fail to understand the story line and view scenes without obvious transitions as separate incidents (Collins, Wellman, Keniston, & Westby, 1978). Young children gradually learn to understand techniques such as fades (Anderson & Smith, 1984) and instant replays (Rice, Huston, & Wright, 1986). However, fast-paced programs that lack clearly defined continuity between scenes still are not understood by 9- and 10-year-olds (Wright et al., 1984). Adult comments can help young children better understand and evaluate television programs (Ball & Bogatz, 1973; Collins, 1983; Watkins, Calvert, Huston-Stein, Wright, 1980).

Television can help children learn. However, there is still no clear consensus on the best format to promote learning. The research on *Sesame Street* appears to indicate that children do learn from this fast-paced program (Ball & Bogatz, 1972). However, Singer and Singer (1979) indicate that programs with a slower pace allow time for children to reflect. Thus, programs such as *Mr. Roger's Neighborhood* may be more effective in stimulating thinking in young children than *Sesame Street*. Lesser (1979) suggests that there may not be one type of television programming that is best for all children. He recommends that a variety of types of programming be available to meet young children's individual differences and learning styles. Parent and teacher co-viewing and discussion of educational programming with children appear to facilitate more learning than if adults are not present and there is no discussion (Abelman, 1984; Ball & Bogatz, 1973; Corder-Bolz, 1980; Salomon, 1977).

Too much television viewing takes time away from other activities that promote learning and creativity (Singer & Singer, 1981, 1983). Extensive television viewing can also prevent children from having the opportunity to engage in reading, play, oral language, and other activities that promote thinking, concentration, and attention spans (Peterson, Peterson, & Carroll, 1986).

In conclusion, it appears that television can promote young children's cognitive, language, and literacy development if (1) programming is appropriate to young children's cognitive development, (2) adults are involved in the viewing process and discuss the program with children, and (3) children have opportunities for other activities that promote cognitive, language, and literacy development.

Computers

Initial research regarding the effects of computers upon young children's cognitive, language, and literacy development indicates that there can be some positive benefits. However, these positive benefits depend on the quality of the software, the attitudes and behaviors of the teacher, the nature of the physical and social environment of the classroom, and the accessibility of the computer (Campbell & Fein, 1986).

Young children can learn about computers and how they work. Interaction with computers in contexts similar to learning centers, where children are free to explore and discover, helps children learn about the nature of computers and develop positive attitudes toward technology (Hofmann, 1986; Kull, 1986).

Computer experiences can be highly sociable, promoting oral language and interaction with both adults and other children (Borgh & Dickson, 1986; Genishi, McCollum, & Strand, 1985; Newman, 1988). Teachers appear to facilitate this interaction by encouraging group participation rather than individual activity, and through their availability to children. In addition, teachers can encourage children to use each other as resources. Teacher awareness of programs and software can help provide information as to when teacher assistance is warranted.

Computer experiences also seem to facilitate divergent and creative thinking in young children. Programs such as Logo seem to provide opportunities for children to express their own learning styles (Kull, 1986). Computer experiences can also provide the opportunity for young children to make discoveries about learning. One study demonstrated that second-graders discovered orthographic and phonetic principles (Hofmann, 1986). Children have also learned about mathematical concepts such as subtraction while using computers (Hofmann, 1986; Kull, 1986).

Computers can also help children develop their writing abilities. Word processing can assist children in more in-depth composing, since they are not burdened with the fine motor task of handwriting. The process of revision can also be enhanced, since word processing makes it easier for children to edit their compositions (Bruce, Michaels, & Watson-Gegeo, 1985; Hoot & Silvern, 1989).

Teachers need to be cautious in selecting software for young children. Just because a program is fun does not always mean that it is a developmentally appropriate or worthwhile learning activity (Burns, Goin, & Donlon, 1990; Clements, 1985). Drill should not be confused with thinking and learning. Teachers must evaluate software for ineffective approaches to instruction for young children, such as isolated drill and activities that resemble workbooks (Fields, Spangler, & Lee, 1991; Kasmoski, 1984). Fields, Spangler, & Lee (1991) caution against high-pressure sales techniques by publishers that encourage schools to spend large amounts of money on inappropriate programs and recommend that

Early childhood professionals need to make certain that computer software is developmentally appropriate for young children.

teachers carefully evaluate all software programs for their developmental appropriateness (see Figure 16.8 for general criteria).

In conclusion, computers demonstrate the potential to promote learning in young children. However, their use must be closely monitored by early childhood professionals. As new information is discovered about young children and computers, more definitive recommendations for facilitating young children's development will become available.

Role of Play in Promoting Cognitive/Language/Literacy Development in 6-, 7-, and 8-Year-Olds

Children in the primary grades are beginning to demonstrate cognitive abilities indicative of concrete operations and emerging social understandings. They are becoming more comfortable with a wide range of social situations and the cognitive, language, and social demands that are placed on them in contexts such as school, home, playground, athletic teams, and community organizations. Piaget (1962), Bruner (1983), and Sutton-Smith (1979, 1986) state that play is significant in the development of children's cognitive abilities to function in

FIGURE 16.8
Criteria for developmentally appropriate software for young children

1. Are children able to boot up the software program independently?
2. Are children able to understand the initial directions? Are the directions presented using a variety of senses (auditory, visual—both words and graphics)?
3. Is the vocabulary used in the program appropriate to the children's developmental level?
4. Do children know when they are correct and incorrect? Are approximations acknowledged/rewarded at appropriate levels?
5. Are the program keyboard functions too complex for young children? Are the participants required to strike one, two, or three keys at one time?
6. Are the program graphics complementary, appropriate, or distracting.
7. Does the program have an audio component? Are the sound levels appropriate for the learning environment (too loud, too soft)? Is the audio component of the program accurate? (Does a bird sound like a bird in the computer program?)
8. Does the program offer children choices? How many? Are the choices appropriate, too simple, or inappropriately complex?
9. Do the program and your computer system foster independence in children or reliance on teacher direction and assistance?
10. Is the computer program congruent with the content and scope of the classroom curriculum, or is "computing" viewed as isolated learning experiences?

novel situations and the development of skills relating to flexibility and adaptability. More recently, Dyson (1990) characterizes young children as eloquent and inventive users of symbols during the primary school years. She suggests that children use a wide range of expressive activities to convey their understanding to peers during social exchanges. At no time in a young child's life are there more opportunities to use language in unique and exciting situations.

Primary grade children have not yet abandoned fantasy play as a means of socialization, communication, and cognitive stimulation among peers. Meanwhile, they are confronted with new educational challenges in formal and informal settings. The opportunities to use symbols in varying contexts appear to be limitless. Six-, seven-, and eight-year-old children regularly express their need to communicate with agemates during creative play situations. However, the increasing complexity of their ideas and occasional misunderstandings between peers require that primary grade children develop ingenious and resourceful communication strategies to foster their social relationships.

Children in the primary grades should be encouraged to use any means possible to express themselves to adults and agemates. Combinations of drawings and various art media, printed words, spoken language, gestures, and movements provide young children with a wide range of communicative expression. The use of these various media and expressive methods should not be restricted to formal classroom settings. Play situations provide primary grade children with exciting opportunities to enhance their symbolic repertoire through extemporaneous social experiences. During these makeshift social exchanges, primary grade children can interact with agemates regarding games, play events, and shared learning experiences. Young children are capable of sharing social

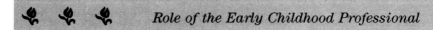

Role of the Early Childhood Professional

Enhancing Cognitive/Language/Literacy Development of Young Children Ages 6 through 8

1. Provide for a continuity of learning experiences from kindergarten to first grade and through the primary grades.
2. Provide developmentally appropriate learning, allowing for individual differences, thus promoting children's self-esteem and positive attitudes about school.
3. Provide learning experiences that are concrete, whole, and integrated rather than ones that are abstract, isolated, or emphasize separate subject matter areas.
4. Provide learning experiences that allow children to interact with materials, other children, and adults.
5. Provide opportunities for child-initiated learning.
6. Be patient and accepting of developmentally appropriate behaviors such as invented spelling, reversals, and counting with fingers.
7. Help parents, other teachers, administrators, and program supervisors to understand developmentally appropriate learning experiences for 6-, 7-, and 8-year-olds.
8. Demonstrate curiosity and interest in learning.
9. Model oral, written, and computer language. Read to children.
10. Use parents as partners in the learning process.
11. Provide appropriate technological and media experiences.
12. Continue to scaffold children's learning.

information and basic knowledge in a manner that is sensitive to the listener and the social context (Corsaro, 1985). When shared social interests exist among peers, young children are capable of expressing their understanding about the texture of wet sand, a colorful butterfly, a new soccer ball, and their anticipation of the climax of a new book.

Pellegrini and Glickman (1990) suggest that playgrounds and play activities provide young children with the best opportunity for peer interaction independent of adult influences. From their study of lower and middle socioeconomic children at play, they suggest that the most reliable means of assessing primary grade children's cognitive abilities, communicative skills, and social competence occurs during spontaneous play activities. Further, they believe that children who engage in social games with rules and related verbal exchanges with peers are more intellectually competent than children who tend to be socially passive. During the primary grades, children develop social skills and communicative abilities that foster positive cognitive, linguistic, and social patterns of behavior. The cognitive and communicative experiences that occur during spontaneous play extend young children's social skills, deepen their empathy toward their friends, and foster their ability to express their understanding of their world.

Key Terms

concrete operations	phonics
formal operations	sight words
meta memory	service words
metacognition	word analysis
cognitive science	configuration
metalinguistic awareness	comprehension
shading	television literacy
registers	

Review Activities/Strategies

1. Interview principals and kindergarten and primary grade teachers in several school districts to determine what is being done to provide a continuum of experience between kindergarten and the primary grades.
2. With several of your classmates, develop a plan for providing such a continuum.
3. Conduct Piagetian conservation experiments with several 6-, 7-, and 8-year-olds. Write up your results.
   a. Note how they compare with 4- and 5-year-olds.
   b. Note differences between the 6-, 7-, and 8-year-olds.
4. Examine some of the curricular materials or software written for first, second, and third grades. Analyze them for:
   a. Developmental appropriateness
   b. Gender bias
   c. Multicultural awareness
5. Collect samples of children's writing from first, second and third grades. Analyze it according to
   a. Content
   b. Form
6. Observe children 6, 7, and 8 years of age working with computers. Analyze their experiences for developmental appropriateness.
7. Read an article on young children and television. Discuss it with your class.

Further Readings

Language and Literacy

Allen, J., & Mason, J. (Eds.). (1989). *Risk makers, risk takers, risk breakers: Reducing the risks for young literacy learners.* Portsmouth, NH: Heinemann.

The contributors of this book suggest policy changes and specific home and classroom practices that can reduce risk in literacy learning. Topics addressed include children and their families, teachers, and administrators.

Gentry, J. R. (1987). *Spel . . . is a four-letter word.* Portsmouth, NH: Heinemann.

This short but interesting book demonstrates how teachers can teach spelling so that children will enjoy learning to spell. Learning to spell is presented as a part of the reading-writing process.

Goodman, K. (1986). *What's whole in whole language?.* Portsmouth, NH: Heinemann.

This short book was written by one of the leaders in the whole language movement. Dr. Goodman describes what whole language is and what it is not. He helps teachers identify aspects of whole language that they are already using, and how to expand on them. He realistically demonstrates how teachers can gradually begin to include more whole language in their classrooms.

Hall, N. (Ed.). (1989). *Writing with reason: The emergence of authorship in young children.* Portsmouth, NH: Heinemann.

The contributing authors of this book are classroom teachers. They show how children ages 3 through 7 write for real audiences and for authentic purposes.

Hoot, J., & Silvern, S. (Eds.). (1989). *Writing with computers in the early grades.* New York: Teachers College Press.

This book discusses the issues and concerns of writing with computers in the early grades. Word processing, types of software, and practical ideas for the classroom are discussed.

Rhodes, L., & Dudley-Marling, C. (1988). *Readers and writers with a difference: A holistic approach to teaching learning disabled and remedial students.* Portsmouth, NH: Heinemann.

The authors share their experiences of using whole language rather than skill-based techniques with learning disabled and remedial students. Rhodes and Dudley-Marling suggest that special children who discover that reading and writing can fulfill their personal needs will continue to use reading and writing throughout life. The authors also encourage teachers to create their own strategies based upon their needs, the needs of the students, and the needs of the setting.

Schwartz, J. I. (1988). *Encouraging early literacy: An integrated approach to reading and writing in N–3.* Portsmouth, NH: Heinemann.

This book describes how to implement a whole language approach from the pre-primary years through grade 3. Theory and research are clearly applied to classroom practice. The importance of basing instruction and use of materials on children's needs rather than grade levels is an important theme throughout this book.

Taylor, D., & Dorsey-Gaines, C. (1988). *Growing up literate: Learning from inner-city families.* Portsmouth, NH: Heinemann.

Taylor and Dorsey-Gaines studied the families of young literate African-American children who came from impoverished urban environments. This book presents new information regarding the strengths of these families, which may change attitudes on the part of some readers.

Cognition

Kamii, C. (1985). *Young children reinvent arithmetic.* New York: Teachers College Press.

Kamii, C. (1989). *Young children continue to reinvent arithmetic, 2nd grade.* New York: Teachers College Press.

These two books are based upon Kamii's study of arithmetic learning in first and second grade classrooms. Based upon Piagetian thought, Kamii demonstrates how young children learn about arithmetic through the process of reinventing. Many ideas for games and activities for the classroom are included.

Katz, L., & Chard, S. (1988). *Engaging the minds of young children: The project approach.* Norwood, NJ: Ablex.

This book describes the project approach to learning with young children. The project approach emphasizes an active, integrated and purposeful approach to learning that is particularly appropriate for children in the primary grades.

Payne, J. (Ed.). (1990). *Mathematics for the young child.* Reston, VA: National Council of Teachers of Mathematics.

This book presents the latest in thinking regarding the development of mathematics in young children. Ideas for more effective teaching of mathematics are presented.

Developmentally Appropriate Practice in Primary Classrooms

Bredekamp, S. (Ed.). (1988). *Appropriate education in the primary grades, a position statement of the National Association for the Education of Young Children.* Washington, DC: The National Association for the Education of Young Children.

This pamphlet describes appropriate and inappropriate practices regarding curriculum, teaching strategies, guidance of social-emotional development, parent-teacher relations, and evaluation. It is useful in helping other adults better understand developmentally appropriate education in the primary grades. Single copies are 50 cents each. One hundred copies are available for $10.00. Request NAEYC #578. National Association for the Education of Young Children, 1834 Connecticut Avenue, N.W., Washington, DC 20009. (800) 424–2460.

Bredekamp, S. (1990). Extra-year programs: A response to Brewer and Uphoff. *Young Children, 46,* (5), 20–21.

Brewer, J. (1990). Transitional programs: Boon or bane? *Young Children, 46*(5), 15–18.

Uphoff, J. (1990). Extra-year programs: An argument for transitional programs during transitional times. *Young children, 46,* (5), 19–20.

These three articles present the current thinking regarding transition classrooms. Developmentally appropriate primary grades, not transition classes, are the answer to appropriate placements.

Katz, L., Evangelou, D., & Hartman, J. (1990). *The case for mixed age grouping in early education.* Washington, DC: National Association for the Education of Young Children.

This book explains mixed age grouping and provides information regarding the social effects and cognitive basis for this type of programming. Concrete examples of successful mixed age settings are included.

SACUS Position Statement on *Continuity of learning for four- to seven-year-old children.* Southern Association on Children Under Six, P.O. Box 5403 Brady Station, Little Rock, AR 72215 (501) 663–0353.

PART SEVEN

A Brief Look Beyond the Early Years: The Effects of Early Development upon Later Development

CHAPTER 17

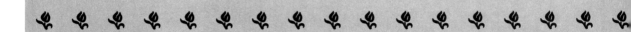

Good teaching, like good parenting, is hard work. There are simply no easy ways to helping children grow and develop into independent, self-confident and responsible adults.

When we instruct children in academic subjects, or in swimming, gymnastics or ballet at too early an age, we miseducate them; we put them at risk for short-term success and long-term personality damage for no useful purpose. There is no evidence that such early instruction has lasting benefits, and considerable evidence that it can do lasting harm.

David Elkind

Later Childhood and Adolescence

After reading and studying this chapter, you will demonstrate comprehension by:

- Describing the major aspects of development in the later childhood years and adolescence.
- Citing research evidence documenting the effects of quality experiences in the early years on later childhood and adolescence.
- Identifying pressures in the early years that can adversely affect development in later childhood and adolescence.
- Describing the role of adults in facilitating the development of older children and adolescents.

■ As Jeremy and Angela move into the later years of childhood and adolescence, what can we expect? What will their development be like? Jeremy has had an almost ideal early childhood. He has had loving and supportive care provided by parents, caregivers, and teachers who were knowledgeable about young children and their developmental needs. He lives in a family free of economic stress. Angela has had a different family experience although it, too, has been full of love and care. Her parents, James and Cheryl, have done the best they could under adverse social and economic circumstances. Even though Angela's birth and first years of life were difficult, the services and support systems available prevented many problems. These services and the love and care of the extended family provided the opportunity for Angela to have a good start in life. ■

An Overview of Later Childhood and Adolescence

The following sections provide a brief description of what to expect in the years of later childhood and adolescence.

Later Childhood

Later childhood refers to the time span of ages 9 through 11. This period is generally characterized by somewhat slower physical development, more even social and emotional behavior than the early childhood years and later adolescence, and the consolidation of cognitive skills begun early in the elementary school years.

During the fourth, fifth, and sixth grades, peers and friends become increasingly important (Hartup, 1983). Children are usually seen in pairs or small groups. Their position in the peer group becomes important (Damon, 1983). Likewise, children become more aware of labels and status within the community and larger society. Involvement in various groups outside the school setting is common. Children in this age group are frequently involved in sports activities, have lessons in the visual and performing arts, and participate in Scout and religious activities. Children in later childhood generally have closest friends of the same gender (Huston, Carpenter, & Atwater, 1986). While their interest in sex continues, it is usually hidden from adults during this period of development.

Even though the peer group has an increasing influence on children in later childhood, the home and family are still important (Furman & Buhrmester, 1985). The home can provide a refuge from the problems encountered within the peer group. Parents also continue to serve as a source of useful social information. Fights with siblings are common during this period of development. Yet, most children of later childhood age are quick to defend their brothers and sisters if others verbally or physically threaten them (Bryant, 1982). Efforts on the part of parents to prepare young children in advance for the birth of a sibling appear to promote positive long-term sibling relationships (Dunn & Kendrick, 1982).

During their ninth through eleventh years, children consolidate their increasing skills in the area of cognitive development (Inhelder & Piaget, 1958; Moshman & Timmons, 1982). They master the symbol systems in reading and math. Their developing reasoning abilities permit them to solve increasingly complex problems. While they are becoming more objective, at times their emotions can control their thinking. They seek more knowledge about the world in general, and become more aware of life, death, bodily processes, and social issues. Moral judgment becomes more flexible (Kohlberg, 1984).

School performance and peer group position contribute to self-concept. Erikson (1963) describes this time as part of the Industry vs. Inferiority stage. Thus, it is important to older children's psychosocial well-being to develop feelings of competence and productivity during this time. Appropriate tasks at home and school that require independent action and behavior can facilitate the development of this feeling of competence and industry.

Physical development usually slows down during this period (Tanner, 1978). Torsos lengthen and many children become slender in appearance. Other children may gain weight and become pudgy. This extra weight gain often sets the stage for rapid growth in height during adolescence. Generally, motor abilities become more refined, as is reflected in increasing participation in sports and

According to Erikson's stage of "Industry vs. Inferiority," it is important for children in later childhood to continue to have opportunities to engage in and successfully complete various tasks and projects.

musical activities. Changes in physical development, indicating the coming of adolescence, can begin during this time. The onset of **puberty** is usually earlier for girls than for boys. It can begin as early as age 8 and generally occurs by age 14. For boys, the age range is from 9 to 15 (Shonkoff, 1984).

Puberty—*the biological developments that result in the ability to produce children.*

Adolescence

Adolescence is a period of dramatic change in all areas of development between the years of childhood and adulthood, generally including the years between ages 12 and 16. Several major changes occur during this period, including rapid growth in height and weight, and sexual development (Tanner, 1978). There are wide individual differences in growth patterns during adolescence, and both early and late maturing adolescents can have difficult adjustments (Peskin, 1967; Simmons & Blyth, 1987).

A major task of adolescence is to establish a personal identity. Erikson (1968) calls this stage of psychosocial development *Identity vs. Role Confusion* (see Figure 17.1). During this time teenagers attempt to sort out their various roles:

Adolescence—*the time of rapid development between the later childhood years and adulthood.*

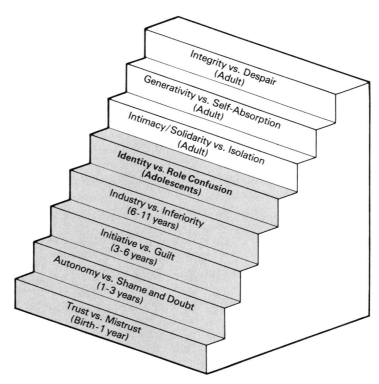

FIGURE 17.1
During later childhood and adolescence Industry vs. Inferiority and Identity vs. Role Confusion are two psychosocial tasks that must be resolved.

gender, racial, familial, religious, peer, and student. Work in developing this identity also involves the trying on of various behaviors of well-known or admired persons.

Adolescents continue to work on establishing a place in the peer group and separating from their parents (Coleman, 1980). Some studies indicate that the separation process may not be as volatile as previously thought (Kandel & Lesser, 1972; Youniss & Smollar, 1985). Parents are also working on separating from their adolescents. Acknowledging the adolescent's increasing independence and sexual maturity often forces parents to deal with their own progression through the life span.

The need for independence and freedom is often unmet because sociocultural freedoms, with the exception of driving, are usually not given until the ages of 18 or 21 (Kett, 1977). Definite ideas and attitudes toward religion, politics, and racial and ethnic groups often appear during adolescence. These can reflect similar attitudes of parents or, in an effort to express independence, can be very different from those of parents (Chand, Crider, & Willits, 1975; Kelley, 1972). At times, some teens can be very concerned about social issues.

They blame adults for these conditions and propose idealistic solutions (Kohlberg, 1984).

Intellectually, adolescents are now able to take on the perspective of another (Inhelder & Piaget, 1958). They view others, peers, parents, and teachers in a critical manner. This critical view of others also causes them to look critically at themselves (Elkind, 1978). As a result, there is a great preoccupation with their own behavior, personality, and physical appearance. Adolescents can now deal with more abstract concepts and can consider and construct multiple alternatives (Keating, 1980). They can distinguish between fact and hypothesis, realism and idealism. Teens can begin to think about and plan for the future, often moving from idealistic to more realistic career goals. School takes on a broader dimension. It is now not only a place to learn but is often the primary place to socialize with the peer group (Simmons & Blyth, 1987).

Coming to terms with sexual development and the need for peer acceptance presents today's adolescents with different situations than the adolescents of earlier years. The epidemic of AIDS, the dramatic increase in teenage pregnancy, and the general adolescent attitude of "it'll never happen to me" create challenges for parents and other adults who work with teens to encourage responsible sexual behavior (National Research Council, 1987). In addition, the availability of drugs, peer pressure to use drugs, and easy money for those who sell drugs can provide temptations to adolescents from all backgrounds (Santrock, 1984).

While there are many changes during later childhood and adolescence, continuity in development is usually the pattern. Thus, in general, children who have done well socially and academically in the early childhood years continue to do well in the later childhood and adolescent years. Positive foundations built in the early years of childhood usually continue through later childhood and adolescence. This phenomenon has been documented through longitudinal research and is one of the major reasons why quality early experiences are important.

Results of Longitudinal Research on Quality Early Childhood Programs

In the early 1960s, three important events occurred that laid the groundwork for the development of new programming for young children. First, Hunt (1961) reported that the nature of environments in the early years has a profound and long-term effect upon learning. Second, Bloom (1964) analyzed previously published studies on learning and concluded that as much as 70 percent of intellectual aptitude as measured by IQ tests and about 50 percent of the reading skill of young adults had been established between the ages of 4 and 9. Third, the research of Piaget documented that young children's cognitive systems and intellectual processing are different from those of older children and adults. These three events, coupled with an increasing awareness of the negative effects of adverse social conditions, provided the impetus for the development of a number of early childhood programs in the 1960s. Some of these programs included Head Start, Follow-Through, the Perry Preschool Project, and the Tuscon Model of Early Childhood Education.

The research on these programs after the first several years looked promising. However, as children who had been in these programs moved into the third and fourth grades, there seemed to be a **washout effect**, in that there was no significant difference in performance between children who had been in these preschool programs and those who had not (Cicerelli, Evans, & Schiller, 1969). There were cries from politicians and others to stop funding these programs. Fortunately, there were a number of scholars who suggested that the final chapter on the real benefits of these programs might not be written until years later, after these children were adolescents or young adults (Berreuta-Clement, Schweinhart, Barnett, Epstein, & Weikart, 1984; Lazar & Darlington, 1982). These farsighted advocates of early childhood education called for and helped implement longitudinal research on the effects of these programs.

As indicated in Table 17.1, this longitudinal research demonstrates that there are rather powerful long-term benefits both to individuals who were in these quality early childhood programs and to society at large. These individuals, when compared with others who were not in quality early childhood programs, had better grades, fewer failing marks, fewer absences from school, required fewer special education classes, and were more likely to graduate from high school and continue their education or enter vocational training. In addition, these individuals also had a higher rate of employment, lower crime rates, less delinquent behavior as juveniles and adults, fewer teenage pregnancies, and a reduced need for public assistance. These quality programs saved school systems and society in general vast sums of money. It is estimated that for every dollar invested in quality preschool education, that there is a savings of $4.75 to $7.00 (Berrueta-Clement, Schweinhart, Barnett, Epstein, & Weikart, 1984; Hechinger, 1986; Lazar, 1983; Royce, Darlington, & Murray, 1983). In addition, as indicated in Table 17.2 (see HIGH/SCOPE column), there is some initial evidence that suggests that individuals who had been in developmentally appropriate pre-primary programs that provided child-initiated activity demonstrated more socially desirable behaviors as adolescents than individuals who had not been in such programs (Schweinhart, Weikart, & Larner, 1986).

There is also some initial research evidence indicating that low-risk children who attend quality preschools also benefit when compared to other low-risk children who did not attend a quality preschool (Larsen & Robinson, 1989). Specifically, these researchers determined that third grade children who attended a developmentally appropriate preschool scored significantly higher on the spelling and language portions of school achievement tests. In addition, 90 percent of these third-graders who attended quality preschool programs participated in music lessons and sports activities, compared with only 68 percent of the children who did not attend preschool. Boys in particular seemed to achieve long-term benefits. This quality preschool program, like those for at-risk children, had a parent education component. Continued data collection in this longitudinal study will eventually provide evidence regarding the possible benefits of quality early childhood programs for low-risk children during adolescence and beyond.

*Washout effect —
the decline of gains
in intelligence and
achievement scores
several years after
the termination of
the intervention
program for young
children.*

TABLE 17.1
Major findings of the Perry Preschool Study

Category	Number[a] Responding	Preschool Group	No-Preschool Group	*p*
Mean IQ at age 15	123	95	83	<.001
Age 15 achievement test	95	122.2	94.5	<.001
% of all school years in special education	112	16%	28%	.039
High school graduation (or equivalent)	121	67%	49%	.034
Post-secondary education	121	38%	21%	.029
Arrested or detained	121	31%	51%	.022
Females only: teen pregnancies per 100	49	64	117	.084
Receiving welfare at age 19	120	18%	32%	.044
Employed at age 19	121	50%	32%	.032

Note: [a]Total *n* = 123.
Source: Barnett, W. S. (1986). *The Perry Preschool Program and its long-term effects: A benefit-cost analysis* (p. 4). Ypsilanti, MI: HIGH/SCOPE Educational Research Foundation. Reprinted with permission.

Inappropriate learning environments and resulting pressures on young children have not only immediate, but long-term negative consequences extending into adolescence.

TABLE 17.2
Social behavior and attitudes reported by curriculum groups at age 15

Variable	Distar	HIGH/SCOPE	Nursery School	*p*
Family relations				
How have you been getting along with your family?				
Great	33%	33%	28%	—
Fair	44%	67%	56%	
Poorly	22%	0%	17%	
How does your family feel about how you're doing?				
Great	0%	6%	6%	.03
All right	67%	94%	89%	
Poorly	33%	0%	6%	
Contribute to household expenses (*N* = 42)	14%	33%	23%	—
Activities				
Participate in sports				
Often	17%	50%	44%	.02
Sometimes	28%	44%	28%	
Never	56%	6%	28%	
In recent weeks, have read				
A book (*N* = 49)	31%	69%	59%	.09
A newspaper	67%	89%	72%	—
A magazine (*N* = 53)	44%	41%	72%	—
Ever done volunteer work	22%	28%	28%	—
School behavior and attitudes				
Appointed to an office or job in school (*N* = 53)	0%	12%	33%	.02
Personal education plans (*N* = 36)				
Postsecondary	50%	77%	64%	—
High school	42%	23%	36%	
Drop out	8%	0%	0%	
Schooling total scale, 19 items, *alpha* = .79	44.3 (9.3)	49.3 (11.1)	45.9 (9.2)	—

Long-Term Effects of Developmentally Inappropriate Experiences

The growing awareness of the importance of education in the early years has caused many well-intentioned but uninformed parents, educators, and policy-makers to create developmentally inappropriate programming for young chil-

TABLE 17.2
continued

Variable	Distar	HIGH/SCOPE	Nursery School	*p*
Learning process subscale, 9 items, *alpha* = .66	21.3 (5.4)	21.5 (5.4)	20.8 (5.8)	—
Teachers subscale, 10 items, *alpha* = .78	23.1 (6.3)	27.8 (6.7)	25.2 (7.6)	—
Mental health				
Perceived number of personal problems (*N* = 52)				—
More than others	17%	11%	11%	
Same as others	33%	33%	50%	
Less than others	50%	56%	39%	
Help sought for a personal problem more than once	11%	41%	22%	—
Self-esteem—Rosenberg scale, 10 items scored 10–40, *alpha* = .70	26.5 (3.2)	28.1 (3.8)	27.7 (3.3)	—
Perceived locus of control—Bialer scale, 23 items, *alpha* = .34	14.6 (2.9)	13.6 (2.7)	13.9 (2.4)	—
Area in which you want to do well				—
School	44%	39%	50%	
Sports	17%	39%	17%	
Family	11%	17%	6%	
Friends	6%	0%	28%	
Other	22%	6%	0%	
Perceived competence in that area				—
Better than others	24%	33%	29%	
The same as others	47%	61%	53%	
Worse than others	29%	6%	18%	

Note: *N* = 54, 18 per group, unless othewise noted. When means are presented, standard deviations are included in parentheses. The probability level of a group difference is reported if it is less than .10; percentages were compared by the chi-square statistic, means by analysis of variance.

Source: Schweinhart, L. J., Weikart, D. P., & Larner, M. B. (1986). Consequences of three preschool curriculum models through age 15. *Early Childhood Research Quarterly, 1*, 79–80. Reprinted with permission.

dren (Black & Puckett, 1987). In addition, parents who want the best for their children often over-program their children into many activities that put inappropriate pressures on them. In an effort to raise test scores, schools also provide inappropriate programs for young children (Bredekamp & Shepard, 1989; Charlesworth, 1989).

Elkind (1981, 1984, 1987) suggests that there may be some rather serious and long-term consequences for these inappropriate pressures and this miseducation of young children. He states, "While miseducation has always been with us—we have always had pushy parents—today it has become a societal norm. If we do not wake up to the potential danger of these harmful practices,

Role of the Early Childhood Professional

Promoting Positive Long-term Development in Children and Adolescents

1. Help parents, other educators, and policymakers become aware of developmentally appropriate practice for young children.
2. Help parents, other educators, and policymakers become aware of the negative short-term effects of developmentally inappropriate practice.
3. Help parents, other educators, and policymakers become aware of the negative long-term effects of developmentally inappropriate practice upon older children and adolescents.

we may do serious damage to a large segment of the next generation" (Elkind, 1987, p. 4). Elkind suggests that inappropriate pressures in the early years can result in suicide and drug problems in later childhood and adolescence.

A study (Hyson, Hirsh-Pasek, & Rescorla, 1989) of 120 children and their mothers in 11 schools indicated that young children ages 3 through 5 who were subjected to formal teaching were less creative upon entering elementary

An important role for the early childhood professional is to educate parents, other educators, and policy makers regarding developmentally appropriate practice, and to make them aware of negative short-term and long-term effects of developmentally inappropriate practice.

school, displayed more test anxiety, and soon lost the academic advantage they had in the beginning. Another investigation (Burts, Hart, Charlesworth, & Kirk, 1990), which examined the frequency of stress behaviors in developmentally appropriate and developmentally inappropriate classrooms, found that there were significantly more stress behaviors in the developmentally inappropriate classroom. Thus it would appear that inappropriate pressures on young children can have rather immediate as well as long-term negative consequences. Therefore, it is critical that early childhood professionals help parents, other educators, and policymakers understand the negative consequences of developmentally inappropriate experiences during the early years.

Key Terms

later childhood   adolescence
puberty   washout effect

Review Activities/Strategies

1. Think back to your teen years.
   a. Make a list of the pressures you encountered.
   b. What were some of the competencies you developed during your adolescence?
   c. What foundations were laid during your early childhood years that helped you in later childhood and adolescence?
2. Make a list of the ways that you can help parents, other educators, and policymakers understand developmentally appropriate practice for young children, and list the possible long-term benefits.

Further Readings

Black, J., & Puckett, M. (1987). Informing others about developmentally appropriate practice. In S. Bredekamp (Ed.), *Developmentally appropriate practice in early childhood programs serving children from birth through age 8*. Washington, DC: The National Association for the Education of Young Children.
    This chapter provides background information on the reasons for developmentally inappropriate practice and why some adults pressure young children. It gives suggestions on how to help adults understand appropriate development of young children.

Elkind, D. (1981). *The hurried child: Growing up too fast too soon*. Reading, MA: Addison-Wesley

Elkind, D. (1984). *All grown up and no place to go: Teenagers in crisis*. Reading, MA: Addison-Wesley

Elkind, D. (1987). *Miseducation: Preschoolers at risk*. New York: Alfred A. Knopf.
    These three books provide background regarding the consequences of developmentally inappropriate experiences for young children on development in later childhood and adolescence. They should be a part of every early childhood professional's library.

Erikson, E. (1968). *Identity: Youth in crisis.* New York: Norton.

This book provides a good description of the psychosocial development in adolescence by the foremost writer about the teen years. It is an invaluable source in helping parents and other adults understand this age group.

Hechinger, F. (Ed.). (1986). *A better start: New choices for learning.* New York: Walker and Company.

This book describes many of the long-term benefits of quality early childhood programming. In addition, there are chapters on the importance of learning in the home and quality child care.

CHAPTER 18

The power to animate all of life's seasons is a power that resides within us.

Gail Sheehy

Early childhood careers can successfully develop using a "path" model of diverse personal growth experiences linked by commitment and concern. Traditional career ladder models are often too rigid.

Political activity ... [must be] the very foundation of our work. ... [It] can benefit young children, their families, ourselves, and all humankind.

Janna Dresden and Barbara Kimes Myers

Developing Adults in the Lives of Developing Young Children

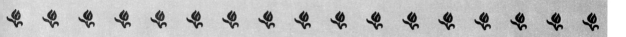

After reading and studying this chapter, you will demonstrate comprehension by:

- Identifying the factors in the dynamics of adult behavior that can promote self-understanding and can facilitate the understanding of other adults in professional relationships: parents, teachers, administrators, and other support staff.
- Describing general adult developmental patterns and the factors that appear to influence adult behaviors.
- Describing the importance of understanding professional development.
- Outlining the process of professional development.
- Describing the role of professional responsibility and ethics in assisting other adults in understanding the unique development and learning styles of young children.
- Describing the relationship between professionalism and advocacy for young children and their families.
- Summarizing the challenges of working with young children.
- Explaining the relationship between understanding how young children develop and learn and implementing developmentally appropriate practice.
- Describing the rewards of becoming a competent early childhood professional by helping young children develop positive self-concepts and attitudes toward learning, two prerequisites for successful, productive lives.

The concept of a person's development extending over the entire life span is relatively recent (Erikson, 1963). For many years, it was assumed that development stopped once one became an adult. Of course, it was acknowledged that there would be changes in physical appearance. Nevertheless, it was assumed that cognitive potential was fixed and did not change through the life span. However, the notion that intelligence continues to develop and change throughout adulthood is now widely accepted (Baltes, Dittman-Kohli, & Dixon, 1984). In addition, not much thought was given to the ongoing social and emotional development of adults until Erikson developed his concept of the Eight Stages of Man (1963). While there are a number of persons who support developmental stages throughout the **life span** (Erikson, 1963; Levinson, 1986; Sheehy, 1976; Vaillant, 1977), recent researchers suggest more complex theories. Before these ideas are presented, you may find it helpful to think about why it is important for an early childhood professional to know about the development of adults.

Life span—the idea that development is a lifelong process and is influenced by biological, environmental, and historical causes.

Importance of Understanding the Dynamics of Adult Development

An awareness of the dynamics of adult development can promote self-understanding. Early childhood professionals need a knowledge of the growth and development of young children in order to be competent professionals. They also need to understand themselves. Self-understanding promotes responsibility and healthy functioning in adults, who must possess positive personalities if they are to be effective with young children.

■ Helen Pope returns to teaching when her children are old enough to be in school. After her eight-year absence from the classroom, Helen is surprised to find that teaching now takes more time, due to increased recordkeeping and paperwork. She also tries to continue doing all the household chores she did when she was at home all day. Pressure and stress mount and she realizes that her family and the children in her classroom are affected by her behavior. Helen comes to the realization that she now has two full-time jobs and that changes need to be made. Including her family in household chores, readjusting the family budget to provide money for food prepared outside the home, and modifying some of her classroom procedures so that the children are more responsible and independent help to relieve stress for Helen, her family, and her classroom.   ■

In addition to self-understanding, an awareness of the dynamics affecting adult behavior and development can help early childhood professionals understand the actions and reactions of other adults in the professional relationship. These adults include parents, other teachers, administrators, and support staff. Understanding others' behavior can produce more empathetic, positive, and productive relationships. Lack of understanding can produce negative and hostile relationships. Consider the following vignette.

■ Remember Ms. Schwartz, the kindergarten teacher who encouraged Kathleen's mother to stay in the classroom until Kathleen adjusted to coming to school? Ms. Schwartz's knowledge of child development and the nature of the separation process was quite helpful in that situation. Her knowledge of adult behavior patterns in the separation process proved invaluable in another incident. When Ms. Bealer came to pick up her daughter Beth from kindergarten one afternoon, Ms. Schwartz asked Ms. Bealer how things were going. In a defensive tone, Ms. Bealer said, "Well you have become the new authority in our house. All Beth says is 'Ms. Schwartz this and Ms. Schwartz that.' " Ms. Schwartz' knowledge of the feelings and behaviors of many parents regarding their child's school entry helped her understand Ms. Bealer's somewhat hostile remarks. Ms. Schwartz knows that Beth is the first child in the Bealer family to come to school and that this is Beth's first extended time away from the home. It is not unusual at this time for parents to feel that they are being replaced in their child's life by another important adult, the teacher. Ms. Schwartz realizes that the developmental milestone of a child entering school can also heighten parental awareness of their progression in the lifespan. Parents, too, are getting older and now must learn new roles and responsibilities as parents of a school-age child. Ms. Schwartz is aware that school entry is a time of new adjustments for the family and that this transition can cause an increased stress level. Consequently, Ms. Schwartz does not take Ms. Bealer's comments personally. Nor does she respond to Ms. Bealer in a negative way or allow the comment to affect her long-term relationship with Ms. Bealer. ■

Trends and Factors Influencing Adult Behaviors

Erik Erikson was the first researcher to promote the concept of sequential stages of adult development (1963). The last three stages of his Eight Stages of Man deal with adult development (see Figure 18.1). Erikson also felt that success in each stage depended upon the successful resolution of the challenges of the preceding stage. The investigations of Levinson (1986) and Vaillant (1977) supported Erikson's notion. Their research was the basis for Gail Sheehy's book *Passages* (1976), which popularized the idea of predictable age-related stages for adults. Sheehy also wrote a sequel entitled *Pathfinders* (1982), which contains exploration of life stages she categorized as the Freestyle Fifties, the Selective Sixties, the Thoughtful Seventies, and the Proud-to-be Eighties.

Life-course—the idea that views development and behavior from birth to death as influenced by major life events, rather than well-defined stages.

More recently, various investigators have suggested that there is great variation in adults at particular ages (Elder, 1982). Therefore, specific stages of adult development may not be reliable indicators of behavior for all adults in particular age ranges. This **life-course** approach suggests the following ideas about adult development:*

• During adolescence most people develop ideas about major events in their life cycle, including the timetable for the unfolding of these events. They plan to assume an occupation, marry, have a family, and retire.

---

*Adapted from Rosenfeld, A., & Stark, E. (1987). The prime of our lives. *Psychology Today, 21*(5), 62–72. Reprinted with permission from Psychology Today Magazine copyright © 1987 (P. T. Partners, L. P.)

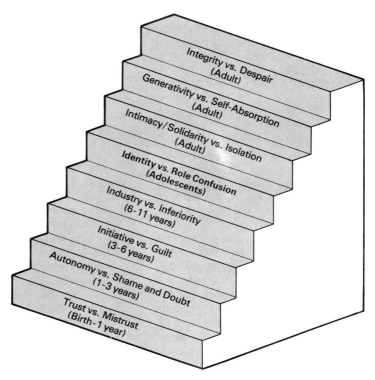

FIGURE 18.1
The last three of Erikson's eight stages deal with adult development.

- There is great individual variation in adults as they move through their adult life. Some men enter the work force at age 18. Others take over a decade to prepare to enter their chosen occupation. Some women become mothers in their mid-teens. Others spend a number of years establishing a career and then choose to become mothers. Others become mothers first, get their children in school, and then focus on career goals. Some may combine career development and raising a family. Others focus upon working at home, and some may choose not to marry or have children.
- Societal changes, often involving economics, affect the timetable for various groups of people in a particular age range and affect how they live their adult lives. Those people who grew up during the Depression often have lived out their lives differently from the adult Baby Boomers.
- Chance events and opportunities can cause wide variation in adult lives. Early retirement, the premature death of a spouse or parent, and the early or unplanned birth of children are chance events that people respond to in a variety of ways.
- People who feel that they are not progressing according to their individual social clock may find their lives more stressful.
- People who find themselves among the first group to be influenced by chang-

During the teen years, most people develop individual timetables regarding when they would like the major events in their lives to occur. Unpredictable life situations may change their plans.

ing societal and economic forces may perceive themselves as being stressed. Two-income families who must find adequate child care for young children and juggle parenting, household, and career responsibilities have been under stress due to traditional male-female role expectations, lack of quality child care options, and the failure of most employers to act in support of the new demands on families.

• There does not appear to be a mid-life crisis for all adults. Some investigators have reinterpreted this event by terming it "mid-life consciousness," in that this is a time for an awakening of thought about the meaning of life and one's place in the life cycle.

• The idea that an adult must successfully resolve the crisis of one developmental stage before moving on to the next is no longer universally accepted.

• Attention must also be paid to cultural variation in expectations regarding the life cycle. Roles and timetables may be gender-specific and different from mainstream thinking of society at large.

In conclusion, it appears that traditional life events still exist in the minds of many adults. However, due to a number of complex factors, both societal and individual, the timetable for the achievement of these events is more varied than in the past. These variations can create options and freedom for some people. For others, these variations can cause stress and crisis.

An awareness of life events and their impact upon parents, other teachers, staff, and administrators is important if the early childhood professional is to establish effective cooperative relationships. The following vignette demonstrates how knowledge of the impact of various events upon the life-course can promote understanding between adults in professional relationships.

■ Three first grade teachers had enjoyed positive, cooperative professional relationships for several years. Linda, who had always been dependable and helpful, began to demonstrate inconsistent and unpredictable behaviors. Elena and Tim could not figure out what was happening. Finally, one day after school, Linda confided that her husband had lost his job and that the family was under great emotional and financial stress. Linda's oldest daughter was planning to start college next year and now it seemed that this would not be financially possible. The crisis of Linda's husband's unemployment upon their life plans and those of their daughter had an adverse impact on Linda's professional behavior. Sharing her problems with Elena and Tim, and their awareness and support, helped Linda to cope. As a result, their working relationships improved. If Tim and Elena had not been aware of the stress caused by the disruption of their co-worker's life, they could have reacted with hostility toward Linda, undermining their positive professional relationship. Eventually, this compounded stress could have affected the nature of Linda's interaction with the children in her classroom. ■

An awareness of the factors influencing the development and behaviors of adults in the life course can serve to foster understanding of self and others and preserve professional relationships. Ultimately, this understanding of the dynamics affecting adults can influence the quality of adult interaction with young children and the nature of the learning environment.

A major theme throughout this book is the dynamic nature of development, which occurs not only in the early childhood years but throughout the life span. Chapter 17 presented a brief overview regarding the continuing development of older children and adolescents. The first part of this chapter discussed the development of adults. We will now discuss the ongoing development of early childhood professionals.

The Importance of Understanding the Developing Early Childhood Professional

An awareness of how teachers develop professionally can also facilitate professional self-awareness and understanding of other professionals. Knowing one's self and understanding others in the professional context can promote a more productive environment. Cooperative professional relationships between adults promote positive climates in which young children can develop and learn (Berger, 1991). Thus, knowledge of professional development is an important com-

An awareness of how teachers develop professionally can facilitate self-awareness and an understanding of other professionals.

ponent of promoting the development of young children. Following is a discussion of several interrelated ideas that appear to influence the developing professional.

The Developing Professional

Some theorists (Erikson, 1963; Havighurst, 1972) have suggested that an important aspect of young adulthood is securing a full-time job. From this perspective, it appears that young early childhood professionals encounter unique problems and concerns that older or experienced professionals may not. Other researchers propose that professionals progress through a sequence of stages (Fuller, 1969; Katz, 1972, 1977). Katz (1972) is one of the few researchers who has examined the development of teachers of young children, and she has identified four stages: survival, consolidation, renewal, and maturity.*

Katz labels the first stage as *survival.* This first stage may last throughout the first full year of teaching. The survival stage finds the teacher focusing on

---

*Adapted with permission from "Developmental Stages of Preschool Teachers" by L. G. Katz, 1972, *The Elementary School Journal, 23,* pp. 50–54. Copyright 1972 by The University of Chicago Press.

how to get through each day and week. Not only are teachers in their early professional development learning basic instructional and management skills, but they are also concerned about acceptance by colleagues and by the parents of the children in their classroom. Discrepancies between the perceived ideal classroom and the realities that emerge can produce anxieties. According to Katz, teachers at this stage need on-site classroom assistance, comfort, guidance, and instruction in specific skills.

Teachers then move into the next stage called *consolidation.* In this stage, teachers' ideas and learning during the survival stage are consolidated. Teachers can begin to focus on the needs of individual children in their classrooms. Teachers in this stage need on-site consultants or experienced teachers to help them strengthen and consolidate their knowledge. The sharing of ideas and information about individual children with these resource people is also helpful during this time.

Katz found that teachers who were in their third or fourth year of teaching often became bored with their past routine of activities in their classrooms. They felt a need for new ideas and different ways of teaching. This stage of *renewal* finds teachers of young children attending conferences and workshops, reading professional magazines and journals, and visiting other classrooms in search of new ideas.

Katz suggests that the last stage, *maturity,* varies from teacher to teacher. Some teachers may reach this stage by their third year of teaching, while others may take five or more years. Teachers who have reached the maturity stage have a need for more in-depth information pertaining to the historical and philosophical basis of the field. They seek out more information about the nature of learning and about the profession. Teachers in the maturity stage frequently pursue advanced degrees, attend conferences and seminars, read extensively about the field, and interact with other mature professionals.

Other researchers (Swick, Brown, & Guddemi, 1986) have determined that personality orientation affects the development of teaching behaviors. Flexible teachers with high self-esteem do not seem to have as many discipline problems as teachers who are rigid, introverted, and have low self-esteem.

A more encompassing view (Heck & Williams, 1984; Lieberman & Miller, 1984) suggests that the development of teacher behaviors is affected by many factors. As seen in Figure 18.2, this ecological perspective takes into account teachers' past experiences, including their own classroom encounters from the early childhood years through teacher training. The environment of the school where they teach, the total school system, the community, and wider societal perspectives on learning influence teachers and their behaviors. Ost (1989) indicates that teachers are continually learning about the subculture of teaching. Like the culture at large, the subculture of teaching is always changing.

Career perspective—the theory that development of early childhood professionals continues throughout their careers and is unique to each person.

While Katz's four developmental stages of teachers ended with reaching the maturity stage at around the fifth year of teaching, a more recent notion suggests that the development of teachers can be viewed from a long-term or **career perspective.** According to Kohl (1984), this career perspective of teaching takes the following into account:

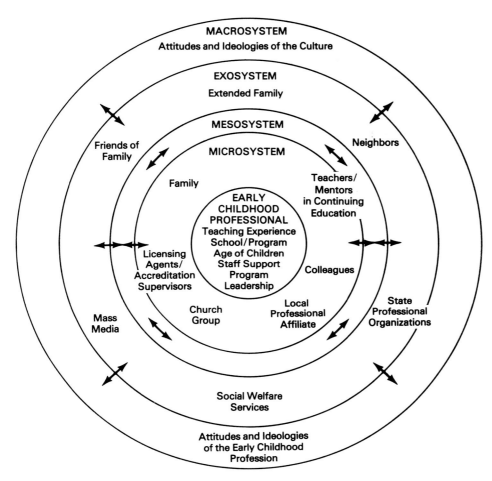

FIGURE 18.2
The development of teachers' behaviors is affected by many factors including prior classroom experiences from the early years of schooling through teacher training, the school where they teach, the total school system, the community, and wider societal perspectives on learning.

- Each teacher's life space, or experiences and background, is unique, just as is each child's.
- Teacher development does not end at one year or five years, but is a long-term process that continues throughout the career.
- The roles of teachers broaden as they develop and may include serving as mentors to younger teachers or assuming other leadership positions.
- Teacher development is facilitated when guided by a plan.

Gehrke (1987) also takes a long-term view of the development of teachers and identifies five stages of teaching: choosing, beginning, learning, continuity,

Career ladder—the idea that the professional's career advancement involves moving up from position to position and that each step up involves increased authority and rewards.

and leaving. Dresden and Myers (1989) suggest that the current emphasis on the **career ladder** may be somewhat limiting. Whereas the career ladder theory implies moving up in the organizational pattern with increased authority and greater renumeration, Dresden and Myers (1989) propose the idea of a **career path.** A career path does not focus on increased authority, but emphasizes the notion of moving to another position that offers opportunities for additional learning and growth (Dresden & Myers, 1989). According to Cunningham (1985), effective schools and professional settings plan for and support the continuing development and renewal of teachers.

Career path—the idea that professional development can involve moving to a different position, which provides new opportunities for learning and growth, rather than increased authority.

Opportunities for Continued Professional Development

Much of the current attention to school reform has focused on teachers (Carnegie Task Force on Teaching as a Profession, 1986; Holmes Group, 1986). The recognition of the first years of teaching as important to teacher effectiveness and retention in the classroom has prompted some states and school districts to mandate induction and orientation programs for beginning teachers. These programs often provide knowledge about various procedures of the school setting and classroom management, and may include support teams or individual mentors who advise and guide beginning teachers (Hawk, 1987; Hawk & Robards, 1987; Huling-Austin, 1986; Lasley, 1986).

Mentor—an experienced early childhood professional who provides support and guidance to a beginning teacher.

Beginning teachers who find themselves in settings that do not have a formalized support system may want to identify a more mature early childhood professional who can serve as a **mentor** and provide needed support. These mentors may be other teachers within or outside the beginning teacher's immediate professional setting. College or university instructors or advisors in early childhood education can also help beginning teachers. In addition, contact with other beginning professionals helps create an awareness of the commonality of concerns and problems encountered by most beginning teachers. Sharing with others who are in similar circumstances also provides support.

Maintaining membership in professional organizations provides another opportunity for further professional development. Professional magazines, journals, and position statements serve to provide developing professionals with current thinking and ideas for their classrooms. Professional organizations also provide conferences, workshops, and seminars, which can be sources of support and continuing education. Serving on professional organization committees, serving as an officer, and making presentations can develop leadership skills.

Master teachers—early childhood professionals who are recognized as outstanding in implementing developmentally appropriate practice.

Another opportunity for continuing professional development is additional training at the graduate level. Information obtained from advanced instruction at the college or university can promote the development of **master teachers,** who are recognized as outstanding teachers of young children. In addition, teachers who seek out advanced training may enter leadership positions that impact policymaking regarding the development and learning of young children. In conclusion, it should be noted that true professionals continue to learn throughout their careers and consciously seek out ways to ensure their continued professional development.

Maintaining membership in professional organizations provides the opportunity for continued professional development.

Professional Responsibility and Ethics

In 1989, the NAEYC Ethics Commission published a new Code of Ethical Conduct and Statement of Commitment (Feeney & Kipnis, 1989) (see Figure 18.3). Several of the ideas and principles contained in this code of **ethics** are particularly relevant concerning the early childhood professional's responsibility in promoting developmentally appropriate practice. Consider the following statements:

Ethics—a set of standards describing the responsibilities in terms of behaviors and conduct with regard to a particular profession.

Above all, we shall not harm children. We shall not participate in practices that are disrespectful, degrading, dangerous, exploitative, intimidating, psychologically damaging, or physically harmful to children. **This principle has precedence over all others in this code.** (P–1.1, p. 26)

To be familiar with the knowledge base of early childhood education and to keep current through continuing education and in-service training. (I–1.1, p. 26)

To base program practices upon current knowledge in the field of child development and related disciplines and upon particular knowledge of each child. (I–1.2, p. 26)

To interpret each childs' progress to parents within the framework of a developmental perspective and to help families understand and appreciate the value of developmentally appropriate early childhood programs. (I–2.5, p. 26)

To help family members improve their understanding of their children and to enhance their skills as parents. (I–2.6, p. 26)

Ethical professional behavior in early childhood education requires that the early childhood professional help others to understand developmentally appropriate practice. Failure to promote developmentally appropriate practice is to promote developmentally inappropriate practice and to be guilty of malpractice. However, before developmentally appropriate practice can be shared by early childhood professionals in an effective way, there are several considerations that need to be addressed.

First, early childhood professionals need to realize that they are part of a relatively small group of people who possess specialized information. In terms of the population at large, there are not many adults who have had training in the development and learning of young children. Many adults who are in leadership positions in educational settings may never have had a course in child development. The National Association of Elementary School Principals has developed *Standards for Quality Programming for Young Children: Early Childhood Education and the Elementary School Principal* to aid principals in implementing appropriate programs for young children and their families. See the Further Reading Section at the end of this chapter for more information.

Adults both inside and outside the education profession may think that it does not take much expertise to work with young children. Or they can be aware of the importance of learning in the early years and think that it should be like learning when they were in first grade, or that it is important to start

FIGURE 18.3
The National Association for the Education of Young Children Statement of Commitment

As an individual who works with young children, I commit myself to furthering the values of early childhood education as they are reflected in the NAEYC Code of Ethical Conduct.

To the best of my ability I will:

- Ensure that programs for young children are based on current knowledge of child development and early childhood education.
- Respect and support families in their task of nurturing children.
- Respect colleagues in early childhood education and support them in maintaining the NAEYC Code of Ethical Conduct.
- Serve as an advocate for children, their families, and their teachers in community and society.
- Maintain high standards of professional conduct.
- Recognize how personal values, opinions, and biases can affect professional judgment.
- Be open to new ideas and be willing to learn from the suggestions of others.
- Continue to learn, grow, and contribute as a professional.
- Honor the ideals and principles of the NAEYC Code of Ethical Conduct.

Note: The Statement of Commitment expresses those basic personal commitments that individuals must make in order to align themselves with the profession's responsibilities as set forth in the NAEYC Code of Ethical Conduct.

formalized learning early so children will do well (Black & Puckett, 1987). Thus, in facilitating the understanding of the development and learning in young children, it is helpful to think about the backgrounds and perspectives of parents, administrators, and other teachers. They have good intentions, but due to a lack of background information they may be unaware of developmentally appropriate education for young children. Therefore, early childhood professionals need to keep in mind that it is their responsibility not only to educate young children, but also to educate adults about the unique development and learning of young children.

After recognizing that most adults are not aware of developmentally appropriate education for young children, the next step is to make these adults aware of your professional training and expertise. You need to help them realize that you possess specific information about how young children develop and learn. It may be that other adults are not even aware that most states require special certifications, endorsements, or training programs for persons who teach young children. Let others know that you have specialized training in how young children learn, that you have a credential that certifies or endorses you to teach young children, that you are a member of early childhood professional organizations, and that you attend professional meetings. If others are aware that you have had training that they do not have, they may be more receptive to what you have to say.

After establishing that you are a professional and have specialized training in the development and learning of young children, you can share information about developmentally appropriate practice. Early childhood professionals must not only know early childhood development and learning but must also be able to articulate what developmentally appropriate practice is. Lay-Dopyera and Dopyera (1987) state that early childhood professionals need to think about what they do in their classrooms and reflect on how it is working. This idea of **reflecting-in-action** behavior comes from Schön (1983).

Sharing information about developmentally appropriate practice with other adults, from the initial employment interview to the first parent conferences, orientation, or parents' meeting, establishes that you are a professional. Observation guidesheets or signs posted at learning centers describing the development and learning taking place can help early childhood professionals articulate developmentally appropriate practice to adults who visit the classroom during the school day. After the children are gone for the day, conferences can be scheduled to answer questions about the nature of developmentally appropriate practice.

Developing a professional resource file or displaying professional materials on a table or counter provides ready access to information when it is needed to share with other adults. Professional organization position statements, textbooks, articles, and brochures with key points highlighted are some of the materials that will prove useful in sharing with other adults. Just as promoting the learning and development of young children in the classroom is ongoing and takes time, educating adults about developmentally appropriate practice also takes time.

Reflecting-in-action—*thinking about one's professional behavior while engaging in that behavior for purposes of evaluation and articulation of developmentally appropriate practice.*

■ A number of parents in Jeremy's first grade class expressed concern about the teacher not correcting their spelling on their daily work. Jeremy's teacher, Ms. Wood acknowledged parental concerns and shared articles on the development of reading and writing with them. She provided examples of children's writing from previous first grade classes so that the parents could anticipate progression. Ms. Wood encouraged the parents to provide writing tools and experiences for the children to write at home. At conferences, Ms. Woods shared samples of the children's writings from their portfolios and noted progression in development.

As the year progressed, the parents could decipher their children's invented spellings and gradually became impressed with the content and length of their writing. The parents of Jeremy's classmates shared this information with parents of other children, educating them about developmentally appropriate education for young children. The principal, Mr. Hibbs, also became very interested in the writing in Jeremy's first grade classroom. In fact, he was so impressed that at the end of the year, he and Ms. Woods made a presentation to the school board and other administrators. As a result, in-service meetings were scheduled throughout the school district to acquaint other first grade teachers of developmentally appropriate practice in promoting the development of writing in young children. ■

Advocacy—actively taking a position that promotes the quality of life for young children and their families.

Ms. Wood helped to promote developmentally appropriate practice beyond her classroom, in the children's homes, and in the school district at large. She demonstrated an awareness of professional ethics and responsibility in influencing policy and decision making. In short, she was aware of the role she could play in **advocacy** on behalf of young children. Following is a brief discussion of the role of advocacy in the development of the early childhood professional.

Professional Responsibility and Advocacy

The NAEYC Code of Ethical Conduct (Feeney & Kipnis, 1989) also addresses the early childhood professional's ethical responsibilities to community and society. Some of these statements pertaining to advocacy include:

To work through education, research, and advocacy toward an environmentally safe world in which all children are adequately fed, sheltered and nurtured. (I–4.3, p. 28)

To work through education, research, and advocacy toward a society in which all young children have access to quality programs. (I–4.4, p. 28)

To promote knowledge and understanding of young children and their needs. To work toward greater social acknowledgement of children's rights and greater social acceptance of responsibility for their well-being (I–4.5, p. 28)

To support policies and laws that promote the well-being of children and families. To oppose those that impair their well-being. To cooperate with other individuals and groups in these efforts. (I–4.6, p. 28)

These ethical behaviors form the basis for early childhood advocacy. Goffin and Lombardi state that

Advocacy on behalf of children needs to be part of the teacher's professional and ethical responsibilities.

advocacy on behalf of children needs to become a part of our professional—and even ethical—responsibilities. Early childhood educators can serve as models of advocacy for those still unaware that the interests of children and society are mutually supportive. Advocacy is a critical vehicle for actualizing our commitment to children. Our caring cannot be restricted to our classrooms or offices if we truly want to improve the lives of children. (Goffin & Lombardi, 1989, p. 2)

Policies affecting children are made at the local, state, and national levels. Our responsibility as early childhood professionals requires that we must become knowledgeable about issues as well as sharing our professional expertise. The media, professional organizations, and appropriate policy- or decision makers can help keep early childhood professionals informed. Goffin and Lombardi (1989) suggest that there are six ways in which early childhood professionals can promote advocacy:

- Sharing our knowledge.
- Sharing our professional experiences.
- Redefining the "bottom line" for children.
- Standing up for our profession.
- Activating parental power.
- Expanding the constituency for children. (pp. 3–5)

In conclusion, true professional behavior is based on a code of ethical responsibility that requires professionals to not only provide children with developmentally appropriate opportunities to develop and learn, but also to educate other adults about young children's development and developmentally appropriate practice. In addition, early childhood professionals advocate for improvement in the lives of young children and their families in arenas outside the classroom and office. Promoting developmentally appropriate practice and advocating for young children requires that the early childhood professional be in a state of continual development and learning. Ward says, "Knowing my capacity to continue to learn throughout life, I shall vigorously pursue knowledge in early childhood education by informal and formal means" (1978, p. 21).

The Challenges of Working with Young Children

■ Ms. Wood encouraged the parents in her first grade classroom to participate in a variety of classroom activities including helping with supplies, sharing hobbies and expertise, and accompanying the class on field trips. Early in the school year, Ms. Wood asked parents to take a personal half-day from work to participate in one of the children's classroom events. Planning early in the year made it possible for a number of parents to have time away from their jobs so they could be in their child's classroom.

After parents had assisted and observed Ms. Wood's skillful interaction with the children, they frequently would remark, "I don't see how you do it with all these children." Or, they would comment, "Your job is certainly more than babysitting a bunch of kids." These comments reflect an awareness on the part of these parents that working with young children is a challenge that requires expertise.   ■

One reason young children are a challenge to work with is that, as the information in this book has demonstrated, young children generally perceive the world and process information differently than older children and adults. In addition, young children do not have the background of experience that older children and adults have. While Katz (1979) suggests that there must be differences between adult-child relationships at home and at school, young children in either context require quality time, support, care, and attention. These needs are demanding on the adults who co-exist with children at home and in settings outside the home. Another challenge in working with young children is helping other adults understand the development and learning of young children and the experiences that promote this development and learning.

Knowledge of How Young Children Develop and Learn

A solid foundation in the development and learning of young children helps early childhood professionals respond to the challenges described above. Early childhood professionals do not think less of young children because they perceive the world differently from older children and adults. Rather, child development information helps them understand these differences, respect children as learners, and provide appropriate opportunities for young children to expand and refine their developing knowledge. Katz says, "Our understanding of the nature of development helps us to answer the *when* questions in curricular planning" (Katz & Ward, 1978, p. 91).

The challenge of being an early childhood professional is great, but the rewards of helping to facilitate the development and learning of healthy and productive human beings is greater.

Early childhood professionals recognize that development is interrelated, and they therefore provide for developmentally appropriate experiences that contribute to young children's growth in all areas: social, emotional, cognitive, language, literacy, and motor. Early childhood professionals who are well grounded in child development and learning can effectively share this knowledge with other adults such as parents, administrators, and policy makers who also influence the lives of young children.

The Rewards of Working with Young Children

Knowing how young children develop and learn, how to implement developmentally appropriate education, and how to articulate this information to other adults helps the early childhood professional support the development of young children's healthy self-concepts and their sense of empowerment as learners, providing the foundation for successful and productive lives. Marshall (1989)

Role of the Early Childhood Professional

Continuing to Develop as a Professional

1. Be aware of the importance of knowledge of the life course and its influence upon self-understanding and the understanding of adults in personal and professional relationships.
2. Be aware of the importance of adult life course events and the impact of these events upon the interrelationships of adults and children in the home and in the learning environment.
3. Be aware of the dynamic process of becoming an early childhood professional.
4. Be aware of professional ethics and responsibility in promoting developmentally appropriate practice for young children.
5. Be aware of professional ethics and responsibility in educating other adults about developmentally appropriate education.
6. Be aware of professional ethics and responsibility in becoming an advocate for improving the lives of young children and their families beyond the classroom and the office.

summarizes research that supports the importance of knowledge of child development and developmentally appropriate practice in facilitating the development of positive self-concepts and sense of control in young children:

- Developmentally appropriate materials that challenge, provide for success, and are accessible promote feelings of competence and confidence in the young children who use these materials (Bredekamp, 1987).
- Developmentally inappropriate experiences can have negative effects on children's self-concepts regarding ability (Marshall & Weinstein, 1984; Rosenholtz & Rosenholtz, 1981; Stipek & Daniels, 1988).
- Low self-concept is associated with lowered academic achievement, emotional problems, and delinquency (Harter, 1983).
- Attempts to help parents understand children's feelings and behavior and to implement practices that promote self-esteem increase children's self-concepts both at the pre-primary and primary grade levels (Summerling & Ward, 1978).
- In mainstream American culture, a sense of control and seeing oneself as a causal agent with the ability to control the environment are dependent upon self-esteem and perceptions of competence (Harter, 1983).

Recall the quote from the beginning of Chapter 1: "There are two lasting gifts we can give our children. . . .one is roots, the other is wings." Knowledge of how children grow and learn helps early childhood professionals promote the development of positive self-concepts, a positive attitude toward learning, and a sense of control in young children—the gifts of roots and wings. The challenge of being an early childhood professional is great, but the rewards and gifts of helping to facilitate the development of healthy and productive human beings are even greater. The authors hope this text has provided you with the foundation for becoming a competent early childhood professional and a knowledge of how young children develop and learn. Best wishes as you continue your development as an early childhood professional.

Key Terms

life span
life course
career perspective
career ladder
career path

mentor
master teacher
ethics
reflecting-in-action
advocacy

Review Strategies/Activities

1. What were the life cycle events you envisioned during your adolescence? Have these events occurred according to your timetable? Why or why not? What kinds of stress have resulted? How did you handle this stress?
2. Interview some early childhood professionals about stressors in their professional lives. How do they cope?
3. Interview several early childhood professionals who have varying amounts of experience. Ask them about their interests and concerns at various times during their career—first year, second year, third through fifth years, and beyond the fifth year.
4. Talk with several experienced early childhood professionals about their career paths. How has each career path provided the opportunity for additional growth and learning?
5. Ask several early childhood professionals how they educate adults (parents, other teachers, and administrators) regarding developmentally appropriate practice.
6. Make a list of the ways you will educate adults about developmentally appropriate practice in your classroom.
7. Invite the public policy chairperson of you local early childhood organization or teacher organization to discuss the advocacy process in your community, your state or the nation.

Further Readings

Development and Life Span

Erikson, E. (1963). *Childhood and society* (2nd ed.). New York: Norton.

Sheehy, G. (1976). *Passages: Predictable crises of adult life.* New York: E. P. Dutton.

Sheehy, G. (1982). *Pathfinders.* New York: E. P. Dutton.
    These three books view adult development from a stage perspective.

Hareven, T. (1982). *Family time and industrial time*. Cambridge: Cambridge University Press.

>This book emphasizes the life course approach to development in adulthood. The influence of family life and work in a New England mill town on lifelong development is depicted.

Lazarus, R. S., & Folkman, S. (1984). *Stress, appraisal, and coping*. New York: Springer.

>This book views adulthood as a series of transitions varying from one individual to another. An examination of the nature of stress caused by these transitions can promote coping and personal growth.

Professional Development

Dresden, J., & Myers, B. K. (January, 1989). Early childhood professionals: Toward self-definition. *Young Children, 44 (2)*, 62–66.

>This article provides information regarding some of the myths of professional development, in particular, the myths of hierarchical power, the career ladder, and lifestyles that exclude other commitments. Political realities are discussed and techniques for empowering early childhood professionals are presented.

Gehrke, N. J. (1987). *On becoming a teacher*. West Lafayette, IN: Kappa Delta Pi Publications.

>This book is an important resource in helping teachers understand the stages in becoming a professional. It provides insight for people who have decided to become teachers and provides needed information for the practicing and beginning teacher.

Katz, L. G. (1977). *Talks with teachers: Reflections on early childhood education*. Washington, DC: The National Association for the Education of Young Children.

>This book discusses the developmental stages of teachers of young children. It presents various approaches to in-service education and describes how to work with young children.

Advocacy

Black, J. K., & Puckett, M. B. (1987). Informing others about developmentally appropriate practice. In S. Bredekamp, (Ed.), *Developmentally appropriate practice in early childhood programs serving children from birth through age 8* (pp. 83–87). Washington, DC: The National Association for the Education of Young Children.

>This chapter helps the reader understand the backgrounds and motivations of those adults who may not be aware of developmentally appropriate practice. Specific suggestions are given to help early childhood professionals promote developmentally appropriate practice among adults who influence the development and learning of young children.

Bredekamp, S. (Ed.). (1987). *Developmentally appropriate practice in early childhood programs serving children from birth through age 8*. Washington, DC: The National Association for the Education of Young Children.

>See the Further Readings section in Chapter 2 for information regarding position statements on developmentally appropriate practice.

Feeney, S., & Kipnis, K. (1989). The National Association for the Education of Young Children Code of ethical conduct and statement of commitment, *Young Children, 45* (1), 24–29.

>This article provides background information regarding the development of NAEYC's Code of Ethical Conduct. The code addresses ideals and principles in four areas: ethical responsibilities to children, ethical responsibilities to parents, ethical respon-

sibilities to colleagues, and ethical responsibilities to community and society. It also includes the Statement of Commitment as presented in Figure 18.3.

Goffin, S. G., & Lombardi, J. (1989). *Speaking out: Early childhood advocacy.* Washington, DC: The National Association for the Education of Young Children.

This book is a must for every early childhood professional. It provides very complete information regarding the advocacy process. Information shared regarding the legislative process, samples of letters, suggestions for phone calls, visits, and testifying are included. Appendices provide information regarding the United States Congress and the path of legislation, the Executive Branch, information to share with decisionmakers, lobbying for non-profits, guides for developing legislation for young children, resources for early childhood advocates, and a list of national organizations concerned with young children.

Jensen, M. A., & Chevalier, L. W. (1990). *Issues and advocacy in early childhood education.* Boston: Allyn & Bacon.

This book is a collection of articles concerning various issues and advocacy in early childhood education. Topics addressed include sex role development and education, television, health and nutrition, abuse, mainstreaming disabled and high-risk children, multicultrual and bilingual education, parent involvement, and individual rights and education. Advocacy for the professional and the profession, including policy and regulations, is also addressed.

Seefelt, C., & Barbour, N. (May, 1988). They said 'I had to . . . :' Working with mandates. *Young Children, 43,* 4–8.

This article discusses mandates and emphasizes the role of early childhood professionals in promoting developmentally appropriate practice. Appropriate procedures for dealing with mandates and resources are provided.

Standards for Quality Programming for Young Children: Early Childhood Education and the Elementary School Principal. (1990). National Association of Elementary School Principals, 1615 Duke Street, Alexandria, VA, 22314. (703) 684-3345.

This publication needs to be in the library of every early childhood professional and given to every elementary school principal. It addresses the development of young children, appropriate curriculum, personnel, accountability, parents and the community, and provides a checklist for applying standards of developmentally appropriate practice in early childhood education programs.

Glossary

Abortion: the ending of a pregnancy, usually during the first trimester.

Accommodation: the cognitive process by which patterns of thought (schemata) and related behaviors are modified to conform to new information or experience (Piaget).

Achievement test: a test that measures what children have learned as a result of instruction.

Acquired Immune Deficiency Syndrome (AIDS): a virus that can be transmitted from the mother to the fetus/embryo via the placenta, and that attacks the immune system, causing death from illnesses that the immune system cannot prevent.

Adaptation: the process by which one adjusts to changes in the environment.

Adipose: the name for tissue in which there is an accumulation of connective tissue cells, each containing a relatively large deposit of fat.

Adolescence: the time of rapid development between the later childhood years and adulthood.

Advocacy: actively taking a position that promotes the quality of life for young children and their families.

Afterbirth: the placenta, after it moves from the uterus and is expelled.

Alphafetoprotein test (AFP): a blood test which can identify disorders in the brain or spinal column in the fetus.

Altruism: intentions to help others without the expectation of reward.

Amniocentesis: a technique that involves extracting amniotic fluid from the uterus for the purpose of detecting all chromosomal and over 100 biomedical disorders.

Anecdotal record: a type of narrative observation describing in detail an incident after it occurs.

Anemia: a condition caused by a lack of red blood cells.

Anomaly: a deviation from the norm.

Anorexia: a severe disorder usually seen in teenage girls which is characterized by self-starvation.

Anoxia: the condition that is caused by the lack of oxygen in the brain of an infant during labor and delivery and can cause brain damage.

Apgar score: a score which rates the physical condition of newborns in the areas of appearance, pulse, grimace, activity, and respiration.

Apnea: absence of breathing for a period of up to 20 seconds.

Approximations: children's attempts at conventional oral or written language which, when produced, are not quite conventional.

Assimilation: the process of incorporating new motor or conceptual learning into existing schemata (Piaget).

Associative play: a loosely organized form of social play that is characterized by overt social behaviors indicating common activities, shared interests, and interpersonal associations.

At-risk: children who have been or are in prebirth or after-birth environments that do not promote typical physical/motor, psychosocial, cognitive, language, and literacy development.

Attachment: a strong emotional relationship between two persons, characterized by mutual affection and a desire to maintain proximity.

Atypical: not typical.

Authoritarian discipline: a child-rearing style in which parents apply rigid standards of conduct and expect unquestioning obedience from the child.

Authoritative discipline: a child-rearing style in which child behavior is directed through rational and reasoned guidance from the adult.

Autonomy: a sense of independence or self-government.

Balance: a body awareness component in which postural adjustments prevent one from falling.

Behavioral theory: the theory that emphasizes the importance of directly observable behavior as influenced by the environment rather than genetic factors or other unobservable forces such as motivation.

Biological Model: the explanation of cognitive development as influenced by biological processes of growth and development in the brain.

Body awareness: the individual's cognizance of his or her body and its parts, and one's internal and external controls over its capabilities.

Bonding: a complex psychobiological connection between the parent and infant.

Book handling knowledge: knowledge of front and back of books, where the story begins, the left-to-right progression of pages, and differences between print and illustrations.

Botulism: an often fatal food poisoning.

Breech birth: a birth in which a part other than the head presents itself for delivery first, usually the buttocks, feet, or in some cases the umbilical cord.

Bulimia: a severe disorder usually seen in teenage girls, which is characterized by binging and then self-induced vomiting.

Career ladder: the idea that the professionals' career advancement involves moving up from position to position and that each step up involves increased authority and rewards.

Career path: the idea that professional development can involve moving to a different position that provides new opportunities for learning and growth, rather than increased authority.

Career perspective: the idea that development of early childhood professionals continues throughout their careers and is unique to each person.

Centration: the preoperational child's inclination to attend to one aspect of a situation.

Cephalocaudal: refers to the head to tail or long axis of the body.

Cerebral cortex: the outer layer of the cerebral hemisphere made up of gray tissue that is mostly responsible for higher nervous functions.

Cervix: the opening of the uterus.

Cesarean: the surgical procedure during which an incision is made through abdominal and uterine walls of the mother to deliver the baby.

Checklist: a list of developmental behaviors that the observer identifies as present or absent.

Chorionic villus test (CVT): a test that analyzes samples of the hair-like projections (chorionic villi) of tissue in the placenta for purposes of determining chromosomal disorders (can be done earlier than amniocentesis).

Chromosomes: ordered groups of genes within the nucleus of a cell.

Classical conditioning theory: the first idea regarding behavior theory, based upon Pavlov's experiment that repeated pairing of two events conditions the same response to either event.

Class inclusion: understanding the relationship between class and sub-class, which occurs during the period of concrete operational thought.

Clostridium botulinum: bacteria that causes botulism.

Cognitive development: the aspect of development that deals with thinking, problem-solving, intelligence, and language.

Cognitive science: the investigation of the knowledge and strategies used in the cognitive process which distinguish expert cognitive processes from novice cognitive processes.

Cognitive theory: the theory that explains the development of learning in terms of how children think and process information, usually associated with Piaget, and more recently, the information process theorists.

Colostrum: first liquid secreted by the mammary glands soon after childbirth.

Comprehension: understanding the meaning of print.

Concept clusters: organization of the tools of the world into categories or patterns of thinking (Vygotsky).

Concrete operational stage: according to Piaget, the stage when children, approximately 7–11 years of age, can use logical reasoning (rather than relying upon perceptions) in situations that are concrete, that is, involve objects and events in the child's immediate environment.

Configuration: the general shape or outline of a word.

Congenital malformations: skeletal or body system abnormalities caused by defective genes within the chromosomes that usually affect the developing embryo during the first 8 weeks of pregnancy.

Conservation: the ability to understand that the physical attributes (e.g., mass and weight) stay the same even if appearance changes.

Constancy of position in space: the notion that letters of the alphabet must have fixed positions if they are to maintain their identity.

Contraction: the movement of the muscles of the uterus, which forces the baby through the cervical opening and into the birth canal.

Conversational conditions and constraints: appropriate behaviors and procedures used during communication, such as taking turns speaking and terminating conversations.

Cooperative play: a well-organized form of social play characterized by well-defined social roles within play groups, influential peer leaders, and shared materials and equipment in order to pursue a well-understood group play theme.

Correlational study: research that attempts to determine a relationship between two or more sets of measurements.

Creative vocabulary: when young children create new words to meet the need for words they have not learned, have forgotten, or for which there is no word in the language system.

Critical period: a time of physiological and/or psychological sensitivity during which the normal development of a major organ or structural system must take place or permanent damage to body structure and/or behavior will result.

Cross sectional study: research that studies children of different ages at the same time.

Deciduous teeth: the first set of teeth, which erupts during infancy; often called temporary or baby teeth. Will later be replaced by a set of 36 permanent teeth.

Defense mechanism: a psychological response to ego threat, frustration, or failure.

Deferred imitation: the ability to imitate behaviors which the child has observed at an earlier time or another place—occurs near the end of the sensorimotor stage.

Deprivation dwarfism: a retardation in physical growth thought to be triggered by insufficient emotional support.

Descriptive: research collected by observing and recording behavior, providing a description of the observed behavior.

Developmental milestones: significant events during the course of growth and development.

Developmental screening test: a test that determines if a child is developing normally.

Developmentally appropriate: pertains to (1) age appropriateness, the universal and predictable patterns of growth and development that occur in children from birth through age eight; and (2) individual appropriateness, the individual rates and patterns of physical/motor, psychosocial, cognition, language and literacy development, personality and learning style, and family and cultural background of each young child.

Developmentally delayed: a course of development that is significantly slower than is typical.

Developmentally inappropriate: pertains to adult expectations that are not age-appropriate or individually appropriate for children from birth through age eight.

Dexterity: quick, precise movements and coordination of the hands and fingers.

Diagnostic test: a test that identifies a child's strengths or weaknesses in a certain area.

Dialects: different forms of language used by various ethnic groups or by people who live in certain geographic regions.

Dilation: the gradual opening of the cervix, which occurs in the first stage of labor.

Directionality: pertains to the perceptual awareness of direction.

Disabilities: conditions in children such as mental retardation, hearing impairments, visual impairments, emotional disturbances, orthopedic impairments, other health impairments, learning disabilities, or multiple disabilities which require special education and services.

Disequilibrium: the imbalance in thinking causing the child to assimilate or accommodate (Piaget).

DNA: deoxyribonucleic acid, the substance in genes that has the information that causes the formation of chains of protein that stimulate the development of tissue and organs and affects other genes and physiological functions.

Dyslexia: a general term for the condition affecting the auditory and visual processes so that print cannot be perceived without distortion.

Early childhood development: the study of the physical/motor, psychosocial, cognitive, language, and literacy development in children from prebirth through age eight.

Echolalia: the infant's babbling of one sound repeated over and over.

Ecological systems theory: the theory that argues that a variety of social systems influences the development of children. (Brofenbrenner)

Egocentrism: the tendency to view the world from one's own perspective; the inability to see another point of view.

Electronic fetal monitor: a device used during labor which is attached to the abdomen of the pregnant woman or the scalp of the fetus, to determine fetal heart rate.

Embryonic stage: the first eight weeks of pregnancy, during which the major organ systems are formed.

Empathy: involves experiencing the feelings or emotions that someone else is experiencing.

Environment: the experiences, conditions, objects, and people which directly or indirectly influence the development and behavior of a child.

Episiotomy: an incision sometimes made in the opening of the vulva to prevent its tearing during birth.

Equilibration: the process of establishing a balance of thinking (Piaget).

Ethics: a set of standards describing the responsibilities in terms of behaviors and conduct with regard to a particular profession.

Event sampling: an observation technique for recording when certain events occur.

Expansions: responses to young children's use of overgeneralizations by using the conventional form in the conversational context.

Experimental study: research that involves treating two or more groups, each in different ways to determine cause-and-effect relationships.

Extensions: responses to children's language that extend the meaning of their language.

Extensors: muscles that act to stretch or extend a limb.

Extinguish: stopping a behavior or response by not reinforcing it over a period of time.

Extrafamilial: actions and behaviors occurring outside the immediate family.

Extrafamilial relationships: those relationships that include people outside the immediate or extended family.

Failure to thrive: a condition in which apparently healthy infants fail to grow normally.

Fast mapping: term used to describe children's rapid learning of language by relating a word to an internalized concept and remembering it after only one encounter with that word.

Fatherese: modification in the father's speech when talking with young children. Can differ from motherese.

Fetal alcohol syndrome (FAS): the physical and mental abnormalities found in babies whose mothers consumed excessive amounts of alcohol during pregnancy.

Fetal stage: the stage that begins after the first eight weeks of pregnancy and continues until birth.

Fetus: the developing human from 9 weeks after conception until birth.

Figure-ground discrimination: the ability to focus on the dominant figure in a picture without being distracted by elements in its background.

Flexors: muscles that act to bend a joint.

Fontanelles: membranous space between cranial bones of the fetus and infant.

Forceps: a surgical instrument similar to tongs, applied to the head of the fetus to speed delivery.

Formal: refers to information gathered about young children, usually through standardized tests.

Formal operations: according to Piaget, the fourth and final stage of cognitive development, which occurs during adolescence, when mental operations can be performed without concrete objects and abstract thinking begins.

Fraternal twins: twins whose development began by the fertilization of two ova (eggs) by two sperm, causing both twins to have different genetic codes.

Functions of language: the various uses of language, which accomplish a variety of communication purposes.

Fundamental movements: coordinations that are basic to all other movement abilities.

Gender: the maleness or femaleness of the zygote as determined by the kind of sperm fertilizing the ovum (Y sperm—genetically male; X sperm—genetically female).

Gender constancy: the realization that one's gender remains the same regardless of age or changes in clothing, hairstyles, or wishes.

Gender identity: one's understanding that one is (biologically) male or female.

Gender role: the public expression of one's gender identity.

Genes: molecules of DNA that store and transmit the characteristics of past generations.

Genetic counseling: information provided to parents or prospective parents regarding the possibility and nature of genetic disorders in their offspring.

Genotype: the combination of genes inherited from both parents and their ancestors.

Gifted: children who give evidence of high performance in various areas of development.

Heredity: the inherited characteristics of humans carried by genes.

Heteronomous morality: a morality that is governed by others rather than self.

Holophrasic: refers to the infant's use of one word to convey a phrase or sentence.

Hypotheses: hunches about the development of young children, usually examined through research.

Identical twins: twins whose development began when the zygote split into two identical halves, thus ensuring that both twins have the identical genetic code.

Identity constancy: the understanding that a person or species remains the same, even though appearance is changed through masks or costumes, which occurs during the late preoperational stage.

Idiosyncratic concepts: ideas of the preoperational child, based on personal experience and overgeneralized to other situations.

Indirect speech act: speech that infers more than the actual uttered words.

Inductive discipline: a positive, nonpunitive form of discipline that relies on reasons and rationales to help children control their behaviors.

Industry: Erikson's psychosocial stage during which the child is mastering social and academic skills sufficient to feel self-assured. The opposite result of this "nuclear crisis" is a sense of inferiority.

Infant mortality: deaths during the first year of life.

Informal: refers to information gathered about young children through approaches other than standardized tests.

Information processing theory: a theory of cognitive development that suggests that the mind is similar to the information processing system of a computer, and unlike Piaget, emphasizes similarities of the thinking of children and adults.

Initiative: the third of Erikson's psychosocial stages, in which the child pursues ideas, individual interests, and activities; when thwarted the child becomes self-critical and experiences guilt.

Inservice: individuals who have completed teacher training programs and have accepted jobs teaching or serving young children.

Intelligence test: a test that measures those abilities designated as a sign of intelligence.

Interactional competence: the repertoire of behaviors that help young children communicate effectively with others.

Interview: asking the child predetermined questions on a one-to-one basis to find out more about the child.

Intrafamilial: actions and behaviors within the immediate family.

Invented spelling: spelling that young children create based upon their own knowledge of sound-symbol relationships and that over a period of time evolves into conventional spelling behaviors.

Irreversibility: the inability of preoperational children to reverse their thinking and to return to their original point of thought.

Isolette: small cribs that provide a controlled environment for newborns who are considered at risk.

Kinesthetic: the sensation of body.

Labor: the three stages of the birth process: dilation, birth of the baby, and discharge of the placenta.

Lamaze method: a method developed by Fernand Lamaze that involves the training of the prospective mother and a partner/coach in breathing and relaxation techniques to be used during labor.

Language acquisition device (LAD): an innate mental mechanism believed by some linguists to make language development possible.

Later childhood: the period of development between the early childhood years and adolescence, ages 9 through 11.

Least restrictive environment: the least specialized classroom, or "regular" classroom, which is viewed as the best learning environment for the student.

Leboyer method: a technique used during childbirth to help the baby in the transition from life inside to outside the uterus; characterized by warm delivery rooms, muted lighting, soothing music, a warm bath, etc.

Left/right dominance: occurs when one or the other side of the body takes the lead in motor coordination activities such as eating or writing.

Levels of processing theory: an information processing model that focuses upon the depth of attention rather than aspects of memory in explaining levels of cognitive performance.

Life-course: the idea that views development and behavior from birth to death as influenced by major life events rather than well-defined stages.

Life span: the idea that development is a life-long process and is influenced by biological, environmental, and historical causes.

Locomotor: the ability to move independently from place to place.

Logico-mathematical knowledge: knowledge that is primarily constructed from children's actions on and interpretations of objects.

Longitudinal study: research that collects information about the same subjects at different ages over a period of time.

Low birth weight: a weight at birth of less than $5\frac{1}{2}$ pounds or 2500 grams.

Low-risk: children who have been and continue to be in settings that facilitate normal physical/motor, psychosocial, cognitive, language, and literacy development.

Mainstream: the practice of incorporating children with disabilities into the regular classroom.

Master teachers: early childhood professionals who are recognized as outstanding in implementing developmentally appropriate practice.

Maturation theory: usually refers to Gesell's theory that suggests that the patterns of growth and development are genetically predetermined and cannot be influenced by environmental stimulation or training to any great degree.

Mental symbols: the behaviors that occur at the beginning of the preoperational stage, including speech, imitation of others, and using one object to represent another.

Mentor: an experienced early childhood professional who provides support and guidance to a beginning teacher.

Metabolic: pertains to the body's complex chemical conversion of food into substances and energy necessary for maintenance of life.

Metacognition: an awareness or knowledge of how one processes information and thought.

Metalanguage: talk about language itself.

Metalinguistic awareness: the ability to think about the forms and meanings of language.

Meta memory: an awareness or knowledge about the ways one's memory processes work.

Moral behavior: the ability to consider the needs and welfare of others and exhibit appropriate behaviors consistent with a set of standards or value orientation.

Moral realism: a morality that focuses on rules and the seriousness of the consequences of an act, rather than the intentions behind the act.

Moral relativism: a morality that focuses on the judgment of situations and intentions underlying individual behavior, rather than focusing solely on consequences of an act.

Morpheme: the smallest unit of meaning in oral or written language.

Motherese: modification in the mother's speech when talking with young children.

Motor fitness: a physical state in which motor coordination facilitates speed, agility, power, and balance.

Multicultural education: Learning experiences that help young children become more aware of and appreciate the commonalities as well as the diversity of various cultural and ethnic groups.

Myelination: the process of covering the nerve cells within the central nervous system with fatty tissue (myelin), which promotes efficient transmission impulses along the neurons.

Narrative observation: a written observation of behavior as it occurs.

Neonatal Behavioral Assessment Scale (NBAS or Brazelton Scale): an assessment of 16 reflexes, responsiveness, state changes, and ability to calm self in the newborn.

Neonatal period: the first four weeks of life.

Neo-Piagetians: researchers who support Piaget's ideas, but are updating his theory according to recent findings about cognitive development.

Nonmaternal care: child care provided by someone other than the child's mother.

Nonparental care: child care provided by someone other than the child's parent.

Norms: average ages of important developmental behaviors or average scores on tests, which according to statistical procedures should be based upon large samples, representative of the whole population.

Object permanence: the realization that objects and people continue to exist even though they may not be visible or detected through other senses.

Operant conditioning: Skinner's term for the voluntary change or modification in behavior as a result of reinforcement or punishment.

Ossify: to convert cartilage or membrane to bone.

Overextension: when young children use a word to refer to a similar but different object, situation, or category.

Overgeneralized speech: the use of a single word or label to represent an entire category of objects similar in use or appearance.

Overnutrition: overconsumption of nutrients needed for growth.

Parallel play: activities in which two or more children play near one another while engaged in independent activities.

Peers: other children who are the same age as a particular child.

Percentile: a statistical measure that ranks subjects from lowest to highest based on a common characteristic or results of an assessment.

Perception: the physiological process by which sensory input is interpreted.

Perceptually bound: young, preoperational children's explanations for certain phenomena because it "looks" that way.

Perceptual motor: interrelationship between perception and motor abilities.

Period of equilibrium: a phase in development during which the child appears to be well-adjusted and reasonably content (Gesell).

Period of disequilibrium: a phase in development during which the child seems less well-adjusted and exhibits tensions and uncertainties (Gesell).

Permissive discipline: a noncontrolling, nondemanding form of discipline in which the child, for the most part, is allowed to regulate his or her own behavior.

Perspective-taking: the ability to understand another's point of view.

Phonics: the sound-symbol relationship of a language system.

Phonology: the speech sounds of a particular language system.

Physical fitness: a physical state in which muscular strength, endurance, flexibility, and the circulatory-respiratory systems are all in optimal condition.

Physical knowledge: knowledge of physical characteristics of objects and events gained through sensorimotor interactions.

Placenta: the organ attached to the wall of the uterus that transmits nutrients from the mother to the embryo/fetus and filters wastes from the embryo/fetus to the mother.

Portfolio: a collection that contains child products, e.g., art, written work, and related materials, all of which are dated and used to document development and learning over a period of time.

Postpartum depression: a period of depression affecting most mothers for a few days and in some cases for weeks and months after childbirth.

Power assertive discipline: a form of discipline in which the "power" of the adult is used to coerce, deprive of privileges or material goods, or use physical punishment to modify a child's behavior.

Predictable books: books that have repeated patterns and predictable text.

Prehension: the coordination of fingers and thumb to grasp.

Premoral: that period in early childhood when the child is unaware of moral rules or values.

Prenatal: the time from conception until birth, an average of 266 days or 38 weeks.

Preoperational: the second of Piaget's stages of

cognitive development, in which children from the ages of 2 to approximately 8 develop the ability to internally represent sensorimotor actions, but cannot engage in the operational or logical thinking of older children and adults.

Pre-primary: the time in young children's lives before they enter primary (first, second, or third) grades.

Preservice: individuals who are in training to teach or serve young children.

Preterm: infants born several weeks before the full term (38 weeks) of pregnancy.

Primary child caregiver: the person from whom the child receives nonparental care and with whom a warm relationship can form.

Primary circular reactions: simple, pleasurable, repetitive acts that are centered on the infant's body.

Primary disabilities: learning disabilities involving attention, memory, and predictable text.

Primitive reflexes: reflexes controlled by subcortical structures in the brain that gradually disappear during the first year of life.

Private speech: speech to oneself that helps direct one's own behavior or communication with oneself.

Private spelling: invented spelling or spelling that young children create to meet their personal communication needs before they learn public or conventional spelling.

Professionals: individuals who have internalized the knowledge base of their particular field and can implement this knowledge in appropriate practice.

Prosocial behavior: behavior that benefits others—helping, sharing, comforting, and defending.

Proximity seeking: the child's attempts to maintain nearness and contact with the attachment figure.

Proximodistal: refers to the direction from body's center outward to the extremities.

Psychoanalytic theory: the ideas of personality development as presented in Freud's psychosexual and Erikson's psychosocial theories.

Psychological state: pertains to conditions of arousal and alertness in infancy.

Psychosexual theory: Freud's theory that suggests that sexual drives play an important role in personality development.

Psychosocial theory: Erikson's theory that argues that social interactions are more important than sexual drives in personality development.

Puberty: the biological developments that result in the ability to produce children.

Public spelling: conventional spelling that children learn over a period of time during the schooling process.

Random: assigning children to experimental and control groups so that each child has the same chance of being selected.

Rating scale: a scale with various traits or categories that allows the observer to indicate the importance of the observed behaviors.

Readiness test: a test that measures what beginning skills children have in order to predict whether they will succeed in a new learning task, e.g., reading.

Recessive gene: a gene that carries a trait that may not appear unless a gene for the same trait is inherited from both parents.

Reflecting-in-action: thinking about one's professional behavior while engaging in that behavior for purposes of evaluation and articulation of developmentally appropriate practice.

Reflexes: unlearned, involuntary response to stimuli.

Registers: variations in the style of speech according to varying social settings.

Reliability: the consistency with which various research methods produce the same results or relatively similar results for each individual from one administration to the next within a short period of time.

Representative sample: a sample of children from approximately the same proportions as are in the population as a whole regarding age, gender, racial and ethnic background, georgraphic location, and socioeconomic level.

Resource persons: persons outside the educational setting who can provide information about young children's development and learning, usually from health-related fields.

Reversals: printing letters or words in reverse.

Rh factor: a treatable condition in the mother that produces antibodies that destroy the red blood cells of her second baby and subsequent babies.

Rich interpretation: the acknowledging that young children know more than they can verbally express and that they use nonverbal behaviors to communicate.

Rubella: virus which can cause birth disorders if the mother contracts during the first three months of pregnancy (also known as German measles).

Running record: a type of narrative observation that records all behavior as it occurs.

Satiation: feeling of fullness or adequate intake of food.

Scaffolding: according to Vygotsky the process of adults or more skilled children facilitating concept development or classification in young children by providing verbal information.

Schemata: mental concepts or patterns, plural for schema (Piaget).

Scripts: the knowledge of a social procedure or event, which includes sequence of events and of roles, often observed in young children in play contexts.

Secondary circular reactions: simple, pleasurable, repetitive acts centered on external objects.

Secondary disabilities: learning disabilities involving thinking and oral language.

Self-actualization: according to Maslow, the process of having basic physical and social/emotional needs met so that individuals can become creative, contributing members of society and feel positive about themselves.

Self-awareness: refers to infant's perception of himself or herself as distinct and separate from other people and objects.

Self-concept: one's sense of oneself as separate and uniquely different from others.

Self-control: the ability to govern one's own behavior.

Self-definition: refers to the criteria by which the self is defined; e.g., age, size, and physical and mental abilities.

Self-esteem: refers to one's positive or negative self-evaluation.

Self-recognition: refers to the infant's ability to recognize his or her image in a mirror, photograph, or other representation.

Semantics: the meaning of language.

Sensorimotor: learning that occurs through the senses and motor activities.

Separation anxiety: fear of being separated from the attachment figure.

Service words: words that help hold a sentence together; e.g., "the" and "to."

Shading: gradually changing the topic of conversation.

Sight words: words that young children recognize immediately.

Signs: internalized representations that are later associated with tools of the world (Vygotsky).

Skeletal age: a measure of physical development based on examination of skeletal x-rays.

Social cognition: the ability to understand the thoughts, intentions, and behaviors of oneself and of others.

Social learning theory: a behavioral theory that argues that learning can also occur through observing others, thus emphasizing the role modeling of other persons the child observes directly and in various types of media.

Sociocentric: the opposite of egocentric; a state in which interests and concerns are focused on others and the person is generally sociable.

Sociocultural Model: the explanation of cognitive development as influenced by various sociocultural experiences within the family, community, and society.

Specimen record: a type of narrative observation that provides detailed information about a particular event, child, or time of day.

Standardized test: a test that is administered and scored according to set procedures and has scores that can be interpreted according to statistical measures representative of the group for which the test was designed.

Stranger anxiety: fear of strangers characterized by avoidance, crying, or other distress signals.

Subcortical: the portion of the brain just below the cerebral cortex responsible for controlling unlearned and reflexive behavior.

Support staff: other persons within the educational setting who support the learning and development of young children; e.g., nurses, social workers, diagnosticians, psychologists, secretaries, cooks, and custodians.

Survival reflexes: reflexes that are essential to basic survival skills.

Syndrome: a group of combined symptoms that characterize a physiological or psychological disorder.

Syntax: the grammar or structure of a particular language system.

Telegraphic speech: children's early speech which, like a telegram, only includes words necessary to understanding meaning.

Television literacy: understanding the specialized symbolic code conveyed through the medium of television.

Temperament: an individual's behavior style.

Teratogens: environmental factors such as viruses and chemical substances that can cause abnormalities in the developing embryo or fetus.

Tertiary circular reactions: reactions in children between 12 and 18 months of age that indicate that the toddlers are experimenting in order to develop knowledge of the environment around them (Piaget's Substage 5 in the sensorimotor period).

Theories: ideas that are organized in a systematic manner based upon observations or other kinds of evidence and are used to explain and predict the behaviors and development of young children, older children, and adults.

Time sampling: an observation technique for recording how often certain behaviors occur over time.

Toilet learning: a gradual maturational process from which the child can gain control over elimination.

Tools of the world: the language and objects of the external world (Vygotsky).

Toxemia: a disease for which the causes are unknown, occurring in the last trimester of pregnancy, which can cause death to both mother and child.

Toxoplasmosis: a microorganism that can be transmitted from cat droppings or raw meat to the mother and to the fetus or embryo via the placenta, causing birth disorders.

Transductive reasoning: according to Piaget, reasoning that occurs in the preoperational stage and involves the young child's attention to the specifics of the immediate situation rather than all aspects of an event.

Transformation: attending to all the states of an event from the beginning to in-between to final stage.

Transitional object: an object, usually a soft, cuddly item, to which a child becomes attached.

Transivity: the ability to representationally seriate or order according to size, which usually occurs in the period of concrete operational thought.

Trimester: the first, second, or third three months of pregnancy.

Ultrasound: a technique that uses sound frequencies to detect structural disorders and the approximate week of pregnancy.

Undernutrition: inadequate intake of nutrients essential for growth.

Validity: the degree to which an instrument or procedure measures what it is intended to measure.

Vernix caseosa: the oily covering that protects the skin of the fetus.

Vocables: early sound patterns used by infants which approximate words.

Washout effect: the decline of gains in intelligence and achievement scores several years after the termination of the intervention program for young children.

Word analysis skills: the ability to analyze words using a variety of strategies; e.g., rhyming words.

Working model: mental construct or image of an event or set of circumstances.

Zone of proximal development: according to Vygotsky, the level of concept development that is too difficult for the child to accomplish alone, but can be achieved with the help of adults or more skilled children.

Zygote: the first cell resulting from the fertilization of the ovum by the sperm.

References

Abelman, R. (1984). Children and TV: The ABC's of TV literacy. *Childhood Education, 60,* 200–205.

Aboud, F. (1988). *Children and prejudice.* Cambridge, MA: Basil Blackwell.

Abramovitch, R., Corter, C., Pepler, D. J., & Stanhope, L. (1986). Sibling and peer interaction: A final follow-up and a comparison. *Child Development, 57,* 217–229.

Ackerman, B. (1982). Contextual integration and utterance interpretation: The ability of children and adults to interpret sarcastic utterances. *Child Development, 53,* 1075–1083.

Ackerman-Ross, S., & Khanna, P. (1989). The relationship of high quality day care to middle-class 3-year-olds' language performance. *Early Childhood Research Quarterly, 4,* 97–116.

Adamson, L. B., & Bakeman, R. (1985). Affect and attention: Infants observed with mothers and peers. *Child Development, 56,* 582–593.

Adickes, E., & Schuman, R. (1981). Fetal muscles and alcohol. *Journal of Pediatric Pathology.*

Adler, R. P., Lesser, G. S., Meringoff, L. K., Robertson, T. S., Rossiter, J. R., & Ward, S. (1980). *The effects of television advertising on children.* Lexington, MA: Heath.

Ainsworth, M. D. S. (1962). The effects of maternal deprivation: A review of findings and controversy in the context of research strategy. In World Health Organization, *Deprivation of maternal care: A reassessment of its effects* (Public Health Paper No. 14, pp. 97–165). Geneva: Author.

Ainsworth, M. D. S. (1967). *Infancy in Uganda: Infant care and the growth of love.* Baltimore: The Johns Hopkins Press.

Ainsworth, M. D. S. (1973). The development of infant-mother attachment. In B. M. Caldwell & H. N. Ricciuti (Eds.), *Review of child development research* (Vol. 3, pp. 1–94). Chicago: University of Chicago Press.

Ainsworth, M. D. S. (1982). Attachment: Retrospect and prospect. In C. M. Parkes & J. Stevenson-Hinde (Eds.), *The place of attachment in human behavior* (pp. 3–30). New York: Basic Books.

Ainsworth, M. D. S., Bell, S. M., & Stayton, D. J. (1974). Infant-mother attachment and social development: Socialization as a product of reciprocal responsiveness to signals. In M. P. M. Richards (Ed.), *The integration of the child into a social world* (pp. 99–135). London: Cambridge University Press.

Ainsworth, M. D. S., Blehar, M. C., Waters, E., & Wall, S. (1978). *Patterns of attachment: A psychological study of strange situations.* Hillsdale, NJ: Erlbaum.

Ainsworth, M. D. S., & Wittig, B. A. (1969). Attachment and the exploratory behavior of one-year olds in a strange situation. In B. M. Foss (Ed.), *Determinants of infant behavior* (Vol. 4, pp. 113–136). London: Methuen.

Alford, B. B., & Bogle, M. L. (1982). *Nutrition during the life cycle.* Englewood Cliffs, NJ: Prentice-Hall.

Allen, J., & Mason, J. M. (Eds.). (1989). *Risk makers, risk takers, risk breakers: Reducing the risks for young literacy learners.* Portsmouth, NH: Heinemann.

Almy, M., & Genishi, C. (1979). *Ways of studying children* (rev. ed.) New York: Teachers College Press.

American Academy of Pediatrics. (1986). *Report of the Committee on Infectious Diseases* (20th ed.). Elk Grove Village, IL: Author.

American Academy of Pediatrics. (1987). Neonatal anesthesia. *Pediatrics, 80,* 446.

American Academy of Pediatrics, Committee on Nutrition. (1976). Commentary on breast feeding and infant formulas including proposed standards for formulas. *Pediatrics, 57,* 278.

American Academy of Pediatrics, Committee on Nutrition. (1979). Commentary on breast feeding and infant formulas, including proposed standards for formulas. In American Academy of Pediatrics, *Nutrition handbook* (pp. 119–138). Evanston, IL: Author.

American Academy of Pediatrics, Committee on Nutrition. (1986). Prudent life-style for children, dietary fat and cholesterol. *Pediatrics, 78,* 521.

American Psychological Association, Committee on Ethical Standards in Psychological Research. (1972, May). Ethical standards for research with human subjects. *APA Monitor,* pp. I–XIX.

Ames, L. B., Gillespie, C., Haines, J., & Ilg, F. L. (1979). *The Gesell Institute's child from one to six.* New York: Harper and Row.

Anderson, D. R., & Smith, R. (1984). Young children's TV viewing: The problem of cognitive continuity. In F. J. Morrison & D. P. Keating (Eds.), *Applied developmental psychology* (Vol. 1, pp. 115–163). Orlando, FL: Academic Press.

Andrews, P. (1981). Children and families: Some basic cultural needs. *Dimensions, 10,* 149–151.

Anselmo, S. (1987). *Early childhood development: Prenatal through age eight.* Columbus, OH: Merrill.

Anson, B. (Ed.). (1966). *Morris' human anatomy* (12th ed.). New York: McGraw-Hill.

Anthony, J., & Benedek, T. (Eds.). (1975). *Depression and human existence.* Boston: Little, Brown.

Apgar, V. A. (1953). A proposal for a new method of evaluation in the newborn infant. *Current Research in Anesthesia and Analgesia, 32,* 260–267.

Apgar, V. A., & Beck, J. (1972). *Is my baby all right?* New York: Trident Press.

Arend, R., Gove, F. L., & Stroufe, L. A. (1979). Continuity of individual adaptation from infancy to kindergarten: A predictive study of ego-resiliency and curiosity in preschoolers. *Child Development, 50,* 950–959.

Asher, S. R., Renshaw, P. D., & Hymel, S. (1982). Peer relations and the development of social skills. In S. G. Moore & C. R. Cooper (Eds.), *The young child: Reviews of research* (Vol. 3, pp. 137–158). Washington, DC: National Association for the Education of Young Children.

Ausubel, D. P., & Sullivan, E. V. (1970). *Theory and problems of child development* (2nd ed.). New York: Grune and Stratton.

Ball, S., & Bogatz, G. A. (1972). Summative research of *Sesame Street:* Implications for the study of preschool children. In A. D. Pick (Ed.), *Minnesota symposium on child psychology* (Vol. 6, pp. 3–17). Minneapolis: University of Minnesota Press.

Ball, S., & Bogatz, G. A. (1973). *Reading with television: An evaluation of Electric Company.* Princeton, NJ: Educational Testing Service.

Baltes, P. B., Dittman-Kohli, F., & Dixon, R. A. (1984). New perspectives on the development of intelligence in adulthood: Toward a dual-process conception and a model of selective optimization with compensation. In P. B. Baltes & O. G. Brim, Jr. (Eds.), *Life-span development and behavior* (Vol. 6, pp. 33–76). New York: Academic Press.

Bandura, A. (1965). Influence of models' reinforcement contingencies on the acquisition for imitative responses. *Journal of Personality and Social Psychology, 1,* 587–595.

Bandura, A. (1977). *Social learning theory.* Englewood Cliffs, NJ: Prentice-Hall.

Bandura, A., Grusec, J. E., & Menlove, F. L. (1967). Vicarious extinction of avoidance behaviors. *Journal of Personality and Social Psychology, 5,* 16–23.

Bank, S. P., & Kahn, M. D. (1982a). Intense sibling loyalties. In M. E. Lamb & B. Sutton-Smith (Eds.), *Sibling relationships: Their nature and significance across the life span* (pp. 251–284). Hillsdale, NJ: Erlbaum.

Bank, S. P., & Kahn, M. D. (1982b). *The sibling bond.* New York: Basic Books.

Barbero, G. J., & McKay, R. J. (1983). Failure to thrive. In R. E. Behrman & V. C. Vaughn, III (Eds.), *Nelson textbook of pediatrics* (12th ed., pp. 253–254). Philadelphia: Saunders.

Barbero, G. J., & Shaheen, E. (1967). Environmental failure to thrive: A clinical view. *Journal of Pediatrics, 71,* 639–644.

Barness, L. A. (1983). Nutrition and nutritional disorders. In R. E. Behrman & V. C. Vaughn, III (Eds.), *Nelson textbook of pediatrics* (12th ed., pp. 136–185). Philadelphia: Saunders.

Baroody, A. J. (1984). The case of Felicia: A young child's strategies for reducing memory demands during mental addition. *Cognition and Instruction, 1,* 109–116.

Bar-Tal, D., Raviv, A., & Goldberg, M. (1982). Helping behavior among children: An observational study. *Child Development, 53*, 396–402.

Baskett, L. M. (1984). Ordinal position differences in children's family interactions. *Developmental Psychology, 20*, 1026–1031.

Baskett, L. M., & Johnson, S. M. (1982). The young child's interaction with parents versus siblings: A behavioral analysis. *Child Development, 53*, 643–650.

Bateson, G. (1955). A theory of play and fantasy. *Psychiatric Research Reports, 2*, 39–51.

Baumrind, D. (1967). Child care practices anteceding three patterns of preschool behavior. *Genetic Psychology Monographs, 75*, 43–88.

Baumrind, D. (1971). Current patterns of parental authority. *Developmental Psychology Monographs, 4*(No. 1, Pt. 2).

Baumrind, D. (1972). Socialization and instrumental competence in young children. In W. W. Hartup (Ed.), *The young child: Reviews of research* (Vol. 2, pp. 202–224). Washington, DC: National Association for the Education of Young Children.

Beaty, J. J. (1990). *Observing the development of the young child* (2nd ed.). Columbus, OH: Merrill.

Beilin, H. (1980). Piaget's theory: Refinement, revision, or rejection? In R. Kluwe & H. Spada (Eds.), *Developmental models of thinking* (pp. 245–261). New York: Academic Press.

Bell, M. J. (1989). Peer leadership and its influence on the outdoor activities of preschool play groups (Doctoral dissertation, The University of Texas at Austin). *Dissertation Abstracts International, 50*, 1554A.

Bell, R. Q., & Chapman, M. (1986). Child effects in studies using experimental or brief longitudinal approaches to socialization. *Developmental Psychology, 22*, 1353–1354.

Bell, S. M., & Ainsworth, M. D. S. (1972). Infant crying and maternal responsiveness. *Child Development, 43*, 1171–1190.

Belsky, J. (1988). The effects of infant day care reconsidered. *Early Childhood Research Quarterly, 3*, 235–272.

Bench, J. (1978). The auditory response. In V. Stave (Ed.), *Perinatal physiology*. New York: Plenum Press.

Benn, R. (1985, April). *Factors associated with security of attachment in dual career families.* Paper presented at the biennial meeting of the Society for Research in Child Development, Toronto.

Ben-Zeev, S. (1977). The influence of bilingualism on cognitive strategy and cognitive development. *Child Development, 48*, 1009–1018.

Berg, W. K., Adkinson, C. D., & Strock, B. D. (1973). Duration and frequency of periods of alertness in neonates. *Developmental Psychology, 9*, 434.

Berger, E. (1991). *Parents as partners in education: The school and home working together* (3rd ed.). Columbus, OH: Merrill.

Bergstrom, J. M. (1984). *School's out—now what?: Creative choices for your children.* Berkeley, CA: Ten Speed Press.

Berk, L. E. (1984). Development of private speech among low-income Appalachian children. *Developmental Psychology, 20*, 271–286.

Berk, L. E. (1985). Why children talk to themselves. *Young Children, 40*(5), 46–52.

Berk, L. E. (1986a). Relationship of elementary school children's private speech to behavioral accompaniment to task, attention and performance. *Developmental Psychology, 22*, 671–680.

Berk, L. E. (1986b, May). Private speech: Learning out loud. *Psychology Today*, pp. 34–42.

Berk, L. E. (1989). *Child development.* Boston: Allyn and Bacon.

Berner, E. S. (1971). *Private speech and role-taking abilities in preschool children.* Unpublished doctoral dissertation, Harvard University.

Bernstein, B. (1972). A critique of the concept of compensatory education. In C. B. Cazden, V. P. John, & D. Hymes (Eds.), *Functions of language in the classroom* (pp. 135–151). New York: Teachers College Press.

Berrueta-Clement, J. R., Schweinhart, L. J., Barnett, W. S., Epstein, A. S., & Weikart, D. P. (1984). Changed lives: The effects of the Perry Preschool Program on youths through age 19. *Monographs of the High/Scope Educational Research Foundation, 8.* Ypsilanti, MI: High/Scope Press.

Bettlelheim, B. (1987). *A good enough parent.* New York: Vintage Books.

Bever, T. G. (1970). The cognitive basis for linguistic structure. In J. R. Hayes (Ed.), *Cognition and the development of language* (pp. 279–362). New York: Wiley.

Bialystok, E. (1986). Factors in the growth of linguistic awareness. *Child Development, 57*, 498–510.

Bijou, S., & Baer, D. (1961). *Child development: Vol.*

1. A systematic and empirical theory. Englewood Cliffs, NJ: Prentice-Hall.

Bissex, G. (1980). *GYNS at work: A child learns to read and write.* Cambridge, MA: Harvard University Press.

Black, J. K. (1979). Formal and informal means of assessing the communication competence of kindergarten children. *Research in the Teaching of English, 13,* 49–68.

Black, J. K. (1981). Are young children really egocentric? *Young Children, 36*(6), 51–55.

Black, J. K. (1984). Beginning readers and beginning teachers. In J. F. Baumann & D. D. Johnson (Eds.), *Reading instruction and the beginning teacher* (pp. 95–120). Minneapolis: Burgess.

Black, J. K., & Martin, R. (1982). Children's concepts about writing at home and school. In J. A. Niles & L. A. Harris (Eds.), *New inquiries in reading research and instruction* (pp. 300–304). Rochester, NY: National Reading Conference.

Black, J. K., & Puckett, M. (1986). *Developmentally appropriate kindergarten reading programs.* Denton: Texas Association for the Education of Young Children.

Black, J. K., & Puckett, M. (1987). Informing others about developmentally appropriate practice. In S. Bredekamp (Ed.), *Developmentally appropriate practice in early childhood programs serving children from birth through age 8* (pp. 83–87). Washington, DC: National Association for the Education of Young Children.

Block, J. H. (1973). Conceptions of sex-role: Some cross-cultural and longitudinal perspectives. *American Psychologist, 28,* 512–526.

Block, J. H. (1983). Differential premises arising from differential socialization of the sexes: Some conjectures. *Child Development, 54,* 1335–1354.

Bloom, B. (1964). *Stability and change in human characteristics.* New York: Wiley.

Bloom, L. (1970). *Form and function in emerging grammars.* Cambridge, MA: MIT Press.

Bloom, L. (1975). Language development review. In F. D. Horowitz (Ed.), *Review of child development research* (Vol. 4). Chicago: University of Chicago Press.

Boggiano, A. K., Klinger, C. A., & Main, D. S. (1986). Enhancing interest in peer interaction: A developmental analysis. *Child Development, 57,* 852–861.

Borgh, K., & Dickson, W. P. (1986). Two preschoolers sharing one microcomputer: Creating pro-

social behavior with hardware and software. In P. Campbell & G. Fein (Eds.), *Young children and microcomputers* (pp. 37–44). Englewood Cliffs, NJ: Prentice-Hall.

Borke, H. (1983). Piaget's mountains revisited: Changes in the egocentric landscape. In M. Donaldson, R. Grieve, & C. Pratt (Eds.), *Early childhood development and education: Readings in psychology* (pp. 254–259). New York: Guilford Press.

Bornstein, M. H. (1984). A descriptive taxonomy of psychological categories used by infants. In C. Sophian (Ed.), *Origins of cognitive skills. The eighteenth annual Carnegie Symposium on Cognition* (pp. 313–338). Hillsdale, NJ: Erlbaum.

Bornstein, M. H. (1985). Human infant color vision and color perception. *Infant Behavior and Development, 8,* 109–113.

Bornstein, M. H. (1988). Perceptual development across the life cycle. In M. H. Bornstein & M. E. Lamb (Eds.), *Developmental psychology: An advanced textbook* (2nd ed., pp. 151–204). Hillsdale, NJ: Erlbaum.

Bower, T. G. R. (1982). *Development in infancy* (2nd ed.). New York: Freeman.

Bowerman, M. (1979). The acquisition of complex sentences. In P. Fletcher & M. Garman (Eds.), *Language acquisition* (pp. 285–305). Cambridge, England: Cambridge University Press.

Bowlby, J. (1969/1982). *Attachment and loss: Vol. 1. Attachment* (2nd ed.). New York: Basic Books.

Bowlby, J. (1973). *Attachment and loss: Vol. 2. Separation: Anxiety and anger.* New York: Basic Books.

Bowlby, J. (1980). *Attachment and loss: Vol. 3. Loss: Sadness and depression.* New York: Basic Books.

Brackbill, Y. (1979). Obstetrical medication and infant behavior. In J. D. Osofsky (Ed.), *Handbook of infant development* (pp. 76–125). New York: Wiley.

Bradley, R. (1985). Review of Gesell School Readiness Test. In J. V. Mitchell, Jr. (Ed.), *Ninth mental measurements yearbook* (Vol. 1, pp. 609–610). Lincoln, NE: Buros Institute of Mental Measurements.

Brady, E., Bowman, B., Cruz, J., Hilliard, A., & Katz, L. (1982). *Early childhood education teacher education guidelines for four- and five-year programs.* Washington, DC: National Association for the Education of Young Children.

Brainerd, C. J. (1978). *Piaget's theory of intelligence.* Englewood Cliffs, NJ: Prentice-Hall.

Brainerd, C. J., & Brainerd, S. H. (1972). Order of acquisition of number and liquid quantity conservation. *Child Development, 43,* 1401–1405.

Braun, E. (1985). *The effects of age at entry and sibling status on peer interaction of four year olds.* Unpublished master's thesis, University of California, Los Angeles.

Brazelton, T. B. (1973). *Neonatal Behavioral Assessment Scale* (Clinics in Developmental Medicine No. 50, Spastics International Medical Publication). Philadelphia: Lippincott.

Brazelton, T. B. (1981). *On becoming a family: The growth of attachment.* New York: Delacorte Press.

Brazelton, T. B. (1984). *To listen to a child: Understanding the normal problems of growing up.* Reading, MA: Addison-Wesley.

Brazelton, T. B., Koslowski, B., & Tronick, E. (1971). Neonatal behavior among urban Zambians and Americans. *Journal of Child Psychiatry, 15,* 97–107.

Brazelton, T. B. (1987). *Working and caring.* Menlo Park, CA: Addison-Wesley.

Brazelton, T. B., & Yogman, M. W. (Eds.). (1986). *Affective development in infancy.* Norwood, NJ: Ablex.

Bredekamp, S. (Ed.). (1987). *Developmentally appropriate practice in early childhood programs serving children from birth through age 8.* Washington, DC: National Association for the Education of Young Children.

Bredekamp, S., & Shepard, L. (1989). How best to protect children from inappropriate school expectations, practices, and policies. *Young Children, 44*(3), 14–24.

Bretherton, I., & Waters, E. (Eds.). (1985). Growing points in attachment theory and research. *Monographs of the Society for Research in Child Development, 50*(1–2, Serial No. 209).

Brinton, B., & Fujiki, M. (1984). Development of topic manipulation skills in discourse. *Journal of Speech and Hearing Research, 27,* 350–358.

Bronfenbrenner, U. (1970, November). *Who cares for America's children?* Keynote address delivered at the Annual Conference of the National Association for the Education of Young Children, Boston.

Bronfenbrenner, U. (1977). Toward an experimental ecology of human development. *American Psychologist, 32,* 513–531.

Bronfenbrenner, U. (1979). *The ecology of human development.* Cambridge, MA: Harvard University Press.

Bronfenbrenner, U. (1986). Ecology of the family as a context for human development: Research perspectives. *Developmental Psychology, 22,* 723–742.

Brooks-Gunn, J., & Lewis, M. (1982). The development of self-knowledge. In C. Kropp & J. Krakow (Eds.), *The child: Development in a social context* (pp. 333–387). Reading, MA: Addison-Wesley.

Brooks-Gunn, J., & Matthews, W. S. (1979). *He and she: How children develop their sex-role identity.* Englewood Cliffs, NJ: Prentice-Hall.

Brown, A. L., Bransford, J. D., Ferrara, R. A., & Campione, J. C. (1983). Learning, remembering, and understanding. In J. H. Flavell & E. M. Markman (Eds.), *Handbook of child psychology: Vol. 3. Cognitive development* (4th ed., pp. 75–166). New York: Wiley.

Brown, D. (1979). *Mother tongue to English: The young child in the multicultural school.* New York: Cambridge University Press.

Brown, R. (1973). *A first language: The early stages.* Cambridge, MA: Harvard University Press.

Brown, R., & Fraser, C. (1963). The acquisition of syntax. In C. N. Cofer & B. S. Musgrave (Eds.), *Verbal behavior and learning: Problems and processes* (pp. 158–209). New York: McGraw-Hill.

Bruce, B., Michaels, S., & Watson-Gegeo, K. (1985). How computers can change the writing process. *Language Arts, 62,* 143–149.

Bruner, J. (1975). The ontogenesis of speech acts. *Journal of Child Language, 3,* 1–19.

Bruner, J. (1983). The acquisition of pragmatic commitments. In R. M. Golinkoff (Ed.), *The transition from prelinguistic to linguistic communication* (pp. 27–42). Hillsdale, NJ: Erlbaum.

Bryan, J. H., Sonnefeld, J., & Greenberg, F. (1981). Children's and parents' views about integration tactics. *Learning Disability Quarterly, 4,* 170–179.

Bryan, T. H., & Bryan, J. H. (1986). *Understanding learning disabilities.* Palo Alto, CA: Mayfield.

Bryant, B. (1982). Sibling relationships in middle childhood. In M. E. Lamb & B. Sutton-Smith (Eds.), *Sibling relationships: Their nature and significance across the life span* (pp. 87–122). Hillsdale, NJ: Erlbaum.

Bryant, B. K. (1985). The neighborhood walk: Sources of support in middle childhood. *Monographs of the Society for Research in Child Development, 50*(3, Serial No. 210).

Bullock, M., & Gelman, R. (1979). Preschool children's assumptions about cause and effect: Temporal ordering. *Child Development, 50,* 89–96.

Burns, S., Goin, L., & Donlon, J. (1990). A computer in my room. *Young Children, 45*(2), 62–67.

Burton, B. T., & Foster, W. R. (1988). *Human nutrition* (4th ed.). New York: McGraw-Hill.

Burts, D. C., Hart, C. H., Charlesworth, R., & Kirk, L. (1990). A comparison of frequencies of stress behaviors observed in kindergarten children in classrooms with developmentally appropriate versus developmentally inappropriate instructional practices. *Early Childhood Research Quarterly, 5,* 407–423.

Calkins, L. M. (1986). *The art of teaching writing.* Portsmouth, NH: Heinemann.

Campbell, P., & Fein, G. (Eds.). (1986). *Young children and microcomputers.* Englewood Cliffs, NJ: Prentice-Hall.

Campos, J. J., Barrett, K. C., Lamb, M. L., Goldsmith, H. H., & Stenberg, C. (1983). Socioemotional development. In M. M. Haith & J. J. Campos (Eds.), *Infancy and developmental psychobiology* (pp. 783–915). New York: Wiley.

Campos, J. J., & Stenberg, C. R. (1981). Perception appraisal and emotion: The onset of social referencing. In M. E. Lamb & L. R. Sherrod (Eds.), *Infant social cognition: Empirical and theoretical considerations* (pp. 273–314). Hillsdale, NJ: Erlbaum.

Carey, S. (1978). The child as word learner. In M. Halle, J. Bresnan, & G. Miller (Eds.), *Linguistic theory and psychological reality* (pp. 264–293). Cambridge, MA: MIT Press.

Carey, S. (1986). Are children fundamentally different kinds of thinkers and learners than adults? In S. F. Chipman, J. W. Segal, & R. Glaser (Eds.), *Thinking and learning skills: Current research and open questions* (Vol. 2, pp. 485–517). Hillsdale, NJ: Erlbaum.

Carle, E. (1979). *The very hungry caterpillar.* New York: Collins.

Carlson-Paige, N., & Levin, D. E. (1985). *Helping children understand peace, war, and the nuclear threat.* Washington, DC: National Association for the Education of Young Children.

Carnegie Task Force on Teaching as a Profession.

(1986). *A nation prepared: Teachers for the 21st century.* New York: Carnegie Corporation.

Caron, A. J., Caron, R. F., & MacLean, D. (1988). Infant discrimination of naturalistic emotional expressions: The role of face and voice. *Child Development, 59,* 604–616.

Carpenter, T. P., Carey, D. A., & Kouba, V. L. (1990). Developing concepts of the operations: A problem-solving approach. In J. Payne (Ed.), *Learning mathematics in early childhood.* Reston, VA: National Council of Teachers of Mathematics.

Carpenter, T. P., Fennema, E., Peterson, P. L., & Carey, D. (1988). Teacher's pedagogical content knowledge in mathematics. *Journal of Research in Mathematics Education, 19,* 345–357.

Carpenter, T. P., Fennema, E., Peterson, P. L., Chiang, C. P., & Loef, M. (1989). Using knowledge of children's mathematical thinking in classroom teaching: An experimental study. *American Educational Research Journal, 26,* 499–531.

Case, R. (1977). Responsiveness to conservation training as a function of induced subject certainty, M-space and cognitive style. *Canadian Journal of Behavioral Science, 9,* 12–15.

Case, R. (1978). Intellectual development from birth to adulthood: A neo-Piagetian approach. In R. S. Siegler (Ed.), *Children's thinking: What develops?* (pp. 37–71). Hillsdale, NJ: Erlbaum.

Case, R. (1984). The process of stage transition: A neo-Piagetian view. In R. J. Sternberg (Ed.), *Mechanisms of cognitive development* (pp. 19–44). New York: Freeman.

Case, R. (1985). *Intellectual development: A systematic reinterpretation.* New York: Freeman.

Case, R., & Khanna, F. (1981). The missing links: Stages in children's progression from sensorimotor to logical thought. In K. W. Fischer (Ed.), *Cognitive development* (New Directions for Child Development No. 12, pp. 21–32). San Francisco: Jossey-Bass.

Case, R., Marini, Z., McKeough, A., Dennis, S., & Goldberg, J. (1986). Horizontal structure in middle childhood: Cross domain parallels in the course of cognitive growth. In I. Levin (Ed.), *Stage and structure: Reopening the debate* (pp. 1–39). Norwood, NJ: Ablex.

Cauley, K., & Tyler, B. (1989). The relationship of self-concept to prosocial behavior in children. *Early Childhood Research Quarterly, 4,* 51–60.

Ceci, S. J., & Bronfenbrenner, U. (1985). "Don't forget to take the cupcakes out of the oven": Prospective memory, strategic time monitoring and context. *Child Development, 56,* 152–164.

Center for Law and Education, Inc. (1988, August). Parents win challenge to kindergarten exam. *NewsNotes,* pp. 2–3.

Chand, I. P., Crider, D. M., & Willits, F. K. (1975). Parent-youth disagreement as perceived by youth: A longitudinal study. *Youth and Society, 6,* 365–375.

Charlesworth, R. (1987). *Understanding child development.* Albany, NY: Delmar.

Charlesworth, R. (1989). "Behind" before they start? Deciding how to deal with the risk of kindergarten "failure." *Young Children, 44*(3), 5–13.

Charlesworth, R., & Hartup, W. W. (1967). Positive social reinforcement in the nursery school peer group. *Child Development, 38,* 993–1002.

Chase, H. P. (1976). Undernutrition and growth and development of the human brain. In J. D. Lloyd-Still (Ed.), *Malnutrition and intellectual development* (pp. 13–38). Littleton, MA: Publishing Sciences Group.

Chess, S. (1967). Temperament in the normal infant. In B. Straub & J. Hellmuth (Eds.), *Exceptional infant: Vol. 1. The normal infant* (pp. 143–162). Seattle, WA: Special Child Publications.

Chess, S., & Thomas, A. (1987). *Origins and evolution of behavior disorders from infancy to early adult life.* Cambridge, MA: Harvard University Press.

Chi, M. T. H. (1978). Knowledge structures and memory development. In R. S. Siegler (Ed.), *Children's thinking: What develops?* (pp. 73–96). Hillsdale, NJ: Erlbaum.

Chi, M. T. H., & Klahr, D. (1975). Span and rate of apprehension in children and adults. *Journal of Experimental Child Psychology, 19,* 434–439.

Chi, M. T. H., & Koeske, R. D. (1983). Network representation of a child's dinosaur knowledge. *Developmental Psychology, 19,* 29–39.

Child Abuse Prevention and Treatment Act of 1975, 42 U.S.C. § 5101 (1974).

Children's Defense Fund. (1988). *A call for action to make our nation safe for children: A briefing book on the status of American children in 1988.* Washington, DC: Author.

Children's Defense Fund. (1989a). *A children's defense budget: FY 1989.* Washington, DC: Author.

Children's Defense Fund. (1989b). *A vision for America's future: An agenda for the 1990's: A children's defense budget.* Washington, DC: Author.

Childs, C. P., & Greenfield, P. M. (1980). Informal modes of learning and teaching: The case of Zinacanteco learning. In N. Warren (Ed.), *Studies in cross-cultural psychology* (Vol. 2). New York: Academic Press.

Chilman, C. S. (1966). *Your child from 6 to 12.* Washington, DC: Children's Bureau, U.S. Department of Health, Education, and Welfare.

Chomsky, C. (1968). *Language and mind.* San Diego, CA: Harcourt Brace Jovanovich.

Chomsky, C. (1969). *The acquisition of syntax in children from five to ten.* Cambridge, MA: MIT Press.

Chomsky, C. (1971). Write first, read later. *Childhood Education, 47,* 296–299.

Chomsky, N. (1980). *Rules and representations.* New York: Columbia University Press.

Christian, J. L., & Gregor, J. L. (1988). *Nutrition for living* (2nd ed.). Menlo Park, CA: Benjamin/Cummings.

Chukovsky, K. (1971). *From two to five* (F. C. Sayers, Ed. and Trans.). Berkeley: University of California Press.

Cicerelli, V. G., Evans, J. W., & Schiller, J. S. (1969). *The impact of Head Start: An evaluation on the effects of Head Start on children's cognitive and affective development* (Vols. 1–2). Athens, OH: Westinghouse Learning Corporation and Ohio University.

Cicourel, A. (1972). Cross-modal communication: The representational context of sociolinguistic information processing. In R. Shuy (Ed.), *Monograph Series on Language and Linguistics: Twenty-third Annual Round Table* (pp. 187–222). Washington, DC: Georgetown University Press.

Clark, E. V. (1978). Strategies for communicating. *Child Development, 49,* 977–987.

Clark, E. V. (1983). Meanings and concepts. In J. H. Flavell & E. M. Markman (Eds.), *Handbook of child psychology: Vol. 3. Cognitive development* (4th ed., pp. 787–840). New York: Wiley.

Clark, M. M. (1976). *Young fluent readers.* London: Heinemann.

Clark, R., & Clark, E. (1977). *Psychology and language.* New York: Harcourt Brace Jovanovich.

Clarke-Stewart, K. A. (1973). Interactions between mothers and their young children: Characteristics and consequences. *Monographs of the Society for Research in Child Development, 38*(6–7, Serial No. 153).

Clay, M. (1975). *What did I write?* Auckland, New Zealand: Heinemann.

Clay, M. (1979). *Sand (concepts about print test).* Auckland, New Zealand: Heinemann.

Clements, D. (1985, April). *Implications of media research for the instructional application of computers with young children.* Paper presented at the annual meeting of the American Educational Research Association.

Clyman, R. B., Emde, R. N., Kempe, J. E., & Harmon, R. J. (1986). Social referencing and social looking among 12-month-old infants. In T. B. Brazelton & M. W. Yogman (Eds.), *Affective development in infancy* (pp. 75–94). Norwood, NJ: Ablex.

Coates, B., Pusser, H. E., & Goodman, I. (1976). The influence of "Sesame Street" and "Mister Rogers' Neighborhood" on children's social behavior in the preschool. *Child Development, 47,* 138–144.

Cohen, M. (1967). *Will I have a friend?* New York: Macmillan.

Cole, M., & Cole, S. (1989). *The development of children.* New York: Freeman.

Coleman, J. (1980). Friendship and the peer group in adolescence. In J. Adelson (Ed.), *Handbook of adolescent psychology* (pp. 408–431). New York: Wiley.

Coll-Garcia, C. T. (1990). Developmental outcome of minority infants: A process-oriented look into our beginnings. *Child Development, 61,* 270–289.

Collins, W. A. (1983). Children's processing of television content: Implications for prevention of negative effects. *Prevention in Human Services, 2,* 53–56.

Collins, W. A., Wellman, H., Keniston, A. H., & Westby, S. D. (1978). Age-related aspects of comprehension and inference from a televised dramatic narrative. *Child Development, 49,* 389–399.

Colon, P. A., & Colon, A. R. (1989). The health of America's children. In F. J. Macchiarola & A. Gartner (Eds.), Caring for America's children. *Proceedings of the Academy of Political Science, 37* (Vol. 2, pp. 45–57). New York: The Academy of Political Science.

Connolly, J. A., & Doyle, A. (1984). Relation of social fantasy play to social competence in preschoolers. *Developmental Psychology, 20,* 797–806.

Copple, C., Siegel, I., & Saunders, R. (1979). *Edu-*

cating the young thinker: Classroom strategies for cognitive growth. New York: Van Nostrand.

Corder-Bolz, C. R. (1980). Mediation: The role of significant others. *Journal of Communication, 30,* 106–118.

Corsaro, W. A. (1985). *Friendship and peer culture in the early years.* Norwood, NJ: Ablex.

Craik, F. I. M., & Lockhart, P. S. (1972). Levels of processing: A framework for memory research. *Journal of Verbal Learning and Verbal Behavior, 11,* 671–684.

Craik, F. I. M., & Tulving, E. (1975). Depth processing and the retention of words in episodic memory. *Journal of Experimental Psychology: General, 104,* 268–294.

Cratty, B. J. (1986). *Perceptual and motor development in infants and children* (3rd ed.). Englewood Cliffs, NJ: Prentice-Hall.

Cross, T. G. (1978). Mother's speech and its association with rate of linguistic development in young children. In N. Waterson & C. E. Snow (Eds.), *The development of communication* (pp. 199–216). New York: Wiley.

Cryan, J. R. (1986). Evaluation: Plague or promise. *Childhood Education, 62,* 344–350.

Cunningham, L. (1985). Leaders and leadership: 1985 and beyond. *Phi Delta Kappan, 67,* 17–20.

Curry, N., & Johnson, C. (1990). *Beyond self-esteem: Developing a genuine sense of human value.* Washington, DC: NAEYC.

Damon, W. (1983). *Social and personality development.* New York: Norton.

Damon, W. (1988). *The moral child: Nurturing children's natural moral growth.* NY: The Free Press.

Damon, W., & Hart, D. (1982). The development of self-understanding from infancy through adolescence. *Child Development, 53,* 841–864.

Darwin, C. (1936). *The origin of species.* New York: Modern Library. (Original work published 1859)

Davis, D. L. (Ed.). (1989). *Biological markers in reproductive and developmental toxicity.* Washington, DC: National Academy of Science Press.

Davis, R. (1990). *A comparison of the reading and writing performance of children in a whole language pre-first grade class and a modified traditional first grade class.* Unpublished doctoral dissertation, University of North Texas, Denton.

DeBoysson-Bardies, B., Sagart, L., & Durand, C. (1984). Discernible differences in the babbling of infants according to target language. *Journal of Child Language, 11,* 1–16.

DeCasper, A. J., & Fifer, W. P. (1980). Of human bonding: Newborns prefer their mothers' voices. *Science*, *208*, 1174–1176.

DeCasper, A. J., & Spence, M. J. (1986). Prenatal maternal speech influences newborn's perception of speech sounds. *Infant Behavior and Development*, *9*, 133–150.

DeMause, L. (Ed.). (1974). *The history of childhood*. New York: Harper and Row.

DeMause, L. (1982). *Foundations of psychohistory*. New York: Creative Roots.

Demos, V. (1986). Crying in early infancy: An illustration of the motivational function of affect. In T. B. Brazelton & M. W. Yogman (Eds.), *Affective development in infancy* (pp. 39–73). Norwood, NJ: Ablex.

Derman-Sparks, L. (1989). *Anti-bias curriculum: Tools for empowering children*. Washington, DC: National Association for the Education of Young Children.

Desmond, M., Wilson, G., Alt, E., & Fisher, E. (1980). The very low birth weight infant after discharge from intensive care: Anticipatory health care and developmental course. *Current Problems in Pediatrics*, *10*, 1–59.

De Vries, R. (1969). Constancy of generic identity in the years three to six. *Monographs of the Society for Research in Child Development*, *34*(3, Serial No. 127).

Diaz, R. M. (1985). Bilingual cognitive development: Addressing three gaps in current research. *Child Development*, *56*, 1376–1378.

Dickinson, D. K. (1984). First impressions: Children's knowledge of words gained from a single exposure. *Applied Linguistics*, *5*, 359–373.

Dietz, W. H. (1986). *Prevention of childhood obesity*. Philadelphia: Pediatric Clinics of North America/Saunders.

Doake, D. (1981). *Book experience and emergent reading in preschool children*. Unpublished doctoral dissertation, University of Alberta, Edmonton.

Dobbing, J. (1984). Infant nutrition and later achievement. *Nutrition Reviews*, *42*, 1–7.

Dollaghan, C. (1985). Child meets word: "Fast mapping" in pre-school children. *Journal of Speech and Hearing Research*, *28*, 449–454.

Donaldson, M. (1979). *Children's minds*. New York: Norton.

Donaldson, M. (1983). Children's reasoning. In M. Donaldson, R. Grieve, & C. Pratt (Eds.), *Early childhood development and education: Readings in psychology* (pp. 231–236). New York: Guilford Press.

Dorr, A. (1983). No shortcuts to judging reality. In P. E. Bryant & S. Anderson (Eds.), *Watching and understanding TV: Research on children's attention and comprehension*. New York: Academic Press.

Dorr, A., Graves, S., & Phelps, E. (1980). Television literacy for young children. *Journal of Communication*, *30*, 71–83.

Dorval, B., & Eckerman, C. (1984). Developmental trends in the quality of conversation achieved by small groups of acquainted peers. *Monographs of the Society for Research in Child Development*, *49*(2, Serial No. 206).

Dresden, J., & Myers, B. K. (1989). Early childhood professionals: Toward self-definition. *Young Children*, *44*(2), 62–66.

Dunn, J. (1984). *Sisters and brothers*. Cambridge, MA: Harvard University Press.

Dunn, J., & Kendrick, C. (1982a). Siblings and their mother: Developing relationships within the family. In M. E. Lamb & B. Sutton-Smith (Eds.), *Sibling relationships: Their nature and significance across the lifespan* (pp. 39–60). Hillsdale, NJ: Erlbaum.

Dunn, J., & Kendrick, C. (1982b). *Siblings: Love, envy, and understanding*. Cambridge, MA: Harvard University Press.

Dunn, J., & Munn, P. (1986). Siblings and the development of prosocial behavior. *International Journal of Behavioral Development*, *9*, 265–284.

Durkin, D. (1966). *Children who read early*. New York: Teachers College Press.

Dyson, A. H. (1981). *A case study examination of the role of oral language in writing processes of kindergartners*. Unpublished doctoral dissertation, The University of Texas at Austin.

Dyson, A. H. (1982). The emergence of visible language: Interrelationships between drawing and early writings. *Visible Language*, *16*, 360–381.

Dyson, A. H. (1983). The role of oral language in the early writing processes. *Research in the Teaching of English*, *17*, 1–30.

Dyson, A. H. (1985). Puzzles, paints and pencils: Writing emerges. *Educational Horizons*, *64*, 13–16.

Dyson, A. H. (1987). Research currents: The emergence of children's written voices. *Language Arts*, *64*, 648–658.

Dyson, A. H. (1990). Symbol makers, symbol weavers: How children link play, pictures, and print. *Young Children, 45*(2), 50–57.

Eaton, W. O., Chipperfield, J. G., & Singbeil, C. E. (1989). Birth order and activity level in children. *Developmental Psychology, 25,* 668–672.

Eaton, W. O., & Von Bargen, D. (1981). Asynchronous development of gender understanding in preschool children. *Child Development, 52,* 1020–1027.

Education Consolidation and Improvement Act of 1981, U.S. Code 1982 Title 20, § 3801 et. seq. Aug. 13, 1981 PL 97–35, 95 STAT. 357, § 551–596.

Eichorn, D. (1979). Physical development: current foci of research. In J. D. Osofsky (Ed.), *Handbook of infant development* (pp. 253–282). New York: Wiley.

Elder, G. H., Jr. (1982). Historical experiences in the later years. In T. K. Hareven & K. J. Adams (Eds.), *Aging and life course transitions: An interdisciplinary perspective* (pp. 75–107). New York: Guilford Press.

Elkind, D. (1974). *A sympathetic understanding of the child from birth to sixteen.* Boston: Allyn and Bacon.

Elkind, D. (1978a). *The child's reality: Three developmental themes.* Hillsdale, NJ: Erlbaum.

Elkind, D. (1978b). *A sympathetic understanding of the child 6 to 16.* Boston: Allyn and Bacon.

Elkind, D. (1978c). Understanding the young adolescent. *Adolescence, 13,* 127–134.

Elkind, D. (1981). *The hurried child: Growing up too fast too soon.* Reading, MA: Addison-Wesley.

Elkind, D. (1984). *All grown up and no place to go: Teenagers in crisis.* Reading, MA: Addison-Wesley.

Elkind, D. (1987). *Miseducation: Preschoolers at risk.* New York: Knopf.

Emde, R. N., & Harmon, R. J. (1972). Endogenous and exogenous smiling systems in early infancy. *Journal of the American Academy of Child Psychiatry, 11,* 177–200.

Endres, J. B., & Rockwell, R. E. (1985). *Food, nutrition, and the young child* (2nd ed.). St. Louis: Times Mirror/Mosby.

England, D. A. (1984). *Television and children* (Fastback Series No. 207). Bloomington, IN: Phi Delta Kappa Educational Foundation.

Erhardt, R. P. (1973). Sequential levels in the development of prehension. *The American Journal of Occupational Therapy, 28,* 592–596.

Erickson, M. F., Stroufe, L. A., & Egeland, B. (1985). The relationship between quality of attachment and behavior problems in preschool in a high risk sample. In I. Bretherton & E. Waters (Eds.), Growing points of attachment theory and research. *Monographs of the Society for Research in Child Development, 50*(1–2, Serial No. 209, pp. 147–166).

Erikson, E. (1963). *Childhood and society* (2nd ed.). New York: Norton.

Erikson, E. (1968). *Identity: Youth and crisis.* New York: Norton.

Ervin-Tripp, S., O'Connor, S., & Rosenberg, J. (1984). Language and power in the family. In J. deWit & W. W. Hartup (Eds.), *Determinants and origins of aggressive behavior* (pp. 347–380). The Hague: Mouton.

Evans, H. J. (1981). Abnormalities and cigarette smoking. *Lancet,* (1), 627–634.

Eveleth, P., & Tanner, J. (1976). *World wide variation in human growth.* Cambridge, England: Cambridge University Press.

Fagot, B. I. (1974). Sex differences in toddlers' behavior and parental reaction. *Developmental Psychology, 10,* 554–558.

Fagot, B. I. (1978). The influence of sex of child on parental reactions to toddler children. *Child Development, 49,* 459–465.

Fagot, B. I. (1982). Sex role development. In R. Vasta (Ed.), *Strategies and techniques of child study* (pp. 273–303). New York: Academic Press.

Fagot, B. I., & Kronsberg, S. J. (1982). Sex differences: Biological and social factors influencing the behavior of young boys and girls. In S. G. Moore & C. R. Cooper (Eds.), *The young child: Reviews of research* (Vol. 3, pp. 193–210). Washington, DC: National Association for the Education of Young Children.

Fantz, R. L. (1961). The origin of form perception. *Scientific American, 204,* 66–72.

Farber, E. A., & Egeland, B. (1982). Developmental consequences of out-of-home care for infants in a low income population. In E. Zigler & E. Gordon (Eds.), *Day care: Scientific and social policy issues* (pp. 102–125). Boston: Auburn House.

Fecter, L., & Mactutos, C. (1983). Carbon monoxide and fetal memory. *Science News, 124,* 387.

Federal Motor Vehicle Safety Standard Act of 1980, 213 U.S.C. (1981).

Feeney, S., & Kipnis, K. (1989). The National Association for the Education of Young Children code of ethical conduct and statement of commitment. *Young Children, 45*(1), 24–29.

Fein, G. (1978). *Child development.* Englewood Cliffs, NJ: Prentice-Hall.

Feldman, D. (1980). *Beyond universals in cognitive development.* Norwood, NJ: Ablex.

Fennema, E., Carpenter, T. P., & Peterson, P. L. (1990). Learning mathematics with understanding: Cognitively guided instruction. In J. E. Brophy (Ed.), *Advances in research on teaching* (Vol. 1). Greenwich, CT: JAI Press.

Ferguson, C. A. (1977). Learning to pronounce: The earliest stages of phonological development in the child. In F. D. Minifie & L. L. Lloyd (Eds.), *Communicative and cognitive abilities: Early behavioral assessment* (pp. 141–155). Baltimore: University Park Press.

Ferrerio, E., & Teberosky, A. (1982). *Literacy before schooling.* Exeter, NH: Heinemann.

Field, D. (1981). Can preschool children really learn to conserve? *Child Development, 52,* 326–334.

Fields, M., & Lee, D. (1987). *Let's begin reading right: A developmental approach to beginning literacy.* Columbus, OH: Merrill.

Field, T. M. (1979). Differential behavioral & cardiac responses of 3-month-old infants to a mirror and a peer. *Infant Behavior and Development, 2,* 179–184.

Field, T. M. (1982). Individual differences in the expressivity of neonates and young infants. In R. Feldman (Ed.), *Development of nonverbal behavior in children* (pp. 279–298). New York: Springer-Verlag.

Field, T. M., Vega-Lahr, N., & Jagadish, S. (1984). Separation stress of nursery school infants and toddlers graduating to new classes. *Infant Behavior and Development, 7,* 277–284.

Fields, M. V., Spangler, K. L., & Lee, D. M. (1991). *Let's begin reading right: Developmentally appropriate beginning literacy.* (2nd ed.). New York: Macmillan.

Fischer, K. W. (1980). A theory of cognitive development: The control and construction of hierarchies of skills. *Psychological Review, 87,* 477–531.

Fischer, K. W., & Pipp, S. L. (1984). Processes of cognitive development: Optimal level and skill acquisition. In R. J. Sternberg (Ed.), *Mechanisms of cognitive development* (pp. 45–80). New York: Freeman.

Fisher, J. J. (Ed.). (1988). *From baby to toddler.* New York: Pergee Books.

Fivush, R. (1984). Learning about school: The development of kindergartners' school scripts. *Child Development, 55,* 1697–1709.

Flavell, J. H. (1963). *The developmental psychology of Jean Piaget.* New York: Nostrand.

Flavell, J. H. (1985). *Cognitive development* (2nd ed.). Englewood Cliffs, NJ: Prentice-Hall.

Flavell, J. H., Friederichs, A. G., & Hoyt, J. D. (1970). Developmental changes in memorization processes. *Cognitive Psychology, 1,* 324–340.

Fleege, P. O. (1990). Stress begins in kindergarten: A look at behavior during standardized testing (Doctoral dissertation, Louisiana State University). *Dissertation Abstracts International, 51,* 3628A.

Flood, J., & Salus, P. (1984). *Language and the language arts.* Englewood Cliffs, NJ: Prentice-Hall.

Fogel, A. (1979). Peer vs. mother directed behavior in 1- to 3-month-old infants. *Infant Behavior and Development, 2,* 215–226.

Fogelman, K. (1980). Smoking in pregnancy and subsequent development of the child. *Child Care, Health and Development, 6,* 233–251.

Forman, G., & Kuschner, D. (1983). *The child's construction of knowledge: Piaget for teaching children.* Washington, DC: National Association for the Education of Young Children.

Forman, M. A., Hetznecker, W. H., & Dunn, J. M. (1983). Psychosocial dimensions of pediatrics: Gender identity and role. In R. E. Behrman & V. C. Vaughn, III (Eds.), *Nelson textbook of pediatrics* (12th ed., pp. 56–58). Philadelphia: Saunders.

Fraiberg, S. (1976). Intervention in infancy: A program for blind infants. In E. Resford, L. Sander, & T. Shapiro (Eds.), *Infant psychiatry: A new synthesis* (pp. 264–284). New Haven, CT: Yale University Press.

Freedman, D. G., & Freedman, N. (1969). Behavioral differences between Chinese-Americans and European-American newborns. *Nature, 224,* 1227.

Freidrich, L. K., & Stein, A. H. (1975). Prosocial television and young children: The effect of verbal labelling and role-playing on learning and behavior. *Child Development, 46,* 27–38.

Freud, S. (1905/1930). *Three contributions to the theory of sex.* New York: Nervous and Mental Disease Publishing. (Original work published 1905)

Freud, S. (1933). *New introductory lectures on psychoanalysis.* New York: Norton.

Freud, S. (1938). The history of the psychoanalytic

movement. In A. A. Brill (Ed. and Trans.), *The basic writing of Sigmund Freud* (pp. 931–977). New York: Modern Library.

Friedman, J., & Koeppel, J. (1990). Pre-K and first grade children: Partners in a writing workshop. *Young Children, 45*(4), 66–67.

Frisch, H. L. (1977). Sex stereotypes in adult-infant play. *Child Development, 48*, 1671–1675.

Fuller, F. F. (1969). Concerns of teachers. *American Educational Research Journal, 6*, 207–226.

Furman, W., & Buhrmester, D. (1985). Children's perceptions of the qualities of sibling relationships. *Child Development, 56*, 448–461.

Fuson, K. C., Secada, W. G., & Hall, J. W. (1983). Matching, counting, and conservation of numerical equivalence. *Child Development, 54*, 91–97.

Gallahue, D. L. (1982). *Developmental movement experiences for children.* New York: Wiley.

Galler, J. R., Ramsey, F., & Solimano, G. (1984). The influence of early malnutrition on subsequent development: 3. Learning disabilities as a sequel to malnutrition. *Pediatric Research, 18*, 309.

Galler, J. R., Ramsey, F., & Solimano, G. (1985). A follow-up study of the effects of early malnutrition on subsequent development: 2. Fine motor skills in adolescence. *Pediatric Research, 19*, 524.

Garbarino, J. (1977). The human ecology of child maltreatment: A conceptual model for research. *Journal of Marriage and the Family, 39*, 731–736.

Gardner, H. (1978). *Developmental psychology: An introduction.* Boston: Little, Brown.

Gardner, H. (1980). *Artful scribbles: The significance of children's drawings.* New York: Basic Books.

Gardner, H. (1983). *Frames of mind: Theory of multiple intelligences.* New York: Basic Books.

Gardner, L. J. (1972). Deprivation dwarfism. *Scientific American, 227*, 76–82.

Gardner, R. A. (1979). *Understanding children.* Cresskill, NJ: Creative Therapists.

Garvey, C. (1977). *Play.* Cambridge, MA: Harvard University Press.

Geber, M. (1958). The psychomotor development of African children in the first year and the influence of maternal behavior. *Journal of Social Psychology, 47*, 185–195.

Gehrke, N. J. (1987). *On being a teacher.* West Lafayette, IN: Kappa Delta Pi Publications.

Gelles, R. J., & Edfeldt, A. W. (1990). Violence toward children in the United States and Sweden. In M. A. Jensen & Z. W. Chevalier (Eds.), *Issues and advocacy in early education* (pp. 133–140). Boston: Allyn and Bacon.

Gelman, R. (1972). Logical capacity of very young children: Number invariance rules. *Child Development, 43*, 75–90.

Gelman, R. (1979). Preschool thought. *American Psychologist, 34*, 900–905.

Gelman, R., & Baillargeon, R. (1983). A review of some Piagetian concepts. In P. H. Mussen (Ed.), *Handbook of child psychology: Vol. 3. Cognitive development* (pp. 167–230). New York: Wiley.

Gelman, R., Bullock, M., & Meck, E. (1980). Preschooler's understanding of simple object transformation. *Child Development, 51*, 691–699.

Gelman, R., & Gallistel, C. R. (1983). The child's understanding of number. In M. Donaldson, R. Grieve, & C. Pratt (Eds.), *Early childhood development and education: Readings in psychology* (pp. 185–203). New York: Guilford Press.

Gelman, R., & Shatz, M. (1978). Appropriate speech adjustments: The operation of conversational constraints on talk to two-year-olds. In M. Lewis & L. A. Rosenblum (Eds.), *Interaction, conversation, and the development of language* (pp. 27–61). New York: Wiley.

Genishi, C., & Dyson, A. H. (1984). *Language assessment in the early years.* Norwood, NJ: Ablex.

Genishi, C., McCollum, P., & Strand, E. (1985). Research currents: The interactional richness of children's computer use. *Language Arts, 62*, 526–532.

Gentry, J. R. (1987). *Spel . . . is a four-letter word.* Portsmouth, NH: Heinemann.

Gerbner, G. (1972). Violence in television drama: Trends in symbolic functions. In G. A. Comstock & E. D. Rubinstein (Eds.), *Television and social behavior: Vol. 1. Media content and control* (pp. 28–187). Washington, DC: U.S. Government Printing Office.

Gerbner, G., & Gross, L. (1980). The violent face of television and its lessons. In E. L. Palmer & A. Dorr (Eds.), *Children and the faces of television: Teaching, violence, selling* (pp. 149–162). New York: Academic Press.

Gerbner, G., & Signorielli, N. (1990). *Violence profile 1967 through 1988–89: Enduring trends.* Philadelphia: University of Pennsylvania, Annenberg School of Communication.

Gesell, A. (1930). *Guidance of mental growth in infant and child.* New York: Macmillan.

Gesell, A. (1954). The ontogenesis of human behavior. In L. Carmichael (Ed.), *Manual of child psychology* (pp. 335–373). New York: Wiley.

Gesell, A., & Amatruda, C. S. (1941). *Developmental diagnosis: Normal and abnormal child development.* New York: Hoeber.

Gesell, A., & Ilg, F. L. (1949). *Child development.* New York: Harper and Row.

Gesell, A., Ilg, F. L., & Ames, L. B. (1974). *The child from five to ten* (rev. ed.). New York: Harper and Row.

Gesell, A., & Thompson, H. (1929). Learning and growth in identical infant twins: An experimental study by the method of co-twin control. *Genetic Psychology Monographs, 6,* 1–125.

Gibson, E. J., & Levin, H. (1975). *The psychology of reading.* Cambridge, MA: MIT Press.

Gilligan, C. (1982). *In a different voice.* Cambridge, MA: Harvard University Press.

Ginsburg, H. (1977). *Children's arithmetic.* New York: Van Nostrand.

Ginsburg, H., & Opper, S. (1979). *Piaget's theory of intellectual development* (2nd ed.). Englewood Cliffs, NJ: Prentice-Hall.

Gleason, J. (1975). Fathers and other strangers: Men's speech to young children. In D. Dato (Ed.), *Developmental psycholinguistics* (pp. 289–297). Washington, DC: Georgetown University Press.

Glover, B., & Shepherd, J. (1980). *The family fitness handbook.* New York: Penguin USA.

Goffin, S. G., & Lombardi, J. (1989). *Speaking out: Early childhood advocacy.* Washington, DC: National Association for the Education of Young Children.

Goldberg, S. (1983). Parent-infant bonding: Another look. *Child Development, 54,* 1355–1382.

Goldfarb, W. (1943). The effects of early institutional care on adolescent personality. *Journal of Experimental Education, 12,* 106–129.

Golinkoff, R. M. (1983). The preverbal negotiation of failed messages: Insights into the transition period. In R. M. Golinkoff (Ed.), *The transition from prelinguistic to linguistic communication* (pp. 57–75). Hillsdale, NJ: Erlbaum.

Gonzalez-Mena, J., & Eyer, D. (1980). *Infancy and caregiving.* Palo Alto, CA: Mayfield.

Goodman, K. (1986). *What's whole in whole language?* Portsmouth, NH: Heinemann.

Goodman, K., & Goodman, V. M. (1983). Reading and writing relationships: Pragmatic functions. *Language Arts, 60,* 590–599.

Goodman, Y. (1980). The roots of literacy. In M. P. Douglass (Ed.), *Claremont Reading Conference forty-fourth yearbook.* Claremont, CA: Claremont Graduate School.

Gordon, A. M., & Browne, K. W. (1985). *Beginnings and beyond.* Albany, NY: Delmar.

Gordon, J. S., & Haire, D. (1981). Alternatives in childbirth. In P. Ahmed (Ed.), *Pregnancy, childbirth and parenthood.* New York: Elsevier.

Gottfried, A. (1984). Touch as an organizer of human development. In C. Brown (Ed.), *The many facets of touch* (pp. 114–120). Skillman, NJ: Johnson and Johnson.

Graves, D. (1983). *Writing: Teachers and children at work.* Exeter, NH: Heinemann.

Green, J. A., Jones, L. E., & Gustafson, G. E. (1987). Perception of cries by parents and nonparents: Relation to cry acoustics. *Developmental Psychology, 23,* 370–382.

Green, M. (1985). The development of metaphoric comprehension and preference (Doctoral dissertation, Boston University). *Dissertation Abstracts International, 46,* 1264A.

Greenspan, S., & Greenspan, N. T. (1985). *First feelings.* New York: Penguin.

Grossmann, K., Grossmann, K. E., Spangler, G., Suess, G. L., & Unzner, L. (1985). Maternal sensitivity and newborns' orientation responses as related to quality of attachment in Northern Germany. In I. Bretherton & E. Waters (Eds.), *Growing points of attachment theory and research. Monographs of the Society for Research in Child Development, 50*(1–2, Serial No. 209, pp. 233–256).

Gruen, G. E., & Vore, D. A. (1972). Development of conservation in normal and retarded children. *Developmental Psychology, 6,* 146–157.

Grusec, J. E., & Abramovitch, R. (1982). Imitation of peers and adults in a natural setting: A functional analysis. *Child Development, 53,* 636–642.

Guthrie, H. (1986). *Introductory nutrition.* St. Louis: Times Mirror/Mosby.

Haith, M. M. (1966). The response of human newborns to visual movement. *Journal of Experimental Child Psychology, 3,* 235–243.

Hakes, D. T., Evans, J. S., & Tunmer, W. E. (1980). *The development of metalinguistic abilities in children.* Berlin: Springer.

Hale, J. (1982). *Black children: Their roots, culture,*

and learning styles. Provo, UT: Brigham Young University Press.

Hale-Benson, J. E. (1986). *Black children: Their roots, culture and learning styles* (rev. ed.). Baltimore, MD: Johns Hopkins University Press.

Halford, G. S., & Boyle, F. M. (1985). Do young children understand conservation of number? *Child Development, 56*, 165–176.

Hall, D. (1985). The outlook for low birth weight babies. *The Practitioner, 229*, 779–783.

Hall, G. S. (1893). *The contents of children's minds.* New York: Kellogg.

Hall, M., Moretz, S., & Statom, J. (1976). A study of early writing. *Language Arts, 53*, 582–585.

Hall, N. (1989). *Writing with reason: The emergence of authorship in young children.* Portsmouth, NH: Heinemann.

Halliday, M. A. K. (1975). *Learning how to mean: Explorations in the development of language.* London: Edward Arnold.

Hareven, T. K. (1982). *Family time and industrial time.* Cambridge, MA: Cambridge University Press.

Haring, N. G., & McCormick, L. (1990). *Exceptional children and youth* (5th ed.). Columbus, OH: Merrill.

Harlap, S., & Shlono, P. H. (1980). Alcohol, smoking, and incidence of spontaneous abortion in the first and second trimester. *Lancet, 2*, 173–176.

Harper, L. V., & Huie, K. S. (1985). The effects of prior group experience, age and familiarity on the quality and organization of preschoolers' social relationships. *Child Development, 56*, 704–717.

Harris, P. L., Donnelly, K., Guz, G. R., & Pitt-Watson, R. (1986). Children's understanding of the distinction between real and apparent emotion. *Child Development, 57*, 895–909.

Harrow, A. J. (1972). *A taxonomy of the psychomotor domain.* New York: Longman.

Hart, C. H., DeWolf, D. M., Royston, K. E., Burts, D. C., & Thomasson, R. H. (1990, Spring). Maternal and paternal disciplinary styles: Relationships to behavioral orientations and sociometric status. Paper presented at the annual conference of the American Educational Research Association, Boston.

Hart, C. H., Ladd, G. W., & Burleson, B. R. (1990). Children's expectations of the outcomes of social strategies: Relations with sociometric status and maternal disciplinary styles. *Child Development, 61*, 127–137.

Harter, S. (1983). Developmental perspectives on the self-system. In E. M. Hetherington (Ed.), *Handbook of child psychology: Vol. 4. Socialization, personality and social development* (4th ed., pp. 275–386). New York: Wiley.

Hartup, W. W. (1977). Peer relations: Developmental implications and interaction in same- and mixed-age situations. *Young Children, 32*(3), 4–13.

Hartup, W. W. (1983). Peer relations. In E. M. Hetherington (Ed.), *Handbook of child psychology: Vol. 4. Socialization, personality and social development* (4th ed., pp. 103–196). New York: Wiley.

Hartup, W. W. (1989). Behavioral manifestations of children's friendships. In T. J. Berndt & G. W. Ladd (Eds.), *Peer relationships in child development* (pp. 46–70). New York: Wiley.

Havighurst, R. J. (1972). *Developmental tasks and education.* New York: McKay.

Hawk, P. (1987). Beginning teacher programs: Benefits for the experienced educator. *Action in Teacher Education, 8*(4), 59–63.

Hawk, P., & Robards, S. (1987). Statewide teacher induction programs. In D. Brooks (Ed.), *Teacher induction: A new beginning* (pp. 33–44). Reston, VA: Association of Teacher Educators.

Hay, D. F. (1979). Cooperative interactions and sharing between very young children and their parents. *Developmental Psychology, 15*, 647–653.

Hay, D. R., Nash, A., & Pederson, J. (1983). Interaction between six-month-old peers. *Child Development, 54*, 557–562.

Healy, J. M. (1987). *Your child's growing mind.* Garden City, NY: Doubleday.

Heath, S. (1982). What no bedtime story means: Narrative skills at home and school. *Language in Society, 11*, 49–76.

Heath, S. B. (1983). *Ways with words: Language life and work in communities and classrooms.* Cambridge, MA: Cambridge University Press.

Hechinger, F. (Ed.). (1986). *A better start: New choices for learning.* New York: Walker.

Heck, S., & Williams, C. R. (1984). *The complex roles of the teacher: An ecological perspective.* New York: Teachers College Press.

Helfer, R. (1982). The relationship between lack of bonding and child abuse and neglect. In M. H. Klaus, T. Leger, & M. A. Truase (Eds.), *Maternal attachment and mothering disorders: A round table* (2nd ed., pp. 21–25). Skillman, NJ: Johnson and Johnson.

Hetherington, E. M., Cox, M., & Cox, R. (1982). Effects of divorce on parents and children. In M. E. Lamb (Ed.), *Nontraditional families* (pp. 233–288). Hillsdale, NJ: Erlbaum.

Hoffman, M. L. (1975). Altruistic behavior and the parent-child relationship. *Journal of Personality and Social Psychology, 31*, 937–943.

Hoffman, M. L. (1988). Moral development. In M. H. Bornstein & M. E. Lamb (Eds.), *Developmental psychology: An advanced textbook* (2nd ed., pp. 497–548). Hillsdale, NJ: Erlbaum.

Hofmann, R. (1986). Microcomputers, productive thinking, and children. In P. Campbell & G. Fein (Eds.), *Young children and microcomputers* (pp. 87–101). Englewood Cliffs, NJ: Prentice-Hall.

Holdaway, D. (1979). *The foundations of literacy*. Sydney: Ashton Scholastic.

Holmes Group. (1986). *Tomorrow's teachers: A report of the Holmes Group*. East Lansing, MI: Author.

Honig, A. S. (1983). Research in review: Sex role socialization in early childhood. *Young Children, 38*(6), 57–70.

Honig, A. S. (1986). Research in review: Stress and coping in children (Part I). *Young Children, 41*(4), 50–63.

Hooker, D. (1952). *The prenatal origin of behavior*. Lawrence: University of Kansas Press.

Hoot, J., & Silvern, S. (Eds.). (1989). *Writing with computers in the early grades*. New York: Teachers College Press.

Hopkins, J., Marcus, M., & Campbell, S. (1984). Postpartum depression: A critical review. *Psychological Bulletin, 95*, 498–515.

Householder, J., Hatcher, R., Burns, W., & Chasnoff, I. (1982). Infants born to narcotic-addicted mothers. *Psychological Bulletin, 92*, 453–468.

Howes, C. (1987a). Peer interaction of young children. *Monographs of the Society for Research in Child Development, 53*(1, Serial No. 217).

Howes, C. (1987b). Quality indicators in infant and toddler child care: The Los Angeles study. In D. A. Phillips (Ed.), *Quality in child care: What does research tell us?* (pp. 81–88). Washington, DC: National Association for the Education of Young Children.

Hudelson, S. (1985). Beginning reading and the bilingual child. *Dimensions, 13*(3), 19–22.

Hudson, J., & Nelson, K. (1983). Effects of script structure on children's story recall. *Developmental Psychology, 19*, 525–635.

Huesmann, L. R., Eron, L. D., Lefkowitz, M. M., & Walder, L. O. (1984). Stability over time and generations. *Developmental Psychology, 20*, 1120–1134.

Hughes, M., & Donaldson, M. (1983). The use of hiding games for studying coordination of points. In M. Donaldson, R. Grieve, & C. Pratt (Eds.), *Early childhood development and education: Readings in psychology* (pp. 245–253). New York: Guilford Press.

Hughes, M., & Grieve, R. (1983). On asking children bizarre questions. In M. Donaldson, R. Grieve, & C. Pratt (Eds.), *Early childhood development and education: Readings in psychology* (pp. 104–114). New York: Guilford Press.

Huling-Austin, L. (1986). Teacher induction programs: What can and cannot reasonably be expected from teacher induction programs. *Journal of Teacher Education, 37*(1), 2–5.

Hunt, C. E., & Brouillette, R. T. (1987). Sudden infant death syndrome: 1987 perspective. *Journal of Pediatrics, 110*, 669–678.

Hunt, J. McV. (1961). *Intelligence and experience*. New York: Ronald Press.

Hunziker, U. A., & Barr, R. G. (1986). Increased carrying reduces infant crying: A randomized controlled trial. *Pediatrics, 77*, 641–648.

Huston, A. C. (1983). Sex-typing. In E. M. Hetherington (Ed.), *Handbook of child psychology: Vol. 4. Socialization, personality and social development* (4th ed., pp. 387–467). New York: Wiley.

Huston, A. C., Carpenter, C. J., & Atwater, J. B. (1986). Gender, adult structuring of activities, and social behavior in middle childhood. *Child Development, 57*, 1200–1209.

Hymel, S., Rubin, K., Rowden, L., & LeMare, L. (1990). Children's peer relationships: Longitudinal prediction of internalizing and externalizing problems from middle to late childhood. *Child Development, 61*, 2004–2021.

Hymes, D. (1971). Competence and performance in linguistic theory. In R. Huxley & E. Ingram (Eds.), *Language acquisition: Models and methods* (pp. 5–28). London: Academic Press.

Hyson, M. C., Hirsh-Pasek, K., & Rescorla, L. (1989). Academic environments in early childhood: Challenge or pressure? Final report to the Spencer Foundation. (Cited in M. Hyson, K. Hirsh-Pasek, & L. Rescorla, The classroom practices inventory: An observation instrument based on NAEYC's guidelines for developmentally appropriate practice for 4- and 5-year-old children. *Early Childhood Research Quarterly, 5*, 1990, 475–492.)

Ingram, D. (1986). Phonological development: Production. In P. Fletcher & M. Garman (Eds.), *Language acquisition* (2nd ed., pp. 223–239). Cambridge, England: Cambridge University Press.

Inhelder, B. (1960). Criteria of stages of mental development. In J. M. Tanner & B. Inhelder (Eds.), *Discussions on child development* (pp. 75–86). New York: International Universities Press.

Inhelder, B., & Piaget, J. (1958). *The growth of logical thinking from childhood to adolescence*. New York: Basic Books.

Isabella, R. A., Belsky, J., & von Eye, A. (1989). Origins of infant-mother attachment: An examination of interactional synchrony during the infant's first year. *Developmental Psychology, 25*, 12–21).

Izard, C. E., & Buechler, S. (1986). Theoretical perspectives on emotions in developmental disabilities. In M. Lewis & L. Taft (Eds.), *Developmental disabilities: Theory, assessment, and intervention*. New York: Medical and Scientific Books.

Jalongo, M. R. (1987). Do security blankets belong in preschool? *Young Children, 42*(3), 3–8.

Jensen, M. A., & Chevalier, Z. W. (1990). *Issues and advocacy in early education*. Boston: Allyn and Bacon.

Jensen, W. A., Heinrich, B., Wake, D. B., & Wake, M. H. (1979). *Biology*. Belmont, CA: Wadsworth.

Jersild, A. T., & Holmes, F. B. (1935a). *Children's fears*. New York: Teachers College Press.

Jersild, A. T., & Holmes, F. B. (1935b). Methods of overcoming children's fears. *Journal of Psychology, 1*, 75–104.

Johnson, D., & Johnson, R. (1984). Classroom learning structure and attitudes toward handicapped students in mainstream settings: A theoretical model and research evidence. In R. L. Jones (Ed.), *Attitudes and attitude change in special education: Theory and practice* (pp. 118–142). Reston, VA: Council for Exceptional Children.

Johnson, J. E., Christie, J. F., & Yawkey, T. D. (1987). *Play and early childhood development*. Glenview, IL: Scott, Foresman.

Johnson, J. E., & Yawkey, T. D. (1988). Play and integration. In T. D. Yawkey & J. E. Johnson (Eds.), *Integrative processes and socialization: Early to middle childhood* (pp. 97–117). Hillsdale, NJ: Erlbaum.

Jones, H. E., & Jones, M. C. (1928). A study of fear. *Childhood Education, 5*, 136–143.

Jones, K. L. (1988). *Smith's recognizable patterns of human malformation*. Philadelphia: Saunders.

Kagan, J. (1971). *Change and continuity in infancy*. New York: Wiley.

Kagan, J. (1982). *Psychological research on the human infant: An evaluative summary*. New York: W. T. Grant Foundation.

Kagan, S. L. (1989). The care and education of America's young children: At the brink of a paradigm shift. In F. J. Macchiarola & A. Gartner (Eds.), Caring for America's children. *Proceedings of the Academy of Political Science, 37* (Vol. 2, pp. 70–83). New York: The Academy of Political Science.

Kail, R. (1984). *The development of memory in children* (2nd ed.). New York: Freeman.

Kamii, C. (1982). *Number in preschool and kindergarten*. Washington, DC: National Association for the Education of Young Children.

Kamii, C. (1985a). Leading primary education toward excellence—beyond worksheets and drill. *Young Children, 40*(6), 3–11.

Kamii, C. (1985b). *Young children reinvent arithmetic*. New York: Teachers College Press.

Kamii, C. (1989). *Young children continue to invent arithmetic: 2nd grade*. New York: Teachers College Press.

Kamii, C. (1990). *Achievement testing in the early grades: The games grown-ups play*. Washington, DC: NAEYC Publications.

Kamii, C., & DeClark, G. (1985). *Young children reinvent arithmetic: Implications of Piaget's theory*. New York: Teachers College Press.

Kamii, C., & DeVries, R. (1978). *Physical knowledge in preschool education*. Englewood Cliffs, NJ: Prentice-Hall.

Kandel, G., & Lesser, G. (1972). *Youth in two worlds: U.S. and Denmark*. San Francisco: Jossey-Bass.

Karmel, M. (1959). *Thank you, Dr. Lamaze: Painless childbirth*. Philadelphia: Lippincott.

Karmiloff-Smith, A. (1979). Language development after five. In P. Fletcher & M. Garman (Eds.), *Language acquisition* (pp. 307–323). Cambridge, England: Cambridge University Press.

Karmiloff-Smith, A. (1986). Stage-structure versus phase-process in modeling linguistic and cognitive development. In I. Levin (Ed.), *Stage and structure: Reopening the debate* (pp. 164–190). Norwood, NJ: Ablex.

Karnes, M. B., & Johnson, L. J. (1989). Training for staff, parents, and volunteers working with gifted young children, especially those with disabilities from low income homes. *Young Children, 44*(3), 49–56.

Kasmoski, K. (1984). Educational computing: The burden of ensuring quality. *Phi Delta Kappan, 66,* 244–248.

Katz, L. G. (1972). Developmental stages of preschool teachers. *The Elementary School Journal, 23,* 50–54.

Katz, L. G. (1977). *Talks with teachers.* Washington, DC: National Association for the Education of Young Children.

Katz, L. G. (Ed.). (1988). Day care [Special issue]. *Early Childhood Research Quarterly, 3*(3–4).

Katz, L. G., & Chard, S. (1988). *Engaging children's minds: The project approach.* Norwood, NJ: Ablex.

Katz, L. G., Evangelou, D., & Hartman, J. (1990). *The case for mixed-aged grouping in early education.* Washington, DC: National Association for the Education of Young Children.

Katz, L. G., & Ward, E. H. (1978). *Ethical behavior in early childhood education.* Washington, DC: National Association for the Education of Young Children.

Katz, P. A. (1976). The acquisition of racial attitudes in children. In P. A. Katz (Ed.), *Towards the elimination of racism* (pp. 125–154). New York: Pergamon Press.

Katz, P. A. (1982). Development of children's awareness and intergroup attitudes. In L. G. Katz (Ed.), *Current topics in early childhood education* (Vol. 4, pp. 17–54). Norwood, NJ: Ablex.

Kaufman, N. (1985). Review of Gesell School Readiness Test. In J. V. Mitchell, Jr. (Ed.), *Ninth mental measurements yearbook* (Vol. 1, pp. 607–608). Lincoln, NE: Buros Institute of Mental Measurements.

Kavale, K. (1982). Meta-analysis of the relationship between visual perceptual skills and reading achievement. *Journal of Learning Disabilities, 15,* 42–51.

Kaye, K., & Marcus, J. (1981). Infant imitation: The sensorimotor agenda. *Developmental Psychology, 17,* 126–134.

Keating, D. P. (1980). Thinking processes in adolescence. In J. Adelson (Ed.), *Handbook of adolescent psychology* (pp. 211–246). New York: Wiley.

Kelley, R. K. (1972). The premarital sexual revolution: Comments on research. *Family Coordinator, 21,* 334–336.

Kellogg, R. (1969). *Analyzing children's art.* Palo Alto, CA: National Press Books.

Kelly, D. H., & Shannon, D. C. (1982). Sudden infant death syndrome and near sudden infant death syndrome: A review of the literature, 1964–1982. In W. Oh (Ed.), *The pediatric clinics of North America* (Vol. 29, pp. 1241–1262). Philadelphia: Saunders.

Kendall, F. E. (1983). *Diversity in the classroom: A multicultural approach to the education of young children.* New York: Teachers College Press.

Kendrick, A. S., Kaufmann, R., & Messenger, K. P. (Eds.). (1991). *Healthy young children: A manual for programs.* Washington, DC: National Association for the Education of Young Children.

Kerwin, M. L. E., & Day, J. D. (1985). Peer influences on cognitive development. In J. B. Pryor & J. D. Day (Eds.), *The development of social cognition* (pp. 211–218). New York: Springer.

Kett, J. F. (1977). *Rites of passage: Adolescence in America 1790 to the present.* New York: Basic Books.

Kirk, R. (1990). Abortion: The Hispanic perspective. *Vista, 1,* 6–8.

Kirk, S., & Chalfant, J. C. (1984). *Academic and developmental learning disabilities.* Denver: Love.

Kitano, M. (1989). The K–3 teacher's role in recognizing and supporting young gifted children. *Young Children, 44*(3), 57–63.

Klaus, M. H., Jerauld, R., Kreger, N., McAlpine, W., Steffa, M., & Kennell, J. H. (1972). Maternal attachment: Importance of the first postpartum days. *New England Journal of Medicine, 286,* 460–463.

Klaus, M. H., & Kennell, J. H. (1976). *Maternal-infant bonding.* St. Louis: Mosby.

Klaus, M. H., & Kennell, J. H. (1982). *Parent-infant bonding* (2nd ed.). St. Louis: Mosby.

Klaus, M. H., & Klaus, P. H. (1985). *The amazing newborn.* Reading, MA: Addison-Wesley.

Klein, D. C. (1958). Kindergarten entry: A study of role transition. In M. Krugman (Ed.), *Orthopsychiatry and the school* (pp. 60–69). New York: American Orthopsychiatric Association.

Kleiman, A. S. (1974). The use of private speech in young children and its relation to social speech (Doctoral dissertation, University of Chicago). *Dissertation Abstracts International, 36,* 472B.

Kohl, H. (1984). *Growing minds: On becoming a teacher.* New York: Harper and Row.

Kohlberg, L. (1966). A cognitive-developmental analysis of children's sex-role concepts and attitudes. In E. E. Maccoby (Ed.), *The development of sex differences* (pp. 82–173). Stanford, CA: Stanford University Press.

Kohlberg, L. (1968, September). The child as a moral philosopher. *Psychology Today,* pp. 63–67.

Kohlberg, L. (1976). Moral stages and moralization: Cognitive-developmental approach. In T. Lickona (Ed.), *Moral development and behavior: Theory, research, and social issues* (pp. 31–43). New York: Holt, Rinehart and Winston.

Kohlberg, L. (1984). *Essays on moral development: Vol. 2. The psychology of moral development.* San Francisco: Harper and Row.

Kohlberg, L., Yaeger, J., & Hjertholm, E. (1968). Private speech: Four studies and a review of theories. *Child Development, 39,* 691–736.

Kolata, G. (1986). Obese children: A growing problem. *Science, 232,* 20–21.

Kopp, C., & Parmelee, A. (1979). Prenatal and perinatal influences on infant development. In J. D. Osofsky (Ed.), *Handbook of infant development* (pp. 29–75). New York: Wiley.

Korner, A. F., Zeanah, C. H., Linden, J., Berkowitz, R. I., Kraemer, H. C., & Agras, W. S. (1985). The relation between neonatal and later activity and temperament. *Child Development, 56,* 38–42.

Krashen, S. (1981). *Second language acquisition and second language learning.* Elmsford, NY: Pergamon Press.

Krauss, R. M., & Glucksberg, S. (1969). The development of communication: Competence as a function of age. *Child Development, 40,* 255–266.

Krebs, D., & Gillmore, J. (1982). The relationship among the first stages of cognitive development, role-taking abilities, and moral development. *Child Development, 53,* 877–886.

Kreutzer, M. A., Leonard, C., & Flavell, J. H. (1975). An interview study of children's knowledge about memory. *Monographs of the Society for Research in Child Development, 40*(1, Serial No. 159).

Kruesi, M. J., & Rapoport, J. L. (1986). Diet and human behavior: How much do they affect each other? *Annual Reviews of Nutrition, 6,* 113–130.

Kull, J. A. (1986). Learning and Logo. In P. Campbell & G. Fein (Eds.), *Young children and microcomputers* (pp. 103–128). Englewood Cliffs, NJ: Prentice-Hall.

Kunjufu, J. (1980). Nutrition for child development. *Black Child Journal, 1,* 6–13.

Labov, W. (1970). The logic of nonstandard English. In F. Williams (Ed.), *Language and poverty* (pp. 153–189). Chicago: Markham.

Labov, W. (1972). *Language in the inner city: Studies in the black English vernacular.* Philadelphia: University of Pennsylvania.

Ladd, G. W., & Golter, B. S. (1988). Parents' management of preschooler's peer relations: Is it related to children's social competence? *Developmental Psychology, 24,* 3–7.

Lamb, M. (1977). The development of mother-infant attachments in the second year of life. *Developmental Psychology, 13,* 639–649.

Lamb, M. E. (1978a). The development of sibling relationships in infancy: A short-term longitudinal study. *Child Development, 49,* 1189–1196.

Lamb, M. E. (1978b). Interactions between 18-month-olds and their preschool-aged siblings. *Child Development, 49,* 51–59.

Lamb, M. E. (1981). The development of father-infant relationships. In M. E. Lamb (Ed.), *The role of the father in child development* (rev. ed., pp. 1–73). New York: Wiley.

Lamb, M. E., Morrison, D. C., & Malkin, C. M. (1987). The development of infant social expectations in face-to-face interaction: A longitudinal study. *Merrill-Palmer Quarterly, 33,* 241–254.

Lamb, M. E., & Sutton-Smith, B. (Eds.). (1982). *Sibling relationships: Their nature across the lifespan.* Hillsdale, NJ: Erlbaum.

Lamme, L. L. (1979). Handwriting in an early childhood curriculum. *Young Children, 35*(1), 20–27.

Lamme, L. L. (1980). Reading with an infant. *Childhood Education, 56,* 285–290.

Lamme, L. L. (1984). *Growing up writing.* Washington, DC: Acropolis Books.

Lamme, L. L., Cox, V., Matanzo, J., & Olson, M. (1980). *Raising readers: A guide to sharing literature with young children.* New York: Walker.

Langlois, J. H., & Down, C. A. (1979). Peer relations as a function of physical attractiveness: The eye of the beholder or behavioral reality? *Child Development, 50,* 409–418.

Langlois, J. H., & Down, C. A. (1980). Mothers, fathers, and peers as socialization agents of sex-typed play behavior in young children. *Child Development, 51,* 1237–1247.

Larson, J., & Robinson, C. (1989). Latter effects of

preschool on low-risk children. *Early Childhood Research Quarterly, 4,* 133–144.

Lasley, T. (Ed.). (1986). Teacher induction: Programs and research [Special issue]. *Journal of Teacher Education, 37*(1).

Lay-Dopyera, M., & Dopyera, J. (1987). Strategies for teaching. In C. Seefeldt (Ed.), *The early childhood curriculum: A review of research* (pp. 13–34). New York: Teachers College Press.

Lazar, I. (1983). Discussion and implications of findings. In Consortium for Longitudinal Studies, *As the twig is bent . . . : Lasting effects of preschool programs* (pp. 461–466). Hillsdale, NJ: Erlbaum.

Lazar, I., & Darlington, R. (1982). Lasting effects of early education: A report from the Consortium for Longitudinal Studies. *Monographs of the Society for Research in Child Development, 47*(2–3, Serial No. 195).

Lazarus, R. S., & Folkman, S. (1984). *Stress, appraisal, and coping.* New York: Springer.

Leahy, R. L., & Shirk, S. R. (1984). The development of classificatory skills and sex trait stereotypes in children. *Sex Roles, 10,* 281–292.

LeBoyer, F. (1975). *Birth without violence.* New York: Knopf.

LeCours, A. R. (1982). Correlates of developmental behavior in brain maturation. In T. Bever (Ed.), *Regressions in mental development.* Hillsdale, NJ: Erlbaum.

Lerner, J. W. (1985). *Learning disabilities: Theories, diagnosis, and teaching strategies* (4th ed.). Boston: Houghton Mifflin.

Lerner, J. W., Mardell-Czudnowski, C., & Goldenberg, D. (1987). *Special education for the early childhood years* (2nd ed.). Englewood Cliffs, NJ: Prentice-Hall.

Lesser, G. S. (1979, March). Stop picking on Big Bird. *Psychology Today,* pp. 57, 60.

Lester, B. M., & Brazelton, T. B. (1982). Cross-cultural assessment in neonatal behavior. In D. A. Wagner & H. W. Stevenson (Eds.), *Cultural perspectives on child development* (pp. 20–53). San Francisco: Freeman.

Leung, E. H., & Rheingold, H. L. (1981). Development of pointing as a social gesture. *Developmental Psychology, 17,* 215–220.

Lever, J. (1976). Sex differences in games children play. *Social Problems, 23,* 478–487.

Levinson, D. J. (1986). A conception of adult development. *American Psychologist, 41,* 3–13.

Levy, G. D., & Carter, D. B. (1989). Gender schema, gender constancy, and gender role knowledge: The roles of cognitive factors in preschoolers' gender-role stereotype attributions. *Developmental Psychology, 25,* 444–449.

Lewis, M., & Brooks, J. (1978). Self-knowledge and emotional development. In M. Lewis & L. Rosenblum (Eds.), *The development of affect* (pp. 205–226). New York: Plenum Press.

Lewis, M., & Brooks-Gunn, J. (1979). *Social cognition and the acquisition of self.* New York: Plenum Press.

Lickona, T. (1983). *Raising good children: Helping your children through the stages of moral development—from birth through the teenage years.* New York: Bantam.

Lieberman, A., & Miller, L. (1984). *Teachers, their world, and their work: Implications for school improvement.* Alexandria, VA: Association for Supervision and Curriculum Development.

Liebert, R. M., Sprafkin, J. N., & Davidson, E. S. (1982). *The early window: Effects of television on children and youth.* (2nd ed.). New York: Pergamon Press.

Lindfors, J. (1980). *Children's language and language learning.* Englewood Cliffs, NJ: Prentice-Hall.

Lindfors, J. (1987). *Children's language and language learning* (2nd ed.). Englewood Cliffs, NJ: Prentice-Hall.

Linn, S., Schoenbaum, S., Monson, R., Rosner, B., Stubblefield, R., & Ryan, K. (1982). Coffee and pregnancy. *New England Journal of Medicine, 306,* 141–145.

Lipsitt, L. P. (1979). Critical conditions in infancy: A psychological perspective. *American Psychologist, 34,* 973–980.

Lipton, M. A., & Mayo, J. P. (1983). Diet and hyperkinesis: An update. *Journal of the American Dietetic Association, 83,* 132.

Lloyd-Still, J. D. (Ed.). (1976). *Malnutrition and intellectual development.* Littleton, MA: Publishing Science Group.

Londerville, S., & Main, M. (1981). Security attachment, compliance, and maternal training methods in the second year of life. *Developmental Psychology, 17,* 289–299.

Loughlin, C., & Martin, M. (1987). *Support literacy: Developing effective learning environments.* New York: Teachers College Press.

Lucariello, J., & Nelson, K. (1985). Slot-filler categories as memory organizers for young children. *Developmental Psychology, 21*, 272–282.

Maccoby, E., & Jacklin, C. N. (1974). *The psychology of sex differences.* Stanford, CA: Stanford University Press.

Maccoby, E., & Jacklin, C. N. (1974/1980). Sex differences in aggression: A rejoinder and a reprise. *Child Development, 51*, 964–980.

Maccoby, E. E., & Martin, J. A. (1983). Socialization in the context of the family: Parent-child interaction. In E. M. Hetherington (Ed.), *Handbook of child psychology: Vol. 4. Socialization, personality and social development* (4th ed., pp. 1–101). New York: Wiley.

MacDonald, K., & Parke, R. D. (1984). Bridging the gap. Parent-child play interaction and peer interactive competence. *Child Development, 55*, 1265–1277.

MacFarlane, A. (1977). *The psychology of childbirth.* Cambridge, MA: Harvard University Press.

MacLaughlin, B. (1978). *Second language learning in children.* Hillsdale, NJ: Erlbaum.

Mahler, M. (1968). *On human symbiosis and the vicissitudes of individuation.* New York: International Universities Press.

Main, M., & Cassidy, J. (1988). Categories of response to reunion with parent at age 6: Predictable from infant attachment classification and stable over 1-month period. *Developmental Psychology, 24*, 415–426.

Main, M., & Weston, D. R. (1981). The quality of the toddler's relationship to mother and father: Related to conflict behavior and the readiness to establish new relationships. *Child Development, 52*, 932–940.

Makin, J. W., & Porter, R. H. (1989). Attractiveness of lactating females' breast odors to neonates. *Child Development, 60*, 803–810.

Malina, R. M. (1982). Motor development in the early years. In S. G. Moore & C. R. Cooper (Eds.), *The young child: Reviews of research* (Vol. 3, pp. 211–229). Washington, DC: National Association for the Education of Young Children.

Mange, A., & Mange, E. (1990). *Genetics: Human aspects.* Sunderland, MA: Sinauer Associates.

Maratsos, M. (1983). Some current issues in the study of the acquisition of grammar. In J. H. Flavell & E. M. Markman (Eds.), *Handbook of child psychology: Vol. 3. Cognitive development* (4th ed., pp. 707–786). New York: Wiley.

Marcus, D. E., & Overton, W. E. (1978). The development of cognitive gender constancy and sex-role preference. *Child Development, 49*, 434–444.

Marion, M. (1991). *Guidance of young children* (3rd ed.). Columbus, OH: Merrill.

Marshall, H. H., & Weinstein, R. S. (1984). Classroom factors affecting students' self-evaluations. *Review of Educational Research, 54*, 301–325.

Marshall, H. H. (1989). The development of self-concept. *Young Children, 44*(5), 44–51.

Martin, C. L., & Halverson, C. F. (1981). A schematic processing model of sex-typing: Theory and research. *Child Development, 52*, 1119–1132.

Martin, C. L., & Halverson, C. F. (1987). The role of cognition in sex role acquisition. In D. B. Carter (Ed.), *Current conceptions of sex roles and sex typing: Theory and research* (pp. 123–137). New York: Praeger.

Maslow, A. (1968). *Toward a psychology of being* (2nd ed.). Princeton, NJ: Van Nostrand.

Maslow, A. (1970). *Motivation and personality* (2nd ed.). New York: Harper and Row.

Masur, E. F., & Gleason, J. B. (1980). Parent-child interaction and the acquisition of lexical information during play. *Developmental Psychology, 16*, 404–409.

Matas, L., Arend, R. A., & Stroufe, L. A. (1978). Continuity of adaptation in the second year: The relationship between quality of attachment and later competence. *Child Development, 49*, 547–556.

Mayhall, P., & Norgard, K. (1983). *Child abuse and neglect.* New York: Wiley.

McDonald, R., & Avery, D. (1983). *Dentistry for the child and adolescent* (4th ed.). St. Louis: Mosby.

McNeill, D. (1970). *The acquisition of language.* New York: Harper and Row.

Mead, M., & Newton, N. (1967). Cultural patterning of perinatal behavior. In S. Richardson & A. Guttmacher (Eds.), *Childrearing: Its social and psychological aspects.* Baltimore: Williams and Wilkins.

Medina, Z., & Neill, D. M. (1988). *Fallout from the testing explosion: How 100 million standardized exams undermine quality and excellence in America's public schools.* Cambridge, MA: National Center for Fair and Open Testing.

Mehan, H. (1982). The structure of classroom events and their consequences for student performance. In P. Gilmore & A. A. Glatthorn (Eds.),

Children in and out of school: Ethnography and education (pp. 59–87). Washington, DC: Center for Applied Linguistics.

Mehler, J. (1985). Language related dispositions in early infancy. In J. Mehler & R. Fox (Eds.), *Neonate cognition: Beyond the blooming buzzing confusion* (pp. 7–28). Hillsdale, NJ: Erlbaum.

Meisels, S. J. (1987). Uses and abuses of developmental screening and school readiness testing. *Young Children, 42*(2), 68–73.

Meisels, S. J. (1989). *Developmental screening in early childhood: A guide* (3rd ed.). Washington, DC: National Association for the Education of Young Children.

Meltzoff, A. N., & Moore, M. K. (1983). Newborn infants imitate adult facial gestures. *Child Development, 54*(3), 702–709.

Melyn, M., & White, D. (1973). Mental and developmental milestones of non-institutionalized Down's syndrome children. *Pediatrics, 52,* 542–543.

Menyuk, P. (1964). Alternation of rules in children's grammar. *Journal of Verbal Learning and Verbal Behavior, 3,* 480–488.

Menyuk, P. (1971). *The acquisition and development of language.* Englewood Cliffs, NJ: Prentice-Hall.

Menyuk, P. (1976). That's another funny, awful way of saying it. *Journal of Education, 158,* 25–38.

Menyuk, P. (1983). Language development and reading. In T. Gallagher and C. Prutting (Eds.), *Pragmatic assessment and intervention issues in language* (pp. 151–170). San Diego, CA: College Hill Press.

Menyuk, P. (1985). Wherefore metalinguistic skills? A commentary on Bialystok and Ryan. *Merrill-Palmer Quarterly, 31,* 253–259.

Menyuk, P. (1988). *Language development: Knowledge and use.* Glenview, IL: Scott, Foresman.

Meredith, H. V. (1968). Body size of contemporary groups of preschool children studied in different parts of the world. *Child Development, 39,* 335–377.

Metzger, M., & Whittaker, C. P. (1991). *The childproofing checklist: A parent's guide to accident prevention.* New York: Doubleday.

Michaels, S. (1981). Sharing time: Children's narrative styles and differential access to literacy. *Language in Society, 10,* 49–76.

Miller, C. S. (1984). Building self-control: Discipline for young children. *Young Children, 40*(1), 15–19.

Miller, N. E., & Dollard, J. (1941). *Social learning and imitation.* New Haven, CT: Yale University Press.

Miller, P. M., Danaher, D. L., & Forbes, D. (1986). Sex-related strategies for coping with interpersonal conflict in children aged five and seven. *Developmental Psychology, 22,* 543–548.

Minkoff, H., Deepak, N., Menez, R., & Fikrig, S. (1987). Pregnancies resulting in infants with Acquired Immune Deficiency Syndrome or AIDS related complex: Follow-up of mothers, children and subsequently born siblings. *Obstetrics and Gynecology, 69,* 288–291.

Moore, B. S., & Eisenberg, N. (1984). The development of altruism. In G. Whitehurst (Ed.), *Annals of child development* (Vol. 1, pp. 107–174). Greenwich, CT: JAI Press.

Moore, K. L. (1983). *Realities in childbearing.* Philadelphia: Saunders.

Morgan, H. (1976). Neonatal precocity and the black experience. *Negro Educational Review, 27,* 129–134.

Morphett, M. V., & Washburne, C. (1931). When should children begin to read? *The Elementary School Journal, 31,* 496–503.

Moshmon, D., & Timmons, M. (1982). The construction of logical necessity. *Human Development, 25,* 309–323.

Musick, J. S., & Householder, J. (1986). *Infant development: From theory to practice.* Belmont, CA: Wadsworth.

Mussen, P. (1979). *The psychological development of the child* (3rd ed.). Englewood Cliffs, NJ: Prentice-Hall.

Myers, B. J. (1982). Early intervention using Brazelton training with middle-class mothers and fathers of newborns. *Child Development, 53,* 462–471.

Nachbar, R. (1989). A K/1 class can work—wonderfully! *Young Children, 44*(5), 67–71.

Naglieri, J. J. (1985). Review of Gesell School Readiness Test. In J. V. Michael, Jr. (Ed.), *Ninth mental measurements yearbook* (Vol. 1, pp. 608–609). Lincoln, NE: Buros Institute of Mental Measurements.

National Academy of Early Childhood Programs. (1984). *Accreditation criteria and procedures.* Washington, DC: National Association for the Education of Young Children.

National Association for the Education of Young Children. (1988). *Position statement on stand-*

ardized testing of young children 3 through 8 years of age. Washington, DC: NAEYC Publications.

National Association for the Education of Young Children. (1990). *Position statement on media violence in children's lives.* Washington, DC: Author.

National Association for the Education of Young Children, & National Association of Early Childhood Specialists in State Departments of Education. (1992). *Guidelines for appropriate curriculum content and assessment in programs serving children 3 through 8 years of age.* Washington, DC: National Association for the Education of Young Children.

National Association of Elementary School Principals. (1990). *Standards for quality programming for young children: Early childhood education and the elementary school principal.* Alexandria, VA: Author.

National Association of State Boards of Education. (1988). *Right from the start: The report of the NASBE Task Force on Early Childhood Education.* Alexandria, VA: Author.

National Center for Fair and Open Testing. (1987, Fall). North Carolina legislature drops exams for 1st, 2nd graders. *Fair Test Examiner,* p. 3.

National Institute of Health. (1982). *Defined diets and childhood hyperactivity* (National Institute of Health Consensus Development Summary, Vol. 4, No. 3). Bethesda, MD: Author.

National Research Council (U.S.). (1987). Panel on adolescent pregnancy and childbearing. In C. Hayes (Ed.), *Risking the future: Adolescent sexuality, pregnancy and childbearing.* Washington, DC: National Academy Press.

Nelson, K. (1973). Structure and strategy in learning to talk. *Monographs of the Society for Research in Child Development, 38*(1–2, Serial No. 149).

Nelson, K. (1979). The role of language in infant development. In M. H. Bornstein & W. Kessen (Eds.), *Psychological development from infancy: Image to intention* (pp. 307–338). Hillsdale, NJ: Erlbaum.

Nelson, K. (1980). *Children's language* (Vol. 1). New York: Gardener Press.

Nelson, K. (1981). Individual differences in language development: Implications for development and language. *Developmental Psychology, 17,* 170–187.

Nelson, K. (1986). *Event knowledge.* Hillsdale, NJ: Erlbaum.

Nelson, K., Carskaddon, G., & Bonvillian, J. D. (1973). Syntax acquisition: Impact of experimental variation in adult verbal interaction with the child. *Child Development, 44,* 497–504.

Nelson, K., & Gruendel, J. (1981). Generalized event representations: Basic building blocks of cognitive development. In M. Lamb & A. Brown (Eds.), *Advances in development psychology* (Vol. 1, pp. 131–158). Hillsdale, NJ: Erlbaum.

Nelson, K., Rescorla, L., Gruendel, J. M., & Benedict, H. (1978). Early lexicons: What do they mean? *Child Development, 49,* 960–968.

Newell, A., & Simon, H. A. (1972). *Human problem solving.* Englewood Cliffs, NJ: Prentice-Hall.

Newman, J. (1988). On line: Logo and the language arts. *Language Arts, 65,* 598–605.

Nilsson, L., Sundberg, A., & Wirsen, C. (1981). *A child is born.* New York: Dell/Seymour Lawrence.

Ninio, A., & Bruner, J. (1978). The achievements and antecedents of labelling. *Journal of Child Language, 5,* 1–16.

Nizel, A. E. (1977). Preventing dental carries: The nutritional factors. In C. Neumann & D. B. Jelliffe (Eds.), *The pediatric clinics of North America* (Vol. 24, pp. 141–155). Philadelphia: Saunders.

Nunner-Winkler, G., & Sodian, B. (1988). Children's understanding of moral emotions. *Child Development, 59,* 1323–1338.

Olney, R., & Scholnick, E. (1976). Adult judgments of age and linguistic differences in infant vocalizations. *Journal of Child Language, 3,* 145–156.

Olson, S. L., Bates, J. E., & Bayles, K. (1984). Mother infant interaction and the development of individual differences in children's cognitive competence. *Developmental Psychology, 20,* 166–179.

Oppenheim, J. F. (1987). *Buy me, buy me! The Bank Street guide to choosing toys for children.* New York: Pantheon.

Orlick, T. D. (1981). Positive socialization via cooperative games. *Developmental Psychology, 17,* 426–429.

Ost, D. H. (1989). The culture of teaching: stability and change. *The Educational Forum, 53,* 163–181.

Owens-Stively, J. (1987). Stress and coping in children. In S. Moore & K. Kolb (Eds.), *Reviews of research for practitioners and parents* (No. 3, pp. 21–33). Minneapolis: University of Minnesota.

Oyemade, U. J., & Washington, V. (1989). Drug

abuse prevention begins in early childhood. *Young Children, 44*(5), 6–12.

Paley, V. (1988). *Bad guys don't have birthdays: Fantasy play at four.* Chicago: University of Chicago Press.

Palkovitz, R. (1984). Parental attitudes and fathers' interactions with their 5-month old infants. *Developmental Psychology, 20,* 1054–1060.

Parke, R. D., & Sawin, D. B. (1977, November). Fathering: It's a major role. *Psychology Today,* pp. 109–112.

Parke, R. D., & Sawin, D. B. (1980). The family in early infancy. In F. Pedersen (Ed.), *One father-infant relationship: Observational studies in a family context.* New York: Praeger.

Parke, R. D., & Sawin, D. B. (1981). Father-infant interaction in the newborn period: A re-evaluation of some current myths. In E. M. Hetherington & R. D. Parke (Eds.), *Contemporary readings in child psychology* (2nd ed., pp. 229–234). New York: McGraw-Hill.

Parten, M. B. (1933). Social participation among preschool children. *Journal of Abnormal Psychology, 27,* 243–269.

Pascual-Leone, J. (1970). A mathematical model for the transition rule in Piaget's developmental stages. *Acta Psychologica, 32,* 301–345.

Pastor, D. L. (1981). The quality of mother-infant attachment and its relationship to toddler's initial sociability with peers. *Developmental Psychology, 17,* 323–335.

Payne, J. N. (Ed.). (1990). *Mathematics for the young child.* Reston, VA: National Council of Teachers of Mathematics.

Pellegrini, A. D., & Glickman, C. D. (1990). Measuring Kindergarteners' Social Competence. *Young Children, 45* (4), 40–44.

Peskin, H. (1967). Pubertal onset and ego functioning. *Journal of Abnormal Psychology, 72,* 1–15.

Peterson, C. C., Peterson, J. L., & Carroll, J. (1986). Television viewing and imaginative problem solving during preadolescence. *Journal of Genetic Psychology, 147,* 61–67.

Petit, G. S., Dodge, K. A., & Brown, M. M. (1988). Early family experience, social problem solving patterns, and children's social competence. *Child Development, 59,* 107–120.

Pflaum, S. W. (1986). *The development of language and literacy in young children.* (3rd ed.). Columbus, OH: Merrill.

Phillips, D. (Ed.). (1987). *Quality in child care: What does research tell us?* Washington, DC: National Association for the Education of Young Children.

Piaget, J. (1926). *The language and thought of the child.* New York: Harcourt, Brace and World.

Piaget, J. (1929). *The child's conception of physical causality.* New York: Harcourt, Brace and World.

Piaget, J. (1952). *The origins of intelligence in children.* New York: Norton.

Piaget, J. (1954). *The construction of reality in the child.* New York: Basic Books.

Piaget, J. (1962). *Play, dreams and imitation in childhood.* New York: Norton.

Piaget, J. (1963). *The psychology of intelligence.* Paterson, NJ: Littlefield, Adams.

Piaget, J. (1965). *The moral judgment of the child.* New York: Norton. (Original work published 1932)

Piaget, J. (1969). *Six psychological studies.* New York: Vintage.

Piaget, J., & Inhelder, B. (1956). *The child's conception of space.* London: Routledge and Kegan Paul.

Piaget, J., & Inhelder, B. (1969). *The psychology of the child.* New York: Basic Books.

Pipes, P. L. (1989). *Nutrition in infancy and childhood* (4th ed.). St. Louis: Times Mirror/Mosby.

Poest, C. A., Williams, J. R., Witt, D. D., & Atwood, M. E. (1989). Physical activity patterns of preschool children. *Early Childhood Research Quarterly, 4,* 367–376.

Pollitt, E., Leibel, R. L., & Greenfield, D. (1981). Brief fasting stress and cognition in children. *American Journal of Clinical Nutrition, 34,* 1526–1533.

Porter, F. L., Miller, R. H., & Marshall, R. E. (1986). Neonatal pain cries: Effect of circumcision on acoustic features and perceived urgency. *Child Development, 57,* 790–802.

Powell, G. J., Yammamoto, J., Romero, A., & Morales, A. (Eds.). (1983). *The psychosocial development of minority children.* New York: Brunner/Mazel.

Press, B., & Greenspan, S. (1985). Ned and Dan: The development of a toddler friendship. *Children Today, 14,* 24–29.

Price, G. G. (1989). Mathematics in early childhood. *Young Children, 44*(4), 53–58.

Province, S., & Lipton, R. C. (1962). *Infants in institutions.* New York: International Universities Press.

Putallaz, M. (1987). Maternal behavior and children's sociometric status. *Child Development, 58,* 324–340.

Queenhan, J., & Queenhan, C. (1978). *A new life.* Boston: Little, Brown.

Radke-Yarrow, M., Zahn-Waxler, C., & Chapman, M. (1983). Children's prosocial dispositions and behavior. In E. M. Hetherington (Ed.), *Handbook of child psychology: Vol. 4. Socialization, personality and social development* (4th ed., pp. 469–545). New York: Wiley.

Ramsey, P. G. (1982). Multicultural education in early childhood. *Young Children, 37*(2), 13–24.

Ramsey, P. G. (1987). *Teaching and learning in a diverse world: Multicultural education for young children.* New York: Columbia University Press.

Read, C. (1971). Pre-school children's knowledge of English phonology. *Harvard Educational Review, 41,* 1–34.

Rebok, G. W. (1987). *Life-span cognitive development.* New York: Holt, Rinehart and Winston.

Reich, P. A. (1986). *Language development.* Englewood Cliffs, NJ: Prentice-Hall.

Rescorla, L. A. (1980). Category development in early language. *Journal of Child Language, 8,* 225–238.

Restak, R. (1984). *The brain.* New York: Bantam Books.

Rheingold, H. L., Hay, D. F., & West, M. J. (1976). Sharing in the second year of life. *Child Development, 47,* 1148–1158.

Rhodes, L. (1981). I can read: Predictable books as resources for reading and writing activities. *The Reading Teacher, 34,* 511–518.

Rhodes, L. K., & Dudley-Marling, C. (1988). *Readers and writers with a difference: A holistic approach to teaching learning disabled and remedial students.* Portsmouth, NH: Heinemann.

Ricciuti, H. N. (1980). Developmental consequences of malnutrition in early childhood. In E. M. Hetherington & R. D. Parke (Eds.), *Contemporary readings in child psychology* (2nd ed., pp. 21–25). New York: McGraw-Hill.

Rice, M. L., Huston, A. C., & Wright, J. C. (1986). Replays as repetitions: Young children's interpretation of television forms. *Journal of Applied Developmental Psychology, 7,* 61–76.

Richardson, J. G., & Simpson, C. H. (1982). Children, gender, and social structure: An analysis of the contents of letters to Santa Claus. *Child Development, 53,* 429–436.

Richardson, L. W. (1981). *The dynamics of sex and gender* (2nd ed.). Boston: Houghton Mifflin.

Riley, S. S. (1984). *How to generate values in young children: Integrity, honesty, individuality, self-confidence, and wisdom.* Washington, DC: National Association for the Education of Young Children.

Robson, K. S. (1967). The role of eye to eye contact in maternal-infant attachment. *Journal of Child Psychology and Psychiatry and Allied Disciplines, 8,* 13–25.

Roedell, W. C., Jackson, N. E., & Robinson, H. B. (1980). *Gifted young children.* New York: Teachers College Press.

Rogers, C. R. (1961). *On becoming a person.* Boston: Houghton Mifflin.

Roopnarine, J. L. (1985). Changes in peer-directed behaviors following preschool experience. *Journal of Personality and Social Psychology, 48,* 740–745.

Rosen, M. (1981). *The rise in caesareans.* Paper presented at the First International Symposium on Computers in Prenatal Medicine, Cleveland, OH.

Rosenfeld, A., & Stark, E. (1987, May). The prime of our lives. *Psychology Today,* pp. 62–72.

Rosenholtz, S. J., & Rosenholtz, S. H. (1981). Classroom organization and the perception of ability. *Sociology of Education, 54,* 132–140.

Rosenthal, M. K. (1982). Vocal dialogues in the neonatal period. *Developmental Psychology, 18,* 17–21.

Rosett, H. L., Snyder, P., Sander, L. W., Lee, A., Cook, P., Weiner, L., & Gould, J. (1979). Effects of maternal drinking on neonate state regulation. *Developmental Medicine and Child Neurology, 27,* 464–473.

Rousseau, J. J. (1955). *Emile.* New York: Dutton. (Original work published 1762)

Royce, J. M., Darlington, R. B., & Murray, H. W. (1983). Pooled analysis: Findings across studies. In Consortium for Longitudinal Studies, *As the twig is bent . . . : Lasting effects of preschool programs* (pp. 411–459). Hillsdale, NJ: Erlbaum.

Rubin, K. H. (1973). Egocentrism in childhood: A unitary construct? *Child Development, 44,* 102–110.

Rubin, K. H. (1982). Nonsocial play in preschoolers: Necessarily evil? *Child Development, 53,* 651–657.

Rubin, K. H., & Everett, B. (1982). Social perspective-taking in young children. In S. G. Moore & C. R. Cooper (Eds.), *The young child: Reviews of research* (Vol. 3, pp. 97–113). Washington, DC: National Association for the Education of Young Children.

Rubin, K. H., Watson, K. S., & Jambor, T. W. (1978). Free play behaviors in preschool and kindergarten children. *Child Development, 49,* 534–536.

Rubin, Z. (1980). *Children's friendships.* Cambridge, MA: Harvard University Press.

Ruble, D. N. (1988). Sex-role development. In M. H. Bornstein & M. E. Lamb (Eds.), *Developmental psychology: An advanced textbook* (2nd ed., pp. 411–460). Hillsdale, NJ: Erlbaum.

Sadker, M., & Sadker, D. (1985, March). Sexism in the schoolroom of the '80's. *Psychology Today,* pp. 54–57.

Saegert, S., & Hart, R. (1976). The development of sex differences on the environmental competence of girls and boys. In P. Burnett (Ed.), *Women in society.* Chicago: Maaroufa Press.

Salk, L. (1974). *Preparing for parenthood.* New York: Bantam Books.

Salkind, N. J., & Ambron, S. R. (1987). *Child development* (5th ed.). New York: Holt, Rinehart and Winston.

Salomon, G. (1977). Effects of encouraging mothers to co-observe "Sesame Street" with their five year olds. *Child Development, 48,* 1146–1151.

Samuels, C. A. (1985). Attention to eye contact opportunity and facial motion by three-month old infants. *Journal of Experimental Child Psychology, 40,* 105–114.

Samuels, M., & Samuels, N. (1986). *The well pregnancy book.* New York: Summit.

Santrock, J. (1984). *Adolescence.* Dubuque, IA: Wm. C. Brown.

Sapon-Shevin, M. (1983). Teaching children about differences: Resources for teaching. *Young Children, 38*(2), 24–31.

Schank, R. C., & Abelson, R. P. (1977). *Scripts, plans, goals, and understanding.* Hillsdale, NJ: Erlbaum.

Schickedanz, J. A. (1986). *More than ABC's: The early stages of reading and writing.* Washington, DC: National Association for the Education of Young Children.

Scholssberg, N. (1970). Adult men: Education or re-education. *Vocational Guidance Quarterly, 19*(1), 36–39.

Schön, D. (1983). *The reflective practitioner: How professionals think in action.* New York: Basic Books.

Schwartz, J. I. (1988). *Encouraging early literacy: An integrated approach to reading and writing in N–3.* Portsmouth, NH: Heinemann.

Schweinhart, L., & Weikart, D. P. (1985). Evidence that good early childhood programs work. *Phi Delta Kappan, 66,* 545–551.

Schweinhart, L. J., Weikart, D. P., & Larner, M. B. (1986). Consequences of three preschool curriculum models through age 15. *Early Childhood Research Quarterly, 1,* 15–46.

Sears, R. R., Maccoby, E. E., & Levin, H. (1957). *Patterns of childrearing.* Evanston, IL: Row, Paterson.

Sears, R. R., & Whiting, J. W. (1953). Some child rearing antecedents of aggression and dependency in young children. *Genetic Psychological Monographs, 47,* 135–236.

Seefeldt, C., & Barbour, N. (1988). "They said I had to . . ." Working with mandates. *Young Children, 43*(4), 4–8.

Selfe, L. (1977). *Nadia: A case of extraordinary drawing ability in an autistic child.* New York: Academic Press.

Selman, R. L. (1976). Social cognitive understanding. In T. Lickona (Ed.), *Moral development and behavior: Theory, research, and social issues* (pp. 219–240). New York: Holt, Rinehart and Winston.

Selman, R. L. (1980). *The growth of interpersonal understanding: Developmental and clinical analysis.* New York: Academic Press.

Selman, R. L. (1981). The child as friendship philosopher. In S. R. Asher & J. M. Gottman (Eds.), *The development of children's friendships* (pp. 242–273). Cambridge, MA: Cambridge University Press.

Sepkowski, C. (1985). Maternal obstetric medication and newborn behavior. In J. W. Scanlon (Ed.), *Prenatal anesthesia.* London: Blackwell.

Shaffer, H. R. (1971). *The growth of stability.* London: Penguin.

Shapiro, J. (1987, January). The expectant father. *Psychology Today,* pp. 36–42.

Shatz, M. (1983). Communication. In P. H. Mussen (Ed.), *Handbook of child psychology: Vol. 3. Cog-*

nitive development (pp. 841–889). New York: Wiley.

Sheehy, G. (1976). *Passages: Predictable crises of adult life.* New York: Dutton.

Sheehy, G. (1982). *Pathfinders.* New York: Bantam Books.

Shepard, L. A., & Smith, M. L. (1986). Synthesis of research on school readiness and kindergarten retention. *Educational Leadership, 44*(3),78–86.

Shepard, L. A., & Smith, M. L. (1987). Effects of kindergarten retention at the end of first grade. *Psychology in the School, 24,* 346–357.

Shirley, M. M. (1961). *The first two years: A study of twenty-five babies.* Minneapolis: University of Minnesota Press.

Shonkoff, J. P. (1984). The biological substrate and physical health in middle childhood. In W. A. Collins (Ed.), *Development during middle childhood: The years from six to twelve* (pp. 24–69). Washington, DC: National Academy Press.

Shriffin, R. M., & Atkinson, R. C. (1969). Storage and retrieval processes in long-term memory. *Psychological Review, 76,* 179–193.

Shultz, T. R., Wright, K., & Schleifer, M. (1986). Assignment of moral responsibility and punishment. *Child Development, 57,* 177–184.

Siegler, R. S. (1981). Developmental sequences within and between concepts. *Monographs of the Society for Research in Child Development, 46*(2, Serial No. 189).

Siegler, R. S. (1983). Information processing approaches to development. In W. Kesson (Ed.), *Handbook of child psychology: Vol. 1. History, theory and methods* (4th ed., pp 129–211). New York: Wiley.

Siegler, R. S. (1986). *Children's thinking.* Englewood Cliffs, NJ: Prentice-Hall.

Siegler, R. S., & Robinson, M. (1982). The development of numerical understandings. In H. W. Reese & L. P. Lipsitt (Eds.), *Advances in child development and behavior* (Vol. 16, pp. 241–312). New York: Academic Press.

Simmons, R., & Blyth, D. (1987). *Moving into adolescence: The impact of pubertal change and school context.* New York: Aldine/Hawthorne.

Singer, J. L., & Singer, D. G. (1979, March). Come back, Mr. Rogers, come back. *Psychology Today,* pp. 56, 59–60.

Singer, J. L., & Singer, D. G. (1981). *Television, imagination, and aggression: A study of preschoolers.* Hillsdale, NJ: Erlbaum.

Singer, J. L., & Singer, D. G. (1983). Psychologists look at television. *American Psychologist, 38,* 826–834.

Skinner, B. F. (1938). *The behavior of organisms.* Englewood Cliffs, NJ: Prentice-Hall.

Skinner, B. F. (1948). *Walden two.* New York: Macmillan.

Skinner, B. F. (1957). *Verbal behavior.* East Norwalk, CT: Appleton-Century-Crofts.

Skinner, B. F. (1974). *About behaviorism.* New York: Knopf.

Skinner, B. F. (1979). *The shaping of a behaviorist.* New York: Knopf.

Smilansky, S. (1968). *The effects of sociodramatic play on disadvantaged preschool children.* New York: Wiley.

Smith, B., & Strain, P. (1988). *Does early intervention help?* (Report No. R188062207).

Smith, C., & Loyd, B. (1978). Maternal behavior and perceived sex of infant: Revisited. *Child Development, 49,* 1263–1266.

Smith, C. A., & Berenberg, W. (1970). The concept of failure to thrive. *Pediatrics, 46,* 661.

Smolak, L. (1986). *Infancy.* Englewood Cliffs, NJ: Prentice-Hall.

Snow, C. E., & Ferguson, C. (Eds.). (1977). *Talking to children: Language input and acquisition.* New York: Cambridge University Press.

Snow, C. E., & Ninio, A. (1986). The contracts of literacy: What children learn from learning to read books. In W. H. Teale & E. Sulzby (Eds.), *Emergent literacy: Writing and reading* (pp. 116–138). Norwood, NJ: Ablex.

Snow, C. E. (1983). Literacy and language: Relationships during the preschool years. *Harvard Educational Review, 53,* 165–189.

Snow, C. W. (1989). *Infant development.* Englewood Cliffs, NJ: Prentice-Hall.

Snyder, M., Snyder, R., & Snyder R., Jr. (1980). *The young child as person: Toward the development of healthy conscience.* New York: Human Sciences Press.

Society for Research in Child Development, Ethical Interest Group. (1975). *Ethical standards for research with children.* Chicago: Society for Research in Child Development.

Solan, L. (1983). *Pronominal reference: Child language and theory of grammar.* Dordreeht, Holland: Reidel.

Spock, B. (1988). *Dr. Spock on parenting.* New York: Simon and Schuster.

Stechler, G., & Halton, A. (1982). Prenatal influences on human development. In B. B. Wollman, G. Stricker, S. J. Ellman, P. Keith-Spiegel, & D. S. Palermo (Eds.), *Handbook of developmental psychology.* Englewood Cliffs, NJ: Prentice-Hall.

Stein, N. L., & Glenn, C. G. (1979). An analysis of story comprehension in elementary school children. In R. O. Freedle (Ed.), *Advances in discourse processing* (Vol. 2, pp. 53–120). Norwood, NJ: Ablex.

Steiner, J. E. (1979). Human facial expressions in response to taste and smell stimulation. In H. Reese & L. Lipsitt (Eds.), *Advances in child development and behavior* (Vol. 13, pp. 257–295). New York: Academic Press.

Stevenson, H. W. (1967). Studies of racial awareness in young children. In W. W. Hartup & N. L. Smothergill (Eds.), *The young child: Reviews of research* (pp. 206–213). Washington, DC: National Association for the Education of Young Children.

Stewart, R. B. (1983). Sibling attachment relationships: Child infant interactions in the strange situation. *Developmental Psychology, 19,* 192–199.

Stewart, R. B., Mobley, L. A., Van Tuyl, S. S., & Salvador, M. A. (1987). The firstborn's adjustment to the birth of a sibling: A longitudinal assessment. *Child Development, 58,* 341.

Stipek, D., & Daniels, D. (1988). Declining perceptions of competence: A consequence of changes in the child or in the educational environment. *Journal of Educational Psychology, 80,* 352–356.

Streissguth, A. P., Martin, D. C., Barr, H. M., & Sandman, B. M. (1984). Intrauterine alcohol and nicotine exposure: Attention and reaction time in 4-year old children. *Developmental Psychology, 20,* 533–541.

Strong, M. (1982). Social styles and second language acquisition of Spanish-speaking kindergarteners. *TESOL Quarterly, 17,* 2.

Stroufe, L. A. (1979). Socioemotional development. In J. D. Osofsky (Ed.), *Handbook of infant development* (pp. 462–516). New York: Wiley.

Stroufe, L. A. (1983). Infant caregiver attachments and patterns of adaptation in preschool: The roots of maladaptation and competence. In M. Perlmutter (Ed.), *Minnesota symposium on child psychology* (Vol. 16, pp. 41–81). Hillsdale, NJ: Erlbaum.

Stroufe, L. A. (1985). Attachment classification from the perspective of infant-caregiver relationships and infant temperament. *Child Development, 56,* 1–14.

Stroufe, L. A. (1988). A developmental perspective on day care. *Early Childhood Research Quarterly, 3,* 283–291.

Stroufe, L. A., Fox, N. E., & Pancake, V. R. (1983). Attachment and dependency in developmental perspective. *Child Development, 54,* 1615–1627.

Stroufe, L. A., Schork, E., Motti, F., Lawroski, N., & LaFreniere, P. (1984). The role of affect in social competence. In C. E. Izard, J. Kagan, & R. Zajonc (Eds.), *Affect, cognition and behavior* (pp. 289–319). New York: Plenum Press.

Sudhalter, V., & Braine, M. D. S. (1985). How does comprehension of passives develop? A comparison of actional and experiential verbs. *Journal of Child Language, 12,* 453–470.

Summerlin, M. L., & Ward, G. R. (1978). The effect of parental participation in a parent group on a child's self concept. *Psychological Reports, 100,* 227–232.

Surber, C. F. (1982). Separable effects of motives, consequences, and presentation order of children's moral judgments. *Developmental Psychology, 18,* 257–266.

Sutton-Smith, B. (1967). The role of play in cognitive development. *Young Children, 22,* 361–370.

Sutton-Smith, B. (1975). A developmental structural account of riddles. In B. Kirschenblatt-Gimblett (Ed.), *Speech play* (pp. 111–119). The Hague: Mouton.

Sutton-Smith, B. (1976). A developmental structural account of riddles. In B. Kirschenbatt-Gimblett (Ed.), *Speech play* (pp. 111–119). The Hague: Mouton.

Sutton-Smith, B. (1979). *Play and learning.* New York: Wiley.

Sutton-Smith, B. (1986). The spirit of play. In G. G. Fein & M. Rivkin (Eds.), *The young child at play* (pp. 3–15). Washington, DC: NAEYC Publications.

Swick, K., Brown, M., & Guddemi, M. (1986). *Personality dimensions of effective teachers.* Columbia: University of South Carolina.

Tanner, J. M. (1970). Physical growth. In P. Mussen (Ed.), *Carmichael's manual of child psychology* (Vol. 2, pp. 77–155). New York: Wiley.

Tanner, J. M. (1971). The regulation of human growth. In H. Munsinger (Ed.), *Readings in child development* (pp. 31–38). New York: Holt, Rinehart and Winston.

Tanner, J. M. (1973). The regulation of human growth. In F. Rebelsky & L. Dorman (Eds.), *Child development and behavior*. New York: Knopf.

Tanner, J. M. (1978). *Fetus into man: Physical growth from conception to maturity*. Cambridge, MA: Harvard University Press.

Taylor, D. (1986). Creating a family story. In W. H. Teale & E. Sulzby (Eds.), *Emergent literacy: Writing and reading* (pp. 139–155). Norwood, NJ: Ablex.

Taylor, D., & Dorsey-Gaines, C. (1988). *Growing up literate: Learning from inner-city families*. Portsmouth, NH: Heinemann.

Teale, W. H. (1981). Parents reading to children: What we know and need to know. *Language Arts, 58*, 902–912.

Teale, W. H. (1984). Reading to young children: Its significance for literacy development. In H. Goelman, A. Oberg, & F. Smith (Eds.), *Awakening to literacy* (pp. 110–121). Portsmouth, NH: Heinemann.

Teale, W. H. (1986). Home background and young children's literacy development. In W. H. Teale & E. Sulzby (Eds.), *Emergent literacy: Writing and reading* (pp. 173–206). Norwood, NJ: Ablex.

Teale, W. H., Estrada, E., & Anderson, A. B. (1981). How preschoolers interact with written communication. In M. L. Kamil (Ed.), *Directions in reading: Research and instruction. Thirtieth yearbook of the National Reading Conference* (pp. 257–265). Washington, DC: National Reading Conference.

Teale, W. H., Hiebert, E., & Chittenden, E. (1987). Assessing young children's literacy development. *The Reading Teacher, 40*, 772–776.

Teale, W. H., & Sulzby, E. (Eds.). (1986). *Emergent literacy: Writing and reading*. Norwood, NJ: Ablex.

Templin, M. C. (1957). Certain skills in children: Their development and interrelationships. *University of Minnesota Institute of Child Welfare Monographs, 26*.

Terman, L. M. (1959). *Genetic studies of genius* (Vols. 1–5). Stanford, CA: Stanford University Press.

Thain, W. S., Casto, G., & Peterson, A. (1980). *Normal and handicapped children: A growth and development primer for parents and professionals*. Littleton, MA: PSG Publishing.

Thomas, A., & Chess, S. (1977). *Temperament and development*. New York: Brunner/Mazel.

Thomas, A., Chess, S., & Birch, H. G. (1968). *Temperament and behavior disorders in children*. New York: New York University Press.

Thomas, A., Chess, S., Birch, H. G., Hertzig, M. E., & Korn, S. (1963). *Behavioral individuality in early childhood*. New York: New York University Press.

Thomas, A., Chess, S., & Korn, S. (1982). The reality of difficult temperament. *Merrill-Palmer Quarterly, 28*, 1–20.

Thompson, J. S., & Thompson, M. W. (1986). *Genetics in medicine*. Philadelphia: Saunders.

Thurman, S. K., & Lewis, M. (1979). Children's responses to differences: Some possible implications for mainstreaming. *Exceptional Children, 45*, 468–470.

Tolstoy, L. N. (1948). *Sobranie khudozhestvennykh proizvedenii [Collected literary works]*. Izd. Pravda (Ogonëk), p. 247.

Tough, J. (1974). *Focus on meaning: Talking to some purpose with young children*. London: George Allen and Unwin.

Tough, J. (1977). *The development of meaning*. London: George Allen and Unwin.

Trelease, J. (1982). *The read aloud handbook*. New York: Penguin.

Tronick, E. Z., Cohn, J., & Shea, E. (1986). The transfer of affect between mother and infant. In T. B. Brazelton & M. W. Yogman (Eds.), *Affective development in infancy* (pp. 11–25). Norwood, NJ: Ablex.

Tunmer, W. E., Bowey, J. A., & Grieve, R. (1983). The development of young children's awareness of the word as a unit of spoken language. *Journal of Psycholinguistic Research, 12*, 567–594.

Tunmer, W. E., & Nesdale, A. R. (1982). The effects of digraphs and pseudo-words on phonemic segmentation in young children. *Journal of Applied Linguistics, 3*, 299–311.

Turiel, E. (1980). The development of social-conventional and moral concepts. In M. Windmiller, N. Lambert, & E. Turiel (Eds.), *Moral development and socialization* (pp. 69–106). Boston: Allyn and Bacon.

United States Congress, Senate Committee on Human Research. (1978). *Obstetrical practices in the U.S.* Washington, DC: U.S. Government Printing Office.

United States Department, Health and Human Services. (1990). *The health consequences of smoking for women: A report of the Surgeon General*. Rockville, MD: Author.

Vaillant, G. E. (1977). *Adaptation to life.* Waltham, MA: Little, Brown.

Vandell, D., & Mueller, E. (1980). Peer play and friendships during the first two years. In H. Foot, A. Chapman, & J. Smith (Eds.), *Friendship and social relations in children* (pp. 181–208). New York: Wiley.

Van Hasselt, V. G. (1983). Social adaptation in the blind. *Clinical Psychology Review, 3,* 87–102.

Vaughn, V. C., III, & Litt, I. F. (1987). The newborn infant. In R. E. Behrman & V. C. Vaughn (Eds.), *Nelson textbook of pediatrics* (13th ed., pp. 7–17). Philadelphia: Saunders.

Vogel, F., & Motulsky, A. G. (1979). *Human genetics: Problems and approaches.* New York: Springer.

Vorhees, C. V., & Mallnow, E. (1987). Behavior teratogenesis: Long-term influences on behavior. In J. D. Osofsky (Ed.), *Handbook of infant development* (2nd ed., pp. 913–971). New York: Wiley.

Vurpillot, E. (1968). The development of scanning strategies and their relation to visual differentiation. *Journal of Experimental Child Psychology, 6,* 632–650.

Vygotsky, L. S. (1962). *Thought and language.* Cambridge, MA: MIT Press. (Original work published 1934)

Vygotsky, L. S. (1978). *Mind in society: The development of higher mental processes.* Cambridge, MA: Harvard University Press.

Vygotsky, L. S. (1987). Thinking and speech. In N. Minick (Trans.), *The collected works of L. S. Vygotsky: Vol 1. Problems in general psychology.* New York: Plenum Press.

Wadsworth, B. (1984). *Piaget's theory of cognitive and affective development.* New York: Longman.

Wallis, C. (1986, January 20). Cocaine babies. *Time,* p. 50.

Wanska, S. K., & Bedrosian, J. L. (1985). Conversational structure and topic performance in mother-child interaction. *Journal of Speech and Hearing Research, 28,* 579–584.

Ward, E. H. (1978). A code of ethics: The hallmark of a profession. In L. G. Katz & E. H. Ward (Eds.), *Ethical behavior in early childhood education* (pp. 17–26). Washington, DC: National Association for the Education of Young Children.

Waters, E. (1985). Review of Gesell School Readiness Test. In J. V. Mitchell, Jr. (Ed.), *Ninth mental measurements yearbook* (Vol. 1, pp. 610–611).

Lincoln, NE: Buros Institute of Mental Measurements.

Watkins, B., Calvert, S., Huston-Stein, A., & Wright, J. C. (1980). Children's recall of television material: Effects of presentation mode and adult labeling. *Developmental Psychology, 16,* 672–674.

Watson, J. B. (1924). *Behaviorism.* New York: Norton.

Watson, J. B. (1928). *Psychological care of infant and child.* New York: Norton.

Watson, J. B., & Rayner, R. (1920). Conditioned emotional reactions. *Journal of Experimental Psychology, 3,* 1–14.

Weber, E. (1984). *Ideas influencing early childhood education.* New York: Teachers College Press.

Webster, L., Wood, R., Eicher, C., & Hoag, C. (1989). A preschool language tutoring project: Family support—The essential factor. *Early Childhood Research Quarterly, 4,* 217–224.

Weir, R. (1962). *Language in the crib.* The Hague: Mouton.

Weiss, C. E., Lillywhite, H. S., & Gordon, M. D. (1980). *Clinical management of articulation disorders.* St. Louis: Mosby.

Weiss, E. (1984). Learning disabled children's understanding of social interactions of peers. *Journal of Learning Disabilities, 17,* 612–615.

Weissburg, J. A., & Paris, S. G. (1986). Young children's remembering in different contexts: A reinterpretation of Istomina's study. *Child Development, 57,* 1123–1129.

Wells, G. (1981). *Learning through interaction: The study of language development.* Cambridge, MA: Cambridge University Press.

Werner, E. E. (1979). *Cross-cultural child development: A view from the planet earth.* Monterrey, CA: Brooks/Cole.

White, B. (1985). *The first three years of life.* Englewood Cliffs, NJ: Prentice-Hall.

White, S. H., & Pillemer, D. B. (1979). Childhood amnesia and the development of a socially accessible memory system. In J. F. Kihlstrom & F. J. Evans (Eds.), *Functional disorders of memory* (pp. 29–73). Hillsdale, NJ: Erlbaum.

Whiting, B. B., & Whiting, J. W. M. (1975). *Children of six cultures: A psychocultural analysis.* Cambridge, MA: Harvard University Press.

Whitley, B. E. (1985). Sex role orientation and psychological well-being: Two meta-analyses. *Sex Roles, 12,* 207–215.

Willert, M. K., & Kamii, C. (1985). Reading in kindergarten: Direct vs. indirect teaching. *Young Children, 40*(4), 3–9.

Williams, J. E., & Morland, J. K. (1976). *Race, color, and the young child.* Chapel Hill: University of North Carolina Press.

Wilson, J. G. (1977). Current status of teratology. In J. G. Wilson & F. C. Fraser (Eds.), *Handbook of teratology* (Vol. 1). New York: Plenum Press.

Winick, B. (1981). Food and the fetus. *American Scientist, 1,* 76–81.

Winick, M. (1976). *Malnutrition and brain development.* New York: Oxford University Press.

Winner, E., Rosenstiel, A. K., & Gardner, H. (1977). The development of metaphoric understanding. *Journal of Learning Disabilities, 10,* 147–149.

Winnicott, D. W. (1953). Transitional objects and transitional phenomena. *International Journal of Psycho-Analysis, 34,* 1–9.

Winnicott, D. W. (1971). *Playing and reality.* London: Tavistock Publications.

Winnicott, D. W. (1977). *The piggle.* New York: International Universities Press.

Wishart, J. G., & Bower, T. G. R. (1985). A longitudinal study of the development of the object concept. *British Journal of Developmental Psychology, 3,* 243–258.

Wolff, P. (1963). Observation on the early development of smiling. In B. Foss (Ed.), *Determinants of infant behavior* (Vol. 2, pp. 113–138). London: Methuen.

Wolff, P. H. (1966). The causes, controls, and organization of behavior in the neonate. *Psychological Issues, 5*(1, Serial No. 17).

Wolfle, J. (1989). The gifted preschooler: Developmentally different but still 3 or 4 years old. *Young Children, 44*(3), 41–48.

Wong-Fillmore, L. (1976). *The second time around: Cognitive and social strategies in second language acquisition.* Unpublished doctoral dissertation, Stanford University.

Wong-Fillmore, L. (1979). Individual differences in second-language acquisition. In C. J. Fillmore, D. Kempler, & W. S. Wang (Eds.), *Individual differences in language ability and language behavior.* New York: Academic Press.

Wong-Fillmore, L. (1981). *Language minority students and school participation: What kind of English is needed?* Paper presented at the Conference on Literacy and Language Use, University of Southern California, Los Angeles.

Wortham, S. C. (1984). *Organizing instruction in early childhood.* Boston: Allyn and Bacon.

Wortham, S. C. (1990). *Tests and measurement in early childhood education.* Columbus, OH: Merrill.

Worthington-Roberts, B., & Williams, S. R. (1989). *Nutrition in pregnancy and lactation* (4th ed.). St. Louis: Times Mirror/Mosby.

Wright, J. C., Huston, A. C., Ross, R. P., Calvert, S. L., Rolandelli, D., Weeks, L. A., Raeissi, P., & Potts, R. (1984). Pace and continuity of television programs: Effects on children's attentions and comprehension. *Developmental Psychology, 20,* 653–666.

Wyden, B. (1971, December 17). Growth: 45 crucial months. *Life,* pp. 93–95.

Yaffee, S. (1980). *Safe sedatives and pregnancy.* Paper presented at the American Association for the Advancement of Science, Washington, DC.

Yammamoto, K. (1972). *The child and his image: The self concept in the early years.* New York: Houghton Mifflin.

Yarrow, L. (1961). Maternal deprivation: Toward an empirical and conceptual re-evaluation. *Psychological Bulletin, 58,* 459–490.

Yarrow, M. R., Scott, P. M., & Zahn-Waxler, C. Z. (1973). Learning concern for others. *Developmental Psychology, 8,* 240–260.

Yarrow, M. R., & Zahn-Waxler, C. Z. (1977). The emergence and functions of prosocial behaviors in young children. In R. C. Smart & M. S. Smart (Eds.), *Readings in child development and relationships* (2nd ed., pp. 77–81). New York: Macmillan.

Youniss, J., & Smollar, J. (1985). *Adolescent relations with mothers, fathers and friends.* Chicago: University of Chicago Press.

Zahn-Waxler, C., Radke-Yarrow, M., & King, R. A. (1979). Child rearing and children's prosocial initiations toward victims of distress. *Child Development, 50,* 319–330.

Zaslow, M. J., & Pedersen, F. A. (1981). Sex role conflicts and the experience of childbearing. *Professional Psychology, 12*(1), 47–55.

Zinchenko, V. P., Chzhi-Tsin, V., & Tarakanov, V. V. (1963). The formation and development of perceptual activity. *Soviet Psychology, 2,* 3–12.

Author Index

Subject Index